Law and Economics

The International Library of Essays in Law and Legal Theory
Second Series
Series Editor: Tom D. Campbell

Titles in the Series:

Freedom of Speech, Volumes I and II
Larry Alexander

Privacy
Eric M. Barendt

Comparative Legal Cultures
John Bell

Contract Law, Volumes I and II
Brian Bix

Corporate Law
William W. Bratton

Law and Democracy
Tom D. Campbell

Legal Positivism
Tom D. Campbell

Administrative Law
Peter Cane

International Trade Law
Ronald A. Cass and Michael S. Knoll

Sociological Perspectives on Law, Volumes I and II
Roger Cotterrell

Intellectual Property
Peter Drahos

Family, State and Law, Volumes I and II
Michael D. Freeman

Natural Law
Robert P. George

Commercial Law
Clayton P. Gillette

Competition Law
Rosa Greaves

Chinese Law and Legal Theory
Perry Keller

International Law, Volumes I and II
Martti Koskenniemi and David Kennedy

Constitutional Law
Ian D. Loveland

Interpretation of Law
D. Neil MacCormick and Fernando Atria

Human Rights
Robert McCorquodale

Anti-Discrimination Law
Christopher McCrudden

Medical Law and Ethics
Sheila McLean

Mediation
Carrie Menkel-Meadow

Environmental Law
Peter Menell

Criminal Law
Thomas Morawetz

Law and Language
Thomas Morawetz

Law and Anthropology
Martha Mundy

Gender and Justice
Ngaire Naffine

Law and Economics
Eric A. Posner

Japanese Law
J. Mark Ramseyer

Justice
Wojciech Sadurski

The Rule of Law
Frederick Schauer

Regulation
Colin Scott

Restitution
Lionel D. Smith

Company Law
David Sugarman

Freedom of Information
Robert G. Vaughn

Tort Law
Ernest J. Weinrib

Rights
Robin West

Welfare Law
Lucy A. Williams

Law and Economics

Edited by

Eric A. Posner

University of Chicago Law School

Ashgate

DARTMOUTH

Aldershot • Burlington USA • Singapore • Sydney

Published by
Dartmouth Publishing Company
Ashgate Publishing Limited
Gower House
Croft Road
Aldershot
Hants GU11 3HR
England

Ashgate Publishing Company
131 Main Street
Burlington, VT 05401-5600 USA

Ashgate website: http://www.ashgate.com

British Library Cataloguing in Publication Data
Law and economics. – (International library of essays in
law and legal theory. Second series)
1. Law and economics 2. Law – Economic aspects
I. Posner, Eric A.
340.1'15

Library of Congress Cataloging-in-Publication Data
Law and economics / edited by Eric A. Posner
p. cm. — (International library of essays in law and legal theory. Second series)
ISBN 0-7546-2098-0 (hb)
1. Law and economics. I. Posner, Eric A. II. Series.

K487.E3 L378 2000
340'.11—dc21 99-055604

ISBN 0 7546 2098 0

Printed and bound in Great Britain by Biddles Short Run Books Ltd, King's Lynn

Contents

Acknowledgements

The editor and publishers wish to thank the following for permission to use copyright material.

American Economic Association for the essay: Isaac Ehrlich (1975), 'The Deterrent Effect of Capital Punishment: A Question of Life and Death', *American Economic Review*, **65**, pp. 397–417.

Columbia University for the essay: Jonathan R. Macey (1986), 'Promoting Public-Regarding Legislation Through Statutory Interpretation: An Interest Group Model', *Columbia Law Review*, **86**, pp. 223–68. This article appeared at *Columbia Law Review*, **86**, p. 223 (1986). Reprinted by permission.

Copyright Clearance Center, Inc. for the essay: Christine Jolls, Cass R. Sunstein and Richard Thaler (1998), 'A Behavioral Approach to Law and Economics', *Stanford Law Review*, **50**, pp. 1471–550.

Georgetown University Law Center for the essay: William N. Eskridge jr and John Ferejohn (1992), 'The Article I, Section 7 Game', *Georgetown Law Journal*, **80**, pp. 523–64. Reprinted with permission of the publishers, Georgetown University and Georgetown Law Journal. Copyright © 1992.

Harvard Law Review Association for the essays: Alan O. Sykes (1988), 'The Boundaries of Vicarious Liability: An Economic Analysis of the Scope of Employment Rule and Related Legal Doctrines', *Harvard Law Review*, **101**, pp. 563–609. Copyright © 1988 Harvard Law Review Association; Lucian Arye Bebchuk (1988), 'A New Approach to Corporate Reorganizations', *Harvard Law Review*, **101**, pp. 775–804. Copyright © 1988 Harvard Law Review Association.

The Journal of Legal Studies for the essays: William M. Landes and Richard A. Posner (1989), 'An Economic Analysis of Copyright Law', *Journal of Legal Studies*, **18**, pp. 325–63. Copyright © 1989 University of Chicago. All rights reserved; Lucian Arye Bebchuk (1996), 'A New Theory Concerning the Credibility and Success of Threats to Sue', *Journal of Legal Studies*, **25**, pp. 1–25. Copyright © 1996 University of Chicago. All rights reserved; Louis Kaplow and Steven Shavell (1994), 'Why the Legal System is Less Efficient than the Income Tax in Redistributing Income', *Journal of Legal Studies*, **23**, pp. 667–81. Copyright © 1994 University of Chicago. All rights reserved; Eric A. Posner (1998), 'Symbols, Signals, and Social Norms in Politics and the Law', *Journal of Legal Studies*, **27**, pp. 765–98. Copyright © 1989 University of Chicago. All rights reserved; Don L. Coursey, Elizabeth Hoffman and Matthew L. Spitzer (1987), 'Fear and Loathing in the Coase Theorem: Experimental Tests Involving Physical Discomfort', *Journal of Legal Studies*, **16**, pp. 217–48. Copyright © 1989 University of Chicago. All rights reserved.

University of Chicago Law School for the essay: Randal C. Picker (1997), 'Simple Games in a Complex World: A Generative Approach to the Adoption of Norms', *University of Chicago Law Review*, **64**, pp. 1225–88.

The Yale Law Journal for the essay: Ian Ayres and Robert Gertner (1989), 'Filling Gaps in Incomplete Contracts: An Economic Theory of Default Rules', *Yale Law Journal*, **99**, pp. 87–130. Reprinted by permission of The Yale Law Journal Company and Fred B. Rothman & Company from *The Yale Law Journal*, **99**, pp. 87–130.

Every effort has been made to trace all the copyright holders, but if any have been inadvertently overlooked the publishers will be pleased to make the necessary arrangement at the first opportunity.

Preface to the Second Series

The first series of the International Library of Essays in Law and Legal Theory has established itself as a major research resource with fifty-eight volumes of the most significant theoretical essays in contemporary legal studies. Each volume contains essays of central theoretical importance in its subject area and the series as a whole makes available an extensive range of valuable material of considerable interest to those involved in research, teaching and the study of law.

The rapid growth of theoretically interesting scholarly work in law has created a demand for a second series which includes more recent publications of note and earlier essays to which renewed attention is being given. It also affords the opportunity to extend the areas of law covered in the first series.

The new series follows the successful pattern of reproducing entire essays with the original page numbers as an aid to comprehensive research and accurate referencing. Editors have selected not only the most influential essays but also those which they consider to be of greatest continuing importance. The objective of the second series is to enlarge the scope of the library, include significant recent work and reflect a variety of editorial perspectives.

Each volume is edited by an expert in the specific area who makes the selection on the basis of the quality, influence and significance of the essays, taking care to include essays which are not readily available. Each volume contains a substantial introduction explaining the context and significance of the essays selected.

I am most grateful for the care which volume editors have taken in carrying out the complex task of selecting and presenting essays which meet the exacting criteria set for the series.

TOM CAMPBELL
Series Editor
The Faculty of Law
The Australian National University

Introduction

Anthologies of essays on law and economics are hazardous undertakings. The field is now so large that it may seem doubtful that any single-volume collection could give the reader a feel for the breadth of the contributions. Indeed, there are several single-volume collections devoted to particular topics within law and economics, such as the law and economics of contracts and the law and economics of torts. A recent 'dictionary' of law and economics, which tries to provide an overview of the entire field, consists of three volumes, 399 entries and more than 2000 pages.

The scale of the field is not the only obstacle presented to the editor of an anthology on law and economics. There is also great methodological diversity. Many essays are technical, but many are informal. Many are theoretical, but some are empirical. Some empirical essays are informal case studies while others rely on rigorous econometric techniques. Many essays adhere strictly to the premises of rational choice theory, while others relax them in diverse directions. The boundary between 'law and economics' and 'economics' is obscure, as is the boundary between 'law and economics' and more mainstream legal scholarship. In the United States some areas of legal scholarship, such as bankruptcy, contracts and commercial law, have been taken over by the economic approach, although others – constitutional law in particular – remain relatively untouched.

All of this means that any anthology of law and economics must omit many important essays, and this volume is no exception. In putting it together, I have allowed myself to be guided by the following constraints. First, I have selected less technical and more informal essays, in anticipation of a readership that is not familiar with the mathematical tools of economics. Second, I have selected shorter essays so that a broad range of topics could be included. Third, I have biased my choice towards more recent essays: the law and economics volumes in the earlier series contain the undisputed classics; more recent essays give a better sense of how the field has been changing and where it is going. Fourth, I have tried to include a diverse group of authors, approaches and styles.

The volume is divided into two Parts. Part I contains more traditional law and economics essays, covering a range of conventional legal topics. This Part will give the novice an indication of the current state of the field and the traditional methods of analysis. Part II contains some more innovative and cross-disciplinary work, which attempt to introduce new methodological techniques and subject-matter concerns to law and economics. It is not yet clear how influential these essays will be, but they give a sense of the field's possible future directions.

Traditional Law and Economics

Contracts

The economic approach to contract law asks how contract rules affect people's incentives to cooperate. Early work pointed out that different damages rules affect people's incentives to breach a contract, or to enter a contract, or to take precautions against contingencies that might change the value of a contract. Ayres' and Gertner's essay (Chapter 1) describes the ways in which contract doctrines also affect people's incentives to disclose information to each other prior to entering a contract.

Ayres and Gertner focus on the case of *Hadley* v. *Baxendale* which held that the victim of breach is entitled to damages only for 'reasonably foreseeable' losses, unless the victim informed the promisor that a breach would result in an unusually high level of damages. They show that this rule, compared to an alternative rule of unlimited liability, may give high-value promisees an incentive to disclose their valuations. When valuations are revealed, the promisor will take more efficient precautions against breach than when valuations are hidden.

But the main interest of the essay is its focus on default rules. When people enter contracts, they usually fail to specify duties when remote contingencies occur. Courts fill the gaps in the contract by relying on rules of contract law, but parties are free to contract around these rules in advance. That is why scholars call these rules 'default rules'. The apparent ease with which parties can evade rules they do not like has led some scholars to argue that contract law doctrines are of minor interest. But this is wrong. If the purpose of contract law is to maximize the value of contracts, then default rules should be designed to give parties the appropriate incentives to engage in contract-related behaviour. When parties negotiate, default rules influence how they bargain, whether they reveal information to each other, and thus whether parties engage in the optimal level of care when they perform their obligations under the contract.

Torts

Just as parties can bargain around the default rules of contract law, they can also bargain around certain rules of tort law. If tort law holds that the employer is liable for the employee's torts ('vicarious liability'), and an employer and employee do not like this rule, they can enter a contract under which the employee must reimburse the employer for any costs resulting from the employee's torts. If tort law holds that the employer is not liable for the employee's torts ('personal liability'), and the employer and employee do not like this rule, they can enter a contract under which the employer agrees to reimburse the employee for any damages. In either case, the employee's wages will be adjusted to reflect any costs taken on by the employer.

Yet as the essay by Alan Sykes (Chapter 2) shows, the choice between liability rules matters. It matters because the cost of bargaining may be high, and it matters because the rules have different consequences for third parties. The latter point is of special interest. When the employee has few assets, both the employer and the employee might prefer a regime of personal liability because, if the employee has insufficient assets, then the employer and the employee do not jointly bear the full costs of negligent behaviour. If the employer and the employee do not bear the full costs of their behaviour, they will engage in socially suboptimal behaviour – in the employee's case, committing torts and, in the employer's case, expanding production beyond the socially optimal level. Hence the case for vicarious liability, which forces the employer to bear the costs of the employee's behaviour, and thus encourages the employer to monitor employees and dismiss those who are likely to commit torts. Although the employee can agree to reimburse the employer, they cannot jointly escape bearing the full costs of their conduct as they can under the rule of personal liability.

Property

The economic analysis of property law initially focused on 'ordinary' property rights, including the right to exclude others from a piece of land. Simplifying greatly, the standard view was that traditional property rights give the owner security to invest in resources. If people did not have property rights, then they would not invest in improving resources under their control, because they could not prevent interlopers from reaping what they had sown. There is a trade-off, however. Often, third parties will be able to use a piece of property more productively than the owner and, when transacting is difficult, a regime of strict property rights can interfere with the creation of value.

Nowhere is this more true than in the field of intellectual property. People have long understood that the expression of an idea or a work of art may be just as valuable as a piece of land. The incentives to invest in a work of art are like the incentives to invest in a piece of land. I will not invest in producing a book if people can copy it without paying me, just as I will not plant crops if others can take them from me without compensating me. But there are important differences. Intellectual property is particularly vulnerable to expropriation: once released in the public domain, it can be copied and resold. This is not true about land and ordinary goods, where possession and easily enforced trespass laws deter the most obvious forms of expropriation. In addition, once intellectual property is in the public domain, someone who can create value by using it may have trouble locating the originator and offering to pay him for a licence to use it. In Chapter 3 Landes and Posner argue that copyright law strikes the right balance between protecting investments in intellectual property and allowing third parties to use that property when contracting with the originator would be costly and the value of third-party use is high.

Criminal Law

The modern economic analysis of criminal law originates with Gary Becker's simple but powerful argument (going back to Bentham and others) that criminal behaviour is just a particular kind of harmful behaviour, and that criminal punishments are best understood as 'prices' that can be used to deter that behaviour. The argument has many testable implications, including the prediction that an increase in criminal punishment will reduce the amount of crime subject to punishment, just as a tax on tomatoes will reduce the number of tomatoes that are consumed.

To some people, this is obvious; to others, it is implausible. The point to understand is that the argument is a hypothesis, and must be tested against the facts. Isaac Ehrlich's essay (Chapter 4) focuses on the question whether capital punishment deters crime. His essay is significant because it is one of the earliest rigorous empirical tests of an argument arising out of the economic analysis of the law. It should also be noted that, in the United States, the conventional wisdom at the time was very much the opposite of the economic position. This wisdom held that crime is a function of social structure, or education or norms, but not a function of the expected cost of criminal punishment. Ehrlich provides evidence that capital punishment does deter crime. His claims are highly controversial, however, and empirical investigation of this issue is ongoing.

Bankruptcy

Bebchuk's essay on bankruptcy (Chapter 5) is notable for its methodological approach. He relies on options theory – a branch of financial economics – to justify a proposal to revise bankruptcy law. Current American bankruptcy law relies heavily on a bankruptcy judge supervising bargaining among the debtor and the creditors. Although the law protects creditors in many ways, it appears that creditors give up value to the debtors even though the debtors are insolvent; moreover, corporate bankruptcy proceedings are frequently delay-filled processes. Bebchuk's elegant options approach would preserve creditors' prebankruptcy contract rights by giving them options on the reorganized firm's value.

Bebchuk's essay is a clear example of the normative side of law and economics. Most of the other essays in this anthology are positive: they explain how the law reflects or deviates from efficiency. By contrast, Bebchuk argues that *the law should be changed, and his argument is that the change would improve the position of all affected people* who have not yet entered credit contracts. Creditors would benefit because it better respects their contractual entitlements than the current system does; and in a competitive credit market they would pass on their savings to debtors, leading to a reduction in the cost of credit.

Procedure

Another selection from Bebchuk (Chapter 6) shows the increasing influence of game theory in law and economics. Game theory is a branch of mathematics that was invented in the middle of the twentieth century, although it has antecedents farther back in time. It entered economics during the 1960s and 1970s, and became influential in the 1980s. It entered law and economics in the late 1980s and early 1990s (although one can find isolated examples in the 1970s). Ayres' and Gertner's essay (Chapter 1) is an example of its use in law and economics. Many scholars in law and economics have expressed scepticism about its usefulness, echoing concerns still heard among economists, but game theory seems to be here to stay. Here, Bebchuk uses standard tools from game theory to analyse why people bring cases whose expected value is less than the expected cost of litigation, and how they are able to extract settlements from defendants. A common example would be a lawsuit for a small amount of money, where legal expenses are high. One might believe that people bring these suits because they are irrational or poorly informed, but Bebchuk shows that this need not be the case. His key point is that, when expenses are spread out over time, the plaintiff may have a credible threat to sue at a later stage – when most of his costs are sunk and the expected gain from winning the lawsuit exceeds the remaining costs. When this is so, the plaintiff can extract a settlement from the defendant at the beginning of the lawsuit.

Statutory Interpretation

An intellectual development parallel to the rise of law and economics is the rise of public choice theory. Where law and economics uses economics to analyse law, public choice theory uses economics to analyse politics. Public choice has focused on the influence of interest groups on political decisions, and one of its recurrent claims is that small, well-organized interest groups expend resources in a wasteful competition for policy outcomes that transfer resources from the disorganized public to the successful interest groups. This is called 'rent-seeking'.

Macey's essay (Chapter 7) uses public choice theory to investigate a legal topic – statutory interpretation. He adopts the public choice view that statutes are frequently the outcome of legislative deals which take value from the public at large and distribute it to well-organized interest groups. He further argues that the techniques of statutory interpretation used by judges, including the reliance on legislative history and on certain canons such as the plain meaning rule, result in the enforcement of the publicly expressed purposes of legislation, rather than the legislators' hidden goals. This judicial practice forces the legislators into a dilemma. If they are open about the legislative deals, courts will enforce them, but the pay-offs to special interest groups will be exposed to the public, which will punish legislators at the polls. If the legislators hide the deals in vague laws that have a public-regarding appearance, then courts will be less able to identify and enforce their deals. But if interest groups cannot depend on courts enforcing the deals they make with legislators, then these deals will not be worth much to them, and they will not invest as much effort in obtaining them. In sum, by forcing legislatures to reveal the purpose of statutes, courts enhance the public's ability to monitor legislatures, and thus discourage rent-seeking by interest groups.

Law and Wealth Redistribution

When writers in law and economics make a normative proposal, they usually justify it on the ground that it promotes efficiency. Bebchuk's bankruptcy reform proposal is an example. Critics of law and economics argue that efficiency is not the only value served by the law, and perhaps not even an important value. Many critics argue that legal rules can be explained and justified by their effect on the distribution of wealth. A common example is the claim that strict liability is superior to negligence because strict liability increases the likelihood that money will end up in the pocket of the victim of an accident, who is likely to be poorer than the large corporations that are so often responsible for torts. The goal of the law should be distributive justice, not efficiency.

Kaplow's and Shavell's essay (Chapter 8) is an important methodological contribution to law and economics, because it justifies the focus on efficiency. The authors show that any inefficient law is inferior – on both efficiency and distributive grounds – to an alternative package consisting of a law that is efficient and an appropriate adjustment to the tax and welfare system. The general point is a familiar one in welfare economics: if you want to help the poor, the most efficient way to do so is through taxation and welfare. But if distributive justice is best pursued through taxation and welfare, then the legal scholar concerned with legal rules ought to focus only on their efficiency effects.

Frontiers

The discussion above shows that even the traditional forms of law and economic analysis display a great deal of methodological cross-fertilization. Law professors are open to ideas in other disciplines, and practitioners of law and economics are no exception. We have already seen examples of the influence of game theory, financial economics and public choice. Part II reveals more radical influences.

Cognitive psychology has cast doubt on the rational actor model underlying law and economics. Although economists have never doubted that people err, and models can account for human error, economics generally assumes that error is random. The cognitive psychologists, however, show that error is often systematic. People display hindsight bias, they underpredict low-probability events, they overpredict events that resemble events they have recently observed and so on. Although cognitive psychology has influenced legal scholarship for a long time, the contribution by Jolls, Sunstein and Thaler (Chapter 9) is the most prominent example of a critical essay from within law and economics (Jolls and Thaler are economists). They do not counsel rejection of law and economics, however. They argue that law and economics would produce better explanations of legal rules, and produce better reform proposals, if it took account of cognitive biases and errors.

Cognitive psychology was stimulated in part by the observation that people's behaviour seems to deviate from that predicted by the rational actor model. It seeks an explanation for these deviations by looking inwards – to human psychology. Another approach has been to look outwards – to society. The most prominent example of this approach is Robert Ellickson's book, *Order Without Law* (1991) which argues that much behaviour is guided by social norms rather than by the law. The essay by Posner (Chapter 10) uses game theory to explain why people conform to social norms, and how the widespread conformity to social norms might affect our understanding of the law. There is an important difference between this approach and that of Jolls and her co-authors. The latter argue that the rational actor model must be modified. Posner adopts the rational actor model, and claims that a great deal of apparently irrational behaviour results from people being concerned about their reputation.

Another recent influence on law and economics is positive political theory – the use of game theory to study political institutions. It resembles public choice theory in its reliance on the rational actor model, but public choice theory, as we saw, focuses not on the structure of political institutions but on the role of interest groups in influencing political outcomes, including legislation. The essay by Eskridge and Ferejohn (Chapter 11) shows how positive political theory can be used to analyse the United States Constitution and court decisions that interpret it. The essay analyses provisions of the Constitution that require bills to be passed by both the House and Senate and presented to the President who may veto them. The authors first show how these rules establish a balance between the power of the President and Congress to influence legislation; then they show how several recent decisions by the United States Supreme Court weaken these rules, and give the President more power to control legislative outcomes than envisioned by the drafters of the Constitution.

The essay by Coursey, Hoffman and Spitzer (Chapter 12) uses experiments to test ideas that are frequently used in law and economics. Experiments have become common in economics and game theory. They have been motivated by the simple fact that many important economic ideas cannot be reliably tested using the aggregated data sets that are available. Experiments typically involve the cooperation of students or other individuals, who are either unpaid or paid a nominal amount. They are asked to bargain with each other, or bid for goods, or engage in exchange – whatever is being investigated. A recurrent question in law and economics is how likely are individuals to trade entitlements. As we saw above, the essays by Ayres and Gertner and by Sykes, place much emphasis on the assumption that people will often (though not always) be able to trade away their legal entitlements. This essay shows how experimentalists investigate this assumption.

Picker's essay (Chapter 13) introduces computer modelling to legal scholarship and law and economics – another way of overcoming the difficulties involved in empirical testing. The power of computers allows the use of somewhat more general models than are typical in economics, because computers enable the testing of the interaction of a variety of parameters.

Picker is interested in understanding the relationship between law and social norms. He uses a very simple model in which people obtain gains by coordinating actions, to show both the robustness of some social norms and the fragility of others. An interesting implication is that state intervention to change norms ('norm-seeding' in Picker's happy phrase) has a high upside and a minimal downside. When existing norms are inefficient, new efficient norms seeded by the state may expand rapidly throughout the population. When existing norms are efficient, and the state mistakenly seeds inefficient norms, the new norms are unlikely to spread throughout the population.

Reference

Ellickson, Robert C. (1991), *Order Without Law*, Berkeley, CA: Harvard University Press.

Part I
Traditional Law and Economics

Contracts

[1]

Filling Gaps in Incomplete Contracts: An Economic Theory of Default Rules

Ian Ayres† and Robert Gertner††

Introduction

The legal rules of contracts and corporations can be divided into two distinct classes. The larger class consists of "default" rules that parties can contract around by prior agreement, while the smaller, but important, class consists of "immutable" rules that parties cannot change by contractual agreement.[1] Default rules fill the gaps in incomplete contracts; they govern unless the parties contract around them. Immutable rules cannot be contracted around; they govern even if the parties attempt to contract around them. For example, under the Uniform Commercial Code (U.C.C.) the duty to act in good faith is an immutable part of any contract,[2] while the warranty of merchantability is simply a default rule that parties can waive by agreement.[3] Similarly, most corporate statutes

---

† Assistant Professor, Northwestern University School of Law; Research Fellow, American Bar Foundation. B.A., Yale University; J.D., Yale Law School; Ph.D. (Economics), Massachusetts Institute of Technology. The support of Northwestern's Corporate Counsel Center is gratefully acknowledged.

†† Assistant Professor, University of Chicago, Graduate School of Business. A.B., Princeton University; Ph.D. (Economics), Massachusetts Institute of Technology. The authors would like to thank Douglas Baird, Randy Barnett, Richard Craswell, John Donohue, Frank Easterbrook, Mark Grady, David Haddock, Steve Harris, Oliver Hart, Ian MacNeil, Joel Rogers, Steve Salop, David Scharfstein, David Van Zandt, Robert Vishny and seminar participants at the University of Chicago, Georgetown, Michigan, Northwestern, and Illinois law schools, and at the U.S. Department of Justice for helpful comments. Rebecca Mitchells and Jerry Richman provided excellent research assistance.

1. *See* B. Black, Corporate Law As Neutral Mutation, (Nov. 1988) (unpublished manuscript on file with authors) (arguing that few corporate laws are immutable). Immutable rules are similar to what Calabresi and Melamed call "inalienable" rules, Calabresi & Melamed, ***Property Rules, Liability Rules, and Inalienability: One View of the Cathedral***, 85 Harv. L. Rev. 1089, 1093 (1972), except that immutable entitlements are created by and conditioned upon contract, while inalienable entitlements exist outside of contract. *See* Schwab, ***A Coasean Experiment on Contract Presumptions***, 17 J. Legal Stud. 237, 239 n.6 (1988) (distinguishing between inalienable and immutable rules).

2. U.C.C. § 1-203 (1976); *see* Morin Bldg. Prod. Co. v. Baystone Constr., Inc., 717 F.2d 413, 414-15 (7th Cir. 1983); Restatement (Second) of Contracts § 205 (1979); R. Posner, Economic Analysis of Law 81 (3d ed. 1986).

3. U.C.C. § 2-314 (1976). U.C.C. § 1-102 (1976) distinguishes between default and immutable rules and states its preference for the former:

> (3) The effect of provisions of this Act may be varied by agreement, except as otherwise provided in this Act and except that the obligations of good faith, diligence, reasonableness and care prescribed by this Act may not be disclaimed by agreement but the parties may by agreement determine the standards by which the performance of such obligations is to be measured if such standards are not manifestly unreasonable.
>
> (4) The presence in certain provisions of this Act of the words "unless otherwise agreed" or

require that stockholders elect directors annually[4] but allow the articles of incorporation to contract around the default rule of straight voting.[5] Statutory language such as "[u]nless otherwise provided in the certificate of incorporation"[6] or "[u]nless otherwise unambiguously indicated"[7] makes it easy to identify statutory default, but common-law precedents can also be divided into the default and immutable camps. For example, the common-law holding of *Peevyhouse v. Garland Coal & Mining Co.*,[8] which limited damages to diminution in value, could be contractually reversed by prospective parties.[9] In contrast, the common law prerequisite of consideration is largely an immutable rule that parties cannot contractually abrogate.[10]

There is surprising consensus among academics at an abstract level on two normative bases for immutability. Put most simply, immutable rules are justifiable if society wants to protect (1) parties within the contract, or (2) parties outside the contract.[11] The former justification turns on parentalism; the latter on externalities. Immutable rules displace freedom of contract. Immutability is justified only if unregulated contracting would be socially deleterious because parties internal or external to the contract cannot adequately protect themselves.[12] With regard to immutable rules, the disagreement among academics is not over this abstract theory, but

---

words of similar import does not imply that the effect of other provisions may not be varied by agreement under subsection (3).

U.C.C. § 1-102 (1976).

4. *See, e.g.*, DEL. CODE ANN. tit. 8, § 211(c) (1974).

5. *See, e.g.*, DEL. CODE ANN. tit. 8, § 214 (1974).

6. DEL. CODE ANN. tit. 8, § 223 (1974).

7. U.C.C. § 2-206 (1976).

8. 382 P.2d 109 (Okla. 1962), *cert. denied*, 375 U.S. 906 (1963).

9. Whether the *Peevyhouse* majority actually intended for prospective parties to be able to choose the "cost of performance measure" is discussed more fully *infra* text accompanying notes 151-61.

10. The consideration requirement is not immutable if written agreements "under seal" serve as a contractual substitute for consideration. *See* U.C.C. § 2-203 (1976) (making inoperative "the law with respect to sealed instruments").

This default rule/immutable rule dichotomy also pervades other areas of the law that have contractual components. In the law of divorce, for example, wealth accrued before marriage is allocated according to default rules that can be altered in pre-nuptial agreements, while income earned after marriage is immutably divided. Similarly, the repayment priorities set by state debtor-creditor law can, like default rules, be reordered through private contract. The laws of intestacy are also default rules: they fill any testamentary gap, but can be contracted around. As discussed below, *infra* text accompanying notes 83-91, one can distinguish between defaults that must be *bilaterally* contracted around and defaults that may be *unilaterally* overcome.

11. *See* I. MACNEIL, CONTRACTS: EXCHANGE TRANSACTIONS AND RELATIONS 346-47 (1978); Calabresi & Melamed, *supra* note 1; Easterbrook & Fischel, *The Economic Structure of Corporate Law*, 89 COLUM. L. REV. (forthcoming 1989) (manuscript at 21-30; on file with authors).

12. Note that even when there are negative externalities, third parties may be able to protect themselves without immutable rules. One implication of the Coase theorem is that in a world with no transaction costs, third parties will have an incentive to contract to reduce externalities to an efficient level. *See* Coase, *The Problem of Social Cost*, 3 J. LAW & ECON. 1 (1960). There are no externalities if the class of parties to the potential contract is defined broadly enough. G. Priest, Internalizing Costs (Yale Law School Program in Civil Liability 1988; working paper no. 93) (explicating pervasiveness of private incentives to internalize costs).

whether in particular contexts parentalistic concerns or externalities are sufficiently great to justify the use of immutable rules.[13]

When the preconditions for immutability are not present, the normative legal analysis devolves to the choice of a default rule. Yet academics have paid little attention about how to choose among possible default rules.[14] The law-and-economics movement has fought long and hard to convince courts to restrict the use of immutable rules,[15] but has lost most of its normative energy in constructing a theory of default choice.[16] Economists seem to believe that, even if lawmakers choose the wrong default, at worst there will be increased transaction costs of a second order of magnitude.[17]

Few academics have gone beyond one-sentence theories stipulating that default terms should be set at what the parties would have wanted.[18]

13. A recent conference (Dec. 9-10, 1988) on "Contractual Freedom in Corporate Law" at Columbia's Center for Law and Economic Studies focused directly on the appropriate application of immutable rules. For example, Jeffrey Gordon argued that having multiple precedents that construe a single legal standard produces positive externalities that might justify imposing an immutable rule. *See* J. Gordon, The Mandatory Structure of Corporate Law (Dec. 2, 1988) (unpublished manuscript on file with authors).

14. Courts or legislatures are inevitably forced to set defaults, because contracts with gaps need to be interpreted. Courts must do something—even if that something is non-enforcement. As discussed *infra* text accompanying notes 51-52, defaults of non-enforcement can play an important role in efficient law.

15. For instance, Anthony Kronman has written:

> [E]x ante arguments for the efficiency of a particular legal rule assume that individuals remain free to contract around that rule, and a legal system that denies private parties the right to vary rules in this way will tend to be less efficient than a system that adopts the same rules but permits contractual variation.

Kronman, *Specific Performance*, 45 U. CHI. L. REV. 351, 370 (1978). *See* Haddock, Macey & McChesney, *Property Rights in Assets and Resistance to Tender Offers*, 73 VA. L. REV. 701, 736 (1987) ("The ability of firms to contract around costly legal rules when lower-cost private alternatives are available must be a feature of any efficient standard-form contract."); *see also* Goetz & Scott, *Liquidated Damages, Penalties and the Just Compensation Principle: Some Notes on an Enforcement Model and a Theory of Efficient Breach*, 77 COLUM. L. REV. 554 (1977) (arguing that "immutable" standards for determining enforceability of liquidated damages clauses should be relaxed). *But see* Clarkson, Miller & Muris, *Liquidated Damages v. Penalties: Sense or Nonsense?*, 1978 WIS. L. REV. 351 (providing efficiency rationale for immutable liquidated-damages rules).

16. For example, Haddock and Macey have suggested that immutable rules against insider trading are inefficient but have remained agnostic about whether corporations wishing to allow their insiders to trade should be forced to "opt out" of an insider trading prohibition, or whether corporations wishing to prohibit insider trading should be forced to "opt in" to such a system. Haddock & Macey, *A Coasian Model of Insider Trading*, 80 NW. U.L. REV. 1449 (1987).

17. *See, e.g.*, Easterbrook & Fischel, *Limited Liability and the Corporation*, 52 U. CHI. L. REV. 89, 102 (1985) ("In light of the ability of firms to duplicate or at least approximate either limited or unlimited liability by contract, does the legal rule of limited liability matter? The answer is yes, but probably not much.").

18. Looking backward to what the present litigants "would have wanted" is analytically analogous to looking forward to what prospective contractors will want. It is to ask (as Lea Brilmayer often does) "who are the prospective parties rooting for?" In both cases the court examines ex ante incentives. While ex post each party will have economic incentives to shift costs to the other side, ex ante the parties have an incentive to place the risks on the least-cost avoider. Kronman, *Mistake, Disclosure, Information and the Law of Contracts*, 7 J. LEGAL STUD. 1 (1978). If a court can identify that ex ante the parties to the contract had identical interests in allocating a certain risk or duty of performance, then it can, in a sense, pierce the ex post adversarial veil. Thus, for example, even if ex post a particular tenant wants to avoid the risk of fire damage, ex ante both landlords *and* tenants may have preferred to have tenants bear this risk as the least-cost avoider. Thus, the fact that after a fire a tenant tries to avoid liability is not dispositive of what prospective tenants would contract for or,

Frank Easterbrook and Daniel Fischel have championed the "would have wanted" theory in a number of articles suggesting that "corporate law should contain the [defaults] people would have negotiated, were the costs of negotiating at arms'-length for every contingency sufficiently low."[19] Similarly, Richard Posner has argued that default rules should "economize on transaction costs by supplying standard contract terms that the parties would otherwise have to adopt by express agreement."[20] Douglas Baird and Thomas Jackson have argued that the default rules governing the debtor-creditor relationship "should provide all the parties with the type of contract that they would have agreed to if they had had the time and money to bargain over all aspects of their deal."[21] While this literature has vigorously examined what particular parties would have contracted for in particular contractual settings,[22] it has failed to question whether the "would have wanted" standard is conceptually sound.[23]

Thus, although the academy recognizes the analytic difference between

---

indeed, of what this particular tenant would have contracted for.

19. Easterbrook & Fischel, *supra* note 11 at 14–15; *see also id.* at 20–21 (default term should be "the term that the parties would have selected with full information and costless contracting"); Easterbrook & Fischel, *Corporate Control Transactions*, 91 YALE L.J. 698, 702 (1982) (default fiduciary duties are derived from a hypothetical contract, imagined by judges, between investors and managers dickering with each other free of bargaining costs); Easterbrook & Fischel, *The Proper Role of a Target's Management in Responding to a Tender Offer*, 94 HARV. L. REV. 1161, 1182 (1981) (corporate law should supply "standard form 'contracts' of the sort shareholders would be likely to choose . . . ."). Calabresi and Melamed's analysis may be an early antecedent of the "would have wanted" analysis. They argue that efficiency-minded law would establish default entitlements as the parties would allocate them in a world without transaction costs. Calabresi & Melamed, *supra* note 1, at 1093–98.

20. R. POSNER, *supra* note 2, at 372; *see also* Schwartz, *Proposals for Products Liability Reform: A Theoretical Synthesis*, 97 YALE L.J. 353, 361 (1988) (offering as default rule "the contract that most well-informed persons would have adopted if they were to bargain about the matter").

21. Baird & Jackson, *Fraudulent Conveyance Law and Its Proper Domain*, 38 VAND. L. REV. 829, 835–36 (1985); *see also* Goetz & Scott, *The Mitigation Principle: Toward a General Theory of Contractual Obligation*, 69 VA. L. REV. 967, 971 (1983) ("Ideally, the preformulated rules supplied by the state should mimic the agreements contracting parties would reach were they costlessly to bargain out each detail of the transaction.").

In Lewis v. Benedict Coal Corp., 361 U.S. 459 (1960), the Supreme Court applied this default-setting standard in deciding whether, in the absence of explicit contractual language, payments to a third-party beneficiary pension fund should be subject to setoff if the union breaches the underlying labor contract. The Court stated, "[i]t may be fair to assume that had the parties anticipated the possibility of a breach by the promisee they *would have provided* that the promisor might protect himself by such means as would be available against the promisee under a two-party contract." *Id.* at 468 (emphasis added). The Court later distinguished what parties to a collective bargaining agreement might have wanted and accordingly established a no-setoff default. *Id.* at 469.

22. *See, e.g.*, Craswell, *Contract Remedies, Renegotiation, and the Theory of Efficient Breach*, 61 S. CAL. L. REV. 629 (1988); *see also infra* text accompanying notes 136–39 (discussing judicial disagreement of Judges Easterbrook and Posner).

23. Charles Goetz and Robert Scott have written one of the more thoughtful examinations of default choice. Goetz & Scott, *The Limits of Expanded Choice: An Analysis of the Interactions Between Express and Implied Contract Terms*, 73 CALIF. L. REV. 261 (1985). Their theory of default rules is based on the idea that a large body of precedent will develop regarding the interpretation and application of a standard-form clause. Parties who contract around a standard-form clause will face the prospect that courts will interpret their contract in a manner that is inconsistent with the parties' initial intentions. Thus, parties who prefer an alternative to the standard-form may accept the latter for fear of misinterpretation.

default and immutable rules, a detailed theory of how defaults should be set has yet to be proposed. Indeed, the lack of agreement over even what to call the "default" concept is evidence of the underdeveloped state of default theory.[24] Default rules have alternatively been termed background, backstop, enabling, fallback, gap-filling, off-the-rack, opt-in, opt-out, preformulated, preset, presumptive, standby, standard-form and suppletory rules.[25]

This Article provides a theory of how courts and legislatures should set default rules. We suggest that efficient defaults would take a variety of forms that at times would diverge from the "what the parties would have contracted for" principle. To this end, we introduce the concept of "penalty defaults." Penalty defaults are designed to give at least one party to the contract an incentive to contract around the default rule and therefore to choose affirmatively the contract provision they prefer. In contrast to the received wisdom, penalty defaults are purposefully set at what the parties would not want—in order to encourage the parties to reveal information to each other or to third parties (especially the courts).

This Article also distinguishes between tailored and untailored defaults. A "tailored default" attempts to provide a contract's parties with precisely "what they would have contracted for." An "untailored default," true to its etymology, provides the parties to all contracts with a single, off-the-rack standard that in some sense represents what the majority of contracting parties would want. *The Restatement (Second) of Contracts'* approach to filling gaps, for example, provides tailored defaults that are "reasonable in the circumstances."[26] "Reasonable" defaults usually entail a tailored determination of what the individual contracting parties would have wanted because courts evaluate reasonableness in relation to the "cir-

---

24. The "default" characterization seems currently in vogue. Professor Robert Clark explains its etymology:

> For those who haven't been exposed to this jargon from the world of computers, "default rules" are the rules that a program follows in "default" of an explicit choice by the user to have some other principle apply. For example, your word processing program may set paper margins of 1 inch on all sides unless you take the trouble to learn the relevant commands and set the margins otherwise.

Clark, *Contracts, Elites, and Traditions in the Making of Corporate Law*, 89 COLUM. L. REV. (forthcoming 1989) (manuscript at 3 n.9; on file with authors).

25. *See* Bebchuk, *Limiting Contractual Freedom in Corporate Law: The Desirable Constraints on Charter Amendments*, 102 HARV. L. REV. 1820 (1989) (using "opt-out" and "opt-in"); Coffee, *The Mandatory/Enabling Balance in Corporate Law: An Essay on the Judicial Role*, 89 COLUM. L. REV. (forthcoming 1989) (using "enabling"); Easterbrook & Fischel, *supra* note 11 (using "standby," "enabling," "presets," and "fallback"); Eisenberg, *The Foundational Model of the Corporation*, 89 COLUM. L. REV. (forthcoming 1989) (using "enabling" and "suppletory" terms); Goetz & Scott, *supra* note 21, at 971 (using "preformulated"); Haddock, Macey & McChesney, *supra* note 15, at 736 (using "default" and "standard-form"); Schwab, *supra* note 1, at 237 (using "presumptive" and "off-the-rack"); Speidel, *Restatement Second: Omitted Terms and Contract Method*, 67 CORNELL L. REV. 785 n.2 (1982) (using "gap-filling").

26. RESTATEMENT (SECOND) OF CONTRACTS § 204 ("Supplying an Omitted Essential Term") (setting default for missing term to be "a term which is reasonable in the circumstances"). *See* Speidel, *supra* note 25, at 792-809.

cumstances" of the individual contracting parties.[27] In contrast, Charles Goetz and Robert Scott have proposed that courts should set untailored default rules by asking "what arrangements would *most* bargainers prefer?"[28]

This Article provides a general theory of when efficiency-minded courts or legislatures should set penalty defaults and how they should choose between tailored and untailored default rules. Some common-law and statutory defaults are flatly at odds with the "would have wanted" principle. Although this Article does not make the full-blown positivist claim that current default rules are efficient, it does offer a more complete explanation of the current diversity of defaults.

An essential component of our theory of default rules is our explicit consideration of the sources of contractual incompleteness. We distinguish between two basic reasons for incompleteness.[29] Scholars have primarily attributed incompleteness to the costs of contracting. Contracts may be incomplete because the transaction costs of explicitly contracting for a given contingency are greater than the benefits.[30] These transaction costs may

27. For example, U.C.C. § 2-306, governing output and requirement contracts, establishes as a default that: In the absence of a stated estimate, "no quantity unreasonably disproportionate . . . to any normal or otherwise comparable prior output or requirements may be tendered or demanded." U.C.C. § 2-306(1) (1976). In determining reasonableness, courts are expressly asked by the U.C.C. to look at specific characteristics of the contracting parties. For example, "[a] shut-down by a requirements buyer for lack of orders might be permissible when a shut-down merely to curtail losses would not." U.C.C. § 2-306(1) comment 2 (1976).

28. Goetz & Scott, *supra* note 21, at 971 (emphasis in original).

29. There are two distinct ways for a contract to be incomplete. First, a contract may fail to specify the parties' duties for specific future contingencies. For example, a contract for the construction of a third floor to a house may not state the parties' respective rights and responsibilities should the entire house burn down before construction is started. Since construction of a third floor is impossible (without the lower two floors), the contract does not cover the contingency of the house burning down.

The second form of contractual incompleteness is more subtle. A contract may also be incomplete in that it is insensitive to relevant future contingencies. Under this second form of contractual incompleteness, parties' duties are fully specified, but the contracts are incomplete because those specified duties are not tailored to economically relevant future events. *See* K. Spier, Incomplete Contracts in a Model with Adverse Selection and Exogenous Costs of Enforcement (Dec. 1988) (unpublished manuscript on file with authors) (discussing causes for such incompleteness). For example, consider a contract that simply obligates one party to construct a garage adjacent to a house. On the face this contract imposes a duty to build a garage whether or not the adjacent house burns down before construction of the garage is complete. The contract is incomplete in this second sense, however, because the duty to build a garage is not sufficiently dependent on future contingencies. If the adjacent house burns down, the parties probably would want to adjust the terms of contract. Such contracts we call insufficiently state-contingent.

Courts recognize the first form of incompleteness and know they must decide how to fill the gap. For instance, non-enforcement is one way courts can fill the gap. Courts seldomly recognize the second form of contractual incompleteness. That is, they are generally unwilling to alter (they strictly enforce) the terms of a contract that is insufficiently state-contingent. The main exception to strict enforcement is the doctrine of impossibility (or economic impracticability) with which courts sometimes refuse enforcement when performance, although literally possible, is not ex post efficient. *See* Posner & Rosenfield, *Impossibility and Related Doctrines in Contract Law: An Economic Analysis*, 6 J. LEGAL STUD. 83, 87 (1977) (discussing legal contours of impossibility doctrine).

30. *See* O. WILLIAMSON, THE ECONOMIC INSTITUTIONS OF CAPITALISM 70 (1985); MacNeil, *Contracts: Adjustment of Long-Term Economic Relations Under Classical, Neoclassical and Relational Contract Law*, 72 NW. U.L. REV. 854, 871-73 (1978); Shavell, *Damage Measures for Breach*

include legal fees, negotiation costs, drafting and printing costs, the costs of researching the effects and probability of a contingency, and the costs to the parties and the courts of verifying whether a contingency occurred. Rational parties will weigh these costs against the benefits of contractually addressing a particular contingency. If either the magnitude or the probability of a contingency is sufficiently low, a contract may be insensitive to that contingency even if transaction costs are quite low.

The "would have wanted" approach to gap filling is a natural outgrowth of the transaction cost explanation of contractual incompleteness. Lawmakers can minimize the costs of contracting by choosing the default that most parties would have wanted. If there are transaction costs of explicitly contracting on a contingency, the parties may prefer to leave the contract incomplete. Indeed, as transaction costs increase, so does the parties' willingness to accept a default that is not exactly what they would have contracted for. Scholars who attribute contractual incompleteness to transaction costs are naturally drawn toward choosing defaults that the majority of contracting parties "would have wanted" because these majoritarian defaults seem to minimize the costs of contracting.

We show, however, that this majoritarian "would have wanted" approach to default selection is, for several reasons, incomplete. First, the majoritarian approach fails to account for the possibly disparate costs of contracting and of failing to contract around different defaults.[31] For example, if the majority is more likely to contract around the minority's preferred default rule (than the minority is to contract around the majority's rule), then choosing the minority's default may lead to a larger set of efficient contracts. Second, the received wisdom provides little guidance about how tailored or particularized the "would have wanted" analysis should be.[32] Finally, the very costs of ex ante bargaining may encourage parties to inefficiently shift the process of gap filling to ex post court determination.[33] If it is costly for the courts to determine what the parties would have wanted, it may be efficient to choose a default rule that induces the parties to contract explicitly. In other words, penalty defaults are appropriate when it is cheaper for the parties to negotiate a term ex ante than for the courts to estimate ex post what the parties would have wanted. Courts, which are publicly subsidized, should give parties incentives to negotiate ex ante by penalizing them for inefficient gaps.

---

of Contract, 11 BELL J. ECON. 466, 468 (1980) ("[B]ecause of the costs involved in enumerating and bargaining over contractual obligations under the full range of relevant contingencies, it is normally impractical to make contracts which approach completeness.").

31. *See infra* Section II.

32. *Id.*

33. Jeffrey Gordon argues that the "would have wanted" approach is also flawed because it shifts risks to the ex ante least-cost avoider but, as applied by most courts, does not in fact compensate the ex post risk bearer. Gordon, *supra* note 13, at 61 (problem with hypothetical bargain argument, "like other Kaldor-Hicks arguments, is that it doesn't guarantee that each party will in fact receive a bigger slice, or a slice of the right size." (citation omitted)).

This Article also proposes a second source of contractual incompleteness that is the focus of much of our analysis. We refer to this source of incompleteness as strategic.[34] One party might strategically withhold information that would increase the total gains from contracting (the "size of the pie") in order to increase her private share of the gains from contracting (her "share of the pie"). By attempting to contract around a certain default, one party might reveal information to the other party that affects how the contractual pie is split. Thus, for example, the more informed party may prefer to have inefficient precaution rather than pay a higher price for the good.[35] While analysts have previously explained incomplete contracting solely in terms of the costs of writing additional provisions, we argue that contractual gaps can also result from strategic behavior by relatively informed parties. By changing the default rules of the game, lawmakers can importantly reduce the opportunities for this rent-seeking, strategic behavior.[36] In particular, the possibility of strategic incompleteness leads us to suggest that efficiency-minded lawmakers should sometimes choose penalty defaults that induce knowledgeable parties to reveal information by contracting around the default penalty. The strategic behavior of the parties in forming the contract can justify strategic contractual interpretations by courts.[37]

Our analysis therefore moves beyond the received wisdom that default rules should simply be what the majority of contracting parties would have wanted. In choosing among default rules, lawmakers should be sensitive to the costs of contracting around, and the costs of failing to contract around, particular defaults. We show that different defaults may lead to different degrees of "separating" and "pooling."[38] In "separating" equilibria, the different types of contracting parties, by bearing the costs of contracting around unwanted defaults, separate themselves into distinct

---

34. See *infra* Section II for examples of strategic incompleteness. A third reason for contractual incompleteness is that some contingencies may simply be unforeseen by all contracting parties. In this case, the default rule will not affect the actions of the parties since by definition they do not consider the contingency in deciding what to do. There will normally be no reason to consider the rule's ex ante effect because it will have none.

There is one caveat to this statement: Behavior may be affected if parties are aware that unforeseen contingencies exist but are unable to ascertain the nature of these contingencies. For example, parties who are aware that a variety of unforeseen contingencies may affect the price at which they should transact may choose a contract that includes a reasonable price clause rather than fixing a price or a price rule as a function of foreseen contingencies. In this way the price can respond to unforeseen contingencies. See D. Kreps, Static Choice in the Presence of Unforeseen Contingencies (Aug. 1988) (unpublished manuscript on file with authors) for a utility-theoretic characterization of behavior in the presence of unforeseen contingencies. The choice of optimal defaults for such unforeseen contingencies is beyond the scope of this article. For a discussion of the appropriate default, see Posner & Rosenfield, *supra* note 29.

35. *See* K. Spier, *supra* note 29 (formalizing this strategic reluctance to reveal information).

36. *See infra* Section I-C.

37. Inefficient strategic behavior will often induce efficiency-promoting counterstrategies by other economic actors. *See* Easterbrook, *Predatory Strategies and Counterstrategies*, 48 U. CHI. L. REV. 263 (1981).

38. *See infra* text accompanying notes 113-16.

contractual relationships. In "pooling" equilibria, different types of contracting parties fail to contract around defaults, thus avoiding transaction costs but bearing the inefficiencies of the substantive default provisions.

In contrast to the majoritarian analysis, our analysis shows that it may be efficient to choose a rule that a majority of people actually disfavor. To set defaults efficiently, lawmakers must not only know what contracting parties want, but how many are likely to get it and at what cost. We recommend a greater and more explicit legal sensitivity toward the ways in which different defaults will affect the resulting contractual "equilibrium."[39]

Finally, before deciding how to fill gaps, courts must decide whether the contract even has a gap. In other words, courts must decide whether the contract already allocates a particular risk or duty. We show that this issue of whether a gap exists is identical to the issue of what is sufficient to contract around a particular default.[40] While the received wisdom is that lawmakers should minimize the costs of contracting around default rules,[41] we suggest that efficiency-minded courts and legislatures may want to intentionally increase these transaction costs to discourage parties from contracting around certain defaults.

The Article has three sections. Section I discusses the possible efficiency of penalty defaults. Section II embeds penalty defaults in a more general model of default choice, a model which suggests when penalty, tailored, or untailored defaults will be efficient. Section III then develops a theory of gap definition that determines what should be sufficient to contract around a given default.

I. Penalty Default Rules

A. *The Zero-Quantity Default*

The diversity of default standards can even be seen in contrasting the law's treatment of the two most basic contractual terms: price and quantity. Although price and quantity are probably the two most essential issues on which to reach agreement, the U.C.C. establishes radically different defaults. If the parties leave out the price, the U.C.C. fills the gap with "a reasonable price."[42] If the parties leave out the quantity, the

39. We will sometimes find it useful to distinguish between situations in which the parties negotiate in ignorance of the default rule and situations in which the parties negotiate in the shadow of the default rule. In the former case, the parties do not know how the courts will decide if the contingency in question occurs, while in the latter case the parties know the legal default (but may not know certain information about the other party). *See infra* text accompanying notes 58-60.

40. *See infra* Section III.

41. *See* Easterbrook & Fischel, *supra* note 11, at 21-30.

42. U.C.C. § 2-305(1) reads: "The parties if they so intend can conclude a contract for sale even though the price is not settled. In such a case the price is a reasonable price at the time for delivery. . . ." U.C.C. § 2-305(1) (1976).

U.C.C. refuses to enforce the contract.[43] In essence, the U.C.C. mandates that the default quantity should be zero.

How can this be? The U.C.C.'s reasonable-price standard can be partly reconciled with the received wisdom that defaults should be set at what the parties would have contracted for.[44] But why doesn't the U.C.C. treat a missing quantity term analogously by filling the gap with the reasonable quantity that the parties would have have wanted? Obviously, the parties would not have gone to the expense of contracting with the intention that nothing be exchanged.

We suggest that the zero-quantity default cannot be explained by a "what the parties would have wanted" principle. Instead, a rationale for the rule can be found by comparing the cost of ex ante contracting to the cost of ex post litigation. The zero-quantity rule can be justified because it is cheaper for the parties to establish the quantity term beforehand than for the courts to determine after the fact what the parties would have wanted.

It is not systematically easier for parties to figure out the quantity than the price ex ante, but it is systematically harder for the courts to figure out the quantity than the price ex post. To estimate a reasonable price, courts can largely rely on market information of the type "How much were rutabagas selling for on July 3?"[45] But to estimate a reasonable quantity, courts would need to undertake a more costly analysis of the individual litigants of the type "How much did the buyer and seller value the marginal rutabagas?"

---

43. U.C.C. § 2-201 states that a "contract . . . is not enforceable under this [provision] beyond the quantity of goods shown. . . " U.C.C. § 2-201(1) (1976). The official comment adds that "[t]he only term which must appear is the quantity term which need not be accurately stated but recovery is limited to the amount stated." U.C.C. § 2-201(1) (official comment) (1978). In some cases, lack of a quantity term will merely be evidence that the parties did not have a meeting of the minds. But even if there are sufficient objective indicia of an intent to contract (and even if the statute of frauds is not raised as an affirmative defense), courts may refuse to enforce the contract because it is indefinite. *See* Jessen Bros. v. Ashland Recreation Ass'n., 204 Neb. 19, 281 N.W.2d 210 (1979) (contract for sod unenforceable for lack of specific quantity term); Burke v. Campbell, 258 Mass. 153, 154 N.E. 759 (1927) (contract unenforceable in part because contract did not state how much stock defendant would receive in exchange for financing corporation); King v. Krischer Mfg. Co., 220 A.D. 584, 222 N.Y.S. 66 (1927) (contract unenforceable because "a quantity of merchandise" too indefinite).

44. A simple "what parties would have wanted" approach has trouble explaining why the parties would choose reasonable price at time of delivery instead of at the time of contracting. There is no reason to think that parties would systematically prefer one risk allocation to the other. However, one can determine the efficient default rule by asking the question, "why didn't the parties explicitly contract for price?" Those parties who wish to allocate the risk of cost fluctuations to the seller will most likely contract for a price at the time of contracting. Those who wish to allocate the risk to the buyer will attempt to contract for a time-of-delivery, cost-based price. Such a clause may be costly to write into the contract explicitly because of the difficulty in measuring the seller's cost exactly. The parties may instead prefer to rely on reaching an agreement in the shadow of the court's reasonable-price default rule.

45. This analysis suggests that courts would be less likely to enforce contracts in "thin" markets in which the market price is not readily ascertainable. *See* Haddock, McChesney & Spiegel, *An Ordinary Economic Rationale for Extraordinary Legal Sanctions*, 78 CALIF. L. REV. (forthcoming 1990) (discussing how efficient legal rules will turn on "thickness" of market).

The U.C.C.'s zero-quantity default is what we term a "penalty default." Because ex ante neither party would want a zero-quantity contract, such a rule penalizes the parties should they fail to affirmatively specify their desired quantity. Because the non-enforcement default potentially penalizes both parties, it encourages both of them to include a quantity term.[46]

B. *Toward a More General Theory of Penalty Defaults*

Penalty defaults, by definition, give at least one party to the contract an incentive to contract around the default. From an efficiency perspective, penalty default rules can be justified as a way to encourage the production of information.[47] The very process of "contracting around" can reveal information to parties inside or outside the contract. Penalty defaults may be justified as 1) giving both contracting parties incentives to reveal information to third parties, especially courts,[48] or 2) giving a more informed contracting party incentives to reveal information to a less informed party.

The zero-quantity default, for instance, gives both contracting parties incentives to reveal their contractual intentions when it would be costly for a court to discover that information ex post. This justification—that ex ante contracting can be cheaper than ex post litigation—can also explain the common law's broader rule that "for a contract to be binding the terms of the contract must be reasonably certain and definite."[49] Similarly, this rationale can explain corporate statutes that give incorporators an incentive to affirmatively declare the number of authorized shares, the address of the corporation for legal process and, indeed, the state of incor-

46. Even if the judicial system were not subsidized, the zero-quantity default might be justified on parentalistic concerns. For example, if private parties are uninformed or systematically underestimate the costs of ex post judicial determination of a "reasonable" quantity, it might be in society's interests to dissuade parties from mistakenly failing to negotiate the contract quantity ex ante.

This rationale for this penalty default depends on the assumption that the private parties pay less than the full costs of their ex post litigation. The parties may lower their transaction costs by shifting the privately funded ex ante negotiations to publicly subsidized ex post litigation. If parties fully internalized ex post litigation costs, at first cut they should be able to choose the cheaper type of negotiation.

47. In encouraging the revelation of information, lawmakers should be sensitive to the influence that defaults can have on the incentives for private parties to acquire information in the first place. *See infra* notes 93-94 and accompanying text.

48. Penalty defaults may be established to provide information to third parties other than the courts. For example, in corporate law certain alterations to the default corporate governance can be accomplished through a by-law amendment, while other alterations can only be made by changing the articles of incorporation. *See infra* note 148 and accompanying text. Requiring certain amendments in the articles of incorporation reveals information to interested third parties, such as creditors, because these articles are publicly filed with the Secretary of State. *See, e.g.*, REVISED MODEL BUSINESS CORP. ACT ANN. § 2.01 (1987) (requiring filing of articles of incorporation).

49. Steinberg v. Chicago Medical School, 41 Ill. App. 3d 804, 807, 354 N.E.2d 586, 589 (1976); *see also* Parks v. Atlanta News Agency, 115 Ga. App. 842, 156 S.E.2d 137 (1967); 1 A. CORBIN, CORBIN ON CONTRACTS § 95 (1952 & Supp. 1989); 1 S. WILLISTON, A TREATISE ON THE LAW OF CONTRACTS § 37 (3d ed. 1957 & Supp. 1978).

poration.[50] Statutes that refuse to enforce corporate charters without these provisions create incentives similar to those created by the common law's refusal to enforce vague or indefinite contracts. In both cases, the parties can make these contractual choices more efficiently ex ante.

Lawmakers should select the rule that deters inefficient gaps at the least social cost. When the rationale is to provide information to the courts, the non-enforcement default is likely to be efficient. Non-enforcement defaults are likely to provide least-cost deterrence because they are inexpensive to enforce and give each party incentives to contract around the rule. It might seem that a penalty default set solely against one side of a contract would be sufficient to get both sides to reveal information. For example, a penalty default that makes the seller sell at one-tenth the market price would certainly encourage sellers to affirmatively fill any price gaps. But one side's penalty may be the other side's windfall. One-sided penalties can create incentives for opportunism.[51] The non-penalized buyer in the above example would have incentives to induce sellers to enter indefinite contracts in order to extract the penalty rent.[52] By taking each party back to her ex ante welfare, the non-enforcement default eliminates this potential for opportunism.

In contrast, when the rationale is to inform the relatively uninformed contracting party, the penalty default should be against the relatively informed party.[53] This is especially true when the uninformed party is also uninformed about the default rule itself. If the uninformed party does not know that there is a penalty default, she will have no opportunistic incentives.

In some situations it is reasonable to expect one party to the contract to be systematically informed about the default rule and the probability of the relevant contingency arising. If one side is repeatedly in the relevant contractual setting while the other side rarely is, it is a sensible presumption that the former is better informed than the latter. Consider, for example, the treatment of real estate brokerage commissions when a buyer breaches a purchase contract. Such contracts typically include a clause which obligates the purchaser to forfeit some given amount of "earnest" money if she breaches the agreement. How should the earnest money be

50. *See* REVISED MODEL BUSINESS CORP. ACT ANN. § 2.02 (1987).

51. Posner defines opportunism (in relation to the common-law contractual duty to act in good faith) as "taking advantage of the vulnerability of the other party to a contract . . . that is due to the sequential character of performance." R. POSNER, *supra* note 2, at 81.

52. Similar opportunistic incentives have been analyzed in other areas of contract law. *See, e.g.*, Clarkson, Miller & Muris, *Liquidated Damages Versus Penalties: Sense or Nonsense?*, 1978 WIS. L. REV. 351 (non-enforcement of penalty clauses prevents opportunistic breach inducement); Goetz & Scott, *supra* note 15, at 586 (mitigation requirement eliminates incentive for opportunism by obligee in case of breach). More generally, the inefficiency of excessive penalties has been detailed in the economics-of-crime literature. *See, e.g.*, R. POSNER, *supra* note 2, at 205–12; Becker, *Crime and Punishment: An Economic Approach*, 76 J. POL. ECON. 169 (1968).

53. *See infra* text accompanying notes 57–73.

split between the seller and the broker if their agency contract does not address this contingency? Some courts have adopted a "what the parties would have wanted" approach and have awarded all the earnest money to the seller.[54] We agree with this outcome, but for different reasons.[55] The real estate broker will more likely be informed about the default rule than the seller. Indeed, the seller may not even consider the issue of how to split the earnest money in case of default.[56] Therefore, if the efficient contract would allocate some of the earnest money to the seller, the default rule should be set against the broker to induce her to raise the issue. Otherwise, if the default rule is set to favor the broker, a seller may not raise the issue, and the broker will be happy to take advantage of the seller's ignorance. By setting the default rule in favor of the uninformed party, the courts induce the informed party to reveal information, and, consequently, the efficient contract results.

Although social welfare may be enhanced by forcing parties to reveal information to a subsidized judicial system, it is more problematic to understand why society would have an efficiency interest in inducing a relatively informed party to a transaction to reveal information to the relatively uninformed party. After all, if revealing information is efficient because it increases the value created by the contract, one might initially expect that the informed party will have a sufficient private incentive to reveal information—the incentive of splitting a bigger pie. This argument ignores the possibility, however, that revealing information might simultaneously increase the total size of the pie and decrease the share of the pie that the relatively informed party receives. If the "share-of-the-pie effect" dominates the "size-of-the-pie effect," informed parties might rationally choose to withhold relevant information.[57]

Parties may behave strategically not only because they have superior

---

54. *See, e.g.*, Dennis Reed, Ltd. v. Goody, 2 K.B. 277 (1950); *see also* J. DUKEMINIER & J. KRIER, PROPERTY 554-55 (2d ed. 1988) (discussing evolution of common-law rule).

55. Earnest money is used to force the purchaser to internalize the cost to the seller of taking the property off the market during the time from the signing of the sale agreement to the closing or, in this case, the breach. Since these costs are largely incurred by the seller, she should receive the compensation. Furthermore, the seller may wish to give the broker incentives to find a buyer who will not default. Allowing the broker to share in the earnest money will lower or eliminate this incentive. One reason, however, that the broker and the seller would ex ante contract for the broker to receive some of the earnest money is that the breach by the initial buyer may necessitate a quick sale which may cause the seller to lower the selling price. This, in turn, would lower the broker's commission. Thus, a "what the parties would have wanted" approach might yield a default in which a risk-averse broker receives a portion of the earnest money.

56. Of course, people hire lawyers in part to ascertain the relevant negotiation issues, contingencies, and default rules. Our argument is therefore most applicable in contractual settings in which lawyers are not employed.

57. Withholding socially valuable private information to obtain private gains is common. Companies may withhold information about innovations from competitors to increase profits; car buyers may withhold information about particular options or accessories that they value if this information signals to car dealers a greater willingness to pay for the underlying automobile; and professional athletes may withhold information about injuries to increase their salaries, even though as a result their team may inefficiently hire reserves.

information about the default, but also because they have superior information about other aspects of the contract. We suggest that a party who knows that a particular default rule is inefficient may choose not to negotiate to change it. The knowledgeable party may not wish to reveal her information in negotiations if the information would give a bargaining advantage to the other side.

How can it be that by increasing the total gains from contracting (the size-of-the-pie effect) the informed party can end up with a smaller share of the gains (the share-of-the-pie effect)?[58] This Article demonstrates how relatively informed parties can sometimes benefit by strategically withholding information that, if revealed, would increase the size of the pie. A knowledgeable buyer, for example, may prefer to remain indistinguishable from what the seller wrongly perceives to be the class of similarly situated buyers. By blending in with the larger class of contractors, a buyer or a seller may receive a cross-subsidized price because the other side will bargain as if she is dealing with the average member of the class. A knowledgeable party may prefer to remain in this inefficient, but cross-subsidized, contractual pool rather than move to an efficient, but unsubsidized, pool. If contracting around the default sufficiently reduces this cross-subsidization, the share-of-the-pie effect can exceed the size-of-the-pie effect because the informed party's share of the default pie was in a sense being artificially cross-subsidized by other members of the contractual class. Under this scenario, withholding information appears as a kind of rent-seeking[59] in which the informed party foregoes the additional value attending the revealed information to get a larger piece of the contractual pie.[60]

58. If, under a given set of default rules, a seller wants to sell a sweater that she values at $50 to a buyer who values it at $150, then without contracting around any of the defaults the parties' agreement will create $100 of value. The total gain from contracting, in other words, will be $100. The parties will split this gain in value between themselves by bargaining for a price between $50 and $150. Suppose, however, that the buyer (and only the buyer) has information that would make the sweater worth $200 to him if the seller would take on a duty that is outside of the default provisions and that would cost the seller $10. The total gains from this non-default exchange would be $140 ($200 - $50 - $10). How could the buyer lose by revealing information that increased the size of the pie by $40? If the parties accept the default provisions and negotiate a $100 price (implying that each party receives a $50 share of the total gains), how can it be that revealing the value-enhancing information—by contracting for the non-default duty—would reduce the buyer's share to less than $50 (implying that the negotiated price would exceed $150 and that the seller's share would exceed $90)?

59. Most broadly, rent-seeking "arises wherever parties have an incentive to expend real resources to capture something of value." V. GOLDBERG, READINGS IN THE ECONOMICS OF CONTRACT LAW 49 (1989). Strategic withholding represents a species of rent-seeking because the relatively informed party commits the real resources of an inefficient contract to capture the cross-subsidization.

60. An equity-minded court might encourage information revelation to foster an equitable distribution of the gains from contracting, even if doing so reduces those gains.

C. *Penalty Defaults in Action*

1. *Uncompensated Damages in* Hadley v. Baxendale

An example of how a penalty default can restrict rent-seeking behavior can be seen in the venerable case, *Hadley v. Baxendale*.[61] In *Hadley* a miller in Gloucester contracted with a carrier to have a broken crank shaft transported to Greenwich. The shipment was delayed, and the miller sued the carrier for consequential damages of the profits lost while the mill was inoperative. The court, holding that only foreseeable consequential damages should be awarded, reversed a damage award and remanded for a new trial.[62]

The holding in *Hadley* operates as a penalty default. The miller could have informed the carrier of the potential consequential damages and contracted for full damage insurance.[63] The *Hadley* default of denying unforeseeable damages may not be consistent with what fully informed parties would have wanted. The miller's consequential damages were real and the carrier may have been the more efficient bearer of this risk. As a general matter, millers may want carriers to compensate them for consequential damages that carriers can prevent at lower cost.[64] The default can instead be understood as a purposeful inducement to the miller as the more informed party to reveal that information to the carrier. Informing the carrier creates value because if the carrier foresees the loss, he will be able to prevent it more efficiently.[65] At the same time, however, revealing

61. 9 Ex. 341, 156 Eng. Rep. 145 (1854). William Bishop has also discussed how the *Hadley* rule could promote efficient revelation of information. *See* Bishop, *The Contract-Tort Boundary and the Economics of Insurance*, 12 J. LEGAL STUD. 241, 254 (1983); L. Bebchuk & S. Shavell, Information and the Scope of Liability for Unusual Damages from Breach of Contract, (March 1983) (unpublished manuscript on file with authors).

62. *Hadley*, 9 Ex. at 356, 156 Eng. Rep. at 151–52.

63. There is some evidence that the miller in fact attempted to inform the carrier of the probable damages. Thus, it may be difficult for parties to contract around the *Hadley* default. For a discussion of how courts can alter the mutability of a default rule by varying the requirements for contracting around it, see *infra* Section III.

64. The efficient risk-sharing agreement between symmetrically-informed shippers (e.g., the miller in this case) and carriers will depend upon their relative attitudes toward risk, the ability of the carrier to prevent the damages, and the ability of the shipper to mitigate damages in case of breach.

Richard Posner and Richard Epstein argue that in many situations there are actions the shipper could take to reduce consequential damages. *See* R. POSNER, *supra* note 2, at 114–15; Epstein, *Beyond Foreseeability: Consequential Damages in the Law of Contract*, 18 J. LEGAL STUD. 105, 121–25 (1989). In such situations the parties would choose to share consequential damages through appropriate liquidated damage clauses. *See* Cooter, *Unity in Tort, Contract, and Property: The Model of Precaution*, 73 CALIF. L. REV. 1, 15 (1985). In Evra Corp. v. Swiss Bank Corp., 673 F.2d 951, 955–59 (7th Cir. 1982), Judge Posner attempts to determine what insurance arrangement the parties would have contracted for. Epstein prefers a less tailored rule that does not require the courts to analyze the relative abilities of both sides to reduce damages.

We proceed under the assumptions that the miller had no economically practical means of reducing the losses from delay (e.g., keeping a spare crankshaft in inventory would have been too expensive) and that both parties were risk-neutral. Under these assumptions the efficient contract is for the carrier who is the least-cost avoider to bear the costs of delay.

65. This is one lesson from Goetz and Scott's analysis of the anxious alumnus: A bus company driving Dean Smith to the Final Four would probably take more efficient precautions if it were

the information to the carrier will undoubtedly increase the price of shipping. Nonetheless, so long as transaction costs are not prohibitive, a miller with high consequential damages will gain from revealing this information and contracting for greater insurance from the carrier because the carrier is the least-cost avoider.

This is not to say that there could not be an equally efficient market response if *Hadley* had gone the other way. If the default required carriers to compensate for unforeseeable consequential damages, low-damage millers would have the incentive to raise the issue of consequential damages. In a competitive industry, the uninformed carrier, in effect, assumes she is facing an average-damage miller and charges a price accordingly. The market price will reflect the expected cost of insuring high-damage millers. A low-damage miller will want to contract for less-than-average insurance and, therefore, a lower price. But the gains from contracting around the default may be insignificant if the proportion of millers with high damages is small. Furthermore, it may be very difficult for a low-damage miller to determine how much of the price is an implicit insurance premium for millers with higher damages.

Thus, there may be situations in which the low-damage millers fail to contract for the low-insurance/low-price contract. In the resulting equilibrium, carriers may charge a price representing their average cost of serving both high- and low-damage millers and take an average amount of precaution (which will be relatively low if there are relatively few high-damage millers).[66] Richard Posner suggests a similar result: If the damage default changed so that manufacturers of photographic film were liable for unforeseen consequential damages, "[t]he manufacturer of the film will probably take no additional precautions . . . because he cannot identify the films whose loss would be extremely costly, and unless there are many of [the high-damage photographers] it may not pay to take additional precautions on *all* the films he develops."[67] Section II formalizes this discussion of *Hadley* to show that low-damage millers might fail to contract around a default that awarded unforeseeable damages while high-damage millers will contract around the *Hadley* rule.[68]

---

warned of how large Dean Smith's consequential damages would be were he to miss the game. Goetz & Scott, *supra* note 15, at 578.

66. The uninformed parties, the carriers, could simply exclude unforeseeable consequential damages from their standard-form contract (thereby contracting around the default at very low cost), and high-damage millers, if they want insurance, could simply contract around the contract default. In other words, if the legal default rule is inefficient, contracting parties may have ways of supplanting it with a default of their own. (This point can also be made with regard to Posner's story about film development; *see infra* text accompanying note 67.) The limits to this contractual response to the contra-*Hadley* default are discussed *infra* notes 70–71 and text accompanying notes 69–71.

67. R. Posner, *supra* note 2, at 114 (emphasis in original).

68. In the economics literature several articles examine situations in which asymmetric information induces inefficient contracting. *See, e.g.*, Akerlof, *The Market for "Lemons": Quality Uncertainty and the Market Mechanism*, 84 Q.J. Econ. 488 (1970); Myerson, *Mechanism Design by an Informed Principal*, 51 Econometrica 1767 (1983).

It is important to consider another channel for information revelation. The uninformed party, the carrier, may attempt to learn the expected damages of the informed parties, the millers, by offering a menu of insurance contracts.[69] The millers might then be induced to self-select the insurance contract that is optimal for their expected damages.[70] The problem faced by uninformed parties trying to induce information revelation, however, is that in many situations the necessary menu is more complicated than in the common carrier example. Devising a menu that induces information revelation may require a great deal of sophistication by the uninformed party and may entail large transaction costs.[71]

The main lesson to draw from our discussion of *Hadley* is that there may be strategic reasons for parties' choosing not to reveal information. If the default rule awarded all consequential damages, to be sure, the low-damage millers would want to distinguish themselves from the high-damage millers. But the high-damage millers may intentionally choose to withhold information that would make their contracts more efficient. An informed party may not realize the full social value of revealing the information and, hence, her private benefits from revealing may diverge from the social benefits of having the information revealed. As elaborated below, by not distinguishing themselves, informed parties may be able to free-ride on the lower-cost qualities of others and thereby contract at a subsidized price. To counteract this strategic behavior, courts should choose defaults that are different from what the parties would have wanted.

Easterbrook and Fischel have argued that courts should choose defaults that "the parties would have selected with full information and costless contracting."[72] Their standard fittingly tracks the two reasons for contractual incompleteness that we have identified—strategic withholding and transaction costs. In a sense, their standard seeks what the parties would have selected if there were no barriers to contractual completeness.[73] We disagree, however, with their conclusion that courts should choose the default that the parties would have selected with "full information." When

69. *See supra* note 66.

70. This is in fact done by many common carriers. The Federal Express standard contract, for example, limits consequential damages to $100 but permits the shipper to buy greater insurance at stated rates. *See* Epstein, *supra* note 64, at 120.

71. *See, e.g., infra* text accompanying note 81 (consumers trying to ascertain information about dealer's expected lost-profit damages may encounter significant resistance in devising menu that encourages dealers to reveal information). For an example of a menu that would require large transaction costs and sophistication on the part of the uninformed party, see Note, *Imperfect Information, The Pricing Mechanism, and Products Liability*, 88 COLUM. L. REV. 1057 (1988) (suggesting that manufacturers should be required to provide menus of warranties so that consumers can judge quality and safety of products)

72. Easterbrook & Fischel, *supra* note 11, at 20-21.

73. Full information by both parties would eliminate any opportunity for strategically withholding information, and costless contracting obviously eliminates transactions costs as an impediment to complete contracting.

relatively informed parties strategically withhold information, courts, to promote information revelation, should choose a default that the informed party does not want. Imposing ex post what completely informed parties would have contracted for may not result in the ex ante revelation necessary for efficient reliance or precaution. For example, we have shown that in *Hadley* fully informed parties may have wanted the carrier to be fully liable for consequential damages. Yet choosing full liability as the damage default may lead carriers to invest suboptimally in accident prevention. *Hadley* is inconsistent with a full-information, "what the parties would have wanted" standard. Instead, *Hadley* penalizes high-damage millers for withholding information that would allow carriers to take efficient precautions.

2. *Goldberg's Solution to the Lost-Profits Puzzle*

Victor Goldberg's analysis of the lost-volume retail seller[74] comports with our discussion of penalty defaults. Goldberg examines what a retailer's damages should be when a customer breaches a contract to buy. The U.C.C. mandates, and other commentators have suggested, that the retailer should receive the lost profits on the good.[75] Goldberg's own analysis suggests that the lost profits approximate the real loss borne by the retailer. But Goldberg instead proposes that courts deny "recovery for lost profits in the absence of explicit contract language to the contrary."[76] In other words, Goldberg proposes that the default damages be zero.

His rationale parallels our rationale for penalty defaults. The zero-damage default is intended to give retailers an incentive to come forward and contract for a nonrefundable deposit or for a liquidated damages clause. Again, the process of contracting around the default apprises the customer of her potential liability. A sales contract gives the consumer an option either to purchase the product or to pay damages. Goldberg's zero-damage default encourages retailers to inform consumers about the price of exercising the option to breach. Consumers will therefore internalize the cost to the retailer of breach and more efficiently take precautions against breach.[77] Furthermore, the consumer may not know the default rule for breach.[78] If a consumer is unaware that the default rule makes

74. Goldberg, *An Economic Analysis of the Lost-Volume Retail Seller*, 57 S. CAL. L. REV. 283 (1984).

75. *See* U.C.C. § 2-708(2) (1976); Goetz & Scott, *Measuring Sellers' Damages: The Lost-Profits Puzzle*, 31 STAN. L. REV. 323, 323 (1979); Speidel & Clay, *Seller's Recovery of Overhead Under UCC Section 2-708(2): Economic Cost Theory and Contract Remedial Policy*, 57 CORNELL L. REV. 681, 694 (1972).

76. Goldberg, *supra* note 74, at 291.

77. In this situation the uninformed party, the consumer, probably could not offer a menu of contracts to the informed retailer to induce revelation of the markup. *See supra* text accompanying notes 69-71. The information requirements, complexity, and transaction costs of such a scheme would be prohibitive.

78. This is similar to our earlier discussion of what the real estate default rule should be for

her liable for lost profits, the seller will have little incentive to bargain about damages.[79] Consumer liability for lost profits can lead to efficient breach and precaution only if consumers know the amount of their liability. The zero-damages penalty default encourages the retailer to reveal her markup.[80]

Although consumers would value this markup information, retailers still have incentives to withhold it.[81] By revealing their profits, retailers may simultaneously reduce their bargaining power. Even Goldberg's penalty default, therefore, could be too weak to induce information disclosure. Retailers may sometimes prefer to take their chances with zero damages for breach rather than disclose a high markup. If the zero-damage penalty default is insufficient to induce information revelation, a stiffer penalty may be necessary to induce the parties to contract for liquidated damages.[82]

3. *Unilateral Defaults as Penalties: The Perverse Incentives of* Lefkowitz

Some contractual rules establish defaults that individual parties may unilaterally change. Consider, for example, the legal effect of offers. The U.C.C.'s mandate that an offer intends any reasonable form of acceptance is a unilateral default that obtains "unless otherwise unambiguously indicated."[83] Consistent with the preceeding analysis, lawmakers may want to set penalty defaults that encourage offerors to reveal information to offerees. Thus, courts may want to choose the default that the offeror does not want.

In *Lefkowitz v. Great Minneapolis Surplus Store, Inc.*,[84] the Minnesota Supreme Court rejected the plaintiff's claim that the defendant, a retailer, had failed to honor two advertised offers that the plaintiff had accepted.[85] In the first offer the defendant had advertised the sale of three

---

splitting earnest money between the seller and the broker when a buyer breaches a purchase contract. *See supra* text accompanying notes 54-56.

79. If the seller raises the issue of damages, thereby revealing her markup, consumers can more efficiently take precautions to avoid breach. Since the consumer will learn she is liable for damages, however, she will insist on a lower price for the good.

80. Similarly, the common-law doctrine of construing ambiguities in contracts against the drafter, *see* I. MACNEIL, *supra* note 11, at 372, can be viewed as a penalty default. The doctrine is not based on the judgment that the parties would have wanted the anti-drafter provision, but that such a penalty encourages drafters to draft more precise contracts.

81. For a fuller discussion of this point, see Ayres & Miller, *"I'll Sell It To You At Cost": Legal Methods to Promote Honest Retail Markup Disclosure*, 84 NW. U.L. REV. (forthcoming 1990) (manuscript on file with authors).

82. It is not necessarily true, however, that retailers will reveal their markups via their choice of liquidated damages. All retailers may uniformly negotiate for minimal liquidated damages that provide no more information than the zero-damage default.

83. U.C.C. § 2-206(1) (1976).

84. 251 Minn. 188, 86 N.W.2d 689 (1957).

85. The court concluded that the newspaper advertisements constituted offers and not merely invitations to make an offer. *Id.* at 192, 86 N.W.2d at 691.

fur coats " 'Worth to $100.00' " for " '$1 Each' "; in the second offer the defendant advertised the sale of one black lapin stole " 'worth $139.50' " for " '$1.00' "[86] The court, following the common-law rule that indefinite contracts are not enforceable, refused to enforce the contract arising out of the first offer but awarded the plaintiff damages for his attempted acceptance of the second.

The court reasoned that the first offer's estimate that the coat was " 'worth to $100' " was too speculative and uncertain to award damages.[87] But in applying the common-law standard that indefinite contracts are unenforceable, the court ignored the likely market response to the non-enforceability default. As argued above, non-enforceability can be viewed as a penalty default that encourages both parties to come forward and fill in the gap;[88] that is, refusing to enforce indefinite contracts drives out indefinite contracts. In *Lefkowitz*, however, the court's refusal to enforce the indefinite *offer* leads to exactly the opposite result.

Ask yourself the simple question: What kind of ad is the Great Minneapolis Surplus Store going to run the week following the court's decision? By lending its imprimatur to the indefinite ad, the court allows retailers to induce inefficient consumer reliance with impunity.[89] The *Lefkowitz* case dramatically illustrates that only by enforcing indefinite offers against the offeror can one drive out indefinite offers.

Lefkowitz was wrongly decided. The defendant's offer was intentionally vague to induce inefficient reliance on the part of the buyer (Lefkowitz incurred the "shoe-leather" costs of traveling to the store). Courts can retain the common law's general reluctance to enforce indefinite contracts so that both parties will have an incentive to make the contracts more definite.[90] But *Lefkowitz* illustrates an exception to this general rule. When the indefiniteness is clearly attributable to one party and induces inefficient reliance from the other party, punitive enforcement may be efficient to drive out inefficient indefinite offers.

D. *Summary*

Penalty defaults stand as stark counter-examples to the proposition that courts should simply choose defaults that the parties would have wanted.[91] Particularly when individual parties have private incentives to withhold

86. *Id.* at 189, 86 N.W.2d at 690.
87. *Id.* at 190, 86 N.W.2d at 690.
88. *See supra* text accompanying notes 49-52.
89. Our argument that consumers will be "suckered" into the store by non-enforceable, indefinite offers assumes that consumers are unable to distinguish between enforceable and unenforceable offers.
90. *See supra* text accompanying note 88.
91. It could be argued that rational contractual parties behind a "veil of ignorance" would want penalty defaults that increase the total gains to contracting. *Cf.* J. RAWLS, A THEORY OF JUSTICE 24-38 (1974) (discussing preferences under utilitarian assumptions of persons behind "veil of ignorance").

information, it may be desirable for the law to give them a nudge. The possibility that efficient defaults will at times be used to reflect what most people want while at other times be used to encourage the revelation of information is analogous to the disparate uses of presumptions in the laws of evidence.[92] In both instances, the law is sometimes chosen to promote the revelation of information.

Finally, having shown that lawmakers will sometimes want to set defaults that encourage one or both parties to reveal information, we now should warn lawmakers that they should sometimes protect the private incentives to become informed. In some instances forcing parties to reveal information will undermine their incentives to obtain the information in the first place.[93] Lawmakers therefore should not impose penalty defaults that have a net effect of reducing the amount of socially useful information. But in some instances, a particular party may need to acquire certain types of information before contracting, so that forcing disclosure would have minimal disincentive effects. For instance, in Goldberg's example of lost-profit damages, retailers naturally knew the profits from a sale. It is hard, therefore, to conceive how forcing retailers to disclose their profits would undermine their private incentives to calculate the profitability of a sale.[94]

---

92. The list of penalty defaults analyzed above is far from exhaustive. For example, the U.C.C. sections which establish implied or default warranties, U.C.C. §§ 2-314 and 2-315, cannot easily be justified as "what the parties would have contracted for." Instead, the defaults, consistent with the foregoing analysis, force sellers to reveal information to consumers about the extent of their coverage. Indeed, one way to identify penalty defaults is to investigate the pervasiveness with which parties contract around them, as is done with the seemingly ubiquitous use of limited warranty disclaimers.

U.C.C. § 2-207 is also inconsistent with "would have wanted" default analysis. This section supplants the common-law mirror-image rule with the default that additional terms in an acceptance that do not materially alter the terms of the offer become part of a contract between merchants. This default cannot be reconciled with a "what the parties would have contracted for" analysis, because there is no reason to think that the merchants would have wanted to include the additional terms of their contract. Instead, the rule places an informational burden on the party with the last clear chance to come forward and notify the other side if the additional terms are objectionable.

Evidentiary presumptions in litigation are sometimes used to reflect a relationship between facts and at other times to place the burden of producing evidence on the party who is more likely to be informed. *See* Allen, *Presumptions in Civil Actions Reconsidered*, 66 Iowa L. Rev. 843, 845 (1981) (suggesting that presumptions are used "to construct rules of decision to avoid factual impasse at trial; to allocate burdens of persuasion; to instruct the jury on the relationship between facts; and to allocate burdens of production").

93. *See* R. Posner, *supra* note 2, at 115; Easterbrook, *Insider Trading, Secret Agents, Evidentiary Privileges, and the Production of Information*, 1981 Sup. Ct. Rev. 309, 359; R. Allen, M. Grady, D. Polsby & M. Yashko, Confidentiality of Legal Affairs (1988) (unpublished manuscript on file with authors); *cf.* Laidlaw v. Organ, 15 U.S. (2 Wheat.) 178 (1817) (permitting relatively informed contracting party to profit by keeping information to himself). Of course, much of patent law is justified as a means of encouraging the private production of information.

94. Anthony Kronman distinguishes "deliberately acquired information" from "casually acquired information." For example, he suggests that if one side to a contract is aware that the other has entered a mistaken bid, the special knowledge of the non-mistaken party "is unlikely to be the fruit of a deliberate search." Requiring disclosure by the knowledgeable party of this casually acquired information will accordingly not undermine incentives to become informed. Kronman, *Mistake, Disclosure, Information, and the Law of Contracts*, 7 J. Legal Stud. 1, 32 (1978) (revealing lost profits from contract can undermine incentives for parties to search for undervalued assets). There may be a tradeoff between inducing efficient search by one party and efficient breach by the other. Retailers do not

II. A General Theory of Default Choice

The prior analysis of *Hadley* can be embedded in a more general model of default choice. To formalize our ideas, we begin by introducing some notation. Let the percentage of millers who had high (unforeseeable) damages be α_H and the percentage of millers who had low (foreseeable) damages be α_L.[95] Let D_H and D_L be the monetary value of damages for the high- and low-damage millers, respectively. The court chooses between two possible defaults: denying or awarding the high, unforeseeable damages. Let the costs of contracting around these defaults be c_H and c_L, where:

c_H = cost of contracting around the *Hadley* default rule that denies awards for unforeseeable consequential damages; and
c_L = cost of contracting around the default rule that awards unforeseeable consequential damages.

We assume that all parties are risk neutral, so the only goal of the insurance aspect of the contract is to induce the carrier to take efficient precaution. As argued above, in a world with full information, both high- and low-damage millers would contract for the carrier to pay for their consequential damages.[96] If the carrier knows the miller's type and bears all damages, she will choose the optimal level of precaution.[97] Let K_H and K_L equal the carrier's optimal investment in precaution for the two types of millers, respectively. Let q_H and q_L equal the probability of damages for each type of miller given the optimal level of precaution for the class.[98]

Before analyzing the likely equilibrium associated with each default, we must say a bit more about the carrier's price. Assume for the moment that the carrier is in a competitive market in which, by definition, there are zero economic profits.[99] Let the competitive price of shipping crankshafts for ***known*** high-damage millers be P_H and for ***known*** low-damage millers be P_L. With this notation, if MC is the marginal cost of shipping with no precaution, then the following equations will hold:

(1) $$P_H = MC + K_H + q_H D_H,$$
(2) $$P_L = MC + K_L + q_L D_L.$$

search for their markup information—in Kronman's terminology it is not "deliberately acquired"—so that information revelation will enhance efficiency.

95. We assume that these are the only types of millers so that $\alpha_H + \alpha_L = 1$. For a similar mathematical model of *Hadley*, see L. Bebchuk & S. Shavell, *supra* note 61.

96. *See supra* text accompanying notes 62-70.

97. We assume that the contract cannot mandate a specific level of precaution because neither the miller nor a court can observe the level of precaution. Otherwise, carriers might sort millers by offering different levels of precaution.

98. Thus, K_H is the level of K that minimizes the expression $K + q(K)D_H$, and K_L is the level of K that minimizes the expression $K + q(K)D_L$, where the function q(K) equals the probability of damages from delay for a given level of precaution, K.

99. Economic profits are the residual earnings after all implicit and opportunity costs are accounted for.

Because of competition, these prices reflect the carrier's marginal cost of shipping, precaution, and expected damages.

What will the market equilibrium look like under the alternative defaults? First consider the *Hadley* low-damage default. Since the carrier is liable only for foreseeable damages, D_L, she will choose a precaution investment of K_L. The probability of damages will therefore be q_L, and the price will be P_L. Now we can ask whether the high-damage millers will contract around the low-damage default for higher insurance. If the high-damage millers fail to contract around the low-damage default, they will pay P_L and, in addition, bear the probability of damage, q_L, multiplied by the uninsured damages $(D_H - D_L)$. Thus, the total expected cost, P_H^{in}, to the high-damage millers if they inefficiently fail to contract around the low-damage default is:

(3) $$P_H^{in} = P_L + q_L(D_H - D_L).$$

But because the carrier invests suboptimally in precaution, the millers' total expected cost in equation (3) must be greater than if the carrier had taken the efficient level of precaution and passed the cost on in the price, P_H:

(4) $$P_H^{in} > P_H.$$ [100]

This difference $(P_H^{in} - P_H)$ represents the inefficiency (f_H) associated with failing to contract for the efficient level of precaution:

(5) $$P_H^{in} - P_H = f_H.$$

"f_H," then, represents the inefficiency cost when high-damage millers fail to contract for greater precaution.[101] High-damage millers effectively pay:

(6) $$P_H^{in} = P_H + f_H$$

when they fail to contract around the *Hadley* low-damage default.

If the high-damage millers contract around this default, they should expect to bear the costs of the increased precaution as reflected in a higher shipping price (P_H rather than P_L) as well as the additional transaction costs of contracting around the default (c_H).[102] This total cost would be:

---

100. From equations (1), (2) and (3):

$$P_H^{in} = P_L + q_L(D_H - D_L) = MC + K_L + q_L D_H, \text{ and}$$
$$P_H = MC + K_H + q_H D_H$$

So that:

$$P_H^{in} - P_H = K_L + q_L(K_L)D_H - (K_H - q_H(K_H)D_H).$$

Because K_H minimizes $K + q(K)D_H$, *see supra* note 98, $K_L + q_L(K_L)D_H$ must be larger than $K_H + q_H(K_H)D_H$. Therefore, the right side of this equation must be positive, and inequality (4) must hold.

101. From the previous note we can calculate the inefficiency cost:

$$f_H = K_L + q_L D_H - (K_H + q_H D_H) = (q_L - q_H)D_H - (K_H - K_L).$$

This latter expression illustrates that the inefficiency of low precaution derives from the fact that the costs of the higher probability of damage, $(q_L - q_H)D_H$, outweigh the lower costs of precaution, $(K_H - K_L)$.

102. The high-damage millers bear all of these additional transaction and precaution costs because competition will keep the carrier's price at marginal cost.

(7) $$P_H + c_H.$$

Thus, the high-damage millers will contract around the low-damage default if the total cost of failing to contract ($P_H + f_H$) exceeds the total costs of contracting ($P_H + c_H$):

(8) $$P_H + f_H > P_H + c_H,$$

or more simply if:

(9) $$f_H > c_H.$$

High-damage millers will contract around the *Hadley*, low-damage default when the cost of inefficient precaution (f_H) is larger than the cost of contracting around the default (c_H). If the additional costs of contracting around the *Hadley* default are sufficiently small, all high-damage millers will contract for the efficient amount of insurance. The high-damage millers will effectively pay $P_H + c_H$ for shipping, while the low-damage millers will pay P_L.

Now consider the non-*Hadley*, high-damage default.[103] If the percentage of high-risk millers, α_H, is sufficiently small, market competition may produce an equilibrium in which no one contracts around the default and the carriers take only low levels of precaution, K_L.[104] If the carriers cannot distinguish between high- and low-damage millers, competition would cause the shipping price to become:

(10) $$P^* = \alpha_L P_L + \alpha_H P_H^{in}.$$

Since in a competitive market, carriers must charge a price equal to the expected average cost of serving both high- and low-damage millers, P^* represents a weighted average of these costs. The low-damage millers cost the carriers P_L, while the high-damage millers cost the carriers P_H^{in} if the inefficient, low level of precaution is taken.[105]

This will be the equilibrium if neither the high- nor the low-damage millers have an incentive to reveal to the carrier their specific type. We might think that the low-damage millers would have an incentive to come forward and reveal their status in order to receive a lower contract price. But they will do so only if:

(11) $$c_L < P^* - P_L.$$[106]

Contracting around the high-damage default will be profitable only if the savings from the reduced shipping price ($P^* - P_L$) are greater than the

103. We assume that the costs to the court of determining the magnitude of unforeseeable consequential damages—i.e., determining whether a given miller is type H or type L—are negligible.

104. If precaution investment is a continuous choice variable (for example, the length of time spent training carriers how to drive safely), its optimal level will be between K_L and K_H. For small α_H the investment will be close to K_L. If there are discrete choices for the level of precaution (for example, use two or three horses) and α_H is small enough, the optimal investment will be K_L.

105. Substituting equations (2) and (3) into equation (10) yields:

$$P^* = MC + K_L + q_L D_L + \alpha_H q_L (D_H - D_L),$$

which, again substituting equation (2), simplifies to:

$$P^* = P_L + \alpha_H q_L (D_H - D_L).$$

106. From the prior footnote, this inequality can be expressed as:

$$c_L < \alpha_H q_L (D_H - D_L).$$

additional transaction cost, c_L. But from equation (10) we see that the equilibrium price, P*, is a positive function of α_H, the percentage of high-damage millers.[107] If this percentage (α_H) is sufficiently low, the transaction costs (c_L) will keep the low-damage millers from contracting around the high-damage default. Note that this is unlike the low-damage default in which the incentives to contract around the default rule are based on the gains to the high-damage millers and are independent of the percentage of the population that has high damages (α_H).

The high-damage millers will not reveal their true status to the carriers because they would be forced to pay more (P_H - P*) but would gain no additional coverage. The high-damage millers fail to distinguish themselves not because of transaction costs, but because they prefer to withhold this information strategically and to receive the subsidized shipping price.[108] The shipping price is subsidized because transaction costs prevent low-damage millers from contracting around the default. Even though the information is socially valuable because it leads to more efficient precaution and even though this value exceeds the transaction costs, the high-damage millers prefer to remain undistinguished from their low-risk counterparts. The high-damage millers do not mind that carriers take inefficiently low levels of precaution because, like all shippers, high-damage millers are fully insured. The low-damage millers bear the costs of this inefficiency, but are not hurt enough individually to distinguish themselves contractually.

Prior analyses of incomplete contracts have suggested that parties fail to contract around inefficient defaults because of transaction costs.[109] Our analysis is striking because it demonstrates the possibility that parties may fail to contract around defaults for strategic reasons.[110] A relatively informed party may strategically withhold information that would increase the joint gains from trade.[111] Moreover, the example illustrates two extreme forms of default equilibria. The *Hadley*, low-damage default caused all high-damage millers to contract around the rule and thus engendered

107. One could imagine situations in which the costs for low-damage millers of contracting around a high-damage default would be small. For example, the Federal Express standard-form contract limits consequential damages if the sender does not contract for more insurance. *See supra* note 70. Such a standard form would allow low-damage millers to cheaply opt for low-damage protection and consequently a lower price.

108. In other words, even if the costs of contracting for higher precaution were zero, the high-damage millers would not reveal their status.

109. *See supra* note 30.

110. In our simplified model, low-damage millers failed to contract around the pooling equilibrium because of transaction costs. *See supra* inequality (11). In a more general model, however, even without transactions costs the informed cross-subsidizing parties (such as the low-damage millers) may fail to contract around pooling equilibria if in doing so they reveal information which reduces their bargaining power. See K. Spier, *supra* note 29 for a more formal demonstration of why similar strategic concerns can keep contracts from being efficiently state-contingent.

111. This, then, is an example in which the "share-of-the-pie effect" exceeds the "size-of-the-pie" effect. *See supra* text accompanying note 57.

what economists sometimes call a "separating" equilibrium in which different types of contracting parties sort themselves through the competitive process into different groups at different prices. In contrast, the non-*Hadley*, high-damage default created a "pooling" equilibrium in which the high- and low-damage millers failed to distinguish themselves to the carriers.[112]

The tension between "pooling" and "separating" equilibria is crucial in choosing the efficient default. Separating equilibria entail the additional transaction costs of causing some parties to contract around the rule; pooling equilibria entail the costs of inefficient reliance or precaution for failing to contract around the rule.[113] In the *Hadley* example the transaction cost of the high-damage millers' contracting around the low-damage default is $\alpha_H c_H$. This is the cost of separating equilibria. The cost of the high-damage default stems from the inefficiently low precaution that carriers take with regard to the high-damage millers, $\alpha_H f_H$. This is the cost of pooling equilibria. If inequality (9) holds (i.e., if $f_H > c_H$), then the costs of pooling exceed the costs of separating, and the *Hadley* default is efficient even though it is not what the high-damage millers would have wanted.

Although the prior section described the *Hadley* rule as a penalty default, it can be alternatively conceived as an untailored default rule that provides what the majority of the parties would want (since under our assumptions, $\alpha_L > \alpha_H$). This reconception suggests that untailored defaults that apply a single rule to different types of contracting parties act as penalty defaults with regard to those parties who disfavor them. Because a majority of the millers had low damages ($\alpha_L > \alpha_H$) and would only want to contract for low damages, one might deduce that the untailored *Hadley* rule is efficient because a majority of the parties prefers it.

But the commonly accepted notion that untailored defaults should be set at what the majority of parties wants does not hold in a more general model of default choice in which the pooling and separating equilibria are not extreme. To extend the *Hadley* model, consider the choice between

112. This analysis is consonant with the economics of insurance literature. *See, e.g.*, Rothschild & Stiglitz, *Equilibrium in Competitive Insurance Markets: An Essay on the Economics of Imperfect Information*, 90 Q.J. ECON. 629, 634-37 (1976) (discussing "separating" and "pooling" equilibria). Low-risk insureds will have incentives to drop out of (or separate from) pools in which they cross-subsidize the premiums of high-risk insureds. *See generally* Priest, *The Current Insurance Crisis and Modern Tort Law*, 96 YALE L.J. 1521 (1987) (arguing that this sort of separation has occurred in third-party insurance pools and is largely responsible for recent "insurance crisis").

113. In this model all millers continue to ship crankshafts regardless of the default rule. If, however, the cross-subsidization of the non-*Hadley* default reduced the consumption of the low-damage millers (who must pay $P^* - P_L$ more) or increased the consumption of the high-damage millers (who have to pay $P_H - P^*$ less), then the pooling equilibria would additionally entail the dead-weight losses associated with inefficient amounts of contracting. *See* Note, *Contract Damages and Cross-Subsidization*, 61 S. CAL. L. REV. 1125 (1988).

two defaults: one and two. As above, there will be a certain percentage of the population of contracting parties for which each default would be preferred, α_1 and α_2, respectively.[114] Again, there will be costs of contracting around each default, c_1 and c_2: let c_1 be the cost of contracting around default two to the default one rule (and define c_2 analogously). The *Hadley* model showed that failing to contract around a default could result in inefficient levels of precaution.[115] Accordingly, let f_1 equal the inefficiency generated if a type one contracting party fails to contract for the type one rule (and analogously define f_2). Most important, in a more general model there may be intermediate amounts of pooling and separation for the different defaults. Accordingly, let:

β_1 = the percentage of type one contracting parties who in equilibrium would actually contract around default two, and
β_2 = the percentage of type two contracting parties who in equilibrium would actually contract around default one.

Thus, while α_1 percent of the contracting parties prefer default one, it is possible that if default two is the rule, a smaller percent ($\beta_1 < \alpha_1$) would contract around it for the efficient amount of precaution. And analogously, some type two contracting parties might not contract around default one if it is the rule ($\beta_2 < \alpha_2$).[116]

The completeness of the *Hadley* pooling equilibrium implies that $\beta_H = \alpha_H$, while the completeness of the non-*Hadley* separating equilibrium implies that $\beta_L = 0$. These extreme results turn on the homogeneity of, for example, f_H and c_H. More generally, if high-damage millers have heterogeneous costs of contracting or of failing to contract, then different defaults may engender intermediate forms of pooling and separating.

In this more general model, each default can engender both costs of contracting and costs of failing to contract. For example, the costs of default one will be:

$$c_2\beta_2 + f_2(\alpha_2 - \beta_2),$$

which equal the transaction costs of those type two contractors who contract around default one ($c_2\beta_2$) and the inefficient reliance or precaution costs for those type two parties who fail to contract around default one ($f_2(\alpha_2 - \beta_2)$). Default one will be optimal only if:

$$c_1\beta_1 + f_1(\alpha_1 - \beta_1) > c_2\beta_2 + f_2(\alpha_2 - \beta_2). \quad (12)$$

This expression establishes the optimal condition for choosing between two untailored defaults. In equilibrium each default may cause a portion of the population to incur the expense of contracting around the default

114. $\alpha_1 + \alpha_2 = 1$.

115. *See supra* text accompanying note 100.

116. Because we assume that parties would never bargain for a less efficient contract, α_1 and α_2 will always be greater than or equal to β_1 and β_2 respectively.

($c_i\beta_i$), and each rule may create costs ($f_i(\alpha_i - \beta_i)$) for those parties that inefficiently fail to contract around it. The efficient default minimizes the sum of these two costs, which, as stated before, are themselves the costs of separation and pooling, respectively:

$$\min_{i=1,2} [c_i\beta_i + f_i(\alpha_i - \beta_i)].$$

In contrast to the majoritarian analysis, condition (12) does not imply that efficiency-minded lawmakers should choose the default rule that most of the parties would want. In other words, condition (12) does not imply that:

$$\alpha_1 > \alpha_2.$$

Indeed, exploiting the fact that $\alpha_2 = 1 - \alpha_1$,[117] one can rearrange condition (12) in terms of α_1. Default one will be efficient if and only if:

$$(13) \qquad \alpha_1 > \frac{f_2 + \beta_2(c_2 - f_2) - \beta_1(c_1 - f_1)}{f_1 + f_2}.$$

The right-hand side of this cumbersome inequality implicitly defines a critical value of α_1^* for choosing between defaults one and two. When α_1 is less than α_1^*, default two is efficient; when α_1 is greater than α_1^*, default one is efficient.

The crude majoritarian criterion ($\alpha_1^* = ½$) only emerges from highly constrained assumptions about β_1, β_2, c_1, c_2, f_1, and f_2. For example, the majoritarian default analysis in the existing contracts literature seems to derive from two divergent sets of assumptions about these crucial variables.[118] One set of majoritarians seems to assume that transaction costs are small enough that no one fails to contract around inefficient defaults ($\alpha_1 = \beta_1$ and $\alpha_2 = \beta_2$) and that the costs of contracting around each default are the same ($c_1 = c_2$).[119] Under these assumptions, the second set of terms in condition (12) drop out of the analysis ($f_i(\alpha_i - \beta_i) = 0$), so that the costs of failing to contract are irrelevant. Inequality (13) can then be simplified to:

$$\alpha_1 > c_2/(c_1 + c_2) = ½,$$

which implies the majoritarian result that default one should be chosen only if a majority of the contracting parties prefers it.

A second set of majoritarians seems to assume that the transaction costs of contracting around a default are so great that no parties will contract around inefficient defaults ($\beta_1 = \beta_2 = 0$) and that the inefficiencies of failing to contract for the right rule are the same ($f_1 = f_2$). Under these assumptions the first terms of condition (12) drop out of the analysis ($c_i\beta_i = 0$), so that inequality (13) can be simplified to:

$$\alpha_1 > f_2/(f_1 + f_2) = ½,$$

117. *See supra* note 114.
118. *See* Craswell, *supra* note 22, at 632-39 (discussing two approaches).
119. *Id.* at 633.

which again implies that default one will be efficient only if a majority prefers it. Majoritarians are forced to make highly restrictive (and sometimes contradictory) assumptions to produce their desired rule. Most fundamentally, the majoritarian analysis errs by looking at only one of the relevant variables, α.

As an alternative, some commentators have suggested that courts fill gaps with the provisions that most parties bargain for in actual contracts.[120] Some academics have labelled this style of gap-filling as "mimicking-the-market."[121] The "mimic-the-market" approach to default rules ignores the fact that the type of parties who contract around a given rule depends upon the rule itself. Parties who dislike a given default rule will contract around it; if we change the default rule to mimic the contracts these parties write, other types of parties may contract around the new default back to the original rule. This process could cycle forever.[122] Set-

120. *See* Epstein, *In Defense of the Contract at Will*, 51 U. Chi. L. Rev. 947, 951 (1984) (a default rule "is normally chosen because it reflects the dominant practice in a given class of cases and because that practice is itself regarded as making good sense for the standard transactions it governs."). Epstein argues that the default for consequential damages should be limited because this "is what the express contracts have typically provided." Epstein, *supra* note 64, at 118. Frank Easterbrook orally suggested a similar standard for choosing corporate default rules at the Columbia conference. *See supra* note 13.

The NLRB has looked at actual collective bargaining agreements in deciding whether there should be a default limiting management's right to transfer work. *See* Milwaukee II, 268 N.L.R.B. Dec. (CCH) 601, 603 (1984) (quoting Ozark Trailers, Inc., 161 N.L.R.B. Dec. (CCH) 561, 570 (1966) (citing M. Chandler, Management Rights and Union Interests 217 (1964))). The Supreme Court has at times looked to actual contracting practices to determine whether a particular issue should be a mandatory subject of bargaining. *See, e.g.*, First Nat'l Maintenance Corp. v. NLRB, 452 U.S. 666, 684 (1981); *see also* Alchian, *Decision Sharing and Expropriable Specific Quasi-Rents: A Theory of* First National Maintenance Corporation v. NLRB, 1 Sup. Ct. Econ. Rev. 235 (1982) (suggesting how "decision sharing" default should be set); Wachter & Cohen, *The Law and Economics of Collective Bargaining: An Introduction and Application to the Problems of Subcontracting, Partial Closure, and Relocation*, 136 U. Pa. L. Rev. 1349, 1364-77 (1988) (suggesting how "default entitlements" in labor market should be set). However, in Lewis v. Benedict Coal Corp., 361 U.S. 459 (1960), discussed *supra* note 21, the Court eschewed any empirical analysis of the private reaction to a particular contract.

121. *See* Schwab, *Collective Bargaining and the Coase Theorem*, 72 Cornell L. Rev. 245, 286-87 (1987).

122. This is not to say that the mimic-the-market rule would never be desirable. If, for instance, filling a particular type of contractual gap is an issue of first impression, it may be reasonable for a court to look at existing contracts as a guide to what the parties would have wanted. If parties were unaware of the default rule when they were contracting, the cycling problem would not arise. If no well-established default exists, many contracting parties may explicitly contract for what they want in order to avoid the penalty of ex post uncertainty. In this case existing contracts provide evidence for what the parties would have done, so mimicking the market may be justified. For example, Epstein uses this approach to argue that one can ascertain the efficient form for workers' compensation legislation by observing the contractual insurance provisions that existed prior to legislation. Epstein, *supra* note 64, at 118-19.

Mimicking the market may also make sense when parties have failed to record any contract. For example, in devising their estates, many parties may not go to the trouble of writing a will, but those that do may restate even well-established intestacy defaults. Thus, looking at actual wills can give some guide to what the general populace wants. But even this argument fails if the contracting sample misrepresents the intestate class. If the reason certain parties fail to contract is related to the substantive provision that those parties want, then the inference between actual and hypothetical contracts is attenuated. For example, if only upper-class people can afford to write wills, then an upper-class preference for children over parents may not be relevant in determining the intestate preferences of

ting defaults that mimic the market therefore will not assure efficiency. A slightly more sophisticated version of mimicking the market would set the default at what most people would contract around another default for. This approach would focus solely on the β's. For example, if a larger percentage of parties were willing to contract around the first default than the second default ($\beta_2 > \beta_1$), then rule two would be chosen as the default. But maximizing the β's suffers the same flaw as maximizing the α's—neither choice rule conforms with the efficiency criterion in inequality (12).[123]

Implementing a complete theory of default choice requires attention to:

1) what the parties want (the α's),

2) whether they will get it (the β's), and

3) the costs associated with getting it (the c's) or not getting it (the f's).

It is especially important that lawmakers ascertain the degree of separating and pooling that each default engenders. For in determining the equilibrium levels of the β associated with each default, the court must estimate the importance of transactional and strategic barriers to contracting around particular default rules, as well as understand the costs associated with failing to strike the efficient contract.

We have shown that at times the efficient default will be one that a majority of contracting parties disfavors. As the number of different types of preferred contracts (and consequently the number of possible defaults) increases, any untailored default is likely to be disfavored by the majority of contractors.[124] Untailored defaults act as penalty defaults with regard to

---

the lower class.

123. Still another partial and inefficient criterion for default choice would attempt to minimize the number of people who failed to contract to their efficient rule. In the model's terminology, this would be equivalent to minimizing $\alpha_i - \beta_i$.

124. The results of this dichotomous model can be extended to a situation in which courts are choosing among more than two default alternatives. In many situations, there will be more than two possible default choices from which the lawmaker may choose. Consider a class of contracts in which tailoring is prohibitively expensive, so that the lawmaker must choose among N (N > 2) possible defaults. Assume that there are different classes of contracting parties for which different rules would be efficient. For example, heterogeneity across buyer risk preferences could lead to a range of optimal risk-sharing rules for different contracts. We assume that when parties contract around a default, they contract for the rule that is efficient for their class. *But see* Schwab, *supra* note 1, at 251 (students sometimes contracted around default to less efficient outcome). A contracting party will be called a type j contracting party if default rule j would be efficient for it. Let:

α_i = the percent of contracting parties who want default i (where $\Sigma_i \alpha_i = 1$);

β_{ij} = the percent of type j contracting parties who will contract around default i (where $\beta_{ii} = 0$);

c_{ij} = the cost for type j parties of contracting around default i; and

f_{ij} = the cost for type j parties of failing to contract around default i (where $f_{ii} = 0$).

Extending the earlier model, we can say that the cost of any default i will be:

$$\sum_{j=1,N} [c_{ij}\beta_{ij} + f_{ij}(\alpha_j - \beta_{ij})].$$

which represents for all contracting types the total costs of contracting around default i or of failing to contract around it. A lawmaker choosing the least-cost default will accordingly want to minimize:

$$\min_{i=1,N} \left\{ \sum_{j=1,N} [c_{ij}\beta_{ij} + f_{ij}(\alpha_j - \beta_{ij})] \right\}.$$

As in the dichotomous model, a penalty default may be the least costly. Even a default x that no one wants, $\alpha_x = 0$, may be optimal if most people contract around the default ($\beta_{xj} \sim \alpha_x$, for all j), and

the classes of contracting parties that disfavor them. As the diversity of contracting types grows, any untailored defaults start to resemble the types of penalty defaults we described in Section I.[125] As the number of possible defaults expands, courts must choose between a penalty default that is efficient within the class of untailored defaults or a tailored default that requires the court to ascertain what individual parties would have wanted. We have analyzed how courts should find the optimal rule within the class of untailored defaults; we now examine whether a tailored default is superior to an untailored default.

With a tailored default the court attempts to determine the default for which the particular parties would have contracted. A major cost of tailored defaults, then, is the cost of this ex post determination.[126] Instead of having the different types of parties separating themselves into different contractual groups ex ante, the court attempts the separation ex post. Instead of contracting costs, the costs of ex post tailoring are the costs of distinguishing between types of contractual parties, where each type would have contracted for a different rule.

These costs of determining what the particular parties would have contracted for can be significant. For example, in *Jordan v. Duff & Phelps, Inc.*,[127] two leading law-and-economics practitioners, Judges Easterbrook and Posner, disagreed about what the particular parties would have wanted. In *Jordan* the Seventh Circuit was called on to fill a gap in a shareholder/employment agreement. The court needed to determine whether the defendant corporation had a duty to disclose material information about a merger to an employee who was about to quit and who was, according to the agreement, thereby required to sell his shares. Predictably, both judges agreed that contractual gaps should be filled with terms that the parties would have wanted.[128]

The judges, however, strongly disagreed about what these terms would have been. Judge Easterbrook, authoring the majority opinion, found it "unwarranted to say that the implicit understanding between Jordan and Duff & Phelps should be treated as if it had such a no-duty clause; we are

---

the costs of contracting around it are low ($C_{xj} \simeq 0$, for all j).

For example, consider our earlier discussion of the zero-quantity default, *supra* text accompanying notes 42-46. The default choice is non-dichotomous. Numerous quantities could be chosen as the default. Although contracting parties would not contract to exchange zero quantity ($x_0 = 0$), most people contract around this default, and the costs of contracting around it are low.

125. Any untailored quantity default would be, except for the smallest proportion of transactions, a penalty default. For example, only the smallest percentage of contracting parties would actually want a default quantity of some randomly chosen number such as, say, 39 or 2003.

126. Richard Epstein criticizes Judge Posner's analysis in EVRA Corp. v. Swiss Bank Corp., 673 F.2d 951, 954 (7th Cir. 1982), because contributory negligence requires costly ex post tailoring by courts. Epstein, *supra* note 64, at 134.

127. 815 F.2d 429 (7th Cir. 1987).

128. *Id.* at 436; *id.* at 446-47 (Posner, J., dissenting).

not confident that this is the clause firms and their employees regularly would prefer."[129]

Judge Posner, in dissent, argued that the parties would have waived any duty of disclosure because waiving such a duty would have "aligned their respective self-interests better than the legal protection that the court devises today."[130] This disagreement between sophisticated jurists suggests that tailoring costs include not only the out-of-pocket litigation expenses but also the potential costs of judicial error. Indeed, if the expected costs of ex post tailoring are sufficiently large, even a tailored rule may give the parties an incentive to contract explicitly ex ante. Ex post tailoring may be more expensive to contracting parties than ex ante contracting. Even if judicial tailoring is accomplished without error, parties may prefer to contract for the same terms that the courts would provide at a higher cost ex post.[131]

But these costs of distinguishing between different types of parties are not the only costs of tailored rules. Because courts do their tailoring after the fact, tailored rules can actually exacerbate the inefficiency of strategic incompleteness. With a tailored rule the relatively informed party—assured that the court will provide the terms that fully-informed parties would want—may have no incentive to reveal her private information to the other party. For example, in our *Hadley* model the high-damage rule was a tailored default that gave each contracting type what they would have contracted for were they fully informed—damages of D_H or D_L, depending on the miller's type. Yet, we have shown conditions under which this tailored high-damage default gives rise to the costs of inefficient reliance or precaution.[132] By not explicitly contracting for damages ex ante, the carrier cannot know if the miller is high-damage or low-damage and therefore may not choose the correct level of precaution. Even if it is costless ex post for the court to determine exactly what two specific parties would have agreed to ex ante, tailored defaults may not be optimal.

In sum, finding the efficient default can involve a complicated inquiry. Knowledgeable parties can leave holes in contracts for strategic reasons—they might prefer to remain in an undifferentiated pool than pay their full freight in an efficient but unsubsidized equilibrium. Efficiency-minded lawmakers must therefore be attuned to the sources of contractual incompleteness and to the attendant costs of pooling and separating associated with their default choice.

129. *Id.* at 436.

130. *Id.* at 448 (Posner, J., dissenting).

131. This point inverts Posner's observation that it may sometimes be "cheaper for the court to 'draft' the contractual term necessary to deal with the contingency if and when it occurs." R. POSNER, *supra* note 2, at 82.

132. *See supra* text accompanying notes 95-103.

III. A Theory of Gaps

The preceding sections have attempted to develop a theory for choosing default rules. But before implementing any default standard, courts need to establish, as a logically prior matter, rules for deciding when a contract is incomplete.[133] Indeed, the litigants in many cases will argue not only about how the gap should be filled but also about whether there is a gap at all.[134]

For example, returning again to *Jordan v. Duff & Phelps*,[135] Judges Easterbrook and Posner disagree not only on how to fill a gap in the employment-stockholding contract but also, and more fundamentally, on whether there was a gap to be filled.[136] Easterbrook's majority opinion concludes that although the fiduciary duty to disclose material information could be contracted around, the parties' agreement did not sufficiently negate this duty: "[T]he possibility that a firm could negotiate around the fiduciary duty does not assist Duff & Phelps; it did not obtain such an agreement, express or implied."[137] Easterbrook's decision then proceeds to fill this disclosure gap with the fiduciary duty default. Posner, in dissent, finds that the "stockholder agreement that defined [the employee's] rights as a shareholder 'with greater specificity' "[138] sufficiently contracted around any default fiduciary duty: "The arrangement that resulted (call it 'shareholder at will') is incompatible with an inference that Duff and Phelps undertook to keep him abreast of developments affecting the value of the firm."[139] In *Jordan*, then, two prominent legal economists disagreed not only about how the gap should be filled but also about what constitutes a gap.

---

133. At an even more basic level, courts will not be able to determine whether a contract has gaps without a prior theory of contract formation. In general, courts will need to determine:

1) whether the parties have formed a contract,
2) whether the contract has gaps, and
3) how the gaps should be filled.

We implicitly assumed in Sections I and II that there were sufficient objective indicia of the parties' meeting of the minds to infer contractual formation. *See* Barnett, *A Consent Theory of Contract*, 86 Colum. L. Rev. 269 (1986) (discussing competing theories of contractual formation). This Section's focus on legal formalities should inform courts' theories of contractual formation and contractual gaps.

134. This point is also made in M. Freed & D. Polsby, Hard Cases Make Bad Law: Employment at Will at the Edge (1988) (unpublished manuscript on file with authors). For example, Freed and Polsby criticize Richard Epstein's analysis, *see* Epstein, *supra* note 120, at 980, that the court supplied the correct "gap-filling" default in Coleman v. Graybar Elec. Co., 195 F.2d 374 (5th Cir. 1952), an employment at will/wrongful termination case: "The contract in *Graybar* was anything but silent . . . . Such an agreement could hardly 'provide otherwise' with more clarity, short of specifically reserving the employer's right to act in bad faith." M. Freed & D. Polsby, *supra*, at 2.

135. 815 F.2d 429 (7th Cir. 1987); *see supra* text accompanying notes 127-31.

136. Judge Posner argued in the alternative. Although he concluded that the contract did not have a gap, *id.* at 449 (Posner, J., dissenting) ("the parties were not silent"), he alternatively found that even if there were a gap, it should be filled differently than the way Easterbrook recommended. *See supra* text accompanying note 129.

137. 815 F.2d at 436.

138. *Id.* at 447 (Posner, J., dissenting) (quoting majority).

139. *Id.*

This question of when a contract is incomplete is identical to the question of what is sufficient to contract around a default. A court's holding that the parties' attempt to contract around a given default is insufficient is identical to a holding that there is still a gap in the contract. By answering one question, the courts necessarily answer the other. Courts need to develop a theory of gaps before they can address how best to fill them.

If the academy has been remiss in developing a theory of default choice, then to an even greater degree it has failed to address what the necessary and sufficient conditions for contracting around defaults should be. In determining these conditions, courts are determining the costs of contracting around a given default.[140] The received wisdom that transaction costs are responsible for contractual incompleteness implicitly suggests that lawmakers should minimize the costs of contracting around defaults so that if any contracting parties do not like the off-the-rack standard, they can inexpensively tailor their corporate or contractual structure to suit themselves.

But legal rules evince a greater diversity than this simple theory suggests.[141] Parties wishing to contract around both statutory and common-law defaults will encounter varying degrees of difficulty. For example, many sections of the U.C.C. establish defaults that are in force "unless otherwise agreed,"[142] but § 2-206 provides that contractual offers shall be construed as inviting any reasonable manner of acceptance "[u]nless otherwise *unambiguously* indicated,"[143] and the Official Comment punctuates this point by saying that this default obtains "unless the offeror has made *quite* clear that it will not be acceptable."[144]

Similarly, in the corporate context the common law of promoter liability requires extraordinary efforts to negate the joint and several liability default. For example, in *Stanley J. How & Assocs. v. Boss*,[145] a promoter was held liable under a contract even though he signed the pre-incorporation agreement: "By: Edwin A. Boss, Agent for a Minnesota Corporation to be formed, who will be the Obligor."[146] The court held that "[w]hile the agreement was not completely clear, the words 'who will be the obligor' are not enough to offset the rule that the person signing for the nonexistent corporation is normally to be personally liable."[147] Con-

140. These costs were represented as c_i in the early model of default choice. *See supra* Section II.

141. *But see* Black, *supra* note 1 (arguing that corporate default rules are trivial). Black's arguments imply that corporate formalities do not impede corporations from establishing tailored forms of corporate governance. But the costs of contracting around some "strong" defaults (that is, fulfilling certain corporate formalities) are likely to give some formalities a more substantive or nontrivial nature. *See, e.g.*, *infra* notes 148–50.

142. *See, e.g.*, U.C.C. § 2-303 (1976).

143. U.C.C. § 2-206 (1976) (emphasis added).

144. *Id.* at Official Comment 1 (emphasis added).

145. 222 F. Supp. 936 (S.D. Iowa 1963).

146. *Id.* at 939.

147. *Id.* at 942. The holding is consistent with the common-law doctrine of construing contractual

tracting around corporate statutes especially exhibits different degrees of difficulty. For example, certain default rules of corporate governance can be changed only in the articles of incorporation, while others can be overcome through less costly bylaw amendments.[148]

At times even seemingly immutable rules can be circumvented at a cost. To be sure, some methods of contracting around legal rules are better described as examples of abuse of the law.[149] But lawmakers at other times seem to allow ostensibly immutable rules to be negated if the private parties structure the transaction properly. For example, the seemingly immutable rule that limited partnerships must have at least one general partner (that is, one partner who retains unlimited personal liability) can be contractually negated in jurisdictions that allow corporate persons to serve as the sole general partner.[150]

A. Peevyhouse *and the Default-Immutable Spectrum*

As the cost of contracting around a default rule becomes extremely large, the default starts to look like an immutable rule.[151] The Oklahoma Supreme Court's classic decision in *Peevyhouse v. Garland Coal & Mining Co.*[152] exemplifies this insight. The Peevyhouses leased their land contemplating that it would be strip-mined. The contract included specific covenants that Garland would restore the land at the end of the lease

---

ambiguities against the drafter. *See supra* note 82.

148. Defaults that may be contracted around only in the articles of incorporation include: Board of directors may be dispensed with entirely in limited circumstances or its functions may be restricted, REVISED MODEL BUSINESS CORP. ACT ANN. § 8.01 (1984); power to compensate directors may be restricted or eliminated, REVISED MODEL BUSINESS CORP. ACT ANN. § 8.11 (1984); special voting groups of shareholders may be authorized, REVISED MODEL BUSINESS CORP. ACT ANN. § 7.25 (1987); and classes of shares may be given more or less than one vote per share, REVISED MODEL BUSINESS CORP. ACT ANN. § 7.21 (1987). Defaults that may be contracted around in either the articles of incorporation or the bylaws include: Number of directors may be fixed or changed within limits, REVISED MODEL BUSINESS CORP. ACT ANN. § 8.03 (1987); qualifications for directors may be prescribed, REVISED MODEL BUSINESS CORP. ACT ANN. § 8.02 (1987); shares may be issued without certificates, REVISED MODEL BUSINESS CORP. ACT ANN. § 6.26 (1987); power of board of directors to amend bylaws may be restricted, REVISED MODEL BUSINESS CORP. ACT ANN. §§ 10.20, 10.22 (1987). *See* REVISED MODEL BUSINESS CORP. ACT ANN. § 2.02 official comment.

149. The field of tax abounds with instances in which clever citizens abusively attempt to contract around tax liabilities in ways that Congress did not foresee or intend. *See, e.g.*, Heintz v. Comm'r, 25 T.C. 132 (1955) (stockholder of merging corporation contractually abrogates seemingly immutable rule for capital gains realization rules); Zuckman v. United States, 524 F.2d 729 (Ct. Cl. 1975) (stockholders of corporation contractually abrogate seemingly immutable rules to carry through losses).

150. In Delaney v. Fidelity Lease Ltd., 526 S.W.2d 543 (Tex. 1975), the Texas Supreme Court voided this contractual attempt to circumvent the general-partner personal-liability rule. The Texas legislature, however, amended its corporations statute to permit a corporation "[t]o be an organizer, partner, member, associate, or manager of any partnership. . . ." TEX. BUS. CORP. ACT ANN. art. 2.02A(18) (Vernon 1989).

151. Conversely, if we admit the possibility of lobbying to change current law, even immutable rules are really defaults where the costs of lobbying to change them are prohibitively expensive. This point was made by Joseph Grundfest at the Columbia conference on December 9-10, 1988, *supra* note 13.

152. 382 P.2d 109 (Okla. 1962), *cert. denied*, 375 U.S. 906 (1963).

period. As it turned out, the restoration "would involve the moving of many thousands of cubic yards of dirt, at a cost estimated by expert witnesses at about $29,000.00."[153] Garland introduced evidence that such restoration would increase the market value of the land by only $300.[154] The court was asked to choose the proper measure of damages: cost of performance ($29,000) or diminution in value ($300).

The majority opinion, which limited the Peevyhouses' damages to diminution in value, clearly claimed that the court's ruling could be contracted around.

> It should be noted that the rule as stated does not interfere with the property owner's right to "do what he will with his own," or his right, if he chooses, to contract for "improvements" which will actually have the effect of reducing his property's value. Where such result is in fact contemplated by the parties, and is a main or principal purpose of those contracting, it would seem that the measure of damages for breach would ordinarily be the cost of performance.[155]

This passage seems to emphasize that, notwithstanding the holding in this particular case, parties retain the right to contract around the diminution-in-value default standard.

The dissenting opinion, however, points to the specific provisions of the contract that had been added to the usual covenants of the defendant's coal mining leases and that seemed to place the duty of restoration on the defendant. In the face of these contractual provisions, the reader of *Peevyhouse* is left with two alternative interpretations. Either the majority opinion is 1) disingenuously creating an immutable rule; or 2) creating a "strong" default rule (that the Peevyhouses' amendments did not sufficiently override).[156] The most straightforward way to distinguish between these competing interpretations is to ask what extra words the Peevyhouses could have added to the contract to "reverse" the majority's

153. *Id.* at 111.

154. Many commentators have criticized the majority's opinion for ignoring the subjective (non-market) value of the land to the Peevyhouses. *See, e.g.*, Muris, *Cost of Completion or Diminution in Market Value: The Relevance of Subjective Value*, 12 J. LEGAL STUD. 379 (1983) (arguing that courts must recognize subjective value to fill compensatory goal of contract law). However, the courts' reliance on market value is probably more a function of the plaintiffs' trial strategy. The Peevyhouses, in trying to focus the jury's attention on cost of performance, may have strategically decided not to introduce any evidence of subjective value. And the court's opinion seems to indicate that evidence of subjective value should be included in diminution damages: "After a careful search of the record, we have found no evidence of a higher figure [than the $300 market diminution], and plaintiffs do not argue in their briefs that a greater diminution in value was sustained." *Peevyhouse*, 382 P.2d at 114. One would predict that in subsequent litigation plaintiffs would begin to introduce subjective value evidence that would be included in diminution damages.

155. *Peevyhouse*, 382 P.2d at 114 (citations omitted).

156. The majority's own use of the word "ordinarily" in the last quoted sentence seems to add some support for the immutability interpretation. After all, is the court suggesting that even if the parties explicitly attempt to contract for cost of performance, there still may be "extraordinary" situations in which the diminution in value standard will apply?

default. If the majority is really doing what it says, we should be able to write such a contract. If we cannot confidently determine what such a contract would need to say, the alternative hypothesis—that *Peevyhouse* really is creating an immutable rule—becomes more compelling.[157]

While the *Peevyhouse* opinion has been criticized for reaching the wrong result,[158] this analysis suggests that the majority also erred by not more clearly establishing what words would be sufficient to contract for the cost of performance damages. Even though the decision (rightly or wrongly) resolved uncertainty about what the default damages would be, it did little to resolve the uncertainty about how one could contract around this default. Even prospective parties who had read *Peevyhouse* and had known that it "does not interfere with the property owner's right to 'do what he will with his own' "[159] would still face considerable uncertainty about how to exercise that right.

This discussion suggests that in many instances decisions should do more than merely decide what the efficient default should be; they should establish "safeharbors" of contractual language that will be sufficient to reach other contractual outcomes.[160] As the *Peevyhouse* case illustrates, by giving prospective parties examples of explicit language, courts can dramatically reduce the uncertainty and costs of contracting around the specific default.[161]

B. *Determining the Efficient Level of Legal Formalities*

There can be good economic reasons for "strong" defaults in which the courts intentionally increase the procedural costs to parties of contracting around the default. These reasons parallel the rationales given in one of the first intuitively economic analyses of contract law, Lon Fuller's classic, *Consideration and Form*.[162] Fuller suggested that legal formalities serve

---

157. Tracking the majority's language, we suggest that prospective parties attempting to overcome the diminution-in-value standard include the following covenant:

> The parties specifically intend and contemplate that the lessee shall restore the land, even if the costs of performance are grossly disproportionate to the diminution in value from failing to restore the land. This is a main and principal purpose of the lease. In writing this provision, we are explicitly contracting around the holding of *Peevyhouse v. Garland Coal*.

If this provision were not sufficient, the *Peevyhouse* rule would, in fact, be immutable.

158. *See, e.g.*, Birmingham, *Damage Measures and Economic Rationality: The Geometry of Contract Law*, 1969 DUKE L.J. 49.

159. *Peevyhouse*, 382 P.2d at 114.

160. Courts may face the constitutional limitation of resolving only "cases or controversies" at issue. U.S. CONST. art. III, § 2, cl. 1. But other decisions have established prospective safeharbors. *See, e.g.*, Miranda v. Arizona, 384 U.S. 436 (1966) (establishing fair and effective warning requirement to persons in police custody).

161. The purpose of such contractual safeharbors should not be to preclude the parties from tailoring other standards. The safeharbor alternatives might additionally provide benefits as common-law interpretations would more fully specify their meanings. *See* J. Gordon, *supra* note 13

162. Fuller, *Consideration and Form*, 41 COLUM. L. REV. 799 (1941). In truth, the fact that the article is claimed by economists (it is, for example, reprinted in A. KRONMAN & R. POSNER, THE ECONOMICS OF CONTRACT LAW 40 (1979)) is as much a tribute to the soundness of its insights as to its nexus with economics.

evidentiary, cautionary and channelling functions. The necessary and sufficient conditions for contracting around a default are examples of formalities that courts require. Our discussion accordingly tracks Fuller's categories.

In Fuller's analysis, the evidentiary function of legal formalities is to provide information to courts in order to lower the costs of subsequent decision making. This analysis is quite resonant with our earlier conclusion that penalty defaults could be justified on efficiency grounds as ways of encouraging the revelation of information.[163] In choosing the necessary conditions (the formalities) for contracting around a default, a court should consider similar informational aspects. We go beyond Fuller though and argue that the evidentiary function of legal formalities can serve to inform not only the courts but the parties within the contract as well.[164] For example, if a penalty default is chosen to encourage one party to reveal information to another, the court may want to regulate the process of contracting around the default so that meaningful information is conveyed.

Structuring formalities to facilitate internal information flows is also related to the cautionary function of legal formalities. Fuller argues that some formalities, such as certain writing requirements, serve a cautionary function by forcing the parties to undertake a minimal amount of reflection before being bound by a contract. But, as already discussed, when the parties to a contract have disparate amounts of information, lawmakers may want to establish formalities that are more directed toward protecting the relatively uninformed. For example, a holding contrary to *Peevyhouse*, in which the courts not only choose cost-of-performance damages as the default but also require extremely explicit language to opt for value diminution damages, might be justified to caution the relatively uninformed landholders of their legal rights.[165] To caution is to give information. Attention to how legal formalities will affect the flow of information should inform lawmakers' theory of gaps as well as their theory of default choice.

Finally, Fuller suggested that legal formalities could serve a chanelling function which, for example, would allow parties to channel their contractual agreements toward legal or non-legal enforcement. Fuller's theory of channelling is highly analogous to our earlier discussion of pooling and especially separating equilibria.[166] As we discussed in our *Hadley* model,

163. *See supra* text accompanying notes 47-60.

164. *See supra* text accompanying notes 53-60.

165. Similarly, if strategic withholding of information explains why employers do not reveal to employees the true probability of future termination, employees may make inefficient investments in goods such as housing and human capital. In such situations it may be efficient for courts not only to make a default rule against termination without cause but also to require employers to state specifically that they wish to be able to fire for even arbitrary reasons. *But see* Epstein, *supra* note 120 (arguing against such a rule); M. Freed & D. Polsby, *supra* note 134

166. *See supra* text accompanying notes 111-14.

different defaults can lead to different degrees of separation.[167] As with chanelling, the separating effect of legal defaults may allow parties to sort themselves into different groups.

There may be situations in which courts should increase the costs of contracting around defaults to force the majority of parties into a particular channel. For example, if a certain type of contract generates a mild externality, we may want to discourage most people from entering this type of contract. But if there is a small class of contracting parties that will be damaged more than society gains if they fail to contract, then courts may want to consider a method of "chanelling" or "separating" the socially beneficial from the deleterious classes of transactions.

One way to do this would be by direct fiat, but there may be ways of encouraging the parties to sort themselves into the correct categories through legal rules. For example, by artificially increasing the costs of contracting around a no-contract default, courts may discourage the low-benefit contractors but not the high-benefit contractors. Although such legal formalisms may engender the efficient types of contracting, they may still be inefficient because the additional transaction costs that the formalities engender are a social cost that could be avoided by simply imposing a tax of an equal magnitude. The tax would be a transfer to the government instead of a dead-weight loss. If courts are constrained from imposing taxes,[168] however, intentionally costly formalisms that increase the cost of contracting around "strong" defaults may be the most efficient rules within their choice set. The channelling function of legal formalities can also be given an informational justification because the very process of self-sorting reveals information about the parties' preferences.[169]

Such intentionally costly formalism would not be used in conjunction with a penalty default. Since the whole point of penalty defaults is to encourage parties to contract around them, formalisms that increase the cost of doing so would be counterproductive. In essence, penalty defaults encourage, and "strong" defaults discourage, contractual mutation.

C. *Legal Responses to Contracting Around Immutable Rules*

An important difference between default and immutable rules is that if parties attempt to contract around a default rule and fail, they will simply

167. *See supra* text accompanying notes 114-16.

168. *See, e.g.*, I. Ayres & P. Schmitt, Court-Ordered Funding of School Desegregation Remedies: Federalism Versus Minority Rights § 3 (1989) (unpublished manuscript on file with authors) (discussing constitutional limits on judicially imposed taxation).

169. The possibility that courts may intentionally want to increase the costs of contracting around a default might potentially explain their refusal to articulate alternative safeharbors. If there is uncertainty about what is sufficient to overcome a particular default, the parties will be discouraged ex ante from even trying. This argument might provide an apology for the *Peevyhouse* holding. However, in *Peevyhouse* the societal externalities of strip-mining militate toward a cost-of-performance default. This channeling explanation is therefore inapposite to the *Peevyhouse* fact pattern.

be bound by the default, whereas if parties attempt to contract around an immutable rule and fail, the law may choose to penalize the attempt by imposing a penalty different from (and, from the parties' ex ante perspectives, worse than) the immutable standard. From an ex ante perspective the possibility of receiving this ex post penalty is just another expected cost of contracting around the default rule.

The legal response to parties who try to contract around immutable rules can also be given a default interpretation. In these cases the courts remove the clauses that transgress the immutable rule and then choose a default to fill the gap. For example, in *Frostifresh Corp. v. Reynoso*,[170] the trial court established an immutable rule that retailers cannot sell at unconscionably high markups. Accordingly, the court struck out the contract's price provision (which was more than three times the retailer's cost), but it then had to decide how to fill the gap. The trial court decided that the reconstructed contract should have a price which only covered the seller's cost. The appellate court reversed and awarded the seller "a reasonable profit" instead of zero profit.[171] The difference in these holdings is very similar to the tension between a tailored default and penalty default. Reconstructing the contract to give the seller a reasonable profit is identical to the U.C.C.'s reasonable-price standard. The zero-profit standard is analogous to a penalty default, in this case imposing the penalty on the seller for trying to contract around a rule, while the penalty defaults discussed earlier penalize parties for not contracting around the rule.

This same tension arises with covenants not to compete. Courts have established an immutable rule that parties cannot make covenants of unreasonable duration. In *Fullerton Lumber Co. v. Torborg*,[172] for example, the Supreme Court of Wisconsin held that a ten-year covenant was unreasonable but then struggled in deciding whether it should reformulate the contract to impose a duty not to compete for a reasonable period or penalize the employer for transgressing the immutable limitation by allowing the former employee to compete immediately.[173]

If the goal of an immutable rule is to discourage people from even attempting to contract around a provision, then it would seem that the penalty reconstruction would be the favored result.[174] This is again analogous

170. 52 Misc. 2d 26, 274 N.Y.S.2d 757 (Dist. Ct. 1966), *rev'd* 54 Misc. 2d 119, 281 N.Y.S.2d 964 (App. Term 1967).

171. Frostifresh Corp. v. Reynoso, 54 Misc. 2d 119, 281 N.Y.S.2d 964 (App. Term 1967).

172. 270 Wis. 133, 70 N.W.2d 585 (1955).

173. The majority reconstructed the contract to have a covenant of "reasonable" duration. 270 Wis. at 146-47, 70 N.W.2d at 592. The dissent would have penalized the employer by allowing the employee to compete immediately. *Id.* at 148-52, 70 N.W.2d at 593-94 (Gehl, J., dissenting).

174. A penalty for even attempting to contract around a legally immutable provision may be necessary to deter attempts in a world where some disputes are not litigated. If all disputes were litigated, attempts to contract around an immutable rule would never succeed. But if some contractual parties fail to challenge unenforceable immutable rules, then imposing a penalty whenever a case does come to court might be justified to prevent underdeterrence. For example, it is widely believed that

to our earlier discussion of penalty defaults, in which we suggested that courts should choose the penalty that provided "least cost deterrence."[175] The difference is that in the earlier discussion the penalties were attempting to deter gaps and here the penalties are attempting to promote gaps (that is, deter contracting around). The preference for penalty defaults to fill the gaps left in unconscionable contracts may justify the common law "blue pencil" test which simply enforces contracts after the offending provision has been struck (with a blue pencil).[176]

CONCLUSION

This article has suggested how efficiency-minded lawmakers should go about filling gaps in contracts. The reasons that parties leave gaps in contracts should strongly inform this decision. Our theory of defaults should, in a sense, be guided by our theories of why there are contractual gaps. Prior theorists have argued that parties leave gaps in contracts because the cost of writing additional terms outweighs the benefit. Accordingly, they have suggested that courts should simply fill in the gap with the term the parties "would have wanted."

This article, however, has articulated a second cause of contractual incompleteness. We have shown that when one party to a contract knows more than another, the knowledgeable party may strategically decide not to contract around even an inefficient default. Because the process of contracting around a default can reveal information, the knowledgeable party may purposefully withhold information to get a larger piece of the smaller contractual pie. This possibility of strategic incompleteness leads us to embrace more diverse forms of default rules. In particular, lawmakers may be able to undercut the incentives for this strategic rent-seeking by establishing penalty defaults that encourage the better informed parties to reveal their information by contracting around the default.

Our analysis does not imply that penalty defaults should be used in all contractual settings. The decision by efficiency-minded courts or legislatures to impose a penalty, untailored majoritarian, or tailored "what the parties would have wanted" default in a particular setting is not a trivial one. The first step in the decision-making process should be to ask "why does the gap exist?" We have suggested that parties may fail to contract around inefficient defaults for strategic as well as transaction cost reasons. When parties fail to contract because they want to shift the ex ante trans-

---

creditors and residential landlords make a practice of including all sorts of illegal clauses in their contracts not because they think the clauses will stand up in court, but because they know that most debtors and tenants have more respect for written contracts than most courts do. The authors are indebted to conversations with Richard Craswell for this point. *See* Craswell, *supra* note 22, at 64–65.

175. *See supra* Section I.B.

176. *See Fullerton*, 270 Wis. at 43, 70 N.W.2d at 590. The "blue pencil" test is the traditional test of severability. If, after removing the unconscionable terms, the contract is still comprehensible in that the parties might have still entered into it, the court will enforce it.

action cost to a subsidized ex post court determination, a penalty default of non-enforcement may be appropriate. When strategic considerations cause a more knowledgeable party not to raise issues that could improve contractual efficiency, a default that penalizes the more informed party may encourage the revelation of information.[177]

Lawmakers should not, however, impose penalty defaults indiscriminately. Even if strategic considerations are established as a significant source of contractual incompleteness, courts or legislatures should consider the costs and benefits of penalty defaults themselves. Since the goal of a penalty default is to induce information revelation, lawmakers should consider the likelihood that the penalty will in fact result in information being revealed,[178] the benefit (in more efficient reliance or precaution) of the revealed information, and the costs of explicitly contracting around the default. If the private information is acquired with economic resources, the value of information revelation must also be weighed against the private incentives to acquire it. Penalty defaults are therefore more likely to be efficient if the private information is acquired passively. In sum, a penalty default should be used if it results in valuable information revelation with low transaction costs.[179]

Throughout the discussion we have cited examples of common-law and statutory rules that are broadly consistent with our theory's categories of penalty, tailored and untailored defaults. But we believe that both courts and legislatures should be more sensitive to the process of contracting. Lawmakers should consider explicitly the informational as well as the contractual equilibria generated by alternative default rules. Different defaults may generate different degrees of pooling and separating. When heterogeneous contracting parties separate themselves into different con-

177. In many settings, such as simple contracts for small transactions, it is easy to point to transaction costs as the source of incompleteness. In other settings, however, parties write complicated, lengthy contracts that are carefully considered by both parties and their lawyers. In these situations a contingency that is not contracted for may be sufficiently important that it is unreasonable to ascribe incompleteness to transaction costs. Some omitted clauses, for example, may be very inexpensive to include from a transaction cost perspective, such as liquidated damage clauses or non-refundable deposits. In such cases courts will find it difficult to point to transaction costs as the source of incompleteness, so penalty defaults should be considered.

178. For example, we suggested that Goldberg's zero-damage penalty default would not sufficiently encourage retailers to contract for liquidated damages, and even if a larger penalty would, the amount of liquidated damages in equilibrium might "pool" at a non-informative low level. *See supra* Section I.C.2. Courts should also consider the possibility that some parties will fail to contract around penalty defaults out of ignorance or oversight.

179. The *Hadley* rule is an example of a penalty default that 1) is cheap to contract around by including a liquidated damage clause, 2) will likely cause damage information to be revealed, and 3) will facilitate more efficient precaution.

We must add an important transitional caveat. A legal change from one default to another can be costly—especially if the move is to a penalty default. Until parties become informed about the new default, there may be transitional costs as the parties continue to bargain in the shadow of an invalid law.

Finally, we note that in many contractual settings, both parties may have private information which they choose to withhold. In such settings of "dual asymmetric information," penalty defaults may not be sufficient to ensure that all private information is revealed.

tractual agreements, they reduce the inefficiencies of strategic pooling but at the cost of increased contracting. Lawmakers need to weigh these costs of pooling and separating in choosing the right rule; but more fundamentally, they need to be able to predict how much pooling and separating different rules are likely to generate.

The analysis of the article is quite general and can be applied to a wide range of legal issues.[180] For example, courts in interpreting statutes are often called upon to fill gaps. A number of scholars have used a "legislation-as-contract" approach to resolve such questions.[181] Jon Macey has proposed a type of penalty default by suggesting that statutory gaps be filled with public-regarding legislation.[182] Macey's default is not what the legislature would have contracted for and thus forces the legislature to make their pork-barrel deals public. Justice Scalia has gone the furthest, however, in articulating a penalty default standard of statutory interpretation.[183] In *Agency Holding Corp. v. Malley-Duff & Assoc.*,[184] the Supreme Court was asked to supply a default statute of limitations for a civil RICO[185] action because the legislation was silent on the issue. While the majority established a four-year limitation as what Congress would have wanted, Justice Scalia argued that there should be no statute of limitation. Scalia was "unmoved by the fear that [this] conclusion might prove 'repugnant to the genius of our laws' "[186] and even suggested that this penalty default might encourage Congress to contract around it: "Indeed, it might even prompt Congress to enact a limitations period that it believes 'appropriate,' a judgment far more within its competence than ours."[187] Ironically, Justice Scalia is arguing for an extreme form of judicial activism. Only by choosing a default that is wholly at odds with Congressional intent can the Court ensure that Congress will reveal its intent. Scalia's ultimate message then is that extreme activism can become a form of disempowering judicial restraint. Examples such as these underscore our primary thesis that efficient defaults may at times deviate from what the parties would have wanted. More importantly, they demonstrate that our

180. *See* discussion *supra* note 10.

181. *See* Easterbrook, *The Supreme Court, 1983 Term—Foreword: The Court and the Economic System*, 98 HARV. L. REV. 4, 15-16 (1984).

182. Macey, *Promoting Public-Regarding Legislation through Statutory Interpretation: An Interest Group Model*, 86 COLUM. L. REV. 223, 236-40 (1986).

183. For a more general discussion of using penalty defaults to force Congress to enunciate the law, see L. Marshall, Let Congress Do It: The Case For an Absolute Rule of Statutory Stare Decisis (1989) (unpublished manuscript on file with authors).

184. 483 U.S. 143, 157 (1987) (Scalia, J., concurring).

185. Racketeer Influenced and Corrupt Organizations Act (RICO), 18 U.S.C. § 1964 (1982 & Supp. V 1987).

186. 483 U.S. at 170 (Scalia, J., concurring) (quoting Occidental Life Ins. Co. v. EEOC, 432 U.S. 355 (1977) quoting Adams v. Woods, 6 U.S. (2 Cranch) 336, 342 (1805)).

187. 483 U.S. at 170.

choice of default must be informed by an understanding of why contracting parties—such as legislatures—leave gaps in their texts.[188]

Finally, we suggest that teachers focus more explicitly on the difference between default and immutable rules. Often students are able to recite the various rules learned in a course without knowing whether they are obligatory or not. Teaching which rules are defaults is not a mere pedagogical conceit. To represent their clients effectively, attorneys need to know not only what the legal rules are, but how, if at all, they can be abrogated to further their clients' interests.[189] A descriptive knowledge of defaults and how to contract around them is a prerequisite of effective advocacy.

188. For example, the statute of limitation gap of RICO in *Malley-Duff* is hard to explain as hidden pork-barrel legislation.

189. In corporate law especially, the mechanism for contracting around the default may be oblique. For example, while corporate statutes do not give the board of directors the right to disapprove a merger, certain "poison pill" plans have the effect of making the board sign off on any hostile bid. *See* Dynamics Corp. of Am. v. CTS Corp., 805 F.2d 705 (7th Cir. 1986) (analyzing economic impact of "poison pill").

Torts

[2]

VOLUME 101 JANUARY 1988 NUMBER 3

HARVARD LAW REVIEW

ARTICLES

THE BOUNDARIES OF VICARIOUS LIABILITY: AN ECONOMIC ANALYSIS OF THE SCOPE OF EMPLOYMENT RULE AND RELATED LEGAL DOCTRINES

*Alan O. Sykes**

"VICARIOUS liability" may be defined as the imposition of liability upon one party for a wrong committed by another party.[1] One of its most common forms is the imposition of liability on an employer for the wrong of an employee or agent.

The imposition of vicarious liability usually depends in part upon the nature of the activity in which the wrong arises. For example, if an employee (or "servant") commits a tort within the ordinary course of business, the employer (or "master") normally incurs vicarious liability under principles of respondeat superior. If the tort arises outside the "scope of employment," however, the employer does not incur liability, absent special circumstances.[2] Roughly speaking, this "scope of employment rule" restricts vicarious liability to tortious conduct that "should be considered as one of the normal risks to be borne by the business,"[3] thereby excluding an employee's "personal" torts.

---

* Assistant Professor of Law, University of Chicago Law School. I have received helpful comments on prior drafts of this Article from Albert Alschuler, Richard Epstein, David Haddock, Fred McChesney, Richard Posner, Stephen Schulhofer, and Steven Shavell, and from the participants in the Law and Economics Workshop of the University of Chicago. I also wish to thank the Lynde and Harry Bradley Foundation, which provided financial support for this research.

[1] Vicarious liability has received increasing academic attention in recent years, much of it from the economic perspective. *See, e.g.*, Kornhauser, *An Economic Analysis of the Choice Between Enterprise and Personal Liability for Accidents*, 70 CALIF. L. REV. 1345 (1982); Kraakman, *Gatekeepers: The Anatomy of a Third-Party Enforcement Strategy*, 2 J.L. ECON. & ORG. 53 (1986); Kraakman, *Corporate Liability Strategies and the Costs of Legal Controls*, 93 YALE L.J. 857 (1984); Landes & Posner, *Joint and Multiple Tortfeasors: An Economic Analysis*, 9 J. LEGAL STUD. 517 (1980); Stone, *The Place of Enterprise Liability in the Control of Corporate Conduct*, 90 YALE L.J. 1 (1980); Sykes, *The Economics of Vicarious Liability*, 93 YALE L.J. 1231 (1984).

[2] *See infra* Part II.

[3] RESTATEMENT (SECOND) OF AGENCY § 229 comment a (1958).

This Article provides an economic analysis of the "scope of employment" rule and related legal doctrines that have evolved to limit vicarious liability in various contexts. Part I develops the theoretical framework by interweaving the economic theory of incentive contracting in principal-agent relationships with the economic interpretation of causation requirements in tort law. Part II applies this framework to a discussion of the two types of tort cases in which the scope of employment is most frequently litigated: "frolic and detour" cases and intentional tort cases. The objective of the analysis is to determine whether the existing disposition of cases tends to promote economic welfare, and, when it does not, to suggest how the law might be modified to that end. Part II also addresses the limited duty of an employer to control employees' conduct that falls outside the scope of their employment and the related line of "negligent hiring" cases. Part II concludes that existing tort doctrine is often consistent with the pursuit of economic welfare but that the law sometimes focuses on factors that are irrelevant to this goal. Accordingly, Part II suggests a number of modifications to existing legal rules.

Part III adapts the theoretical framework developed in Part I to analyze the liability of a motor vehicle owner for the tort of someone who borrows the vehicle, the liability of a premises owner for the tort of an intruder, and the liability of an employer for the sexual harassment of one employee by another. Like Part II, Part III concludes that the approach of current law to these issues is often reasonably efficient but that several aspects of existing doctrine should be modified.

I. Economic Principles

The analysis throughout this Article contemplates the choice between a rule of personal liability, under which the employee alone is liable for his wrongs,[4] and a rule of vicarious liability, under which the employer and employee are jointly and severally liable. The objective of the analysis is to identify the circumstances under which each rule is "efficient" — that is, the circumstances under which each rule best promotes economic welfare. The concept of economic welfare that underlies the analysis is by now familiar: liability rule A will be said to be "efficient" relative to liability rule B if rule A is *potentially* Pareto superior to rule B from the perspective of society as a whole.[5]

[4] The use of masculine pronouns throughout is for convenience only and is not intended to convey any assumption about gender identity.

[5] This measure of economic welfare is sometimes known as the "potential compensation test," which serves as the basis for much of the modern literature on applied welfare economics and cost-benefit analysis. Conceptually, the test inquires whether those who benefit from a change

A. The Efficiency of Vicarious Liability for Employment-Related Wrongs

In most cases in which an employee commits a tort during the ordinary course of duties, no question arises as to whether the employee acted within the scope of employment. The wrongful conduct is plainly a consequence of the employment relationship and represents the materialization of a risk that is normally attendant upon such employment relationships.

The efficiency of imposing vicarious liability on the employer under these conditions has been studied at some length. In a previous article,[6] I analyzed the choice between personal liability and vicarious liability for torts clearly within the scope of employment and developed several principles for assessing which rule best promotes economic welfare. Because these principles also bear upon the efficiency of vicarious liability in cases in which the scope of employment is in question, it is useful to summarize them here.[7]

1. The Significance of the Choice Between Personal Liability and Vicarious Liability. — Economic theory suggests that between any employer and employee there exists an optimal allocation of the risk of financial loss attendant upon any judgment against the employee. This allocation must take into account each party's attitude toward risk-bearing, the employee's incentives to avoid whatever conduct might lead to a judgment against him, and the incentives available to the employer to monitor the employee or otherwise to guard against the occurrence of a wrong.

If the assumption of liability by the employer is efficient from the perspective of the employer and the employee, and the employer agrees to bear all or part of the risk of a particular judgment, that agreement represents part of the employee's total compensation package, and other components of total compensation are reduced commensurately. In general, the employer will agree to bear all or part of the risk of a judgment if and only if the expected cost to him of doing so (including perhaps a risk premium if the employer is risk averse) is less than the reduction in the other components of the

---

in policy can compensate those who suffer and still remain better off themselves. Thus, any change in policy that satisfies the test is potentially Pareto superior — if compensation is actually paid to those who suffer, no one will be worse off than before and some will be better off. *See* H. VARIAN, MICROECONOMIC ANALYSIS 218 (1st ed. 1978). All technical problems with the measure, such as its possible circularity in exceptional cases due to wealth effects, are assumed away. The use of the potential compensation test is now quite routine in economic studies of tort law. *See, e.g.*, W. LANDES & R. POSNER, THE ECONOMIC STRUCTURE OF TORT LAW 16–17 (1987).

[6] *See* Sykes, *supra* note 1.

[7] For a complete exposition of these results, see *id.* at 1233–59.

employee's compensation package that the employee will accept in exchange for the employer's promise.

Absent transaction costs for private risk-allocation agreements, the optimal allocation of risk does not depend upon where the law initially places liability. If the employer would bear the risk in an optimal agreement but a rule of personal liability prevails, then the employer and the employee will contract voluntarily for the employer to reimburse the employee in the event of a judgment. On the other hand, if the employee would bear the risk in an optimal agreement but a rule of vicarious liability prevails, then the employee will contract to reimburse the employer for any amount that the employer pays to a successful plaintiff.

In short, regardless of who bears liability initially, private contracting between the employer and the employee can ensure that the ultimate liability of each party accords with the optimal allocation of risk. Such analysis suggests that the choice between a rule of personal or vicarious liability may be unimportant.[8]

This conclusion rests, however, upon two critical assumptions. First, it assumes that the sum of the payments to the plaintiff by the employer and the employee is the same under both rules of liability. If the plaintiff's judgment exceeds the employee's assets, however, as may often be the case, then the plaintiff will collect more under vicarious liability. Private contracting cannot achieve the same allocation of risk under either liability rule in these circumstances because the magnitude of the risk to be allocated changes with the liability rule. Either the employee, the employer, or both the employer and employee must pay more under vicarious liability.

Second, as suggested at the outset, the proposition that the choice of liability rule does not affect the ultimate incidence of liability depends upon an assumption that the transaction costs of negotiating and enforcing a private risk-allocation contract are small enough to permit the employer and the employee profitably to enter into such a contract. In fact, the costs of risk-allocation agreements may be considerable, and a reallocation of liability by contract thus may be infeasible or at least quite costly.

Hence, the choice between vicarious liability and personal liability is a significant one whenever the employee is unable to pay judgments in full under a rule of personal liability or the costs of negotiating and enforcing a private risk-allocation contract between the employer and the employee are significant. Both circumstances arise frequently in practice and, as suggested below, both lead to significant inefficiencies under personal liability that vicarious liability sometimes will eliminate.

---

[8] This proposition is also developed in some detail in Kornhauser, *supra* note 1, at 1347, 1357–61.

2. *The Potential Inefficiencies of Personal Liability.* — Assume for the moment that the employee's tort is not related to any voluntary business transaction with the employer's business (thus, for example, the victim is not a customer or a fellow employee). This assumption ensures that the probability of a tort will not affect consumer willingness to pay for the goods and services of the enterprise and will not affect the wage demands of fellow employees. I will relax this assumption below as required.

The possibility that employees may be unable to pay judgments against them in full creates three possible inefficiencies under a rule of personal liability. First, because the employee does not bear the full (expected) cost of his wrongs, his incentive to avoid committing a wrong, either accidentally or intentionally, often (though not always[9]) will be inefficiently small. As a result, the incidence of wrongdoing increases to an inefficiently high level.

Second, because the employer's business does not bear the full cost of the compensable wrongs attendant upon its operation[10] (either directly through liability payments or indirectly through wages paid to employees who make liability payments[11]), its profitability is inflated relative to what it would be if the employee could pay judgments in full. In a competitive market, the employer is then likely to expand production beyond the socially optimal level because his private marginal costs of production are lower than the social marginal costs of production.[12]

---

[9] Conceivably, even if an employee cannot pay judgments in full, the prospect of a judgment that would exhaust his assets might motivate an inefficiently *high* level of care. Specifically, a highly risk-averse employee may exercise great care to avoid bankruptcy and might exercise more care than would be cost effective if, for example, all liability were efficiently allocated to a risk-neutral employer.

[10] As Coase recognized long ago, however, injuries are also a cost of *victims'* activities. *See* Coase, *The Problem of Social Cost*, 3 J.L. & ECON. 1 (1960). This fact and its implications for the choice between personal and vicarious liability are discussed at length at pp. 579–81 below.

[11] This problem does not arise if employees can pay judgments in full, because employees will then bear the full costs of compensable wrongs either directly or indirectly. Obviously, employers do not pay judgments directly under a rule of personal liability unless they agree to "insure" their employees against liability. If an employer does not provide such "insurance," however, employees will take that fact into account in choosing among alternative employment opportunities. Employees will then require higher wages to accept positions that require them to bear a greater risk of liability, and employers will bear costs of liability *indirectly* through wage payments. If employees can pay all judgments against them in full, their wage demands will reflect the full expected value of prospective liability judgments. Business enterprises will then fully internalize the expected costs of liability through wage payments even if liability judgments are fully paid by employees and transaction costs preclude express bargaining between employers and employees over the allocation of the risk of judgments against the employees.

[12] The social marginal costs of production include all marginal costs to the enterprise — labor, materials, liability judgments paid, and so on — plus the marginal costs of wrongs to injured parties that are properly attributable to the business enterprise but that go uncompen-

Third, when employees are potentially insolvent, they may be dissuaded from entering optimal risk-allocation agreements with their employers. An effective risk-sharing agreement requires the employer and the employee to pay the full value of the judgment against the employee, which clearly reduces their expected wealth relative to a regime in which part of the judgment goes unsatisfied.[13] The existence of this added "cost" to risk-sharing may dissuade risk-sharing — indeed, it may motivate employers to seek out insolvent employees to bear the risk of dangerous activities — despite the fact that the employer is often the better risk bearer.[14]

In addition to these three inefficiencies, inefficiencies may arise under a rule of personal liability even when employees *are* able to pay all judgments in full if there are significant costs to employers and employees in negotiating and enforcing risk-allocation agreements. Specifically, if the employer is the better risk bearer, such costs may prevent the employer from assuming the risk of judgments against the

---

sated. Part I.B. below considers the issue of which costs are "properly attributable" to the enterprise. *See infra* pp. 571–79.

[13] Suppose, for example, that the employer is risk neutral and the employee is risk averse. Suppose further that the probability of the tort is 0.1 and that this probability cannot be reduced through precautionary measures by the employee — there is no moral hazard problem if the employer assumes the risk of liability. If the employee could pay all judgments in full, optimal risk-sharing would then require the employer to assume the risk of liability in its entirety to shield the risk-averse employee from any prospect of an adverse judgment. The employer would be compensated by the opportunity to reduce wages by an amount greater than or equal to the actuarial value of the risk that he assumes.

Suppose, however, that the potential liability of the employee is $1 million and that the employee has only $10,000 in assets. To provide the risk-averse employee with protection against loss of his assets in the event of an adverse judgment, the employer must agree to pay not $10,000, but $1 million. The first $990,000 assuredly will go to the plaintiff, and only amounts in excess of that will provide the employee with protection from the prospect of insolvency. In effect, if the employer is to offer insurance to the risk-averse employee, he must also offer insurance to the plaintiff. (This discussion properly assumes that the employee cannot obtain a discharge in bankruptcy and *then* collect an insurance payment from the employer — the prospective payment from the employer would be treated as an asset by the bankruptcy court and could not be withheld from the plaintiff). Yet only the employee can compensate the employer for insurance through a wage reduction, and the amount of compensation that he will offer may be far short of that necessary to justify the insurance.

In this example, the expected payment from the employer to the plaintiff under an insurance arrangement to protect the employee against the loss of his $10,000 would equal (0.1) x $1 million = $100,000. Hence, the employer could only come out ahead if wages fell by more than $100,000, but that amount probably exceeds the total wages of the employee and far exceeds anything that he would be willing to pay for $10,000 worth of insurance.

[14] Other things being equal, the employer is likely to be the better risk bearer if he can more readily insure against the risk of liability; if he can diversify the risk by virtue of a large pool of employees who each present similar risks; or if he is a corporation as to which the risk of judgments against employees is a diversifiable risk for the stockholders. The employer may also be a better risk bearer simply because the employer is wealthier than the employee and thus may be less averse to risks of a given magnitude.

employee that exist under personal liability. Alternatively, the employer and the employee will have to incur the costs of an agreement to shift the risk of liability to the employer.

3. The Effects of Vicarious Liability. — Vicarious liability reduces or eliminates *some* of the inefficiencies that can arise under personal liability.[15] First, because vicarious liability ensures that any judgment against the employee will be paid to the limit of the combined assets of the employer and the employee, any inefficient expansion of the scale of business activity that results when the employee cannot pay judgments is avoided, or at least lessened. Second, vicarious liability often will improve the efficiency of risk-sharing by eliminating the incentive that may exist under personal liabilty to leave liability on the employee in order to take advantage of his inability to pay judgments. Moreover, if the employer is the better risk bearer, vicarious liability can eliminate transaction costs that the employer and the employee might otherwise incur in negotiating and enforcing a private agreement under which the employer assumes the risk of liability.

The ultimate efficiency or inefficiency of vicarious liability also depends, however, on its effect upon employees' incentives to avoid wrongful conduct. The effect of vicarious liability on such incentives depends in turn upon the devices available to the employer to induce careful behavior and the costs of those devices.

One such device is direct observation of the employee's activities. If the employer can cheaply observe precautionary behavior (or deliberately tortious behavior) by each employee, the employer can simply announce a desired standard of conduct, observe subsequent employee behavior, and penalize employees who fail to meet the desired standard.[16] This type of incentive system is usually inexpensive to design

---

[15] As noted above, this discussion is limited to wrongs against parties outside the employment relation whose injury is not related to any voluntary business transaction with the employer's business. The analysis can easily be extended to other types of injuries, such as injuries to customers or fellow employees. *See* Sykes, *supra* note 1, at 1256–59.

For example, suppose that employees occasionally commit torts against customers of their employers. If customers are fully informed *ex ante* about the probability of a tort and the prospects of compensation at each business and take that information fully into account in their purchase decisions, then their willingness to pay for the goods and services of each business will adjust perfectly to reflect the prospect of an uncompensated injury. Businesses will then be unable to externalize liability by employing judgment-proof agents. The efficiency of vicarious liability will therefore depend primarily upon whether it improves risk allocation between the employer and the employee in the presence of transaction costs. *See id.* at 1258.

By contrast, if customers have no information about the risk of torts associated with their voluntary business transactions, their willingness to pay will not reflect risks of uncompensated injury. The existence of the customer relationship is of no signficance to the analysis of vicarious liability in such cases. *See id.* at 1257.

Various intermediate cases of "imperfect information" may also be postulated. For analysis of the information conditions in particular settings and their implications, see Parts III.B. and III.C. below.

[16] For example, suppose that injuries at a construction project can be easily avoided by the

and to implement (assuming that observation is inexpensive) and often provides the employer with the ability to avert employee misconduct altogether.

The employer's influence over advancement and compensation decisions often provides another important incentive device. If the employee desires a long-term relationship with the employer, the employer can exploit this desire through policies under which the employee's prospects for advancement and pay raises, and even the employee's continued employment, depend in part upon the employee's avoidance of any misconduct that might result in harm. Such incentives are also fairly inexpensive to implement in many cases[17] and, as long as the employee values the employment relationship, these incentives can act as an effective constraint on the employee's behavior even if the employer cannot cheaply observe that behavior. Moreover, because these incentives affect the employee's current and future stream of earnings, they may motivate the employee to avoid wrongful conduct better than the prospect of a liability judgment, which will only be paid to the limit of the employee's *current* assets (if the judgment is dischargeable in bankruptcy).

The ability of the employer to affect the employee's incentives is much more limited, however, when the employee's behavior is not easily observed or when the employee has no interest in maintaining a long-term employment relationship. Under these conditions, perhaps the only device available to dissuade misconduct is the threat of an indemnity action against the employee in the event that the employer incurs vicarious liability. Such actions can be quite costly to pursue, however, and may not be cost effective if the employee's assets are modest.[18] When the threat of an indemnity action is the only device for the maintenance of incentives, therefore, a rule of vicarious liability actually may reduce employees' incentives to avoid wrongful conduct and reduce economic welfare.[19]

---

erection of a barricade to shield an excavation. Knowing the need for such a precaution, the employer can simply order employees to erect it and observe whether or not they comply. Such an observation will usually require little expenditure of time or effort by the employer.

[17] *See* Sykes, *supra* note 1, at 1253–55.

[18] The limited empirical evidence suggests that the employer's right to indemnity is rarely exercised. *See* Sykes, *supra* note 1, at 1243. Whether this may reflect an optimal assumption of risk by employers or the costs of indemnity actions is difficult to determine.

[19] If an employee's assets are too meager to justify the pursuit of indemnity by the employer under vicarious liability, then a prospective plaintiff may also find it unprofitable to bring suit under personal liability. If so, then the imposition of vicarious liability will not dilute the employee's incentives to avoid wrongdoing. Plaintiffs may find it worthwhile to file suit, however, even if the employer does not. Unlike the employer, the plaintiff may have an emotional or dignitary interest in filing an action. Alternatively, the employer may decline to pursue indemnity in order to avoid the disruption of otherwise amicable relations with the workforce — an indemnity action that sends an employee into personal bankruptcy could send

B. *The Causal Relation Between Business Activity and Employee Wrongs*

The analysis to this point has assumed that the wrong committed by the employee is properly viewed as a cost of the employer's business. For example, the proposition that the evasion of liability judgments by an insolvent agent may lead to an inefficient expansion in the scale of business activity clearly rests on this assumption or, to put it slightly differently, on an assumption that the business is the "cause" of the wrongs that lead to the judgments. These notions warrant further elaboration.

1. A Definition of "Enterprise Causation." — The legal meaning of the term "cause" depends upon context. In tort law, for example, one often distinguishes "cause in fact" from "proximate cause" and other forms of "causation,"[20] and a variety of definitions exist for each concept.[21]

This Section introduces a definition of causation that captures the relationship between the existence of an employer's business and the occurrence of a wrong by an employee. To distinguish this concept of causation from similar concepts in the law and in the literature, it will be termed "enterprise causation."

Initially, it is necessary to define the term "wrong" as it is used in the analysis that follows:

> Definition: A "wrong" is an injurious act that leads to liability of a given magnitude.

For example, a particular act of negligence that a person commits while driving a motor vehicle, resulting in a tort that creates liability of $1 million, might constitute a "wrong."[22]

---

a signal to the workforce that the employer has little interest in the personal welfare of his employees, affecting morale and productivity adversely.

Finally, even if an indemnity action is worthwhile for the employer, such actions are costly. Also, vicarious liability adds an additional party to litigation and thus may increase litigation costs significantly. Unless these costs are offset by some other benefit of vicarious liability, a shift from personal liability to vicarious liability will reduce economic welfare.

[20] *See e.g.*, W. KEETON, D. DOBBS, R. KEETON & D. OWEN, PROSSER AND KEETON ON THE LAW OF TORTS 263–321 (5th ed. 1984) [hereinafter PROSSER & KEETON].

[21] For a recent survey of the causal inquiry, see Wright, *Causation in Tort Law*, 73 CALIF. L. REV. 1735 (1985).

[22] Such a definition of "wrong" is to be distinguished from narrower definitions that, for example, might distinguish among otherwise identical "wrongs" according to the identity of the victim or to the time and place at which the wrong occurs, and from broader definitions that might not, for example, distinguish among wrongs according to the magnitude of liability.

This definition is chosen because the analysis to follow focuses on the degree to which the employment relation affects the expected social costs of torts. To capture those effects, it is useful to consider the effect of the employment relation on the probability distribution of each possible "wrong" as here defined.

The remaining definitions capture the "causal" connection between the existence of the employment relation and the occurrence of employees' wrongs. The crucial variable in this analysis is the extent to which the employment relation increases the probability of each wrong.

> Definition: An enterprise "fully causes" the wrong of an employee if the dissolution of the enterprise and subsequent unemployment of the employee would reduce the probability of the wrong to zero.[23]

For example, consider the case of a service station attendant who negligently performs improper repairs on a customer's vehicle, resulting in an accident and a judgment against the attendant. The accident is fully caused by the service station enterprise under the above definition if the dissolution of the service station enterprise and the subsequent unemployment of the attendant would reduce the probability of an accident attributable to negligent repairs by the attendant to zero.

By contrast, suppose that the same attendant occasionally commits acts of wife-beating and that the incidence of such acts bears no relation to the attendant's employment or unemployment. Then, the tort of wife-beating is not caused by the service station enterprise, because its dissolution and the employee's subsequent unemployment would not reduce the probability of the tort.

To be sure, intermediate cases exist. The probability of wife-beating, for example, might be increased by certain stressful occupations. Such cases motivate a further refinement of the definition of enterprise causation.

> Definition: An enterprise "partially causes" the wrong of an employee if the dissolution of the enterprise and subsequent unemployment of the employee would reduce the probability of the wrong but not eliminate it.

One component of the definitions of both full and partial enterprise causation is the "subsequent unemployment" of the employee after dissolution of the enterprise. Thus, to assess enterprise causation in the service station example above, one assumes that after the dissolution of the service station agency the attendant does not go to work for another service station or open his own repair business.

---

[23] This definition of causation is closely related to the concept of "probabilistic causation" developed in Shavell, *An Analysis of Causation and the Scope of Liability in the Law of Torts*, 9 J. LEGAL STUD. 463, 468–69 (1980), and to the analysis of causation developed in Landes & Posner, *Causation in Tort Law: An Economic Approach*, 12 J. LEGAL STUD. 109 (1983). Calabresi was perhaps the first to suggest the economic signficance of probabilistic notions of causation. *See* Calabresi, *Concerning Cause and the Law of Torts*, 43 U. CHI. L. REV. 69 (1975).

To be sure, if the service station agency were in fact to dissolve, the employee might well move to a position with another employer. The probability of wrongful behavior in that new position (whether or not in the same line of business) might be less than, equal to, or greater than the probability of wrongful behavior in the former position. Nonetheless, the appropriate benchmark for the comparison of probabilities in the analysis to follow is the subsequent unemployment of the employee. That comparison is the appropriate one because, as the economic discussion will indicate, the efficiency of resource allocation is enhanced if each business enterprise bears the incremental social costs associated with its operation. By measuring those incremental costs with reference to the social costs that would otherwise arise if the resources used by the enterprise were unemployed, a resulting competitive equilibrium will tend to generate an efficient allocation of resources among alternative enterprises and alternative (nonenterprise) uses for the resources (such as leisure).[24] To be sure, this proposition is subject to a number of caveats relating to the theory of the second-best, many of which are linked to matters discussed below (cost externalization due to insolvency, the infeasibility of cost internalization by both injurers and victims, and so on).[25]

Note finally that the definitions of full and partial enterprise causation leave open the possibility that the dissolution of the enterprise and subsequent unemployment of the employee may increase the probability that the former employee will commit some other wrong.[26]

2. The Implications of Enterprise Causation. — (a) Passive Victims. — Assume initially that the victims of wrongs are "passive," in the sense that they cannot or will not take cost-effective measures to protect themselves against wrongs either by adopting precautions or by curtailing activities that might expose them to potential wrongdoers.[27] The importance of enterprise causation may now be illus-

---

[24] To give a simple example that suggests why the "subsequent unemployment" benchmark is appropriate, suppose that an individual will commit a wrong that causes $10,000 worth of harm with probability 0.1 if he is unemployed. If he is employed by either Sears or Wards, the probability of the same wrong rises to 0.2. Thus, if the individual is hired by either company, an incremental social cost of (0.2–0.1) x $10,000 = $1,000 results from his activities as an employee. If his employment is to be economically efficient, it must generate enough value to cover this cost in addition to his wages and all other costs of hiring him. Yet if the incremental costs of wrongs by workers at Sears were measured with reference to the probability of wrongs by workers at Wards, one would conclude that these incremental costs were zero — the probability of the wrong is the same at either company. And if, as a result, neither Sears nor Wards were required to bear the $1,000 incremental cost associated with hiring the worker, both would tend to hire an inefficiently high number of employees and to expand to a point at which the social marginal costs of their activities exceeded the social marginal benefits.

[25] *See infra* pp. 579–81.

[26] The implications of this possibility are explored in note 34 below.

[27] This assumption is relaxed below. The analysis in this Section encompasses instances in which victims cannot take measures to reduce their exposure to injury; instances in which it is

trated with variations on the following hypothetical. An enterprise produces a good that many consumers value well in excess of its marginal capital, labor, and materials costs. The good is priced competitively, thereby yielding substantial consumer (and perhaps producer) surplus. Suppose, however, that some of the employees who produce the good tend to commit assaults that result in civil liability. By hypothesis, neither the probability that an employee will commit an assault nor the magnitude of the resulting liability depends upon the employee's wealth, upon whether he is employed or unemployed, or upon any characteristic of his employment. In addition, by hypothesis, no incentive mechanism exists that would enable the employer to reduce the incidence of employee assaults.

To hold the employer vicariously liable for such employee assaults, regardless of when or where they occur or the identity of the assault victim, is almost certainly inefficient. The employer cannot affect the number of assaults or the total amount of damages. Thus, to the extent that vicarious liability imposes additional costs on the enterprise, it may drive the enterprise out of business or at the very least cause it to shrink as the marginal costs of production increase. Society then will lose at least some of the economic surplus from the production of the enterprise.[28]

Employers might recoup some of their losses through indemnity actions, and when they did not, the costs of vicarious liability to the employer would be mitigated by a decline in the wages paid to employees — if an employer were forced to "insure" his employees against liability for assaults that are unrelated to the enterprise, employees would reduce their wage demands by the expected value to them of the "insurance" provided by their employers. In a perfectly informed labor market in which employees could pay all judgments against them, and neglecting the effects of risk aversion, this reduction in wage demands would result in a wage that was lower by precisely the expected value of the liability borne by the employer. The marginal costs of production would be unaffected, and no loss of surplus would arise.

This conclusion, however, assumes away the familiar problems of employee insolvency and transaction costs. Employees who cannot

---

inefficient for victims to take such measures; and instances in which victims, because of "bounded rationality" (for example, a failure to perceive the risk of injury or the opportunity to take precautionary measures), systematically neglect the opportunity to reduce their exposure to injury.

[28] One caveat relates to the possibility that vicarious liability provides risk-sharing benefits that are unattainable in its absence due to transaction costs. Although it seems highly improbable, because of the moral hazard problem, that an optimal risk-allocation agreement between the employer and the employee would call for the employer to assume liability for the employee's assaults, it is conceivable that employers are better risk bearers than assault victims. Vicarious liability might then enhance the efficiency of risk-sharing when employees are judgment-proof.

pay judgments in full may not value "insurance" provided by employers at its full expected cost to the employer. Their wage demands thus will not fall by the full expected value of the "insurance," and a decline in wages will not fully compensate the employer for increased liability. In addition, as noted above, various transaction costs tend to increase when employers are held vicariously liable, and these costs will add to the marginal costs of production. Hence, the imposition of vicarious liability under the circumstances hypothesized here appears inefficient because it leads to higher costs of production, higher prices, and a loss of consumer and producer surplus, but in no way reduces the expected costs of employee misconduct.

This analysis suggests the general proposition that vicarious liability for a given wrong is probably inefficient if (a) the enterprise does not cause the wrong, even partially; and (b) the enterprise cannot reduce the probability of the wrong through incentive contracts with its employees.[29]

A second proposition can be illustrated with a slight modification of the above hypothetical. Continuing with the assumption that the employer cannot reduce the incidence of assaults through incentive devices, suppose that the employee is more likely to commit assaults in the workplace than elsewhere, so that his employment increases the probability that an assault will occur. The probability of a wrong thus depends upon whether the employee is employed or not, but (by hypothesis) cannot be affected by the employer once the employee has been hired. An employee with an intrinsically stressful job may be more likely to commit an assault, for example, but the employer's only effective means of reducing the probability of an assault may be to terminate the employment relationship.

In this situation, it is inefficient to impose vicarious liability on the enterprise for the full value of the wrong, because the scale of the enterprise's activity will tend to contract excessively. Yet it is also inefficient to allow the enterprise to escape liability altogether — if the employee is insolvent, the resulting scale of enterprise activity will be excessive. Efficient resource allocation thus requires the enterprise to bear liability for part, but not all, of the cost of the wrong.[30] If

[29] Previous writers have suggested similar propositions, but without considering the availability of effective incentive devices. *See* Calabresi, *Some Thoughts on Risk Distribution and the Law of Torts*, 70 YALE L.J. 499, 514 (1961) (arguing that "resource allocation militates strongly against allocating to an enterprise costs not closely associated with it"); Smith, *Frolic & Detour*, 1923 COLUM. L. REV. 444, 461 (suggesting that an enterprise should bear risk only if the enterprise is a contributing factor).

[30] Although the computation of the appropriate judgment against the enterprise may be complex (perhaps infeasible) in practice, it is conceptually straightforward — the value of the judgment against the employer must ensure that the enterprise directly or indirectly bears a cost of production with an expected value exactly equal to the increment in the expected value of the wrong attributable to the enterprise.

the imposition of partial liability is infeasible for institutional reasons — if vicarious liability must be imposed on an all or nothing basis — then the liability rule is inevitably "second-best." Other things being equal, the greater the extent to which the employment relation "causes" the wrong, the more likely it is that vicarious liability for the entire judgment will be second-best efficient.[31]

A third proposition may be illustrated with a further variation of the assumptions above. Again suppose that the employer cannot reduce the incidence of assaults with incentive devices and that the probability of an assault depends solely upon the employment or unemployment of the employee. Assume further that the probability of an assault would be *zero* if the employment relationship were dissolved and the employee remained unemployed thereafter. Thus, the enterprise fully causes the assault. It follows that the injury attributable to the assault is a cost that is fully attributable to the operation of the enterprise — the enterprise will operate at an efficient level of output only if it bears, directly or indirectly, all liability for the employee's assault. The imposition of vicarious liability is plainly efficient under these circumstances because, by hypothesis, it can have no adverse effect on the incentives of the employee to engage in tortious conduct.

The analysis becomes more complex if incentive devices can reduce the probability of the wrong or if the assumption of liability by the employer may affect the propensity of the employee to commit the assault. To continue with the previous hypothetical, suppose that the probability of an assault is not directly affected by the employment or unemployment of the employee — and thus the enterprise does not even "partially cause" the assault — but that the employer can reduce the probability of an assault through some appropriate incentive device, for example, by threatening to discharge the employee if he commits an assault or by observing the employee's behavior in advance of an assault and intervening to prevent the assault before it occurs. Obviously, the employer has no reason to use such an incentive device under a rule of personal liability. The question thus arises whether vicarious liability may enhance economic welfare even though the enterprise does not cause the wrong.

---

[31] Formally, to determine the second-best rule in a competitive market, one must weigh the loss of economic surplus under personal liability (owing to the fact that the social marginal costs of production would exceed the private marginal costs of production, which would result in an equilibrium market price below social marginal costs) against the loss of surplus under vicarious liability (owing to the fact that the private marginal costs of production would exceed the social marginal costs, which would result in an equilibrium market price that exceeded social marginal costs). Of course, this "second-best" rule may well be impossible to identify in practice, at least on a case-by-case basis. Probably the best that can be done is to choose between vicarious liability and personal liability in general classes of cases, based upon a rough analysis of the economic costs and benefits of each rule.

To examine this issue, suppose first that the costs to the enterprise of using the incentive device are zero and that the incentive device always prevents the assault — thus, the enterprise never actually pays damages under a rule of vicarious liability. Vicarious liability is clearly efficient under these circumstances, because it eliminates any possibility of an assault at no cost to the enterprise.[32]

Now suppose that the incentive device reduces but does not eliminate the probability of the assault and that the reduction of the expected damages from assaults when the incentive device is utilized exceeds the costs of the incentive device. If the prospective victims knew of their impending assault, they would offer the enterprise, and the enterprise would accept, a side payment to use the incentive device. The marginal costs of production for the enterprise would not increase, and the incidence of assaults would decline with no adverse effect on the level of enterprise activity.

Of course, such side payment schemes are unlikely to arise in practice. In their absence, perhaps the only way to motivate the employer to utilize the incentive device is to hold him liable for any judgment against the employee. Under a strict liability theory, the employer would always incur joint and several liability with the employee. Under a negligence theory, the employer could avoid liability with a showing that the assault occurred despite the fact that he utilized the appropriate incentive device.

Usually, vicarious liability in employment relationships (conventional respondeat superior liability) is "strict" — the employer cannot successfully defend the action by proving that he exercised all reasonable means to dissuade the employee from committing the wrong.[33] In the present hypothetical, strict liability will indeed induce the employer to utilize any and all incentive devices that are cost effective in reducing his liability. Because the employer is not compensated for the costs of the incentive devices as he would be under an idealized side-payment scheme, however, and because he bears liability for judgments against the potentially impecunious employee, the marginal costs of production for enterprise output increase and the scale of enterprise activity contracts to a point at which the prevailing price exceeds the social marginal costs of production. To determine whether vicarious liability has reduced or enhanced economic welfare, the resulting loss of consumer and producer surplus must be weighed against the reduction in the expected value of losses from assaults. The welfare effects of vicarious liability are more favorable the greater

[32] If workers value the opportunity to commit assaults and incorporate this factor into their wage demands, however, or if monitoring behavior by employers imposes some disutility on the workforce, workers may require higher compensation from enterprises that discourage assaults. To this extent, no incentive device may be costless from the perspective of the employer.

[33] *See* PROSSER & KEETON, *supra* note 20, at 501–02.

the degree to which the incentive device reduces the probability of assaults and the lower the costs to the enterprise of implementing the incentive device.

An alternative approach to employer liability, as noted, is to impose liability on the employer only if he is negligent and fails to use the desired incentive device. Hereafter, this policy will be termed "vicarious liability based on negligence" — a term that may suggest that liability is not really vicarious at all, but that I employ here for expositional convenience. In the present hypothetical, this approach is unambiguously superior to strict vicarious liability, because the employment of the tortfeasor does not increase the probability of the wrong, and hence the associated liability is not properly included in the social marginal costs of enterprise production. If the costs to the enterprise of using the incentive device are significant, however, the welfare consequences of vicarious liability based on negligence are still ambiguous. Although the enterprise escapes liability if it uses the incentive device, the costs of using it will become part of the marginal costs of production for the enterprise. Price will rise and consumer and producer surplus will fall. Again, to determine the net effect on social welfare, this reduction of surplus must be weighed against the benefits of the incentive device to potential assault victims. Other things being equal, the lower the cost of using the incentive device, and the greater its effectiveness, the more favorable are the welfare effects of vicarious liability.[34]

The analysis developed above also applies, with only minor modifications, to vicarious liability outside the employment relationship. Whenever an individual or business can dissuade wrongdoing at little or no cost through the adoption of incentives that affect the behavior of potential wrongdoers,[35] the imposition of vicarious liability can

---

[34] One final complication relates to the possibility that unemployment may be the "cause" of certain types of wrongs. Specifically, workers who are unemployed may commit any number of intentional or accidental wrongs, the probability of which declines or disappears once they are employed. The employment relationship thereby creates a social benefit for which employers *may* not be compensated: in an ideal world, employees' wage demands would be reduced to the extent that their employment eliminates the possibility of certain liability judgments against them. Employers thereby would be "compensated" for this ancillary benefit of employment. Even if employees take such factors into account in their wage demands, however, those demands will not fall by the full amount of the expected liability averted by employment if the employees cannot pay judgments against them.

Clearly, such a benefit is difficult to incorporate into the design of a liability rule, but its existence may in some cases weigh against the imposition of vicarious liability because vicarious liability will increase the costs of production for business enterprises and lead to a reduced level of production and employment.

[35] For a slight variation in the analysis, suppose that an employer has advance notice that his employee is about to commit a murder and can avert the murder by reporting the employee to the police — an arguably inexpensive "incentive device" from the employer's perspective. It probably would be efficient to impose a duty upon the employer to make the report. Of course,

motivate the adoption of such incentive devices and will be efficient whenever the benefit of reduced malfeasance exceeds the social costs of those incentive devices.[36] When the "causal" relationship between the activities of the entity subject to vicarious liability and the prospective wrong is weak, however, vicarious liability based on negligence is superior to strict vicarious liability.

The one caveat to this proposition relates to administrative costs, which are an important consideration in any economic analysis of liability rules. One must always be alert to the possibility that one liability rule may be cheaper to administer than another or may tend to produce fewer meritless suits. With respect to the choice between strict vicarious liability and vicarious liability based on negligence, the negligence approach probably leads to incrementally higher administrative costs associated with the need to litigate the employer's negligence, whereas the strict liability approach probably leads to incrementally higher administrative costs associated with a higher number of lawsuits.[37] The analysis to follow (except where noted) assumes that these costs roughly cancel out, so that the administrative cost factor does not weigh substantially in favor of either regime.

(b) Second-Best Issues: Victims Who Are Not Passive. — Suppose now that tort victims can take precautions to guard against being victimized and that they can (and will) curtail whatever activities expose them to the possibility of a wrong. Under these assumptions, no conventional tort liability rule can induce both injurers and victims to behave optimally (if the victim is not a party to a voluntary transaction with the business enterprise, as assumed above).[38]

Specifically, either a negligence regime or a strict liability regime, coupled with an appropriate contributory negligence defense or its equivalent, arguably can induce both injurers and victims to take cost-effective precautions during the course of their activities (assuming no insolvency on the part of either). Despite the exercise of such precautions, however, some injuries may occur. The frequency of injuries might be reduced if injurers and victims reduced their participation in activities that create a risk of injury. Indeed, an efficient

---

there is no reason to limit such a duty to employers; anyone who has advance notice of the prospect of a serious crime, and can avert the crime at little cost to himself by informing the police, arguably should have a duty to inform. The imposition of liability for failure to report is one way, though certainly not the only way, to encourage the desired behavior.

[36] To be sure, the value that society places on individual liberty and autonomy may constrain the degree to which vicarious liability is imposed under these conditions. To put it another way, any undesirable infringement of individual liberty and autonomy that might result from the imposition of vicarious liability and the resultant monitoring of some individuals by others is properly viewed as an economic cost.

[37] *See, e.g.*, W. LANDES & R. POSNER, *supra* note 5, at 65–66 (comparing the costs of administering strict liability and negligence standards).

[38] *See* Shavell, *Strict Liability Versus Negligence*, 9 J. LEGAL STUD. 1 (1980).

adjustment in such activity levels *will* occur on the part of any party who bears the full costs of the injuries that occur despite the exercise of due care. Yet it is impossible (with conventional liability rules) for all parties to bear those costs. Under negligence, victims bear such costs, and injurers avoid them; the opposite result occurs under strict liability. Hence, whichever regime prevails, either victims or injurers will fail to make an efficient adjustment in their activity levels.[39]

As a result, the choice between strict liability and negligence is an exercise in "second-best" analysis. If it is more efficient for injurers to internalize losses when everyone exercises due care, a rule of strict liability with a contributory negligence defense is superior; if it is more efficient for victims to bear losses when everyone exercises due care, a rule of negligence with a contributory negligence defense is superior.[40]

Related second-best issues arise when the injurer is judgment-proof and a court must decide whether to impose vicarious liability on the injurer's employer — the choice between personal liability and vicarious liability under these circumstances plainly affects the degree of cost internalization by injurers and victims. Putting aside the effects of the liability rule on the efficiency of risk-sharing and precautionary behavior, a rule of personal liability, which induces victims to curtail their activities, may sometimes be more efficient than a rule of vicarious liability, which leads employers to curtail their activities (or their employee's activities). The reverse possibility also exists if it is more efficient for employers to reduce activities than for victims to do so.

Thus, once the assumption of passivity on the part of victims is relaxed, the choice between personal liability and vicarious liability becomes considerably more complicated *if employees are judgment-proof.* Vicarious liability then affects the balance of cost internalization by injurers and victims, and it may be quite unclear how this balance should be struck, just as it may be unclear whether negligence or strict liability is the better rule to govern the liability of the employee.

Of course, if employees are able to pay judgments in full, vicarious liability will not affect the amount of compensation paid to victims.[41] Victims' behavior — their choice of precautions and activity levels —

---

[39] Of course, if "contributory negligence" existed whenever the victim failed to engage in the "first-best" activity level, in addition to those instances in which the victim failed to exercise due care, and if "negligence" existed whenever the injurer failed to engage in the "first-best" activity level, then either strict liability or negligence with a contributory negligence defense might achieve a first-best outcome. Judgments about the first-best activity level are presumably beyond the competence of the courts in all but exceptional cases, however, and ordinarily are not addressed in the analysis of negligence or contributory negligence.

[40] *See* Shavell, *supra* note 38.

[41] This assumes that the computation of damages will not be affected, for example, by the presence of a "deep-pocket" defendant.

will then be unaffected by the choice between personal liability and vicarious liability, and the analysis can proceed as if the victims are "passive."

Furthermore, even if employees are judgment-proof, classes of cases arise in which cost internalization by injurers and their employers is clearly more efficient than cost internalization by victims.[42] In these cases, the analysis can also proceed as if victims are "passive," because the greater degree of cost internalization by employers under vicarious liability is unambiguously beneficial. Alternatively, vicarious liability may considerably improve the efficiency of risk-sharing or the efficiency of precautionary behavior by injurers, and these efficiencies may outweigh any inefficiencies of vicarious liability resulting from reduced cost internalization by victims.

In addition, observe that if the choice between vicarious liability and personal liability does not affect the amount of damages awarded to victims (although it obviously may affect how much of any award they can collect), then vicarious liability results in the same cost internalization by enterprises that cause injuries, and the same cost internalization by victims, that would result if all employees who cause injuries could pay judgments against them in full. Thus, if one supposes that the degree of cost internalization by injurers and victims is roughly efficient when employees can pay judgments in full, vicarious liability is an attractive method of promoting that degree of cost internalization.

Finally, whether or not victims are "passive," and irrespective of the appropriate degree of cost internalization by injurers and victims, the implications of enterprise causation remain much the same. The more the employment relationship contributes to the probability of the wrong, the greater the economic benefits (if any) of strict vicarious liability, other things being equal. Similarly, if the enterprise does not even partially cause the wrong, strict vicarious liability is inferior to vicarious liability based upon negligence. Vicarious liability based upon negligence may in turn be inferior to personal liability, depending upon such factors as the cost and effectiveness of the incentive devices available to the employer.

II. The Scope of Employment Rule

The law places agency relationships into several categories, and the rules governing the vicarious tort liability of an employer or "principal" depend critically upon the category into which the agency falls. Most employer-employee relationships are "master-servant" re-

---

[42] For example, victims may perceive the risk of injury as *de minimis* and thus ignore it in deciding on their activity levels. *See infra* note 53; *supra* note 27.

lationships, in which the master controls or has the right to control the physical conduct of the servant in the performance of the servant's duties.[43] Absent the requisite degree of control, however, the employee may be classified as an independent contractor or other nonservant agent.[44] Under the doctrine of respondeat superior, masters are liable for torts that their servants commit within the scope of employment. If the tortfeasor is an independent contractor or nonservant agent, however, with some exceptions, the principal or employer is not liable for the tort.[45]

The discussion to follow focuses upon respondeat superior and specifically upon the scope of employment limitation to the master's liability. The *Restatement (Second) of Agency* defines the "scope of employment" as follows:

> (1) Conduct of a servant is within the scope of employment if, but only if:
>
> (a) it is of the kind he is employed to perform;
> (b) it occurs substantially within the authorized time and space limits;
> (c) it is actuated, at least in part, by a purpose to serve the master, and
> (d) if force is intentionally used by the servant against another, the use of force is not unexpectable by the master.
>
> (2) Conduct of a servant is not within the scope of employment if it is different in kind from that authorized, far beyond the authorized time or space limits, or too little actuated by a purpose to serve the master.[46]

According to the *Restatement*, masters are not liable for torts committed by their servants outside the scope of employment unless:

> (a) the master intended the conduct or the consequences, or (b) the master was negligent or reckless, or (c) the conduct violated a non-

[43] *See* RESTATEMENT (SECOND) OF AGENCY § 2(1)–(2) (1958); PROSSER & KEETON, *supra* note 20, at 501–08.

[44] *See* RESTATEMENT (SECOND) OF AGENCY § 2(3) (1958); PROSSER & KEETON, *supra* note 20, at 509–16.

[45] *See* RESTATEMENT (SECOND) OF AGENCY § 219 (1958); RESTATEMENT (SECOND) OF TORTS § 409 (1965); PROSSER & KEETON, *supra* note 20, at 501–16; H. REUSCHLEIN & W. GREGORY, HANDBOOK ON THE LAW OF AGENCY AND PARTNERSHIP 99–104 (1979); W. SELL, AGENCY 84–91 (1975). The economic basis for the distinction between "servants" and "independent contractors," and the basis for the various exceptions to the independent contractor rule, are discussed at length in Sykes, *supra* note 1, at 1259–79.

[46] RESTATEMENT (SECOND) OF AGENCY § 228 (1958); *see also id.* § 229 (kind of conduct within scope of employment); *id.* § 230 (acts forbidden by master); *id.* § 231 (criminal or intentionally tortious acts); *id.* § 232 (failure to act); *id.* § 233 (time of service); *id.* § 234 (area of service); *id.* § 235 (conduct not for purpose of serving master); *id.* § 236 (conduct actuated by dual purpose); *id.* § 237 (re-entry into employment).

delegable duty of the master, or (d) the servant purported to act or to speak on behalf of the principal and there was reliance upon apparent authority, or he was aided in accomplishing the tort by the existence of the agency relation.[47]

The commentators offer somewhat simpler definitions.[48] Seavey, for example, suggested that a tort is within the scope of employment if "it can be said rationally that the employment is the primary cause of the tort."[49] According to Prosser and Keeton, the scope of employment encompasses "acts which are so closely connected with what the servant is employed to do, and so fairly and reasonably incidental to it, that they may be regarded as methods, even though quite improper ones, of carrying out the objectives of the employment."[50]

All of these characterizations are somewhat ambiguous and provide only modest insight into the application of the scope of employment rule in practice. To facilitate concrete discussion of the rule and its economic consequences, this Part considers two groups of cases: cases involving torts by servants during a purported "frolic and detour" from their employment and cases involving intentional torts by servants. The analysis concludes with a brief discussion of the duty of a master to control conduct of a servant that is outside the scope of employment.

A. Frolic and Detour

A "frolic" or "detour" from employment occurs when an employee, while on travel for the employer, deviates from his assigned tasks for personal errands or other personal business. Not surprisingly, most frolic and detour cases involve motor vehicle torts. Thus, it is instructive to review the economic issues that arise with respect to motor

---

47 *Id.* § 219(2).

48 In addition to efforts to define the scope of employment, several commentators have advanced suggestions for reform or rationalization of the scope-of-employment limitation. In an article on frolic and detour cases, Smith suggests limiting the scope of employment to a "zone of risk" — vicarious liability would be imposed only if the enterprise is a "contributing cause" of the tort and the deviation from the servant's regular employment that led to the tort was "probable" in light of what the servant was employed to do. *See* Smith, *supra* note 29, at 724–25, 728. James argues for the imposition of vicarious liability for all reasonably foreseeable risks incidental to the enterprise. *See* James, *Vicarious Liability*, 28 TUL. L. REV. 161, 174–80 (1954). Morris criticizes any limitation of liability to foreseeable risks on the ground that most enterprises purchase insurance; insurance actuaries, Morris suggests, estimate risks by generalizing from the experience of many entrepreneurs with many types of risks, so that the ability of a particular entrepreneur to foresee a particular risk is irrelevant. *See* Morris, *Enterprise Liability and the Actuarial Process — The Insignificance of Foresight*, 70 YALE L.J. 554 (1961).

49 W. SEAVEY, HANDBOOK OF THE LAW OF AGENCY 148 (1964).

50 PROSSER & KEETON, *supra* note 20, at 502.

vehicle torts when no issue of enterprise causation is present.[51] Suppose, for example, that a truck driver negligently causes an accident while making a delivery for his employer. If the driver precisely followed the route suggested by the employer, and undertook no personal business during the trip, then the accident is fully caused by the employer's enterprise.[52]

As earlier analysis suggests, the choice between personal liability and vicarious liability is arguably immaterial if the truck driver carries enough insurance to pay any judgment against him in full. The compensable costs of accidents are fully internalized by the enterprise (the truck driver's wages must compensate him for the cost of the insurance necessary to cover on-the-job accidents). Furthermore, vicarious liability will not enhance the efficiency of risk-sharing because the driver's insurance company is at least as efficient a risk bearer as the employer.

In many instances, however, the driver will not have insurance, or the insurance that he does have will be inadequate to pay the judgment in full, particularly if the judgment is large. Vicarious liability then has two obvious benefits. First, it will force the enterprise to bear a greater proportion of the cost of the accidents that it "causes." Second, it will shift risk from the driver and accident victim, who are probably relatively poor risk bearers, to the employer or his insurance company, who are likely to be superior risk bearers.

Even if the employer will not seek indemnity from the employee, vicarious liability is unlikely to reduce significantly the driver's incentives to avoid the commission of motor vehicle torts. The widespread existence of private automobile insurance policies suggests that the efficiencies that accompany the shifting of risk to a superior risk bearer outweigh any moral hazard problem attendant upon insurance for motor vehicle accidents. Similar efficiencies in risk-bearing should arise when the employer "insures" the driver.

One question remains: does reduced cost internalization by victims under vicarious liability, and a resulting inefficient increase in their activity levels as drivers or pedestrians, offset the other benefits of vicarious liability? This result seems improbable, as there is no apparent reason why cost internalization by the victims of motor vehicle torts should be systematically preferred to cost internalization by injurers. Indeed, although cost internalization may induce an efficient adjustment in the activity levels of employees who are potential in-

[51] Such issues are discussed at some length in Sykes, *supra* note 1, at 1268–71.

[52] That is, if one assumes that unemployed people engage in approximately the same amount of personal driving as employed people, then the incremental probability of injuries in the course of business-related driving done by a truck driver is entirely attributable to the business enterprise.

jurers, it may have little impact on the activity levels of potential victims acting in their personal capacity.[53]

How does the analysis change if the tort is not "caused" by the enterprise? Suppose, for example, that an employee has an accident while shopping for groceries on his own time over the weekend — an activity clearly unrelated to the enterprise. Under these circumstances, the imposition of vicarious liability would place a cost on the enterprise that was not related to any wrong "caused" by its activities.[54] The price of the enterprise's goods or services would rise inefficiently, and consumer and producer surplus would decline. Vicarious liability would then be inefficient *unless* (a) it caused the employer to adopt incentive devices that produced a reduction in the incidence of motor vehicle torts by employees that was substantial enough to offset the inefficiencies of imposing added costs on the enterprise, or (b) it resulted in an increase in the efficiency of risk-sharing that offset those inefficiencies.

As to possibility (a), it is doubtful that an employer could reduce significantly the number of motor vehicle torts committed by employees on personal business. Obviously, the employer cannot deter such torts cost effectively by observing and correcting negligent behavior in advance of an accident. In addition, because many motor vehicle torts probably are attributable to carelessness or momentary lapse of attention rather than to calculated risk-taking, the ability of an employer to affect substantially the probability of motor vehicle torts through threats of discharge or other such incentives within the employment relationship is quite limited. It thus seems improbable, or at least highly conjectural, that the benefits of a reduced accident rate under vicarious liability would be substantial enough to justify the imposition of added costs on the business enterprise.

With regard to possibility (b), any risk-sharing benefits would also

[53] Businesses are interested in overall profitability. The imposition of additional costs on a business will affect profitability and thus affect investment decisions concerning the scale of business activity. Hence, one would expect that cost internalization by businesses, particularly large businesses for which periodic accident liability is highly probable, will have a systematic impact on their activity levels.

In the case of individuals, however, a slightly greater or lesser degree of cost internalization with respect to fairly low-probability events may have little impact on decisionmaking. The activity of walking, for example, may not be greatly affected by the choice between vicarious liability and personal liability, because the slightly greater risk of uncompensated injury (for example, by a negligent driver) under personal liability may be so small that individuals do not consider this risk in choosing whether to walk. If so, then no inefficiencies could arise from the reduction in cost internalization by pedestrians under a rule of vicarious liability; in effect, such victims are "passive."

[54] An indemnity action to recover that cost would itself be costly, and thus enterprise costs will increase even with an indemnity action.

be offset at least in part by the inefficiency of imposing costs on the enterprise that are unconnected to its operation and by added costs of litigation.[55] Moreover, many (though not all) of the costs of personal injuries are covered by first-party insurance policies and, to that extent, risk-sharing is reasonably efficient even without transferring losses to the employer. Thus, the imposition of vicarious liability probably could not be justified simply as a means of increasing the efficiency of risk-sharing.

The law is basically consistent with this analysis. A motor vehicle tort committed by an employee while on a personal shopping trip on his day off, for example, is unquestionably outside the scope of employment, and his employer will escape liability under the scope of employment rule.[56] In most reported frolic and detour cases, however, the tort occurs while the employee is on "company time" but is at least arguably engaged in personal business. The analysis of such cases is only slightly more difficult.

For example, assume that an employee runs a personal errand during a business trip and commits a motor vehicle tort during the personal errand. Assume further, however, that the employee would run an identical personal errand on his own time even if he had no affiliation with the employer. Under this assumption, the existence of the employment relationship has no effect on the ex ante probability of the tort. For the reasons given above, therefore, it is probably inefficient to impose liability on the employer. Indeed, in reaction to the imposition of vicarious liability, an employer might attempt to discourage employees from performing personal errands while on company business. Yet society may actually benefit if employers permit employees to perform such errands, because the employee's total company and personal travel will decline, thereby reducing the overall likelihood of a tort, as well as the cost of travel.

On the other hand, some torts committed during personal errands are "caused" by the enterprise. If an agent travels on business to a distant city, for example, and his lack of familiarity with the city streets considerably increases the probability of an accident, any resulting tort is to a considerable extent "caused" by the enterprise.

Hence, the following principle would, in theory, provide a reason-

---

[55] The creation of a social insurance fund to compensate motor vehicle tort victims who cannot recover fully from tortfeasors is probably a superior policy alternative. Such a fund could achieve comparable risk-sharing benefits without the high transaction costs of the tort system (although, to be sure, taxes to finance such a fund might have their own misallocative effects). Such funds already exist to some extent in many states in the form of state-administered "uninsured motorist" funds and are financed in part by a vehicle registration tax on all owners of motor vehicles who fail to present evidence of a minimum level of insurance coverage.

[56] *See* PROSSER & KEETON, *supra* note 20, at 503–05.

ably efficient disposition of the frolic and detour cases involving motor vehicle torts. If a motor vehicle tort occurs during a personal errand of the employee, the employer incurs vicarious liability for the tort only if (a) the tort arose during an errand of the sort that probably would not have occurred absent the existence of the employment relationship, or (b) for some other reason, the probability of the tort was substantially increased by the existence of the employment relationship — for example, the tort occurred because the employee was unfamiliar with the area in which he was required to travel.

The courts' approach to frolic and detour cases, however, is often quite different. In many cases, the courts focus on the length of the detour from the employee's business travel route as the test for vicarious liability — the employer is only liable for torts committed when the employee makes "short" detours.[57] Such a focus seems inefficient because the relationship between enterprise causation and the magnitude of the departure from an assigned route appears quite weak. An employee may stop for personal business that he would transact anyway without any significant departure from his route, and an employee who travels across country on business may make an extensive detour for sightseeing that he would not undertake absent his business travel.[58]

Other courts focus on the foreseeability of the employee's deviation from his route as the test for vicarious liability.[59] This approach might seem reasonable, as employers can hardly undertake to deter behavior that they cannot foresee. Yet it is the foreseeability of the *tort* that is important to the design of whatever incentives the employer might wish to utilize, not the foreseeability of its *location*, and motor vehicle torts by traveling agents are almost always foreseeable. More importantly, the degree of enterprise causation bears no apparent relationship to the foreseeability of the employee's detour. Hence, the foreseeability test that is applied in many frolic and detour cases also seems economically unsound.

---

[57] *See, e.g.*, Riley v. Standard Oil Co., 231 N.Y. 301, 132 N.E. 97 (1921) (imposing vicarious liability for a four-block departure from the assigned route); RESTATEMENT (SECOND) OF AGENCY § 234 (1958). *See generally* W. SEAVEY, *supra* note 49, at 151–52 (discussing various detour cases).

[58] To be sure, it may be desirable from the employer's perspective to permit his employees to take short detours while on company time — the benefit to the employee may well outweigh the slight cost to the employer and thereby allow for a more than offsetting reduction in the employee's compensation. Yet the mere fact that the employer implicitly authorizes short detours should not result in liability for accidents that occur in the course of such detours. As noted earlier, that policy may simply motivate the employer to prohibit personal errands on company time altogether, with a resulting *increase* in the overall likelihood of torts.

[59] *See, e.g.*, Kohlman v. Hyland, 54 N.D. 710, 210 N.W. 643 (1926); PROSSER & KEETON, *supra* note 20, at 504–05.

B. Intentional Torts

The basic principles that govern the efficiency of vicarious liability for intentional torts are developed in Part I above, through the various hypotheticals involving employee assaults.[60] In analyzing the case law with respect to these principles, it is instructive to divide intentional torts by employees into two categories: torts that arise from the employee's purely personal motivations, and torts that occur when the employee acts to serve the principal. This division highlights important distinctions in existing law as well as important distinctions in the effects of vicarious liability on resource allocation.

As to the first category, vicarious liability is likely to be efficient (subject to the usual second-best caveats concerning victims' incentives), even if an intentional tort has a seemingly personal motivation,[61] when two conditions hold. First, the tort must be "caused," at least in large part, by the employment relationship. Second, the imposition of liability on the employer must not excessively reduce the employee's incentives to avoid wrongful conduct.[62]

The second of these conditions for efficiency is familiar. The first condition, however, requires further discussion. Suppose, for example, that an intentional tort occurs because the existence of the enterprise causes the employee to encounter unusual circumstances that he would not otherwise encounter. Intrinsically stressful occupations, for

---

[60] *See supra* pp. 573–79.

[61] It is important to recognize that vicarious liability provides fewer risk-sharing benefits in the case of intentional torts than in the case of unintentional torts, because intentional torts involve fewer uncertainties. Specifically, suppose that employees are never held liable for intentional torts that they do not commit, that employees never "accidentally" commit intentional torts, and that the employee can accurately foresee the amount of the judgment that will result from a tortious act. Then, there is no risk to share between the employer and the employee — the employee knows that tortious behavior will result in a claim against him in a certain amount and that otherwise no claim will arise. Risk is nonexistent for him because there is a deterministic relationship between his behavior and the judgment.

With respect to potential tort victims, however, risk still exists. Hence, opportunities for beneficial risk-sharing between employers and tort victims may still arise.

[62] In one sense, the tortious conduct of an intentional tortfeasor is often "observable" by a vicariously liable employer because intentional torts usually result in judgments against the tortfeasor about which the vicariously liable employer will have knowledge. Indeed, if tortious behavior always leads to a judgment, then the employer's awareness of the existence or nonexistence of a judgment is tantamount to awareness of the existence or nonexistence of tortious behavior. This situation is quite distinct from most unintentional torts; an employee can exceed the speed limit a thousand times, for example, but never have an accident.

The "observability" of the employee's behavior in this sense may not help the employer to deter his torts. A distinction must be drawn between direct observation of tortious conduct and inferential "observation" based on the existence of a judgment. In the latter case, the observation of behavior is necessarily *subsequent* to the tort. Thus, the employer cannot intervene to discourage the commission of the tort but can only exact an ex post penalty. As discussed earlier, ex post penalties, such as costly indemnity actions, may be quite inferior to ex ante penalties based upon observation of potentially tortious behavior.

example, may precipitate intentional torts. In such cases, the business enterprise "causes" the tort even though the employee's tortious behavior may evince a purely personal motivation.

Most hornbook statements of the law suggest that vicarious liability will not apply if an agent acts out of personal ill will. Rather, the employee must act out of a purpose to serve the employer.[63] Recent case law, however, reflects a more flexible approach that appears consistent with the efficiency analysis. For example, one California court upheld the imposition of vicarious liability against a building subcontractor for his drunken employee's assault of two employees of the general contractor.[64] The court reasoned that the tort resulted from the tortfeasor's perception of his rights as an employee.[65]

Similarly, the D.C. Circuit has held that a jury could impose vicarious liability on a trucking company whose deliveryman raped a customer.[66] Crucial to the holding was the court's observation that the deliveryman's "badge of employment" enabled him to secure entry to the victim's premises.[67] This result appears efficient if one assumes that the probability of a rape was considerably enhanced by the deliveryman's employment status.

Finally, in *Ira S. Bushey & Sons, Inc. v. United States*,[68] the Second Circuit affirmed the imposition of vicarious liability upon the Coast Guard for vandalism by a drunken sailor. Observing that "the proclivity of seamen to find solace for solitude by copious resort to the bottle while ashore has been noted in opinions too numerous to warrant citation,"[69] Judge Friendly suggested that vicarious liability was appropriate because the tort was caused by the nature of the tortfeasor's employment.[70]

---

63 *See, e.g.*, RESTATEMENT (SECOND) OF AGENCY § 228 (1958); PROSSER & KEETON, *supra* note 20, at 505–06; W. SEAVEY, *supra* note 49, at 157.

64 *See* Rodgers v. Kemper Constr. Co., 50 Cal. App. 3d 608, 124 Cal. Rptr. 143 (1975).

65 *See id.* at 621–22, 124 Cal. Rptr. at 151.

66 *See* Lyon v. Carey, 533 F.2d 649 (D.C. Cir. 1976).

67 *See id.* at 651–52.

68 398 F.2d 167 (2d Cir. 1968).

69 *Id.* at 172.

70 The following passage from Judge Friendly's opinion supports the interpretation of the case as implicitly resting on notions of enterprise causation:

> One can readily think of cases that fall on the other side of the line. If Lane [the sailor] had set fire to the bar where he had been imbibing or had caused an accident on the street while returning to the drydock, the Government would not be liable; the activities of the "enterprise" do not reach into areas where the servant does not create risks different from those attendant on the activities of the community in general. . . . We agree with the district judge that if the seaman "upon returning to the drydock, recognized the Bushey security guard as his wife's lover and shot him," . . . vicarious liability would not follow; the incident would have related to the seaman's domestic life, not to his seafaring activity, . . . and it would have been the most unlikely happenstance that the confrontation with the paramour occurred on a drydock rather than at the traditional spot.

Id. (citations omitted).

The other major class of intentional tort cases — in which the tort occurs at least in part because the agent seeks to further the interests of his principal — raises entirely familiar issues. In these cases, there is rarely any question that the existence of the agency "causes" the tort.[71] Hence, subject to the previously discussed danger that vicarious liability may reduce the incentives of employees to avoid wrongful conduct or necessitate a spate of costly indemnity actions, the greater willingness of courts to impose vicarious liability in these cases[72] is economically sound.

C. Duty of a Master To Control Conduct of a Servant That Is Outside the Scope of Employment

Section 317 of the *Restatement (Second) of Torts* provides:

> A master is under a duty to exercise reasonable care so to control his servant while acting outside the scope of his employment as to prevent him from intentionally harming others or from so conducting himself as to create an unreasonable risk of bodily harm to them, if
>
> (a) the servant
> (i) is upon the premises in possession of the master or upon which the servant is privileged to enter only as his servant, or
> (ii) is using a chattel of the master, and
>
> (b) the master
> (i) knows or has reason to know that he has the ability to control his servant, and
> (ii) knows or should know of the necessity and opportunity for exercising such control.[73]

Under certain conditions, section 317 seemingly imposes vicarious liability on employers for tortious acts committed by employees that are not "caused" by the enterprise. Interestingly, however, vicarious liability will arise only if the employer is negligent — if he breaches his duty to exercise reasonable care. Thus, section 317 differs from conventional respondeat superior liability, which is strict. As noted earlier, strict vicarious liability is less efficient than vicarious liability based on negligence if the enterprise does not cause the tort. To this extent, if the scope of employment is circumscribed to encompass only

---

[71] *See* Straiton v. Rosinsky, 183 Pa. Super. 545, 133 A.2d 257 (1957) (imposing vicarious liability on a theatre after an usher struck an unruly child with a flashlight); Howard v. Zaney Bar, 369 Pa. 155, 85 A.2d 401 (1952) (refusing to impose vicarious liability on a bar when a bartender shot a patron who harassed a female customer).

[72] *See, e.g.*, *Straiton*, 183 Pa. Super. at 547–48, 133 A.2d at 259; PROSSER & KEETON, *supra* note 20, at 505–06; W. SEAVEY, *supra* note 49, at 157. *But see Howard*, 369 Pa. 155, 85 A.2d 401.

[73] RESTATEMENT (SECOND) OF TORTS § 317 (1965).

those torts substantially "caused" by the business enterprise, section 317's approach to torts committed outside the scope of employment is clearly efficient.

Section 317's requirement that the employer know or have reason to know that he has the ability, opportunity and need for control is also efficient. If the employer lacks such knowledge, vicarious liability imposes additional costs on the enterprise that lead to higher prices for enterprise goods and services without any attendant benefits to tort victims.

The requirement that the employee be on the employer's premises or be using the employer's chattels, however, is somewhat suspect. Perhaps one could argue that under such conditions the employer is more likely to be able to dissuade misconduct cheaply. Yet even if employees are on the employer's premises, close supervision of workers is sometimes quite costly; so too may be the supervision of an employee who uses a chattel at a considerable distance from the employer's premises. In addition, this requirement prevents the imposition of liability on the employer in some cases in which the employer can dissuade misconduct quite cheaply. To return to the example of the drunken sailor, an officer drinking at the same bar as an enlisted man may be able to dissuade the enlisted man's behavior quite easily. Yet, because the enlisted man is away from his boat and is not using his employer's chattel, the employer would escape liability under the *Restatement*.

The application of section 317 in practice, however, is much more limited than its language might suggest. Cases citing section 317 or its earlier incarnation in the first *Restatement*, as well as the cases that the *Restatement* cites as the basis for section 317, primarily involve acts that would not have occurred absent the existence of the enterprise. Such cases do not raise issues of enterprise causation and might be better handled by treating the tort as within the scope of employment.[74] Moreover, cases that rely on section 317 generally involve rather obvious acts of negligence on the part of the employer — for example, the knowing retention of an incompetent employee or the knowing allowance of dangerous practices by an employee even though relatively inexpensive measures could have stopped the practices.[75]

[74] *See, e.g.*, Fletcher v. Baltimore & Potomac R.R., 168 U.S. 135 (1897) (finding that the employer knowingly allowed workers to throw firewood off moving trains); McCrink v. City of New York, 296 N.Y. 99, 71 N.E.2d 419 (1947) (holding that the city knowingly retained policeman with propensity for drunkenness who later shot two people while intoxicated on duty); Hogle v. H.H. Franklin Mfg. Co., 199 N.Y. 388, 92 N.E. 794 (1910) (finding that the employer allowed employees to throw objects out of a factory window). These cases are cited in the Reporter's notes to Section 317. *See* RESTATEMENT (SECOND) OF TORTS § 317 appendix, at 24 (1965); *id.* at 25–27 (listing court citations to the first *Restatement*).

[75] *See, e.g.*, cases cited *supra* note 74.

One area that raises more difficult issues, however, is the growing line of cases imposing liability on employers for "negligent hiring." Typically, though not always, these cases involve intentional torts by employees with a history of criminal conduct or violent behavior that purportedly suggests unfitness for the job that they are employed to perform.

Vicarious liability may be efficient in these cases if the job subjects the tortfeasor to unusual stress or temptation or otherwise places him in circumstances that are especially conducive to repetition of past misbehavior. For example, it seems quite imprudent for a landlord to hire a convicted rapist as a security guard and give him a pass key to tenants' apartments. If a rape occurs as a result, the imposition of liability on the landlord is probably efficient, as the employment relationship seemingly facilitated ("caused") the tort. Even if the employer can do little to control the behavior of the guard after he is hired, liability will encourage the employer to perform a careful background check on applicants for such positions and to reject those applicants whose backgrounds are unsuitable.[76]

Vicarious liability is potentially inefficient, however, if the nature of the employment does not increase the likelihood of misbehavior, unless the employer has an opportunity cheaply and effectively to dissuade misconduct through monitoring or supervision. Cases that impose liability upon the employer for an assault by an employee against a co-worker or customer, principally because the employer had knowledge that the tortfeasor had committed assaults or other crimes in the past,[77] are quite troubling. Absent a showing that the employer

---

[76] Few cases are so easy. Suppose, for example, that a background check of the applicant reveals that he once was discharged for sleeping on the job, that he had an arrest record for minor crimes, and that a female co-worker had once complained that he "made eyes at her." *See* Easley v. Apollo Detective Agency, 69 Ill. App. 3d 920, 926–27, 387 N.E.2d 1241, 1244–45 (1979) (reviewing a claim of attempted sexual assault by a security guard who used his pass key to gain access to the tenant's apartment). The employer in this case was held liable for compensatory damages under an Illinois statute that imposed liability on detective agencies for the misconduct of their employees. *See* ILL. REV. STAT., ch. 38, para. 201-10b(10) (1975) (repealed 1984).

The employee's background would not have signaled to most employers that he might commit a rape. Nonetheless, security guards may face exceptional temptation and opportunity for malfeasance. The imposition of strict vicarious liability on employers of security guards who use their positions to facilitate criminal or tortious activity, as was accomplished by the Illinois statute in *Easley*, may then be justified because much of their malfeasance is arguably "caused" by their employment status.

[77] *See, e.g.*, Najera v. Southern Pac. Co., 191 Cal. App. 2d 634, 639 n.3, 13 Cal. Rptr. 146, 149 n.3 (1961) (citing cases recognizing "the common law liability of employers for their direct negligence in hiring or retaining in their employ persons with known characteristics which might subject other persons to danger"); Tatham v. Wabash R.R., 412 Ill. 568, 107 N.E.2d 735 (1952) (holding that a complaint alleging that the employer knowingly employed a dangerous man to work with the plaintiff stated a cause of action in negligence under the Federal Employers' Liability Act).

was in a position to intervene to prevent the assault and neglected to do so, the imposition of liability in these cases may simply cause the costs of production for the employer's enterprise to increase with no offsetting reduction in the incidence of wrongdoing. Alternatively, and much more probably, employers will choose not to hire individuals with a criminal record or other history of antisocial behavior.[78] Society then loses the value of the labor services of such individuals, and their resulting inability to find gainful employment may well increase their propensity to commit wrongs.[79]

III. Other Applications

The economic principles developed above adapt readily to the study of the efficiency of vicarious liability in other areas. This Part

---

[78] Arguably, if an employer has knowledge of an employee's violent propensities, he should at least have a duty to disclose those propensities to other employees to enable them to protect themselves. The difficulty with such a duty to disclose, however, is that disclosure may make it difficult or impossible for the individual who is the subject of the disclosure to work productively with fellow employees. As a consequence, prospective employers may simply decline to hire individuals with any history of violent behavior, with the adverse consequences discussed in the text.

[79] An interesting and novel application of the "negligent hiring" doctrine is found in Di Cosala v. Kay, 91 N.J. 159, 450 A.2d 508 (1982). In that case, the employer — a Boy Scout camp — allegedly knew that its employee owned firearms and kept them in his living quarters on the grounds of the camp. During a social visit by the employee's nephew, his mother, and a 19-year-old camp counselor, the counselor found a loaded handgun and accidentally shot the employee's nephew. The New Jersey Supreme Court held that the plaintiff should have been allowed to reach the jury on the issue of negligent hiring or supervision.

The weakness of the causal relation between the injury and the employment relation in *Di Cosala* is clear. The injury occurred during a social visit by the plaintiff to his uncle's house, a visit that could just as easily have taken place with the same unfortunate outcome in the absence of the employment relation.

In addition, the case differs dramatically from most negligent hiring cases in that no intentional misconduct by the employee was involved (the employee was not even present at the time of the accident), and no question was raised about the employee's character or fitness for his position. Rather, the plaintiff's theory was simply that the employer had knowledge that the firearms were present and should have refused to allow them to be kept in living quarters that the employer had supplied to the employee on the grounds of the camp.

Despite the rather unusual circumstances of this case, vicarious liability is at least arguably efficient. Given the propensity of children to play with firearms, and the serious danger of resulting accidents, it is perhaps negligent to store them at all at a Scout camp, at least without special precautions. Although the principal danger created by such negligence is that of injury to a camper, the possibility of injury to a social guest also plainly exists. An employer with actual knowledge that the firearms are in the possession of an employee under these conditions can insist that they be removed from the camp or be safely stored. The implementation of such a policy probably costs the employer very little (simply the effort of issuing a verbal command), and employees ordinarily can be expected to abide by the policy. The case thus seemingly presents an instance in which, despite the weakness of the causal relation between the tort and the employment relation, vicarious liability is justified because the employer has an opportunity to dissuade misconduct cheaply and effectively through supervision.

explores the vicarious liability of motor vehicle owners who lend their cars to third parties who cause injury, of premises owners whose guests or tenants suffer torts committed by intruders, and of employers whose employees are sexually harassed by their supervisors or co-workers. These topics introduce new twists to the analysis, such as the significance of contractual relationships between the party to be charged with vicarious liability and the injured party (in the premises liability and sexual harassment cases). Like the cases analyzed in Section II, these cases also raise interesting questions about causation.

A. The Vicarious Liability of Motor Vehicle Owners

A motor vehicle owner's liability for torts committed by a driver who borrows the owner's vehicle varies considerably among jurisdictions.[80] In some states, the owner only incurs liability for a tort committed by the other driver when the owner himself committed some act of negligence, such as entrusting the vehicle to a driver known to be incompetent, or allowing a driver to drive recklessly while the owner is riding as a passenger.[81] The modern trend, however, is toward an expansion of owners' liability for the negligence of other drivers, with an increasing prevalence of strict vicarious liability in many jurisdictions. Some states permit plaintiffs to argue that an owner who rides as a passenger retains a right of control over the driver that creates a "master-servant relationship," thereby subjecting the owner to liability under a theory of respondeat superior.[82] One state imposes strict liability on the theory that because the automobile is a "dangerous instrumentality," the owner incurs liability for the negligence of anyone to whom he entrusts it.[83] Another basis for strict vicarious liability is the "family purpose doctrine," under which family members are deemed "agents" of the owner when using the automobile for a "family purpose."[84] Finally, about a dozen states have imposed strict vicarious liability through "automobile consent" statutes.[85] These statutes generally hold automobile owners liable for the negligence of anyone who uses the automobile with the owner's express or implied permission.

As with any form of vicarious liability, imposing liability on automobile owners would have no economic consequences if the drivers could always pay judgments against them in full (with or without the aid of insurance) and if drivers and owners could costlessly negotiate

[80] For a reasonably complete survey of motor vehicle owners' liability across jurisdictions, see PROSSER & KEETON, cited in note 20 above, § 73, at 522–28.

[81] *See id.* at 523.

[82] *See id.*

[83] *See id.* at 524.

[84] *See id.*

[85] *See id.* at 527.

between themselves to allocate the risk of civil liability. The ultimate incidence of liability would then be determined by agreement between drivers and owners, without regard to who bears liability under the law.

Plainly, however, many drivers are incapable of paying judgments against them, and customized risk-allocation agreements between owners and drivers are rarely negotiated because they are costly. The imposition of vicarious liability on the owners of automobiles thus raises a number of issues closely related to the issues that arose in the earlier analysis of the frolic and detour cases, such as the extent of causation and the cost and effectiveness of incentive devices.

If someone borrows a motor vehicle for personal use and commits a tort, no obvious relationship to any business enterprise is present — a fact that might seem to distinguish the frolic and detour cases. Even so, the concept of enterprise causation remains relevant. For example, suppose that a tort occurs when a parent sends his child on an errand for the parent. The tort is then "caused" by the parent's activities, and the risk of the tort should be taken into account by the parent in deciding whether to undertake the activity himself or to send his child to undertake it. The parent's calculus in this respect is analogous to that of a business, which takes into account the costs attendant upon its operation in determining the scale at which to operate.

Alternatively, suppose that the parent lends an automobile to a child so that the child can run a personal errand of his own. In that capacity, the parent functions much like an auto rental agency, except that the child likely does not pay for the use of the vehicle — the parent's returns are psychic rather than monetary. Just the same, the costs of the tort are "caused" by the family "business" that provides the child with an automobile for personal use. Those costs should be taken into account in determining the scale at which to operate that "business" — the number of vehicles to purchase and the extent to which children may use them — and in designing incentives within the family to encourage the child to drive carefully when parents grant permission to use a vehicle.

With these observations in mind, consider now the alternative approaches of various jurisdictions to the liability of motor vehicle owners for torts committed by a driver who borrows the vehicle.

1. Negligence. — Not surprisingly, all jurisdictions provide a right of action against negligent automobile owners, even if the driver is also negligent. Beyond question, such a right of action is efficient. Whether the owner entrusts an automobile to an incompetent driver, provides a driver with a negligently maintained vehicle, or fails to exercise opportunities to dissuade negligent driving while riding as a passenger, the imposition of liability is appropriate to deter owners from such careless behavior. Of course, the driver must also be liable for his own negligence, and it may often be efficient for owners to have a right to indemnity from the negligent driver who causes the tort.[86]

Some jurisdictions, however, limit the right of action against the owner to circumstances in which the owner has been negligent. This policy is suspect. When drivers are judgment-proof, a variety of inefficiencies arise if the drivers alone are liable for their torts. Their inability to pay judgments may reduce their incentive to drive with care and lead them to undertake activities that require driving even if the (partially externalized) costs of those activities exceed their benefits. In addition, insolvent drivers may have little incentive to purchase liability insurance because a successful plaintiff cannot collect from them, and the efficiency of risk-sharing will suffer.

2. *Variations of Strict Vicarious Liability.* — Strict vicarious liability can mitigate the inefficiencies that arise if the owner is held liable only when negligent. First, it motivates the owner of the vehicle to employ certain worthwhile incentive devices that might encourage the driver to exercise care and that might not be required by the due care standard in a negligence regime. Parents, for example, can condition the continued use of the family automobile by a child upon the avoidance of accidents. Moreover, as suggested in the analysis of the frolic and detour cases, any moral hazard attendant upon shifting liability from the driver to the owner is likely to be modest even if the owner does not pursue indemnity or employ some other incentive device to motivate the driver. As noted earlier, the widespread prevalence of liability insurance for automobile accidents (usually with risk-related insurance premiums) suggests that the moral hazard problem is not unmanageable. Second, the imposition of liability upon the owner may encourage him to deny use of the automobile when the activity of driving is not worth the risk. If the owner is a rental agency, for example, the efficient level of driving activity will result when the agency charges a rental rate that covers its expected costs of operation, including its expected liability. If the owner is a parent, the efficient level of driving activity will result when the parent limits each child's driving to occasions of sufficient importance to justify the risk. Third, the imposition of liability on the owner will encourage the purchase of liability insurance, especially if other drivers are unable to pay judgments themselves. Risk will then be shifted to an efficient risk bearer.

This analysis lends support to the "family purpose doctrine." The most common application of that doctrine — the imposition of liability

---

[86] *See* Landes & Posner, *supra* note 1, at 527–28 (arguing that *B* should have a right of indemnity against *A* any time either one acting alone could have avoided an accident but *A* could have done so more cheaply than *B*).

on parents for torts by their children — arises in situations in which the tortfeasor is generally quite impecunious.

By contrast, the limitation of strict vicarious liability in some jurisdictions to circumstances in which the owner is present as a passenger is more difficult to justify. Vicarious liability in such cases may well be efficient: the presence of the owner in the vehicle may provide the owner with an opportunity to dissuade the driver from negligence, and the occurrence of a tort might indicate that the owner has negligently failed to do so. Alternatively, perhaps the presence of the owner suggests that the activity of driving is necessitated by the owner's personal business, and this causal relation to the owner's personal activities warrants vicarious liability just as a causal relation to an employer's business enterprise often warrants vicarious liability in the frolic and detour cases. Nevertheless, the *limitation* of vicarious liability to circumstances in which the owner is present seems ill-advised. Such a limitation will bar liability in some instances in which the economic case for vicarious liability is strong, as when a parent lends an automobile to an impecunious child.

Finally, the consent statutes, the broadest extension of strict vicarious liability, are arguably efficient. To be sure, these statutes increase the transaction costs of the tort system by adding additional parties to litigation even in cases in which vicarious liability provides few benefits. Yet if an important benefit of vicarious liability is improvement in the efficiency of risk-sharing, other transaction costs may be reduced by the approach of the consent statutes, which allow plaintiffs to reach the insurance coverage on the injurer's *vehicle* without regard to the insurance coverage of the injurer himself — if the state wishes to ensure a minimum level of insurance coverage to compensate the injured party in any accident, enforcing compliance with respect to each registered vehicle may be cheaper than enforcing compliance by each driver, because the number of drivers considerably exceeds the number of vehicles. Transaction costs may also be reduced by the existence of a bright-line rule of vicarious liability that avoids the need for litigation over the circumstances in which vicarious liability provides clear economic benefits. Such efficiencies may indeed justify the approach of the consent statutes.

B. The Vicarious Liability of Premises Owners for Torts by Intruders

Increasingly, premises owners incur vicarious liability for intentional torts (usually criminal acts) commited by intruders.[87] Landlords

[87] *See generally* Brown & Doyle, *Growing Liability for Premises Owners*, A.B.A. J., Mar. 1, 1986, at 64.

may incur liability for torts against tenants[88] and innkeepers may incur liability for torts against guests.[89] The liability of premises owners in these cases usually rests on a negligence theory, a claim that the premises owner failed to provide adequate security against intruders.[90] Courts that accept this theory typically hold that the premises owner owes a duty to take reasonable precautions against a foreseeable risk of crime.[91] To my knowledge, no court has gone beyond the negligence approach to impose strict vicarious liability on premises owners for intentional torts committed by intruders.

These cases differ from the cases previously analyzed because of the existence of a contractual relationship between the injured party and the premises owner. The intruder cases also raise a number of interesting economic questions about the "cause" of the tortious activity at issue, as well as the social utility of security measures.

Suppose, for example, that a motel chain builds a motel in the midst of a business district with a low and stable crime rate. Suppose further that the motel cannot take precautions to reduce the incidence of crime against guests of the motel. After the motel is built, all variables that affect the crime rate remain constant, and the crime rate remains unchanged from the period before the motel was constructed. Nonetheless, a few guests of the motel are victimized by criminal activity for which a remedy lies in tort.

Under the assumed conditions, the motel is plainly not the "cause" of any crime or tort. The construction of the motel has not affected the incidence of crime, and it is merely happenstance that guests of the motel are occasionally victimized — if the motel did not exist, criminals would simply locate other victims. The costs of crimes against guests, therefore, are not attributable to the motel and, given that the motel cannot take precautions, it would be inefficient to require the motel to bear tort liability for crimes against guests. This is true for the same reasons that it is generally inefficient to hold employers liable for torts by employees that are not "caused" by the employment relationship or whose probability the employer cannot reduce through incentive devices. Even if the guests' willingness-to-

---

[88] *See, e.g.*, Kline v. 1500 Mass. Ave. Apartment Corp., 439 F.2d 477 (D.C. Cir. 1970); Pippin v. Chicago Hous. Auth., 78 Ill. 2d 204, 399 N.E.2d 596 (1979). *See generally* Annotation, *Landlord's Obligation to Protect Tenant Against Criminal Activities of Third Persons*, 43 A.L.R.3D 331 (1972).

[89] *See, e.g.*, Garzilli v. Howard Johnson's Motor Lodges, Inc., 419 F. Supp. 1210 (E.D.N.Y. 1976); Gray v. Kircher, 193 Cal. App. 3d 1069, 236 Cal. Rptr. 891, 892–93 (1987). *See generally* Annotation, *Liability of Hotel or Motel Operator for Injury to Guest Resulting from Assault by Third Party*, 28 A.L.R.4TH 80 (1984).

[90] *See* PROSSER & KEETON, *supra* note 20, at 442–43.

[91] *See id.* ("A growing number of courts have imposed . . . duties of reasonable protection upon landlords to protect their tenants, and to protect others perhaps as well, from criminal attack, provided that such assaults are reasonably foreseeable and preventable.").

pay rose by the value of the "insurance" provided by the motel chain, vicarious liability would still be inefficient because it would foster unnecessary litigation.

Now suppose that the motel can reduce the incidence of crimes against guests through investment in additional security measures: dead-bolt locks, patroling watchmen, and the like. Assume further that the costs of these security measures are less than the associated reduction in the expected costs of crimes against guests. Hence, motel guests collectively would be willing to pay the motel operator an amount in excess of the cost of the security measures. In a world of perfect information, the operator would undertake such measures voluntarily, knowing that he could raise room rates to recoup the cost without losing customers. Yet guests may not possess the information necessary to factor the quality of security into their willingness-to-pay for a room, and thus a market solution may not materialize.

Nonetheless, the law should not necessarily impose a duty on the proprietor to undertake the security measures. The private value of security measures (as between the motel and its guests) may considerably exceed their social value. If security measures do not reduce the incidence of crime but merely redirect criminals to easier targets, then the added safety of motel guests is offset by reduced safety for others in the neighborhood. In this case, the optimal contract from the perspective of the motel and its guests is not socially optimal, and the security measures are inefficient from a societal perspective. On the other hand, if security measures deter crime altogether, their private and social value will converge. The imposition of a duty upon motel operators to undertake cost-effective security measures may then be efficient.[92]

For yet another variation in the analysis, suppose that a motel is constructed in a dangerous neighborhood, making its guests natural targets for crime and increasing the crime rate. An argument could then be made for *strict* vicarious liability on the theory that the motel "caused" the wrongs against its guests; if guests are poorly informed about security so that no market penalty is exacted for the dangerous location, the imposition of vicarious liability for crimes that are caused by the decision to locate in a dangerous neighborhood will help to provide efficient locational incentives and to discourage the construction of motels where the resulting crimes against guests may impose a cost that exceeds the surplus from the services of the motel. To be sure, some sort of contributory negligence defense would still be nec-

---

[92] Such a duty may be inefficient, however, for another reason. If the market fails to provide adequate security measures because of poor consumer information, the adoption of legally mandated security measures may not increase consumer willingness-to-pay. The result may be a decline in consumption of motel services with a resultant loss of economic surplus that may partially offset the benefits of the security measures.

essary to ensure that guests take precautions themselves (such as locking their rooms).[93]

In sum, if the existence of the motel creates a special temptation for criminals or otherwise leads to an increase in the total number of crimes, then strict vicarious liability *might* be efficient; otherwise, motel operators should incur liability only for failure to utilize cost-effective security measures. This principle raises the question what measures are "cost effective" and highlights the possible distinction between the private and social value of security measures. If security measures have no social value, then a duty to undertake them is inefficient *a fortiori*.

As noted earlier, modern case law on premises liability for the intentional torts of intruders, whether applied to motel operators, apartment landlords, or other premises owners (except private homeowners), applies a negligence standard. It imposes a duty on the premises owner to take reasonable security measures against foreseeable risks of crime or tort but stops short of strict liability. This approach is efficient if (1) premises owners do not "cause" intentional torts by intruders to a substantial degree; (2) premises owners can nonetheless deter such torts through cost-effective security measures that protect persons on their premises without simply redirecting the tortfeasor to an easier mark; and (3) because of information costs or other transaction costs, the efficient use of security measures will not result by contract.

The first two assumptions are at least plausible in most premises liability cases and, as suggested above, the third is also plausible with respect to cases involving innkeepers. The third assumption is far less plausible, however, for another important class of premises liability cases — suits by tenants against their landlords.

The leading case of *Kline v. 1500 Massachusetts Ave. Apartment Corp.*[94] is illustrative. A tenant was assaulted and robbed in a common hallway, presumably (though not certainly) by an intruder. The victim had been a tenant in the building for approximately seven years prior to the assault. During that time, a number of security measures in the building had been discontinued — the desk attendant in the lobby was no longer present on a regular basis, the building no longer had a doorman, an entrance to the garage was no longer guarded regularly, and the rear entrance was no longer kept locked at all times. The D.C. Circuit, in a 2-1 decision, held that the

[93] Note that vicarious liability probably would not have much effect on the incentives of criminals to commit crimes — the motel would have a right to indemnity against any criminal with significant financial assets, and criminal penalties would still apply to all criminals who were apprehended.

[94] 439 F.2d 477 (D.C. Cir. 1970).

defendant-landlord had breached his duty of reasonable care to protect tenants from assaults by third parties.

Specifically, the majority concluded that a duty to provide security for the entrances and common areas of the building should be imposed on the landlord because the landlord had exclusive control over them and because he had reason to anticipate that assaults would occur without adequate security. To satisfy that duty, the court held that the landlord was obliged to maintain the "same relative degree of security" that was in effect at the time the plaintiff became a tenant in the building, because she "was led to expect that she could rely upon this degree of protection."[95]

The dissent, among other things, suggested in effect that the court should not second-guess the market.[96] Its argument was simple — tenants can select a building and a neighborhood according to their willingness-to-pay for security, location, and other amenities. The dissent argued that the court imprudently substituted its judgment about the appropriate level of security for the collective judgment of the landlord and the tenants as reflected in their leases and in the level of security customarily provided by the landlord.[97] Such a substitution was especially inappropriate, the dissent maintained, when the tenant of seven years was well-informed about the level of security.[98]

Upon reflection, the argument of the dissent is compelling. As noted above, the plausible rationale for the imposition of negligence-based vicarious liability on innkeepers includes an assumption that their guests are imperfectly informed about the dangers of the neighborhood and the need for security, and perhaps the quality of the security that innkeepers offer. As a consequence, customers may place insufficient value on security, and their willingness to pay may not compensate the innkeeper for instituting efficient security measures. The incentive to provide them is then lost.

Because the landlord-tenant relation typically extends over a much longer period of time than the innkeeper-customer relation, however, tenants can develop information about the need for security in the neighborhood. Moreover, because most tenants anticipate a stay of some months or years, it pays for them to invest in the acquisition of information about the safety of a neighborhood before moving into it. They are then in a position to assess the value of security measures in their rental alternatives. Landlords recognize this behavior of tenants and have every incentive to provide security services for which

---

95 *Id.* at 486.

96 *See id.* at 492–93 (MacKinnon, J., dissenting).

97 *See id.* at 492.

98 *See id.*

prospective tenants are willing to pay through higher rents[99] — by definition, all efficient security measures.[100]

Thus, the trend in the case law toward expanded landlord liability for assaults by intruders is disquieting.[101] Whatever the merits of innkeeper liability, the liability of landlords is perhaps best left to the realm of contract.[102] This conclusion is reinforced by the observation above that the private value of security measures may exceed their social value, so that even the security measures required by contract may be economically excessive. Under these circumstances, it seems

---

[99] A possible objection to this analysis is that landlords can reduce the quality of security in a rental building, up to a point, without inducing existing tenants to leave. Moving is costly, and tenants will not move out until the cost imposed upon them by a decline in security exceeds the cost of finding and moving into another apartment. Thus, it might be argued, landlords can entice tenants to a building by providing the efficient level of security initially and then reduce the level of security later without penalty.

This argument presupposes, however, that natural turnover in rental units is low. Setting aside the complications of rent control, *see infra* note 103, most landlords must continually fill vacancies by attracting new tenants. Even if existing tenants are perhaps unlikely to move out solely in response to a decline in security, the fact that the landlord must fill vacancies that arise for other reasons provides him with a strong incentive to offer and to maintain adequate security measures. *Cf.* Schwartz & Wilde, *Intervening in Markets on the Basis of Imperfect Information: A Legal and Economic Analysis*, 127 U. PA. L. REV. 630 (1979) (arguing that a relatively low percentage of consumers who comparison shop actively can generate efficient competitive equilibria). There can be no assurance that this process will operate perfectly in all cases, but neither can a case be made for systematic judicial intervention, especially in light of the possibility that the level of security that emerges by contract may be economically excessive due to a divergence of the private and social values of security measures.

[100] The analysis of the majority in no way undermines this proposition. To be sure, if security measures are to be instituted at all with respect to building entrances and common areas, the landlord must put them in place. Even if such measures are in the interests of the tenants collectively, no single tenant will purchase them on his own, and collective action to purchase them is probably too costly. Yet as the analysis in the text suggests, landlords do have an incentive to supply security measures that cost less than their value to the tenants (measures that are cost effective from the tenants' perspective) because they can then raise rents by more than enough to compensate.

As for the suggestion that the plaintiff was led to rely on the security measures in place six years before the assault, the response of the dissent is a proper one: the decline in security over time was obvious to the plaintiff, yet she continually renewed her month-to-month tenancy. It is thus incorrect to suggest, as the majority opinion implied, that the decline in security was somehow a breach of an implicit contractual obligation.

[101] *See, e.g.*, Samson v. Saginaw Professional Bldg., 393 Mich. 393, 224 N.W.2d 843 (1975) (imposing a duty of care on a landlord for an assault by a mental patient of a tenant upon the employee of another tenant); Johnston v. Harris, 387 Mich. 569, 198 N.W.2d 409 (1972) (holding that a landlord may be negligent in creating conditions conducive to third-party criminal activities); *see also* Frances T. v. Village Green Owners Ass'n, 42 Cal. 3d 490, 723 P.2d 573, 229 Cal. Rptr. 456 (1986) (en banc) (holding that a condominium association may be liable for an assault by an intruder upon a unit owner).

[102] The role of tort, if any, should be limited to the redress of breaches of "implied contract." For example, *Kline* would be a different case if the assault had resulted from a sudden and unanticipated discontinuation of security services that the landlord had expressly or impliedly agreed to provide (such as the failure of the doorman to show up for his shift).

especially ill-advised to impose upon landlords a duty to take greater precautions against intruders than their contractual obligations require.[103]

C. The Vicarious Liability of Employers for Acts of Sexual Harassment by Employees Against Subordinates or Co-workers

1. Legal Background. — Sexual harassment in the workplace may constitute a common law intentional tort. Depending upon the nature of the harassment and the jurisdiction, an action may lie for intentional infliction of emotional distress, wrongful discharge, assault, battery, invasion of privacy, or interference with contract.[104] In any such tort action, the plaintiff may seek a judgment against the employer of the offending individual. Common law tests for vicarious liability will then apply; the plaintiff must normally demonstrate that the offending individual was a "servant" and that the tort occurred within the scope of his employment.

Some acts of sexual harassment also constitute discrimination on the basis of sex in violation of title VII of the Civil Rights Act of 1964.[105] Thus, instead of a common law tort action, or perhaps in addition to one, some victims of sexual harassment may file a complaint with the Equal Employment Opportunity Commission (EEOC). If the EEOC fails to resolve the complaint satisfactorily through conciliation within a specified period, the complainant may bring an action in federal court.[106] In practice, the backlog of cases at the EEOC virtually ensures that the conciliation period will elapse before the complaint is resolved, and hence most complainants ultimately

---

[103] This process breaks down in the presence of rent control, which may prevent landlords from raising the rent to capture the greater willingness-to-pay that results from improved security and may greatly reduce the natural turnover in rental units that forces landlords to maintain security in order to attract new tenants. *See supra* note 99. Indeed, one of my students, who lived in northwest Washington, D.C. at the time of the *Kline* decision, conjectures that the deterioration of security measures at 1500 Massachusetts Ave. may well have followed the imposition of rent control. I have been unable to confirm or refute this hypothesis.

[104] *See, e.g.*, Monge v. Superior Court *ex rel.* Crown Gibraltar, 176 Cal. App. 3d 503, 508, 222 Cal. Rptr. 64, 66 (1986) (recognizing causes of action for intentional infliction of emotional distress, wrongful termination of employment, and breach of implied covenant of good faith and fair dealing between employer and employee); Drinkwalter v. Shipton Supply Co., 732 P.2d 1335, 1338 (Mont. 1987) (holding that sexual harassment may constitute a breach of the employment contract's covenant of good faith and fair dealing and may also give rise to actions for wrongful discharge on public policy grounds).

[105] The Supreme Court held that sexual harassment can violate a person's civil rights under title VII in Meritor Sav. Bank v. Vinson, 106 S. Ct. 2399 (1986). The Court based its holding on 42 U.S.C. § 2000e-2(a)(1) (1982), which prohibits employers from discriminating "against any individual with respect to his compensation, terms, conditions, or privileges of employment, because of such individual's . . . sex."

[106] *See generally* B. SCHLEI & P. GROSSMAN, EMPLOYMENT DISCRIMINATION LAW 421–29 (2d ed. 1983).

have the option to bring suit. The remedies for a successful action include lost pay and injunctive relief but do not include certain compensatory damages[107] (such as damages for emotional distress) or punitive damages.

Victims must sue the "employer," which is defined to include agents of the employer.[108] Thus, a critical issue in sexual harassment cases under title VII, as in cases brought in tort, is the existence of an agency that would establish employer liability. Indeed, under title VII, employer liability is an absolute prerequisite to suit.

The Supreme Court addressed the standards for employer liability in sexual harassment suits under title VII in *Meritor Savings Bank v. Vinson*.[109] In *Meritor*, the Court distinguished three types of sexual harassment: (a) "quid pro quo" harassment, whereby supervisory personnel seek sexual favors in return for promotions, raises, and the like; (b) "hostile environment" harassment by supervisory personnel, whereby a supervisor seeks sexual favors from a subordinate without expressly offering any quid pro quo (the situation in *Meritor*) and does so with sufficient frequency or offensiveness that the harassment becomes actionable under title VII; and (c) hostile-environment harassment by co-workers, without participation by supervisory personnel.[110]

The Court suggested that a rule of strict vicarious liability will generally apply to quid pro quo harassment by supervisory personnel. Such a rule had already been adopted by a number of courts and was set forth in the EEOC guidelines on sexual harassment.[111] As to hostile-environment harassment by supervisory personnel, the Court declined to set forth a standard for employer liability and instead suggested that the issue should be resolved case by case through the application of common law agency principles.[112] By implication, common law agency principles will also guide cases of hostile-environment

---

[107] *See id.* at 1452.

[108] *See* 42 U.S.C. § 2000e(b) (1982). Although the law on this point is sketchy, it appears that the liability of co-defendants (for example, the company and its offending "agent") is joint and that the court may apportion damages between them as it sees fit. *See, e.g.*, Russell v. American Tobacco Co., 528 F.2d 357 (4th Cir. 1975) (holding the union and employer jointly liable), *cert. denied*, 425 U.S. 935 (1976). An unsuccessful defendant has no right to contribution (or, presumably, indemnity) against a party who might have been joined as a defendant in the original action but was not. *See* Northwest Airlines, Inc. v. Transport Workers Union, 451 U.S. 77 (1981). At the time of the original action, however, defendants can seek to join other parties as co-defendants and assert cross-claims against them. *See* B. SCHLEI & P. GROSSMAN, *supra* note 106, at 647–51.

[109] 106 S. Ct. 2399 (1986).

[110] *See id.* at 2405–08.

[111] *See id.* at 2407–08 (citing Brief for United States and Equal Employment Opportunity Commission as *Amicus Curiae* at 22, 26, *Meritor* (No. 84-1979)); 29 CFR § 1604.11(c) (1985).

[112] *See Meritor*, 106 S. Ct. at 2408.

harassment by nonsupervisory personnel, although *Meritor* was not directly concerned with such harassment.

Finally, the Court's analysis made clear that the employer's liability may be predicated on his negligence. Negligence may exist if the employer fails to adopt a policy against sexual harassment and to provide an effective grievance procedure for victims of harassment or has actual knowledge of harassment and fails to take remedial action.[113] Lower courts had previously adopted a rule of liability based on the employer's negligence that typically required actual or constructive knowledge of harassment on the part of the employer in addition to a failure to take remedial action.[114]

In a concurring opinion, Justice Marshall argued that the application of agency principles to hostile-environment harassment by supervisory personnel should almost always lead to a finding of agency and thus to employer liability.[115] Justice Marshall reasoned that harassment by a supervisor is facilitated by the supervisor's position in the company hierarchy, whether or not a quid pro quo is offered. He therefore found no justification for a different standard of employer liability in these two types of cases.

2. *Economic Analysis.* — The efficiency of vicarious liability in sexual harassment cases involves the same economic issues as the efficiency of vicarious liability in intentional tort cases. What distinguishes the harassment cases from many cases involving intentional torts by employees, however, is the existence once again of a contractual relationship between the injured party and the employer of the wrongdoer.

The significance of this contractual relationship is unclear. If potential targets of harassment are fully informed of the risk of harassment prior to accepting employment, employers must compensate workers subject to a greater risk of harassment with higher wages. Employers then have an incentive to adopt workplace policies that reduce the costs of harassment and will do so to the point at which the reduction in those costs (as measured by the decline in wages of prospective targets of harassment) is at the margin equal to the costs of further antiharassment measures. In addition, to the extent that some harassment remains after the adoption of all cost-effective measures against it, victims of harassment will be compensated by higher wages, and the costs of workplace harassment will be borne by the employer through the wage bill.

Yet the underlying premise of this analysis may be incorrect. In practice, prospective employees may have little information about the

---

113 *See id.* at 2408–09.

114 *See, e.g.*, Tomkins v. Public Serv. Elec. & Gas Co., 568 F.2d 1044, 1048–49 (3d Cir. 1977).

115 *See Meritor*, 106 S. Ct. at 2409–11 (Marshall, J., concurring).

probability and seriousness of workplace harassment prior to accepting employment. Of course, once the costs of harassment become apparent, a victim of harassment can always quit and find a different job, but the costs of doing so (search costs, forfeit of returns to nontransferable investments in training, and so on) may outweigh the benefits. Even if the victim does quit, significant injury to the victim already may have occurred, and the employer may simply hire another ill-informed employee at the same wage rate. Hence, it is doubtful that a market solution to the problem of sexual harassment will emerge systematically.[116]

If a market solution does not materialize, employers will not bear the costs of harassment "caused" by their business enterprise or adopt cost-effective policies to discourage harassment, absent the imposition of civil liability. The analysis can then proceed as if acts of harassment are committed against strangers rather than against individuals who have a contractual relationship to the employer. In this case, the principles developed in Part I apply directly.[117] If the harassment is "caused" by the employer's enterprise, this fact weighs in favor of strict vicarious liability. Liability based on negligence is more efficient if the causal relation between the enterprise and the harassment is weak but the employer can nonetheless adopt inexpensive, effective incentive devices to dissuade employees from misconduct. Consider now the various forms of sexual harassment and their legal treatment after *Meritor*.

(a) Sexual Harassment by Supervisory Employees. — A strong argument can be made that harassment by supervisory employees is "caused" by the employer's enterprise, whether or not a quid pro quo is part of the harassment. To be sure, some supervisory employees would commit acts of harassment irrespective of their position but, as Justice Marshall suggested in *Meritor*, sexual harassment by supervisors is often facilitated by a position of authority.[118] Absent the

---

[116] Contrast this analysis to the analysis of landlord liability for intruders in *Kline*. *See supra* pp. 600–03. The difference there lies in the ability of prospective tenants to obtain information about the safety of the neighborhood and to observe the quality of security measures before they move into a rental building. Landlords then have an incentive to provide the security measures that tenants collectively regard as cost effective, with the expectation that the cost can be recouped through higher rents. Concomitantly, a failure to provide cost-effective security measures will lower the willingness-to-pay of prospective tenants by an amount that exceeds the cost savings to the landlord. A "market solution" to the problem of sexual harassment is much less likely to emerge, because prospective employees will often have little or no information about the risks of sexual harassment before they accept a new position.

[117] Moreover, in any cases in which information problems are overcome and the market solution does materialize, nothing is lost, save perhaps the transaction costs of litigation, by applying the same standard of employer liability to those cases as is applied in other cases — an implication of the Coase Theorem. *See* Coase, *supra* note 10.

[118] *See Meritor*, 106 S. Ct. at 2410–11 (Marshall, J., concurring).

existence of a supervisor-subordinate relationship, the supervisor would have no leverage over the subordinate, and the likelihood of sexual harassment would be significantly reduced. Of course, the causal relation to the enterprise is strongest in quid pro quo cases, because such harassment cannot occur absent the enterprise hierarchy. Therefore, the case for strict vicarious liability is strongest for quid pro quo harassment but may also be quite strong for hostile-environment harassment by supervisory personnel.

A possible objection to strict vicarious liability is that it might lead to increased harassment by reducing the incentive for supervisory employees to behave responsibly. This objection seems unfounded. To be sure, employers probably cannot observe acts of harassment very frequently and thus cannot intervene to prevent it. But they can (and do) promulgate policies under which employees who commit acts of harassment are discharged or otherwise penalized with regard to advancement, salary increases, and the like. Such incentives are potentially effective for all employees who value long-term relationships with their employers.[119]

Another possible objection to strict vicarious liability for sexual harassment by supervisors is that it may lead to meritless lawsuits. When an employee is fired, for example, the employee may be tempted to fabricate a sexual harassment claim to save face. Arguably, this is a serious problem, because sexual harassment suits often turn solely on an assessment of the credibility of the witnesses. As a result, the chances of success in a meritless lawsuit may be significant.

Yet it is important not to exaggerate this concern. Just as the difficulties of proof may enhance the chances of success and settlement value of meritless suits, they also reduce the chances of success in meritorious suits, especially given that the plaintiff bears the burden of proof. Moreover, victims of sexual harassment may be reluctant to file suit or even to report incidents to their employers for fear of reprisal or a tainted reputation in the labor market. In sum, whatever incentives exist for meritless suits are substantially counterbalanced by incentives against meritorious suits, which will reduce the aggregate costs to employers of sexual harassment suits to a level that may well fall below the true costs of harassment in the workplace.

Thus, assuming that some combination of incentives will enable the employer to reduce the incidence of sexual harassment (or at least to avoid a significant increase in harassment), and assuming that the problem of meritless suits is not a terribly serious one, a strong argument can be made for strict vicarious liability for acts of harassment

---

[119] Indemnity actions may provide yet another disincentive to harassment, albeit a highly imperfect one. Indemnity is apparently not available under title VII. *See* Anderson v. Local Union No. 3, 582 F. Supp. 627, 633 (S.D.N.Y. 1984). At present, the development of an indemnity action would be a useful addition to the incentive devices available to the employer.

against subordinates by supervisory employees. The causal relation between such acts and the employer's enterprise is probably quite strong, and the market is unlikely to produce an efficient solution to the problem of sexual harassment in many cases, notwithstanding the contractual relationship between the employer and the injured party.

(b) Sexual Harassment by Nonsupervisory Co-Workers. — The causal relation to the enterprise is clearly weaker in cases of harassment by nonsupervisory co-workers. These co-workers have no leverage to exert over the individual who is the object of harassment, and individuals prone to commit acts of harassment in the absence of any leverage may well do so irrespective of their occupation, position, employment, or unemployment. Hence, the probability that they will engage in harassment may be unaffected, or affected only slightly, by their employment relationship. Strict vicarious liability for such harassment will almost certainly be inefficient. Vicarious liability based on negligence may be efficient, however, if employers are capable of significantly reducing the incidence of sexual harassment through inexpensive incentive devices.

Interestingly, as noted earlier, the rule of employer liability applied by most courts in these cases requires actual or constructive knowledge of harassment on the part of the employer, coupled with a failure by the employer to take remedial action.[120] This rule may well be efficient if one supposes that the employer cannot cost effectively diminish sexual harassment except by announcing a policy against it and taking disciplinary action under that policy after receiving knowledge of specific incidents of harassment — a highly plausible assumption.

Thus, more or less consistent with existing law, perhaps the best rule for cases involving harassment by nonsupervisory co-workers is to impose a duty on employers to announce policies against sexual harassment and to provide channels through which victims of harassment can complain to the employer. Once such a policy is in place, the failure of an employee to report harassment to the employer should act as a bar to vicarious liability unless the employer can be shown to have knowledge of the harassment through other channels. The employer should also escape liability if, despite a report of harassment, the employer makes a good faith judgment that the report lacks credibility or is unable to remedy the problem despite reasonable efforts to do so.

CONCLUSION

This Article has extended the previous economic treatment of vicarious liability, which focused on risk-sharing, cost internalization,

[120] *See supra* p. 605.

and incentive maintenance in the employment relationship as the key economic issues, to incorporate probabilistic notions of causation. The scope of employment limitation upon respondeat superior liability may be understood in many instances as a way to limit the employer's liability to torts that are "caused" by the business enterprise. Yet some of the rules that have developed to define the scope of employment, particularly in the frolic and detour cases, are difficult to reconcile with a view of the tort law as promoting efficiency.

The economic principles developed here are also useful in the study of vicarious liability outside the employment relationship and outside the common law of torts. Given certain plausible empirical assumptions, many aspects of the law concerning the liability of motor vehicle owners for torts by another driver, the liability of premises owners for torts by intruders, and the liability of employers for sexual harassment by one employee against another may also be understood as an effort to promote efficiency, although other aspects of the law, such as the growing liabilty of landlords for torts by intruders, are harder to justify on economic grounds.

Property

[3]

AN ECONOMIC ANALYSIS OF COPYRIGHT LAW

*WILLIAM M. LANDES and RICHARD A. POSNER**

INTELLECTUAL property is a natural field for economic analysis of law,[1] and copyright is an important form of intellectual property. Yet while there are good introductions to the economics of copyright law, and a number of excellent articles on the economics of copying (as distinct from copyright *law*),[2] no article examines the field of copyright as a whole, discussing the evolution and major doctrines in the law from an economic standpoint. This article, which is in the spirit of our recent articles on the economics of trademark law, tries to fill this gap—although the field is so vast that our analysis cannot be exhaustive. As in most of our work, we are particularly interested in positive analysis, and specifically in the question to what extent copyright law can be explained as a means for promoting efficient allocation of resources.

* Landes is Clifton R. Musser Professor of Economics at the University of Chicago Law School. Posner is a Judge of the United States Court of Appeals for the Seventh Circuit and a Senior Lecturer at the University of Chicago Law School. We thank Steven Shavell, George Stigler, and participants in the law and economics workshops at Columbia Law School and Harvard Law School for many helpful comments on a previous draft.

[1] See, for example, our articles Trademark Law: An Economic Perspective, 30 J. Law & Econ. 265 (1987), and The Economics of Trademark Law, 78 Trademark Rptr. 267 (1988); and Edmund W. Kitch, Graham v. John Deere Co.: New Standards for Patents, 1966 Sup. Ct. Rev. 293.

[2] See, for example, Stanley M. Besen & Sheila Nataraj Kirby, Private Copying, Appropriability and Optimal Copying Royalties, J. Law & Econ. (in press); William R. Johnson, The Economics of Copying, 93 J. Pol. Econ. 158 (1985); S. J. Liebowtiz, Copying and Indirect Appropriability: Photocopying Journals, 93 J. Pol. Econ. 945 (1985); S. J. Leibowitz, Copyright Law, Photography, and Price Discrimination, J. Res. Law & Econ. 181 (1986); S. J. Leibowitz, Some Puzzling Behavior by Owners of Intellectual Products, 5 Contemp. Policy Iss. 44 (1987); Ian E. Novos & Michael Waldman, The Effects of Increased Copyright Protection: An Analytical Approach, 92 J. Pol. Econ. 236 (1984); Michael O'Hare, Copyright: When Is Monopoly Efficient? 4 J. Policy Analysis & Mgmt. 407 (1985). Notable early studies are Arnold Plant, The Economic Aspects of Copyright in Books, 1 Economica (n.s.) 167 (1934); Arnold Plant, The New Commerce in Ideas and Intellectual Property (1953); Robert M. Hurt & Robert N. Schuchman, The Economic Rationale of Copyright, 56 Am. Econ. Rev. Papers & Proc. 42 (1966).

[*Journal of Legal Studies*, vol. XVIII (June 1989)]
 0047-2530/89/1802-0004$01.50

A distinguishing characteristic of intellectual property is its "public good" aspect. While the cost of creating a work subject to copyright protection—for example, a book, movie, song, ballet, lithograph, map, business directory, or computer software program—is often high, the cost of reproducing the work, whether by the creator or by those to whom he has made it available, is often low. And once copies are available to others, it is often inexpensive for these users to make additional copies. If the copies made by the creator of the work are priced at or close to marginal cost, others may be discouraged from making copies, but the creator's total revenues may not be sufficient to cover the cost of creating the work. Copyright protection—the right of the copyright's owner to prevent others from making copies—trades off the costs of limiting access to a work against the benefits of providing incentives to create the work in the first place. Striking the correct balance between access and incentives is the central problem in copyright law. For copyright law to promote economic efficiency, its principal legal doctrines must, at least approximately, maximize the benefits from creating additional works minus both the losses from limiting access and the costs of administering copyright protection.

Section I develops the basic economic model of copyright protection, including an analysis of the optimal degree of that protection. Section II applies the model to the principal doctrines of copyright law. It considers such questions as the originality requirement for copyright protection, the distinction between ideas and expression, the absence of copyright protection for utilitarian works, the protection of derivative works, and issues of fair use.

I. The Basic Economics of Copyright

We begin with the factors—including, of course, copyright protection—that determine the number of works created. Then we examine the exploitation of the created work—the number of copies and the price per copy. Last, we incorporate the important features of our discussion into a model of the optimal degree of copyright protection.

A. Number of Works as a Function of Copyright and Other Factors

1. General Considerations

The cost of producing a book or other copyrightable work (we start by talking just about books and later branch out to other forms of expression) has two components. The first is the cost of creating the work. We assume that it does not vary with the number of copies produced or sold, since it consists primarily of the author's time and effort plus the cost to the publisher of soliciting and editing the manuscript and setting it in type. Consistent with copyright usage we call the sum of these costs the "cost of expression."

To simplify the analysis, we ignore any distinction between costs incurred by authors and by publishers, and therefore use the term "author" (or "creator") to mean both author and publisher. In doing this we elide a number of interesting questions involving the relation between author and publisher. For example, do such principles as *droit moral*, entitling authors to reclaim copyright from assignees after a fixed period of years or entitling artists to royalties on resales of their art by initial (or subsequent) purchasers,[3] increase or reduce the incentive to create new works? The answer suggested by economic analysis is that, contrary to intuition, such principles reduce the incentive to create by preventing the author or artist from shifting risk to the publisher or dealer. A publisher (say) who must share any future speculative gains with the author will pay the author less for the work, so the risky component of the author's expected remuneration will increase relative to the certain component. If the author is risk averse, he will be worse off as a result. However, we do not explore such matters in this article.

The second component of the cost of producing a work increases with the number of copies produced, for it is the cost of printing, binding, and distributing individual copies. The cost of expression does not enter into the making of copies because, once the work is created, the author's efforts can be incorporated into another copy virtually without cost.

For a new work to be created, the expected return—typically, and we shall assume exclusively, from the sale of copies—must exceed the expected cost. The demand curve for copies of a given book is, we assume, negatively sloped because there are good but not perfect substitutes for a given book.[4] The creator will make copies up to the point where the marginal cost of one more copy equals its expected marginal revenue. The resulting difference between price and marginal cost, summed over the number of copies sold, will generate revenues to offset the cost of expression. Since the decision to create the work must be made before the demand for copies is known, the work will be created only if the difference between expected revenues and the cost of making copies equals or exceeds the cost of expression. If we assume that the cost of creating

[3] See generally Michael E. Horowitz, Note: Artists' Rights in the United States: Toward Federal Legislation, 25 Harv. J. Legis. 153 (1988).

[4] We maintain throughout our analysis the assumption of a downward-sloping demand curve for copies of a given work.

(equivalent) works differs among authors, the number of works created will increase until the returns from the last work created just covers the (increasing) cost of expression.

Two qualifications should be noted. First, for many types of intellectual property some price discrimination may be possible because individual works are not perfect substitutes and arbitrage is preventable. Thus, a book publisher will commonly charge higher prices for hardcover editions and later reduce the price for persons willing to wait for the paperback edition to appear. Similarly, the prices charged by exhibitors for first-run movies will generally be higher than the prices in the aftermarket (cable viewing, video cassettes, and network television). Price discrimination increases revenue and thus the number of works produced, though it may not increase the number of copies of each work.[5] Second, the demand for copies of a given work depends not only on the number of copies but on the number of (competing) works as well. The greater the number of such works (past and present), the lower the demand for any given work. Thus, the number of works and the number of copies per work will be determined simultaneously, and the net effect of this interaction will be to reduce the number of works created.

This description of the market for copies and the number of works created assumes the existence of copyright protection. In its absence anyone can buy a copy of the book when it first appears and make and sell copies of it. The market price of the book will eventually be bid down to the marginal cost of copying, with the unfortunate result that the book probably will not be produced in the first place, because the author and publisher will not be able to recover their costs of creating the work. The problem is magnified by the fact that the author's cost of creating the work, and many publishing costs (for example, editing costs), are incurred before it is known what the demand for the work will be. Uncertainty about demand is a particularly serious problem with respect to artistic works, such as books, plays, movies, and recordings. Even with copyright protection, sales may be insufficient to cover the cost of expression and may not even cover the variable cost of making copies. Thus, the difference between the price and marginal cost of the successful work must not only cover the cost of expression but also compensate for the risk of failure. If a copier can defer making copies until he knows whether the work is a success, the potential gains from free riding on expression will be even greater, because the difference between the price and mar-

[5] The effect of (imperfect) price discrimination on output is normally assumed to be indeterminate. See, for example, F. M. Scherer, Industrial Market Structure and Economic Performance 316, 321 (2d ed. 1980).

ginal cost of the original work will rise to compensate for the uncertainty of demand, thus creating a bigger profit potential for copies. So uncertainty generates an additional disincentive to create works in the absence of copyright protection.

Practical obstacles limit copying the original works of others even in the absence of any copyright protection. But these obstacles, while serious in some cases, can easily be exaggerated. When fully analyzed, they do not make a persuasive case for eliminating copyright protection.

1. *The copy may be of inferior quality, and hence not a perfect substitute for the original.* In the case of books and other printed matter, the copier may not be able to match the quality of paper or binding of the original or the crispness of the printing, and there may be errors in transcription. None of these is an important impediment to good copies any longer, but in the case of works of art—such as a painting by a famous artist—a copy, however accurate, may be such a poor substitute in the market that it will have no negative effects on the price of the artist's work. Indeed, the copy may have a positive effect on that price, by serving as advertising for his works. On the other hand, it may also deprive him of income from selling derivative works—the copies of his paintings—himself. (More on derivative works shortly.) To generalize, when either the cost of making equivalent copies is higher for the copier than for the creator or the copier's product is a poor substitute for the original, the originator will be able to charge a price greater than his marginal cost, even without legal protection. And, obviously, the greater the difference in the costs of making copies and in the quality of copies between creator and copier (assuming the latter's cost is higher or quality lower), the less need there is for copyright protection.

2. *Copying may itself involve some original expression—as when the copy is not a literal copy but involves paraphrasing, deletions, marginal notes, and so on—and so a positive cost of expression.* The copier may incur fixed costs as well, for example costs of rekeying the words from the copy he bought or of photographing them. Still, we would expect the copier's average cost to be lower than the creator's because it will not include the author's time or the cost of soliciting and editing the original manuscript. Nevertheless, when the copier cannot take a completely free ride on the creator's investment in expression and his other fixed costs, the need for copyright protection is reduced.

Between the literal copier and the author who makes no use whatever of previous works, three additional types of producer can be distinguished. One is the author who makes at least some, but perhaps modest, use of previous works; most authors are of this type. Next is the author of a derivative work, that is, a work that draws very heavily on previous works, though the derivative work involves some original elements. Third is the unoriginal copier who nevertheless tries to complicate the author's task of proving infringement by differentiating the copied work from the original in minor ways. Derivative works and infringement are discussed in Section II; the author who makes some use of previous works figures prominently in our formal analysis, along with the literal copier.

3. *Copying takes time, so there will be an interval during which the original publisher will not face competition.* This point, which is related to the first because generally the cost of production is inverse to time,[6] has two implications for the analysis of copyright law. First, because modern technology has reduced the time it takes to make copies as well as enabled more perfect copies to be made at low cost, the need for copyright protection has increased over time. Second, for works that are faddish—where demand is initially strong but falls sharply after a brief period—copyright protection may not be as necessary in order to give the creator of the work a fully compensatory return.

4. *There are contractual alternatives to copyright protection for limiting copying.* One is licensing the original work on condition that the licensee not make copies of it or disclose it to others in a way that would enable them to make copies. But contractual prohibitions on copying may, like trade secrets, be costly to enforce and feasible only if there are few licensees. Where widespread distribution is necessary to generate an adequate return to the author or where the work is resold or publicly performed, contractual prohibitions may not prevent widespread copying. Thus, the greater the potential market for a work, the greater the need for copyright protection. The development of radio, television, and the phonograph has expanded the market for copies and thereby increased the value of copyright protection.

5. *Since a copier normally must have access to a copy in order to make copies, the creator may be able to capture some of the value of copies made by others by charging a high price for the copies he makes and sells.* For example, a publisher of academic journals may be able to capture part of the value that individuals obtain from copying articles by charging a higher price for the journal—especially to libraries; or a record company may be able to charge a higher price because of home taping.[7] Although this possibility limits the need for copyright protection, it does not eliminate it. If one can make many copies of the first copy, and many copies of subsequent copies, the price of copies will be driven down to marginal cost and the creator will not be able to charge a sufficiently

[6] See Armen A. Alchian, Costs and Outputs, in Readings in Microeconomics 159, 165 (William Breit & Harold M. Hochman eds., 2d ed. 1971).

[7] This point is stressed by Liebowitz, Copying, *supra* note 2.

higher price for his copy to capture its value in allowing others to make more copies; no one (except the first copier and the most impatient readers) will buy from him rather than from a copier.

6. *Many authors derive substantial benefits from publication that are over and beyond any royalties.* This is true not only in terms of prestige and other nonpecuniary income but also pecuniary income in such forms as a higher salary for a professor who publishes than for one who does not,[8] or greater consulting income. Publishing is an effective method of self-advertisement and self-promotion. The norms against plagiarism (that is, against copying without giving the author credit) reinforce the conferral of prestige by publishing; to the extent that those norms are effective, they ensure that the author will obtain recognition, if not always royalties, from the works he publishes.

Such points have convinced some students of copyright law that there is no need for copyright protection.[9] Legal rights are costly to enforce—rights in intangibles especially so—and the costs may outweigh the social gains in particular settings. Perhaps copyright in books is one of them. After all, the first copyright law in England dates from 1710 (and gave much less protection than modern copyright law), yet publishing had flourished for hundreds of years in England despite censorship and widespread illiteracy.[10] The point is a little misleading, however. In the old days, the costs of making copies were a higher fraction of total cost than they are today, so the problem of appropriability was less acute. Also, there were alternative institutions for internalizing the benefits of expression.[11] And before freedom of expression became generally applauded, publishing was often believed to impose negative externalities—so there was less, sometimes no, desire to encourage it. Finally, while it may be difficult to determine whether, on balance, copyright is a good thing, it is

[8] Compare Howard P. Tuckman & Jack Leahey, What Is an Article Worth? 83 J. Pol. Econ. 951 (1975).

[9] See Plant, *supra* note 2; compare Stephen G. Breyer, The Uneasy Case for Copyright: A Study of Copyright in Books, Photocopies, and Computer Programs, 84 Harv. L. Rev. 281 (1970). But see Barry W. Tyerman, The Economic Rationale for Copyright Protection of Published Books: A Reply to Professor Breyer, 18 UCLA L. Rev. 1100 (1971).

[10] On the history of copyright law—which appears to have emerged first in fifteenth-century Venice—see Bruce W. Bugbee, The Genesis of American Patent and Copyright Law, ch. 2 (1967); Brander Matthews, Books and Play-Books, ch. 1 (1895); Comment, Copyright: History and Development, 28 California L. Rev. 620 (1940); and references in note 11 *infra*.

[11] In England, the Stationers' Company had long enjoyed a monopoly of printing, and this gave the company the equivalent of copyright protection. With the decline of the company, a need for a copyright law was felt, leading to the passage of the first general copyright law (in England) at the beginning of the eighteenth century, as mentioned. See Benjamin Kaplan, An Unhurried View of Copyright, ch. 1 (1967); Philip Wittenberg, The Protection of Literary Property, ch. 1 (1968).

easy to note particular distortions that a copyright law corrects. Without copyright protection, authors, publishers, and copiers would have inefficient incentives with regard to the timing of various decisions. Publishers, to lengthen their head start, would have a disincentive to engage in prepublication advertising and even to announce publication dates in advance, and copiers would have an incentive to install excessively speedy production lines. There would be increased incentives to create faddish, ephemeral, and otherwise transitory works because the gains from being first in the market for such works would be likely to exceed the losses from absence of copyright protection. There would be a shift toward the production of works that are difficult to copy; authors would be more likely to circulate their works privately rather than widely, to lessen the risk of copying; and contractual restrictions on copying would multiply.

A neglected consideration—one that shows not that copyright protection may be unnecessary but that beyond some level copyright protection may actually be counterproductive by raising the cost of expression—will play an important role both in our model and in our efforts to explain the salient features of copyright law. Creating a new work typically involves borrowing or building on material from a prior body of works, as well as adding original expression to it. A new work of fiction, for example, will contain the author's expressive contribution but also characters, situations, plot details, and so on, invented by previous authors. Similarly, a new work of music may borrow tempo changes and chord progressions from earlier works. The less extensive copyright protection is, the more an author, composer, or other creator can borrow from previous works without infringing copyright and the lower, therefore, the costs of creating a new work. Of course, even if copyright protection effectively prevented all unauthorized copying from a copyrighted work, authors would still copy. But they would copy works whose copyright protection had run out, or they would disguise their copying, engage in costly searches to avoid copying protected works, or incur licensing and other transaction costs to obtain permission to copy such works. The effect would be to raise the cost of creating new works—the cost of expression, broadly defined—and thus, paradoxically, perhaps lower the number of works created.[12]

[12] A parallel analysis (independent of ours) of the novelty requirement in patent law is found in Suzanne Scotchmer & Jerry Green, Novelty and Disclosure in Patent Law (Berkeley and Harvard, unpublished manuscript, May 12, 1988). The authors point out that the more stringent the requirement, making it harder to get a patent, the greater the gains from patenting but the less information useful to other inventors will be disclosed (patent applicants must disclose their inventions in the application).

Copyright holders might, therefore, find it in their self-interest, ex ante, to limit copyright protection. To the extent that a later author is free to borrow material from an earlier one, the later author's cost of expression is reduced; and, from an ex ante viewpoint, every author is both an earlier author from whom a later author might want to borrow material and the later author himself. In the former role, he desires maximum copyright protection for works he creates; in the latter, he prefers minimum protection for works created earlier by others. In principle, there is a level of copyright protection that balances these two competing interests optimally—although notice that the first generation of authors, having no one to borrow from, will have less incentive to strike the optimal balance than later ones.[13] We shall see in Section II that various doctrines of copyright law, such as the distinction between idea and expression and the fair use doctrine, can be understood as attempts to promote economic efficiency by balancing the effect of greater copyright protection—in encouraging the creation of new works by reducing copying—against the effect of less protection—in encouraging the creation of new works by reducing the cost of creating them.

2. A Formal Model of the Effect of Copyright Protection on the Creation of Works

The basic economics of copyright protection can be brought out more clearly by a formal model. We assume for the sake of simplicity that authors and copiers produce quality-adjusted copies that are perfect substitutes.[14] Let p equal the price of a copy, $q(p)$ the market demand for copies of a given work, x and y the number of copies the author and the copiers produce, respectively (so $q = x + y$), c the author's marginal cost of a copy (assumed to be constant), and e the author's cost of creating the work (that is, the cost of expression). To simplify further, we ignore the other fixed costs of creating and publishing a work and assume that demand is not subject to uncertainty. We denote the level of copyright protection by $z \geq 0$ where $z = 0$ means no copyright protection. The level of copyright protection involves such considerations as the necessary degree of similarity between two works before infringement can be found,

[13] Later generations of authors may also differ among themselves on where to set the level of copyright protection. Authors expecting to borrow less than they are borrowed from will prefer more copyright protection than those expecting to be net borrowers. Ex ante, however, before anyone knows whether he is likely to be a net "debtor" or "creditor," authors should be able to agree on the level of copyright protection.

[14] For example, a copier might produce a copy half as good as one produced by the author. On a quality-adjusted basis, two copies of the copier would count as one quality-adjusted copy.

the elements in a work that are protected, and the period of time for which the work is protected. For purposes of our formal model, we assume that all these factors can be incorporated into a single index of copyright protection, z.

We assume that copiers, like fringe firms in a market with a dominant firm, supply copies up to the point where price equals marginal cost, and that their marginal cost increases (not necessarily steeply) as both the number of copies and the level of copyright protection increase.[15] We can thus write the copiers' supply curve as

$$y = y(p, z) \tag{1}$$

with $y_p > 0$ and $y_z < 0$.[16]

The author's profits are

$$\Pi = (p - c)x - e(z), \tag{2}$$

and substituting for x, we have

$$\Pi = (p - c)[q(p) - y(p, z)] - e(z), \tag{3}$$

where $e(z)$ denotes the author's cost of expression, which is higher the greater copyright protection is.[17]

[15] Given our earlier assumption that the author's marginal cost (c) is constant, increasing marginal cost for copiers is a necessary assumption; otherwise copiers will produce all copies (in which event, the work will not be created) or no copies (in which event, the degree of copyright protection is not an interesting question). There is also a substantive reason to expect increasing marginal cost for copiers. Recall that the copying that takes place for a given level of z is lawful. Some of it will be by consumers (for example, home taping of television programs) and some will be by producers who incorporate the author's work into their product (for example, fair use copying). To be sure, the higher the level of z, the smaller the amount of such lawful copying. At a given level of z, however, there will be some types of copying that require consumers and firms to use only a small amount of their own resources. In effect, there will be a lot of free riding on the author's work, so the cost of copying will tend to be low. Other types of copying will require relatively larger amounts of resources by the copier. Here free riding will be less important, so costs will tend to be greater. Such differences should generate differences in the cost of copying among copiers and lead to rising marginal costs.

[16] We can derive the copiers' supply curve from their cost as follows. Let the total cost of copying for copiers equal $M = M(y, z)$ where $M_y > 0$ (= marginal cost), $M_{yy} > 0$, $M_z > 0$, $M_{zz} \geq 0$, and $M_{yz} > 0$. That is, marginal cost is positive and increases with the number of copies. We assume that z increases both the total and marginal cost of copies (M_y) because, as z increases, the amount of protected material in a given work will rise, so that copiers must add more of their own material or make greater alterations in the copy to avoid infringement. This factor will tend to make copying more costly. To simplify, we assume that $\partial M_{yy}/\partial z = 0$—that is, that the rate of change in marginal cost is independent of z. Since copiers operate where $p = M_y(y, z)$, we have $y_p = \partial y/\partial p = 1/M_{yy} > 0$ and $y_z = \partial y/\partial z = -M_{yz}/M_{yy} < 0$. Note that y_z denotes the shift to the left in the copier's supply curve as z increases, so that at each price copiers make fewer copies.

[17] Our model is similar to one used by Salop and Scheffman to analyze how a dominant firm selects strategies that raise both its and its rivals' costs. See Salop & Scheffman, Cost-

Let the author's gross profits, R in our notation, equal his revenue from selling copies minus the cost of making those copies, or $(p - c)x$. We show later that R increases as z increases. The author will create a work only if

$$R \geq e(z) \tag{4}$$

since otherwise his profits (eq. [2]) would be negative.

Let N equal the total number of (equivalent) works created. Our assumption that the cost of expression $[e(z)]$ will differ among authors—some authors will be more efficient at creating equivalent works and so their costs will be lower than other authors'—implies that with free entry of authors into the business of creating new works, N will rise until the cost of expression of the marginal author equals R. The supply of works will equal

$$N = N(R, z), \tag{5}$$

where $N_R > 0$ and $N_z < 0$.

The net effect on N of an increase in copyright protection (z) depends on the balance between two effects, because the increase leads to both a movement up the supply curve of works (as R increases) and a shift of the supply curve to the left as z drives up the cost of expression. In symbols, $dN/dz = N_R(dR/dz) + N_z$. At low levels of z the revenue-enhancing effect of limiting copying by free riders should dominate, so that $dN/dz > 0$. For example, when z is very low, few or no works will be created, since free riding by copiers may prevent any author from covering his cost of expression.[18] So N will increase as z increases, at least up to some level, say $\bar{z}$. Beyond $\bar{z}$ we assume that increases in the cost of expression to marginal authors will dominate, so that the number of works will begin to fall. That is, $dN/dz > 0$ for all $z < \bar{z}$, $dN/dz = 0$ at $\bar{z}$, and $dN/dz < 0$ for all $z > \bar{z}$.

The intuition behind these results is straightforward. Some copyright protection is necessary to generate the incentives to incur the costs of creating easily copied works, but too much protection can raise the costs of creation for subsequent authors to the point where those authors cannot cover them even though they have complete copyright protection for their own originality. The key issue is how the level of protection, z, here

---

Raising Strategies, 36 J. Indus. Econ. 19 (1987). In our model, copyright protection is like a strategy that raises both the rivals' (copiers') marginal cost and the dominant firm's fixed cost (the author's cost of expression). Salop and Scheffman's framework was helpful to us in developing our formal model.

[18] If, however, the copier's marginal cost is much greater than the creator's marginal cost, copyright protection may not be necessary for the creator to be able to cover his full cost of expression. In such a case, the principal effect of increasing z, even at lower levels, will be to raise the cost of expression and thus lower N.

modeled as a single index, is set along several dimensions. In general, the modern law of copyright makes intelligent estimates when it withholds legal protection from ideas as opposed to their expression, when it gives copyright holders rights over derivative works, when it creates a limited fair use exception, and when it sets the term of a copyright at life plus 50 years. Each of these topics is considered in the second part of this article.

B. *The Exploitation of a Work*

Optimal copyright protection depends not only on the number and the cost of works but also on the number and the cost of copies of each work. The latter cost is the focus of this part of the article. Once created, a work can be exploited in many ways and they need not be mutually exclusive. The author (or publisher, remember) of a novel may sell copies, sell to a magazine prepublication rights to publish selections, and license derivative works such as a play, musical, movie, translation, or condensation. Similarly, he may license the characters in his novel for a comic book or television series, or for a line of clothes. Later we distinguish between copiers who simply make identical copies of the novel and those who create derivative works (since, for example, one might expect that the disincentive to create the novel would be greater in the former than in the latter instance). For now, we treat all different ways to exploit a work identically and call them the making and selling of copies.

1. The Price of a Copy

The author will choose the price that maximizes his profits, Π in equation (2). This requires that p satisfy the equation

$$[q(p) - y(p, z)] + (p - c)(q_p - y_p) = 0, \tag{6}$$

which can be rewritten as

$$p\{1 - F/[\epsilon^d + \epsilon^s(1 - F)]\} = c, \tag{7}$$

where F is the share (that is, fraction) of copies made by the author, $1 - F$ is the share of copies made by copiers, ϵ^d is the elasticity of demand for copies, and ϵ^s is the elasticity of supply of the copiers [$\epsilon^s = y_p(p/y)$]. The price per copy will be greater the less elastic the demand for copies, the less elastic the copiers' supply curve, and the larger the author's share of copies relative to that of copiers, which in turn will be larger the lower the author's cost of making copies relative to that of copiers.[19]

[19] We assume that the second-order condition for a maximum is satisfied—that is, that

$$\partial^2\Pi/\partial p^2 = 2(q_p - y_p) + (p - c)(q_{pp} - y_{pp}) < 0.$$

We can determine the effect on price of changes in the level of copyright protection (z), and in the author's marginal cost of copying, by totally differentiating p in equation (6) with respect to z and c. This yields

$$dp/dz = y_z/S > 0, \tag{8}$$

$$dp/dc = (q_p - y_p)/S > 0, \tag{9}$$

where S equals $\partial^2\Pi/\partial p^2$, which is negative (from the second-order condition for profit maximization). Increases in z and c increase the price of a copy and reduce the total number of copies sold—provided, of course, that copiers' output is still positive. If not, increases in z will have no effect on the price and output or the number of copies; the author will be a monopolist and will not need any further copyright protection.

We are also interested in the effect of changes in z on the author's gross profits (that is, before deducting the cost of expression) and on the number of copies made by author and copiers (again assuming that copiers have a positive output). The change in gross profits (R) from a small change in z is given by

$$dR/dz = -(p - c)y_z > 0.\text{[20]} \tag{10}$$

Since y_z in equations (8) and (9) denotes the reduction in the quantity supplied by copiers as z increases (holding p constant), the change in the author's gross profits for a small increase in z will equal the difference between price and the author's marginal cost multiplied by the increased number of copies he supplies, an increase that in equilibrium will just match the reduction in copies supplied by copiers.

Although the author's gross profits will increase with greater copyright protection until copiers cease making copies—after which additional copyright protection can yield no benefit since there are no more competitors to exclude—net profits need not rise. The cost of expression to authors of copyrighted works increases as copyright protection increases. The less material an author (not a copier) can borrow from other copyright holders without infringing their copyrights, the greater will be the cost of creating his work. Formally, the change in net profits from in-

[20] We have dR/dz equals

$$d(p - c)x/dz = xdp/dz + (p - c)\{q_p(dp/dz) - [y_p(dp/dz) + y_z]\}.$$

Collecting terms yields

$$d(p - c)x/dz = dp/dz[x + (p - c)(q_p - y_p)] - (p - c)y_z.$$

Since $x + (p - c)(q_p - y_p) = 0$ from the first-order profit-maximizing condition, the first term in the above expression vanishes, which then leaves the expression in the text.

creases in z will be positive or negative depending on whether

$$-(p - c)y_z - e_z \gtrless 0. \tag{11}$$

The sign of equation (11) bears on the earlier question of whether an increase in copyright protection will raise or lower the number of works created. A positive sign for the marginal work (or author) means that an increase in z increases gross profits by more than the cost of expression, so net profits will rise and the number of works will increase. A negative sign means that greater copyright protection will reduce the number of works.

We speculated earlier that at low levels of z the revenue-enhancing effect would dominate, while at higher levels (above $\bar{z}$) the cost-enhancing effect would dominate. Equation (11) allows us to be more explicit about the factors affecting the relationship between z and the number of works. Since gross profits equal the cost of expression for the marginal author, we can rewrite (11)—the condition for whether z increases or decreases the number of works—in percentage terms:

$$-\tilde{y}_z(y/x) - \tilde{e}_z \gtrless 0, \tag{12}$$

where "~" denotes the percentage change in the variable-per-unit change in z. Equation (12) is more likely to be negative the smaller the copiers' share relative to the author's share (that is, the smaller is y/x). Since the copiers' share will fall and the author's rise as z increases, equation (12) is more likely to be negative at higher than at lower levels of copyright protection. So, consistent with our earlier speculation, the revenue-enhancing effect of additional copyright protection diminishes as the level of protection increases.

Although there is no obvious relationship between $\tilde{y}_z$ and the level of copyright protection, $-\tilde{y}_z$ will be greater the larger the increase in the copiers' marginal cost as z increases and the smaller the rate of increase in marginal cost with respect to a change in the number of copies—that is, the smaller the copier's supply elasticity.[21] This has two implications:

1. *The more difficult it is for copiers to avoid infringing the author's copyright by substituting other inputs for the protected part of the author's work, because the protected part is bigger, the larger will be the increase in the copiers' marginal cost.* The greater, therefore, will be the increase in the author's gross profit, and so the more likely it will be

[21] From note 16, recall that $-y_z = M_{yz}/M_{yy}$ where M_y denotes the copiers' marginal cost. Hence, $-\tilde{y}_z$ will tend to be greater the bigger the increase in the copiers' marginal cost as z increases and the smaller the increase in their marginal cost as y increases (that is, the flatter or more elastic the copiers' marginal cost curve).

that the number of works will increase as copyright protection expands. If the copying is exact, there will be, by definition, no other inputs to substitute for the author's work, and therefore an increase in z will tend to have a large positive effect on the copier's marginal cost curve and so on the number of works created.

2. *The smaller the difference in efficiency or cost of copying among copiers (which depends in turn on the similarity of the uses that copiers make of the author's work), the more elastic the copiers' supply or marginal cost will be and the larger, therefore, the increase in the author's gross profit as* z *increases.* This, too, makes it more likely that expanding copyright protection will increase the number of works created. Alternatively, if copiers use the author's work in diverse ways, the marginal cost of copying is likely to be less elastic and, hence, an increase in copyright protection will have a smaller effect on the author's gross profits.

What happens to the number of copies produced by copiers and by the author as the level of copyright protection rises? Since price will rise, the total number of copies will fall. The change in the copiers' output (y), however, will depend on the net effect of two offsetting effects. As z rises the copiers' supply curve will shift to the left ($y_z < 0$), reducing y; but the increase in p will lead to a movement up the supply curve, increasing y.

Turning to the number of copies sold by the author (x), and recalling that $x = q - y$, one sees that since an increase in copyright protection raises price and lowers the total number of copies sold, the author will sell more copies only if y declines by more than the reduction in q. That is indeed the most likely outcome, however. Since an increase in z raises the residual demand faced by the author, he would normally be expected to sell more. But if the elasticity of the residual demand curve declines sufficiently as it shifts outward, the author may produce less at the new equilibrium price. This is simply an illustration of the well-known proposition that an increase in demand may reduce the optimal output of a monopolist if the elasticity of demand declines sufficiently with the increase.

2. Some Welfare Effects of Copyright Protection

Let w equal the standard measure of economic welfare (the sum of consumer and producer surplus) in the market for copies of a single work before the cost of creating the work is deducted:

$$w = \int_{p^*}^{\infty} q(p)dp + (p^* - c)[q(p^*) - y(p^*, z)] + \int_{p^0}^{p^*} y(p, z)dp. \quad (13)$$

The first term in the equation is consumer surplus at p^* (the profit-maximizing price set by the author), the middle term is the author's gross profits, and the last term is the copiers' profits.[22]

Net welfare equals $w - e(z)$, where $e(z)$ is the cost of creating the particular work and is a function of the scope of copyright protection. The change in net welfare with respect to change in z equals

$$\partial[w - e(z)]/\partial z = (p^* - c)\{q_p(dp^*/dz) - [y_p(dp^*/dz) + y_z]\} + \int_{p^0}^{p^*} y_z dp - e_z \gtreqless 0.^{23} \quad (14)$$

This complicated expression has a simple interpretation. The first term is the change in the author's surplus from changing the scope of copyright protection. It depends on the difference between price and the author's marginal cost and on the change in the number of copies he sells; for the term in brackets is merely the difference between the change in total copies and the number of copies sold by copiers. Normally the author will sell more copies when z increases, because the copiers' marginal costs will rise. Notice that at the margin, copiers generate no consumer or producer surplus because they equate marginal cost to price. As for the last two terms in equation (14), $\int_{p^0}^{p^*} y_z dz$ is negative because an increase in z increases the total cost to copiers of the copies they produce, and $-e_z$ is also negative because the cost of expression increases with the amount of copyright protection.

An increase in copyright protection is likely to reduce the welfare benefits (consumer plus producer surplus) generated by a given work—assuming it will be created. Both the increase in the cost of creating the work and the increase in the cost to copiers reduce welfare, and only rarely will these increases be offset by cost savings resulting from the shift

[22] Notice that p_0 is the minimum price at which copiers are willing to produce a copy. Since we assume that copiers incur no fixed costs, the number of copies at p_0 is zero—that is, $y(p_0, z) = 0$.

[23] From eq. (13) we have

$$\partial w/\partial z = -q(p^*)(dp^*/dz) \quad \text{(i)}$$

$$+[q(p^*) - y(p^*, z)](dp^*/dz) + (p^* - c)[q_p(dp^*/dz) - (y_p(dp^*/dz) - y_z)] \quad \text{(ii)}$$

$$+ y(p^*, z)(dp^*/dz) - y(p^0, z)(dp^0/dz) + \int_{p^0}^{p^*} y_z dp, \quad \text{(iii)}$$

where (i) denotes the reduction in consumer surplus ($dp^*/dz > 0$); (ii) the change in the author's profits which depend on both the change in price and the change in the number of copies he produces (which may be positive or negative); and (iii) the change in the copier's surplus, which depends on the increase in price, the increase in his costs, and the change in the number of copies he produces. Combining the terms in $\partial w/\partial z$ yields eq. (14).

in producing copies from copiers to the author, a shift that will be larger the lower the author's marginal cost relative to that of the copiers. For the cost savings are obtained only on the additional units produced by the author, while the cost increase affects all copies produced by copiers plus the cost of expression.

Total welfare, however, which we analyze next, depends on the number of works created as well as on the consumer and producer surplus generated by a given work, assuming it is created; and the number of works may rise as copyright protection expands even though welfare per work falls. The traditional view stresses the trade-off between the benefits of copyright protection in encouraging the production of works and the losses from reducing access to the works by consumers. If one defines "access" as the sum of consumer and producer surplus generated by a single work, access is indeed likely to fall as copyright protection increases. But it falls because of factors—the increase in copiers' costs *and* in the cost of expression—that are ignored in the traditional view. That view stresses losses to consumers from higher prices—a factor that drops out of our analysis.

C. *The Optimal Level of Copyright Protection*

Let total welfare equal

$$W = W[N, w, E(N, z)]. \tag{15}$$

W will be an increasing function of both N, the number of (equivalent) works created, and w, the consumer and producer surplus per work before deducting the cost of creating the work, and will be a decreasing function of E, the total costs of creating works (including the cost of administering and enforcing the copyright system). In turn, E will be an increasing function of both N and z (that is, $E_N > 0$ and $E_z > 0$).[24] We assume for convenience that (15) can be written as

$$W = f(N)w - E(N, z), \tag{16}$$

[24] Note that $E_{NN} > 0$ because authors will differ in the costs of creating works and, as the economic return from creating works increases, higher-cost authors will find it economical to create works. $E_{Nz} > 0$ because increasing copyright protection will raise the cost to all authors of creating works. Administrative and enforcement costs are likely to rise both with the number of works created, holding constant z, and with the level of copyright protection, holding constant N, since more works will be registered and more infringement suits brought. One possible offset, however, is that an increase in copyright protection will deter some infringers. In that event, the number of suits may fall despite the greater incentive to pursue infringement claims as z increases.

where $f_N > 0$ and $f_{NN} < 0$—that is, there is diminishing marginal utility as the number of works created increases.

Maximizing W with respect to z yields

$$\partial W/\partial z = f_N N_z w + f(N) w_z - (E_N N_z + E_z) = 0, \tag{17}$$

or, equivalently,

$$N_z(f_N w - E_N) = -f(N) w_z + E_z, \tag{18}$$

where $N_z = (\partial N/\partial R)R_z + (\partial N/\partial z)$ and $w_z = (p^* - c)(dx/dp)(dp/dz) + \int_{p^0}^{p^*} y_z dp$ (see eq. [14]).[25] We denote by z^* the level of z that maximizes w. The right-hand side of equation (18) will be positive at z^* in the typical case, because an increase in z will lower producer and consumer surplus per work (that is, w_z is negative) and raise the cost of expression for all works and increase administrative and enforcement costs ($E_z > 0$).[26]

N_z measures the response of the number of works created to an increase in copyright protection. As we saw earlier, it can be either positive or negative. However, when z is set optimally, N_z will be positive. For suppose that N_z were negative at z^*. Since the same level of N could be attained at a lower z (because N increases initially and then falls as z rises), a lower z would yield a higher level of W. Not only would $E(N, z)$ be lower (since it is a positive function just of z when N is unchanged, and z would now be lower), but w (consumer and producer surplus per work before deducting the cost of expression) would be higher at a lower z for reasons explained in the previous section.

We can therefore eliminate from our analysis levels of z at which $N_z < 0$. The only exception would be where w *fell* as z fell—that is, the loss in producer surplus from substituting copies made by copiers for those made by authors exceeded the reduction in the cost of copiers as z fell—provided that, in addition, this effect was large enough to offset the reduction in E as z fell. We showed earlier, however, that w is likely to rise as z falls. Moreover, if total welfare were maximized when N_z was negative, this would turn the traditional rationale for copyright protection upside down. Instead of encouraging the production of works, copyright would discourage them in equilibrium; and instead of reducing access, it would increase access (defined, as before, in terms of welfare per work).

Another consideration, not captured in our formal model but working in

[25] We assume that the second-order condition for a maximum is satisfied, that is, $\partial^2 W/\partial z^2 < 0$.

[26] The right-hand side of eq. (18) could be negative in the unlikely event that w increased and enforcement costs decreased as z increased, and these changes more than offset the increased cost of expression. In that event, z^* would be at a level sufficient to eliminate all copying.

the same direction, is that, as N rises, a point may be reached where further increases in N will raise each author's cost of expression and hence E_N, the marginal cost of expression. With more and more copyrighted works, the amount of public-domain material—unappropriated materials suitable for inclusion in a new work—remaining will fall, and it will cost more to create a new work. This problem would be particularly serious if "ideas" (in the sense used in copyright law) as well as expression were copyrightable. They are not, as we shall see, and our explanation will be based on the relation between z and N developed in this section.

D. *Implications*

Our analysis of optimal copyright protection has a number of implications.

1. At z^*, the amount of producer and consumer surplus per work (w) weighted by f_N must exceed the cost of creating the marginal work;[27] otherwise the left-hand side of (18) would be negative. This implies that the optimal amount of copyright protection is greater for classes of work that are more valuable socially (that is, higher w is relative to the cost of creating the work). The left-hand side of (18) would rise, initially, relative to the right-hand side, requiring an increase in z to restore equilibrium.

2. Optimal copyright protection requires that z^* be set *below* the level that maximizes the number of works created. The latter would require that $N_z = 0$ (assuming that N increases initially and later decreases as z increases), which would make the left-hand side of equation (18) zero. Differently stated, strengthening copyright protection beyond z^* would increase the incentive to create more works ($N_z > 0$) but would not be worth the costs in reduced welfare per work, the higher costs of expression (for works that would have been created anyway at a lower value for z), and the greater administrative and enforcement costs.

3. From (18) it follows that the greater the responsiveness of N to an increase in z (that is, the greater N_z at each level of z), the greater the optimal value of copyright protection must be to reach equilibrium. In turn, N_z will be greater as z increases, the greater the increase in gross profits (R) (which is greater the greater the difference between p and c and the bigger the reduction in copies made by copiers as z increases), the smaller the increase in the cost of expression for the marginal author, and the smaller the rate of increase in the marginal cost of expression as N

[27] E_N also includes the incremental cost of administering and enforcing the copyright system that results from an increase in N. Note that since $E_{NN} > 0$, w will also exceed the full cost of creating each work at z^*.

increases (and hence the smaller the difference among authors in the cost of creating works).

4. We know that the optimal extent of copyright protection tends to rise with the value of a work (w) and that w will be greater the greater the demand for the work and the lower the marginal cost of making copies. Hence if, over time, growth in income and technological advances enlarge the size of the market for any given work, and the cost of copying declines, copyright protection should expand.

5. Suppose that w falls only slightly as copyright protection expands. Then the right-hand side in equation (18) will be smaller, and the optimal level of copyright protection will rise. Put differently, the less that welfare per work is affected by copyright protection, the higher will be the optimal level of that protection because of the benefits of copyright in increasing the number of works.

6. The more that the cost of expression rises as z increases (that is, the greater is E_z), the lower will be the optimal degree of copyright protection. This suggests that, if it is feasible to differentiate in infringement proceedings between individuals who make literal copies and those who use copyrighted material to create new, albeit derivative, works, there will be broader copyright protection against the former group than against the latter.

7. Finally and obviously, our analysis implies that the lower the cost of administering and enforcing a copyright system is and the more responsive authors are to pecuniary incentives, the greater will optimal copyright protection be.

II. Applications

A. *The Nature of Copyright Protection*

Our task now is to use our model to explain the principal features of copyright law. We begin with the nature of the protection that a copyright gives its owner. In contrast to a patent, a copyright merely gives protection against copying; independent (that is, accidental) duplication of the copyrighted work is not actionable as such. In speaking of "independent [accidental, inadvertent] duplication" we are addressing only the problem of an independent *recreation* of the original copyrighted work. The accidental *use* of someone else's work might be thought of as duplication, but in that context liability for infringement is strict, much as it is for the trespass on a neighbor's land made by a person who thinks that he owns it.

The more difficult question is to explain why duplication in the sense of independent recreation is not actionable. Our analysis suggests two possible explanations. The first is the added cost to the author of checking countless numbers of copyrighted works to avoid inadvertent duplication. The costs (if actually incurred—a qualification whose significance will become apparent shortly) would increase $e(z)$ and lower social welfare because both net welfare per work $[w - e(z)]$ and the number of works created would fall. True, the author's gross revenues might rise if the reduction in the amount of accidental duplication raised the demand for copies or made that demand less elastic.[28] But since accidental duplication of copyrighted works is rare (except in the area of popular music, discussed below), the net effect of making it unlawful would be to lower social welfare.

In contrast to copyright, accidental infringements of patents are actionable, and the difference makes economic sense. A patent is issued only after a search by the applicant and by the Patent Office of prior patented inventions. This procedure is feasible because it is possible to describe an invention compactly and to establish relatively small classes of related inventions beyond which the searchers need not go. The procedure makes it relatively easy for an inventor to avoid accidentally duplicating an existing patent.

No effort is made by the Copyright Office to search copyrighted works before issuing a copyright, so copyright is not issued but is simply asserted by the author or publisher. There are billions of pages of copyrighted material, any one page of which might contain a sentence or paragraph that a later writer might, by pure coincidence, duplicate so closely that he would be considered an infringer if he had actually copied the words in question or if copying were not required for liability. What is infeasible for the Copyright Office is also infeasible for the author. He cannot read all the copyrighted literature in existence (in all languages, and including unpublished works!) in order to make sure that he has not accidentally duplicated some copyrighted material.

The cost of preventing accidental duplication would be so great, and the benefits in terms of higher revenues (and so the amount of damages if such duplication were actionable) so slight because such duplication is rare, that even if it were actionable no writer or publisher would make much effort to avoid accidental duplication, so the increase in the cost of expression would probably be slight. But social welfare would be reduced somewhat. At best we would have a system of strict liability that had no

[28] If we include in y the copies made by accidental duplication, then expanding the scope of copyright protection to make each "copying" unlawful would shift upward the copiers' supply curve and raise the residual demand curve of the author.

significant allocative effective; and as explained in the literature on negligence and strict liability in tort law, the costs of enforcing such a regime are socially wasted because their only product is an occasional redistribution of wealth (here that would be from the accidental "infringer" to the first author or publisher of the material duplicated).[29]

The second reason we expect accidental duplication not to be made unlawful derives from the economic rationale for copyright protection, which is to prevent free-riding on the author's expression. Accidental duplication does not involve free-riding. Since the second work is independently created, its author incurs the full cost of expression. If the works are completely identical—a remote possibility, to say the least[30]—competition between the two works could drive the price of copies down to marginal cost and prevent either author from recovering his cost of creating the work. It is more likely that significant differences between the two works will remain, so that both authors may be able to earn enough to cover their respective costs of expression—particularly if neither author is the marginal author, whose gross revenues would just cover the cost of expression in the absence of accidental duplication.

Although for simplicity our analysis focuses on copyright protection for literature and other written works, it is applicable, mutatis mutandis, to other forms of expression as well. A significant difference between literary and musical copyright is that courts hold that accidental duplication may infringe a songwriter's copyright if his song has been widely performed.[31] Since most popular songs have simple melodies and the number of melodic variations is limited, the possibility of accidental duplication of several bars is significant. Widespread playing of these songs on the radio makes it likely that the second composer will have had access to the original work, which both increases the likelihood of accidental duplica-

[29] See William M. Landes & Richard A. Posner, The Economic Structure of Tort Law 70, 115–16 (1987).

[30] Recall Learned Hand's remark in Sheldon v. Metro-Goldwyn Pictures, 81 F.2d 49 (2d Cir. 1936), that "if by some magic a man who had never known it were to compose anew Keats' Ode on a Grecian Urn, he would be an author, and, if he copyrighted it, others might not copy that poem, though they might of course copy Keats." Hand, of course, thought such accidental duplication a remote possibility. The probability of accidental duplication of Keats' poem word for word is too small to justify courts in treating it as a litigable question, that is, one fairly open to doubt.

[31] For example, in ABKO Music, Inc. v. Harrisongs Music, Ltd., 722 F.2d 988, 998-99 (2d Cir. 1983), the court found that George Harrison's "My Sweet Lord" had infringed "He's So Fine," recorded by the Chiffons. "He's So Fine" had been one of the most popular songs in the United States and England during the same year that Harrison (a former member of the Beatles) composed "My Sweet Lord." The court found an infringement even though it also found that Harrison had copied the Chiffons' song unconsciously rather than deliberately.

tion and reduces the cost of avoiding it. If proof of intentional duplication were required for infringement, composers of popular songs would have little copyright protection and social welfare would fall.

This result may appear to show that musical copyright follows the pattern of patent law rather than of literary copyright, but the appearance is deceptive. Two forms of "accidental" duplication of a copyrighted work must be distinguished. The first is independent creation: the duplicator makes no use, direct or indirect, of the copyrighted work. Such a duplicator is never an infringer. The second is unconscious borrowing. Unlike the independent creator, the unconscious borrower is a free rider, and is therefore properly deemed an infringer. Musical copyright is special only in that unconscious borrowing is more likely in the musical than in the literary realm.

To distinguish between copying and independent duplication, the courts use an implicit indifference-curve analysis in which access is traded off against similarity. Where there is a strong showing of similarity, it is more likely that the original work was copied and less likely that it was independently created (particularly for complicated works, in contrast to, say, a few bars of a popular melody). In such a case, the copyright owner can prevail even if he presents only weak evidence that the defendant had access to the original work. On the other hand, where the differences between the original work and its "copy" are substantial, the copyright owner will normally have to provide strong evidence of access to rebut the defense of independent creation.

B. *The Scope of Protection*

The most difficult economic questions about copyright law have to do with the scope of legal protection. We shall discuss these under the headings of (1) idea versus expression, (2) derivative works. and (3) fair use.

1. Idea versus Expression

i) *The economic rationale for not protecting ideas.* A copyright protects expression but not ideas.[32] Postponing to the next section the problem of distinguishing between the two, we offer several reasons for the difference in treatment.

a) Suppose that the N works in our model express the same idea differently; for example, each work might be a different novel about a

[32] Ideas may sometimes be protected in other ways. For example, if A discloses an idea to B on the implicit understanding that if B uses the idea he will pay A, A will be protected under the doctrine of quasi contract or unjust enrichment. See Minnear v. Tors, 266 Cal. App. 2d 495 (1968).

romance between young people who belong to different social classes or religious faiths and whose parents are feuding. If copyright protected the first author's idea, the cost of expression to each of the remaining $N - 1$ authors would increase, because each would have to invest time and effort in coming up with an original idea for his work, or to substitute additional expression for the part of his idea that overlapped the first author's, or to incur licensing and other transaction costs to obtain the right to use the first author's idea.[33] The net effect of protection would be to reduce the number of works created—in the limit, to one, although the Coase Theorem makes this outcome unlikely—so that social welfare in equation (16) would fall. Granted, the copiers' cost would also rise if a copyright protected ideas, because copiers use not only the author's expression but also his ideas. However, this offset is likely to be small. Copiers are copying expression either unlawfully, in which case the marginal deterrence from protecting ideas is likely to be small, or lawfully, for example, because their copying is deemed a fair use. In either case, copyright protection for ideas would have a negligible effect on the copier's cost of copying. Even if protection did increase the gross profits of the $N - 1$ authors and thus offset partially the reduction in N, social welfare would fall because both N and welfare per work would fall.

The traditional explanation for protecting only expression emphasizes the welfare losses from monopoly of an idea. We emphasize the increase in the cost of creating works and the reduction in the number of works rather than the higher price (per copy) that is normally associated with monopoly. In a more complicated model the demand for copies would depend not only on the number of copies (our model) but also on the number of competing works. In that case, protecting ideas would raise the price of copies.

b) The author is both a user of ideas developed by others and a creator of new ideas. Suppose our N authors did not know which one would be the first to come up with an idea that the other $N - 1$ authors would use. Since (as we shall see in the next section) the costs involved in coming up with the kind of new idea normally embodied in an expressive work usually are low relative to the costs in time and effort of expressing the idea, and since the originator of the idea will probably obtain a normal return in one form or another from being first in the market even without receiving copyright protection, the N authors, behind a veil of ignorance,

[33] More formally, the full cost of creating a work would equal $e(z) + i$, where i is the cost of obtaining the ideas used in the work. Normally, i would not depend on the level of copyright protection. However, if copyright law protected ideas (call this protection z^i to distinguish it from z), then i would rise. In addition, e would probably rise because the author would substitute e for i.

probably would agree unanimously (or nearly so) to a rule that protected expression but not ideas. If so, then that rule would be Pareto optimal.

c) Another objection to copyright protection of ideas is that it would encourage rent seeking. Since the costs of developing a new idea are likely to be low in most cases relative to the potential reward from licensing the idea to others, there would be a mad rush to develop and copyright ideas. Resources would be sucked into developing ideas with minimal expression, and the ideas thus developed would be banked in the hope that a later author would pay for their use. Although the development of new ideas would be accelerated, the dissemination of ideas might not be.

d) A final concern is with the administrative costs involved in defining rights in ideas. Courts would have to define each idea, set its boundaries, determine its overlap with other ideas, and, most difficult of all, identify the idea in the work of the alleged infringer. Yet the total administrative and enforcement costs of operating a copyright system might actually shrink if ideas were protected, because of the significant reduction in the number of works created. Since the optimal level of copyright protection for expression takes account of the costs of enforcement, our first point—the decline in social welfare from fewer works—incorporates the savings in administrative and enforcement costs from few works. The present point, therefore, concerns the increase in these costs if the number of works is held constant.

ii) *Distinguishing ideas from expression.* Although the line between expression and idea is often hazy, there are clear cases on both sides of it. If an author of spy novels copies a portion of an Ian Fleming novel about James Bond, he is an infringer. If, inspired by Fleming, he decides to write a novel about a British secret agent who is a bon vivant, he is not an infringer. If an economist reprints Professor Coase's article on social cost without permission, he is an infringer; but if he expounds the Coase Theorem in his own words, he is not.

In both of these cases the original work (novel or article) is the joint output of two types of input, only one of which is protected by copyright law. In the case of the novel, the reason for the limited protection is easily seen.[34] The novelist creates the novel by combining stock characters and situations (many of which go back to the earliest writings that have survived from antiquity) with his particular choice of words, incidents, and dramatis personae. He does not create the stock characters and situations, or buy them. Unlike the ideas for which patents can be obtained, they are not new and the novelist acquires them at zero cost, either from observation of the world around him or from works long in the public

[34] See Richard A. Posner, Law and Literature: A Misunderstood Relation, ch. 7 (1988).

domain. Most works of fiction that anyone would want to copy are intended for a mass audience—which means they *must* use stock characters and situations in order to be understood. To give the author of a work embodying such characters or situations ("idea" in copyright lingo) copyright protection beyond the form in which he molds them into a particular novel or story ("expression") would increase the cost of expression of later authors without generating offsetting benefits.

This discussion helps to show why, in the first part of our discussion of ideas versus expression, we disparaged the welfare benefits from creating property rights to ideas. What passes for "ideas" in the case of most expressive writing normally is not comparable to the sort of inventions, costly to develop, that receive protection under the patent laws. An alternative to distinguishing between ideas and expression, therefore, would be to confine copyright protection to original works, or to a work insofar as it was original, much as in the case of patent law. The problem is that originality or novelty is an even more debatable quality of fiction than of mechanical and other technical processes. If copyright protection depended on originality, authors and publishers would find it hard to know in advance of litigation whether they actually had a property right.

In the case of Professor Coase, the reason for confining copyright protection to the form in which he expressed the Coase Theorem, and not extending it to the theorem itself, is less obvious. The theorem was not obtained at zero cost but reflected extensive education and thought. Also, it is clearly original. But precisely because the theorem is a powerful analytical construct, copyright protection would yield the inventor a very large income over and above the considerable nonpecuniary (as well as indirect pecuniary) income that accrues to a major theoretician. The total income would, in all likelihood, exceed the cost of inventing the theorem, thus creating a problem of rent seeking. Moreover, the cost of copyright enforcement would be much greater than in the case where the article itself was copied. It would often be hard to tell whether an article in economics was really using the Coase Theorem; the author (if he did not want to pay a royalty) would make every effort to explain his results in different terms. Furthermore, mathematical and scientific (including social scientific) ideas often are discovered simultaneously, or nearly so; this would make it difficult to determine whether an alleged infringer was a copier or an independent inventor.

iii) *The merger of ideas and expression.* By this locution we refer to cases where there are only a few ways of expressing an idea, so that protecting expression fully would, as a practical matter, prevent anyone but the author from using the idea. In such cases, copyright protection is construed narrowly, as we would predict. The classic case is *Baker v.*

Selden.[35] Selden had published a book describing a bookkeeping system that he had invented, and he illustrated the book with blank bookkeeping forms. Baker copied the forms, rearranging columns and using different headings, and sold them to people who wanted to use Baker's system. This was held not to be infringement, since otherwise Selden would have had a monopoly over his bookkeeping system that he could have exploited by insisting that anyone wanting to use the system buy the forms necessary for using it from him.

It might seem that without copyright protection Selden could not have prevented Baker even from copying Selden's book, but this is not correct. If Baker had published a book in which he copied verbatim (or by close paraphrase) the expository portions of Selden's book, he would have been guilty of infringement. If he wanted to sell the forms together with explanatory material, he had to write that material himself. The expressive part of Selden's book was protected.

Is this the optimal result? On the one hand, denying Selden the right to copyright his forms may have prevented him from recouping the expense in time and effort of inventing a new bookkeeping system. On the other hand, there are other ways he could have cashed in on such a notable commercial innovation; and granting him such copyright protection might have overcompensated him (and thus created a danger of rent seeking)—as well as have created deadweight losses in the market for account forms, by raising the price of those forms above their cost by the amount of royalty that he charged for permission to use his copyright.

The scope of the rule of *Baker v. Selden* is an issue in the current controversy over whether copyright protection for computer software extends to the visual "desktop" on which the computer operator views "icons" representing documents, files, programs, and so on, and to the organization and sequence by which the operator is led through a program. Because a given desktop display or program sequence can be generated by a variety of different programs, the program copyright itself does not cover these visual aspects of computer use. The question is whether they are separately copyrightable by analogy to a painting—a visual display that could be generated by a variety of different processes too. The argument against copyrightability is that the visual aspects in question have become so standardized in the computer market that copyright protection would enable the copyright holder as a practical matter to exclude competing manufacturers of computers. The counterargument is

[35] 101 U.S. 99 (1879); see also Morrisey v. Procter & Gamble Co., 379 F.2d 675 (1st Cir. 1967), where the rationale for denying copyright protection is explained in terms highly congruent with our analysis.

that the "idea" is the display of documents or other data, or sequences of stops, on a screen, and the "expression" the particular visual symbology. The mere fact that a particular set of symbols has become the industry standard is a tribute to the expressive skills of the particular manufacturer and should not be deemed to convert expression into idea.

We hope the debate will be resolved not by the semantics of the words "idea" and "expression" but by the economics of the problem and, specifically, by comparing the deadweight costs of allowing a firm to appropriate what has become an industry standard with the disincentive effects on originators if such appropriation is forbidden. These disincentive effects may be small. The probability that a particular display format will become the industry standard is small; presumably there are significant returns over and above copyright to a firm that achieves such a position; and the narrowly expressive aspects of the display are protected, thus limiting the effect of free riding.

Another contemporary application of *Baker v. Selden* concerns copyright of architects' plans. The plans themselves can be copyrighted, and if they are then copied without authorization the copier is an infringer. But what if someone copies not the blueprints but the building built from them? Is he an infringer? The law's answer is "no."[36] The economic explanation is that a building is functional as well as formal or decorative, so that if the architect could prevent the copying of the design elements visible in the building he would have much fuller property-right protection than copyright law (with its very long term) envisages. The analogy to the principle that denies trademark protection to "functional" trademarks (for example, trademarks in features, such as shape, that may be essential to the operation as well as appearance of the trademarked product) should be evident.[37] Notice the close analogy to the computer-software problem. The building built without the aid of the architect's plans corresponds to the desktop display generated without access to the originator's software. In both cases, the originator's property right is measured by the savings in cost of duplication that the copier could obtain by taking out a license from the originator.

Returning once more to the Coase example, notice that while in *Baker v. Selden* expression was incidental to idea, that is not true of Coase's article, in which, besides announcing the theorem, Coase gave illustra-

[36] See, for example, Imperial Home Corp. v. Lamont, 458 F.2d 895, 898 (5th Cir. 1972); Demetriades v. Kaufmann, 680 F. Supp. 658 (S.D.N.Y. 1988).

[37] See Landes & Posner, Trademark Law: An Enforcement Perspective, *supra* note 1, at 297–99.

tions of it, compared it with previous approaches, defended it, and discussed its implications for law, economics, and public policy.

A difficult problem in distinguishing ideas from expression is posed by technique, which we view as intermediate between idea and expression. The main illustrations are in literature and the arts, and include the sonnet form, stream-of-consciousness writing, the five-act play, perspective in painting, the pointed arch, and serial composition in music.[38] The law assimilates techniques to idea and so denies copyright protection. Another reason besides the monopoly profits that such protection would yield in many cases is that technique is harder to copy well than a work embodying the technique. It is easy to copy someone else's sonnet—but try writing one! With copies likely to be costly, slow to appear, and imperfect, the originator of a technique will be able to recoup some and perhaps all of his fixed costs even if he has no property right in the technique, as opposed to a right in his own works embodying the technique.

In between works of fiction on the one hand, and works in which expression is largely or entirely merged into ideas (*Baker v. Selden*) on the other hand, are works of nonfiction. The facts that form the subject matter of such a work may or may not dictate the expression; if they do it is a case of merger, and copyright protection should be denied. The classic example is narrative history. The first author of a history of the United States should not be allowed to copyright the sequence of events narrated, since that would preclude any subsequent author from writing a narrative history of the United States covering the same period as the first author. The argument against copyright protection in this case is even stronger than in a case like *Baker v. Selden*. The historian has not, of course, invented the facts of history that constitute the subject matter of his work—although it would not be correct to say that he acquired them at zero cost; he may have made a substantial investment in research and study.

2. Derivative Works

A derivative work is translation into a different language or medium. Illustrations include a German translation of an English play, the movie version of a play, photographs of a painting, a wind-up Mickey Mouse doll, and a porcelain plate with scenes taken from a movie. The owner of a copyrighted work has a right to prevent the making of a derivative work and

[38] See Posner, *supra* note 34, ch. 7.

thus can sue the maker of an unauthorized derivative work for infringement of the original. He can also copyright the derivative work. Thus he has a monopoly of works derived from his copyrighted work. If, however, the original work is in the public domain, the creator of the derivative work can obtain a copyright of the derivative work, though not, of course, of the original.

The case for giving the owner of a copyrighted work a monopoly of its derivative works as well is a subtle one. It is not, as it might seem to be, to enable the original author, publisher, and so on, to recoup his fixed costs. By definition, the derivative work is an imperfect substitute; often it is no substitute at all. A person who is in the market for an original painting priced at $20,000 will not be interested in a $50 photograph of the painting. A German who cannot read English will not buy the English original if there is no German translation. There are exceptions, of course; for example, a movie based on a book might reduce or, more likely, expand the demand for the book. Even where there is no element of substitution or complementarity—that is, where the derivative work is not part of the copiers' supply curve (see eq. [15]), so that the demand faced by the author for the original is independent of the demand for the derivative work—giving the original author the exclusive right over derivative works will enhance his income. But the conferral of the right is not necessary in order to prevent his sales from being driven to zero. And since it is not certain that *any* copyright protection is necessary to enable authors and publishers to recover their fixed costs, it would be speculative to conclude that without control over derivative works authors and publishers would not be able to cover the fixed costs of the original work—though no doubt some works would not be created without the expectation of revenues from derivative works, just as some products would not be produced if producers were forbidden to price discriminate.

To understand the best economic case for giving the owner of the original control over derivative works, even if the demand for the work is unrelated to the demand for the original, one must first consider why derivative works should be copyrightable. Imagine the situation of the translator who was not permitted to obtain copyright protection for his contribution to the derivative work, viewed as the joint product of him and the original author. To translate *The Brothers Karamazov* into English is an enormously time-consuming task. If the translator could not obtain a copyright of the translation, he might be unable to recover the cost of his time; for anyone would be free to copy the translation without having incurred that cost and could undersell him at a profit.

This analysis may seem to imply that the derivative, not original, author should be allowed to copyright the derivative work. Not so. Such a rule could distort the timing of publication of both the original and derivative works. The original author, eager to maximize his income from the work, would have an incentive to delay publication of the original work until he had created the derivative work as well (or arranged for its creation by licensees), in order to gain a head start on any would-be author of such a work.[39]

Another reason for giving the original author a monopoly of derivative works is to reduce transaction costs. Suppose Dostoevsky's heir owned the copyright on the original Russian version of *The Brothers Karamazov,* but some American owned the copyright on the English translation. A publisher who wanted to bring out a new edition of that translation would have to deal with two copyright holders. Transaction costs would be reduced if one person owned both copyrights. Of course, even if they were separately owned to begin with, one of the owners could buy the other's copyright. But this transaction, with its attendant costs, can be avoided if the law places the power to obtain both copyrights in the same person to begin with—and that is, in effect, what the law does.

If it is optimal for the original author to have the right to copyright derivative works, why not just forbid copyright in derivatives of copyrighted works? A copyright is just the right to exclude; if no one can copyright a derivative work, anyone who makes such a work is an infringer of the original work—except, of course, the author of the original work. Therefore, a rule that derivative works are not copyrightable would give the original author the same legal protection he would enjoy under a rule that allowed only the original author to copyright a derivative work. Not quite, however. First, if the derivative work is made shortly before the expiration of the copyright on the original work, the author may lack an adequate incentive to create the derivative work unless it can be copyrighted. Second, proof of infringement is simplified if the author can enforce a copyright in a derivative work, for then there is no need to decide whether the infringer's derivative work is similar enough to the original to be infringing. Third, by enabling the author's property right to be subdivided, the copyrightability of derivative works facilitates transactions (compare time-sharing and other subdividings of more conventional property rights). We give an example below.

For obvious reasons, the derivative work must have some expressive elements not found in the original work; otherwise it would be identical to

[39] Here is an analogy from another area of copyright law. The fair use privilege (of which more shortly) is narrower in the case of unpublished than published works. See Harper & Row, Publishers, Inc. v. Nation Enterprises, 471 U.S. 539 (1985). If there were a broad fair use privilege for unpublished works, authors would have an incentive to incur heavy expenditures to prevent anyone from gaining access to the works.

the original work. Suppose the derivative work is a wind-up Mickey Mouse doll that looks just like the copyrighted Mickey Mouse comic strip character;[40] the commercial success of the doll depends on its being an exact replica of the Walt Disney character. Since this mechanical "translation" of the figure into a new medium involves no expression, copyright protection is not required to prevent free riding by third parties, as it was in our example of an English translation of Dostoevsky.

Now consider derivative works based on works in the public domain—for example, a modern edition of Adam Smith's *Wealth of Nations*. Here the case for granting copyright protection to the derivative work is stronger, so we would expect a weaker requirement of incremental expression than for derivatives of copyrighted works. Since in such a case the original author (or his heirs), lacking copyright, is not able to prevent free riding on the expression contained in the derivative work, the incentive to create the derivative work will be seriously impaired if the work is not copyrightable. In contrast, if the original author's copyright has not run out, no one can copy from the derivative work without also copying from the original when the derivative work adds very little in expression to the original, so the author of the derivative work (normally the original author or his licensee) is protected. Moreover, the problems associated with multiple copyright holders are somewhat reduced when the derivative work is based on public domain material. So arguments based on administrative and enforcement costs against granting copyright protection are also weaker.

To determine the presence of incremental and, hence, copyrightable expression requires comparison between the original and the derivative. Some courts have required that the increment be significant, worrying that if it is set too low, and if the original and derivative copyrights happen to be in different hands (recall that one reason for allowing the copyrighting of derivative works is to allow an unbundling of the original author's rights), the costs of determining infringement could be prohibitive.[41] If the derivative work is only trivially different from the original, it may be impossible to determine whether an infringing work was copied from (and hence infringed) the derivative work, the original, or both. In addition, if the original and derivative works are barely distinguishable (for example, translating John Steinbeck into "modern" American prose), the benefits

[40] Divided ownership may arise by contract when that is efficient. For example, consider a movie based on a book. The producers of the movie will invariably own the copyright on the movie, because they are best able to exploit derivative uses of the movie (for example, video cassettes, adaptations for television, posters, advertisements, colorization); concentrating ownership in the book publisher would impede such exploitation.

[41] See, for example, Gracen v. Bradford Exchange, 698 F.2d 300 (7th Cir. 1983).

of legal protection in encouraging the creation of new and distinct works may be trivial. But in making this point we are abstracting from the case, illustrated by photography of works of art, where the creativity of the derivative work consists precisely in the fidelity with which it reproduces the impression created by the original.

3. Fair Use

"Fair use" is a doctrine that allows some copying of a copyrighted work without deeming the copier an infringer, even though the copyright holder has not authorized the copying.[42] The conventional view is that no general theory can explain the cases that invoke the doctrine. Such a view is reinforced by Section 107 of the Copyright Act, which codified the fair use doctrine for the first time.[43] Section 107 identifies a series of factors—drawn from prior judicial decisions—to be considered, such as purpose and character of use, nature of copyrighted work, amount and substitutability of portion used, and effect on potential market for copyrighted work, but leaves open the question of their relative importance and how one uses them to determine whether a use is fair. Our economic model, however, explains the major applications of the fair use principle.

i) *The high-transaction-cost case.* Suppose that the costs of a voluntary exchange are so high relative to the benefits that no such exchange is feasible between a user of a copyrighted work and its owner. User A might be willing to pay B (the copyright holder) a sum that B would gladly accept to consent to the use of the work, but the cost of negotiating such a license may be prohibitive if, for example, all A wants to do is quote a brief passage from B's work. A fair use privilege creates a clear benefit to A but does not harm B. The copier here is neither a firm selling copies nor a potential purchaser of copies, so his projected use affects neither the supply of copies nor the demand for them.

Several qualifications are in order, though none undermines this important justification for fair use. First, although transaction costs are prohibitive in our example, we could substitute for the existing property-rights approach (which in the absence of the fair use doctrine would prevent A from making any use of B's work) a liability rule under which the user would not have to negotiate with the copyright holder but would merely be required to pay damages (if any) ex post. However, the transaction

[42] It is an immensely important doctrine, as illustrated by the fact that it has its own treatise; see William F. Patry, The Fair Use Privilege in Copyright Law (1985), as well as a large journal literature well illustrated by William W. Fisher III, Reconstructing the Fair Use Doctrine, 101 Harv. L. Rev. 1659 (1988).

[43] 17 U.S.C. § 106.

costs of this approach would also be high relative to the potential benefits, such as the extra incentive to create the work. Often, users are numerous, and this would make for a high cost of arranging compensation and a large number of legal proceedings. Also, the potential fee (or damages) per user might be so small—perhaps zero—that enforcement proceedings would be infeasible. A compulsory licensing scheme might be possible, but any such government regulation would be likely to entail substantial costs.

Second, fair use, if too broadly interpreted, might sap the incentive to develop innovative market mechanisms that reduce transaction costs and make economic exchanges between copyright holders and users feasible. The American Society for Composers, Authors, and Publishers (ASCAP) (or Broadcast Music, Inc. [BMI], the other performing-rights organization) is an illustrative market response to copyright problems caused by high transaction costs. The number of users (radio and TV stations, night clubs, and so on) of copyrighted music makes individual negotiations with copyright holders to acquire performance rights infeasible. This problem is eliminated when ASCAP acquires nonexclusive rights from copyright holders and offers a blanket license to users for an annual fee; this allows users to perform any songs in ASCAP's repertory. Since performance distributions from ASCAP are an important part of composers' incomes, a fair use exception for performance would greatly reduce the pecuniary incentive to compose music.

Third, even if there are many users and it is too costly to negotiate individual licenses for part of the work, some users might be willing to purchase the entire work. Suppose you want to photocopy a chapter from a book. Although individual negotiations may be infeasible, you might, if forbidden to photocopy the chapter, purchase the entire book.

These are not arguments against the fair use doctrine. They are arguments for construing it narrowly. Only if the benefits of the use exceed the costs of copyrighted protection—as they do *not* in the performing-right case, given the economical method of conferring copyright through performing-rights organizations, and possibly not in the chapter-photocopying case as well—is the no right/no liability solution of fair use defensible on pure transaction-cost grounds.

ii) *Book reviews.* A standard example of fair use is the book review that quotes brief passages from the book being reviewed. Conventional legal analysis conceives the doctrine as striking a balance between the author's interest in royalties and the interest of the reviewer and his readers in free access to limited portions of the work. The first stage of economic analysis reconceives the doctrine as economizing on transaction costs, though they need not be prohibitive as in our previous discussion. Since book reviews are a substitute for advertising, the publisher presumably would "license" reviewers to quote brief passages from the book for free. By giving reviewers, in effect, an automatic license, the fair use doctrine avoids the costs of explicit transactions between publishers and reviewers that would yield the identical outcome. This is the theory by which "time-shifting" home video recordings of copyrighted television programs were held in the *Betamax* case to be protected by the fair use doctrine.[44]

A second stage of economic analysis begins by noting that a book or movie is an experience good rather than an inspection good, so that accurate pre-use information about product quality is likely to enlarge demand for these products. Yet if there were no fair use doctrine, a publisher might not allow quotation by reviewers apt to review a particular book unfavorably, or (what amounts to the same thing) might condition the license on the reviewer's deleting "excessively" critical portions of the review. But it does not follow that publishers, as a class, would be better off under such a regime, since readers would tend to discount favorable reviews, knowing there was some probability that the favor had been procured by permission to quote the book. Ex ante, publishers are better off if reviewers are free to quote without permission; it makes reviews a credible form of book advertising.[45] Even if publishers were made better off by retaining legal control over reviews, the consumers of books would be worse off. The suppression of an unfavorable review would be comparable to concealment by an ordinary seller of a defect in his goods.

iii) *Parody*. One stage beyond the review is the parody, which copies the distinctive features of the original work in order to recall it to the reader. The reminding function is essential; without the reader's awareness of the original, the parody will not be recognized as such and so will fall flat. One could view the parody as a derivative work, and give the author of the original work control over it, but this would enable the author of the original work to stifle what is often a particularly effective form of criticism—ridicule.

A difficult case is that of the noncritical parody, perhaps better described as "burlesque" and well illustrated by Jack Benny's famous bur-

[44] See Sony Corp. of America v. Universal City Studios, Inc., 464 U.S. 417 (1984); Wendy J. Gordon, Fair Use as Market Failure: A Structural and Economic Analysis of the Betamax Case and Its Predecessors, 82 Colum. L. Rev. 1600 (1982).

[45] Consistent with this view, reviewers may not take so much from the original work that the review itself serves as a substitute for the work. Yet it is lawful for the criticism in the review to destroy the market for the work. The latter is an aspect of the provision of information on experience goods. This information tends, on balance, to increase the demand for such goods, though in particular instances it will reduce it.

lesque of *Gas Light*.[46] Benny was not attacking *Gas Light* any more than Abbott and Costello were attacking *Frankenstein* in *Abbott and Costello Meet Frankenstein*. Humorous but not ridiculing versions of the original, these burlesques are derivative works in a pure form, and modern copyright law gives the copyright holder the exclusive right to make such works. A derivative work is a substitute, though an imperfect one, for the original; it may therefore siphon revenues from the original work not by disparaging that work but by satisfying part of the demand for it. So maybe the law should try to distinguish between parody and burlesque and treat the latter but not the former as infringing. The difficulty of doing this should be obvious. Yet the law may already be doing it implicitly by the emphasis it places on whether the allegedly infringing work is fulfilling the demand for the original work (which a parody does not do); if so it is a derivative work and infringing.[47]

iv) *Reducing the cost of creating works.* The question of fair use arises in another setting involving the permissible use that later authors can make of earlier works: deciding whether an allegedly infringing work is "substantially similar" to the work which it is said to infringe. Answering this question requires a court to sort out the contribution to the new product of the original copyright holder and the alleged infringer. The inputs into a work of fiction (including movies, television plays, and so on) include characters, situations, plot details, and so on, invented by previous authors and not yet so standard or hackneyed that they are considered part of the elementary repertory of stock characters and situations on which all authors should be free to draw. When "substantial similarity" is defined narrowly, the later author will be allowed to use these inventions without having to negotiate with the copyright holder. Courts refer to this as a *productive* fair use, as distinct from simply a *reproductive* use. A productive use is one that lowers the cost of expression and tends to increase the number of works, while a reproductive one simply increases the number of "copies" of a given work, reduces the gross profits of the author, and reduces the incentives to create works. Not surprisingly, a fair use defense for a productive use is looked on more favorably than such a defense for a reproductive use.

Striking the right balance was a critical issue in our formal model, where we saw that if all borrowing from previously copyrighted works were deemed infringement, the number of new works (N) might fall.

[46] See Benny v. Loew's Inc., 239 F.2d 532 (9th Cir. 1956), affirming a judgment against Benny.

[47] See, for example, Berlin v. E. C. Publications, Inc., 329 F.2d 541 (2d Cir. 1964; Fisher v. Dees, 794 F.2d 432, 437–38 (9th Cir. 1986).

Whether the law has struck the right balance is not readily determinable, but the fact that the law denies protection for ideas and requires substantial, rather than some, similarity for infringement[48] is evidence of implicit awareness of the problem.

C. *The Optimal Term of a Copyright*

The usual economic argument for limiting the duration of a right in intellectual property is twofold. First, such a limitation reduces the potential monopoly profits (hence, rent seeking and resource misallocation) from ownership of such a right.[49] Second, it reduces tracing costs. Both reasons loom large in the patent area, which is why patents expire much sooner than either copyrights or trademarks. Patents confer larger potential gains than copyrights or trademarks, and (a related point) patented inventions are hard to keep track of over a long period of time because an invention (for example, the wheel) may eventually become embodied in a vast range of different products. Trademarks rarely confer any monopoly power. And they pose no tracing problem, because to be valid a trademark must be used in conjunction with a specific product that is actually being sold in the market; hence the term of a trademark is indefinite (that is, until abandonment—just as with real property and other tangible products).

Copyrights, too, rarely confer monopoly power, but there are two types of tracing problem, though neither is serious. First, it is hard to keep track of heirs over many generations. This is a potential problem with real estate as well, but is solved by having a registry of land titles. A similar system could be instituted for copyrights. Second, books may go out of print and older works in general may not be easily available. But this problem is solved by having a registry—the Copyright Office—which retains copies of all copyrighted works. Moreover, since copyright just protects against copying, not independent duplication, a book or other work that is not widely available is simply less likely to be copied. Nevertheless, since the tracing cost is positive and grows with the amount of time that has elapsed since the publication of the copyrighted work, there is an argument for limiting the term of a copyright to the point at which the incentive effects of copyright become negligible because of the time value of money. Income prospects that lie twenty-five years in the future have

[48] See, for example, Nichols v. Universal Pictures Corp., 45 F.2d 119, 121 (2d Cir. 1930) (L. Hand, J.); 3 Nimmer on Copyright § 13.03[A] (1986).

[49] See William Nordhaus, Invention, Growth and Welfare, ch. 5 (1969), for a formal model of the optimal life of a patent that depends on the trade-off between incentive creation and resource misallocation.

little effect on present decisions, though not zero since people do make provisions for retirement more than twenty-five years in advance. The prospect of royalties in one hundred years, however, would have no effect on most authors' incentives.

It might seem that more than tracing costs are at stake in the decision to impose a time limit on copyrights. The longer the term, the fewer the number of works that are in the public domain, and therefore the higher that E (the cost of expression) will be. This is true, but the higher cost must be discounted along with the higher income of copyright holders. Thus, if the question were whether to increase the term of copyright from fifty to sixty years, not only would the additional revenues to the authors have to be discounted to present value but so would the additional costs to the authors of new works. This assumes, however, that the increase in term is prospective only. If the increase applies retroactively, that is, to existing works as well as to works not yet produced, the increased incentive to create will be limited to a subset of the affected works (those not yet produced), while the increase in the cost of expression will apply to borrowing from all works, existing and not yet produced. This is a strong argument against making increases in copyright term retroactive.

If we are right that copyrights should be time-limited to save on tracing costs, it might seem to follow that all property rights should similarly be limited. But this is wrong. Even one hundred years from now it will be desirable to have a given parcel of land owned by someone, in order to prevent overuse—and why not the heirs of the present owner unless they sell it before then? There is no congestion externality in the case of information, including the text of a book, and hence no benefit (yet potentially substantial costs) in perpetuating ownership beyond the period necessary to enable the author or publisher to recoup the fixed costs of creating the work. After that, it is fine to dump the copyrighted work into the public domain. As we do not intend land ever to be in the public domain, we cannot economize on the costs of administering property rights by placing a time limit on these rights in land.

This point can be sharpened by contrasting the copyright situation with that of "publicity rights" (rights to the commercial exploitation of a person's name or likeness), where there *is* a congestion externality. Suppose an insurance company wants to use a picture of George Washington in its logo and an heir of George Washington appears and objects, claiming that the right of publicity is a descendible right. The heir could not argue that the recognition of such a right almost two hundred years after the death of a public figure is necessary to recoup the investment in becoming a public figure, but he could argue that, unless there is a property right in the public figure's name and likeness, there may be congestion, resulting in a loss of value. This is the economic insight behind the growing movement toward making publicity rights inheritable[50] and also behind state antidilution statutes.[51] The advertising value of a name and likeness may be diminished if anyone can use them. That is not a problem with books, art works, and other copyrighted items.[52]

The current length of a copyright is the author's lifetime plus fifty years. This reflects a long trend toward lengthening the term of copyright (as well as expanding its scope, for example, by including derivative works, which in this country has gone from twenty-eight years in 1790 (a fourteen-year initial term renewable for another fourteen years) to forty-two years in 1831 (a twenty-eight year initial term renewable for fourteen years) to fifty-six years in 1909 (a twenty-eight-year initial term renewable for twenty-eight years) to the present term in 1976. This trend is consistent with the fact that the cost of copying has fallen over this period, for we showed earlier that the lower the cost of copying the greater the optimal scope of copyright protection.

The present term may seem both too long—the author who publishes a work at age thirty and dies at age eighty has one hundred years of copyright protection, and even in the unlikely event that the work will still generate a substantial income in the one hundredth year, the present value of that expectation will be virtually zero—and arbitrary in making the term of the copyright depend on the author's longevity. But maybe the term is neither too long nor arbitrary. A point stressed in the legislative history of the 1976 act is that, by making the death of the author the determining date for copyright protection, "all of a particular author's works, including successive revisions of them, would fall into the public domain at the same time, thus avoiding the present problems of determining a multitude of publication dates and of distinguishing 'old' and 'new' matter in later editions."[53] And we know that bequest motives play a role in people's decisions to work, save, and so on, and those motives depend on the altruistic feelings that people have, primarily for members of their family, including descendants. This feeling is attenuated with regard to remote descedants, but the fifty-year term after death cuts them off.

[50] See Timothy P. Terrell & Jane S. Smith, Publicity, Liberty, and Intellectual Property: A Conceptual and Economic Analysis of the Inheritability Issue, 34 Emory L. J. 1 (1985).

[51] See Landes & Posner, Trademark Law: An Economic Perspective, *supra* note 1, at 306–09.

[52] An exception, however, is when the absence of property rights in an earlier work discourages someone today from incurring the cost necessary to rediscover and popularize the work.

[53] H. R. Rep. No. 1476, 94th Cong., 2d Sess. 134 (1976).

Criminal Law

[4]

The Deterrent Effect of Capital Punishment: A Question of Life and Death

By Isaac Ehrlich*

Debate over the justness and efficacy of capital punishment may be almost as old as the death penalty itself. Not surprisingly, and as is generally recognized by contemporary writers on this topic, the philosophical and moral arguments for and against the death penalty have remained remarkably unchanged over time (see Thorsten Sellin (1959, p. 17), and (H. A. Bedau, pp. 120–214). Due in part to its essentially objective nature, one outstanding issue has, however, become the subject of increased attention in recent years and has played a central role in shaping the case against the death penalty. That issue is the deterrent effect of capital punishment, a reexamination of which, in both theory and practice, is the object of this paper.

The multifaceted opposition to capital punishment relies partly upon ethical and aesthetic considerations. It arises also from recognition of the risks of errors of justice inherent in a legal system, errors occasionally aggravated by political, cultural, and personal corruption under certain social regimes. Such errors, of course, are irreversible upon application of this form of punishment. But the question of deterrence is separable from subjective preferences among alternative penal modes and can be studied independently of any such preferences. Of course, the verification or estimation of the magnitude of the deterrent effect of the death penalty—the determination of the expected tradeoff between the execution of a murderer and the lives of potential victims it may help save—can, in turn, influence evaluation of its overall desirability as a social instrument even if that evaluation is largely subjective.

Recent applications of economic theory have presented some analytical considerations and empirical evidence that support the notion that offenders respond to incentives and, in particular, that punishment and law enforcement deter the commission of specific crimes. Curiously, two of the most effective opponents of capital punishment, Beccaria in the 18th century and Sellin in recent years, have never to my knowledge questioned analytically the validity of the deterrent effect of punishment in general. Beccaria even recognizes explicitly the probable existence of such a general effect. What has been questioned by these scholars is the existence of a *differential* deterrent effect of the death penalty over and above its most common practical alternative, life imprisonment (see Beccaria, pp. 115–17). Sellin has presented extensive statistical data that he and others have interpreted to imply, by and large, the absence of such an effect (see Sellin (1959, 1967)).

Whether, in fact, the death penalty constitutes a more severe punishment than

* University of Chicago and National Bureau of Economic Research. I have benefitted from comments and suggestions from Gary Becker, Harold Demsetz, Lawrence Fisher, John Gould, Richard Posner, George Stigler, and Arnold Zellner. I am particularly indebted to Randall Mark for useful assistance and suggestions and to Walter Vandaele and Dan Galai for helpful computational assistance and suggestions. This paper is a reduced version of a more complete and detailed draft (see the author 1973b). Financial support for this study was provided by a grant to the NBER from the National Science Foundation, but the paper is not an official NBER publication since it has not been reviewed by the board of directors.

life imprisonment for the average potential offender cannot be settled on purely logical grounds, although crime control legislation, ancient and modern, clearly answers this question affirmatively. Observation that convicted offenders almost universally seek and welcome the commutation of a death sentence to life imprisonment is consistent with the intuitive ranking of the death penalty as the harshest of all punishments. Still, one may argue that the differential deterrent effect of capital punishment on the incentive to commit murder may be offset by the added incentive it may create for those who actually commit this crime to eliminate policemen and witnesses who can bring about their apprehension and subsequent conviction and execution.

The existence of the differential deterrent effect of capital punishment is ultimately an empirical matter. It cannot, however, be studied effectively without thorough consideration of related theoretical issues. The crucial empirical question concerns the kind of statistical test to devise in order to accept or reject the relevant null hypothesis. Since the inquiry concerns a hypothetical deterrent effect, the null hypothesis should be constructed in a form that permits testing of the relevant set of behavioral relations implied by a general theory of deterrence. That includes the deterrent effects of law enforcement activities in general. Moreover, even if a negative effect of capital punishment on the rate of murder is established through systematic empirical research, there still remains the question of the existence of a *pure* deterrent effect distinct from a potential preventive or incapacitating effect associated with this form of punishment. An effect of the second type might be expected since execution eliminates categorically the possibility of recidivism.

Contrary to previous observations, this investigation, although by no means definitive, does indicate the existence of a pure deterrent effect of capital punishment. In fact, the empirical analysis suggests that on the average the tradeoff between the execution of an offender and the lives of potential victims it might have saved was of the order of magnitude of 1 for 8 for the period 1933–67 in the United States. Two related arguments are offered in this context of which only the second will be elaborated in this paper. First, it may be argued that the statistical methods used by Sellin and others to infer the nonexistence of the deterrent effect of capital punishment do not provide an acceptable test of such an effect and consequently do not warrant such inferences. Second, it is argued that the application of the economic approach to criminality and the identification of relevant determinants of murder and their empirical counterparts permit a more systematic test of the existence of a differential deterrent effect of capital punishment. The theoretical approach, emphasizing the interaction between offense and defense—the supply of and the (negative) social demand for murder—is developed in Section I. Section II is devoted to the empirical implementation of the model. Some implications of the empirical evidence are then presented and discussed in Section III.

I. An Economic Approach to Murder and Defense Against Murder

A. *Factors Influencing Acts of Murder and Other Crimes Against Persons*

The basic propositions underlying the approach to murder and other crimes against the person are 1) that these crimes are committed largely as a result of hate, jealousy, and other interpersonal conflicts involving pecuniary and nonpecuniary motives or as a by-product of crimes against property; and 2) that the propensity to perpetrate such crimes is influenced by the prospective gains and losses associated with their commission. The abhorrent, cruel, and occasionally pathological nature of murder notwithstanding, available evidence is at least not inconsistent with these basic propositions. Victimization data reveal that most murders, as well as other crimes against the person, occur within the family or among relatives, friends, and other persons previously known to one another, and are not committed as a rule by strangers on the street (see President's Commission on Law Enforcement and Administration of Justice (*PCL*), pp. 14, 15, 81, and 82). Indeed, hate and other interdependencies in utility across persons as well as malevolent and benevolent exchanges would seem more likely to develop among groups that exercise relatively close and frequent social contact than among groups that exercise little or no contact. There is no reason a priori to expect that persons who hate or love others are less responsive to changes in costs and gains associated with activities they may wish to pursue than persons indifferent toward the well-being of others.

More formally, assume that person o's utility from a consumption prospect C_o, depends upon his own consumption c_o, and consumption activities involving other persons c_j, $j=1, \ldots n$, or

$$(1) \qquad U_o(C_o) = U_o(c_o, c_j)$$

where the sign of $\partial U_o/\partial c_j$ indicates the direction in which o's utility is affected by consumption activities pursued by others. The key feature of this consumption model involving interdependent preferences[1] is that it provides a framework for analyzing positive or negative transfers of resources by one person (here identified with person o) that modify the levels of consumption enjoyed by others while simultaneously determining his own consumption level. Such modifications are constrained generally by the pertinent transfer production functions, by the endowments of resources possessed by person o and other relevant persons, and by potential awards and penalties that are conditional upon o's benevolent or malevolent actions with varying degrees of uncertainty.[2]

This framework can be applied to analysis of the incentive to commit murder and other crimes against the person by explicitly incorporating into the model the uncertainties associated with the prospective punishments for crime. Specifically, murder can be considered a deliberate action intended by an offender o to inflict severe harm on a victim v by setting c_v equal to, say, zero. The offender undergoes some direct costs of planning and executing the crime, and bears the risk of incurring detrimental losses in states of the world involving apprehension, conviction, and punishment.[3] Assuming the offender

[1] For a more complete discussion of this model, see Harold Hochman and James Rodgers, and Gary Becker (1974).

[2] It might be argued that although the wish to harm other persons cannot be rejected on economic grounds, nonetheless the execution of such desires (as opposed to benevolent actions) must be considered irrational in the sense of violation of Pareto optimality conditions. If there were no bargaining, transfer, or enforcement costs associated with mutually acceptable and enforceable contracts between a potential offender o and his potential victim v, and if v's wealth constraint were not binding, then it would always be optimal for v to offer compensation to o for not committing a crime against him and for o to seek such compensation or extortion. The reason is that a reduction in v's consumption level is thus achieved by o without incurring the direct costs of committing a crime and the prospective cost of legal sanctions. Indeed, there exists some range of compensations that would increase both o's and v's utilities relative to their expected utilities if crime is committed by o against v. Many crimes against persons, and some cases of property crimes as well, may occasionally be avoided by such arrangements; successful extortions involving kidnapping or hijacking constitute obvious examples. Yet in many situations compensations may be too costly to pursue or to enforce, just as fully effective private or public protection against murder may be too costly to provide. The incidence of murder must then be expected on purely economic grounds.

[3] The case in which crime is committed in pursuit of material gains has been analyzed explicitly by the

TABLE 1

Event		State s	Probabilities π_s	Consumption Prospect C_s
Apprehension	conviction of murder	execution	$(Pa)(Pc\|a)(Pe\|c)$	C_d: $(c_o=0;\ c_v=0)$
		imprisonment for murder	$(Pa)(Pc\|a)(1-Pe\|c)$	C_c: $(c_o=c;\ c_v=0)$
	conviction of a lesser offense or acquittal	other punishment	$Pa(1-Pc\|a)$	C_b: $(c_o=b;\ c_v=0)$
No Apprehension		no punishment	$1-Pa$	C_a: $(c_o=a;\ c_v=0)$

behaves as if to maximize expected utility, a necessary and sufficient condition for murder to occur is that o's expected utility from crime exceeds his expected utility from an alternative (second best) action:

$$(2)\quad U^*_{om}(C^m_o \mid c_v = 0) \equiv \sum_{s=a}^{S} \pi_s U_o(C_{os}) > U^*_{ol}(C^l_o \mid c_v = c^l_v),$$

where $s=a, \ldots, S$ denote a set of mutually exclusive and jointly exhaustive states of the world including all the possible outcomes of murder; c_{os} denote the offender's consumption levels, net of potential punishments and other losses, that are contingent upon these states; π_s denote his subjective evaluation of the probabilities of these states; and C^m_o and C^l_o denote, respectively, his consumption prospect in the event he commits murder or takes an alternative action.

To illustrate the behavioral implications of the model via a simple yet sufficiently general example, assume the existence of just four states of the world associated with the prospect of murder as summarized in Table 1. In Table 1, Pa denotes the probability of the event of apprehension and $1-Pa$ denotes its complement—the probability of escaping apprehension; $Pc|a$ denotes the conditional probability of conviction of murder given apprehension, and $1-Pc|a$ denotes its complement—the probability of conviction of a lesser offense (including acquittal); finally, $Pe|c$ and $1-Pe|c$ denote, respectively, the conditional probabilities of execution and of other punishments given conviction of murder. The (subjective) probabilities of the set of states introduced in Table 1 are equal by definition to the relevant products of conditional probabilities of sequential events that lead to this more final set of states. The last column in Table 1 lists the consumption levels that are contingent upon the occurrence of these states. Economic intuition suggests that the relevant consumption levels can be ranked according to the severity of punishment imposed on the offender; that is, $C_a > C_b > C_c > C_d$.

In the preceding discussion the incidence of murder has been viewed to be motivated by hate. As hinted earlier in the discussion, however, murder could also be a by-product, or more generally, a complement of other crimes against persons and property. Since the set of states of the world underlying the outcomes of these other crimes also includes punishment for murder, the decision to commit these would also be influenced by factors determining the probability distribution of outcomes considered in Table 1. In turn, the incidence of murder would be influ-

author (1973a). Note that the victim's level of consumption need not directly enter the offender's utility function in this case.

enced by factors directly responsible for related crimes. In general, behavioral implications concerning the effect of various opportunities on the incidence of murder ought to be analyzed within a framework that includes related crimes as well. For methodological simplicity and because data exigencies rule out a comprehensive empirical implementation of such a framework, the following discussion emphasizes the effect of factors directly related to murder and the direct effect on murder of general economic factors like income and unemployment. In practice, however, the effect of these latter factors on murder may be due largely to their systematic effects on particular crimes against property.

1. *The Effects of Probability and Severity of Punishment*

An immediate implication of the model that is independent of the specific motives and circumstances leading to an act of murder is that an increase in the probability or severity of various punishments for murder decreases, relative to the expected utility from an alternative independent activity, the expected utility from murder or from activities that may result in murder. These implications have been discussed at length elsewhere (see the author (1970, 1973a)) but the somewhat more detailed formulation of the model adopted in this paper makes it possible to derive more specific predictions concerning the relative magnitudes of the deterrent effects of apprehension, conviction, and execution that expose the theory to a sharper empirical test. Specifically, given the ranking of the consumption levels in states of the world involving execution, imprisonment, other punishment, and no punishment for murder, as assumed in the preceding illustration, and given the level of the probabilities of apprehension and the conditional probabilities of conviction and execution, it can be shown that the partial elasticities of the expected utility from crime with respect to these probabilities can be ranked in a descending order as follows:

$$\epsilon_{Pa} > \epsilon_{Pc|a} > \epsilon_{Pe|c} \tag{3}$$

where $\epsilon_P = -\partial \ln U^* / \partial \ln P$ for $P = Pa$, $Pc|a$, $Pe|c$.[4] The interesting implication of condition (3) is that the more general the event leading to the undesirable consequences of crime, the greater the deterrent effect associated with its probability: a 1 percent increase in the (subjective) probability of apprehension Pa, given the values of the conditional probabilities $Pc|a$ and $Pe|c$, reduces the expected utility from murder more than a 1 percent increase in the conditional (subjective) probability of conviction of murder $Pc|a$ (as long as $Pc|a<1$), essentially because an increase in Pa increases the overall, i.e., unconditional, probabilities of three undesirable states of the world: execution, other punishment for murder, and punishment for a lesser offense, whereas an increase in $Pc|a$ raises the unconditional probability of the former two states only. A fortiori, a 1 percent increase in $Pc|a$ is expected to have a greater deterrent effect

[4] Differentiating equation (2) with respect to Pa, $Pc|a$, and $Pe|c$, using the contingent outcomes of murder as illustrated in Table 1, it can easily be demonstrated that:

$$\epsilon_{Pa} = -\frac{\partial U^*_{om}}{\partial Pa}\frac{Pa}{U^*_o} = \frac{1}{U^*_o}\{Pa(1 - Pc|a) \cdot [U(C_a) - U(C_b)] + PaPc|a(1 - Pe|c) \cdot [U(C_a) - U(C_c)] + PaPc|aPe|c \cdot [U(C_a) - U(C_d)]\} > 0$$

$$\epsilon_{Pc|a} = -\frac{\partial U^*_{om}}{\partial Pc|a}\frac{Pc|a}{U^*_o} = \frac{1}{U^*_o}\{PaPc|a(1-Pe|c) \cdot [U(C_b) - U(C_c)] + PaPc|aPe|c \cdot [U(C_b) - U(C_d)]\} > 0$$

$$\epsilon_{Pe|c} = -\frac{\partial U^*_{om}}{\partial Pe|c}\frac{Pe|c}{U^*_o} = \frac{1}{U^*_o}\{PaPc|aPe|c \cdot [U(C_c) - U(C_d)]\} > 0$$

Clearly, $\epsilon_{Pa} > \epsilon_{Pc|a} > \epsilon_{Pe|c} > 0$.

than a 1 percent increase in $Pe|c$ as long as $Pe|c$ is less than unity. If there exists a positive monotonic relation between an average person's subjective evaluations of Pa, $Pc|a$, and $Pe|c$ and the objective values of these variables, and between an average person's expected utility from crime and the actual crime rate in the population, equation (3) would then amount to a testable theorem regarding the partial elasticities of the murder rate in a given period with respect to objective measures of Pa, $Pc|a$, and $Pe|c$. On the basis of this analysis, it can be predicted that while the execution of guilty murderers deters acts of murder, *ceteris paribus*, the apprehension and conviction of guilty murderers is likely to have an even larger deterrent effect.

Analogous to the effects of the probabilities of various punishments for murder, an increase in the severity of these punishments, their probabilities held constant, is generally expected to decrease the expected utility from murder and so to discourage its commission. Due to lack of space, other implications concerning the effect of severity as well as probability of punishment on the elasticities ϵ_{Pa}, $\epsilon_{Pc|a}$, and $\epsilon_{Pe|c}$ are omitted here. For a more complete analysis, see the author (1973b).

2. *Effects of Employment Opportunities, Income, and Demographic Variables*

The model developed in this section suggests that the incentive to commit murder or other crimes that may result in murder in general would depend on permanent income (or wealth), the relevant opportunities to extract related material gains as well as on direct opportunities for malevolent actions, including the direct costs involved in effecting the production of malevolent transfers. The means for a direct implementation of the effect of these latter opportunities are not readily available (see, however, the discussion in fn. 14). In contrast, variations in legitimate and illegitimate earning and income opportunities may be approximated by movements in the rate of unemployment and of labor force participation, U and L, respectively, and in the level and distribution of permanent income Y_p in the population.

The relevance of the latter set of variables has been discussed in detail elsewhere (see the author (1973a)), particularly in connection with crimes against property, some of which involve murder. However, the level and distribution of income within a community may also exert a direct influence on the incentive to commit murder because of their impact on the individual demand for malevolent actions. In addition, although the decision to commit murder is presumably derived from considerations related to lifetime utility maximization, the timing of murder may be affected by variations in the opportunity cost of time throughout the life cycle, because the typical punishment for murder involves a finite imprisonment term. Thus, to the extent that earning opportunities are imperfectly controlled in an empirical investigation, it may be important to investigate the independent effects of variations in demographic variables, such as the age and racial composition of the population, A and NW, respectively. Controlling for variations in age composition may also be important because of the differential treatment of young offenders under the law.

B. *Defense Against Murder*

1. *Factors Determining Optimal Law Enforcement Activity*

Following the approach used by Becker (1968), I shall attempt to derive implications concerning law enforcement activity against murder on the assumption that law enforcement agencies behave as if they seek to maximize a social welfare function by minimization of the per capita loss from murder. Losses accrue from three main elements: harm to victims net of gains to offenders; the direct costs of law enforcement by police and courts; and the net social costs associated with penalties. The behavior of enforcement agencies is assumed to be in accordance with the general implications of the deterrent theory of law enforcement.

The main elements of the social loss function can be summarized by:

$$(4)\quad L = D(q) + C(q, Pc) + \gamma_1 Pc\ Pe \mid c\ qd + \gamma_2 Pc(1 - Pe \mid c)qm$$

The term $D(q)$ represents the net social damage resulting from the death of victims and other related losses, where $q \equiv Q/N$ denotes the rate of murder in the population. The term $C(q, Pc)$ represents the total cost of apprehending, indicting, prosecuting, and convicting offenders. The aggregate output of these law enforcement activities can be summarized by the fraction of all murders that are "cleared" by the conviction of their alleged perpetrators (assuming a fixed proportional relation between the number of murders and their perpetrators). This fraction θ may be viewed as an objective indicator of the probability that a perpetrator of murder will be convicted of his crime, $Pc = Pa(Pc \mid a)$ with one qualification: since the overall probability of error of justice, π—that of apprehending and convicting an innocent person—is greater than nil, the true probability of conviction $0 < Pc < 1$ will be systematically lower than θ. However, to abstract the analysis from a separate determination of the optimal value of ϵ, it is henceforth assumed that Pc and θ are proportionally related, so that C can be defined as a direct function of Pc.[5] The rate of murder q is introduced as a separate determinant of C because of the argument and evidence that the costs of producing a given value of θ are higher for higher levels of q. The larger is q, the larger the number of suspects that must be apprehended, charged, and convicted in order to achieve a given value of θ. Both D and C are assumed to be monotonically increasing, continuously differentiable, and concave functions in each of their respective arguments.

The third and fourth terms in equation (4) represent the per capita social costs of punishing guilty and innocent convicts through execution and imprisonment (or other penalties), respectively. The variables d and m denote the private costs to victims and their families from execution and imprisonment, and the multipliers γ_1 and γ_2 indicate the presence of additional costs or gains to the rest of society from administering and otherwise bearing the respective penalties of execution and imprisonment that are imposed on guilty and innocent convicts.[6] For methodologi-

[5] Pc and θ would be proportionally related if the number of arrests of innocent and guilty persons were proportionally related and if the probability of legal error remained constant as more resources were spent on enforcement activity through arrests and prosecutions. Alternatively, it might be argued that Pc and θ are highly (positively) correlated because of the well-known proposition that at any given level of evidence presented in court in reference to the defendant's guilt or innocence, the probability of legal or type I error, α (that of convicting the innocent), is negatively related to the probability of type II error, β (that of acquitting the guilty). Hence α might be negatively correlated with $Pc \mid ch \equiv 1 - \beta$ where $P_c \mid ch$ denotes the conditional probability that a guilty offender will be convicted once he is charged. However, the assumption that Pc and θ, or $Pc \mid ch$ and α, are mutually dependent is made mainly for methodological convenience without affecting the basic implications of the following analysis. More generally, the direct costs of law enforcement activity C may be specified as a function including Pc and the unconditional probability of legal error ϵ as independent arguments so that optimal values of these probabilities may be determined separately via appropriate expenditures.

[6] More specifically, $\gamma_1 = b_1 + \lambda\beta_1$ and $\gamma_2 = b_2 + \lambda\beta_2$, where λ is a coefficient relating Pc to the fraction of murders cleared by convicting innocent persons π and b and β indicate the respective net social costs from

cal convenience, the costs of execution and imprisonment can be combined, and equation (4) can be rewritten as:

$$(5) \qquad L = D(q) + C(q, Pc) + \gamma_1 Pcfq$$

where $f = (Pc|c)d + \gamma_2(1 - Pc|c)m/\gamma_1$ is a measure of the average social cost of punishment for murder.

Equation (5) identifies the unconditional probability of conviction Pc, and the expected social cost of punishment f, as the main control variables underlying law enforcement activity. Given the harshness of the method of execution, the length of imprisonment terms, and other factors determining d and m (changes in these factors occur slowly in practice) the magnitude of f is largely a function of the conditional probability of execution $Pe|c$. The values of $0 < Pc < 1$ and $0 < Pe|c < 1$ that locally minimize equation (5) must then satisfy the following pair of equilibrium conditions:

$$(6) \quad \left[D_q + C_q + C_p \frac{1}{q_p} + \gamma_1 Pcf(1 - Ep) \right] q_p = 0$$

$$(7) \qquad [D_q + C_q + \gamma_1 Pcf(1 - Ef)] q_f f_e = 0$$

where

$$Ep \equiv - \frac{\partial Pc}{\partial q} \frac{q}{Pc} \equiv \frac{1}{\varepsilon_{Pc}}$$

$$Ef \equiv - \frac{\partial f}{\partial q} \frac{q}{f} \equiv \frac{1}{\varepsilon_f}$$

$$f_e \equiv \frac{\partial f}{\partial Pe|c} = \left(d - \frac{\gamma_2}{\gamma_1} m \right)$$

and the subscripts p, f, and e associated with the variables C and q denote the partial derivatives of the latter with respect to Pc, f, and $Pe|c$, respectively. The product $\gamma_1 f_e$ indicates the difference between the social costs of execution and imprisonment.

In equation (7) the term $-(D_q + C_q)q_f f_e$ represents part of the marginal revenue from execution: the value of the lives of potential victims saved, and the reduced costs of apprehending and convicting offenders due to the differential deterrent effect of execution on the frequency of murder. The term $\gamma_1 Pcf(1 - Ef)q_f f_e$ represents the net marginal social cost of execution: the value to society of the life of a person executed at a given probability of legal error, plus all the various costs of effecting his execution (including mandatory appeals) net of imprisonment costs thereby "saved." Because in equilibrium, the two must be equated, the optimal value of $Pe|c$ need not be unity—capital punishment may not always be imposed even when it is legal—and would depend on the relative magnitude of the relevant costs and gains. A similar interpretation applies to equation (6).

Inspection of the equilibrium conditions given by equations (6) and (7) reveals a number of interesting implications. First, it may be noted that if an increase in $Pe|c$ unambiguously raises the social cost of punishment for murder, that is, if $\gamma_1 f_e = \gamma_1 d - \gamma_2 m > 0$, then in equilibrium, the deterrent effect associated with capital punishment must be less than unity, or $\varepsilon_{P|e} < \varepsilon_f < 1$.[7] Put differently, executions must only decrease the rate of murders in the population but not the rate of persons executed, for otherwise the marginal cost of execution would be negative and a corner solu-

punishing guilty and innocent convicts through execution, denoted by the subscript 1, or imprisonment, denoted by the subscript 2. The conditional probability of execution given conviction is implicitly assumed to be equal for all convicts.

[7] By definition,

$$\varepsilon_{Pe|c} \equiv -(\partial q/\partial Pe|c)(Pe|c/q)$$
$$\equiv \varepsilon_f(\partial f/\partial Pe|c)(Pe|c/f) \equiv \varepsilon_f \varepsilon_{fe}$$

Clearly,

$$\varepsilon_{fe} = Pe|c[d - (\gamma_2/\gamma_1)m]/\{(\gamma_2/\gamma_1)m + Pe|c[d - (\gamma_2/\gamma_1)m]\}$$

is lower than unity if $[d - (\gamma_2/\gamma_1)m] > 0$. Under this condition, and the assumption that $\gamma_1 > 0$, $\varepsilon_{Pe|c} < \varepsilon_f < 1$.

tion would be achieved at $Pe|c=1$. However, equation (7) does not have the same implications regarding the value of ε_{Pc}. More specifically, equation (6) shows that the marginal costs of conviction include the marginal costs of apprehending and convicting offenders, in addition to the marginal costs of punishing those convicted. Therefore, the overall marginal revenue from convictions must also be higher than that from executions. Indeed, by combining equations (6) and (7), it can readily be shown that in equilibrium, $\varepsilon_{Pc} > \varepsilon_f > \varepsilon_{Pe|c}$;[8] that is, the deterrent effect associated with Pc must exceed the differential deterrent effect associated with $Pe|c$. This proposition is essentially the same as that derived regarding the response of offenders to changes in Pc and $Pe|c$ (see equation (3)). The compatibility of the implications of optimal offense and defense under the assumption that both offenders and law enforcement agencies regard execution to be more costly than imprisonment insures the stability of equilibrium with respect to both activities. It also provides the basis for a sharp empirical test of the theory.

2. *The Interdependencies Among the Murder Rate and the Probabilities of Conviction and Execution*[9]

Any exogenous factor causing a decrease in the severity of punishment for murder via a decrease in $Pe|c$ can be shown to increase the value of Pc because it tends to decrease the marginal costs of conviction and increase its marginal revenue. More specifically, given the values of d and m, an increase in social aversion toward capital punishment or in the costs of the related due process, measured by γ_1, can be shown to produce a decline in the optimal value of $Pe|c$ and a simultaneous increase in the optimal value of Pc. This analysis is consistent with an argument often made regarding the greater reluctance of courts or juries to convict defendants charged with murder when the risk of their subsequent execution is perceived to be undesirably high. Conviction and execution thus can be considered substitutes in response to changes in the shadow price of each. Indeed, the empirical investigation reveals that at least over the period between 1933 and 1969, in which the estimated annual fraction of convicts executed for murder in the United States, denoted by PXQ_1, fell from roughly 8 percent to nil, the national clearance ratios of reported murders, denoted by P^0a, and the fraction of persons charged with murder who were convicted of murder, denoted by $P^0c|a$, on the whole, moved in an opposite direction. The zero order correlation coefficient between PXQ_1, and P^0a is found to be -0.028, while that between PXQ_1 and $P^0c|a$ is found to be -0.19. (In principle, the product $P^0aP^0c|a$ approximates the value of Pc.) The general implication of this analysis is that the simple correlation between estimates of the murder rate and the conditional probabilities of execution cannot be accepted as an indicator of the true differential deterrent effect of capital punishment, because the simple correlation is likely to confound the offsetting effects of opposite changes in Pc and possibly also in the probability and severity of alternative punishments for murder.

Just as convictions and executions are expected to be substitutes with respect to changes in the shadow cost of each activity, they can be expected to be complementary with respect to changes in the severity of damages from crime, essentially because such changes increase the marginal revenues from both activities. Since an

[8] By like reasoning and some simplifying assumptions, it can also be shown that in equilibrium, $\varepsilon_{Pa} > \varepsilon_{Pc|a} > \varepsilon_{Pc|c}$.

[9] Proofs to the theorems discussed in this section can be developed through an appropriate differentiation of equations (6) and (7) with respect to the relevant variables.

exogenous increase in the rate of murder is expected to increase the marginal social damage D_q, and, indirectly, the marginal costs of apprehension and conviction C_q, it is expected to induce an increase in the optimal values of both Pc and $Pe|c$. This analysis demonstrates the simultaneous relations between offense and defense and suggests that the deterrent effects of conviction and execution must be identified empirically through appropriate simultaneous equation estimation techniques.

II. New Evidence on the Deterrent Effect of Capital Punishment

A. *The Econometric Model*

In the empirical investigation an attempt is made to test the main behavioral implications of the theoretical model. The econometric model of crime and law enforcement activity devised by the author (1973a) is applied to aggregate crime statistics relating to the United States for the period 1933–69. The model treats estimates of the murder rate and the conditional probabilities of apprehension, conviction, and execution as jointly determined by a system of simultaneous equations. Since data limitations rule out an efficient estimation of structural equations relating to law enforcement activities or private defense against murder, the following discussion focusses on a supply-of-murders function actually estimated in this study.

1. *The Murder Supply Function*

It is assumed that the structural equations explaining the endogenous variables of the model are of a Cobb-Douglas variety in the arithmetic means of all the relevant variables. The murder supply function is specified as follows.

$$(8)\quad \left(\frac{Q}{N}\right) = CPa^{\alpha_1} Pc|a^{\alpha_2} Pe|c^{\alpha_3} U^{\beta_1} L^{\beta_2} Y_p^{\beta_3} A^{\beta_4} \exp(v_1)$$

where C is a constant term and v_1 is a disturbance term assumed to be subject to a first-order serial correlation. The regression equation thus can be written as:

$$(9)\quad y_1 = Y_1 A_1' + X_1 B_1' + v_1$$

where

$$(10)\quad v_1 = \rho v_{1-1} + e_1$$

The variables y_1, Y_1, and X_1 denote, respectively, the natural logarithms of the dependent variable, other endogenous variables, and all the exogenous variables entering equation (8); ρ denotes the coefficient of serial correlation, and the subscript -1 denotes one-period lagged values of a variable. The coefficient vectors A_1' and B_1' have been estimated jointly with ρ and the standard error of e_1, σ_e, via a nonlinear three-round estimation procedure proposed by Ray Fair.

2. *Variables Used*

The dependent variable of interest (Q/N) is the true rate of capital murders in the population in a given year. The statistic actually used, $(Q/N)^0$, is the number of murders and nonnegligent manslaughters reported by the police per 1,000 civilian population as computed from data reported by the FBI *Uniform Crime Report* (*UCR*)[10] and the Bureau of the Census. This statistic can serve as an efficient estimator of the true Q/N if the two were related by:

$$(11)\quad \left(\frac{Q}{N}\right) = k\left(\frac{Q}{N}\right)^0 \exp \mu$$

where k indicates the ratio of the true number of capital murders committed in a given year relative to all murders reported to the police, and μ denotes random

[10] I am indebted to the Uniform Crime Reporting Section of the FBI for making available their revised annual estimates of the total number of murders and other index crimes in the United States during the period 1933–65.

errors of reporting or identifying murders. It should be noted, however, that the fraction of capital murders among all murders may have been subject to a systematic trend over time. Indeed, the theory developed in Section IA suggests that the decrease in the tendency to apply the death penalty in the United States over time may have led to an increase in the fraction of capital murders among all murders. More important, the number of reported murders may have decreased systematically over time because of the decrease in the fraction of all attempted murders resulting in the death of the victims due to the continuous improvement in medical technology. To account for such possible trends, the term k in equation (11) can be defined as $k=\delta \exp(\lambda T)$, where δ and λ are constant terms and T denotes chronological time. Upon substitution of $(Q/N)^0$ for (Q/N) in equation (8), the inverse values of δ and μ would be subsumed under the constant term C and the stochastic variable v, respectively, and $\exp(-\lambda T)$ would emerge as an additional explanatory variable. Thus, the natural value of T is introduced in equation (9) as an independent exogenous variable.[11]

The matrix of endogenous variables associated with Y_1 in equation (9) includes the conditional probabilities that guilty offenders be apprehended, convicted, and executed for murder. These probabilities have been approximated by computing objective measures of the relevant fractions of offenders who are apprehended, convicted, and executed. The following paragraphs contain a brief discussion of these measures.

Pa is measured by the national "clearance rates" as reported by the FBI *UCR*, which are estimates of the percentage of all murders cleared by the arrest of a suspect. It is denoted by P^0a. The conditional probability $Pc|a$ is identically equal to $Pch|a \cdot Pc|ch$—the product of the conditional probabilities that a person who committed murder be charged once arrested, and that he be convicted once charged. Statistical exigencies preclude the estimation of a complete series of $Pch|a$, but $Pc|ch$ is estimated by the fraction of all persons charged with murder who were convicted of murder in a given year as reported by the FBI *UCR*. This fraction, denoted by $P^0c|a$, may serve as an efficient estimator of the overall true probability $Pc|a$, provided that $Pch|a$ were either constant over time, or proportionally related to the probability of arrest Pa.

The actual measures of $Pe|c$ consist of alternative estimates of the expected fractions of persons convicted of murder in a given year who were subsequently executed, $P^0e|c$. Because no complete statistics on the disposition of murder convicts by type of punishment are available, however, $P^0e|c$ has been estimated indirectly by matching annual time-series data on convictions and executions. Over most of the period considered in this investigation (up to 1962), executions appear to lag convictions by 12 to 16 months on the average. An objective measure of $P^0e|c$ in year t, therefore, may be the ratio of the number of persons executed in year t+1 to the number convicted in year t or $PXQ_1=E_{t+1}/C_t$.[12] It must be pointed

[11] Another important reason for introducing chronological time as an exogenous variable in equation (8) is to account for a possible time trend in missing variables, in particular, the average length of imprisonment for both capital and noncapital murders for which no complete time-series is available. Scattered evidence shows rising trends in the median value of prison terms served by all murder convicts over a large part of the period considered in this investigation, but this increase may have been largely technical. With executions being imposed less frequently over time, the frequency of life imprisonment sentences for murder convicts may have risen accordingly, thus increasing the mean or median time spent in prisons by these convicts.

[12] Execution figures are based on *National Prisons Statistics Bulletin* (*NPS*) statistics. Conviction figures are derived by $C_t=Q_t^0P^0a_tP^0c|a_t$. Statistics on the time elapsed between sentencing and execution can be found in *NPS* numbers 20 and 45.

out, however, that the number of persons executed in year t+1, and hence PXQ_1, is, of course, unknown in year t and must be forecast by potential offenders. Even if expectations with respect to PXQ_1 were unbiased on the average, the actual magnitude of PXQ_1 is likely to deviate randomly from its expected value in year t. The effect of such random noise would be to bias the regression coefficient associated with PXQ_1 toward zero. I have therefore constructed four alternative forecasts of the desired variable: $PXQ_{1_{-1}}=E_t/C_{t-1}$; $PXQ_2=E_t/C_t$; $TXQ_1=$ the systematic part of PXQ_1 computed via a linear distributed lag regression of PXQ_1 on three of its consecutively lagged values; and $PDL_1=$ the systematic part of PXQ_1 computed via a second degree polynomial distributed lag function relating PXQ_1 and four of its consecutively lagged values. The advantage of using these alternative estimates of the expected $P^0e|c$ is that all being based on past data, they may be treated largely as predetermined rather than as endogenous variables. Alternatively, PXQ_1 is treated as an endogenous variable along with P^0a and $P^0c|a$, and its systematic part is computed via the reduced form regression equation (see Table 3).

Two difficulties associated with the use of the proposed estimates of $P^0e|c$ as measures of the true conditional probability of execution warrant special attention. First, it may be argued that the fraction of convicts executed for murder may represent only the fraction of those convicted of *capital* murders among all murder convicts. Variations in PXQ_1 or in other related estimates might then be entirely unrelated to the probability that a convict liable to be punished by the death penalty will be actually executed, and the expected elasticity of the murder rate with respect to these estimates might be nil. However, the significant downward trend in PXQ_1 between 1933 and 1967 suggests, especially during the 1960's, that it may serve as a useful indicator of the relative variations in the true $Pe|c$. Second, it should be noted that the relative variation in the reported national murder rate relates to the United States as a whole, whereas the measures of $P^0e|c$ relate to only a subset of states which retained and actually enforced capital punishment throughout the period considered. Thus, the empirical estimates of the elasticities of the national murder rate with respect to $P^0e|c$ may, on this ground, be expected to understate the true elasticities of the murder rate in retentionist states only.

The matrix of exogenous variables associated with X_1 in equation (9) includes annual census estimates of the labor force participation rate of the civilian population 16 years and over (calculated by excluding the armed forces from the total noninstitutional population) L; the unemployment rate of the civilian labor force U; Milton Friedman's estimate of real per capita permanent income (extended through 1969)[13] Y_p; the percentage of residential population in the age group 14–25, A; and chronological time T. Other exogenous variables assumed to be associated with the complete simultaneous equation model of murder and law enforcement X_2 are one-year lagged estimates of real expenditure on police per capita $XPOL_{-1}$ and annual estimates of real expenditure by local, state, and federal governments per capita $XGOV$. Real expenditures are computed by deflating *Survey of Current Business* estimates of current expenditures by the implicit price deflator for all governments. In addition, X_2 includes the size of the total residential population in the United States N, and the percent of nonwhites in

[13] I am indebted to Edi Karni for making available to me his updated calculations of the permanent income variable.

residential population NW. The reason for including NW in the list of variables subsumed under X_2 is discussed below in Section IIB. A list of all the variables used in the regression analysis is given in Table 2.

B. *The Empirical Findings*

An interesting finding which poses a challenge to the validity of the analysis in Section I is that over the period 1933–69, the simple correlation between the reported murder rate and estimates of the objective risk of execution given conviction of murder is positive in sign. For example, the simple correlation coefficients between $(Q/N)^0$ and PXQ_1, $PXQ_{1_{-1}}$, and PXQ_2 are found to be 0.140, 0.096, and 0.083, respectively. However, the results change substantively and are found to be in accordance with the theoretical predictions and statistically meaningful when the full econometric framework developed in the preceding section is implemented against the relevant data. Despite the numerous limitations inherent in the empirical counterparts of the desired theoretical constructs, the regression results reported in Tables 3 and 4 uniformly exhibit a significant negative elasticity of the murder rate with respect to each alternative measure of the probability of execution. More importantly, the regression results also corroborate the specific theoretical predictions regarding the effects of apprehension, conviction, unemployment, and labor force participation.

Table 3 shows that the estimated elasticity of the murder rate with respect to the conditional probability of execution is

TABLE 2—VARIABLES USED IN THE REGRESSION ANALYSIS, ANNUAL OBSERVATIONS 1933–69

	Variable	Mean (Natural Logarithms)	Standard Deviation (Natural Logarithms)	Arithmetic Mean
y_1	$(Q/N)^0$ = Crime rate: offenses known per 1,000 civilian population.	−2.857	0.156	0.058
Y_1	P^0a = Probability of arrest: percent of offenses cleared.	4.997	0.038	89.835
	$P^0c\|a$ = Conditional probability of conviction: percent of those charged who were convicted of murder.[a]	3.741	0.175	42.733
	$P^0e\|c$ = Conditional probability of execution; PXQ_1 = the number of executions for murder in the year t+1 as a percent of the total number of convictions in year t.[b]	0.176	1.749	2 590
X_1	L = Labor force participation: fraction of the civilian population in the labor force.	−0.546	0.030	0.579
	U = Unemployment rate: percent of the civilian labor force unemployed.	1.743	0.728	7.532
	A = Fraction of residential population in the age group 14–24.	−1.740	0.118	0.177
	Y_p = Friedman's estimate of (real) permanent income per capita in dollars.	6.868	0.338	1012.35
	T = Chronological time (years): 31–37.	2.685	0.867	19.00
X_2	NW = Fraction of nonwhites in residential population.	−2.212	0.063	0.110
	N = Civilian population in 1,000s.	11.944	0.161	155,853
	$XGOV$ = Per capita (real) expenditures (excluding national defense) of all governments in million dollars.	−7.661	0.501	.000532
	$XPOL_{-1}$ = Per capita (real) expenditures on police in dollars lagged one one year.[a]	2.114	0.306	8.638

[a] The figures for $P^0c|a$ (1933–35) and $XPOL$ (all the odd years 1933–51) were interpolated via an auxiliary regression analysis.

[b] The actual number of executions 1968, 1969, and 1970 was zero. However, the numbers were assumed equal to 1 in each of these years in constructing the value of PXQ_1 in 1967–69.

TABLE 3—MODIFIED FIRST DIFFERENCES OF MURDER RATES (IN NATURAL LOGARITHMS) REGRESSED AGAINST CORRESPONDING MODIFIED FIRST DIFFERENCES OF SELECTED VARIABLES SET I (1933–69)

($\hat{\beta}/S_{\hat{\beta}}$ in parentheses)

Effective Period / D.W. Statistic	$\hat{\rho}$(CORC) / $\hat{\sigma}_e$	C (Constant)	$\Delta^* \hat{P}^o a$	$\Delta^* \hat{P}^o c\|a$	Alternative $\Delta^* P^o e\|c$: $\Delta^* PXQ_1$	$\Delta^* PXQ_2$	$\Delta^* PXQ_{1-1}$	$\Delta^* L$	$\Delta^* A$	$\Delta^* Y_p$	$\Delta^* U$	$\Delta^* T$
1. 1935–69	0.257	−3.176	−1.553	−0.455	−0.039			−1.336	0.630	1.481	0.067	−0.047
1.84	0.052	(−0.78)	(−1.99)	(−3.58)	(−1.59)			(−1.36)	(2.10)	(4.23)	(2.00)	(−4.60)
2. 1935–69	0.135	−4.190	−1.182	−0.386		−0.068		−1.277	0.481	1.318	0.062	−0.047
1.82	0.042	(−1.25)	(−1.83)	(−3.85)		(−3.69)		(−1.59)	(2.19)	(4.86)	(2.38)	(−6.61)
3. 1935–69	0.077	−4.419	−1.203	−0.374			−0.065	−1.405	0.512	1.355	0.068	−0.047
1.81	0.045	(−1.25)	(−1.78)	(−3.59)			(−3.29)	(−1.63)	(2.26)	(4.88)	(2.55)	(−6.54)
					$\Delta^* TXQ_1$	$\Delta^* PDL_1$	$\Delta^* P\hat{X}Q_1$					
4. 1937–69	0.291	−2.447	−1.461	−0.487	−0.049			−1.393	0.524	1.295	0.063	−0.044
2.00	0.046	(−0.61)	(−2.03)	(−3.38)	(−2.26)			(−1.58)	(1.94)	(3.90)	(2.09)	(−4.93)
5. 1939–69	−0.207	6.868	−2.225	−0.850		−0.062		−0.457	0.059	0.580	0.014	−0.032
2.15	0.050	(1.39)	(−3.04)	(−4.124)		(−3.82)		(−0.50)	(0.23)	(1.70)	(0.43)	(−4.09)
6. 1935–69	0.208	−3.503	−1.512	−0.424			−0.059	−1.368	0.485	1.455	0.064	−0.050
1.86	0.051	(−0.85)	(−1.94)	(−3.38)			(−1.73)	(−1.38)	(1.42)	(4.25)	(1.93)	(−4.87)

Note: All variables except T are in natural logarithms. The definitions of these variables are given in Table 2. The term $\Delta^* X$ denotes the linear operation $X - \hat{\rho} X_{-1}$. The value of $\hat{\rho}$ is estimated via the Cochrane-Orcutt iterative procedure (*CORC*). The term $\hat{\sigma}_e$ is defined in Section IIA1. The terms $\Delta^* \hat{P}a$ and $\Delta^* \hat{P}c|a$ in equations 1–5 are computed via a reduced form regression equation including: C(constant), Q/N_{-1}, Pa_{-1}, $Pc|a_{-1}$, $P^oe|c$, L, A, Y_p, U, T, $P^oe|c_{-1}$, L_{-1}, A_{-1}, Y_{p-1}, U_{-1}, $XPOL_1$, $XGOV$, NW, N. The terms $\Delta^* \hat{P}a$, $\Delta^* \hat{P}c|a$, and $\Delta^* \hat{P}XQ_1$ in equation 6 are computed via the same reduced form with $PXQ_1(P^oe|c)$ excluded.

lowest in absolute magnitude when the objective measure of $Pe|c$, PXQ_1, is treated in the regression analysis as if it were a perfectly forecast and strictly exogenous variable. The algebraic value of the elasticity associated with PXQ_1 is −0.039 with upper and lower 95 percent confidence limits (calculated from the normal distribution) of 0.008 and −0.086. The corresponding elasticities associated with the alternative measures of $Pe|c$, PXQ_{1-1}, PXQ_2, TXQ_1, $\hat{P}XQ_1$, and PDL_1

TABLE 4—MODIFIED FIRST DIFFERENCES OF MURDER RATES (IN NATURAL LOGARITHMS) REGRESSED AGAINST CORRESPONDING MODIFIED FIRST DIFFERENCES OF SELECTED VARIABLES SET II: ALTERNATIVE TIME PERIODS AND OTHER TESTS

($\hat{\beta}/S_{\hat{\beta}}$ in parentheses)

Effective Period / D.W. Statistic	$\hat{\rho}$(CORC) / $\hat{\sigma}_e$	C (Constant)	$\Delta^* \hat{P}^o a$	$\Delta^* \hat{P}^o c\|a$	$\Delta^* P^o e\|c$: $\Delta^* PXQ_{1-1}$	$\Delta^* TXQ_1$	$\Delta^* L$	$\Delta^* A$	$\Delta^* Y_p$	$\Delta^* U$	War Years Dummy (1942–45)	$\Delta^* T$
1. 1935–69[a]	0.059	−4.060	−1.247	−0.345	−0.066		−1.314	0.450	1.318	0.068		−0.046
1.80	0.044	(−1.00)	(−1.56)	(−3.07)	(−3.33)		(−1.49)	(2.20)	(4.81)	(2.60)		(−6.54)
2. 1937–69[a]	0.287	−2.568	−1.435	−0.474		−0.049	−1.388	0.526	1.289	0.063		−0.044
1.99	0.046	(−0.61)	(−1.87)	(−3.22)		(−2.31)	(−1.57)	(1.94)	(3.91)	(2.10)		(−4.96)
3. 1936–69[b]	—	−3.608	−1.385	−0.345		−0.064	−1.218	0.482	1.348	0.068		−0.047
1.49	0.046	(−1.03)	(−2.12)	(−3.25)		(−3.52)	(−1.40)	(2.13)	(4.94)	(2.59)		(−6.69)
4. 1935–69	0.061	−4.882	−1.172	−0.383	−0.069		−1.487	0.477	1.393	0.077	0.018	−0.048
1.84	0.046	(−1.32)	(−1.73)	(−3.20)	(−3.22)		(−1.61)	(1.89)	(4.30)	(1.95)	(0.31)	(−5.76)
5. 1937–69	0.250	−2.086	−1.634	−0.508		−0.055	−1.444	0.406	1.334	0.077	0.035	−0.045
2.08	0.048	(−0.51)	(−2.16)	(−2.83)		(−2.36)	(−1.51)	(1.23)	(3.73)	(1.80)	(0.50)	(−4.72)
6. 1941–69	−0.164	3.025	−1.744	−0.714	−0.074		−1.008	0.141	0.734	0.028		−0.036
2.21	0.048	(0.57)	(−2.21)	(−3.70)	(−3.70)		(−1.04)	(0.56)	(2.06)	(0.91)		(−4.40)
7. 1941–69	−0.029	3.752	−1.947	−0.723		−0.066	−0.962	0.152	0.771	0.0311		−0.036
2.13	0.048	(0.68)	(−2.38)	(−3.69)		(−3.34)	(−0.99)	(0.55)	(2.00)	(0.96)		(−4.13)
8. 1933–66	−0.001	−5.678	−0.564	−0.265	0.055		−2.111	0.283	0.922	0.036		−0.036
1.90	0.033	(−2.21)	(−1.10)	(−3.49)	(−3.72)		(−3.18)	(1.65)	(4.16)	(1.74)		(−6.30)
9. 1939–66	0.016	−2.601	−0.946	−0.360		−0.051	−1.766	0.212	0.780	0.027		−0.033
1.96	0.037	(−0.598)	(−1.38)	(−1.984)		(−3.23)	(−2.254)	(1.03)	(2.920)	(1.11)		(−4.99)

Note: same references as in Table 3 but the reduced form used to compute $\Delta^* \hat{P}^o a$ and $\Delta^* \hat{P}^o c|a$ does not include N.

[a] Same as equations 3 and 4 in Table 3 with the missing data pertaining to $XPOL_{-1}$ interpolated via a smoothing procedure.

[b] Same as equation 4 in Table 3 with $\hat{\rho}$ assumed to be zero (level regression).

vary between −0.049 and −0.068 with upper and lower 90 percent confidence limits ranging between −0.01 and −0.10. These results have been anticipated by the analysis of Section IIA2 where it was suggested that the regression coefficient associated with PXQ_1 is likely to be biased toward zero due to the effect of random forecasting errors. In addition, since the analysis of optimal social defense against murder suggests that an exogenous change in (Q/N) may change the socially optimal value of $Pe|c$ in the same direction, the coefficient associated with PXQ_1 may be biased toward a positive value because of a potentially positive correlation between (Q/N) and the unsystematic part of PXQ_1. This simultaneous equation bias is expected to be eliminated when the systematic part of PXQ_1 is estimated via the reduced form regression equation $(\hat{P}XQ_1)$. It is noteworthy that the estimated elasticities of $(Q/N)^0$ with respect to alternative measures of $Pe|c$ are found generally low in absolute magnitude. This, perhaps, is the principal reason why previous studies into the effect of capital punishment on murder using simple correlation techniques and rough measures of the conditional risk of execution have failed to identify a systematic association between murder and the risk of execution.

The regression results regarding the effects of P^0a, $P^0c|a$, and $P^0c|c$ constitute perhaps the strongest findings of the empirical investigation. Not only do the signs of the elasticities associated with these variables conform to the general theoretical expectations, but their ranking, too, is consistent with the predictions in Section I. Table 3 shows that the elasticities associated with P^0a range between −1.0 and −1.5, whereas the elasticities associated with $P^0c|a$ in the various regression equations range between −0.4 and −0.5. And, as indicated in the preceding paragraph, the elasticities associated with $P^0e|c$ are lowest in absolute magnitude. Consistent with predictions and evidence presented in Section IB regarding a negative association between $P^0e|c$ on the one hand and P^0a and $P^0c|a$ on the other, introduction of the latter variables in the regression equation is found to be particularly useful in isolating the (negative) deterrent impact of estimates of $P^0e|c$. Of similar importance is the introduction of the time trend T.

The estimated values of the elasticities associated with the unemployment rate U, labor force participation L, and permanent income Y_p in Table 3 are not inconsistent with the theoretical expectations discussed in Section IA. Of particular interest is that the effects of equal percentage changes in $P^0e|c$ and U are found to be nearly alike in absolute magnitude. Because murder is often a by-product of crimes involving material gains, the positive effect of U on $(Q/N)^0$ may be attributed in part to the effect of the reduction in legitimate earning opportunities on the incentive to commit such crimes. Indeed, preliminary time-series regression results show that the elasticities of robbery and burglary rates with respect to the unemployment rate are even larger in magnitude than the corresponding elasticities of the murder rate. These results conform more closely to theoretical expectations than do the results in a cross-state regression analysis (see the author (1973a)). The reason, presumably, is that due to their higher correlation with cyclical variations in the demand for labor, changes in U over time measure the variations in both involuntary unemployment and the duration of such unemployment more effectively than do variations in U across states at a given point in time. The estimated negative effect of variations in the labor force participation rate on the murder rate can be explained along similar lines. Theoretically, variations in L are likely to reflect opposing income and substitution effects of changes in market earning opportunities. However, with measures of both permanent income Y_p, and the rate of unemployment introduced in the regression equation as independent explanatory variables, changes in L may reflect a pure substitution effect of changes in legitimate earning opportunities on the incentive to commit crimes both against persons and property.[14] Finally, the positive association between Y_p and $(Q/N)^0$ need not imply a positive income elasticity of demand for hate and malice since changes in the *level* of the personal distribution of income may be strongly correlated with payoffs on crimes against property. If legitimate employment opportunities are effectively accounted for by U and by L, changes in Y_p may be highly correlated with similar changes in the incidence of crimes against property. Such a partial correlation is indeed observed across states and in a time-series regression analysis of crimes against property now in progress.

The positive effect of variations in the percentage of the population in the age group 15–24, A, on the murder rate is consistent with the cross-state evidence concerning the correlation between these variables. A possible explanation for this finding was already offered in Section IIA2. Additional analysis, not reported herein, indicated that the effect of the percentage of nonwhites in the population NW becomes statistically insignificant when the time trend T is introduced as an independent explanatory variable in the regression equation. Consequently, this variable is excluded from the regressions estimating the supply of murders function. This result stands in sharp contrast to the ostensibly positive effect of NW on the murder rate across states. I have argued elsewhere in this context that the apparently higher participation rate of nonwhites in all criminal activities may result largely from the relatively poor legitimate employment opportunities available to them (see the author (1973a)). Since, over time, variations in these opportunities may be effectively accounted for by the variations in U and L, the estimated independent effect of NW may indeed be nil. The negative partial effect of T on $(Q/N)^0$ reported in Tables 3 and 4 is not inconsistent with the predictions advanced in Section IIA2.

The regression results are found to be robust with respect to the functional form of the regression equation. In addition, estimating the regression equations by introducing the levels of the relevant variables rather than their modified first differences (that is, assuming no serial correlation in the error terms) artificially reduces the standard errors of the regression coefficients as would be expected on purely statistical grounds (see Table 4, equation (3)). The results are further insensitive as to the specific estimates of expenditures on police used in the reduced form regression equation. The data for this variable are not available for all the odd years between 1933 and 1951 and the missing statistics were interpolated either via a reduced form regression analysis ($XPOL$) or a simple smoothing procedure. The results are virtually identical (compare equations (1) and (2) in Table 4 with equations (3) and (4) in Table 3). The introduction of a dummy variable

[14] A possible explanation for the significant negative association between labor force participation and particularly crimes against the person is that interpersonal frictions and social interactions leading to acts of malice occur mostly in the nonmarket or home sector rather than at work. An increase in the total time spent in the nonmarket sector (a reduction in L) might then generate a positive scale effect on the incidence of murder. This *ad hoc* hypothesis is nevertheless supported by FBI *UCR* evidence on the seasonal pattern of murder. This crime rate peaks twice a year: around the holiday season (December) and around the summer vacation season (July–August) in which relatively more time is spent out of work. It is also supported by evidence that the frequency of murders on weekends is significantly higher than on weekdays (see William Graves, p. 327).

distinguishing the World War II years (1942–45) from other years in the sample has no discernible effect on the regression results, while the effect of the dummy variable itself appears to be statistically insignificant.

Of more importance, the qualitative results reported in Table 3 are for the most part insensitive to changes in the specific interval of time investigated in the regression analysis, as indicated by the results reported in Table 4. However, the absolute magnitudes of some of the estimated elasticities, especially those associated with P^0a, $P^0c|a$, $P^0e|c$, U, and L do change when estimated from different subperiods. Finally, the time-series estimates of the supply-of-murders function appear quite consistent with independent estimates derived through a cross-state regression analysis using data from 1960. A detailed discussion of related issues is included in the author (1973b).

III. Some Implications

A. *The Apparent Effect of Capital Punishment: Deterrence or Incapacitation?*

It has already been hinted in the introduction to this paper that an apparent negative effect of execution on the murder rate may merely reflect the relative preventive or incapacitating impact of the death penalty which eliminates the possibility of recidivism on the part of those executed. An estimation of the differential preventive effect of execution relative to imprisonment for capital murder has been attempted in this study through an application of a general model of the preventive effect of imprisonment developed in the author (1973a). In this application of the model, execution is identified with an imprisonment term Te, which is equal to the life expectancy of an average offender imprisoned for murder. The differential preventive impact of execution is estimated by taking account of the alternative average sentence served by those imprisoned for capital murder Tm, the fractions of potential murders executed and imprisoned, and the rate of population growth.

Derivation of the expected partial elasticity of the murder rate with respect to the fraction of convicts executed, $\sigma_{P^0e|c}$, is omitted here for lack of space. I shall point out only that estimates of $\sigma_{P^0e|c}$ derived on the basis of the extremely unrealistic assumption that any potential murderer at large (outside prison) commits one murder each and every year and for values of Te and Tm estimated at 40, and between 10 and 16 years, respectively, vary between 0.020 and 0.037 (see the author (1973b)). These estimates, therefore, do not account for the full magnitudes of the absolute values of the elasticities of the murder rate with respect to estimates of the fraction of convicts executed that are reported in Tables 3 and 4. Moreover, according to the model of law enforcement involving only preventive effects, the partial elasticity of the murder rate with respect to the fraction of those apprehended for muder P^0a is expected to be identical to the corresponding elasticity with respect to the fraction of those apprehended and charged with murder who were convicted of this crime, $P^0c|a$. The reason, essentially, is that equal percentage changes in either P^0a or $P^0c|a$ have the same effect on the fractions of offenders who are incapacitated through incarceration or execution, and thus should have virtually equivalent preventive effects on the murder rate. This prediction is ostensibly at odds with the significant positive difference between empirical estimates of the murder rate with respect to P^0a and $P^0c|a$. In contrast, the latter findings are consistent with implications of the deterrent theory of law enforcement (see equation (3)). In light of these observations one cannot reject the hypothesis that punishment in general, and execution in particular, exert a unique deterrent effect on potential murderers.

B. *Tentative Estimates of the Tradeoff Between Executions and Murders*

The regression results concerning the partial elasticities of the reported murder rate with respect to various measures of the expected risk of execution given conviction in different subperiods $\hat{\alpha}_3$, can be restated in terms of expected tradeoffs between the execution of an offender and the lives of potential victims that might thereby be saved. For illustration, consider the regression coefficients associated with $\hat{P}XQ_1$ and $PXQ_{1_{-1}}$ in equations (6) and (3) of Table 3. These coefficients, -0.06 and -0.065, respectively, may be considered consistent estimates of the average elasticity of the national murder rate, $(Q/N)^0$, with respect to the objective conditional risk of execution, $P^0e|c=(E/C)^0$, over the period 1935–69. Evaluated at the mean values of murders and executions over that period, $\bar{Q}=8{,}965$ and $\bar{E}=75$, the marginal tradeoffs, $\Delta Q/\Delta E=\hat{\alpha}_3\bar{Q}/\bar{E}$, are found to be 7 and 8, respectively. Put differently, an additional execution per year over the period in question may have resulted, on average, in 7 or 8 fewer murders. The weakness inherent in these predicted magnitudes is that they may be subject to relatively large prediction errors. More reliable point estimates of the expected tradeoffs should be computed at the mean values of all the explanatory variables entering the regression equation (hence, also the mean value of the dependent variable) because the confidence interval of the predicted value of the dependent variable is there minimized. The mean values of the dependent variable and the explanatory variable used to calculate the value of $\hat{\alpha}_3$ in equation (3) of Table 3 are found to be nearly identical with the actual values of these two variables in 1966 and 1959, respectively. The corresponding values of murders and executions in these two years were $Q(1966)=10{,}920$ and $E(1959)=41$; the marginal tradeoffs between executions and murders based on the latter magnitudes and the elasticity $\hat{\alpha}_3=-0.065$ are found to be 1 to 17.

It should be emphasized that the expected tradeoffs computed in the preceding illustration mainly serve a methodological purpose since their validity is conditional upon that of the entire set of assumptions underlying the econometric investigation. In addition, it should be pointed out that the 90 percent confidence intervals of the elasticities used in the preceding illustrations vary approximately between 0 and -0.10 implying that the corresponding confidence intervals of the expected tradeoffs in the last illustration range between limits of 0 and 24. As the above illustrations indicate, however, although the estimated elasticities $\hat{\alpha}_3$ reported in Tables 3 and 4 are low in absolute magnitude, the tradeoffs between executions and murders implied by these elasticities are not negligible, especially when evaluated at relatively low levels of executions and relatively high levels of murder.[15]

Finally, it should be emphasized that the tradeoffs discussed in the preceding illustrations were based upon the partial

[15] A decrease in the number of executions in 1960 from 44 to 2 (the actual number of executions in 1967), which implies a decline of 95 percent in the value of $Pe|c$ in that year, would have increased the murder rate that same year by about 6.2 percent from 0.05 to 0.053 per 1,000 population if the true value of α_3 were equal to 0.065. The implied increase in the actual number of murders in 1960 would have been from 9,000 to 9,558. For comparison, note that the actual murder rate in 1967 was 0.06 per 1,000 population and the number of murders was 12,100. The values of other explanatory variables associated with the supply of murders function were, of course, quite different in these two years. By this tentative and rough calculation, the decline in $Pe|c$ alone might have accounted for about 25 percent of the increase in the murder rate between 1960 and 1967.

elasticity of $(Q/N)^0$ with respect to measures of $P^0e|c$ and thus, implicitly, on the assumption that the values of all other variables affecting the murder rate are held constant as the probability of execution varies. In practice, however, the values of the endogenous variables Pa and $Pc|a$ may not be perfectly controllable. The theoretical analysis in Section IB suggests that exogenous shifts in the optimal values of $Pe|c$ may generate offsetting changes in the optimal values of Pa and $Pc|a$. Indeed, consistent estimates of the elasticities of the reported murder rates with respect to alternative measures of $P^0e|c$ that were derived through a reduced form regression analysis using as explanatory variables only the exogenous and predetermined variables included in the supply of offenses function and other structural equations (X_1 and X_2 in Table 2) are found to be generally lower than the elasticities reported in Table 3.[16] The actual tradeoffs between executions and murders thus depend partly upon the ability of law enforcement agencies to control simultaneously the values of all the parameters characterizing law enforcement activity.

IV. Conclusions

This paper has attempted to present a systematic analysis of the relation between capital punishment and the crime of murder. The analysis rests on the presumption that offenders respond to incentives. Not all those who commit murder may respond to incentives. But for the theory to be useful in explaining aggregate behavior, it is sufficient that at least some so behave.

Previous investigations, notably those by Sellin, have developed evidence used to unequivocally deny the existence of any deterrent or preventive effects of capital punishment. This evidence stems by and large from what amounts to informal tests of the sign of the simple correlation between the legal status of the death penalty and the murder rate across states and over time in a few states. Studies performing these tests have not considered systematically the actual enforcement of the death penalty, which may be a far more important factor affecting offenders' behavior than the legal status of the penalty. Moreover, these studies have generally ignored other parameters characterizing law enforcement activity against murder, such as the probability of apprehension and the conditional probability of conviction, which appear to be systematically related to the probability of punishment by execution. In addition, the direction of the causal relationship between the rate of murder and the probabilities of apprehension, conviction, and execution is not obvious, since a high murder rate may generate an upward adjustment in the levels of these probabilities in accordance with optimal law enforcement. Thus the sign of the simple correlation between the murder rate and the legal status, or even the effective use of capital punishment, cannot provide conclusive evidence for or against the existence of a deterrent effect.

The basic strategy I have attempted to follow in formulating an adequate analytic procedure has been to develop a simple economic model of murder and defense against murder, to derive on the basis of this model a set of specific behavioral implications that could be tested against available data, and, accordingly, to test those implications statistically. The theoretical analysis provided sharp predictions concerning the signs and the relative mag-

[16] The elasticities associated with PXQ_1, $PXQ_{1_{-1}}$, TXQ_1, and PDL_1 in this modified reduced form regression analysis relating to the period 1934–69 are found equal to −0.0269 (−0.83), −0.0672 (−2.29), −0.0414 (−1.99), and −0.052 (−5.81), respectively, where the numbers in parentheses are the ratios of the coefficients to their standard errors.

nitudes of the elasticities of the murder rate with respect to the probability of apprehension and the conditional probabilities of conviction and execution for murder. It suggested also the existence of a systematic relation between employment and earning opportunities and the frequency of murder and other related crimes. Although in principle the negative effect of capital punishment on the incentive to commit murder may be partly offset, for example, by an added incentive to eliminate witnesses, the results of the empirical investigation are not inconsistent with the hypothesis that, on balance, capital punishment reduces the murder rate. But even more significant is the finding that the ranking of the elasticities of the murder rate with respect to Pa, $Pc|a$, and $Pe|c$ conforms to the specific theoretical predictions. The murder rate is also found negatively related to the labor force participation rate and positively to the rate of unemployment. None of these results is compatible with a hypothesis that offenders do not respond to incentives. In particular, the results concerning the effects of the estimates of the probabilities of apprehension, conviction, and execution are not consistent with the hypothesis that execution or imprisonment decrease the rate of murder only by incapacitating or preventing apprehended offenders from committing further crimes.

These observations do not imply that the empirical investigation has proved the existence of the deterrent or preventive effect of capital punishment. The results may be biased by the absence of data on the severity of alternative punishments for murder, by the use of national rather than state statistics, and by other imperfections. At the same time it is not obvious whether the net effect of all these shortcomings necessarily exaggerates the regression results in favor of the theorized results. In view of the new evidence presented here, one cannot reject the hypothesis that law enforcement activities in general and executions in particular do exert a deterrent effect on acts of murder. Strong inferences to the contrary drawn from earlier investigations appear to have been premature.

Even if one accepts the results concerning the partial effect of the conditional probability of execution on the murder rate as valid, these results do not imply that capital punishment is necessarily a desirable form of punishment. Specifically, whether the current level of application of capital punishment is optimal cannot be determined independently of the question of whether the levels of alternative punishments for murder are optimal. For example, one could argue on the basis of the model developed in Section IA that if the severity of punishments by means other than execution had been greater in recent years, the apparent elasticity of the murder rate with respect to the conditional probability of punishment by execution would have been lower, thereby making capital punishment ostensibly less efficient in deterring or preventing murders. Again, this observation need not imply that the effective period of incarceration imposed on convicted capital offenders should be raised. Given the validity of the analysis pursued above, incarceration or execution are not exhaustive alternatives for effectively defending against murders.[17] Indeed, these conventional punishments may be considered imperfect means of deter-

[17] Ironically, the argument that capital punishment should be abolished because it has no deterrent effect on offenders might serve to justify the use of capital punishment as an ultimate means of prevention of crime, since the risk of recidivism that cannot be deterred by the threat of punishment is not eliminated entirely even inside prison walls. In contrast, since the results of this investigation support the notion that execution exerts a pure deterrent effect on offenders, they can be used to suggest that other punishments, even those which do not have any preventive effect, can in principle serve as substitutes.

rence relative to monetary fines and other related compensations because the high "price" they exact from convicted offenders is not transferrable to the rest of society. Moreover, the results of the empirical investigation indicate that the rate of murder and other related crimes may also be reduced through increased employment and earning opportunities. The range of effective methods for defense against murder thus extends beyond conventional means of law enforcement and crime prevention. There is no unambiguous method for determining whether capital punishment should be utilized as a legal means of punishment without considering at the same time the optimal values of all other choice variables that can affect the level of capital crimes.

REFERENCES

C. B. Beccaria, *An Essay on Crimes and Punishments*, London 1767, originally published in 1764.

H. A. Bedau, *The Death Penalty in America*, Garden City 1967.

G. S. Becker, "Crime and Punishment: An Economic Approach," *J. Polit. Econ.*, Mar./Apr. 1968, *78*, 169–217.

———, "A Theory of Social Interactions," *J. Polit. Econ.*, Nov./Dec. 1974, *82*, 1063–93.

I. Ehrlich, "Participation in Illegitimate Activities: An Economic Analysis," unpublished doctoral dissertation, Columbia Univ. 1970.

———, (1973a) "Participation in Illegitimate Activities: A Theoretical and Empirical Investigation," *J. Polit. Econ.*, May/June, 1973, *81*, 521–65.

———, (1973b) "The Deterrent Effect of Capital Punishment: A Question of Life and Death," Nat. Bur. Econ. Res. working pap. series no. 18, 1973.

R. C. Fair, "The Estimation of Simultaneous Equation Models with Lagged Endogenous Variables and First Order Serially Correlated Errors," *Econometrica*, May 1970, *38*, 507–16.

W. F. Graves, "The Deterrent Effect of Capital Punishment in California," in H. A. Bedau, ed., *The Death Penalty in America*, Garden City 1967.

H. M. Hochman and J. D. Rodgers, "Pareto Optimal Redistribution," *Amer. Econ. Rev.*, Sept. 1969, *59*, 542–57.

T. Sellin, *The Death Penalty*, Philadelphia 1959.

———, *Capital Punishment*, New York 1967.

President's Commission on Law Enforcement and Administration of Justice *(PCL)*, *Crime and Its Impact—An Assessment*, Task Force Reports, Washington 1967.

U.S. Department of Justice, Bureau of Prisons, *National Prisons Statistics Bulletin (NPS)*, various numbers; published prior to 1950 by Bureau of Census, Washington.

———, Federal Bureau of Investigation, *Uniform Crime Report (UCR)*, Washington, various years.

U.S. Office of Business Economics, *The National Income and Product Accounts of the United States, 1929–65, Statistical Tables, Surv. Curr. Bus.*, supp., Washington 1966.

———, *Business Statistics, Surv. Curr. Bus.*, Washington, various years.

Bankruptcy

[5]

A NEW APPROACH TO CORPORATE REORGANIZATIONS

*Lucian Arye Bebchuk**

In this Article, Professor Bebchuk proposes a new method of dividing the reorganization pie among the participants in corporate reorganizations. This method, he argues, can address the substantial efficiency and fairness problems that afflict the existing process of division. Under the proposed method, participants will receive certain rights with respect to the reorganized company's securities; these rights will be designed so that, whatever the reorganization value is, no participant will have a basis for complaining that he is receiving less than the value to which he is entitled. Although Professor Bebchuk proposes the method as a basis for law reform, he shows that it also can be used under the existing reorganization rules.

I. Introduction

THE concern of this Article is the way in which corporate reorganizations divide the reorganization pie. The Article puts forward a new method for making the necessary division. This method can address some major efficiency and fairness problems long thought to be inherent in corporate reorganizations. Although the method is proposed as a basis for law reform, it can also be used under the existing rules.

Reorganization is one of the two routes that a corporation in bankruptcy may take. When a corporation becomes insolvent and bankruptcy proceedings are commenced, the corporation is either liquidated or reorganized. In liquidation, which is governed by chapter 7 of the Bankruptcy Code,[1] the assets of the corporation are sold, either piecemeal or as a going concern. The proceeds from this sale are then divided among those who have rights against the corporation, with the division made according to the ranking of these rights.

---

* Assistant Professor of Law, Harvard Law School, and Faculty Research Fellow, National Bureau of Economic Research. I gratefully acknowledge the valuable comments of Bob Clark, Scott Edelman, Dan Fischel, Ron Gilson, Henry Hansmann, Tom Jackson, Louis Kaplow, William Klein, Louis Kornhauser, Reinier Kraakman, Saul Levmore, Roberto Romano, Hal Scott, and Steve Shavell. I also benefited from the helpful comments of participants in a conference at Harvard Law School and a workshop at the University of Pennsylvania Law School. Finally, I would like to thank the National Science Foundation (grant SES-8708212) and the Harvard Law School Program in Law and Economics for their financial support.

A mathematical derivation of all the elements of this Article's analysis is included in the discussion paper version of the Article, which was issued as Discussion Paper #37, January 1988, Program in Law and Economics, Harvard Law School.

[1] 11 U.S.C. §§ 701–786 (1982 & Supp. IV 1986).

Reorganization, which is governed by chapter 11 of the Bankruptcy Code,[2] is an alternative to liquidation. Reorganization is essentially a sale of a company to the existing "participants" — all those who hold claims against or interests in the company. This "sale" is of course a hypothetical one. The participants pay for the company with their existing claims and interests; in exchange, they receive "tickets" in the reorganized company — that is, claims against or interests in this new entity.

Why is the reorganization alternative necessary? The rationale commonly offered is that a reorganization may enable the participants to capture a greater value than they can obtain in a liquidation.[3] In particular, reorganization is thought to be especially valuable when (i) the company's assets are worth much more as a going concern than if sold piecemeal, and (ii) there are few or even no outside buyers with both accurate information about the company and sufficient resources to acquire it. In such situations, liquidation might well leave the participants with less than the going-concern value of the company's assets; consequently, the participants will have more value to split if they retain the enterprise and divide it among themselves.

The development of U.S. Bankruptcy law in this century suggests that public officials have long believed that reorganization is indeed desirable in an important set of cases. In 1938, Congress adopted chapter X of the Chandler Act[4] to provide a detailed set of rules to govern reorganizations. Chapter 11 of the Bankruptcy Code replaced these rules in 1978.[5] Throughout this period, many corporations in financial distress, including major Fortune 500 corporations, have taken the reorganization route.[6]

This Article takes as given the existence (and significant use) of the reorganization alternative to liquidation. Professors Baird and Jackson have recently challenged the conventional wisdom that it is desirable to have the corporate reorganization alternative; in their view, it might well be desirable to eliminate the reorganization alternative and resort to liquidation in the case of each insolvent corporation.[7] This Article does not enter that debate. Although the Article

---

2 *Id.* §§ 1101–1174.

3 *See, e.g.*, Clark, *The Interdisciplinary Study of Legal Evolution*, 90 YALE L.J. 1238, 1252–54 (1981).

4 Pub. L. No. 75-696, 52 Stat. 840 (1938) (repealed 1978). Earlier, Congress had amended the Bankruptcy Act of 1898, 30 Stat. 544, by adopting section 77, 47 Stat. 1467, 1474–82 (1933), to govern railroad reorganizations, and section 77B, 48 Stat. 912, 912–22 (1934), to govern other reorganizations.

5 *See* The Bankruptcy Reform Act of 1978, 11 U.S.C. §§ 1101–1174 (1982 & Supp. IV 1986).

6 *See, e.g.*, *LTV Corp. Files for Bankruptcy: Debt is $4 Billion*, N.Y. Times, July 18, 1986, at A1, col. 1. At the time of filing, LTV was ranked as the 43rd largest industrial company in the U.S. *See id.* at D4, col. 1.

7 *See* T. JACKSON, THE LOGIC AND LIMITS OF BANKRUPTCY ch. 9 (1986); Baird, *The Uneasy Case for Corporate Reorganizations*, 15 J. LEGAL STUD. 127 (1986).

seeks to improve the reorganization process, it does not advance, or indeed take any position on, the proposition that having reorganizations is desirable. Rather, it advances only the proposition that as long as reorganizations remain, the best method for dividing the reorganization pie is the one put forward below.

Part II of this Article briefly describes the problems that have long afflicted the division process in corporate reorganizations. Because no objective figure is generally available for the value of the reorganized enterprise, the law has consigned the division of the reorganization pie to a process of bargaining and litigation among the various classes of participants. This process of bargaining and litigation frequently results in substantial deviations from participants' entitlements, commonly involves significant delays and litigation costs, and often produces an inefficient capital structure for the reorganized company.

Part III describes the proposed method of dividing the reorganization pie. The new method involves no bargaining or litigation, nor does it require that the value of the reorganized company be identified. Under the method, the participants in a reorganization would receive a set of rights with respect to the securities of the reorganized company. These rights are designed so that, whatever the reorganization value, the participants will never end up with less than the value to which they are entitled.

Part IV demonstrates the perfect consistency of the method's outcome with the entitlements of all participants. In particular, I show that the method will be effective even if the market is inaccurate in pricing the value of the rights distributed to the participants. Whether or not the market's pricing is accurate, no participant will have a justifiable basis for complaining about the method's outcome.

Part V discusses the implementation of the proposed method. Reorganization law, I suggest, should be reformed to facilitate and require use of the method in every corporate reorganization. Under such a regime, the division process will be effected swiftly, fairly, and efficiently. Moreover, the proposed method can be used even under the existing rules. Some participants will likely find it in their interest to use the method as a basis for reorganization plans filed for confirmation under the existing rules.

In describing the operation and effectiveness of the proposed method, Parts III and IV use a simple example for convenience of exposition. Part VI shows how the proposed method can be adapted to deal with complex real-world features that are not present in that example.

II. The Division Problem in Corporate Reorganization

The division problem in corporate reorganization, on which this Article focuses, may be stated briefly as follows. Given the set of all claims by participants, each claim defined by its size and relative priority, how should the reorganization pie (that is, the value of the reorganized company) be divided among the participants?

It is true that this issue of division, although central, is not the only element in corporate reorganizations. A reorganization inevitably must also include the preliminary process of determining the size and relative priority of the participants' claims. For example, it might be necessary to determine the amount the company owes to the holders of a certain bond issue or to certain business partners, as well as the relative priorities of these debts. Although this preliminary, inevitable process of determining the size and ranking of claims often involves significant delay and litigation costs, I will not discuss it. Rather, I will focus on the division problem, and to this end I will largely assume that the size and ranking of the participants' claims are already known.

As explained below, the existing reorganization process resolves the problem of division in a way that suffers from substantial imperfections. These imperfections are all rooted in a problem of valuation. It is generally impossible to place an objective and indisputable figure on the value that the reorganized company will have (the "reorganization value").[8] If such a figure were available, the distribution of tickets in the reorganized company would be easy to determine. Without such a figure, however, it is difficult to decide where, down the rank of creditors and preferred shareholders, it is necessary to stop issuing tickets in the newly reorganized entity.

This problem of valuation obviously does not exist in a liquidation, when actual sale to an outsider takes place. The liquidation results in an exchange of the company's assets for cash (or cash equivalents, such as marketable securities). Whether or not this cash represents the true value of the assets sold, there is no question as to the monetary value of the total pie available for distribution. The receiver running the liquidation thus can start by paying creditors that are most senior, until either no money is left or their claims are paid in full; the receiver then will pay money to creditors in the next tier, again until no money is left or their claims are paid in full; and the receiver will continue in this fashion until all the money runs out.

In contrast to liquidation, the sale of the company's assets in a reorganization is fictional. Consequently, no objective figure is available for the total monetary value to be distributed or, as a result, for the monetary value of the various tickets in the reorganized company. Although agreement over this reorganization value would be hard to achieve even among impartial observers, the clear conflict of interest

[8] *See, e.g.* Roe, *Bankruptcy and Debt: A New Model for Corporate Reorganization*, 83 COLUM. L. REV. 527, 547–48 (1983).

among the participants makes it all the more difficult. Senior creditors have an incentive to advance a low valuation, because a low valuation would entitle them to a larger fraction of the tickets in the reorganized company.[9] For a similar reason, equityholders have an incentive to advance a high valuation.[10] It is of course possible to ask courts to estimate the reorganization value, and courts indeed sometimes must make such estimates. But no one suggests that we can rely on such judicial estimates to be generally accurate.[11]

The law has always dealt with this valuation problem by leaving the division of tickets in the reorganized company to a process of bargaining among the participants.[12] The law has sought only to provide a set-up for this bargaining and to establish constraints within which the division must take place. Under existing rules, a plan of reorganization generally will obtain judicial confirmation if all the classes of participants approve it.[13] The legal rules governing this approval process prescribe how participants may be grouped into classes, how their votes are to be solicited, and what majority counts as class approval.[14] The rules constrain the bargaining process by prescribing the limits within which the classes may bargain. In particular, the rules limit the concessions that a class may elect to make: the class may vote to make concessions but it may not, without unanimous agreement among the members of the class, concede to receive less than the class would get in a liquidation.[15] Similarly, the rules also limit the amount that a class can hope to extract in conces-

---

[9] Suppose, for example, that the senior creditors are owed $100 and that the reorganized company will have 100 common shares. Then, if the value of the reorganized company is determined to be $100, the senior creditors will be entitled to all of the reorganized company's shares. But if the value is determined to be $1000, then the senior creditors will be entitled to only 10% of the company's shares.

[10] For example, imagine that the company owes $100 to all of the creditors and that the reorganized company will have 100 common shares. Then, if the value of the reorganized company is determined to be $100, the equityholders will be entitled to nothing. But if the value is determined to be $1000, the equityholders will be entitled to 90% of the company's shares.

[11] The difficulties involved in judicial estimates of a reorganized company's value are apparent to any reader of cases in which judges have to make such estimates. *See, e.g., In re* King Resources Co., 651 F.2d 1326, 1335–38 (10th Cir. 1980); *In re* Evans Products Co., 65 Bankr. 870, 875–76 (S.D. Fla. 1986).

[12] For a description of the evolution of reorganization law in the last fifty years, see Coogan, *Confirmation of a Plan under the Bankruptcy Code*, 32 CASE W. RES. L. REV. 301, 303–05, 309–26 (1982).

[13] *See* 11 U.S.C. § 1129(a) (1982 & Supp. IV 1986). For a discussion of the conditions for confirming a reorganization plan, see Trost, *Business Reorganizations Under Chapter 11 of the New Bankruptcy Code*, 34 BUS. LAW. 1309, 1328–37 (1979).

[14] *See* 11 U.S.C. §§ 1122, 1125, 1126 (1982 & Supp. IV 1986); Coogan, *supra* note 12, at 328–36.

[15] This limitation arises from the "best interest of the creditors" test established by 11 U.S.C. § 1129(a)(7) (1982). *See* Coogan, *supra* note 12, at 344–45.

sions from other classes: a plan will be confirmed in spite of the objection of a class if it can be shown that the value the class is receiving meets a certain standard.[16]

This process of bargaining and litigation is quite imperfect. First, and most importantly, the reorganization process often produces a division that substantially deviates from the participants' entitlements. Sometimes the deviation is unintentional, the result of inaccurate evaluation. Sometimes the deviation is deliberate: participants might use their power to delay in order to extract a reorganization plan that gives them more than the value to which they are entitled. For example, equityholders, it is generally believed, often use their delaying power to extract a substantial value even in instances in which the creditors are entitled to all of the reorganization value.[17]

Second, the reorganization process often results in the choice of an inefficient capital structure for the reorganized company. The company's capital structure should be chosen solely to maximize the reorganized company's value. But under the existing system, the choice of the capital structure is often substantially affected by various strategic factors.[18]

Third, putting aside the severe shortcomings of the outcome of the division process, the process itself has substantial costs. The process usually involves significant litigation costs and frequently produces delay (beyond the time necessary to determine the size and ranking of the participants' claims). This delay might result from a genuine failure of the participants to reach an agreement, but it also might be caused deliberately by some participants whose interest would be served by a postponement.[19] The resulting delay commonly involves significant costs, some obvious and some subtle. For one thing, the company usually cannot function efficiently during the reorganization period.[20]

---

[16] A court will approve a plan over the objection of a class if the value given to the class satisfies the "absolute priority" standard. This possibility is established by the "cramdown" provision of 11 U.S.C. § 1129(b) (1982). *See* Coogan, *supra* note 12, at 352–57.

[17] *See, e.g.*, Trost, *Corporate Bankruptcy Reorganization: For the Benefit of Creditors or Stockholders?*, 21 UCLA L. REV. 540, 550 (1973).

[18] For a discussion of the ways in which strategic factors shape the choice of the capital structure, see Roe, cited in note 8 above, at 536–46.

[19] In particular, a delay often might be in the interest of equityholders. When the value of the reorganized company is lower than the total value of creditors' claims, the equityholders might have nothing to lose and something to gain from a delay.

[20] Potential business partners, for example, might be reluctant to do business with the company or might be willing to conduct business only on special terms. Furthermore, management decisions during the reorganization period are afflicted with serious conflict-of-interest problems. The company is usually run by the pre-reorganization management, which represents the equityholders. The interests of the equityholders in an insolvent corporation are likely to be served by courses of action that may not be value maximizing. For example, it likely will be in the interest of the equityholders for the company to take risks, even if taking such risks

Observers of the corporate reorganization process have long been painfully aware of its substantial imperfections.[21] In 1978, Congress tried to alleviate some of the widely perceived problems by making significant changes in reorganization law. The 1978 changes, for example, sought to provide more room for bargaining by giving classes the power to make greater concessions to each other.[22] It is unclear, however, whether the changes have made matters better or worse. Whether or not the new rules are an improvement, there seems to be a consensus on one thing — that although the division process can perhaps be improved, it is bound to remain significantly imperfect, because of the impossibility of accurate judicial valuation and the inevitable shortcomings of bargaining and litigation.[23]

Indeed, this perception concerning the inherent imperfection of the division process in reorganizations has been the main basis for the view, recently expressed by Professors Baird and Jackson, that it might be desirable to eliminate the reorganization alternative altogether and resort only to liquidation.[24] As explained below, however, this perception is wrong: the reorganization process can be greatly improved.

III. The Proposed Method

A. The Example

To describe and assess the proposed method, it will be useful to consider it in the context of a concrete and simple example. Consider a publicly traded company that has three classes of participants. Class *A* includes 100 senior creditors, each owed $1. Class *B* includes 100

---

would not be value maximizing. Taking a risky course of action will likely benefit the equityholders of an insolvent corporation, because they might well have little to lose from a downward turn in the company's fortunes and more to gain from an upward turn.

[21] *See, e.g.*, D. BAIRD & T. JACKSON, CASES, PROBLEMS, AND MATERIALS ON BANKRUPTCY Ch. 9 (1985); Blum, *The Law and Language of Corporate Reorganization*, 17 U. CHI. L. REV. 565, 571–72 (1950); Brudney, *The Investment-Value Doctrine and Corporate Readjustments*, 72 HARV. L. REV. 645 (1959); Roe, *supra* note 8, at 536–49.

[22] For a discussion and assessment of the 1978 changes, see Coogan, cited in note 12 above, and Trost, cited in note 13 above.

[23] Indeed, the perception that the division process is inherently imperfect is held even by Professor Roe, who has put forward an important proposal for reforming the process. *See* Roe, *supra* note 8. Although Roe's proposal would in my view be a substantial improvement over the existing process, it would not perform as well as the method proposed in this Article. *See infra* p. 790.

[24] *See* T. JACKSON, *supra* note 7, ch. 9; Baird, *supra* note 7, at 127–48.

junior creditors, each owed $1. Class C includes 100 equityholders, each holding one unit of equity.[25]

The company is now in bankruptcy proceedings and is to be reorganized. The Reorganized Company, which I will call RC, is going to have a capital structure that for now I will assume to be given. For any chosen capital structure, it is of course possible to divide the securities of RC into 100 equal units. For example, if RC will have 100 shares of common stock and 50 shares of preferred stock, then each of the 100 RC units will consist of 1 common share and 1/2 preferred share. The question for the reorganization process is how to divide the 100 units of RC among the three classes of participants.

B. *Dividing the Pie Supposing its Size is Known*

Let us denote the value of the reorganized company RC as V per unit. Thus, $100V$ is the total size of the pie to be distributed. As already noted, the division of the pie would be a straightforward matter if we could measure its size exactly (that is, if we could estimate V with precision). In such a case, we would simply proceed according to the ranking of the various classes involved.

Consider first the case in which the figure placed on V is no higher than $1. In this case, the total pie is no greater than $100, which is the full value of class A's claims. Therefore, all the 100 units of RC should be given to the senior creditors (and divided among them pro rata).

Consider next the case in which the figure placed on V is greater than $1 but no greater than $2. In this case, the total pie is no greater than $200, which is the full value of the claims of the senior and junior creditors, and it thus should be divided only among the creditors. Because there is enough to pay the senior creditors in full, they should receive a value of $100, which can be accomplished by giving them $100/V$ units. Dividing these units among senior creditors pro rata, each senior creditor would receive $1/V$ units worth $1. The junior creditors should receive the remaining value of $100V - \$100$, which can be accomplished by giving them the remaining $100 - (100/V)$ units. Dividing these units among the junior creditors, each would end up with $1 - (1/V)$ units.[26]

---

[25] As will be apparent, the method would also apply well to companies whose stock is not publicly traded, because the method's effectiveness does not hinge on the presence of market trading. Similarly, the other simplifying features of the example are not essential for the method's effectiveness. In particular, Part VI will show how the method might be adapted to situations in which the company has more than three classes of participants, secured creditors, and/or a class whose claims are concentrated in one hand.

[26] For example, if V is $1.25, then class A should receive 80 shares (100/1.25), with each senior creditor receiving 0.8 shares; and class B should receive 20 shares (100 − 100/1.25), with each junior creditor receiving 0.2 shares.

Finally, consider the case in which the figure placed on V is higher than \$2. In this case, there is more than enough to pay both class A and class B in full. To be paid in full, the senior creditors as a class should receive $100/V$ units, with each senior creditor getting $1/V$ units. The junior creditors, also paid in full, should also receive $100/V$ units total, or $1/V$ units each. And the equityholders should receive the remaining value of $100V - \$200$. This would be accomplished by giving them — and dividing among them pro rata — the remaining $100 - (200/V)$ units (that is, $1 - (2/V)$ units for each equityholder).[27]

The conclusions of the above analysis — showing how the reorganization pie should be divided if we could measure V precisely — are summarized in Table 1 below.[28]

TABLE 1

DISTRIBUTION OF UNITS SUPPOSING V IS KNOWN

Value of V	Distribution of Units	
$V \leq 1$	Senior Creditors:	1 unit each (worth V)
	Junior Creditors:	nothing
	Equityholders:	nothing
$1 < V \leq 2$	Senior Creditors:	$1/V$ unit each (worth \$1)
	Junior Creditors:	$1 - (1/V)$ unit each (worth $V - \$1$)
	Equityholders:	nothing
$V > 2$	Senior Creditors:	$1/V$ unit each (worth \$1)
	Junior Creditors:	$1/V$ unit each (worth \$1)
	Equityholders:	$1 - (2/V)$ unit each (worth $V - \$2$)

[27] For example, if V is \$2.50, then the senior creditors should get 40 shares (0.40 shares each), the junior creditors should get 40 shares (0.40 shares each), and the equityholders should get 20 shares (0.20 shares each).

[28] Another way of expressing participants' entitlements as a function of V is by using the mathematical notation min(., .) and max(., .). (This notation has the following meaning: $\min(x, y)$ denotes the smaller of the values x and y; similarly, $\max(x, y)$ denotes the greater of the values x and y.)

As we have seen, a senior creditor is entitled to receive the smaller of (i) \$1, the full value of his claim, and (ii) V, his pro rata share of the reorganization value. Thus, a senior creditor is entitled to $\min(\$1, V)$.

A junior creditor is entitled to receive no less than the smaller of (i) \$1, the full value of his claim, and (ii) his pro rata share of the value left, if any, after the senior creditors are paid in full, which is $\max(0, V - \$1)$. Thus, the junior creditor is entitled to $\min(\$1, \max(0, V - \$1)$.

Finally, an equityholder is entitled to no less than his pro rata share of the value left, if

C. Participants' Entitlements as a Function of Reorganization Value

The question of division thus would pose no problem if we could measure V with precision. As already emphasized, however, the value of V — and thus also the monetary value to which each participant is entitled — cannot be determined with indisputable accuracy. But even though we cannot identify precisely the value to which each participant is entitled, we can precisely express this value as a function of V, the reorganized company's per unit value.

Consider first the senior creditors. As the analysis above has shown, a senior creditor is entitled to a value of V if $V \leq \$1$ and a value of \$1 if $V > \$1$. Alternatively put, a senior creditor is entitled to a value of \$1 unless the reorganization value is less than \$100, in which case the senior creditor is entitled to his pro rata share of the reorganization value (that is, to one unit of *RC*).

Consider next the junior creditors. A junior creditor, we have seen, is entitled to nothing if $V \leq \$1$, is entitled to $V - \$1$ if $\$1 < V \leq \$2$, and is entitled to \$1 if $V > \$2$. Alternatively put, a junior creditor is entitled to a value of \$1 unless the reorganization value is less than \$200, in which case he is entitled to his pro rata share of the value that is left, if any, after the senior creditors are paid in full.

Finally, an equityholder is entitled to nothing if $V \leq \$2$, and to $V - \$2$ if $V > \$2$. Alternatively put, an equityholder is entitled to his pro rata share of the value that is left, if any, after the senior and junior creditors are paid in full.

Table 2 below summarizes these conclusions concerning participants' entitlements as a function of the reorganization value.

TABLE 2

PARTICIPANTS' ENTITLEMENTS AS A FUNCTION OF V

	$V \leq \$1$	$\$1 < V \leq \$2$	$V > \$2$
Senior Creditor	V	\$1	\$1
Junior Creditor	0	$V - \$1$	\$1
Equityholder	0	0	$V - \$2$
TOTAL	V	V	V

any, after the senior and junior creditors are paid in full. Thus, the equityholder is entitled to max(0, $V - \$2$).

To summarize, the participants' entitlements are as follows:

Senior Creditors: min(\$1, V)
Junior Creditors: min(\$1, max(0, $V - \$1$))
Equityholders: max(0, $V - \$2$).

D. The Proposed Approach

The idea underlying the proposed method is simple. Even though we do not know *V* and consequently do not know the value of participants' entitlements in terms of dollars or *RC* units, we do know precisely what participants are entitled to as a function of *V* (that is, for any value that *V* might take). With this knowledge, it is possible to design and to distribute to the participants a set of rights concerning *RC*'s units such that, for any value that *V* might take, these rights would provide participants with values perfectly consistent with their entitlements.

Before describing the proposed approach, a preliminary remark on implementation is in order. As will be seen presently, each of the rights distributed to participants will have an "option" component.[29] In principle, the options should be for immediate exercise. However, because the participants might need a little bit of time to understand the terms of the options given to them, it might well be desirable to provide them with such time. The exercise date of the options, then, will be shortly after the distribution of the rights. For concreteness, I will assume below that the reorganized company will start its life and distribute the rights to participants on January 1; and that the exercise date for all the rights distributed will be four days later, on January 5.

Thus, on January 1, the reorganized company will start its life. But, under the proposed method, the units of *RC* will not be distributed at this point but rather will be retained by the company until January 5. Instead of receiving *RC* units, on January 1 the participants will get the following rights with respect to *RC* units.

1. Senior Creditors. — Each senior creditor will receive one type-*A* right. A type-*A* right may be redeemed by the company on January 5 for $1. If the right is not redeemed, its holder on January 5 will be entitled to receive one unit of *RC*.[30]

To get some sense at this stage of the value to senior creditors of receiving type-*A* rights, consider a creditor that holds his type-*A* right until January 5. If the right is redeemed, then the creditor will be paid in full. If the right is not redeemed, then the creditor will receive a value of *V*. And indeed, the senior creditor is never entitled to receive more than either $1 or *V* (see Table 2).

---

[29] As economists have recognized, it is often useful to break a security into its option components. Many securities can be described usefully as a set of certain options with respect to the assets of the issuing firm. *See, e.g.*, R. BREALEY & S. MYERS, PRINCIPLES OF CORPORATE FINANCE chs. 20, 23 (2d ed. 1984).

[30] In the terminology of options, a type-*A* right is equivalent to the following position: having one (call) option on one *RC* unit with an exercise price of $0, plus being short one (call) option on one *RC* unit with an exercise price of $1.

2. *Junior Creditors.* — Each junior creditor will receive a type-*B* right. The company may redeem a type-*B* right on January 5 for $1. If the right is not redeemed, its holder will have the option on January 5 to purchase one unit of *RC* for $1. To exercise this option, the holder of the right must submit it to the company by January 5 accompanied by a payment of the $1 exercise price.[31]

Again, it might be worthwhile to describe briefly how receiving a type-*B* right will provide a junior creditor with the value to which he is entitled. If the creditor holds on to the type-*B* right and the right is redeemed, then the creditor will be paid in full. If the right is not redeemed, exercising it will provide the creditor with a value of $V - \$1$. And indeed, the creditor is never entitled to receive a value higher than both $1 and $V - \$1$ (see Table 2).

3. *Equityholders.* — Each equityholder will receive one type-*C* right. A type-*C* right may not be redeemed by the company. The holder of a type-*C* right will have the option to purchase one *RC* unit on January 5 for $2. To exercise this option, the holder must submit the right to the company by January 5 accompanied by a payment of the $2 exercise price.[32]

Note that if an equityholder holds on to his right until January 5 and then chooses to exercise it, he will get a value $V - \$2$. And indeed, the equityholder is never entitled to a positive value exceeding $V - \$2$ (see Table 2).

These three types of rights will all be transferable. Thus, between January 1 and January 5, there will presumably be public trading in the rights. A participant that is given any one of the rights may thus either sell it on the market or retain it until the exercise date of January 5.

Table 3 below summarizes the terms of the rights to be distributed to participants.

E. The Exercise of Rights

Adding up the obligations that *RC* will have toward the holders of type-*A*, type-*B*, and type-*C* rights shows that the net obligation of *RC* is to distribute 100 *RC* units on January 5, which is exactly what is available for distribution. Thus, *RC* should have no problem meeting all its obligations toward the holders of the three types of rights. Nonetheless, it is worth going through the mechanics of the process in detail.

---

[31] In the terminology of options, one type-*B* right is equivalent to the following position: having one (call) option on one *RC* unit with an exercise price of $1, plus being short one (call) option on one *RC* unit with an exercise price of $2. If the option on which the holder is short is not exercised, he will simply end up with an option to purchase one *RC* unit for $1. If the option on which the holder is short is exercised, he will end up with $1 (purchasing one *RC* unit for $1 and selling it for $2).

[32] In the terminology of options, one type-*C* right is equivalent to one (call) option on one *RC* unit with an exercise price of $2.

TABLE 3

THE DISTRIBUTION OF RIGHTS

Senior Creditors

Each senior creditor receives one type-*A* right. A type-*A* right may be redeemed by the company on January 5 for $1. If the right is not redeemed, on January 5 its holder will be entitled to receive one unit of *RC*.

Junior Creditors

Each junior creditor receives one type-*B* right. A type-*B* right may be redeemed by the company on January 5 for $1. If the right is not redeemed, on January 5 its holder will have the option to purchase one unit of *RC* for $1.

Equityholders

Each equityholder receives one type-*C* right. A type-*C* right may not be redeemed by the company. The holder of such a right on January 5 will have the option to purchase one unit of *RC* for $2.

Suppose first that all of the holders of type-*C* rights wish to exercise their options to buy *RC* units and that they submit a total of $200 to the company. *RC* then will provide them with all 100 units of *RC* (one unit for each right submitted), and it will use the $200 received from them to redeem all of the type-*A* and type-*B* rights.

Suppose now that no type-*C* rights are submitted for exercise, but that all holders of type-*B* rights wish to exercise their options to buy *RC* units at $1 and therefore submit a total of $100 to the company. In this case, *RC* will give all of the *RC* units to the holders of these type-*B* rights, and it will use the $100 received from them to redeem all of the type-*A* rights.

Next, suppose that no type-*B* or type-*C* rights are submitted for exercise. The mechanics of this case will be simpler still: the 100 units of *RC* will be distributed to the holders of type-*A* rights (one *RC* unit per right).

Finally, it remains to consider situations in which only a fraction of the type-*B* or type-*C* rights are submitted for exercise. Such situations are unlikely to arise if there is public trading in the rights.[33]

[33] To see why such situtations are unlikely, imagine for example that as January 5 arrives, some holders of type-*B* rights (the "optimists") submit the rights for exercise while other holders of type-*B* rights (the "pessimists") do not submit their rights. The optimists' behavior indicates that they believe that *V* exceeds $1. The pessimists, as long as they do not intend to use their rights in any way, should be happy to sell them for any negligible positive price. Thus, as long

But in any event, given the design of the rights — in particular, the fact that the total net obligation of the company toward all right holders is to distribute 100 units of *RC* — such situations will present no special problem for the execution process.

For example, suppose that only 50 type-*B* rights (and presumably no type-*C* rights)[34] are submitted for exercise. Then, those who submitted type-*B* rights will receive 50 units of *RC* (one unit per submitted right). The $50 submitted by them will be used for pro rata redemption of type-*A* rights. Consequently, each holder of a type-*A* right will end up with $0.50 and 0.50 units of *RC*.

More generally, *RC* will proceed in situations of partial submission of rights as follows. The money received from the exercise of type-*C* rights will be used half for pro rata redemption of type-*A* rights and half for pro rata redemption of type-*B* rights. The money received from the exercise of (unredeemed and submitted) type-*B* rights will be used for pro rata redemption of type-*A* rights. The 100 *RC* units will be given to those submitting type-*C* rights, those submitting type-*B* rights that are not going to be redeemed, and those holding type-*A* rights that are not going to be redeemed.[35]

IV. Consistency with Participants' Entitlements

This Part demonstrates that the outcome of the proposed method of division will be perfectly consistent with the entitlements of the

---

as some shares are held by pessimists who are not going to use them, the market price of type-*B* rights must be negligible. But at such a market price, the optimists would buy the rights and submit them to the company for exercise. Alternatively put, if the optimists, but not the pessimists, view the rights as having some value and use, then, in the presence of market trading, the rights should all end up at the hands of the optimists, who would use them; no rights would remain idle in the hands of pessimists to whom the rights are of no use.

[34] If some type-*B* rights are not submitted for exercise, then the market price of such rights must be negligible. In such a case, no holder of a type-*C* right will have a reason to submit it. If the holder did submit a type-*C* right, he would have to pay $2 to get one *RC* unit. Therefore, even if the holder does believe that *V* exceeds $2, he will still be better off not using his type-*C* right but instead purchasing a type-*B* right for the negligible market price, and then using this right to purchase an *RC* unit for only $1.

[35] To consider a more complex example than the one above, suppose that only 50 type-*C* rights and all of the type-*B* rights are submitted for exercise. Those who submitted type-*C* rights will receive 50 *RC* units. The $100 received from them will be used for a pro rata redemption of 50 type-*A* and 50 type-*B* rights: each holder of a type-*A* or a type-*B* right will have half of his right redeemed. The 50 remaining *RC* units will be divided among the holders of the 50 unredeemed, submitted type-*B* rights. The $50 received by the company from the exercise of these 50 type-*B* rights will be used to redeem the remaining 50 type-*A* rights. In sum, the units of *RC* will end up half in the hands of those submitting type-*C* rights and half in the hands of those holding type-*B* rights.

participants. As emphasized earlier, the problems of the division process arise from the difficulties involved in determining the monetary value of the reorganized company. The proposed method, however, makes no attempt to estimate this monetary value, nor does it require even a rough sense of the monetary value of the rights that the participants will receive. Although we may not know how much these rights are worth, we can be confident that whatever their worth is, they will provide the receiving participants with no less than the value to which they are entitled.

A. The Significance of Not Relying on Accurate Market Pricing

The rights given to the participants will be traded on the market in the brief period between the issue date and the exercise date. As the analysis below will indicate, if the market does not underestimate the reorganized company's value, then the market price of any type of right will be no less than the value to which the participants receiving the right are entitled; consequently, the participants will be able to capture the value of their entitlement by immediately selling their rights on the market. Thus, the conclusion concerning the method's effectiveness follows immediately if one assumes that the market will not undervalue the distributed rights. As this Part shows, however, such an assumption is not necessary to reach this conclusion: the method's effectiveness does not hinge on the market's not undervaluing the rights or even on the presence of market trading in the rights.

This feature of the method is very important. Many may believe that capital market prices are efficient not only in most cases but also in the particular case of companies in financial distress. But whatever one's views on the merits of this question, one must recognize that many public officials and commentators believe that the market often errs (and usually in the direction of undervaluation) in appraising the value of companies that emerge out of reorganization.[36] Indeed, the primary rationale for the existence of the reorganization alternative to liquidation is the concern that the market often undervalues such companies; if the market could be relied on to price such companies perfectly, there would be no reason to expect that a reorganization would ever provide the participants with a greater value than they would get from a going-concern sale effected through a chapter 7 liquidation proceeding. Thus, any examination of the best reorganization method should take into account the concern that the market's estimate might be inaccurate. It is therefore a significant advantage

[36] *See, e.g.*, Citibank, N.A. v. Baer, 651 F.2d 1341, 1347–48 (10th Cir. 1980); *In re* Interstate Stores, Inc., SEC Corporate Reorganization Release No. 322, 13 S.E.C. Docket 757, 786–87 (1977); Blum, *supra* note 21, at 566–67; Brudney, *supra* note 21, at 673–75.

of the proposed method that an inaccurate market pricing of the rights will not provide participants with a basis for objecting to the method's outcome.

This feature of the method is the main reason why it is superior to the method of division put forward by Professor Roe five years ago.[37] Roe was the first to seek, as I do in this Article, a method of division that would not be based on the problematic process of bargaining among the various classes of participants. He proposed to estimate the value of the reorganized company by selling ten percent of the reorganized company's securities on the market and then extrapolating the company's value from the sale price for these securities. Although Roe's method is, in my view, superior to the existing process of bargaining among classes, the method's reliance on market pricing makes it, as Roe himself recognized,[38] substantially imperfect. First, the method does not address the concerns of those who believe that the market might not perceive accurately the value of companies in reorganization. Second, even if the market's perceptions are accurate, selling a sample of the company's securities might produce an inaccurate figure, because some participants will have an incentive to manipulate the sale price. Third, Roe's method is inapplicable to companies whose securities are not publicly traded. Because the method that I propose does not hinge on the existence of accurate market pricing, it does not suffer from any of these problems.

Before proceeding to a detailed demonstration, it is worth stating briefly why accurate market pricing of the rights is not essential for the proposed method's effectiveness. Although participants may sell their rights on the market, they can always choose to retain them until the exercise date. If they do so, then, as is shown below, they will not end up with less than the value to which they are entitled. Consequently, even assuming that a given participant does not have, or attaches no value to, the opportunity to sell his rights on the market, the participant will have no basis for complaining about the method's outcome.

B. The Outcome in the Example

To demonstrate the method's effectiveness, I wish first to show that, in the example used in Part III, no participant has any basis for complaining about the method's outcome. Consider first the senior creditors. If they retain the type-*A* rights given to them, they will end up in one of two positions. First, their rights may be redeemed for $100 (if the holders of the type-*B* or type-*C* rights choose to exercise them). In this case, the senior creditors surely cannot complain about

---

[37] *See* Roe, *supra* note 8.

[38] *See id.* at 575–80.

the outcome, as their claims will be paid in full. Alternatively, the senior creditors' rights may not be redeemed, in which case the creditors will end up holding all 100 units of *RC*. Again, they will have no basis for complaining, for they will be getting the whole reorganization pie: there is nothing more that could be given to them.

Now, the senior creditors surely might be unhappy about the way in which the market assesses the value of *RC* units and therefore also the value of type-*A* rights. Suppose that the senior creditors believe *V* to be $0.90, and suppose that the market believes the value of *V* to be only $0.50. In this case, the senior creditors will not be able to sell their type-*A* rights for more than $0.50. Similarly, if and when they get the units of *RC*, they will be able to sell them for only $0.50. But the fact that others are unwilling to pay the senior creditors more than $0.50 for what in their view is worth $0.90 does not provide the senior creditors with a basis for complaining that the reorganization's outcome deprives them of the value to which they are entitled — for they will receive from the reorganization process all that there is to distribute. They can complain about the market ("oh, the market is not what it is supposed to be") but not about the method's way of dividing *RC* units among the participants.

Consider now the junior creditors. If the junior creditors do not sell their type-*B* rights, they can end up in one of two positions. First, their rights may be redeemed by the company at $1 per right (if the type-*C* rights are submitted for exercise). In this case, the junior creditors will be paid in full and clearly have no reason to complain. Alternatively, the junior creditors may end up with options to purchase *RC* units at $1 per unit. The value of these options is by definition not lower than the value to which the creditors are entitled — for the junior creditors are entitled to no more than the value that is left, if any, after the senior creditors are paid in full. And having the option to receive all of the reorganization pie by paying the senior creditors' prior $100 claim makes the above value accessible to the junior creditors.

Again, the junior creditors might be unhappy about the way in which the market assesses the value of *RC* units and thus the value of their type-*B* rights. Suppose for example that the junior creditors believe that *V* is $1.90 and that the value to which they are entitled is thus $90 (the reorganization value of $190 minus the senior creditors' claims of $100). Suppose further that the market estimates *V* at $1.50 and thus prices the junior creditors' type-*B* rights at $0.50. The junior creditors will have no basis for complaining that the rights given to them have a $50 value, which is less than the $90 to which they are entitled. It would be inconsistent for them to assert both (i) that *V* is $1.90 and they are thus entitled to $0.90 each, and (ii) that the value of their options is only $0.50 each. If *V* is $1.90, then the value of an option to buy an *RC* unit at $1 is $0.90; this value can be realized simply by exercising the option. The junior creditors thus should not sell their type-*B* rights to the unappreciative market; if they do sell, they will have only themselves to blame.

Finally, consider the equityholders. If they do not sell their type-*C* rights, they will on the exercise date have options to purchase *RC* units at $2. These options will make accessible to them the very value to which they are entitled — which is all that is left, if anything, after the claims of the senior and junior creditors are paid in full.

Again, the equityholders may claim that the market undervalues the value of *RC* units and thus the value of their type-*C* rights. But then they should not sell their rights; rather they should retain and exercise them. Their perception (whether accurate or not) that such undervaluation takes place will provide them with no basis for complaining about the method's outcome — for reasons similar to those that have been discussed above with respect to the junior creditors.

C. A More General Defense

Having examined in detail the method's outcome in our example, I now wish to state in general terms why any given participant will have no basis for complaining that the method's outcome is inconsistent with his entitlement. Suppose first that a given participant retains the right distributed to him until the exercise date. For him to assert that he has received less than the value to which he is entitled, he has to assert either (i) that those above him in priority (or those who bought their rights) have received too much, or (ii) that those below him in priority (or those who bought their rights) have received too much.

Those below the participant in priority (or those who bought their rights) will be able to capture any value only if they pay in full all the claims of those above them — including the participant's own claim. Thus, the participant will never have a basis for complaining that he is receiving too little because those below him are getting too much.

Similarly, the participant will be unable to complain that those above him in priority (or those who bought their rights) are getting too much — that is, that they are paid more than in full. By exercising the option given to him, the participant can ensure that, as far as his pro rata share of the company is concerned, those above him will not get more than the full value of their claims. The option automatically makes accessible to him his pro rata share of the value left after the preceding claims are paid in full — and he is entitled to no more.[39]

---

[39] To illustrate the above reasoning, consider the position of a junior creditor in our example. For the creditor to have a justifiable complaint, he must assert either that the senior creditors

Thus, assuming that the participant's right is not transferable and that he must retain it until the exercise date, he will not end up with less than the value of his entitlement. And, clearly, he cannot be made worse off by the ability to sell his right, if he so wishes, in the period preceding the exercise date: if he believes that the market undervalues his right, he need not sell but rather can retain his right until the exercise date. Indeed, the ability to sell may improve the participant's situation: if he believes that the market accurately prices his right or overvalues it, he presumably will benefit from having the opportunity to sell.

D. *Addressing the Problem of Differing Estimates*

An alternative way of explaining the proposed method's effectiveness is by showing how it addresses the valuation problem, which may be referred to as the problem of divergent estimates. Because no objective, indisputable figure is available for the reorganized company's value, participants may advance different estimates of this value. If the participants could all be expected to advance the same estimate, the question of division would be straightforward: their common estimate could be used to divide the reorganized company's securities. The division question is difficult only because participants may well differ in the estimates they advance. Such differences may result from either strategic manipulation or genuine disagreement.

1. *Strategic Manipulation.* — Under the existing method of division, even if all participants actually share the same estimate of the reorganized company's value, they may well have strategic reasons for advancing different estimates. In the bargaining between any class and the classes preceding it, the preceding classes have an incentive to advance a low estimate whereas the junior class has the opposite interest.

Suppose, for instance, that the junior creditors and the senior creditors in our example have the same estimate of *V*; and consider what estimates they will find it in their interest to advance during bargaining and litigation under the existing method of division. The senior creditors will generally find it in their interest to advance an estimate below the participants' common estimate, for a low value of *V* would entitle them to a larger fraction of *RC*'s securities. The

are getting too much or that the equityholders are getting too much. The junior creditor cannot complain that the equityholders are getting too much, because they will get something only in the event that the junior creditor's type-*B* right is redeemed, in which case he will be paid in full. Similarly, the junior creditor's possession of a type-*B* right should prevent him from complaining that the senior creditors are receiving too much — that is, more than $100, the full value of their claims. For, by exercising his right, the junior creditor can ensure that, as far as his pro rata share of the company is concerned, the senior creditors will not receive more than the full value of their claims.

junior creditors will generally find it in their interest to advance an estimate exceeding the participants' common estimate, for a high value of *V* would entitle them to a larger fraction of *RC*'s securities.

Under the proposed method, however, no class will be able to benefit from strategic manipulation of estimates. The division of securities will in no way depend on what the participants or anyone else *claim V* is. The division depends only on what the participants *do* with their rights. And the participants' decisions whether to exercise their rights will necessarily reflect their true judgment concerning *V*. In particular, the junior creditors in our example will not be able to get any value simply by asserting that *V* exceeds $1; the only way for them to get any value is by exercising their rights (which of course they will do only if they estimate *V* to exceed $1). Similarly, the senior creditors will not be able to get a higher value by strategically advancing a low estimate of *V*; what they will end up with depends only on what the junior creditors elect to do with their rights.

2. *Genuine Disagreement.* — Strategic manipulation is not the only reason for the different estimates that parties may advance under the existing reorganization process. Parties also may differ in their estimates due to genuine disagreement. Such differences may exist not only among classes but also among the participants in any given class.

The proposed method addresses the possibility of different subjective estimates by enabling each participant to decide individually, based on his *own* estimate of the reorganized company's value, whether to exercise his rights. Consequently, each participant will get no less, and may indeed get more, than the value to which he believes he is entitled based on his *own* estimate of the reorganization value.

Consider, for instance, a junior creditor in our example. If the creditor believes that *V* is less than $1, then the value of his entitlement based on his estimate of *V* is zero (see Table 2). If the creditor keeps his right, which he will have to do if the right's market price is zero, he will not exercise it and indeed will end up with no value. But if others are more optimistic and believe that *V* exceeds $1, then the market price of type-*B* rights will be positive, and the creditor will be able to sell his right for this positive market price.

Next, suppose that the creditor believes that *V* is between $1 and $2 — $1.50 for instance — and that he thus believes that the value of his entitlement is $0.50 (see Table 2). By retaining and exercising his right, the junior creditor can capture a value that equals his own estimate of the value of his entitlement. If other parties are more optimistic and have higher estimates of *V*, however, the creditor will be able to capture a value that exceeds his own estimate of his entitlement. In such a case, the market price of his type-*B* right will exceed its $0.50 value to him, and he will sell his right for this higher market price.

Finally, if the junior creditor believes that V exceeds \$2, then the value of his entitlement based on his estimate of V will be \$1 (a payment in full of his claim) (see Table 2). If others also believe that V exceeds \$2, then, because type-C rights will be exercised, type-B rights will be redeemed at \$1 (and will trade at \$1 beforehand). In such a case, the creditor will end up with a value that equals in his eyes the value of his entitlement. But if others are more pessimistic and believe that V is below \$2, then the participant's type-B right will not be redeemed, and by exercising it, he will end up with a value exceeding in his eyes the value of his entitlement.

E. Note on Participants' Information and Financial Resources

A question that some may raise is whether one can object to the proposed method by arguing that participants lack sufficient information or financial resources.

1. Information. — Under the proposed method, as well as under the existing process of division, participants must make decisions on the basis of whatever information they have concerning the reorganized company's value. Therefore, it is necessary to examine whether, in comparison to the existing process, the proposed method might either increase the amount of information that participants need or decrease the amount of information that they possess.

The proposed method does not increase the participants' need for information. Under the existing process, each class of participants must make its bargaining and litigation decisions on the basis of whatever estimate of the reorganized company's value it happens to have. Assuming that participants will not have less information under the proposed method than under the existing process, they will be able to use the same estimate to make the necessary decisions about their rights.

Indeed, under the proposed method, participants will not even need to make a judgment, as they must under the existing process, concerning their best estimate of the reorganized company's value. They will only have to make the much more limited judgment whether the reorganized company's value exceeds the estimate that is implicit in the market price of their rights (that is, whether the value of their rights exceeds the rights' market price).

Finally, there is no reason to assume that participants will have less information under the proposed method than under the existing process. Indeed, the proposed method provides an important additional source of information — the market pricing of rights. To be sure, the proposed method may still reduce the amount of information that participants will have if it substantially decreases the extent to which participants take advantage of the available sources of information. Such a decrease may arguably take place because of collective action problems: under the proposed method, participants will act individually rather than collectively, and they may have less incentive or ability to look for information. But the proposed method will not prevent participants from acquiring information as a class rather than individually when there are some advantages in doing so: in such cases, the committee representing the class will likely engage in information acquisition (say, by hiring an investment banker to do the job) and then disseminate its conclusions to individual class members.

2. *Financial Resources and Willingness to Invest.* — Another possible objection to the method arises from the fact that the method will require some participants to invest in the enterprise to capture the value to which they are entitled. Participants in an insolvent company, so the argument might go, may reasonably be reluctant to make such an investment or may lack the necessary financial resources.

It should initially be noted that most participants will not need to put in any money to capture the value of their entitlements. For one thing, many participants will have their rights redeemed by the company. Furthermore, even participants whose rights are not redeemed by the company will not have to put in any money if they believe that the market does not underestimate the reorganized company's value; in such a case, they can capture the value to which they believe they are entitled by selling their rights on the market. Thus, a given participant will need to invest money to capture the value of his entitlement only when the company does not redeem his rights and he believes that the market is underestimating the reorganized company's value.

Consider a junior creditor in our example who believes that V is \$1.50 (in other words, that buying an *RC* unit at \$1.50 will provide an "adequate" rate of return) — and who thus believes that he is entitled to \$0.50. Suppose also that the market estimates V to be only \$1.30 and thus prices the creditor's type-*B* right at \$0.30. The creditor will be able to capture the value to which he believes he is entitled only if he invests the \$1 necessary to exercise his right.

Let us first suppose that the amount at stake constitutes a small fraction of the creditor's wealth. In such a case, the creditor's need to put in \$1 will not provide him with a basis for complaint, for if V is equal to \$1.50 in his judgment, then from his perspective purchasing a unit worth V for \$1 must be equivalent to his getting \$0.50. To see this equivalency, observe that purchasing a unit for \$1 is equivalent to receiving \$0.50 plus being required to purchase an *RC* unit for \$1.50. Given that the amount at stake is small relative to the creditor's wealth and that the creditor values the *RC* unit at \$1.50, the creditor should be indifferent to the requirement that he purchase a unit for \$1.50.

Thus, if the amounts that participants need to invest to exercise their rights are small relative to their wealth, which I suspect is the case for most participants in reorganizations of publicly traded corporations, then the need to invest will pose no problem. If participants' wealth is not sufficiently large relative to the amount at stake, however, problems may arise. Suppose, for instance, that the junior creditor in the example discussed above does not have the $1 necessary to exercise his right. In such a situation, the creditor may complain that his lack of funds forces him to sell his type-*B* right for a price below the value of his entitlements: given the undervaluation of *RC*'s units by the market, he will end up with only $0.30 rather than the $0.50 to which he believes he is entitled.

Even when such a liquidity problem does arise, it commonly can be eliminated or at least substantially alleviated by the participant's ability to borrow. In a well-functioning capital market, the junior creditor's borrowing power will be augmented by his ability to use as collateral the very *RC* unit that he will buy. In the example under consideration, if the market estimates the value of an *RC* unit at $1.30, then a junior creditor will be able to borrow the $1 necessary to exercise his option by pledging the purchased *RC* unit as a collateral.[40]

In sum, although the need to invest funds might pose some problems to the effectiveness of the proposed method, these problems appear to be quite limited. Most participants will not need to invest any amount in order to capture the value to which they believe they are entitled, because their rights will be either redeemed or valued sufficiently by the market. Furthermore, those who will need to invest will have no basis for complaining as long as the amount at stake is small relative to their wealth. Finally, as for those whose rights will be neither redeemed nor sufficiently valued by the market and whose wealth is not sufficiently large relative to the amount at stake, any problem resulting from the need to invest will be mitigated by their ability to borrow.

V. Implementation

A. Under a New Reorganization Regime

The proposed method of division is put forward as the basis for reform of reorganization law. The optimal reorganization regime, I

[40] Lack of sufficient financial resources, then, may pose a problem only if the market's estimate of V is lower than not only the creditor's estimate but also the $1 that the creditor needs to exercise his right. For example, if the market estimates V at $0.80, then the junior creditor will not be able to borrow the full $1 necessary to exercise his right by pledging the unit as collateral.

suggest, is one that requires and facilitates the use of this method in every case of reorganization.

The proposed reorganization regime will include, as any reorganization regime must, a preliminary process of determining the size and ranking of participants' claims; this process may be straightforward at times, but it also may be complex and time-consuming at other times. Once the participants' claims are identified, however, the process of division will proceed smoothly and quickly.

Although the process of division will largely follow automatically from the method's principles, a reorganization plan will be necessary to fix some limited elements of the reorganized company's features. In particular, the plan would fix the reorganized company's capital structure.[41] Several possible parties can be charged with designing a reorganization plan for confirmation by the supervising court. Possible candidates include a trustee appointed by the court, incumbent management (which presumably represents the equityholders), or the committee representing a certain class of creditors. Note that assigning the role of designing the plan to representatives of a given class of participants will not create a conflict-of-interest problem. Given the way in which the proposed method operates, the choice of capital structure cannot be used to divert value from one class of participants to another. Therefore, in choosing the capital structure, the party charged with designing the reorganization plan will aim solely at maximizing the value of the reorganized company.

Because of the limited elements that the reorganization plan will cover, designing it and receiving the court's confirmation will presumably take relatively little time. Once the capital structure is specified, the division will proceed automatically and swiftly: rights to the reorganized company's securities will be distributed to participants in accordance with the method, the securities themselves will be distributed shortly afterwards as the rights are exercised, and the company will be out of the reorganization process, hopefully on its way to a bright future.

This regime will best address the efficiency and fairness problems that have thus far afflicted the division process in corporate reorganizations. First, the outcome will always be in accordance with the entitlements of all the participants involved. Second, the choice of capital structure will be value maximizing. Third, the delay and litigation costs under the new regime will be the smallest possible under any reorganization regime (largely consisting of the unavoidable delay and costs involved in determining the size and ranking of claims).

---

[41] As Part VI will explain, the plan may also include a few other elements, such as the treatment of secured claims and the reinstatement of some contracts with favorable terms.

B. Under Existing Law

The proposed method may be useful even under the existing reorganization rules. Some parties should find it in their interest to use the method as a basis for the reorganization plans that they file.

Under the existing rules, the equityholders usually have the exclusive right for a specified period of time to file (and seek confirmation of) a reorganization plan.[42] Subsequently, any participant may file a reorganization plan.[43] To obtain confirmation of a reorganization plan, its proponents must achieve either (i) acceptance of the plan by every class, or (ii) if a class objects, a judicial overruling of this objection on the grounds that the plan provides the class with no less than its entitlement.[44] Achieving either (i) or (ii) is often problematic or at least time-consuming: securing class approval involves the complications of bargaining; and obtaining a judicial determination that the plan provides the class with the value of its entitlement involves the difficult problems of valuation.

Once the period in which the equityholders have exclusive right to propose plans has passed, it will be in the interest of the senior creditors to file a plan based on the proposed method. The proposed method will provide the senior creditors either with the full value of their claims or at least with all of the reorganized company's securities, which is all they can hope for. Furthermore, they will be able to secure confirmation of such a plan relatively quickly; given the way in which the method is designed, they should face no difficulty in demonstrating to the court that their plan provides all other classes with no less than the value to which these classes are entitled.

Using the method will free the senior creditors from the threat of strategic behavior by participants junior to them. At present, juniors may seek more than the value to which they are entitled by threatening to oppose the plan and create protracted litigation. The proposed method will eliminate this threat by enabling the senior creditors to demonstrate easily that their plan provides all participants with a value consistent with their entitlements.

If parties do use the proposed method in their confirmation plans, some of the potential benefits of the method will be obtained even under existing rules. First, and most importantly, outcomes will come closer to those suggested by the participants' entitlements. Second, parties using the method as a basis for their reorganization plans will choose a capital structure solely on the basis of their judgment as to which structure would be value maximizing. Third, delays and litigation costs will decrease significantly.

---

[42] *See* 11 U.S.C. § 1121(b) (1982); Trost, *supra* note 13, at 1325–26.

[43] *See* 11 U.S.C. § 1121(c) (1982 & Supp. IV 1986).

[44] *See id.* § 1129(a)(7)(A), (b)(1); Trost, *supra* note 13, at 1328–44.

VI. EXTENSIONS

The analysis in Parts III and IV used a concrete example for convenience of illustration. This Part drops the simplifying assumptions used in constructing that example and considers four important complications that are present in reorganizations. I first show how the method can be adjusted easily to apply to situations in which there are more than three classes. I then discuss three issues that may arise and require treatment under any reorganization regime — contracts with favorable terms that are worth reinstating, secured claims, and concentration of claims in one hand. As I explain, the proposed method of division is consistent with any way that reorganization law might wish to treat these issues. Consequently, the potential presence of these problems does not undermine my earlier conclusion that the proposed method offers the best way of dividing the reorganization pie.

A. More Than Three Classes

The example used above consisted of a company with three consecutively ranked classes, each with 100 units of membership. The method, however, can be applied easily in the general case of a company with any number of consecutively ranked classes, each with any number of membership units. Describing the operation of the method in general terms, applicable to any such case, the rights distributed to participants will be as follows.

Each unit of membership in the most senior class will entitle its holder to receive a right that the company may redeem for the participant's pro rata fraction of the class' total claim. If this right is not redeemed, it will entitle its holder to receive (without any payment) his pro rata fraction of the reorganized company's securities.[45]

Each unit of membership in any intermediate class (any class below the most senior one and above the most junior one) will entitle its holder to a right that may be redeemed by the company for the participant's pro rata fraction of the class' total claim. If the right is not redeemed, it will entitle its holder to purchase his pro rata fraction of the company's securities for a price equal to his pro rata fraction of the total claim of the classes above his class.[46]

---

[45] For example, if the total claim of the senior class is $300, then each member of the class will receive, for each $1 debt that he is owed, a right that may be redeemed by the company for $1 and, if not redeemed, will entitle its holder to receive 1/300 of the reorganized company's securities.

[46] Consider, for example, a situation in which the total claim of a given intermediate class of creditors is $200 and the total claim of the classes above it is $540. In this case, any member of this intermediate class will receive, for each $1 debt that he is owed, a right that may be redeemed by the company for $1 and, if not redeemed, will entitle him to purchase 1/200 of the company's securities for a price equal to $2.70 (1/200 of the total preceding claims of $540).

Finally, each unit of membership in the class of residual claimants (the most junior class) will entitle its holder to receive a right that may not be redeemed by the company. This right will entitle its holder to purchase his pro rata fraction of the company's securities for a price equal to his pro rata fraction of the total claim of all the classes above the residual claimants' class.[47]

B. Contracts with Favorable Terms

Prior to entering the reorganization stage, a company presumably has a whole set of outstanding contracts. To the extent that such contracts are breached or discontinued by the reorganization process or by preceding events, the other parties to the contracts are likely to have claims against the company. Some of the contracts, however, may be at terms that appear favorable to the company, given the information available at the reorganization stage. The breach or discontinuation of these contracts will not be in the interest of any participants except the parties with whom the company has the contracts; the pie available to the other participants will be maximized by "reinstating" these contracts, that is, by having the reorganized company maintain them.

A typical case of a contract that is worth reinstating is one providing the company with a long term loan at an interest rate that at the time of reorganization appears favorable to the company. Consider a company that took from a bank a $100,000 long term loan with an interest rate of 5% and suppose that by the time of the reorganization interest rates have risen to 10%. In this case, the bank may wish to have the loan declared in default and consequently get a claim of $100,000 against the reorganizing company. But the pie available to the other participants may well be maximized by reinstating the loan contract, because, given the contract's 5% interest rate, the present value of the future installments on the loan will be much less than $100,000.

Any reorganization regime must determine whether and under what conditions reinstatement of contracts is allowed.[48] Existing reorganization law, for example, includes a detailed arrangement concerning the possibility of reinstating some contracts; participants whose contracts with the company are reinstated do not need to

---

[47] For example, suppose that the total claim of the classes preceding the residual claimants' class is $1800 and that the residual claimants' class includes 200 units. Then, each unit in this class will entitle the holder to a right to purchase 1/200 of the reorganized company's securities for $9 ($1800/200).

[48] For a discussion of some of the policy issues that are involved in this determination, see T. JACKSON, cited in note 7 above, at 35–44.

approve the reorganization plan because their claims are "unimpaired."[49]

Whichever approach we wish reorganization law to take to the issue of reinstating contracts, the operation of the proposed method of division will be consistent with that approach. Given the regime's rules concerning which contracts can be reinstated, the reorganization plan filed under the proposed method will specify those contracts that the plan's designers elected to reinstate (as well as the means of reinstating them). For the reasons noted earlier,[50] the designers of the plan presumably will choose to reinstate only those contracts whose reinstatement will maximize the pie available to the rest of the participants. The parties to the reinstated contracts will have claims that are not impaired and they therefore will not participate in the division of rights. The reorganized company, however, will be subject to the reinstated contracts, and the value of its securities will be affected by this fact. The division of rights among the participants whose claims are impaired will then proceed smoothly according to the proposed method.

C. Secured Claims

Thus far the analysis has assumed that the priority of a given claim over other claims necessarily applies to all assets of the debtor company. Some claims, however, are secured claims, which means that their priority over other claims is with respect only to a specific subset of the debtor's assets. Secured claims are often present in reorganizations.

In the presence of secured claims, any reorganization regime (and indeed any liquidation regime as well) must resolve two issues. First, the regime must choose both a method for deciding whether a claim secured by a given asset is *fully* secured (a method that may include estimating the asset's value) and, for claims that are not fully secured, a method for dividing these claims into fully secured and unsecured parts. Second, the regime must determine whether the holder of a secured claim has an *in rem* right to have the asset sold to pay his claim or only a right to be paid the appraised value of the asset. The existing reorganization regime includes an arrangement governing these issues,[51] and commentators have been debating the merits of this arrangement as well as possible reforms.[52]

---

[49] *See* 11 U.S.C. §§ 1124, 1126(f) (1982 & Supp. IV 1986).

[50] *See supra* p. 798.

[51] *See* 11 U.S.C. §§ 506, 1111(b) (1982 & Supp. IV 1986).

[52] *See, e.g.*, Baird & Jackson, *Corporate Reorganizations and the Treatment of Diverse Ownership Interests: A Comment on Adequate Protection of Secured Creditors in Bankruptcy*, 51 U. CHI. L. REV. 97 (1984); Eisenberg, *The Undersecured Creditor in Reorganizations and the Nature of Security*, 38 VANDERBILT L. REV. 931 (1985).

Whichever arrangement we wish to apply to secured claims, the proposed method of division will be consistent with it. The arrangement will govern the identification of fully secured claims and their treatment under the reorganization plan.[53] The units of the reorganized company's securities that will then be available for distribution will be divided among the holders of unsecured claims and interests according to the proposed method of division.

D. Concentration of Claims in One Hand

The last complication to be discussed, which appears less frequently than those discussed above, is the possibility of a concentration of claims in one hand. Suppose, for instance, that 60% of the units in Class *A* in our simple example (the class of senior creditors) are held by a given bank. In such a case, if the type-*A* rights are not redeemed by the company, the bank will get 60% of the company's securities while the other members of the class will get 40% of these securities. The rights given to the bank will be worth more per right than those given to the other senior creditors, because shares in a controlling block are worth more than minority shares. Consequently, the value given to the senior class will be divided disproportionately, with the bank getting more than the value of its entitlement and the other members of the class getting less than the value of their entitlements.

Such a problem can arise, however, in any reorganization regime that divides the reorganized company's securities among the participants.[54] As long as the division proceeds under the assumption that any two shares of the reorganized company are worth the same amount, a concentration of claims may lead to a given participant's receiving a controlling block; as a result, this participant will end up with more than the value of his entitlement, whereas others will receive less than the value of theirs. Because this problem may arise and require a solution under any reorganization regime, its potential presence does not weaken my earlier conclusion that the proposed method is the best way of dividing the reorganization pie.

Although the problem of concentrated claims is unlikely to arise frequently and is in no way unique to the proposed method, I do wish to note what appears to be the best means of addressing it.[55] If the

---

[53] If the arrangement requires or suggests making some immediate payments to the holders of the secured claims, then the reorganization plan may include provisions for selling assets or raising funds in some other way. For the reasons noted earlier, *see supra* p. 798, the designers of the plan presumably will seek to adopt that allowable method of treating secured claims that will maximize the pie available to the rest of the participants.

[54] Thus, for example, Roe, in discussing his proposed reorganization regime, recognized the existence of this problem. *See* Roe, *supra* note 8, at 575–76.

[55] The endorsed approach is that suggested by Roe, cited in note 8, at 575–76.

exercise of rights provides someone with a controlling block of the reorganized company's equity, then the holder of this controlling block should be required to dispose of his controlling position — by selling enough shares to go below a specified control threshold — within a specified period of time. Under such a rule, those who exercise rights will be able to count on receiving shares that, at least after a specified period of time, will not be minority shares.

VII. Conclusion

This Article has put forward a new method of division for corporate reorganizations. This method can eliminate certain efficiency and fairness problems that have been long viewed as inherent to the reorganization process. Under the method, once the size and relative priority of the participants' claims are determined, the division of the reorganization pie will be resolved quickly and efficiently — and in perfect consistency with the entitlements of all the participants. The method is put forward as a basis for law reform: the optimal reorganization regime is one that requires and facilitates the application of the proposed method in every reorganization case. Furthermore, the method can be used even under the existing legal rules, as a basis for reorganization plans that participants may want to file. It is hoped that the method will indeed prove useful to public officials overseeing corporate reorganizations and to participants in such reorganizations.

Procedure

[6]

A NEW THEORY CONCERNING THE CREDIBILITY AND SUCCESS OF THREATS TO SUE

*LUCIAN ARYE BEBCHUK**

ABSTRACT

Negative-expected-value (NEV) suits are ones in which the expected litigation costs exceed the expected judgment. This article offers a new theory for the credibility and success of plaintiffs with NEV suits. The theory is based on recognizing that litigation costs are generally not incurred all at once but rather over time; this divisibility of the litigation process is shown to play a crucial strategic role. The analysis identifies the conditions under which a plaintiff with an NEV suit will have a credible threat and succeed in extracting a settlement. It is demonstrated that plaintiffs have credible threats in a much wider set of cases—including in numerous small-stakes cases—than has been suggested by prior economic analysis of the subject.

I. Introduction: What Can Make NEV Suits Credible?

A. *The Puzzle*

A negative-expected-value (NEV) suit is one in which the plaintiff would obtain a negative expected return from pursuing his suit all the way to trial, that is, one in which the plaintiff's expected litigation costs would exceed the expected judgment. An NEV suit need not be one in which the plaintiff is unlikely to win; it may be one, for example, in which the plaintiff is certain to win but the needed litigation costs exceed the amount that could be won.

* Professor of Law, Economics, and Finance, Harvard Law School. An earlier version of this article was circulated in 1991 under the title "The Credibility and Success of Suits Known to Be Made Solely to Extract a Settlement Offer." I am indebted to Omri Ben-Shahar for his valuable assistance and suggestions throughout my work on this project. For helpful comments and conversations, I am grateful to David Friedman, Andrew Guzman, Bruce Hay, Christine Jolls, Louis Kaplow, Mitch Polinsky, Bill Landes, Avery Katz, Lewis Kornhauser, Steve Shavell, Kathy Spier, Lars Stole, and workshop and conference participants at the University of Chicago and Harvard University. I wish to thank the University of Chicago Law School for its hospitality during a period in which I worked on this article. Finally, for their financial support, I am grateful to the National Science Foundation and to the Harvard Law School Program in Law and Economics (which is supported by the John M. Olin Foundation).

[*Journal of Legal Studies*, vol. XXV (January 1996)]
 0047-2530/96/2501-0001$01.50

It is clear that NEV suits are abundant. For one thing, NEV suits arise in a large fraction, if not the overwhelming majority, of small-stakes cases. Because the costs of legal proceedings are unlikely to be negligible even if the amount pursued is small, a party that has a justifiable claim to a small amount might well have a potential NEV suit.

A plaintiff will pursue an NEV suit only if he expects to extract a positive settlement offer from the defendant.[1] The question, however, is, Why would a defendant agree to pay any settlement amount to a plaintiff with an NEV suit? To be sure, the defendant may prefer such a settlement to a trial. But why would the defendant believe that, in the absence of a settlement, the plaintiff would pursue his suit rather than drop it? The critical issue, therefore, concerns the credibility of the plaintiff's threat. The defendant would not agree to any positive settlement amount unless she found the plaintiff's threat to litigate credible. However, forced to choose between litigating his case all the way to judgment or dropping it, a rational plaintiff with an NEV suit would choose to drop his suit. Thus, it is necessary to understand what could make the plaintiff's threat credible in the eyes of the defendant.

Resolving whether and when NEV suits are credible is important for understanding the effects of the legal system. There are numerous instances in which legal rules provide parties with entitlements that are worth less than what it would cost to litigate them. If plaintiffs do not have credible threats to pursue legal action, the ability to litigate these entitlements will play little role in shaping the outcomes of such cases. Whatever plaintiffs get in these cases would have to result from other factors, such as defendants' integrity or defendants' caring about their reputations. But if threats to sue may be credible and successful even in NEV cases, then plaintiffs' power to seek legal remedies does affect the outcomes in these numerous cases.

B. The Literature

The early economic literature on litigation, beginning in the early 1970s with papers by Landes, Gould, and Posner,[2] has largely avoided the puz-

[1] In some situations, a plaintiff can expect to get, at some intermediate point during the litigation process, some additional information about his chances. Getting favorable information may turn an NEV suit into one that has positive expected value. See Bradford Cornell, The Incentive to Sue: An Option Pricing Approach, 19 J. Legal Stud. 173 (1990); William M. Landes, Sequential versus Unitary Trials: An Economic Analysis, 22 J. Legal Stud. 99 (1993). My focus in this article, however, is on suits in which the expected judgment is expected to be lower than the plaintiff's total litigation costs even if things turn out favorably for the plaintiff.

[2] William M. Landes, An Economic Analysis of the Courts, 14 J. Law & Econ. 61 (1971); John P. Gould, The Economics of Legal Conflicts, 2 J. Legal Stud. 279 (1973); Richard A. Posner, An Economic Approach to Legal Procedure and Judicial Administration, 2 J. Legal Stud. 399 (1973).

zle of NEV suits by focusing on settlement decisions in positive-expected-value (PEV) suits. In particular, looking at the papers written in the 1980s to model pretrial negotiation in the presence of asymmetric information,[3] one finds that they have all assumed that the parties are certain about one thing: that the plaintiff's suit has a positive expected value.[4] Only in recent years has research also focused on NEV suits.

One explanation for NEV suits that I gave in an earlier paper focuses on the effects of imperfect information.[5] The defendant may not know whether the plaintiff's expected value of litigation is positive or negative. Consequently, the defendant cannot be certain that, in the absence of a settlement, the plaintiff would drop his suit. To avoid the risk of incurring litigation costs, the defendant therefore may elect to offer a positive settlement amount. This uncertainty model cannot explain, however, the success of suits that defendants know to be NEV suits. And there are clearly many cases of NEV suits which defendants can identify as such. For example, most small-stakes situations will be recognized by defendants as NEV suits.

Another explanation that was given by Rosenberg and Shavell[6] does apply to some NEV suits that are identified by defendants as such. Rosenberg and Shavell considered a situation in which, after the plaintiff files a suit at little or no cost, the defendant must incur some significant costs of responding (because failure to respond would lead to default or summary judgment against the defendant) before the plaintiff has to incur any costs. In this situation, even if the defendant knows that the plaintiff will drop the case once the defendant responds, the defendant will be willing to pay a settlement amount of up to the costs of responding in order to avoid incurring these costs. Although the Rosenberg-Shavell explanation may be relevant in some cases, it is applicable only to situations in which the defendant must incur substantial responding costs before the plaintiff incurs any meaningful litigation costs. Furthermore, un-

[3] See, for example, Lucian A. Bebchuk, Litigation and Settlement under Imperfect Information, 15 RAND J. Econ. 404 (1984); Jennifer F. Reinganum & Louis L. Wilde, Settlement, Litigation and the Allocation of Litigation Costs, 17 RAND J. Econ. 557 (1986); Barry Nalebuff, Credible Pretrial Negotiation, 18 RAND J. Econ. 198 (1987).

[4] Nalebuff's paper, *supra* note 3, illustrates especially well the analysts' focus on PEV suits. His paper emphasizes how plaintiffs structure their settlement strategies to rule out the possibility of their learning from the defendant's response that their suit is an NEV one.

[5] See Lucian A. Bebchuk, Suing Solely to Extract a Settlement Offer, 17 J. Legal Stud. 437 (1988). The imperfect information explanation was subsequently examined also by Avery Katz, The Effect of Frivolous Lawsuits on the Settlement of Litigation, 10 Int'l Rev. L. & Econ. 3 (1990).

[6] David Rosenberg & Steven Shavell, A Model in Which Suits Are Brought for Their Nuisance Value, 5 Int'l Rev. L. & Econ. 3 (1985).

der the Rosenberg-Shavell model, what the plaintiff can get in an NEV suit bears no connection to the expected judgment but depends only on the defendant's costs of responding.

C. *The Proposed New Approach*

This article offers a new explanation for the credibility and success of NEV suits. The explanation is based on the recognition that litigation costs are not incurred all at once but are spread over a period of time, with bargaining possibly taking place on numerous occasions throughout this period. The credibility of an NEV suit can arise from the fact that bargaining in "late" rounds occurs after some of the plaintiff's litigation costs are sunk. There may arrive a stage at which a threat to continue all the way to judgment becomes credible by virtue of the small fraction of the litigation costs that remains to be incurred. At this stage, it is rational for the defendant to agree to a settlement. The expectation that this will occur, it is shown, can lend credibility to the plaintiff's threat to proceed in earlier stages.

The analysis in the article identifies both the conditions under which an NEV suit will succeed and the amount that such a suit will extract in settlement. Whether the threat to sue is credible—and if so, what settlement it would produce—depends on the relationship between the two sides' litigation costs in a way that fits our intuition. Similarly, the credibility and success of the suit also depend on the expected judgment—again, in a direction that fits our intuition.

The explanation that this article offers applies to a large set of circumstances. In particular, it applies to cases that cannot be explained by the existing literature. Consider the numerous small-stakes cases in which the plaintiff's suit is known to be an NEV one and in which the plaintiff cannot force the defendant to incur large up-front litigation costs. The analysis shows that when the plaintiff's litigation costs are sufficiently divisible, and when bargaining can occur throughout the litigation process, the plaintiff's threat in these cases may nevertheless be credible.

While the article focuses on explaining the success of NEV claims, it also seeks to make a methodological contribution to the analysis of settlement decisions. The article highlights the strategic importance of the fact that litigation costs, including the costs of conducting a trial, are generally incurred in a divisible fashion. This divisibility might play an important role in settlement bargaining, and it might have a considerable effect on the parties' positions and their final payoffs.

Before proceeding, it is worth emphasizing that, throughout, the focus of the analysis is on positive issues—on understanding when potential plaintiffs will be able to extract settlements from potential defendants. The analysis demonstrates that plaintiffs have a greater ability to extract settlements than has been previously suggested. While this conclusion has normative implications (is this greater ability to extract settlements socially desirable?), analysis of these implications is deferred to another occasion.

The article is organized as follows. Section II begins with an informal analysis that demonstrates the main results of the article through simple numerical examples. Section III develops a model of sequential bargaining between a plaintiff and a defendant, demonstrates in general the effect of divisibility on the plaintiff's ability to extract a settlement, and identifies the settlement amount. Section IV further explores the conditions under which NEV suits will succeed. Section V examines the effects of divisibility under the British (fee-shifting) rule of litigation finance. Section VI considers some extensions and generalizations of the analysis. Finally, Section VII offers concluding remarks.

II. Informal Analysis

A. *The One-Stage Case*

Consider a suit in which the expected judgment (the probability of the plaintiff prevailing, times the magnitude of the judgment that he will get if he prevails) is 100. If the parties proceed all the way to judgment, each party will incur litigation costs of 140. This is an NEV suit since the plaintiff's expected gain is $100 - 140 = -40 < 0$. Suppose, initially, that there is only one litigation stage in which all of the parties' litigation costs are incurred in a lump-sum fashion, with bargaining taking place prior to that stage.

In this scenario, the plaintiff does not have a credible threat. If the defendant refuses to settle, the plaintiff would choose to drop his case and get zero rather than litigate the case and suffer an expected loss. Anticipating this, the defendant would refuse to settle for any positive amount. The suit has no credibility, and it thus cannot succeed.

B. *How Two-Stage Division Can Bolster Credibility*

Let us change the above example and suppose that the parties' litigation costs of 140 each are incurred not in a lump-sum fashion, but rather in two equal-cost stages. Suppose also that the parties can negotiate a settlement between stages. As will be shown below, the division of the suit into two stages might well make the plaintiff's threat to sue credible, and it may thus enable the plaintiff to extract a settlement offer from the defendant.

In analyzing this case, as well as subsequent cases, we are going to apply "backward induction." This approach is the standard method used by economists for analyzing strategic interactions in which parties make decisions over several time periods.[7] According to this approach, an analysis of how parties decide at any one point in time must be preceded by an analysis of the decisions at later points in time. This is so because the consequences of a decision at any one time depend on the decisions to be made at later times. Parties' choices among actions depend on what they expect future decisions to be.

Thus, the backward induction approach suggests that the analysis should start by examining what parties will decide in the final stage. In this last stage, expectations about future decisions no longer play a role, and we can analyze the parties' decision given any set of circumstances in which they may find themselves (circumstances that may result, in part, from earlier decisions). Equipped with this understanding, we can proceed to analyze what will happen one stage earlier. Knowing what the parties will do in the last stage, we can determine their decisions for any set of circumstances in which they may find themselves in the stage before last. We can continue to proceed backwards in this way, identifying the decision that will be reached in each stage based on the understanding of the future consequence of each action. The analysis is complete once we reach the initial stage.

In the example that we consider now, the parties can negotiate and decide whether or not to settle at two points in time: before the first stage of litigation, and between the two stages—assuming they reach this point. Following the approach of backward induction, let us begin by considering the later point, the time between the two stages. Assuming that the parties reach this bargaining round, the plaintiff will have a credible threat to proceed to judgment. At this stage, the cost of the first stage of litigation is already sunk. Going all the way to judgment would involve an additional cost of only 70 and provide an expected judgment of 100.

Thus, if the parties somehow reach the bargaining round between the two stages, the plaintiff will have a credible threat and will be able to extract a settlement. For the plaintiff, any settlement amount exceeding 30 will be preferable to proceeding to trial. For the defendant, given that she will incur an additional cost of 70 if the case proceeds to trial, any

[7] For a technical presentation of the backward induction principle, see Drew Fudenberg & Jean Tirole, Game Theory 96–99 (1991). For a less technical approach, see David M. Kreps, A Course in Microeconomic Theory 399–402 (1990).

settlement below 170 will be preferable to proceeding to trial. Thus, the parties can be expected to settle somewhere between 30 and 170. If, for example, they have equal bargaining power, we can expect them to settle for 100 (the midpoint amount).

Having determined what will happen in the second round of negotiations, we can now take the analysis one step back in time. At the initial round, before the litigation costs of the first stage are incurred, the parties will recognize that if they reach the second round—after spending 70 each—the plaintiff will have a credible threat to proceed and will extract a settlement. If the parties expect this later settlement amount to be greater than 70, then the plaintiff will have a credible threat to proceed through the first stage. Proceeding through the first stage will cost the plaintiff 70, but it will provide him with the opportunity to extract a settlement exceeding 70. Because the plaintiff has a credible threat to proceed at the initial negotiations round, the parties can be expected to settle at that time.

The settlement amount agreed upon at the initial round will be shaped by the parties' costs at the first stage and by the settlement amount that is expected to be agreed on if the parties were to reach the second bargaining round. Suppose, for example, that the parties have equal bargaining power. Then, as explained, if they were to reach the point between the two stages, they would settle for 100. Given that the first stage litigation costs are 70 for each side, the settlement range in the bargaining that precedes the first stage is between 30 and 170. Parties with equal bargaining power will thus settle before the first stage at the midpoint of the settlement range, that is, for 100.

C. *How Multistage Division Can Further Bolster Credibility*

We have seen that a two-stage division can provide the plaintiff with a credible threat even if, without such division, the plaintiff would not have had a credible threat. We will show now that a division into more than two stages further expands the set of situations in which the plaintiff has a credible threat and thus can extract a settlement offer.

Consider the following example. Continue to assume that the expected judgment is 100, but suppose now that each party's total litigation costs are 300. In this case, even if the litigation had two equal-cost stages, the plaintiff would not have a credible threat to proceed. For even if the parties somehow passed the first stage, the plaintiff would not have a credible threat to proceed. Proceeding into the second stage would cost him 150 and would provide an expected judgment of only 100. Thus, if the parties reached the second stage, the plaintiff would not be able to extract a settlement offer. Anticipating this, the plaintiff will not have a credible threat prior to the first stage of litigation. Thus, in the two-stage case of this example, the plaintiff will not be able to extract any settlement offer.

Suppose, however, that the litigation is expected to be divided into not two but 10 equal-cost stages and that bargaining can take place prior to each stage. In this case, the plaintiff may have a credible threat and may be able to extract a settlement offer.

To see this, let us suppose that both sides have equal bargaining power and let us pursue the analysis by backward induction. What would the parties do at the last round of the bargaining (just prior to the tenth litigation stage) if they reached this point? The plaintiff would have, at this round, a credible threat to proceed to judgment through the last stage. At this round, the cost of proceeding to judgment is 30 (the other 270 are already sunk), and the expected judgment is 100. Given that the plaintiff has a credible threat, and that settlement can save each party a cost of 30, the settlement range is between 70 and 130. Thus, parties with equal bargaining power can be expected to settle prior to the tenth litigation stage for (the midpoint amount of) 100.

Now, let us go one stage back in time. What would the parties do at the bargaining round just prior to the ninth litigation stage, assuming they reached this point? Here, again, the plaintiff has a credible threat to proceed to the next stage. Proceeding to the next stage would cost him only 30 (the cost of one stage of litigation), and—in light of the analysis above—proceeding can be expected to result in a settlement of 100 at the tenth round. Thus, given that the plaintiff has a credible threat at the ninth round, we can calculate the expected settlement amount at this round. A settlement at the ninth round can save each party 30, whereas failing to settle in this round will result in a settlement of 100 at the tenth round. Thus, assuming that the parties reach the ninth round, and assuming that they have equal bargaining power, the parties can be expected to settle in this round for 100.

We can now proceed one stage backwards, to the eighth round, and so forth. Conducting the analysis in this way, we find that, prior to each stage, the plaintiff would have a credible threat to proceed to the next stage and therefore would be able to extract a settlement. And the fact that he would be able to extract this settlement provides credibility to the plaintiff's threat one stage earlier in time.

Specifically, in this example, the plaintiff will have a credible threat to proceed at the outset—prior to the first stage of litigation—and the parties can be expected to settle immediately. The expected settlement amount will be 100, a reflection of the assumption that the parties have equal litigation costs and equal bargaining power.

D. *Not All Threats to Sue Are Credible*

We have illustrated how the divisibility of the litigation process can expand the set of circumstances in which a plaintiff with an NEV suit has a credible threat and can therefore extract a settlement. Before proceeding with the article's general analysis, it is important to emphasize that divisibility will not always provide a credible threat. There are cases of NEV suits in which, no matter how finely the litigation process is divided, the plaintiff does not have a credible threat and cannot extract a settlement offer.

Reconsider the example examined above, in which the expected judgment is 100 and the parties have equal bargaining power. Let us change the parties' litigation costs: assume that the plaintiff's litigation costs are 500 and the defendant's litigation costs are 100. Even assuming a very fine division of the litigation process (into, say, 100 equal-cost rounds), the plaintiff will not have a credible threat to sue.

To see this, let us start by considering the situation of the parties if they were to reach the last, 100th stage. At this stage, the plaintiff will have a credible threat to proceed to judgment; for the expected judgment is 100 and the remaining costs at this point are only 5. Given that the plaintiff has a credible threat, if the parties were to reach the 100th round (which, we will see, does not happen), a settlement will take place. But what is important to notice is the expected settlement amount. Since a settlement at the 100th round saves the plaintiff 5 in litigation costs and the defendant only 1, the settlement range is between 95 and 101. Assuming that the parties have equal bargaining power, the expected settlement at the 100th round is 98, 2 below the expected judgment in the case.

Now, let us go one stage back in time, to the bargaining round before the 99th stage. At this round, the parties will recognize that proceeding one more stage will cost the plaintiff 5 and the defendant 1 and will produce an expected settlement of 98 at the 100th round. Thus, the settlement range at the 99th round is between 93 and 99, and the expected settlement is 96, 4 below the expected judgment in the case.

Continuing backwards in time in similar fashion, we will find that, at any given round, if the parties were to reach this round, it can be calculated that the expected settlement will be lower than the expected settlement that the parties would agree on if they were to reach the next round. In particular, if the parties were to reach the 53rd round, it can be calculated that the expected settlement will be only 4. But this implies that the plaintiff will not have a credible threat to proceed at the 52nd round. For at this point, proceeding through another stage would cost the plaintiff 5 and would produce an expected settlement of only 4. Thus, given that the plaintiff will not have a credible threat to proceed at the 52nd round, the plaintiff will not be able to extract any positive amount from the defendant. And this implies that the plaintiff will not have a credible threat to proceed also at the 51st round, or at any other earlier round.

Hence, divisibility can bolster the plaintiff's strategic position but cannot guarantee that the plaintiff will always have a credible threat. Whether the plaintiff has a credible threat or not depends, as the analysis below will demonstrate, on the relationship between the following parameters: the expected judgment, the plaintiff's litigation costs, the defendant's litigation costs, and the way in which the parties' costs are spread throughout the litigation process. Indeed, a principal purpose of the analysis below is to identify the circumstances under which plaintiffs with NEV suits have or do not have credible threats to sue.

III. The Model

A. *Framework of Analysis*

A party, to whom we will refer as the plaintiff, has a potential suit against another party, to whom we will refer as the defendant. If the suit is pursued all the way to judgment, the plaintiff will win an award of J with probability π; thus, the expected judgment is $W = \pi J$.

Litigation imposes costs, and the total costs incurred by the plaintiff and the defendant, if the suit proceeds all the way to judgment, are C_p and C_d, respectively. Initially, it will be assumed that the allocation of litigation costs is governed by the American rule. Under this rule, each party bears his or her own litigation costs regardless of the outcome of the trial. Section V extends the analysis to the case in which the British rule of fee-shifting applies.

It is assumed throughout that the suit is an NEV suit. That is, we assume that $W < C_p$.

A central feature of the model is the structure of the parties' expenditures over time. It is assumed that C_p and C_d are not incurred all at once, but are spread over a number of stages. Specifically, it is assumed that there are $n > 1$ stages between the filing of a suit and the judgment. At each stage $i = 1, 2, \ldots, n$, each party incurs a fraction of his or her total litigation costs. Let c_p^i and c_d^i denote the costs incurred in stage i by the plaintiff and the defendant, respectively. In addition, define

$C_p^i = \Sigma_{j=i}^n c_p^j$ and $C_d^i = \Sigma_{j=i}^n c_d^j$. C_p^i and C_d^i denote the remaining litigation costs once stage i is reached, that is, what each party has to incur from stage i to judgment.

Because the parties' costs are spread over many stages, bargaining can take place after some but not all litigation costs have been incurred. Specifically, it is assumed that the parties may bargain prior to each of the n stages in which costs may be incurred.

At any given bargaining round, if this round is reached, either the plaintiff or the defendant will make a settlement offer; the identity of the party that can make the settlement offer at any given round is assumed to be determined randomly just prior to that, and each party is equally likely to be the offeror.[8] (Section VI will consider the case in which one party has superior bargaining power and is therefore more likely to be the offeror at any given round.) After the offer is made, the other party may either accept it (that is, a settlement is reached) or reject it. In the event that the offer is rejected, the plaintiff will either drop the suit or proceed through the next stage of litigation, in which case the parties incur another fraction of their litigation costs.

It is assumed that the parties have no commitment mechanisms (such as ones grounded in reputation) that would enable them to bind themselves to a particular cause of action. For the credibility of NEV suits to be an interesting problem, this must be the case. For if the plaintiff could credibly commit himself to go to trial in case the defendant refused to settle, then the plaintiff (even though he has an NEV suit) would always be able to extract a settlement offer. Conversely, if the defendant could commit herself credibly not to settle, the plaintiff would always be discouraged from initiating a suit.

For simplicity, both parties are assumed to be risk-neutral. It is also assumed that π, J, $\{c_p^i\}$, and $\{c_d^i\}$ are common knowledge. Finally, the parties are assumed to have identical discount rates. All money values at periods $i > 0$ are expressed in terms of their present value at $i = 0$. In particular, J, $\{c_p^i\}$ and $\{c_d^i\}$ are all expressed in terms of their present value at $i = 0$.

Before proceeding with the analysis, let us consider what would have happened if n were equal to 1, that is, if litigation costs were all incurred in a lump-sum fashion. In this case, the plaintiff's having an NEV suit implies that the plaintiff would not be able to extract a positive settlement from the defendant. There would be only one possible bargaining point—

[8] In modeling a multiperiod bargaining, it is conventional to assume that in every period each party is equally likely to be the offeror. The alternative conventional formulation, in which the two parties alternate roles, would produce similar results.

just before the single stage of litigation. And, at this point, the defendant would neither propose, nor agree to accept, any positive settlement amount. The defendant will recognize that pursuing the suit would yield a negative payoff for the plaintiff. Therefore, if a settlement is not reached, the plaintiff will drop the suit rather than pursue it. This is true regardless of the relative magnitude of the defendant's costs. In this case, the plaintiff's threat to proceed to trial and to impose litigation costs on the defendant is simply not credible, and this threat therefore cannot extract a settlement. Thus, when litigation costs are indivisible, NEV suits cannot succeed. As we will now examine, however, when litigation costs are divisible, the set of credible threats—and, thus, of the NEV suits that succeed in extracting a settlement—is expanded.

B. The Bargaining

As explained, to analyze the considered game we should reason by backward induction, beginning with the last round of the bargaining. Suppose that the parties reach round n. Regardless of the identity of the party making an offer at this round, the defendant will agree to pay a positive settlement amount only if the plaintiff has a credible threat to proceed to the terminal stage—judgment—in the absence of a settlement. The plaintiff's threat to proceed to judgment will be credible if and only if[9]

$$W \geq c_{\mathrm{p}}^{n}. \tag{1}$$

This condition can be satisfied for an NEV suit if the fraction of the costs borne in the nth stage is small enough, that is, if the costs are sufficiently divisible.

If the plaintiff's threat to proceed is credible, then the defendant will agree to settle, and we should examine the expected value of the settlement. When the plaintiff makes the settlement offer, his offer, denoted by S_{p}^{n}, will equal the highest value that the defendant will be willing to accept:

$$S_{\mathrm{p}}^{n} = W + c_{\mathrm{d}}^{n}. \tag{2a}$$

However, if the defendant is the one who makes the offer, her offer, denoted by S_{d}^{n}, will equal the lowest value acceptable to the plaintiff:

$$S_{\mathrm{d}}^{n} = W - c_{\mathrm{p}}^{n}. \tag{2b}$$

[9] It is assumed throughout that in the event of indifference between proceeding and not proceeding, the plaintiff will proceed.

Since each party is equally likely to be making the offer at round n, the expected value of the settlement, conditional on the parties reaching round n, will be

$$S^n = \tfrac{1}{2}(S_p^n + S_d^n) = W + \tfrac{1}{2}(c_d^n - c_p^n). \quad (3)$$

This settlement will be reached prior to the parties' spending their stage n expenditures.

Now consider rounds prior to the last round. At each such round, the plaintiff's threat to proceed through the following stage of litigation will be credible if and only if the cost he must incur in *the following stage* is lower than the expected settlement amount that he can expect to obtain at the next bargaining round. Thus, if any round $i < n$ is reached, the plaintiff's threat to proceed through the following litigation stage will be credible if and only if

$$S^{i+1} \geq c_p^i. \quad (4)$$

If the plaintiff's threat is not credible, the defendant will not agree to any positive settlement amount, and S^i will be equal to 0. If the plaintiff's threat is credible, the settlement offer depends on whether the plaintiff or the defendant makes the offer, and it will be either

$$S_p^i = S^{i+1} + c_d^i \quad (5a)$$

or

$$S_d^i = S^{i+1} + c_p^i. \quad (5b)$$

The expected value of period i's settlement is thus

$$S^i = S^{i+1} + \tfrac{1}{2}(c_d^i - c_p^i), \quad (6)$$

which yields

$$S^i = W + \tfrac{1}{2}(C_d^i - C_p^i). \quad (7)$$

Notice that expression (7) is the expected settlement *conditional* on the plaintiff's round i threat being credible, which itself depends on the plaintiff's threat being credible in all future periods. Expression (7) says that in any given round, if the plaintiff can credibly threaten to proceed, the parties can be expected to settle in the midpoint of the settlement range. The settlement range for a given round reflects the costs of litigating this stage, as well as the expected settlement in the next round. And since the values of the expected settlements in the next and later rounds are determined in a similar way, it turns out that the settlement range at any given round reflects the expected judgment and the litigation costs that remain.

C. The Outcome

The above backward induction analysis is complete once we reach the first round of the bargaining. The following Proposition summarizes the outcome of the bargaining:

PROPOSITION. (*a*) An NEV suit will be settled if and only if the plaintiff has, before each stage of the litigation process, a credible threat to proceed to the next stage, which is the case if and only if

$$c_p^i \leq W + \tfrac{1}{2}(C_d^{i+1} - C_p^{i+1}) \quad \text{for every } i = 1, 2, \ldots, n. \tag{8}$$

b) If an NEV suit is settled, the settlement will take place at $i = 1$, and its expected value will be

$$S^* = W + \tfrac{1}{2}(C_d - C_p). \tag{9}$$

REMARKS. (*a*) *The Credibility of Threats.* While the bargaining game is resolved instantly, it will end with a positive settlement only if the plaintiff has a credible threat to proceed in all subsequent rounds. If the plaintiff does not have a credible threat in some round *j*, then the defendant will refuse to settle in this round, at which point the plaintiff will drop the suit rather than proceed. The anticipation that this will occur undermines the credibility of the plaintiff's threats in all previous rounds. Consequently, the defendant will not be willing to settle for any positive sum. Therefore, the conditions stated by the Proposition for an NEV suit to succeed are those ensuring that the plaintiff's threats are credible in all rounds.

b) *The Early Resolution.* As one would expect in a bargaining game with perfect information, a settlement, if reached, will occur in the first round of negotiations. This result is reached because there is no asymmetric information in the game and, therefore, the outcome of the game can be anticipated by both parties. Since delay imposes costs, the outcome would not be a settlement in later rounds. For if the parties expected such a settlement, they would be able to structure a settlement in the first round that would make both of them better off.[10]

[10] To account for the possibility of long, costly, pretrial negotiations that produce a settlement in later rounds, asymmetric information must be introduced. In a model with asymmetric information, parties' uncertainty about each other's costs, the expected judgment at trial, or even the length of the game, may delay their reaching a settlement. See Kathryn E. Spier, The Dynamics of Pretrial Negotiation, 59 Rev. Econ. Stud. 93 (1992). For a general discussion of bargaining models with incomplete information, see Martin J. Osborne & Ariel Rubinstein, Bargaining and Markets 91–106 (1990); A. E. Roth, Game Theoretic Models of Bargaining (1985).

c) Divisibility Might Enable NEV Suits to Succeed. The Proposition implies that the divisibility of litigation costs might provide the plaintiff with a credible threat, even though the plaintiff has an NEV suit. There are clearly cases in which, even though $C_p > W$, the conditions for credibility specified in the Proposition are satisfied. The next section will explore the circumstances under which this will happen.

d) Greater Divisibility Can Only Bolster Credibility. The fact that divisibility is the feature that bolsters credibility can be highlighted by examining the effect of increased divisibility. If we take any stage k and break it into two, such that the cost in that stage, c_p^k, is now divided between the two substages, with a bargaining round taking place in between, credibility can only be bolstered. If the plaintiff had a credible threat in round k, he would continue to have such a threat in each of the two subrounds that now exist. If the plaintiff did not have a credible threat in round k, however, the split into two subrounds might produce a credible threat. The cost of pursuing each of the two substages is now just a fraction of the cost of stage k. Consequently, the plaintiff might have prior to each of the two substages a credible threat to proceed even though he did not have a credible threat before the division.[11]

e) The Division of Settlement Gains. Finally, let us comment on the expected settlement amount in those cases in which the divisibility of the litigation process provides the NEV plaintiff with a credible threat. In these cases, the surplus produced by avoiding a trial, that is, the saving of litigation costs, is divided equally between the two parties. This equal division is to be expected, since the model is one of symmetry in the parties' bargaining power: the plaintiff and the defendant have equal opportunities to make offers. This equal division thus would not occur in a case in which the parties have unequal bargaining power, a case that will be examined in Section VI.

IV. Exploring the Conditions for a Credible Threat

The analysis thus far enables us to determine in general whether an NEV suit is credible, and if so, what settlement it can extract. This section takes a closer look at the conditions identified above to explore further how the credibility of the threat depends on the various parameters involved. To explore this question, we shall consider different cases concerning the way in which litigation costs are divided over time.

[11] A formal demonstration that greater divisibility can only bolster credibility is provided in a companion, more technical piece. See Lucian A. Bebchuk, Of Divisibility and Credibility: An Analysis of Negative-Expected-Value Suits (mimeographed, Harvard University 1995).

A. *The Case of Equal-Cost Stages*

We begin by focusing on a simple case in which the parties' costs are distributed uniformly across the litigation stages. That is, there are n equal-cost stages, with $c_p^i = C_p/n$ and $c_d^i = C_d/n$. Later, we will extend the analysis to include patterns in which the costs are spread unevenly over time.

1. The Conditions for Credibility

COROLLARY 1. In the case of equal-cost stages, the plaintiff's threat is credible and an NEV suit will succeed if

(i) $W \geq C_p/n$,

and

(ii) $W + \frac{n-1}{2n}(C_d - C_p) \geq C_p/n.$

Proof. Condition (i) is clearly necessary, as it must hold for the threat to be credible at $i = n$. When (i) is satisfied, condition (ii) (that the threat at $i = 1$ is credible) turns out to be sufficient. Together, the two conditions guarantee that there is no intermediate round in which the threat is not credible. To verify this, note that for all i, $C_p/n \leq S^{i+1}$ holds if

$$W + \frac{n-i}{2n}(C_d - C_p) \geq C_p/n.$$

If $C_p \leq C_d$, then condition (i) is sufficient to make this inequality satisfied for all i. If $C_p > C_d$, then the left-hand side increases with i, so condition (ii) guarantees that the inequality is satisfied. Q.E.D.

Corollary 1 states that, in the considered case of equal-cost stages, it is sufficient to have credible threats in the first and last rounds. This is not because the other rounds are irrelevant but rather because credibility in these intermediate rounds is implied by the two "boundary" conditions of credibility at $i = 1$ and $i = n$.

The conditions specified in Corollary 1 illustrate well how greater divisibility bolsters credibility. Observe that, as costs become more divisible, that is, as n grows larger, the two conditions in Corollary 1 are more likely to hold. In particular, when n becomes very large, these two conditions collapse into the condition specified in the following Corollary.

COROLLARY 2. When the litigation process has a sufficiently large number of equal-cost stages, the condition for the plaintiff's threat to be credible and for the NEV to succeed can be approximated by

$$W + \tfrac{1}{2}(C_d - C_p) > 0. \qquad (10)$$

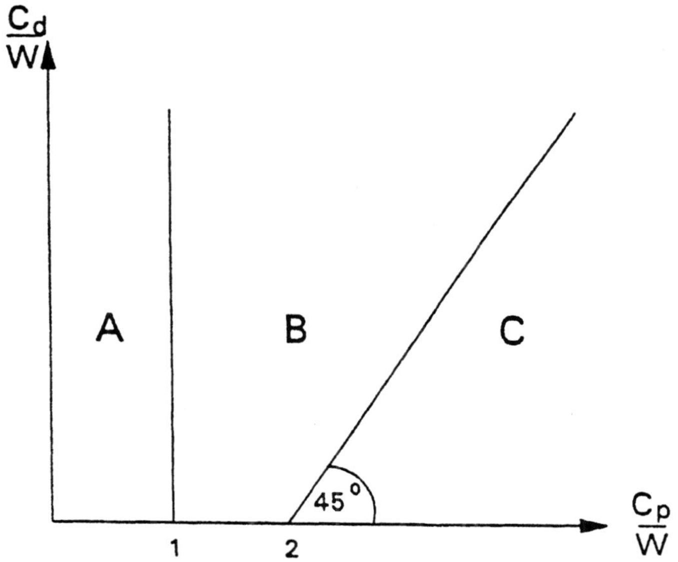

FIGURE 1

The analysis to follow examines condition (10) to draw conclusions about how the success of an NEV suit depends on the parameters of the case.

2. The Relative Magnitude of C_p and W

A suit is an NEV suit if $C_p/W > 1$. Condition (10) implies that the plaintiff's threat is credible and an NEV suit will therefore succeed if

$$\frac{C_p}{W} < 2 + \frac{C_d}{W}. \tag{11}$$

This condition can be illustrated in Figure 1, which partitions the universe of cases into three areas. Area A contains all the suits that have a positive expected value ($C_p < W$). All the suits in areas B and C are NEV suits. Area B contains all the NEV suits in which the plaintiff can succeed in obtaining a positive settlement amount. Area C contains the NEV suits in which the plaintiff does not have a credible threat to proceed and therefore will not succeed in extracting a settlement.

Finally, it is worth noting that, regardless of the size of C_d, an NEV suit will succeed as long as $C_p < 2W$. In particular, even if the defendant has no litigation costs (that is, $C_d = 0$), a settlement will take place whenever the plaintiff's litigation costs are no more than twice the expected judgment.

3. The Relative Magnitude of C_p and C_d

Condition (10) indicates that an NEV suit will succeed if

$$\frac{C_p}{C_d} < 1 + 2\frac{W}{C_d}. \quad (12)$$

That is, no matter how small the stakes are, the plaintiff will be able to extract a positive settlement offer as long as his litigation costs are lower than the defendant's ($C_p/C_d < 1$). This result fits our intuition. When $C_p < C_d$, the defendant has "more to lose" from litigation than the plaintiff. This helps the plaintiff's position and enables him to extract a settlement.

B. On the Case of Nonuniform Division

Subsection *A* explored the conditions for credibility in situations in which costs are distributed uniformly across stages. This subsection considers situations in which some stages are more costly than others. For simplicity, we will consider below only the simple case in which the parties have identical "time profiles"—that is, the distributions of their costs over time have the same form. Thus, my assumption is that $c_p^i/C_p = c_d^i/C_d$ for every i, and let us denote by θ_i the fraction of total costs that is incurred by each side in stage i. The more complex case, in which each party has a different time profile, is analyzed in a companion, more technical paper.[12]

Applying the Proposition established in Section III to this case, we find that for threats to be credible, the following conditions must hold:

$$\theta_i C_p \leq W + \tfrac{1}{2}\left(\sum_{j=i+1}^{n} \theta_j\right)(C_d - C_p) \quad \text{for every } i = 1, 2, \ldots, n. \quad (13)$$

If we assume that the cost in each stage i is sufficiently small, then we can establish, by the reasoning used earlier, the following Corollary:

COROLLARY 3. In the identical time profiles case, if the plaintiff's litigation costs in each stage are sufficiently small, then the condition for the plaintiff's threat to be credible can be approximated by

$$W + \tfrac{1}{2}(C_d - C_p) > 0. \quad (10)$$

[12] See *id.* It is worth noting that the conditions for credibility identified in this companion work for the case of nonidentical time profiles differ from the conditions specified in Corollary 3 below for the case of identical time profiles.

REMARK. The condition for credibility that Corollary 3 identifies is the same as the one that applies to the uniform distribution case. Thus, all the conclusions reached in Subsection *A*, concerning the effects of the different parameters, hold also in the case in which stages have different costs but the parties still have identical time profiles.

V. THE BRITISH RULE

The analysis has thus far assumed that the allocation of litigation costs is governed by the American rule, that is, that each party bears his or her litigation costs regardless of the outcome at trial. We now turn to consider the success of NEV suits under the British rule, which requires the losing party to reimburse the winner's costs.

Under the British rule, the plaintiff incurs no litigation costs if he wins but must bear both parties' litigation costs if he loses.[13] Since the probability of the plaintiff losing is $(1 - \pi)$, his expected litigation costs are $(1 - \pi)(C_p + C_d)$. As before, my focus is on such NEV suits. Under the British rule, a plaintiff's suit has a negative expected value if the expected litigation costs of $(1 - \pi)(C_p + C_d)$ exceed the expected judgment of W, or, equivalently, if

$$C_p + C_d > \frac{W}{1 - \pi}. \tag{14}$$

The analysis of the previous sections can easily be adjusted to the British rule case. Specifically, litigation under the British rule is equivalent to litigation under the American rule with the adjustment that the expected judgment in the British rule case is not W but rather W^*, defined as[14]

$$W^* = W + \pi C_p - (1 - \pi)C_d. \tag{15}$$

Thus, the analysis of whether an NEV suit will succeed can proceed in the same way as in the previous section, with W^* replacing W. As before, for an NEV suit to succeed, the plaintiff must have a credible threat in all rounds. Consequently, the conditions for a credible threat are the n conditions stated in (8), with W^* replacing W.

[13] It is assumed throughout the analysis in this section that reimbursement under the British rule takes place only if the case reaches the judgment stage. In a model of multiround litigation, there is another version of the British rule that may be considered, in which the defendant is entitled to reimbursement if the plaintiff drops the suit after the litigation commenced. The analysis below can be adjusted to apply to this alternative version.

[14] This equivalence was first identified in Bebchuk, *supra* note 3.

In the identical time profiles case, the conditions for credibility reduce to the two conditions stated in Corollary 1, with W^* replacing W. When the litigation costs are sufficiently divisible, these two conditions can be approximated by

$$W + \pi C_p - (1 - \pi) C_d > 0 \tag{16a}$$

and

$$W + (\pi - 1/2)(C_d + C_p) > 0. \tag{16b}$$

A sufficient condition for (16a) and (16b) to be satisfied is that

$$\pi > \frac{C_d}{C_p + C_d} \tag{17a}$$

and

$$\pi > 1/2. \tag{17b}$$

Thus, in the identical time profiles case, if $\pi > 1/2$ and $C_d < C_p$, the plaintiff's threat will be definitely credible. These conditions, it should be emphasized, are sufficient but not necessary for credibility, and the plaintiff might thus have a credible threat even if they are not met.

VI. Extensions and Generalizations

A. Cost-Free Stages

The analysis has thus far assumed that in each stage of the bargaining process the plaintiff must incur some (possibly very small) cost. That is, there is no stage in which the defendant incurs some cost whereas the plaintiff incurs no cost. This subsection examines the consequences of having such a "cost-free" stage. The main result is that the existence of a cost-free stage might bolster the credibility of the plaintiff's threat, and it may thus expand the set of cases in which a plaintiff with an NEV suit will be able to extract a settlement offer.

To see this, consider a case in which there is a cost-free stage k. Suppose that at some round after k, there is no credible threat to proceed.[15] Without the cost-free stage, the lack of a credible threat in a subsequent

[15] If the threats to proceed to judgment are credible in all rounds subsequent to k, then the existence of the cost-free stage would not have the bolstering effect that is identified below.

round would completely eliminate the plaintiff's ability to extract a settlement at an earlier stage. However, even though there is no credible threat after stage k, in the bargaining just prior to the cost-free stage k the plaintiff will have a credible threat. In this stage, the plaintiff has nothing to lose by proceeding to the next round, even if the expected settlement at the next round, S^{k+1}, is 0 (that is, the suit will be dropped at $k + 1$). Thus, if round k is reached, the defendant will be willing to settle, to avoid her stage k litigation costs (recall, the defendant does incur some costs at stage k). Moving backwards to round $k - 1$, the plaintiff might now be able to make a credible threat even if $c_p^{k-1} > 0$, because S^k is now positive. Thus, the plaintiff will be able to extract a settlement offer if he has a credible threat in all rounds prior to k, that is, if

$$c_p^i \leq \tfrac{1}{2}\left(\sum_{j=i+1}^{k} c_d^j - \sum_{j=i+1}^{k} c_p^j\right) \quad \text{for every } i = 1, 2, \ldots, k - 1. \tag{18}$$

Even though threats after stage k are not credible, and the plaintiff cannot threaten to pursue his case all the way to judgment, he might still have prior to stage k credible threats to pursue the case up to the cost-free stage k and drop it then. If condition (18) holds, and the plaintiff's threats have credibility only because of the presence of a cost-free stage, then a settlement will be reached in round 1, and the expected settlement amount will be

$$S^* = \tfrac{1}{2}\left(\sum_{j=1}^{k} c_d^j - \sum_{j=1}^{k} c_p^j\right). \tag{19}$$

Notice that the expected settlement in this case is independent of the expected judgment, W. This occurs because possibility of reaching the judgment stage is never relevant to the parties' considerations. When credibility is gained only because of the presence of a cost-free round, the settlement amount will depend only on the relative sizes of the parties' litigation costs up to that stage.[16] If the defendant's cumulative expenses are expected to exceed the plaintiff's cumulative expenses all the

[16] This result generalizes the analysis of Rosenberg & Shavell, *supra* note 6. Their analysis focusses on the special case in which the very first stage of the process is a cost-free stage for the plaintiff. They conclude that the plaintiff will be able to extract a settlement reflecting the defendant's litigation costs at that initial round.

way up to the cost-free stage, then the plaintiff will have a credible threat in all the rounds preceding the cost-free stage and will be able to extract a positive settlement amount.[17]

B. Different Bargaining Power

The analysis has thus far supposed that the parties have equal bargaining power. This assumption implies that in each round, each party has an equal chance of being the one that makes the take-it-or-leave-it offer.

The model can be adjusted, however, to apply to the case in which the parties might differ in their bargaining power. To cover this general case, suppose that in each round the plaintiff makes the take-it-or-leave-it offer with probability α and the defendant makes the take-it-or-leave-it offer with probability $1 - \alpha$. Since a take-it-or-leave-it offer gives the party offering it a bargaining advantage, the cases in which $\alpha < 1/2$ are those in which the defendant has stronger bargaining power, and the cases in which $\alpha > 1/2$ are those in which the plaintiff has stronger bargaining power.

With this adjustment, the analysis can proceed as in Sections III–IV. In particular, it can be established that the plaintiff will have a credible threat and will be able to extract a settlement offer if

$$c_p^i \leq W + \alpha C_d^{i+1} - (1 - \alpha) C_p^{i+1} \quad \text{for every } i = 1, 2, \ldots, n. \tag{20}$$

In this case, the expected settlement amount will be

$$S^* = W + \alpha C_d - (1 - \alpha) C_p. \tag{21}$$

In the case of identical time profiles, and with sufficient divisibility, the conditions for credibility can be approximated by the condition

$$W + \alpha C_d - (1 - \alpha) C_p > 0, \tag{22}$$

[17] How would the analysis change under the British rule? If fee-shifting takes place only in the event that judgment is rendered, there will never be fee shifting in this situation, because the plaintiff will not proceed beyond stage k. Therefore, the parties' costs are the same as under the American rule, and the analysis above carries over. However, if the other version of the British rule applies (under which, if the plaintiff drops his case at any point, the plaintiff has to reimburse the defendant for the costs she has already incurred) the outcome is different. Here, even if the plaintiff has a stage in which $c_p^k = 0$, proceeding to the next stage is no longer cost-free for the plaintiff. His real cost of proceeding, given that he expects to drop subsequently the suit, will equal the defendant's cost at that stage. Thus, there are no cost-free stages under this version of the British rule.

or, after rearrangement,

$$\alpha > \frac{C_p - W}{C_p + C_d}. \tag{23}$$

Note that the right-hand side of (23) is always positive and smaller than one, and that its positive value can be very small in the case of some NEV suits. Thus, as long as the plaintiff has some chance of making an offer (α is positive), some NEV suits can succeed. As can be expected, an increase in α (which represents an increase in the plaintiff's power) expands the set of circumstances in which the plaintiff will be able to extract a settlement offer and raises the expected value of the settlement amount. Conversely, a decrese in α contracts the set of circumstances in which an NEV can succeed.

Thus, as long as the plaintiff has any bargaining power ($\alpha > 0$), the important conclusions obtained earlier remain: divisibility of litigation costs continues to play a major role in shaping the outcome of settlement bargaining; NEV suits might consequently succeed; and greater divisibility can only bolster the credibility of the plaintiff's threat and thus make more likely the success of his NEV suit.

VII. Concluding Remarks

A. *The Wider Set of Credible-Threat Cases*

One contribution of this article is to point out that plaintiffs have credible threats—and can extract settlement offers—in a much wider set of circumstances than has been suggested by the prior economic literature.

The implications of the analysis in this respect are quite substantial because there are numerous cases in which defendants know (or suspect with a high probability) that the plaintiff has an NEV suit in his hands. To start with, in the universe of small-stakes cases, there are numerous instances in which defendants recognize that the small amount at stake is smaller than the litigation costs needed to pursue it. In addition, there are likely to be many high-litigation-costs cases in which the amount at stake is not small but the needed litigation costs would clearly be large enough to exceed it.

Under the prior understanding of the subject, plaintiffs with such NEV suits face great difficulties in getting any amount from the defendant. On this understanding, if the plaintiff cannot bind himself to pursue the suit (which would likely be the case in any one-shot situation), the plaintiff would lack a credible threat.[18] To be sure, defendants in such cases might still pay plaintiffs because of the defendants' moral convictions or their concern for reputation, but they would have no "economic" reason to pay.

The analysis of this article, however, suggests a very different picture for the numerous cases in which plaintiffs have, and can be recognized to have, an NEV suit. If the litigation process in these cases is sufficiently divisible, this divisibility might by itself provide plaintiffs with a credible threat, and it therefore might provide the defendant with an "economic" reason to pay. Thus, the force of the law in these cases is significantly greater than has been suggested by prior analysis.

B. The Key Role of Divisibility

A key feature of the situation that was analyzed is that litigation costs are incurred not all at once but in stages. Thus, the practical importance of the conclusions depends on whether such divisibility commonly exists. The following observations suggest that this is indeed the case.

One important part of litigation costs is payment for lawyers' time. By definition, lawyers' investment of time is incurred as time goes by. That this might lead to divisibility of litigation costs is especially visible in the common case in which lawyers charge hourly fees. In that case, the plaintiff's litigation costs would go up with each hour that the lawyer works (and would not increase—a cost-free period—in each hour in which the lawyer does not work).

In addition, divisibility may be facilitated by the fact that rules of procedure often separate the litigation process into stages. It is not uncommon for the legal process to involve considerable delays between stages. This enables the parties to engage in extensive bargaining between stages, when some of their costs have yet to be accrued.[19]

[18] According to the prior literature on the subject, this is generally true unless the case falls into the special circumstances identified in the Rosenberg-Shavell analysis (*supra* note 6 and Section I*B*).

[19] It may be worth noting the analysis in the model assumes not only that the litigation process is divided into stages but also that bargaining can take place between these stages. Surely, if the defendant could commit herself not to receive or entertain a settlement offer, she would in fact eliminate the plaintiff's ability to extract a settlement in an NEV suit. However, such a commitment is equivalent to a commitment to reject any settlement offer made by the plaintiff. And the focus of this article (see Section III*A*) is on situations in which mechanisms for such a commitment are unavailable (as are mechanisms that commit the plaintiff to go to trial).

In this connection, it is worthwhile noting that the law does not facilitate the making of commitments to reject settlement offers. In particular, Rule 1.4 of the American Bar Association Model Rules of Professional Conduct requires lawyers to keep their clients reasonably informed, so as to permit the clients to make decisions regarding the representation. The

Divisibility, we have seen, can play a major strategic role in settlement bargaining. This article has sought to highlight and analyze this role. Economic analysis in the field of litigation and settlement should recognize and pay close attention to the strategic importance of divisibility.

official comment to that rule specifies that lawyers must pass any settlement offer that they receive to the side they represent.

Statutory Interpretation

COLUMBIA LAW REVIEW

VOL. 86 MARCH 1986 NO. 2

PROMOTING PUBLIC-REGARDING LEGISLATION THROUGH STATUTORY INTERPRETATION: AN INTEREST GROUP MODEL

*Jonathan R. Macey**

INTRODUCTION

We live in a time of widespread dissatisfaction with the legislative outcomes generated by the political process.[1] Too often the process seems to serve only the purely private interests of special interest groups at the expense of the broader public interests it was ostensibly designed to serve. While the current distrust of government represents a major shift away from the dominant public perception of "government as helper"[2] that existed from the time of the New Deal until the present decade, the current attitude is not new by any means. As Professor Sunstein has observed, "[t]he problem of faction has been a central concern of constitutional law and theory since the time of the American Revolution."[3] In fact, a basic justification offered by the framers for their new Constitution centered around its usefulness in controlling interest groups.[4]

Academics, however, have only recently applied the tools of

* Assistant Professor of Law, Emory University School of Law and Senior Academic Member, Emory Law & Economics Center. A.B. Harvard University, 1977; J.D. Yale Law School, 1982. I thank Bruce A. Ackerman, Harold J. Berman, Evan H. Caminer, William J. Carney, Philip P. Frickey, David D. Haddock, Howard O. Hunter, Henry G. Manne, William T. Mayton, Richard A. Posner, and Cass R. Sunstein who contributed useful ideas and made helpful suggestions on a previous draft of this Article. I also received valuable comments from participants at an Emory Law School Faculty Colloquium, a University of Virginia Legal Studies Workshop, and a University of Chicago Law & Economics Workshop. Jack Winsbro, Emory Law School class of 1987, provided valuable research assistance.

1. See Sunstein, Interest Groups in American Public Law, 38 Stan. L. Rev. 29, 29 (1985).

2. This conception of government is also known as the public interest theory of legislation. It is a theory more often assumed than articulated. Posner, Theories of Economic Regulation, 5 Bell J. Econ. & Mgmt. Sci. 335, 335 n.1 (1974). The public interest theory of legislation was developed and formally set forth in the economics literature by Baumol and Pigou. See W. Baumol, Welfare Economics and the Theory of the State (2d ed. 1965); A. Pigou, The Economics of Welfare (4th ed. 1950). Baumol and Pigou perceive legislation as designed to correct imperfections in the functioning of the market economy. For example, free-rider problems might thwart private efforts at obtaining optimal pollution control. Baumol and Pigou would argue that the government can increase societal wealth by enacting legislation that taxes those who pollute.

3. Sunstein, supra note 1, at 29.

4. See infra notes 92–94 and accompanying text.

microeconomics to predict the effect such groups will have on the lawmaking process.[5] According to the so-called interest group or economic theory of legislation,[6] market forces provide strong incentives for politicians to enact laws that serve private rather than public interests, and hence statutes are supplied by lawmakers to the political groups or coalitions that outbid competing groups.[7] The widespread acceptance of interest group theory has led to suspicion about much of what Congress does, creating, in turn, a climate hospitable to judicial interference with legislative outcomes.

Much has been written of the circumstances under which courts should strike down legislative enactments.[8] As a practical matter, however, the Constitution is rarely used to invalidate a statute, especially an economic one.[9] This judicial restraint has led economists to conclude erroneously that the concept of an independent judiciary is only an illusion and that federal judges, as agents of the legislative branch, simply "enforce the 'deals' made by effective interest groups with earlier

5. The economics of legislation applies the laws of supply and demand to the provisions of economic legislation. "The 'interest group' theory asserts that legislation is a good demanded and supplied much as other goods, so that legislative protection flows to those groups that derive the greatest value from it, regardless of overall social welfare . . . ." Posner, Economics, Politics, and the Reading of Statutes and the Constitution, 49 U. Chi. L. Rev. 263, 265 (1982).

6. The development of the economic theory of legislation can be traced to two seminal publications: J. Buchanan & G. Tullock, The Calculus of Consent (1966), and Stigler, The Theory of Economic Regulation, 2 Bell J. Econ. & Mgmt. Sci. 3 (1971). The theory is now almost universally accepted among economists. See Kalt & Zupan, Capture and Ideology in the Economic Theory of Politics, 74 Am. Econ. Rev. 279 (1984).

The theory is also referred to as "public choice" theory and as "rent-seeking." Public choice has its antecedents in the literature of game theory. Rent-seeking refers to the attempt to obtain economic rents (i.e., payments for the use of an economic asset in excess of the market price) through government intervention in the market. A classic example of rent-seeking is a corporation's attempt to obtain monopolies granted by government. Such monopolies allow firms to raise prices above competitive levels. The increased income is economic rent from government regulation.

7. As interest group theory has developed, it has gained increasing academic support. See R. Posner, The Federal Courts 271 (1985) (describing "the shift in scholarly thinking about legislation from a rather naive faith in the public-interest character of most legislation to a more realistic understanding of the importance of interest groups in the legislative process"). The shift away from a public interest view of the legislative process is not tied to any particular political perspective. The interest group theory of legislation is "[e]spoused by an odd mixture of welfare state liberals, muckrakers, Marxists, and free-market economists." Posner, supra note 2, at 335.

8. One commentator has noted that "the question of the legitimacy of judicial review has claimed more discussion and more analysis than any other issue in constitutional law." P. Bobbitt, Constitutional Fate 3 (1982); see, e.g., A. Bickel, The Least Dangerous Branch (1962).

9. See Landes & Posner, The Independent Judiciary in an Interest-Group Perspective, 18 J.L. & Econ. 875, 895–901 (app.) (1975). Between 1789 and 1972, only 97 acts of Congress were held unconstitutional. Id. at 895.

legislatures."[10]

The reluctance of article III courts to strike down interest group legislation as unconstitutional finds its source in two seeemingly irreconcilable components of American constitutional theory, both derived from the separation of powers embodied in articles I, II, and III.[11] The first is the system of checks and balances, which is intended to raise the decision costs of government by requiring that the various branches share power.[12] The second is the basic constitutional premise, embodied in article I, that the legislature has the power to make law. These two constitutional principles, taken together, imply that judicial interpretation is consistent with the constitutional scheme only if two conditions are satisfied: the interpretive act must (1) result in making legislation more public-regarding by serving as a check on legislative excess, and it must (2) not intrude on the constitutional authority of the legislature to make law.

Condition Two ensures that the Constitution's allocation of the lawmaking function to the legislature will remain intact,[13] while Condition One reflects the constitutional premise that federal courts improve the operation of the democratic process by serving as a structural check on the tendency of Congress to engage in factionalism.[14] Condition One is justified by the need to mitigate the harmful effects of interest group domination of the political process. Condition Two is justified by the basic principle of democratic theory that the power to make law ultimately should reside in representative institutions such as

10. Id. at 894; see also id. at 877 ("[T]he independent judiciary is . . . essential to the interest-group theory of government.").

11. See Aranson, Gellhorn & Robinson, A Theory of Legislative Delegation, 68 Cornell L. Rev. 1, 2 (1982) (first three articles of the American Constitution "plainly embod[y] a system of separation of powers"). The Federalist Nos. 47 and 48 (J. Madison) articulated the justification for the version of separation of powers ultimately adopted in the Constitution. The arguments for separation of powers "find their most complete expression in Montesquieu." Aranson, Gellhorn & Robinson, supra, at 2.

12. See Aranson, Gellhorn & Robinson, supra note 11, at 2–3; Sunstein, supra note 1, at 44.

13. When a federal court declares an act of Congress unconstitutional, it is encroaching on the legislature's authority to make law. A. Bickel, supra note 8, at 16–17. This observation caused Bickel to dismiss Federalist 78, which advocates giving judges the power of judicial review. See The Federalist No. 78, at 468 (A. Hamilton) (C. Rossiter ed. 1961) ("[W]here the will of the legislature, declared in its statutes, stands in opposition to that of the people, declared in the Constitution, the judges ought to be governed by the latter rather than the former.").

Whatever one's position may be on the question of judicial review, judicial review is not now a major obstacle to special interest legislation. See Mashaw, Constitutional Deregulation: Notes Toward a Public, Public Law, 54 Tul. L. Rev. 849, 849 (1980).

14. For the purposes of the argument that follows, it is important to distinguish between Condition One, which is an implied condition inherent in the structure of the Constitution, and Condition Two, which is explicit in article I. This distinction strengthens the argument that the judicial function of serving as a check on the legislature (Condition One) is an institutional by-product of the act of judging.

Congress.[15]

These conditions appear to be irreconcilable. On one hand, any action by a court to check the legislature appears to intrude on the constitutional authority of the legislature to make law. On the other hand, a refusal to check the legislature seems to be an unconstitutional abdication of the judiciary's obligation to curb legislative excess.

As developed in this Article, these two constitutional features may be reconciled by recognizing that the constitutional requirement that the judiciary serve as a check on Congress' excesses often is fulfilled by the very act of statutory interpretation itself. The judiciary, using traditional methods of statutory interpretation, *inevitably* checks legislative excess by serving as a mechanism that encourages passage of public-regarding legislation and impedes passage of interest group bargains.[16] In other words, there need not be overt confrontation between the judicial branch and the legislative branch in order for checking and balancing to take place. As shown below, checking legislative abuse is an institutional by-product of the judiciary's traditional role as interpreter of statutes in the resolution of specific legal disputes.

When called upon to interpret a statute, a court has three alternatives. First, it can look beyond the terms of the statute and seek to enforce the terms of the deal between the interest group and the legislature. This "legislation-as-contract" method of statutory interpretation is the approach advocated recently by Judge Frank Easterbrook.[17] I will argue that this approach to statutory interpretation is illegitimate because it violates the first condition described above. Specifically, it denies the federal judiciary its proper role in the constitutional scheme as a check on factionalism and legislative excess.

Conversely, a court can identify what it perceives to be a special interest group bargain and strike the deal down on constitutional grounds. Variations of this activist approach to non-public-regarding statutes are advocated by Jerry Mashaw,[18] Bernard Siegan,[19] and Richard A. Epstein,[20] among others.[21] While this approach satisfies the

15. See A. Bickel, supra note 8, at 19.

16. See infra notes 129–44 and accompanying text.

17. See Easterbrook, The Supreme Court, 1983 Term—Foreword: The Court and the Economic System, 98 Harv. L. Rev. 4 (1984).

18. Mashaw, supra note 13.

19. B. Siegan, Economic Liberties and the Constitution (1980).

20. Epstein, Taxation, Regulation, and Confiscation, 20 Osgoode Hall L.J. 433, 438 (1982); Epstein, Toward a Revitalization of the Contract Clause, 51 U. Chi. L. Rev. 703 (1984); Epstein, Needed: Activist Judges for Economic Rights, Wall St. J., Nov. 14, 1985, at 32, col. 4.

21. See, e.g., Gunther, The Supreme Court, 1971 Term—Foreword: In Search of Evolving Doctrine on a Changing Court: A Model for a Newer Equal Protection, 86 Harv. L. Rev. 1, 20–21, 23 (1972); Michelman, Politics and Values or What's Really Wrong with Rationality Review?, 13 Creighton L. Rev. 487, 500–02 (1979); Sunstein, Naked Preferences and the Constitution, 84 Colum. L. Rev. 1689 (1984).

terms of Condition One by constraining the legislature, as Alexander Bickel observed, it violates Condition Two by usurping the lawmaking prerogatives of Congress.[22]

Finally, there is what is best called "the traditional approach," which, as the name implies, refers to the classic, time-honored methods of statutory interpretation that judges actually employ to decide cases. This approach differs from Easterbrook's approach in that it counsels judges to interpret statutes based on what the statutes actually say, rather than on what the judges believe the bargain was between the interest group and the legislature. The traditional approach, I will argue, encourages more public-regarding legislation by frequently transforming statutes designed to benefit narrow interest groups into statutes that in fact further the public's interests. Unlike the other two approaches, this one enables the judiciary to serve as a check on Congress without interfering with Congress' constitutionally granted authority to make law.

Important constraints upon the legislature, this Article argues, derive from aspects of the judicial process other than judicial nullification of legislative enactments on constitutional grounds. Given the constraint on Congress that derives from the interpretive act of judging, the reluctance of the judiciary to declare statutes unconstitutional does not suggest that the judicial process is not a significant obstacle to the pursuit of special interest legislation. Although legislative acts are only infrequently declared unconstitutional, more subtle constraints are imposed upon the legislature by the judicial process itself. The thesis of this Article, then, is that the very act of statutory construction often transforms statutes designed to benefit narrow interest groups into statutes that in fact further the public interest.

After describing the economic theory of legislation in Part I, this Article considers alternative theories of statutory interpretation as they relate to rival constitutional theories. Using economic analysis, the Article posits that the Constitution was designed to serve public rather than private interests and explains how the traditional method of statutory interpretation is an integral part of this design. The final section suggests ways in which judges can improve the operation of the legislative process through the traditional approach to statutory interpretation.

I. The Economic Theory of Legislation

Interest group theory treats statutes as commodities that are purchased by particular interest groups or coalitions of interest groups that outbid and outmaneuver competing interest groups.[23] The cur-

22. See A. Bickel, supra note 8, at 16 (The "ineluctable reality" is that "judicial review is a counter-majoritarian force in our system.").

23. See supra note 6.

rency through which laws are bought and sold consists of political support, promises of future favors, outright bribes, and whatever else politicians value.[24]

The arguments in this Article do not hinge on an assumption that all legislation is best explained as self-serving behavior narrowly construed. Indeed, they assume not only that laws are passed for a wide variety of reasons, but also that, as a general matter, it is impossible for judges to reconstruct the complex array of motives that prompted the passage of a particular statute. Some legislation serves the public interest by maximizing society's welfare from an economic perspective.[25] Some legislation serves legitimate, public-regarding, noneconomic goals.[26] Other legislation seems to defy any rational explanation and can only be based on "public sentiment rather than on either an objective weighing of demonstrable pros and cons or on cartel-like pressures for redistributing wealth."[27] Hence, some legislation serves the public interest, while some can only be described as "amorally redistributive."[28] One purpose of the third branch is to serve as a natural filter through which public-regarding legislation[29] passes undisturbed, while

24. See Landes & Posner, supra note 9, at 877. A subtle yet fundamental confusion exists in the public choice literature regarding the precise identity of the suppliers of interest group legislation. If one imagines simple supply-and-demand curves for interest group legislation, everyone agrees that it is the interest groups themselves that are making the demands for favorable legislation. The as yet unanswered question pertains to the supply side of the equation. According to Landes and Posner, interest group legislation is supplied by the legislators. See id. McCormick and Tollison argue, however, that it is the public that supplies the favorable legislation; the legislators act only as brokers in the transaction, taking a commission for their efforts. See R. McCormick & R. Tollison, Politicians, Legislation and the Economy: An Inquiry into the Interest-Group Theory of Government (1981).

25. See Posner, supra note 5, at 270.

26. See id.

27. Id. at 271.

28. Id. at 268. Posner uses the term "amorally redistributive" not to refer to every legislatively imposed transfer of wealth from one group to another, but only to wealth transfers enacted by legislators that are inefficient in the Kaldor-Hicks sense; that is, if it makes one group better off but makes some other group worse off by an even greater amount. It would be efficient for the second group to pay the first group in order to prevent the transfer from being made. Because of the impossibility of making interpersonal comparisons of utility, it is difficult to specify with certainty which wealth transfers are amorally redistributive and which are morally redistributive.

29. The term "public-regarding" is taken from Mashaw, supra note 13, at 868. One of the central arguments made in this Article is that courts are not competent to judge whether a particular statute is public-regarding or not because statutes designed to benefit narrow interest groups are often couched in public interest language. See infra notes 47–48 and accompanying text. If a precise, easily applied definition of the term "public-regarding" could be devised, then a constitution would best serve the public if it simply required that judges declare all statutes not meeting this test to be unconstitutional. It is precisely because it is so difficult to decipher legislative motive and to determine public-regardingness that constitutional theory is an interesting and difficult discipline.

Although the phrase "public-regarding" is admittedly rather vague, it is not com-

rent-seeking legislation is cast aside. But this filtering process must be accomplished in such a way that the courts do not intrude on the law-making authority of the legislature. To see how this filtering process works to decrease the relative incidence of amorally redistributive legislation requires an understanding of the process by which special interest groups tend to dominate the legislative process.

A. *The Assumptions of the Economic Theory of Legislation*

The high information and transaction costs associated with representative government enable interest groups to obtain wealth transfers from society as a whole to themselves. Information costs are incurred by an individual or group in the process of discovering the impact of an issue on the wealth of that individual or group, as well as the costs of identifying similarly situated individuals or groups who are likely to share the costs of obtaining political action.[30] Transaction costs, which include, inter alia, the cost of overcoming free-rider incentives,[31] are the costs of organizing these similarly situated individuals into effective political coalitions.[32] Pre-existing coalitions and groups of allied individuals will be more effective than dispersed individuals in obtaining transfers of wealth from society as a whole to themselves.

Because some groups enjoy lower information and transaction costs than others, they will succeed in obtaining wealth transfers to themselves at the expense of other groups.[33] These differential costs are the sine qua non of rent-seeking. It is costly to acquire and disseminate information about these wealth transfers, and any gains from ef-

---

pletely devoid of meaning. Legislation may be said to be public-regarding if it serves some purpose other than obtaining for particular legislators the pecuniary advantage of the political support of some narrow interest group, even if this purpose is the transfer of wealth from one group to another.

Public-regardingness is best thought of in procedural terms. If the statute in question is the result of a reified, deliberative congressional process in which conceptions of the public good were considered, then the statute is public-regarding. If, however, the statute simply represents legislative acquiesence to raw political power, it is not public-regarding. The advantage of this process-oriented approach to public-regardingness is that it avoids the pitfall of selecting among statutes solely on the basis of outcome. At the same time, if a statute promotes the general welfare or if it serves the interest of a group that is not well organized and has no access to the political process (such as poor people), it is likely that the statute will be found to be public-regarding under a process-based definitional approach. On the other hand, it is improbable that a statute that distributes wealth on an ad hoc basis to a group that is well organized and can fend for itself in the marketplace without legislative protection is public-regarding. Regulations that protect commercial banks from competition or erect barriers to entry to the profession of optometry fall into this category. In any event, the analysis presented in this Article applies regardless of what conception of public-regardingness is adopted.

30. R. McCormick & R. Tollison, supra note 24, at 17.

31. See M. Olson, The Rise and Decline of Nations 18 (1982).

32. R. McCormick & R. Tollison, supra note 24, at 16.

33. Id. at 25 ("[D]ifferential organization costs among individuals and groups are the basis for wealth redistribution . . . .").

forts in this regard must be shared with everyone. Consequently, rational members of the public will not try to acquire information about these transfers even though it would be in the interests of the public as a whole that they do so.[34]

This analysis suggests that politicians can advance their own private interests by identifying and helping enact legislation that transfers wealth from groups with high information and transaction costs to groups with low information and transaction costs. Interest groups will be willing to "pay" politicians up to the amount of the wealth transfer for such brokerage services.[35]

B. *The Mechanics of Interest Group Theory*

The major implications of interest group theory are that legislation transfers wealth from society as a whole to those discrete, well-organized groups that enjoy superior access to the political process, and that government will enact laws that reduce societal wealth and economic efficiency in order to benefit these economic groups. The economic theory of legislation does not predict that all laws will enrich the few at the expense of the many, but it does predict that this will be the dominant outcome and that there will be a trend in this direction.[36]

Interest groups influence the political process by such overt methods as promises of political support, campaign contributions, and outright bribes, and by slightly more subtle methods such as investing in congressional retirement funds.[37] Another common method of influence is paying congressmen honoraria for speaking engagements.[38] Interest groups also impose their will upon the general public by controlling the flow of information to legislators on particular issues.[39] This control of information, particularly regarding complex issues, en-

34. See M. Hayes, Lobbyists and Legislators: A Theory of Political Markets 69–70 (1981) ("Members of the mass public will generally find it irrational to obtain the information necessary to identify their interests on any given issue and moreover will be ill equipped to interpret any information they do obtain . . . ."); RePass, Issue Salience and Party Choice, 65 Am. Pol. Sci. Rev. 389 (1971) (Voters generally show interest in only one or two issues of immediate concern to them but remain apathetic and uninformed on most others.).

35. See M. Hayes, supra note 34, at 18–25.

36. The principal exponent of this trend is Mancur Olson, who has attempted to demonstrate this implication empirically. See M. Olson, supra note 31, at 75–117.

37. See G. Easterbrook, What's Wrong With Congress?, The Atlantic, Dec. 1984, at 57, 70–72.

38. See id. Payments for speaking engagements are desirable because they do not have to be filtered through a campaign fund. The payments can be quite substantial: in 1983, 11% of United States senators earned more from speaking fees than from their salaries; 21% earned more than $50,000 from speaking fees. Id.

39. See N. Ornstein & S. Elder, Interest Groups, Lobbying and Policymaking 75–76 (1978); see also G. Wilson, Interest Groups in the United States 113–14 (1981) (quoting senator remarking on the essential function of lobbying groups in supplying information, particularly on technical subjects).

ables interest groups "to distort congressmen's thinking on an issue—normally all an interest group needs to achieve its ends."[40] Those affected by the regulation (the general public) cannot overcome the free-rider problem that prevents the presentation of information favorable to the public interest.[41] Thus, the cost of obtaining and disseminating information about legislative issues often results in passage of special interest legislation by legislators who really believe they are acting in the public interest.[42]

The economic theory of legislation predicts that laws are likely to benefit the few at the expense of the many, because no one has an incentive to enact laws that benefit the people in general.[43] This is the classic "free-rider" problem that inevitably plagues public interest legislation in a representative democracy.[44] Because the benefits of such legislation are spread among everyone in the population, individual members of the public lack sufficient incentives to promote public interest laws since all the costs of such promotion must be absorbed by the promoters themselves. Hence, the laws that are enacted will tend to benefit whichever small, cohesive special interest groups lobby most

40. G. Easterbrook, supra note 37, at 70.

41. See M. Olson, supra note 31, at 17–19.

42. As such, the popular use of words like "deal" and "contract," which appear in the academic literature to describe interest group type legislation, is somewhat misleading. The economic theory of legislation describes statutes the passage of which represents a conscious decision by legislators to support legislation favoring some interest group as a quid pro quo for political or financial support as well as statutes for which legislative support is obtained because legislators erroneously believe the statute will advance the public interest. While terms such as "deal" and "contract" are misleading for these latter statutes because they imply the existence of an agreement when in fact none exists, the terms are not wholly inaccurate. To achieve passage of either type of statute, interest groups must spend resources in the legislative arena in exchange for favorable legislation. If interest groups do not spend resources on political or financial support, then they must spend resources on things such as "information campaigns," "fact sheets," and "position papers" to achieve their goals.

The analysis of the interplay between statutory interpretation and interest group behavior set forth in this Article applies with particular force to situations where legislators act with benign motives yet produce amorally redistributive statutes. In such cases, the traditional process of statutory interpretation provides legislators with useful information as to the true consequences of their actions. See infra notes 145–54 and accompanying text; see also infra notes 129–33 and accompanying text (describing traditional approach to statutory interpretation).

43. M. Olson, supra note 31, at 41–47.

44. See P. Aranson, American Government: Strategy and Choice 79–82 (1981). By definition, the benefits from public spirited legislation fall on the public generally. As such, it is extremely unlikely that any individual will find it advantageous to devote privately the necessary resources to obtain such legislation. Those members of the public who spend nothing will have a free ride at the expense of those who invest in public-regarding legislation. Since any gain goes to the group as a whole, those who contribute nothing benefit just as much as those who have contributed a great deal. Thus it pays for each individual to do nothing and to hope that others will make an effort upon which he can "free ride."

effectively.[45] To use a familiar illustration, everyone who buys milk is harmed by milk price supports, but the small cohesive lobby of milk producers nonetheless is able to obtain these subsidies.[46]

The most disturbing feature of interest group theory is that the cost to the legislature of supplying favorable laws to special interest groups appears to be quite low. All of the tangible expenses incurred in the process are borne by the taxpayer. The only costs to the legislators consist of the loss of support from individuals and groups who are aware that they are harmed by the legislation, plus the opportunity costs of the legislators' time.

Where it is difficult to discern the nature of the wealth transfer embodied in a particular statute, loss of public support will be a small part of a legislator's cost calculation. Interest groups and politicians have incentives to engage in activities that make it more difficult for the public to discover the special interest group nature of legislation. This often is accomplished by the subterfuge of masking special interest legislation with a public interest facade.[47] To the extent that this can be carried out successfully, the political costs to legislators of enacting special interest legislation will decline.

Thus, statutes generally can be divided into three distinct categories. The first are those designed to advance some public purpose, such as protection of the environment or providing for national defense. Besides these public interest statutes, there are two types of special interest statutes—"open-explicit" statutes and "hidden-implicit"

45. This is because small groups can more easily resolve the free-rider problems described above. See M. Olson, supra note 31, at 41 ("Members of 'small' groups have disproportionate organizational power for collective action . . . ." (emphasis omitted)); Posner, supra note 2, at 345 ("[T]he fewer the prospective beneficiaries of a regulation, the easier it will be for them to coordinate their efforts to obtain the regulation.").

46. See 7 U.S.C. § 1446(c), (d) (1982) (authorizing milk price supports). Even regulations that have long been thought to accomplish such worthy goals as improving the environment recently have been shown to benefit special interests. See B. Ackerman and W. Hassler, Clean Coal/Dirty Air 44–48, 98–100 (1981); Kalt, The Costs and Benefits of Federal Regulation of Coal Strip Mining, 23 Nat. Resources J. 893, 908–09 (1983); Maloney & McCormick, A Positive Theory of Environmental Quality Regulation, 25 J.L. & Econ. 99 (1982); Pashigian, The Effect of Environmental Regulation on Optimal Plant Size and Factor Shares, 27 J.L. & Econ. (1984).

47. "[T]he question [of] whether the legislative action has a public purpose is always one that the legislature purports to have decided affirmatively." Mashaw, supra note 13, at 868.

Legislators have incentives to search for issues in which the winners (special interest groups) are easily identified, while the losers (the general polity) cannot be easily identified. See R. McCormick & R. Tollison, supra note 24, at 17. By masking the true purpose of a statute and claiming that it is actually in the public interest, legislators and interest groups lower the cost of passing statutes that transfer wealth to themselves. Cf. M. Olson, supra note 31, at 35 (Passage of costly legislation protecting the professions has been facilitated by the "susceptibility of the public to the assertion that a professional organization . . . ought to be able to determine who is 'qualified' to practice the profession.").

statutes. Open-explicit statutes are naked, undisguised wealth transfers to a particular, favored group. By contrast, hidden-implicit statutes are couched in public interest terms to avoid the political fallout associated with blatant special interest statutes.

Hidden-implicit statutes exist because the political costs of enacting them is lower than the political costs of enacting open-explicit statutes. We observe open-explicit statutes because they are less ambiguous and therefore more likely to be enforced in precisely the way the relevant interest groups prefer. As described below, in deciding whether to lobby for one type of statute or another, interest groups must make a trade-off between the higher political costs associated with open-explicit statutes and the greater uncertainty associated with hidden-implicit statutes.[48]

Where statutes are accompanied by extensive committee hearings and debates that extol the advantages of the statute from the public perspective, reliance on such public statements is likely to lead judges to take the legislature at its word, and to interpret the statute in the way the legislature said that it wanted. Thus, the traditional reliance on legislative history raises the political cost of special interest legislation by increasing the probability of nullification. This in turn forces the legislature to be explicit about the deals it is making, if it wants to be sure those deals will ultimately be enforced.

II. The Judiciary As Enforcer of Legislative Deals: Legislation as Contract

The previous section set forth the basic premises of the economic theory of legislation. This theory of legislation makes strong predictions about the efficacy of interest groups in determining outcomes generated by ordinary political processes. But the legislative process cannot be analyzed in a vacuum. The Constitution plays a large role in determining the total mix of interest group and public interest statutes. After all, the Constitution establishes the procedure for enacting statutes, and thus formulates the rules of the game for politicians and interest groups. This section considers one view, developed by Landes and Posner, that the Constitution was designed to promote interest group domination of the legisative process and that the judiciary, by enforcing the deals struck by such groups, was part of this design. The section then describes an approach to statutory interpretation developed by Judge Easterbrook that complements this theory by providing a guide for judicial conduct that provides assurance to interest groups that the "deals" they strike will be enforced.

The historical champion of the interest group theory of the Constitution was Charles Beard, whose well-known view was that the Constitution was an antimajoritarian act in which a small number of well-

48. See infra notes 136–44.

organized economic interest groups "successfully strangled our popular revolution."[49] Writing in the Beardian vein, William Landes and Richard Posner claim that the establishment of an independent federal judiciary is evidence of the triumph of special interest groups at the constitutional level.[50] They assert that "the independent judiciary is not only consistent with, but essential to, the interest-group theory of government."[51]

Viewing legislation as the result of bargains struck between special interest groups and lawmakers,[52] Landes and Posner observe that if the parties to a contract believe that the bargain they are striking is unenforceable, the value of that contract will be significantly diminished. Thus, special interest groups and politicians have a strong incentive to ensure the enforceability of the deals they make.[53] According to Landes and Posner, the independent judiciary facilitates interest group activity by providing the "stability or continuity necessary to enable interest-group politics to operate in the legislative arena."[54] The ability of legislators to offer special interest groups permanent, rather than short-term, deals increases demand for the legislators' services and increases the income of legislators who enact such rules. Thus, according to Landes and Posner, interest group theory best explains why the framers enacted article III. Because the costs imposed by an independent judiciary in the form of uncertainty are less than the benefits to the legislature of longevity, value-maximizing legislators and interest groups will thus prefer an independent judiciary. The insight of

49. This description of Beard's outlook on the Constitution is contained in Ackerman, The Storrs Lectures: Discovering the Constitution, 93 Yale L.J. 1013, 1015 (1984).

50. See Landes & Posner, supra note 9, at 894 (The Court's role is to enforce the special interests protected by the Constitution.).

51. Id. at 877. The assertion that an independent judiciary is essential to the operation of interest groups or to the interest group theory of government is demonstrably false. As Gordon Tullock has shown, interest groups thrive under dictatorships, which of course do not have independent judiciaries. See Tullock, Rent Seeking in Dictatorships (unpublished manuscript) (on file at the offices of the Columbia Law Review). Perhaps Landes and Posner mean that rent-seeking is less costly in governmental systems in which the judiciary is independent than in governmental systems in which it is not. They do not provide any support for this hypothesis, however, nor is there support for this theory in the literature. See id.

52. See Landes & Posner, supra note 9, at 877 (presenting a model in which "legislation is 'sold' by the legislature and 'bought' by the beneficiaries of the legislation [and] [p]rivate sales, and other private contracts, carry legal sanctions for non-performance"); see also id. at 879 (describing the buying and selling by Congress of legislation for dairy industry).

53. Id.

54. Id. at 878. This stability or continuity enables a member of the current legislature to capture his full share of the present value of an entitlement scheme designed to run in perpetuity, even if he plans to leave the legislature at the end of the current session. See Aranson, Judicial Control of the Political Branches: Public Purpose and Public Law, 4 Cato J. 719, 731–32 (1985) (describing the Landes & Posner theory).

Landes and Posner was that the existence of an independent judiciary is not necessarily inconsistent with an interest group theory of politics.[55]

Landes and Posner observe that the judiciary enhances the efficacy of interest group statutes by providing the stability, continuity, and assurance of enforcement necessary to maximize the value of legislative enactments that transfer wealth to interest groups. They fail, however, to provide any model of judicial behavior beyond judicial reluctance to declare legislation unconstitutional. The legislation-as-contract approach espoused by Judge Frank Easterbrook provides the model of judicial behavior that the Landes-Posner model lacks. Judge Easterbrook suggests that a good judge is one who interprets the law in the way the legislature *really meant* for it to be interpreted, not in the way that the legislature *says* that it is to be interpreted.[56] This is referred to

55. As Landes and Posner themselves recognize, their explanation of article III fails to account fully for all of the constraints imposed by an independent judiciary on deals enacted by Congress. Their test is empirical, not theoretical, and their sole measure of judicial independence is the number of times that the Supreme Court has nullified acts of Congress as unconstitutional. Landes & Posner, supra note 9, at 895. In their own words: "Nullification is an extreme example of judicial unreliability, and for this reason is likely to be deficient as an overall measure of the costs of judicial independence." Id.

The incidence of judicial nullification of legislation on nonconstitutional grounds dwarfs the incidence of judicial nullification on constitutional grounds. See infra text accompanying notes 129–72 (cataloguing nonconstitutional ways that an independent judiciary thwarts the deals made between interest groups and the legislature); see also G. Calabresi, A Common Law for the Age of Statutes (1982):

> Constitutional adjudication and use of the passive virtues, though not unusual reactions to anachronistic laws, are not the most common judicial responses. The traditional judicial weapon in dealing with statutes has always been interpretation of what the written law means. Just as the increasing prevalence of statutes gave a new impetus . . . to constitutional adjudication, so interpretation has been totally recast in the twentieth century to increase its capacity to deal with statutorification of the American legal system.

Id. at 31.

There are several additional shortcomings to the measure of judicial independence that Landes and Posner use. When a federal court declares a state statute unconstitutional, it will be clear that the same statute would also be unconstitutional if enacted by Congress. Thus, observed nullifications of state statutes signal Congress that its authority to make deals is limited. As Landes and Posner themselves point out: "If nullification of a *particular* law can be anticipated, legislators and groups are likely to be deterred from enacting that law in the first place, thereby saving the costs of enactment." Landes & Posner, supra note 9, at 895 n.41 (emphasis added).

Landes and Posner also observe that when lower court rulings "gut the law in question, a Supreme Court bent on nullification may accomplish this purpose simply by not granting certiorari." Id. As they point out, this phenomenon also tends to bias their study so as to provide a deficient measure of the costs of judicial independence on legislative deals. In sum, the test of constitutionality that Landes and Posner use to measure judicial independence does not come close to measuring the true extent of the constraints imposed by the third branch on legislative deal-making.

56. See Easterbrook, supra note 17, at 14–18, 42–60. Actually, Easterbrook advocates a dual approach to statutes. He argues that judges should interpret public interest statutes in the traditional manner advocated in this Article. But when judges are called upon to interpret special interest statutes, he believes that judges "should take the

as the "legislation-as-contract" approach to statutory interpretation because it calls upon the judge who is interpreting a statute to engage in the same sort of interpretive exercise as the judge who is interpreting a private contract between two parties.[57] Judge Easterbrook concludes that the quality of a judge construing a statute is determined by his ability to seek out and enforce the nature of the original agreement between the legislature and the special interest group.[58]

Recognizing that many legislative special interest bargains are enacted as legislation with a public interest mask (what I call "hidden-implicit legislation"), Judge Easterbrook suggests three methods of discovering the rent-seeking purpose of such legislation. According to him, once judges discover this purpose they will be able to interpret the statutes "correctly." The first method is to inquire whether the statute is general or specific. The more general the statute, the more likely it is to be in the public interest; the more detailed the law, the more evidence of interest group compromise.[59] Courts should look for such clues as limitations on entry, subsidies from one group to another, and the inability of the parties to contract around the provisions of a new statute.[60] Finally, Judge Easterbrook urges his fellow judges to look at the process by which the particular bill became law. Of particular interest are the identities of the lobbyists and even "[w]hat deals were struck in cloakrooms."[61]

Following his chosen approach to statutory interpretation, Judge Easterbrook evaluates Supreme Court cases of the 1983 term, praising or condemning them on the basis of whether they conform to his own interpretation of the terms of the original bargains between the legislators and the interest group that produced the statutes.[62] *Norfolk Redevelopment and Housing Authority v. Chesapeake & Potomac Telephone Co.*[63]

---

beady-eyed contractual approach." Id. at 15. Easterbrook is dismayingly vague as to the normative basis for his approach to statutory construction. Implicit in his argument that judges should treat special interest statutes like contracts is the erroneous premise that article III judges are agents of the legislature. See id. at 60 ("Judges must be honest agents of the political branches."). Judges are not agents of the legislature: they are agents of the people. See The Federalist No. 78, at 464–72 (A. Hamilton) (C. Rossiter ed. 1961) ("[W]here the will of the legislature, declared in its statutes, stands in opposition to that of the people, declared in the Constitution, the judges ought to be governed by the latter rather than the former . . . ."); id. at 468. In fact the reason federal judges are given life tenure rather than periodic appointments renewable by the executive or the legislature is to avoid "improper complaisance" to whichever branch was given such power. Id. at 471.

57. Easterbrook, supra note 17, at 15.

58. See id. at 60; see also supra note 42 (discussing use of the word "contract" in reference to legislation).

59. See Easterbrook, supra note 17, at 60.

60. Id. at 17.

61. Id.

62. Id. at 54–58.

63. 464 U.S. 30 (1983).

wins praise because "the Court did not set off in search of the 'purpose' of the legislators. The Court instead looked to see what coalition of interests had obtained the statute."[64]

On the other hand, Judge Easterbrook criticizes the Court for its decision in *Securities Industry Association v. Board of Governors (Bankers Trust)*,[65] because it failed to recognize the nature of the special interest group bargain incorporated in the Glass-Steagall Act.[66] While a persuasive argument can be made that the Glass-Steagall Act is in fact a special interest statute,[67] one cannot reach this conclusion by examining either the statute itself[68] or its legislative history.[69] The statute is framed conspicuously in public interest terms, its stated purpose being to promote bank safety and to eliminate conflicts of interest in the delivery of banking services.[70]

Judge Easterbrook, however, counsels judges to ignore the stated objectives of the Glass-Steagall Act and to decide instead whether the plaintiff, a special interest group called the Securities Industry Association, could properly claim "the spoils of victory in the legislative process."[71] Because the Court evaluated the Glass-Steagall Act as a public interest statute rather than as an interest group statute, Judge Easterbrook calls it "the most troubling economic decision of the Term."[72]

---

64. Easterbrook, supra note 17, at 54.

65. 104 S. Ct. 2979 (1984).

66. The Glass-Steagall Act is the popular name for the Banking Act of 1933, ch. 89, 48 Stat. 162 (codified in scattered sections of 12 U.S.C.); see Easterbrook, supra note 17, at 57–58.

67. See Macey, Special Interest Groups Legislation and the Judicial Function: The Dilemma of Glass-Steagall, 33 Emory L.J. 1, 15–21 (1984).

68. Sections 16, 20, 21, and 32 of the Glass-Steagall Act, Pub. L. No. 73-66, 48 Stat. 162 (codified in scattered sections of 12 U.S.C.), deal with the separation of commercial banking and investment banking. These sections are "usually the intended reference when the name Glass-Steagall Act is used." Note, A Banker's Adventures in Brokerland: Looking Through Glass-Steagall at Discount Brokerage Services, 81 Mich. L. Rev. 1498, 1501 n.12 (1983).

69. See Operation of the National and Federal Reserve Banking Systems: Hearings on S. 71 Before the Subcomm. on Banking of the Senate Comm. on Banking and Currency, 71st Cong., 3d Sess. (1931); 75 Cong. Rec. 9887 (1932) (remarks of Sen. Glass, principal drafter of the Glass-Steagall Act); id. at 9913 (remarks of Sen. Bulkley). Senator Bulkley's remarks "have been treated as authoritative by courts, in part because he was addressing Congress on the subject of the separation of commercial and investment banking at the specific request of the chairman of the Senate Banking Committee, Senator Glass." Note, A Conduct-Oriented Approach to the Glass-Steagall Act, 91 Yale L.J. 102, 105 n.19 (1981).

70. The most complete analysis of the legislative intent behind the Glass-Steagall Act, and a classic example of what this Article calls the "traditional" method of statutory interpretation is contained in Investment Co. Inst. v. Camp, 401 U.S. 617 (1971).

71. Easterbrook, supra note 17, at 57.

72. Id. The Court's decision in fact seems benign. The narrow holding did not itself bar the entry of commercial banks into the business of investment banking, and the resultant competition in the delivery of investment banking services undoubtedly benefitted the public. The Court held that commercial paper was a "security" for the

The flaw in Judge Easterbrook's approach is that it diminishes the legitimate role of the judiciary as a check on legislative excess. Where a special interest group has negotiated a low-cost, hidden-implicit deal with the legislature, there is no reason why it should receive the benefits of the more expensive open-explicit deal. Indeed, to award such benefits encourages a shift toward the vague sort of legislation that increases the information costs the public faces in evaluating legislation. As compared with the traditional approach, the legislation-as-contract approach leads not only to more special interest legislation, but also to legislation that is less honest as to its special interest antecedents. The allocation between the two types of interest group statutes—open-explicit and hidden-implicit—will depend on the relative costs to the interest groups of getting these statutes enacted. As the cost of hidden-implicit deals goes up, the relative value of open-explicit deals goes up.[73] Thus, under the traditional approach to statutory interpretation, there will be not only less special interest legislation than under Judge Easterbrook's approach, but also the percentage of special interest deals that are hidden-implicit will decline because of the higher probability that they will not be enforced by the judiciary.[74]

---

purposes of the Glass-Steagall Act. See *Bankers Trust*, 104 S. Ct. at 2981. This holding appears to be consistent with the theory that the federal judiciary acts as enforcer of interest group bargains, because the holding endorsed the position of the plaintiff—the Securities Industry Association—which was a special interest group trying to keep commercial banks from competing with investment banks for commercial paper business. The Court, however, left open the question of whether the defendant, Bankers Trust Company, was "underwriting" commercial paper as that term is defined by Glass-Steagall. See id. at 2992 n.12. Subsequently, the Board of Governors of the Federal Reserve System held that commercial banks could engage in a wide variety of sales activities without being deemed to be underwriting. This ruling made it possible for commercial banks to enter the commercial paper market and compete with investment banks. See Nash, Fed. Backs Sale of Paper, N.Y. Times, June 5, 1985, at D1, col. 6. Recently, however, Bankers Trust Company's sale of commercial paper was held to be a "distribution" of securities for the purposes of the Glass-Steagall Act, and the bank was prohibited from selling commercial paper. See Securities Indus. Assoc. v. Federal Reserve Board, 1986 Fed. Sec. L. Rep. (CCH) ¶ 92,456 (D.D.C. Feb 4, 1986). Even if the district court's decision is ultimately upheld, which is subject to doubt, Bankers Trust was able to enter the commercial paper market and compete for nine years. Thus, the traditional approach used by the Supreme Court permitted, at least for a time, the entry of commercial banks into the commercial paper market. Judge Easterbrook's approach, which counsels seeking out and enforcing the special-interest group bargain, would arrive at an opposite conclusion, resulting in less competition for the delivery of investment banking services.

73. This is because open-explicit and hidden-implicit legislation are substitutes for one another. Interest groups will seek the type of legislation that provides the greatest benefit for the least cost. If hidden-implicit and open-explicit deals are equally likely to be enforced in the courts, then there will be no open-explicit deals because the political cost of such deals is higher.

74. As courts become more unreliable as enforcers of hidden deals, fewer such deals will be made. Some interest groups will find it advantageous to make open deals. Others will abandon the legislative process as a source of income, and resort to market processes. The switch from the legislature to the market is clearly preferable, since all

Even if the legislation-as-contract approach could be legitimized, it is beyond the competence of the judiciary to conduct the kind of inquiry advocated by Judge Easterbrook.[75] Judges interpret statutes; they are not investigative reporters. The idea that Congress passes statutes "with a wink," and that courts should dig behind the scenes to find out the "real story," is both unwarranted and dangerous. The danger lies in the fact that judges may mistakenly interpret public interest statutes as special interest statutes. When this occurs, some interest group receives a windfall at the expense of the public. Where judges make mistakes in the other direction, interpreting a special interest statute as being in the public interest, the public rather than an interest group receives the windfall.

On the other hand, when an interest group bargain is explicit, courts should uphold the bargain. It is well settled that it is illegitimate for judges to impose their own values in place of those of the legislature, because such a substitution thwarts Congress' constitutional authority to make law. The legislature, and not the judiciary, is the forum through which societal preferences are aggregated. Statutory decisions are legitimate only when judges enforce the law as enacted by the legislature. This general maxim that judges must respect the legislature's will is subject only to the judicial power to review statutes for constitutional infirmity.[76]

The interest group nature of a statute will not generally be available on the statute's face or in the legislative history.[77] The tobacco price support system, which is a patent wealth transfer to the tobacco industry, is the exception and not the rule. The interest group roots of most other laws are not so clear.

This ambiguity is not accidental. The cost of a statute that is a pure wealth transfer to some well-organized special interest group is much higher than the cost of a wealth transfer that is masked in public interest terms. For this reason, many of the statutes that Judge Easterbrook identifies as unambiguous private interest statutes are couched just as unambiguously in public interest terms.[78] Where a statute is

market transactions are efficient while many legislative deals are not. Market transactions (transactions characterized by voluntary, uncoerced exchange) are efficient because both parties to such a transaction are by definition at least as well off as they were prior to the transaction or else the transaction would not have occurred. Government regulation, which by definition is coercive, often will not be efficient in this sense. Cf. Posner, An Economic Theory of the Criminal Law, 85 Colum. L. Rev. 1193, 1195 (1985) ("[T]he market is a more efficient method of allocating resources than forced exchange.").

75. See Posner, supra note 5, at 272.

76. See Marbury v. Madison, 5 U.S. (1 Cranch) 137 (1803) (establishing the power of judicial review).

77. See infra text accompanying notes 133–44.

78. See, e.g., supra notes 65–70, infra notes 136–44 and accompanying text (discussing Judge Easterbrook's treatment of Silkwood v. Kerr-McGee Corp., 464 U.S. 238

framed in public interest terms it should be treated by courts as a public interest statute.

By taking Congress at its word when interpreting the terms of a statute, courts inevitably serve as obstacles to the goals of the rent-seekers. Although Judge Easterbrook sees this as a failure of the judiciary, it is, I will argue, precisely the result the constitutional structure was designed to produce. The very presence of an independent judiciary serves as an inevitable and legitimate obstacle to the interest group's objectives. The value to the public of this obstacle will be significantly diminished if judges begin to act as investigative reporters or economists rather than as judges.

The understanding that much lawmaking is the outcome of struggles among interest groups does not lead to the conclusion that the lawmaking process should be unbridled. True, the economic approach to legislation clearly suggests that statutes can be viewed as contracts between special interest groups and Congress, but it does not follow from this that it is the job of article III judges to substitute microeconomic principles for statutory language and legislative history in order to seek out and enforce interest group bargains.

III. An Alternative Vision: Private-Regarding Statutes and Public-Regarding Constitutions

Judge Easterbrook's approach complements the conclusion of Landes and Posner that the framers intended article III judges to act as agents of the legislature by enforcing the interest group bargains forged there. Nonetheless, there is clear evidence that the Constitution was designed to discourage special interest legislation through institutions such as the independent judiciary. This section will argue that the purpose of the constitutional separation of powers is to raise the very costs that Judge Easterbrook advocates lowering. A fundamental precept of constitutional law is that the separation of powers built into the first three articles is "designed to limit the power of self-interested groups or factions by ensuring that government power would be exercised in accordance with certain predetermined constraints."[79] While

(1984), and Securities Indus. Ass'n v. Board of Governors, 468 U.S. 137 (1984), both of which treated statutes that are couched unambiguously in public interest terms and that are deemed by Easterbrook to be special interest statutes). While I happen to agree with Judge Easterbrook's assertion that these statutes are in fact special interest statutes, the fact remains that there is no proof of this assertion.

79. Sunstein, supra note 21, at 1691; cf. The Federalist No. 48, at 308 (J. Madison) (C. Rossiter ed. 1961) (discussing the particular tendency of legislatures to usurp the powers of the other branches). The most complete expression of the value of the separation of powers in this regard is contained in B. de Montesquieu, The Spirit of the Laws 151–52 (T. Nugent trans. 1949). There is evidence that Montesquieu's ideas influenced the framers. See, e.g., The Federalist No. 9, at 76 (A. Hamilton) (C. Rossiter ed. 1961) (quoting Montesquieu); id. No. 78, at 466 (A. Hamilton) (citing Montesquieu); id. No. 47, at 301 (J. Madison) (same).

the framers' view of the nature and sources of legislation may have been less economically sophisticated than our own, it can hardly be said that they were unaware of the problems posed by coalitions of interest groups. In fact, as Gordon Wood has pointed out,[80] and as *The Federalist Papers* themselves make clear,[81] the views of the framers were influenced to a significant extent by the problem of factions that plagued the state legislatures of the day.

A. *The Activist Approach*

Starting with the premise that legislation is or should be public-regarding, the activists would empower the courts to declare unconstitutional legislation that subordinates the interests of the public to the interests of a special interest group.[82] I will not attempt to summarize the voluminous literature rejecting this approach,[83] because since 1937 courts have refused to nullify economic regulation on constitutional grounds.[84]

The activists' view of the Constitution as vesting in the federal courts broad authority to strike down special interest statutes has not explained why judges are any better than legislators at regulating. The activist theory embodies the premise that legislators frequently use their lawmaking power to serve private rather than public interests. Yet without any theory to predict how judges would deal with the unbridled power to declare special interest statutes unconstitutional, the activist theory is incomplete.

Alexander Bickel argued that, however telling the criticisms heaped upon the legislative process may be, alternative processes and

80. See G. Wood, The Creation of the American Republic 273–82 (1969); see also Mashaw, supra note 13, at 858 ("It is commonplace that the 'founding fathers' did not wholly trust legislatures." (citations omitted)).

81. See The Federalist No. 48, at 310–13 (J. Madison) (C. Rossiter ed. 1961). Interestingly, Hamilton in Federalist 17 and Madison in Federalist 45 express the fear that the states will be more likely to encroach on the national government than the national government on the states. See id. No. 17, at 118–22 (A. Hamilton); id. No. 45, at 288–94 (J. Madison). History has proven them wrong.

82. The spokesman-in-chief for the opposition view that preaches judicial restraint was Alexander Bickel. See A. Bickel, supra note 8, at 16–17; Ackerman, supra note 49, at 1014. Bickel's criticism of judicial activism was based on the fact that legislators represent a majoritarian force in society, because they are elected, whereas federal judges, who are merely appointed, do not. Any judicial attempt to invalidate an act of Congress is thus subject to what Bickel termed the "counter-majoritarian difficulty."

83. See, e.g., McCloskey, Economic Due Process and the Supreme Court: An Exhumation and Reburial, 1962 Sup. Ct. Rev. 34.

84. G. Gunther, Cases and Materials on Constitutional Law 472 (11th ed. 1985) ("The modern Court has turned away due process challenges to economic regulation with a broad 'hands off' approach. No such law has been invalidated on substantive due process grounds since 1937." (citation omitted)); Mashaw, supra note 13, at 849 ("The Supreme Court has said . . . often and loudly ever since 1937 [that] '[s]ubstantive due process' is dead where 'economic' issues are concerned.").

rival institutions such as the judiciary are likely to be even worse at ordering public preferences. After all, the Constitution places the power to make law in the legislature, and allowing the courts to trump legislative acts on constitutional grounds would usurp this authority:

> [N]othing can finally depreciate the central function that is assigned in democratic theory and practice to the electoral process; nor can it be denied that the policy-making power of the *representative institutions*, born of the electoral process, is the distinguishing characteristic of the system. Judicial review works counter to this characteristic.[85]

Thus, just as Judge Easterbrook's approach to statutory interpretation is likely to be ignored because it gives too much power to Congress, the activist approach, by ignoring the separation of powers, is likely to be ignored because it usurps congressional authority and creates harmful friction between the branches. Because the federal judiciary depends on Congress for its jurisdictional authority (indeed the lower federal courts depend on Congress for their very existence),[86] it is simply unrealistic to think that Congress would permit the courts systematically to eradicate the rents it receives from interest groups.

The implication is that—quite apart from the real or imagined merits of judicial activism—it is highly improbable that the Constitution will be the major instrument courts use to mitigate the problem of special interest legislation.[87] This does not mean that the power of judicial review ought never to be used; but rather that it is a complement to, rather than a substitute for, the traditional judicial techniques discussed below.[88]

B. *The Constitution as a Public-Regarding Document*

Inasmuch as the public is often adversely affected by special interest legislation, it has a strong incentive to devise institutional mechanisms—like constitutions—that make passage of such legislation more

85. A. Bickel, supra note 8, at 19 (emphasis added).

86. See U.S. Const. art. III, § 1 ("The judicial Power of the United States, shall be vested in one Supreme Court, and in such inferior Courts as the Congress may from time to time ordain and establish."); see also P. Bator, P. Mishkin, D. Shapiro & H. Wechsler, Hart and Wechsler's The Federal Courts and the Federal System 11 (2d ed. 1973) ("[I]t seems to be a necessary inference from the express decision that the creation of inferior federal courts was to rest in the discretion of Congress that the scope of their jurisdiction, once created, was also to be discretionary.").

87. The framers, by vesting the power to make law in the legislature, did not envision the courts exclusively using the Constitution as a weapon with which to hack away at interest group deals. It is well known that the Constitution does not even specifically confer upon judges the power of judicial review. See G. Gunther, supra note 84, at 13; see also The Federalist No. 78, at 470 (A. Hamilton) (C. Rossiter ed. 1961) ("[I]t is not with a view to infractions of the Constitution only that the independence of the judges may be an essential safeguard against the effects of occasional ill humors in the society.").

88. See supra notes 129–44 and accompanying text.

difficult.[89] Because of the information and transaction costs described above,[90] mechanisms to constrain interest group behavior must be installed, if at all, at the constitutional level.[91] In the legislative arena, interest group pressures are likely to prevail in a struggle to implement constraints on the efficacy of rent-seeking.

Before one can gauge whether a constitution is designed to promote the general welfare of the public by impeding the efficacy of interest groups or to advance the interests of particular groups or classes within society, it is necessary to establish guidelines by which the "public-regardingness" of a constitution can be evaluated. There are two ways to make such an evaluation. The first is to examine the stated intentions of the framers as those intentions are preserved in the public record. A second, more objective means of evaluating a constitution is to examine the actual effects of the document on interest group behavior. If the constitution establishes mechanisms that facilitate rent-seeking and interest group activity, it is reasonable to infer that the framers intended to encourage this result. If, on the other hand, the constitution establishes mechanisms that retard such activity by making it more costly, one can also infer that these costs were intended.

Madison's formal, publicly articulated pronouncements indicate that controlling the ability of interest groups to achieve anti-majoritarian outcomes in the legislature was a primary goal of the new Constitution.[92] Perhaps the most familiar is his statement in Federalist 10 that "[a]mong the numerous advantages promised by a well-constructed Union, none deserves to be more accurately developed than its tendency to break and control the violence of faction."[93] Indeed, a dominant theme of *The Federalist Papers* is the desirability of adopting

89. See R. McCormick & R. Tollison, supra note 24, at 126–27.

90. See supra notes 30–35 and accompanying text.

91. See Ackerman, supra note 49, at 1013–31.

92. See Sunstein, supra note 1, at 39–40.

93. The Federalist No. 10, at 77 (J. Madison) (C. Rossiter ed. 1961). See also Federalist 55, which indicates the desire to design a constitution that will not be "an unsafe depository of the public interests . . . [and] will sympathize least with the feelings of the mass of people and be most likely to aim at a permanent elevation of the few on the depression of the many." Id. No. 55, at 341 (J. Madison); cf. id. No. 78, at 468 (A. Hamilton) (indicating the possibility that the will of the legislature sometimes "stands in opposition to that of the people").

The argument that the Constitution serves to prepare the way for a time of politics as usual by setting up constraints on special interest groups is a theory developed most fully by Bruce Ackerman. See Ackerman, supra note 49, at 1020–31. Ackerman emphasizes, however, the constitutional authority of courts in this regard. See id. at 1029–30 ("Given the danger that normal government will be captured by partisans of narrow special interests, Publius proposes to consolidate the Revolutionary achievements of the American people through the institution of judicial review."). This Article shares Ackerman's premise that the Constitution was designed to promote "public-regardingness" in politics, but argues that this is done through traditional methods of statutory interpretation, rather than through constitutional judicial review. See infra notes 129–44 and accompanying text.

the Constitution as a means of controlling interest groups.[94]

As we see from examining hidden-implicit legislation, however, it is often impossible to draw conclusions about the intentions of those who make law simply by evaluating their public pronouncements. This is particularly true when the lawmakers, who spoke a long time ago, did so not as individuals but as a collective body. Thus while the framers made it absolutely clear in their public pronouncements that reducing the political power of factions was a central feature of their constitutional design, an even more convincing indication that the Constitution was intended to promote the public interest is found by examining the *results* of the framers' work.

One who observes the impressive success of interest groups in obtaining favorable legislation might be tempted to conclude either that the Constitution has failed in its attempt to impede interest groups or that it was not designed to impede their activities in the first place.[95] The first part of this section explains why such a conclusion is erroneous. The second part suggests economic reasons why constitutions are more likely to promote the public interest than are ordinary laws. Finally, the section evaluates the United States Constitution to determine whether it is designed to impede the success of interest groups or to facilitate interest group bargains.

1. *Agency Costs and Representative Government.* — The formation of a representative democracy, where voters elect legislators to run the enterprise of government, establishes what economists refer to as an "agency relationship." An agency relationship calls for one person or group of people (the principal) to hire another person or group of people (the agent) to perform services and make decisions on the principal's behalf.[96] The contract is successful from the standpoint of the contracting parties if it accurately anticipates likely postcontractual problems and establishes mechanisms to deal with these problems in cost-effective ways.

In a representative democracy, the contract that initiates this agency relationship is its constitution. The principals are the citizens, and the agents are the officials they elect. Assuming that elected officials, like all agents, are rational economic actors, they are inevitably more concerned with maximizing their own utility than with maximizing the utility of their principals. This divergence of interests (called "agency costs")[97] is an unwanted but inevitable feature inherent in any

94. See Sunstein, supra note 1, at 29.

95. Cf. id. at 221 ("It is clear that constituent pressures play a significant role in many legislative decisions and that the federalist idea of national responsibility to a national constituency does not exist in practice.").

96. Jensen & Meckling, Theory of the Firm: Managerial Behaviour, Agency Costs and Ownership Structure, 3 J. Fin. Econ. 305, 308 (1976).

97. Id. In the context of public corporations, Jensen and Meckling define "agency costs" as the sum of (1) monitoring expenditures by the principal (in the political pro-

principal-agent relationship—including, perhaps especially, the one that exists between voters and their elected representatives.

The study of agency costs, particularly in publicly held corporations, has generated an enormous literature in the field of economics. An important segment of this literature describes the innovative mechanisms that market forces have developed to reduce the magnitude of agency costs by more closely aligning the interests of principals and agents.[98]

The agency costs inherent in representative democracy manifest themselves in the side bargains between interest groups and legislators described above.[99] Because of the high cost of monitoring the behavior of elected officials, the expected costs to the officials of such behavior is low, and the benefits are high. The goal of a public-regarding constitution, then, is to establish mechanisms (such as the separation of powers)[100] and institutions (such as the independent judiciary)[101] that make rent-seeking by interest groups more costly by reducing the benefits that legislators can realize. However, there are inevitable costs associated with establishing the very mechanisms and institutions that retard rent-seeking.[102]

Because rent-seeking cannot be eliminated without cost, one cannot conclude that a constitution seeks to facilitate rent-seeking merely because it fails to eliminate it entirely. Such criticism suffers from the fallacy noted first by Ronald Coase, and characterized by Harold Dem-

cess this is the cost of contributions to legislative "watchdog" organizations plus the net cost of keeping informed about political affairs); (2) the bonding expenditures by the agent (this is the cost to politicians of putting their assets in a blind trust and the cost—in foregone opportunities—of campaign promises and pledges; when politicians pass laws making political bribery illegal they are bonding their behavior); and (3) the residual loss.

The residual loss from rent-seeking is likely to be quite large. This is due to the fact that it consists of not only the extra income of the legislators from political favors, but also the value of the wealth distributions made to interest groups.

98. See K. Arrow, Essays in the Theory of Risk Bearing 223–28 (1974); Fama, Agency Problems and the Theory of the Firm, 88 J. Pol. Econ. 288 (1980); Klein, Crawford & Alchian, Vertical Integration, Appropriable Rents, and the Competitive Contracting Process, 21 J.L. & Econ. 297 (1978); Smith & Warner, On Financial Contracting: An Analysis of Bond Covenants, 7 J. Fin. Econ. 117 (1979); Smith & Watts, Incentive and Tax Effects of Executive Compensation Plans, 7 Austl. J. Mgmt. 139 (1982).

99. See supra notes 30–48 and accompanying text.

100. See supra note 11 and accompanying text.

101. See infra notes 129–44 and accompanying text.

102. One such cost is the danger that the institutional arrangements imposed will filter out "good" (public-regarding) law along with "bad" (special interest) law. The framers were aware of this cost and believed that the benefits of reducing the amount of special interest legislation outweighed it. See The Federalist No. 73, at 444 (A. Hamilton) (C. Rossiter ed. 1961); infra note 118. In addition, there are costs associated with having an independent judiciary that must evaluate and interpret statutes, and to having an executive with the power to veto laws passed by Congress.

setz as the "Nirvana" form of analysis.[103] In fact, rational principals will expend resources to control the behavior of their agents only up to the point at which the marginal costs of such expenditures equals the marginal benefit in terms of reduced rent-seeking.[104]

The test of whether the framers intended to eliminate rent-seeking, then, should not be whether the Constitution eliminates all rent-seeking, but how effectively it provides mechanisms that align the interest of elected representatives with those of the public generally.[105] As we shall see, under this test, the mechanisms and institutions established in the United States Constitution indicate a purpose to minimize special interest bargains.

2. *The Economics of Constitutional Creation.* — Recently, public choice theorists have suggested economic reasons why constitutions are likely to be more public-regarding than other forms of law. One is that special interest groups are unlikely to agree to constitutional rules that make life easier for other special interest groups. Rules that facilitate rent-seeking generally are likely to cost each separate special interest group more in the way of wealth transfers to other groups than the group itself can expect to receive from the transfers it obtains.[106]

Individual members of a particular special interest group are hurt as much as any member of the general public by any special interest legislation not specially designed to benefit their group. For example, the airline industry, which strongly advocates anticompetitive regulation for itself,[107] is hurt as much as the general public by other protectionist regulation. Other groups that enjoy the protection of an anticompetitive regulatory environment for their own industries are harmed by the higher air fares that result from the regulation of air-

---

103. See Coase, Discussion, 54 Am. Econ. Rev. (Papers & Proc.) 194–97 (1964); Demsetz, Information and Efficiency: Another Viewpoint, 12 J.L. & Econ. 1 (1969). The reduction in societal wealth caused by rent-seeking, like any other form of agency cost, is " 'non-optimal' or inefficient only in comparison to a world in which we could obtain compliance of the agent to the principal's wishes at zero cost or in comparison to a *hypothetical* world in which the agency costs were lower." Jensen & Meckling, supra note 96, at 327–28 (emphasis in original).

104. Jensen & Meckling, supra note 96, at 326–28.

105. See Fama & Jensen, Agency Problems and Residual Claims, 26 J.L. & Econ. 327, 327 (1983) ("An important factor in the survival of organizational forms is control of agency problems.").

106. See, e.g., R. McCormick & R. Tollison, supra note 24, at 127 ("[W]e would expect the consumer-taxpayer to play a larger role in constitutional processes than in normal political processes.").

107. See, e.g., Regulatory Reform in Air Transportation: Hearings on S2551, S3346, and S3536 Before the Subcomm. on Aviation of the Senate Comm. on Commerce, 94th Cong., 2d Sess. 516 (1976) (statement of Albert V. Casey, Chairman and President, American Airlines, Inc.); id at 582 (statement of Frank Borman, President and Chief Executive Officer, Eastern Airlines, Inc.) On the application of the economics of legislation to deregulation, see Jarrell, Change at the Exchange: The Causes and Effects of Deregulation, 27 J.L. & Econ. 273 (1984); Macey & Haddock, Shirking at the SEC: The Failure of the National Market System, 1985 U. Ill. L. Rev. 315.

lines. Thus, even special interest groups that might benefit from some specific, discrete legislative wealth transfers are likely to object to general constitutional provisions that facilitate rent-seeking.

Finally, since the life of a constitutional rule is much longer than the effective life of a statute, the present value of the cost to the public of a constitutional rule that is not public-regarding will be much greater than the cost of an identical statutory rule. This greater cost will tend to mitigate the free-rider problem that plagues the public in the normal legislative arena.[108]

3. *The United States Constitution.* — If the United States Constitution was designed to facilitate rent-seeking, Judge Easterbrook's approach to statutory interpretation would lead to outcomes entirely consistent with this constitutional design. But if the Constitution was constructed to promote public, rather than private, interests by establishing a system of government that retards interest group activity, Judge Easterbrook's approach to statutory interpretation inevitably would produce results contrary to the goals of the framers. The evidence about the nature of the United States Constitution that follows strongly suggests that the Constitution was enacted to curb rather than promote narrow interest group behavior, and therefore that, unlike the traditional approach to statutes, Judge Easterbrook's approach to statutes is inconsistent with the constitutional design.

Bruce Ackerman has pointed out that the great insight of the framers of the United States Constitution was "to recognize that the future of American politics will not be one long, glorious reenactment of the American Revolution."[109] According to Ackerman, the principal defense given in *The Federalist Papers* for ratification of the new Constitution was that it laid the "foundations for a different kind of politics—where well organized groups try to manipulate government in pursuit of their narrow interests."[110] As described below, these foundations consist of the establishment of constitutional mechanisms and institutions that raise the costs of rent-seeking without imposing burdens on society greater than the savings derived from the diminution in such rent-seeking.

Support for the hypothesis that the Constitution is a public-regarding document, structured to favor the general polity over special interest groups can be derived from article I, which sets forth the size and

108. See R. McCormick & R. Tollison, supra note 24:

> [W]e would expect the citizen-consumer-taxpayer to play a larger role in constitutional processes than in normal political processes . . . [because] the individual voter's stake is . . . larger when considering constitutional issues. At the relevant margins of behavior, then, we expect more voter impact on constitutions than on regular elections.

Id. at 127.

109. Ackerman, supra note 49, at 1020.

110. Id.

composition of the Senate and the House of Representatives.[111] Building on the theoretical work of James Buchanan and Gordon Tullock,[112] Robert McCormick and Robert Tollison have demonstrated empirically that for a fixed number of total legislators, interest groups fare better in the market for legislation where the legislators are distributed equally between the two houses of a bicameral legislature.[113] Therefore, if the Constitution was designed to make interest group bargains less costly, we would expect article I to require the House and Senate to be of equal size. Yet, consistent with a public-regarding view of the Constitution, article I plainly envisions a wide disparity in membership size between the House and the Senate.[114]

In addition, as Buchanan and Tullock have shown,[115] where the members of each house of a bicameral legislature represent different constituencies, and where the two houses must concur to pass a law, it is more difficult for discrete factions to ensure the passage of legislation that furthers their interests. Thus the Constitution has imposed what is, in effect, a supermajority voting rule,[116] which raises decision costs and makes favorable treatment less likely for special interest groups.[117] The same analysis applies to the executive veto, which enables the executive branch to act as a third house of the legislature, thus further raising the cost to interest groups of obtaining favorable legislation.[118]

The provision in article I, section 2, allowing for the growth of the House of Representatives as the population grows, up to the point at which there is one representative for every thirty thousand people, is also consistent with the view that the Constitution impedes factional-

111. U.S. Const. art. I, § 2, cl. 3 ("The Number of Representatives shall not exceed one for every thirty Thousand . . . ."); id. § 3, cl. 1 ("The Senate of the United States shall be composed of two Senators from each State, chosen by the Legislature thereof, for six Years . . . .").

112. J. Buchanan & G. Tullock, supra note 6, at 43.

113. R. McCormick & R. Tollison, supra note 24, at 45–57.

114. See supra note 111.

115. See J. Buchanan & G. Tullock, supra note 6, at 233–48.

116. Id.

117. Id. at 244.

118. Id. Structural features such as the bicameral legislature, the relative sizes of the house and senate, and the executive veto raise the costs of passing all legislation. The benefit of such a system is that it reduces the efficacy of interest group activity. The cost is that it makes it more difficult to pass public-regarding legislation. The framers were aware of this cost, and believed the benefit to be greater:

> It may perhaps be said that the power of preventing bad laws includes that of preventing good ones; and may be used to the one purpose as well as to the other. But this objection will have little weight with those who can properly estimate the mischiefs of that inconstancy and mutability in the laws, which form the greatest blemish in the character and genius of our governments . . . . The injury which may possibly be done by defeating a few good laws will be amply compensated by the advantage of preventing a number of bad ones.

The Federalist No. 73, at 443–44 (A. Hamilton) (C. Rossiter ed. 1961).

ism.[119] Because rent-seeking is expected to increase as the population grows larger,[120] and to become more difficult as the legislature grows, a constitutional proviso that ties growth of the legislature to growth of the population is consistent with a public-regarding view of the Constitution.

The first amendment's free speech and press guarantees also support the hypothesis that the Constitution was designed to impede rather than advance rent-seeking. As Alexander Meiklejohn[121] and Robert Bork[122] have observed, the first amendment was designed to protect the integrity of the political process "so that the country may better be able to adopt the course of action that conforms to the wishes of the greatest number, whether or not it is wise or is founded in truth."[123] In addition, the commerce clause, the privileges and immunities clause, the equal protection clause, the due process clause, the contract clause, and the eminent domain clause have all been shown to be "united by a common theme and focused on a single underlying evil: the distribution of resources or opportunities to one group rather than another solely on the ground that those favored have exercised raw political power to obtain what they want."[124]

In sum, the idea that the Constitution was designed to impede interest groups from obtaining economic advantage through political means is "the most promising candidate for a unitary theory of the Constitution."[125] The fact that the Constitution establishes a multitude of mechanisms to deter the efficacy of interest groups is strong evidence that the framers intended this deterrence. Even the process by which the Constitution was enacted ensured that it would be a public-regarding document. Unlike statutes, which are enacted by a representative body, the Constitution was adopted by a direct democratic process.[126] The framers recognized (and here the italics are in the original) that the Constitution "was to be submitted to *the people them-*

119. See The Federalist No. 55, at 343–44 (J. Madison) (C. Rossiter ed. 1961).

120. See R. McCormick & R. Tollison, supra note 24, at 42–45.

121. See A. Meiklejohn, Free Speech and Its Relation to Self Government 93–95 (1948).

122. Bork, Neutral Principles and Some First Amendment Problems, 47 Ind. L.J. 1, 20 (1971).

123. A. Bickel, The Morality of Consent 62 (1975) (summarizing the views of Bork and Meiklejohn); see also id. at 83 (quoting Madison's characterization of the reporter as "a sentinel over public rights").

124. Sunstein, supra note 21, at 1689.

125. Id. at 1732.

126. A topic of some debate at the constitutional convention was whether the Constitution should be ratified by the state legislatures or by the people. See 5 The Debates in the Several State Conventions on the Adoption of the Federal Constitution 157–59, 352–56 (J. Elliot ed. 1866 & photo. reprint 1941). The mode chosen was ratification by "conventions of the people" rather than by state legislatures. Id. at 352. This mode was selected because it would "ground the new Constitution in a popular sovereignty, while at the same time making the ratification a federal rather than a national act." Mayton,

selves,"[127] and that "the disapprobation of this supreme authority would destroy it forever."[128] Thus, it is likely that the influence of interest groups on the content of the United States Constitution was less than the influence of such groups on the content of ordinary, day-to-day legislation.

The following section of this Article explores more fully how the presence of an independent judiciary makes it more difficult for interest groups to press for costly and nonproductive transfers of wealth. Despite the fact that interest group statutes are seldom struck down on constitutional grounds, the judiciary, through its traditional approach to statutory interpretation, imposes important constraints on special interests.

IV. The Subtle Virtues of the Traditional Approach to Statutory Interpretation: Legislative Subterfuge and Judicial Mistake

The classic exposition of the traditional approach to statutory interpretation is Benjamin Cardozo's *The Nature of the Judicial Process*,[129] which describes how judges in fact go about deciding cases and interpreting statutes. Judges interpret statutes by starting with the language and reaching a decision that applies that language to a particular set of facts in a way that is consistent with the publicly articulated purpose of the statute. That publicly articulated purpose will almost invariably be a public-regarding purpose. Thus, while the traditional approach encompasses a wide variety of judicial styles, all of these styles share the same goal—to discover what the enacting legislators say they intended to accomplish by passing the statute and then to render decisions designed to attain the lawmakers' stated objectives. An essential principle of statutory interpretation is that judges ought not to look beyond the legislature's stated purpose when interpreting statutes. Justice Cardozo pointed to "a wise and ancient doctrine that a court will not inquire into the motives of a legislative body or assume them to be wrongful. . . . The process of psychoanalysis [should not be carried into such] unaccustomed fields" as statutory interpretion.[130]

The traditional approach conforms to the common sense notion about what judges do, and needs no lengthy elaboration. Henry M. Hart and Albert Sachs provide the best capsule description when they admonish judges to "assume, unless the contrary unmistakably appears, that the legislature was made up of reasonable persons *pursuing*

Seditious Libel and the Lost Guarantee of a Freedom of Expression, 84 Colum. L. Rev. 91, 96 n.26 (1984) (citation omitted).

127. The Federalist No. 40, at 253 (J. Madison) (C. Rossiter ed. 1961).

128. Id.

129. B. Cardozo, The Nature of the Judicial Process (1949).

130. United States v. Constantine, 296 U.S. 287, 298–99 (1935) (Cardozo, J., dissenting).

reasonable purposes reasonably."[131] As an English judge remarked over four hundred years ago in *Heydon's Case*,[132] "the office of all judges is always to make such construction as shall suppress the mischief, and advance the remedy" that "Parliament hath resolved and appointed to cure the disease of the Commonwealth."[133]

While at first it may appear that the traditional approach to statutory interpretation will simply rubber-stamp special interest legislation, in fact the traditional method poses considerable constraints on such legislation.[134] This is because where a sharp divergence between the stated public-regarding purpose of the legislature and the true special interest motivation behind a particular statute, courts will, under the traditional approach, resolve any ambiguities in the statute consistently with the stated public-regarding purpose. Judges using the traditional approach will not look beyond this publicly stated purpose to try to discover a special interest deal.

The reason special interest legislation is so often drafted with a public-regarding gloss is because this gloss raises the costs to the public and to rival groups of discovering the true effect of the legislation.[135] This, in turn, minimizes the major cost to the legislator of supporting narrow interest group legislation—the loss of support from groups that are harmed by the legislation—and thus reduces the cost to special interest groups of persuading the legislature to vote for the special interest legislation. Special interest statutes may also be passed with public-regarding facades because special interest groups often control the flow of information to lawmakers. Congress, relying on this information, may pass statutes that it believes are unambiguously in the public interest, but which in fact are riddled with incidental benefits to interest groups.

---

131. H. Hart & A. Sacks, The Legal Process: Basic Problems in the Making and Application of Law 1415 (10th ed. 1958) (emphasis added).

132. 76 Eng. Rep. 637, 638 (Ex. 1854).

133. Id. at 638.

134. Hamilton, the principal advocate in *The Federalist Papers* for the constitutional establishment of an independent judiciary, based his defense of this branch of government on its ability to control legislative excess, not through judicial review alone but through the "firmness of judicial magistracy" in its role as interpreter of statutes:

> But it is not with a view to infractions of the Constitution alone that the independence of judges may be an essential safeguard against the effects of occasional ill humors in the society. . . . [T]he firmness of the judicial magistracy is of vast importance in mitigating the severity and confining the operation of such laws. It not only serves to moderate the immediate mischiefs of those which may have been passed but it operates as a check upon the legislative body in passing them; who, perceiving that obstacles to the success of an iniquitous intention are to be expected from the scruples of the courts, are in a manner compelled, by the very motives of the injustice they mediate, to qualify their attempts.

The Federalist No. 78, at 470 (A. Hamilton) (C. Rossiter ed. 1961).

135. This involves engrafting a "public value" onto a statute in order to "justify the exercise of governmental power." Sunstein, supra note 21, at 1697.

The traditional method of statutory interpretation imposes a constraint on such legislative subterfuge. Judges employing the traditional method of statutory interpretation, by giving a statute its public rather than private meaning, may reach a result that serves the public interest, but fails to honor the terms of the original deal between the legislature and the interest group. It is significant that the traditional method of interpretating statutes, unlike other approaches to statutory interpretation, and indeed unlike judicial review itself, do not require that judges determine which statutes are public-regarding and which are not. Indeed, under the traditional approach judges treat all statutes the same way. A good example of a case where the court reached a result that serves the public interest but failed to honor the original deal is *Silkwood v. Kerr-McGee Corp.*[136] The case presented the issue of whether the Atomic Energy Act of 1954,[137] which established a comprehensive system of federal regulation of the manufacture and use of radioactive materials, preempted state tort law. Karen Silkwood, a Kerr-McGee employee, was contaminated by radiation when she was exposed to plutonium that the company fabricated into rods for use in nuclear reactors. After her estate received a jury award of ten million dollars in punitive damages against Kerr-McGee for using deficient safety procedures in the plant, the company and the Nuclear Regulatory Commission appealed on the ground that the federal statutory scheme of insurance and regulation under the Atomic Energy Act of 1954 protected the company against such state law tort claims, thereby precluding an award of punitive damages.

On its face, the Act appears unambiguously to be a public interest statute. It was ostensibly designed to improve plant safety and encourage "widespread participation in the development and utilization of atomic energy for peaceful purposes."[138] But, as Judge Easterbrook notes, the statute in actuality "favors incumbents—those who generate power or make reactors—at the expense of potential entrants and con-

136. 464 U.S. 238 (1984).

137. 42 U.S.C. § 2011–2296 (1982).

138. Id. § 2013(d). With regard to the issue of safety, "Congress' decision to prohibit the States from regulating the safety aspects of nuclear development was premised on its belief that the [Nuclear Regulatory] Commission was more qualified to determine what type of safety standards should be enacted in this complex area." *Silkwood*, 464 U.S. 238, 250 (1984); see also H.R. Rep. No. 1125, 86th Cong., 1st Sess. 3 (1959) (Certain types of regulation were not to be turned over to the states because "the technical safety considerations are of such complexity that it is not likely that any State would be prepared to deal with them.").

The ostensible concerns about participation and utilization were incorporated directly into the statute itself. See 42 U.S.C. § 2013(d) (1982); see also *Silkwood*, 464 U.S. at 257 (citing cases that interpret § 2013(d)). It is difficult to imagine how a statute that lowers the recovery permitted plaintiffs against producers of nuclear power at common law *encourages* such producers to act with greater caution or concern for safety. It is even more difficult to see how a statute that limits entry through licensing encourages "widespread participation" in the industry.

sumers."[139] The Act does this by forbidding firms from using or refining certain materials without a federal license. Such licensing statutes are a hallmark of special interest legislation,[140] protecting current participants from new entrants.

As the dissent pointed out, the ten million dollar award imposed by the jury under state law was one hundred times greater than the maximum fine the Nuclear Regulatory Commission (NRC) could impose under the circumstances.[141] Thus the punitive damage award was in direct conflict with the special interest goal of favoring incumbents by limiting the tort liability of those supplying nuclear power. Because Congress sold the Atomic Energy Act to the public as a safety regulation, the award of punitive damages did not seem to the Court to be inconsistent with the legislative scheme. The majority in the Supreme Court took Congress at its word, and therefore upheld the punitive damage award.

Congress could have been more explicit in its favoritism for the nuclear power industry when it passed the Act, but not without cost. If the Act had been clear on its face that it was designed to enrich producers of atomic energy at the expense of the rest of the population, then only a holding that barred punitive damage awards against producers of atomic energy would be consistent with such legislative purpose. But the costs of organizing the public to wage a battle against a statute of this sort would be reduced because information costs would be less and, as a result, the costs to the special interest group of getting Congress to enact such a law in the face of public opposition would be increased.

As *Silkwood* illustrates, the cost to special interest groups of legislative subterfuge is the probability that a court will be unable to discern, or will refuse to recognize, the underlying bargain and will therefore fail to enforce the legislative compromise. Legislative subterfuge thus leads inevitably to what interest groups might consider to be judicial mistake, and the possibility of mistake imposes costs on the efficacy of special interest bargains. Even a judiciary that wholeheartedly desires to serve the interests of Congress cannot do so when the interests of that body are intentionally vague.[142]

The chance that special interest goals, disguised by the legislature, will survive interpretation by the third branch is diminished further by the judiciary's traditional insistence on reason, analytical coherence, and principled judgment in the judicial process. This historical com-

139. Easterbrook, supra note 17, at 45.

140. Id. ("The [Atomic Energy] Act is a licensing statute, and licensing statutes are the playgrounds of interest groups.").

141. *Silkwood*, 464 U.S. at 263 (Blackmun, J., dissenting).

142. See supra notes 39–42 and accompanying text; cf. R. Posner, supra note 7, at 271 ("[A]ll statutes have an ostensible public-interest justification, and even where the fig leaf is thin it is difficult for the courts to see through it.").

mitment to neutral principles is reinforced by the tradition that judges issue written opinions that justify and explain their decisions. The drafting exercise itself frequently will prompt a judge (or his clerks) to see the incoherence behind the articulated purpose of a statute, and to see the difficulty of justifying a particular result on the grounds that the statute serves the public interest goals identified by the legislature.[143] Consequently, judges often need not willfully substitute their opinions for those of the legislature in order to serve as an obstacle to rent-seeking. The very presence of an independent judiciary is a structural device that raises the cost to private interest groups of enacting statutes that defeat the public interest.

Even in a situation where Congress seeks to serve the public interest but instead passes a special interest statute because interest groups control the flow of information to the legislature, the process of judicial interpretation promotes the public interest by informing the legislature about the true nature of the legislation it has passed. Lobbyists are likely only to inform the legislature about the benefits of a particular legislative scheme. Judicial interpretation, however, helps fill this information gap in that the litigation process often brings the costs of legislative schemes to light. This publicity provides information to prompt those affected by the legislation to organize coalitions to protest it. These individuals may not have opposed the legislation initially because they were unaware that it was pending or because they misconstrued the effects it would have on them. In addition, litigation may provide Congress itself with new information about the costs of the scheme it enacted.

When the legislature has passed a statute that claims to be in the public interest but in fact benefits an interest group, that interest group may meet with frustration in the courts when it tries to enforce the statute. The statute is unlikely to serve the ends it claims to serve and at the same time enrich a particular group. When the court interprets the statute so as to serve the public, the court may, as it did in the *Silkwood* case, inadvertently invalidate a legislative bargain. But when this happens it is all to the common good.

The benefits of traditional statutory review extends far beyond particular plaintiffs. Society as a whole benefits, because the lower the probability of enforcement of special interest statutes with public pur-

---

143. See A. Bickel, The Supreme Court and the Idea of Progress (1970):

> The restraints of reason tend to ensure also the independence of the judge, to liberate him from the demands and fears—dogmatic, arbitrary, irrational, self- or group-centered—that so often enchain other public officials. They make it possible for the judge, on some occasions, at any rate, to oppose against the will and faith of others, not merely his own will or deeply-felt faith, but a method of reaching judgments that may command the allegiance, on a second thought, even of those who find the result disagreeable.

Id. at 82.

pose facades, the lower their value to the special interest groups. The further a statute strays from its articulated purpose, the lower the value will be because of the greater chance that the courts will fail to carry out any hidden interest group orientation that may exist. The interest group pressing for enactment of a special interest statute can always go back to Congress after an unfavorable judicial ruling to have the statute clarified. But the costs of this second bite at the legislative apple will be considerable. In addition to the normal cost of getting legislation passed, the publicity that surrounds any congressional overruling of a court decision will make it easier for opposing groups to mobilize.[144] Consequently, when special interest groups find it disadvantageous to press for explicit statutes in the first place, they are even more likely to find it disadvantageous in the future.

In addition to decreasing the overall quantity of special interest legislation, traditional statutory interpretation encourages Congress to be more explicit about the true special interest purposes of the special interest statutes it does pass. As described above, there are two types of special interest statutes: open-explicit statutes which represent the naked, undisguised transfer of wealth to some group, and hidden-implicit statutes which disguise their special interest orientation by shrouding it in public interest terms. Hidden-implicit statutes are less costly to enact initially, but the underlying deals are ultimately less likely to be enforced in the courts. Open-explicit deals have a higher probability of being enforced but are more costly politically. An interest group will select the type of statute that maximizes its own net benefit.

Inevitably, there will be an equilibrium between open-explicit and hidden-implicit statutes. Any technique of statutory interpretation that decreases the probability of a judicial nullification of hidden-implicit statutes will result in more of this type of statute relative to the number of open-explicit statutes. Under Easterbrook's contractarian approach, therefore, because judges actively seek to discover the disguised terms in hidden-implicit statutes, we would expect to observe a lower proportion of open-explicit statutes relative to the total number of interest group statutes. By contrast, under the traditional approach to statutory interpretation espoused here, legislative subterfuge is less likely to be successful, and as a result, at the margin we will observe a higher percentage of open-explicit statutes relative to hidden-implicit statutes. Therefore, the traditional approach to statutory interpretation results not only in less special interest legislation, but in special interest legislation that is more candid as to its true nature and purpose. Increased candor will improve the operation of the judicial process by encourag-

144. See infra notes 145–54 and accompanying text (discussing the value of publicity for making statutes more "public-regarding").

ing simpler statutes and by affording litigants the benefits of greater predictability.

V. Institutional Constraints

The preceding discussion advocates the use of traditional methods of statutory interpretation as the best means of addressing the problem of special interest group legislation. This section describes more fully how this method imposes a constraint on special interest legislation and suggests ways of enhancing the tendency of the traditional method of adjudication to further the public interest.

A. *The Federal Courts and the Value of Publicity*

One of the primary reasons for the public's failure to rise up in indignation at the special interest nature of certain pieces of legislation is simply the cost of discovering what Congress is doing.[145] As this cost goes down, the public will be able to place more pressure on the legislature to serve the public good. Thus, even when a federal court upholds a bargain between an interest group and the legislature, the publicity attending the court's decision in an important case serves the valuable function of informing the public about the kinds of things Congress is doing. The publicity value of Supreme Court decisions is particularly high. Important Court decisions are the beginnings of conversations between the Court and the people and their representatives.[146] The publicity surrounding a major decision provides information that would not otherwise be available to the polity.

One tactic for getting publicity that was frequently used by Justice Felix Frankfurter might best be described as "judicial blackmail."[147] Frankfurter, when faced with special interest group statutes, chose "a narrow, harsh interpretation of those laws on the ground that such a reading would break the log jam of interests and force the legislative hand."[148] As Dean Calabresi has pointed out,[149] nowhere is Frankfurter's use of this device more apparent than in his interpretations of the Jones Act,[150] a legislative scheme remarkably similar to the Atomic Energy Act reviewed in the *Silkwood* case.[151]

---

145. Cf. M. Olson, The Logic of Collective Action 126–27 (1971) (discussing interests of voters and groups in primarily their own welfare); R. McCormick & R. Tollison, supra note 24, at 16–17 (explaining how the activities of voters seeking to affect political decisions depend on the nature of the information available and the costs of organizing into political coalitions entailed).

146. See Bickel & Wellington, Legislative Purpose and the Judicial Process: The Lincoln Mills Case, 71 Harv. L. Rev. 1 (1957).

147. G. Calabresi, supra note 55, at 34.

148. Id.

149. Id. at 33–34.

150. Ch. 250, 41 Stat. 988 (1920) (codified in scattered sections of 46 U.S.C.).

151. Silkwood v. Kerr-McGee Corp., 464 U.S. 238 (1984); see supra notes 136–43 and accompanying text.

Just as the Atomic Energy Act sought to rewrite the common law of damages by setting an upper bound on the recovery of those injured by producers of nuclear energy, the Jones Act set an upper limit on the common law recovery available to persons injured at sea. Like the Court in *Silkwood*, the Court evaluating the Jones Act was skeptical of the value of the Act where it curtailed the common law rights of sailors to recover for maritime injuries. Unlike the majority in *Silkwood*, Frankfurter would have upheld the terms of the special interest group bargain, but he would have done so in such a way as to bring public excoriation upon the lawmakers responsible for the wealth transfer.[152]

The Frankfurter approach has particular appeal where the terms of the special interest group bargain are explicit. By enforcing a statute but refusing to seek out a public interest purpose where none exists, judges using traditional methods of interpretation such as those used by Frankfurter impose costs on legislative bargains that lobbyists must reckon with when entering the legislative arena.

The publicity generated by court decisions provides not only the public but also legislators with information. Because interest groups often control the flow of information to Congress, statutes that benefit particular interest groups may be passed by legislators who believe they are acting in the public interest.[153] Over time, statutory interpretation tends to educate Congress about the actual effects of the statutes they pass and serves the public interest by improving the deliberative nature of the legislative process.[154]

B. *The Logical Impossibility of Consistent Decisions*

As we have seen, special interest group bargains are less valuable to the contracting parties if the parties are uncertain as to whether the bargains will ultimately be enforced by the courts.[155] Nonetheless, as Judge Easterbrook elegantly has demonstrated, the Supreme Court, through no fault of its own, "continues to hand down inconsistent decisions, to dishonor precedents, and to change the weight attached to particular . . . statutory provisions or the values derived from them."[156] Pointing out these inconsistencies has long been a way of criticizing the Court, since, after all, "[e]veryone thinks that the Court should be consistent."[157] But elementary public choice theory illustrates that

---

152. G. Calabresi, supra note 55, at 34. See also United States v. Bethlehem Steel Corp., 315 U.S. 289 (1942), in which the Court's construction of the statute in question provoked a rapid legislative revision. See W. Murphy, Elements of Judicial Strategy 129-31 (1964).

153. See supra notes 39-42 and accompanying text.

154. See Sunstein, supra note 1, at 52-53 (describing the nature of legislators' "deliberative responsibility").

155. See supra notes 141-44.

156. Easterbrook, Ways of Criticizing the Court, 95 Harv. L. Rev. 802, 812 (1982).

157. Id. at 811.

achievement of even basic consistency is in fact impossible for the Court. Judge Easterbrook's point is that the "[p]lurality opinions, concurring opinions, shifting coalitions, frequent overrulings (not many acknowledged as such), inconsistent lines of precedent—in other words the manifold institutional failings of appellate courts in general and the Supreme Court in particular—are . . . primarily consequences of the fact that a court is an electoral body."[158]

Following Arrow's Impossibilty Theorem, Easterbrook demonstrates that under certain conditions beyond the power of the justices to control, it is not only likely, but inevitable that Supreme Court opinions will be inconsistent.[159] But Arrow's Theorem also implies that, where there is unanimity among the justices, consistency *is possible.*[160] Arrow's Theorem further suggests that consistency is possible in simple cases where there are only two possible outcomes.[161] Regarding specific issues, consistency can be achieved even in complex cases where multiple outcomes are possible, if there is unanimity among the justices as to either preference or the ranking of preferences.[162]

---

158. R. Posner, supra note 7, at 242 (discussing Posner's reading of Easterbrook).

159. See Easterbrook, supra note 156, at 823–31. Arrow's Theorem, for which Arrow won the Nobel Prize, sets out five conditions (which are paraphrased below), and proves that no voting system can satisfy all five simultaneously:

1. Unanimity Rules: If all voters prefer alternative *A* to alternative *B*, then alternative *A* will be selected.
2. No Veto by Any Individual: No one's preferences control the actions of the other voters.
3. Range of Alternatives: There must be at least three admissible alternatives, and every voter must be free to select among these alternatives as he chooses.
4. Independence of Irrelevant Variables: The choice between two alternative variables must depend solely on a comparison of those two variables.
5. Transitivity: If the collective decision selects *A* over *B* and *B* over *C*, it must also select *A* over *C*. This is the requirement of logical consistency.

See id. at 823 (setting out Arrow's five conditions in slightly different form).

In short, Arrow's Theorem shows that no voting system can satisfy all of these conditions simultaneously. Thus, where conditions one through four are met, transitivity and thus logical consistency is not possible. Easterbrook's argument is that the Court's decisions are inconsistent because conditions one through four hold for the Court, thus making condition five impossible. See id. at 824–31.

For a relatively accessible proof of Arrow's Theorem, see D. Mueller, Public Choice 186–88 (1980). Mueller's book also contains an untechnical survey of the literature of public choice.

160. See Easterbrook, supra note 156, at 814–23.

161. Consistency is out of the reach of the Supreme Court only where there are at least three possible decisions open to the Court. See supra note 159; see also Easterbrook, supra note 156, at 825–29 (discussing the "Range Condition" of Arrow's Theorem).

162. See Easterbrook, supra note 156, at 825–29. This conclusion can also be derived from Condorcet. See M. Condorcet, Essai sur l'application de l'analyse à la Probabilité des Décisions Rendues à la Pluralite des Voix (New York photo reprint 1972) (Paris 1785). Easterbrook's article on voting procedure in the Supreme Court contains an excellent example of the application of Condorcet's voting paradox to

For a variety of reasons, a hidden-implicit statute enacted to aid a special interest group but masked as a public interest statute is likely to be subject to a wider variety of interpretations than either a purely public interest statute or an open-explicit statute. First, it is always possible to read the statute in a way that is consistent with its ostensible public purpose. Second, it will be possible to read the statute as a private interest bargain, and to refuse to enforce it. Finally, following the Easterbrook legislation-as-contract approach, it is possible to read the statute as a private interest bargain and to agree to enforce it as such.[163] Where statutes are subject to three or more possible interpretations, Arrow's Theorem suggests that consistency is not possible. Of course some public interest statutes also will be subject to more than two interpretations. The discussion here is necessarily limited to tendencies and not absolutes. Special interest statutes are likely to be more ambiguous and complex and therefore subject to a wider variety of conditions and interpretations. According to Arrow's theorem, this complexity makes inconsistency more likely.[164]

The above discussion is limited to the hidden-implicit type of special interest statute. Open-explicit statutes are likely to be enforced logically and consistently by courts, because these statutes, like public interest statutes, by definition make no effort to hide their true purposes.[165] Thus, like public-regarding statutes, these statutes are not likely to be subject to more than two interpretations. But, as demonstrated above, these open-explicit statutes can only be passed at a relatively high political cost to legislators.[166]

Consequently, the inconsistency of Supreme Court decisions ought not be viewed as an unmitigated evil. While inconsistency is detrimental when it leads to the misapplication of public interest statutes,

---

Supreme Court voting behavior on establishment clause issues. See Easterbrook, supra note 156, at 815–17; cf. A. MacKay, Arrow's Theorem, The Paradox of Social Choice (1980) (discussing Arrow's five conditions and their relevance to the design of institutions that make decisions collectively).

163. See Easterbrook, supra note 17, at 54–58.

164. A complex statute is one in which judges have a wide range of plausible choices about how the statute should be interpreted. Arrow's range condition presumes complexity because it presumes that decisionmakers have more than two choices. As the number of choices increases, the range of choices is likely to increase and thus the likelihood of consistency (condition 5) being attained is diminished. Cf. Easterbrook, supra note 156, at 825–26 ("Multi-peakedness becomes more and more likely as the number of dimensions of choice increases.").

165. While both the discussion and the underlying theory are complex, most of the insights of the theory can be usefully summarized by the simple aphorism that "it is easy to reach agreement on easy cases." Id. at 805. When the legislature makes no attempt to hide the true purpose of the legislation it passes statutes will be easier to construe than when there is an attempt at subterfuge. As Judge Posner has observed: "To the extent that legislators use Aesopian language to deceive potential opponents of the interest groups behind legislation, they may fool the courts as well and thereby limit the political power of those interest groups." Posner, supra note 5, at 273.

166. See supra notes 47–48, 129–44 and accompanying text.

it is beneficial when it results in nullification or misapplication of special interest group bargains.

C. *Judicial Willfulness*

The above discussion has assumed that courts invariably attempt to interpret statutes so as to achieve the publicly articulated goals of the legislature. It is also true that judges will at times ignore or deliberately misread statutes in order to thwart the will of the legislature. As Justice Frankfurter chose to embarrass Congress by a highly literal interpretation of the Jones Act, Justice Black reacted to the same statute by misreading it.[167]

There are sanctions that Congress can impose on a willful judiciary. While the salaries of sitting judges technically cannot be reduced,[168] Congress has the power to withhold raises, which, during inflationary periods, amounts to salary reduction.[169] When this sanction is imposed, however, it punishes both those judges who are faithful servants and those who are not. Hence it is an ineffective tool for disciplining judges or groups of judges, especially since such measures may cause dissension even among the ranks of the most faithful. Congress also has the authority to curtail the jurisdiction of the courts,[170] thereby making the work that judges do less interesting and less important. But if Congress seriously curtailed the jurisdiction of the federal courts, it would have no reliable institution to enforce its enactments. True, legislative bargains could be enforced by state courts, but Congress has even less ability to control state judges than federal judges. Congress would face similar problems if it tried more subtle sanctions, such as refusing to appropriate funds for judges' support personnel. Again, these sanctions apply to faithful judicial agents as well as unfaithful ones.

A further reason why legislative sanctions on the judiciary are likely to be futile lies in the fact that much judicial willfulness is subconscious.[171] Justice Cardozo observed that the forces that shape the decisions of judges "are seldom fully in consciousness . . . . Deep below consciousness are other forces, the likes and the dislikes, the predilections and the prejudices, the complex of instincts and emotions and habits and convictions which make the man, whether he be litigant or

167. See G. Calabresi, supra note 55, at 34.

168. See U.S. Const. art. III., § 1.

169. R. Posner, supra note 7, at 29–47, especially at 37 (discussing judges' salaries and showing chart of federal judicial salaries in constant (1983) dollars from 1800 to 1983).

170. See U.S. Const. art. III, § 1. Congress is not even compelled to *create* any lower federal courts. See supra note 86.

171. See B. Cardozo, supra note 129, at 167–77 (describing the subconscious forces that lead judges to the decisions they make).

judge."[172] Regardless of the sanctions that Congress might impose on the judiciary, it is surely powerless to curb subconscious willfulness.

The point here is not to praise or defend judicial willfulness, but merely to point out its inevitability, and to observe that this willfulness, while deplorable in particular cases, serves to lower the present value of rent-seeking to interest groups.

VI. Some Suggestions For Making Law More Public-Regarding

For much of the nation's history, the prevailing school of statutory interpretation counseled that it was wise to restrict legislative enactments as narrowly as possible.[173] After a relatively brief hiatus during the New Deal, the dominant attitude about legislative enactments is now shifting back to this earlier incarnation.[174] This recent trend reflects a more realistic conception of the negative outcomes that the legislative process frequently generates and is consistent with the approach to statutes that existed when the framers enacted the Constitution, as well as with the approach advocated in this Article.

Accordingly, the suggestions that follow about statutory interpretation frequently counsel returning to the older approaches to statutes that fell into disuse during the past fifty years. If used properly, these

172. Id. at 167.

173. In the first edition of Justice Sutherland's famous treatise on statutory construction he opined that:

> The natural tendency and growth of the law is towards system and towards certainty, towards modes of operation at once practical and just, by the process of its intelligent judicial administration; but this process is impaired by overwork and legislative interference.

J. Sutherland, Statutes and Statutory Construction iii (1st ed. 1891). This approach to statutory interpretation was the dominant approach at the time of the framing of the Constitution, and met with approval in *The Federalist Papers* as a means of controlling factions. See The Federalist No. 78, at 470 (A. Hamilton) (C. Rossiter ed. 1961). Common law courts in England never had the power of judicial review that developed early on in the United States. But, as societal attitudes about statutes became more benign, judicial attitudes about statutory construction also changed. Thus, in 1943, when Horack wrote the preface to the new edition of Sutherland's treatise on statutory interpretation, he observed that: "The third edition reflects the growing acceptance of statutes as a creative element in the law rather than, as Sutherland suggested in the first edition, as 'legislative interference.' " 1 J. Sutherland, Statutes and Statutory Construction vi (3d ed. 1943).

174. See R. Posner, supra note 7, at 271 (describing "shift in scholarly thinking about legislation from a rather naive faith in the public-interest character of most legislation to a more realistic understanding of the importance of interest groups in the legislative process"); see also Sunstein, supra note 1, at 29–30 (current "dissatisfaction" with American scheme of government traceable to problems produced by interest groups); supra text accompanying notes 1–6; cf. G. Calabresi, supra note 55, at 31–43 (arguing that judges be given the power to alter statutes not in conformity with the predominant legal topography); Easterbrook, Statutes' Domains, 50 U. Chi. L. Rev. 533, 544 (1983) (statutes' domains should be restricted unless Congress plainly gives courts right to expand its scope).

suggestions will improve the performance of the legislature by increasing its incentives to act in the public interest. The common feature of the suggestions is that they do not require judges to pick and choose among particular statutes on the basis of whether the judges think the statute benefits the public rather than a special interest group. These suggestions, like the traditional approach, counsel judges to take a consistently neutral approach to all statutes. The result of this approach will be to raise the costs of enacting hidden-implicit legislation without intruding on the legislature's authority to make law.

A. *The Use of Legislative History*

A core premise of the traditional method of statutory interpretation is that the legislature should be taken at its word when it enacts a statute. Judge Easterbrook's approach to statutory interpretation seems to call upon judges to ignore legislative histories, and to invoke instead principles of economics in order to apply statutes according to the terms of the bargain struck with or between interest groups. But this approach blurs an important distinction that must be made between two types of special interest statutes: those that are unabashedly special interest in nature, and those that masquerade as public interest statutes.[175]

While courts have an obligation to enforce otherwise constitutional statutes, they have no obligation to encourage rent-seeking. The traditional method of statutory construction calls upon judges to refer to the legislative history—including floor debates and committee hearings and reports—for clarification of complex statutes.[176] The federal courts "have made increasing use of legislative history materials."[177] Today the courts use such materials in virtually every case where statutory interpretation is required. This practice, when used in conjunction with the traditional method of statutory interpretation, will act as a brake on the efficacy of special interest legislation so long as such materials are used with sensitivity to the issue of public-regardingness as described below.

By contrast, the use of nonpublic or off-the-record statements of legislative intent is inconsistent with the analysis presented here. The constraints of the political marketplace, which impose costs on legislators who fail to act in the public interest, do not affect legislators who make nonpublic or off-the-record statements about a statute. Such statements, although they might reveal the special interest nature of a

175. See supra notes 47–48 and accompanying text.

176. See Posner, supra note 5, at 272. For a more penetrating look into the use of these documents, particularly the use of legislative history, see Dickerson, Statutory Interpretation: A Peek into the Mind and Will of a Legislature, 50 Ind. L.J. 206 (1975); Radin, Statutory Interpretation, 43 Harv. L. Rev. 863 (1930).

177. Johnstone, An Evaluation of the Rules of Statutory Interpretation, 3 U. Kan. L. Rev. 1, 4 (1954).

legislative enactment, should not be relied upon by courts. Reliance would lead only to windfalls for special interest groups.

The same analysis applies to postenactment remarks by legislators: these cannot "be treated simply as impartial interpretations of the law" by anyone who "takes seriously the interest-group theory of politics."[178] Under the Easterbrook legislation-as-contract approach, such statements would be of value because they can provide insights into the special interest nature of statutes,[179] but under the traditional approach these statements should be accorded no weight.

Isolated statements such as public remarks by individual legislators read into the *Congressional Record* should also be ignored by judges. Such individual remarks often will reflect an appeal to a particular congressman's own constituency rather than an honest attempt to clarify a statute.

By way of illustration, suppose a statute can be interpreted in two ways. One interpretation will result in reading the statute as affecting a public purpose. The other interpretation will benefit a special interest group. While Congress may have passed the law with an intent to benefit the public, a particular congressman, whose district is controlled by the interest group that will benefit from a skewed interpretation may have a strong incentive to make isolated statements claiming the statute was designed solely to benefit his local interest group. The congressman suffers no cost in making such statements while enjoying the significant benefit of support from the relevant interest group.

For a similar reason, the commonly held view that prior interpretations of statutes by administrative agencies should be afforded great deference should be reconsidered. This is an implication of "capture theory," a primitive version of the economic theory of regulation which predicts "that over time regulatory agencies come to be dominated by the industries regulated."[180] While this theory has little value where a single agency regulates separate industries with conflicting interests[181] and ignores the influence of consumer groups on regulatory agencies,[182] the fact remains that administrative agencies, like legislatures, are subject to substantial interest group influence. When courts rubber stamp their interpretations of legislation, they ignore political reality and abdicate their role as a check on the legislature. Just as legislators can avoid political ramifications of their actions by passing hidden-implicit statutes, so too can they avoid such ramifications by giving broad authority to administrative agencies that they expect to be captured by

178. Posner, supra note 5, at 275.

179. California state courts have begun to permit legislators to give courtroom testimony about their past legislative intent. See Comment, Statutory Interpretation in California: Individual Testimony as an Extrinsic Aid, 15 U.S.F.L. Rev. 241 (1981).

180. Posner, supra note 2, at 341 (footnote omitted).

181. Id. at 342.

182. Id.

interest groups. Agency officials, who lack lifetime appointments, are subject to political pressures from which judges are immune. As a result, blind deference to agencies should be abandoned and courts should subject agency action to rationality review and means-ends analysis.

B. *Using the Canons of Statutory Construction*

The canons of statutory construction,[183] while they elicit little modern commentary, are frequently invoked by judges.[184] There are so many canons that most questions of statutory interpretation fall within the domain of more than one canon.[185] As Professor Llewellyn once observed, for every canon a judge might bring to bear in interpreting a statute one way, there is another canon that suggests the opposite outcome.[186] As a result, the canons of statutory construction enhance, rather than limit, the power of judges to engage in willful statutory interpretation. A judge who invokes a canon of construction to defend a particular reading of a statute masks his willfulness under a cloak of legitimacy, because he appears to be using a neutral, rather than a result-oriented, source to support his result.

Nonetheless, the canons can be ranked and ordered by judges on the basis of which best fulfill the two conditions of public-regardingness and legitimacy set forth above.[187] Perhaps the best example of a valuable canon is the venerable (but still popular) "plain meaning rule" which commands judges to begin their inquiry into the meaning of a statute with the actual words of the statute, and only to stray from this approach if absolutely necessary. Closer adherence to this method of statutory interpretation would diminish judges' present need to instantly refer to legislative history in order to decide cases. It would also force legislators to spell out the nature of their intentions much more clearly on the face of the statutes they pass. In addition, the canon that statutes in derogation of the common law should be narrowly construed,[188] limits the scope of inefficient statutes by protecting the do-

183. See 4 J. Sutherland, Statutes and Statutory Construction 1–3 (C. Sands 4th ed. 1975) (listing and describing the canons of construction).

184. R. Posner, supra note 7, at 276.

185. See K. Llewellyn, The Common Law Tradition: Deciding Appeals 521–35 (1960); Wald, Some Observations on the Use of Legislative History in the 1981 Supreme Court Term, 68 Iowa L. Rev. 195, 215–16 (1983) ("[I]n the present state of the law, the various approaches to statutory construction are drawn out as needed, much as a golfer selects the proper club when he gauges the distance to the pin or the contours of the course.").

186. K. Llewellyn, supra note 185, at 521; see also R. Posner, supra note 7, at 202 (Canons of construction are "fig leaves covering decisions reached on other grounds, often grounds of public policy.").

187. See supra p. 225.

188. See Norfolk Redevelopment & Housing Authority v. Chesapeake & Potomac Tel. Co., 464 U.S. 30, 35 (1983). Interestingly, Judge Easterbrook seems to endorse the

main of efficient common law rules from encroachment by ill-conceived, special interest statutes.[189] Were this canon invoked with regularity, Congress would be forced to be much more explicit about the nature of the statutes it adopts. This is especially true if this canon were applied along with the rule that statutes should be interpreted according to their "plain meaning" even if that interpretation is contrary to Congress' actual purpose.[190] By forcing the legislature to spell out more clearly the terms of its bargains with special interest groups, these canons strengthen the separation of powers and limit special interest legislation. These methods of interpretation are a legitimate exercise of judicial power, because they do not obstruct the ability of the legislature to make law, and they do not allow judges to pick and choose between statutes they like and statutes they do not like.

In contrast, some other canons enhance the efficacy of hidden special interest bargains by increasing the probability that the bargains will be enforced in the courts. Prominent among these is the rule that remedial statutes are to be broadly construed.[191] Often, "remedial" statutes do not actually remedy anything, but are used as a guise for the transfer of wealth to some favored group. The Interstate Commerce Act[192] and the Glass-Steagall Act[193] are remedial statutes that have come to be seen as promoting the narrow interests of particular industry groups.[194] When judges are called upon to apply such remedial

use of this canon, at least when special interest statutes are being construed. The basis for his endorsement is that special interest groups are entitled only to the exact terms of the deal they reached with the legislature and no more. A judge should seek out the bargain and enforce it, but only as a "faithful agent" of the legislature, not with "enthusiasm." Easterbrook, supra note 17, at 15.

189. There is a growing literature on the efficiency of the common law. See Cooter & Kornhauser, Can Litigation Improve the Law Without the Help of Judges?, 9 J. Legal Stud. 139 (1980); Goodman, An Economic Theory of the Evolution of Common Law, 7 J. Legal Stud. 393 (1978); Landes & Posner, Adjudication as a Private Good, 8 J. Legal Stud. 235, 238–40 (1979); Priest, The Common Law Process and the Selection of Efficient Rules, 6 J. Legal Stud. 65 (1977); Rubin, Why is the Common Law Efficient?, 6 J. Legal Stud. 51 (1977); Terrebonne, A Strictly Evolutionary Model of Common Law, 10 J. Legal Stud. 397 (1981).

190. A "milder version" of this canon "holds that in interpreting a statute one should begin, though perhaps not end, with the words of the statute." R. Posner, supra note 7, at 277; see also International Brotherhood of Teamsters v. Daniel, 439 U.S. 551, 558 (1979) ("'The starting point in every case involving construction of a statute is the language itself.'" (quoting Blue Chip Stamps v. Manor Drug Stores, 421 U.S. 723, 756 (1975) (Powell, J., concurring))); Massachusetts Bonding & Ins. Co. v. United States, 352 U.S. 128, 138 (1956) (Frankfurter, J., dissenting) ("Of course, one begins with the words of a statute to ascertain its meaning, but one does not end with them.").

191. See SEC v. C.M. Joiner Leasing Corp., 320 U.S. 344, 353 (1943).

192. Interstate Commerce Act of 1887, ch. 104, 24 Stat. 379 (codified as amended in scattered sections of 49 U.S.C.).

193. The Glass-Steagall Act is the popular name for the Banking Act of 1933, ch. 89, 48 Stat. 162 (codified in scattered sections of 12 U.S.C.).

194. See Macey, supra note 67, at 15–21 (Glass-Steagall Act); Posner, supra note 5, at 271 (Interstate Commerce Act).

statutes they often will find that the statutory language makes little sense in light of their stated public interest objectives. Such statutes must be narrowly construed. Otherwise, they will be devoid of meaning and impossible to apply coherently.[195]

While none of the canons of construction intrudes absolutely on the authority of the legislature to make law, some canons serve the public interest better than others because they provide better incentives for Congress to pass public-regarding legislation. Thus, sensitivity to the economics of legislation leads to normative conclusions in favor of canons of construction that encourage legislative honesty and raise the costs of passing special interest legislation. The use of these canons enables judges to fulfill their function within the constitutional scheme as a check on legislative abuse without requiring that they attempt to determine on a case by case basis which statutes are public-regarding and which are not. Other canons, such as the broad construction of remedial statutes, that make legislative subterfuge less costly, do not satisfy the requirement that article III courts should serve as a check on rent-seeking in the legislature.[196]

Conclusion

Examining the independent judiciary from an interest group perspective sheds new light on what Alexander Bickel described as the

195. It is important to observe that the ordering of the canons of construction does not require judges to pick and choose among statutes on the basis of whether the statute is public-regarding or not. Rather, the rank ordering is based simply on the *general recognition that at least some unspecifiable number of statutes* are special interest in nature. The basis for the ordering of the canons suggested here is that the preferred canons are realistic about the dual nature of legislation and exert pressure on Congress to enact public-regarding statutes, by raising the cost of enacting special interest statutes.

It has been argued that the canon regarding remedial statutes would be a "sound working rule" if every statute were public-regarding. See R. Posner, supra note 7, at 278; see also Easterbrook, supra note 17, at 15 ("If statutes generally are designed to . . . replace the calamities produced by unguided private conduct with the ordered rationality of the public sector, then it makes sense to use the remedial approach to the construction of statutes . . . ."). But, as argued above, see supra note 165 and accompanying text, judges do not need much help to interpret public-regarding statutes, because in such statutes the nature of the legislature's objective is plain. These statutes do not have to be construed more broadly or more narrowly than Congress intended in order to give them a fixed meaning.

196. This argument can perhaps best be seen in light of the argument made by Judge Easterbrook that judges, when construing interest group legislation, should give interest groups precisely what they bargained for, no more and no less. Easterbrook, supra note 17, at 15. Viewed from the ex ante perspective that Judge Easterbrook himself advocates, the approach to the canons of construction taken here does precisely that. When a bargain between a legislature and a special interest group is struck, there will be, ex ante, some probability (greater than zero) that the bargain ultimately will be abrogated in the courts. Once the new rules of the game are made clear, nothing will change except that the present value of rent-seeking in the legislature will go down, and on the margin fewer such bargains will be made.

counter-majoritarian difficulty of judicial review. The analysis here suggests that, as an institution, the independent judiciary places subtle pressures on Congress to act in ways that benefit the public. In addition, the third branch imposes costs on the interest groups that seek to transfer wealth to themselves from the rest of society. Most important, the judiciary can accomplish these ends in ways that enhance, rather than diminish, the constitutional separation of powers and the lawmaking authority of elected officials.

The conclusions in this Article are a testament to Edmund Burke's views on the enduring value of society's traditional institutions.[197] As an institution, the federal judiciary is subject to two fundamental criticisms. First, those who benefit from legislative outcomes are likely to complain that any judicial interference with statutory enactments conflicts with the principle of majority rule. Those who lack access to the legislative process can respond that the Constitution is committed not only to the principle of majority rule but also to the principle, envisioned by the separation of powers, that the lawmaking process must be checked. The absence of obvious checking by courts leads to the second criticism—that judges should control legislative excess. The imperative that judges steer a course between these two constitutional principles inexorably mitigates against absolutes. Individual rights are threatened rather than enhanced by judges who seek to impose their ideas of the common good upon the rest of us. Thus, where statutes are naked wealth transfers to special interest groups—what has been described here as "open-explicit" bargains—the choice is between two unappealing alternatives. The first is to enforce the statute so as to maintain the terms of a bargain that is clearly not in the public interest. The second, which is to invalidate the rule for some reason or other, has a surface appeal, because it seems to serve the public interest. In reality, however, this alternative is not likely to be invoked by judges or tolerated by Congress where it is invoked. But the conclusion that judges cannot, on constitutional grounds, substitute their own notions of the public good for the will of the legislature does not mean that they must shrink from their responsibility to constrain legislative excess. Such constraints are vital, but they must be imposed without upsetting the balance created by the separation of powers.

The value of the independent judiciary does not lie in its unbridled capacity to seek out and do good. As the framers envisioned, the value of the judiciary is institutional rather than episodic in nature. The judiciary is most valuable to society when judges take the "traditional" approach to the interpretation of statutes.

This Article makes no claim that the Constitution is the most effi-

197. See Burke, Reflections on the Revolution in France, *in* 3 The Works of the Right Honourable Edmund Burke 19 (1792); see also P. Magnus, Edmund Burke (1939) (describing the nature of Burke's philosophy); J. Morley, Burke (1887) (same). Burke's ideas are brilliantly summarized in A. Bickel, supra note 123, at 23–30.

cient mechanism possible for restraining rent-seeking. Nonetheless, the Constitution permits judges, using traditional methods of statutory interpretation, to play a role in regulating the activities of special interest groups. The suggestions set forth here may appear to be disturbingly modest weapons with which to confront the seemingly awesome problem posed by special interest groups. But the alternative is to abandon representative democracy in favor of either the anarchy of direct participation or the tyranny of judicial despotism.

Law and Wealth Redistribution

[8]

WHY THE LEGAL SYSTEM IS LESS EFFICIENT THAN THE INCOME TAX IN REDISTRIBUTING INCOME

*LOUIS KAPLOW and STEVEN SHAVELL**

In economic analysis of law, normative judgments about legal rules are usually based on the rules' efficiency, regardless of their effects on the distribution of income. As a consequence, the economic approach is often criticized. Such criticism would be moot if the income tax system—understood here to include possible transfer payments to the poor—could be used freely to achieve any desired distribution of income. But income taxes and transfer payments distort incentives to work, limiting the degree to which it is socially desirable to employ the income tax system to redistribute income. The question therefore arises whether legal rules[1] should be used to take up some of the slack and promote distributional objectives,[2] even if at a sacrifice to efficiency.

In this article, we develop the argument that redistribution through legal rules offers no advantage over redistribution through the income tax system and typically is less efficient.[3] The reason is that using legal

* Professors, Harvard Law School, and Research Associates, the National Bureau of Economic Research. We are grateful for comments from Jennifer Arlen, Reuven Avi-Yonah, David Charny, A. Mitchell Polinsky, Alvin Warren, and participants in a workshop at Georgetown University Law Center.

[1] For purposes of this article, the term "legal rules" refers to rules other than those that define the income tax and welfare system.

[2] Our discussion concerns the overall distribution of income or wealth, not entitlement to payment based on desert.

[3] The first model establishing this point is in Steven Shavell, A Note on Efficiency vs. Distributional Equity in Legal Rulemaking: Should Distributional Equity Matter Given Optimal Income Taxation? 71 Am. Econ. Rev. 414 (1981). A related argument is made in Aanund Hylland & Richard Zeckhauser, Distributional Objectives Should Affect Taxes but Not Program Choice or Design, 81 Scand. J. Econ. 264 (1979). (For extensions and further applications, see Louis Kaplow, Should the Government's Allocation Branch Be Concerned about the Distortionary Cost of Taxation and Distributive Effects? (Discussion Paper No. 137, Harvard Law School Program in Law and Economics 1993).)

It does not appear, however, that the point is understood in legal academia. See, for

[*Journal of Legal Studies*, vol. XXIII (June 1994)]
 0047-2530/94/2302-0001$01.50

rules to redistribute income distorts work incentives fully as much as the income tax system—because the distortion is caused by the redistribution itself—and also creates inefficiencies in the activities regulated by the legal rules.

To illustrate, suppose that high-income individuals are subject to an income tax of 30 percent and that, in principle, further redistribution to the poor would be desirable. Would we want to adopt an inefficient legal rule because it redistributes an additional 1 percent of high earners' income to the poor? Under such a regime, high-earning individuals would surrender 31 percent of each additional dollar of income: 30 percent would go to the tax authority, and 1 percent would be taken by the legal system. Now assume, instead, that an efficient legal rule is retained and the income tax rate for high earners is raised to 31 percent. Then they would be in the same position and would be induced to work the same amount as under the inefficient regime. (The increase in the tax rate from 30 to 31 percent does not reduce their incentive to work because it is offset by the 1 percent decrease in the implicit tax that was associated with the inefficient legal rule.) The added tax revenue could be given to the poor, just as under the regime with the inefficient legal rule. Hence, redistribution using the 31 percent income tax and the efficient legal rule differs in only one respect from redistribution using the inefficient legal rule with the 30 percent income tax: because redistribution is accomplished in the presence of an efficient legal rule, resources would, by definition, be saved. With this savings, all individuals could be made better off (for example, by reducing taxes and increasing payments to the poor).

---

example, Guido Calabresi, The Pointlessness of Pareto: Carrying Coase Further, 100 Yale L. J. 1211, 1224 n.36 (1991) ("far from obvious that, as a general matter, tax and welfare programs *are* more efficient than a mixture of these and of other rules of law"); Duncan Kennedy, Distributive and Paternalist Motives in Contract and Tort Law, with Special Reference to Compulsory Terms and Unequal Bargaining Power, 41 Md. L. Rev. 563, 613 (1982) (inefficiencies from compulsory terms and from redistribution through taxation "involve exactly the same kinds of waste," leaving a difficult empirical question as to which is preferable); Anthony T. Kronman, Contract Law and Distributive Justice, 89 Yale L. J. 472, 508 (1980) (because taxation and contractual regulation both have efficiency costs, determining the preferable means of redistribution raises an empirical question that "must be resolved on a case-by-case basis, in the light of detailed information about the circumstances likely to influence the effectiveness of each method of redistribution"). In addition, Jennifer Arlen does not take into account the existence of the income tax system in arguing that legal rules should reflect parties' wealth. See Jennifer H. Arlen, Should Defendants' Wealth Matter? 21 J. Legal Stud. 413 (1992) (discussed in note 14 *infra*); see also *id.* at 428 (noting that basing liability on defendants' wealth would affect incentives to accumulate wealth, but claiming that "no matter what the outcome of [further analysis of the issue], it is clear that the conventional analysis . . . is not theoretically sound").

More generally, we show that, *even though the income tax distorts work incentives, any regime with an inefficient legal rule can be replaced by a regime with an efficient legal rule and a modified income tax system designed so that every person is made better off.* In Section I, we present the analysis leading to this conclusion. In Section II, we discuss briefly the general role of legal rules in redistribution and when, if ever, it is efficient for legal rules to take into account parties' wealth.

I. Analysis

We provide here an informal demonstration of our result: given any regime with an inefficient legal rule (notably, one intended to help achieve a redistributive goal), there exists an alternative regime with an efficient legal rule and a modified income tax system in which all individuals are better off. For concreteness, we will use a specific example in our analysis, but it will be clear that our argument does not depend on the particulars of the example. (For a formal proof, and discussion of certain qualifications, see the Appendix.)

Suppose that individuals engage in an activity that may cause accidents, the likelihood of which may be reduced by potential injurers' exercise of care. It is a familiar result that the strict liability rule—under which individuals pay for the harm they cause—leads to efficient behavior. Suppose that each individual's expected net accident costs under this rule, denoted $\hat{a}$, are \$1,000. These equal the cost of care, harm suffered, and damages paid, less damages received.

Compare this efficient legal rule to an inefficient one that redistributes income from higher- to lower-income individuals. (Redistribution might be accomplished, for example, by setting damages higher when the injurer is wealthy and lower when the injurer is poor. Such a redistributive legal rule would be inefficient: it would induce the wealthy to take more care and the poor to take less care than is efficient.) Let us denote the net expected accident costs—the cost of care, harm suffered, and damages paid, less damages received—individuals bear under this rule by $a(y)$; that is, an individual's accident costs are a function of his income, y. (Expected accident costs must be a function of income if the rule is to redistribute income relative to a rule under which everyone's accident costs are the same.)

In particular, suppose that relative to the efficient rule the poorest (those with income of \$0) benefit by \$500 and the richest (those with income of \$100,000) lose \$1,000, with a linear relationship in between. Figure 1 depicts accident costs under this inefficient rule and also under the efficient strict liability rule. Relative to the efficient rule, the ineffi-

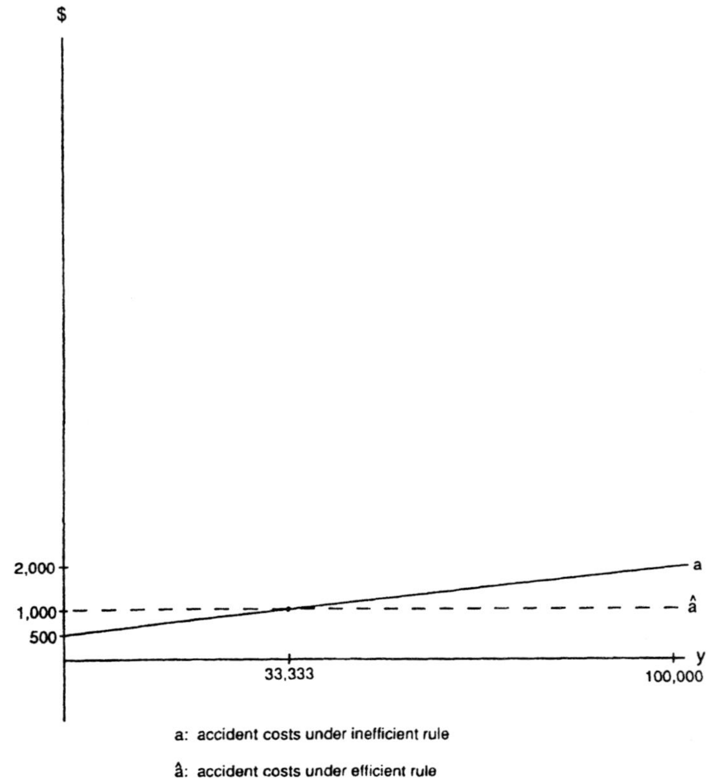

FIGURE 1

cient legal rule redistributes from those with incomes over $33,333 to those with lower incomes.

To complete the description of the regime with the inefficient rule, assume that there is an income tax with a rate of 20 percent. In particular, individuals pay tax on 20 percent of their income to the extent it exceeds $10,000; individuals with income under $10,000 receive transfer payments equaling 20 percent of the difference (so those earning no income receive $2,000).[4] This tax system, denoted t, is illustrated by the solid line in Figure 2.

In Figure 2, we also show a dashed line for $t + a$, which represents individuals' total payments under the tax system and on account of accidents in the regime with the inefficient legal rule. It is this combination that determines an individual's welfare level and work incentives. With

[4] This may be familiar to some readers as a negative income tax. It also is analogous to a conventional income tax combined with a welfare system.

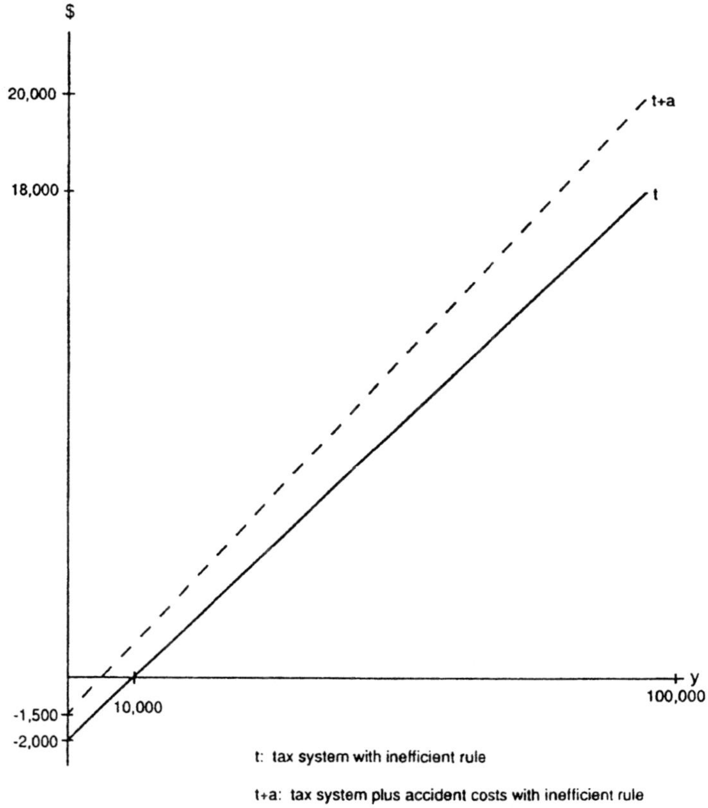

FIGURE 2

regard to the latter, we emphasize that when an individual with income *y* contemplates earning additional income by working harder, his total marginal expected payments equal the sum of his marginal tax payment and the expected marginal cost on account of accidents.[5]

Having described the regime under the inefficient legal rule, we will demonstrate that all individuals can be made better off in a regime with the efficient legal rule and an altered income tax system. Consider the

[5] Of course, the extent to which individuals accurately perceive both their marginal tax rate and the amount implicitly taxed by the legal system is an empirical question. We think it plausible that if the legal system redistributed a significant amount of income, individuals would take this into account. (After all, individuals often would not need to understand the effects of legal rules; rather, they might simply observe, for example, the resulting high prices of products bought disproportionately by the rich.) If they misestimated the extent of redistribution, there is no compelling reason to assume that their guesses would be too low rather than too high.

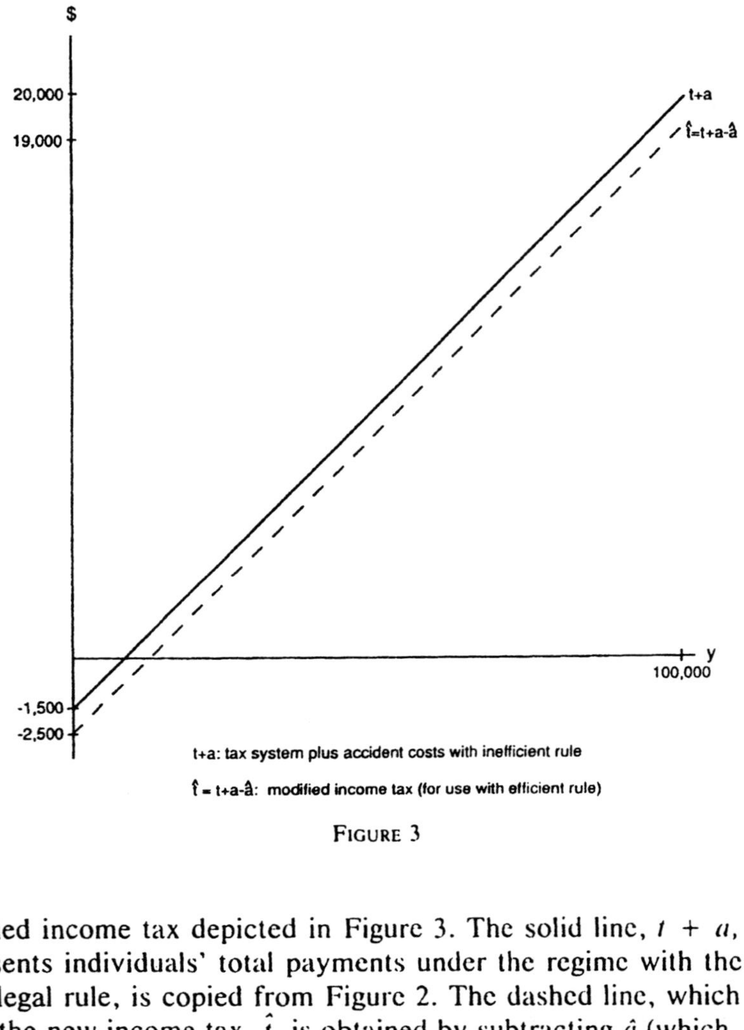

FIGURE 3

modified income tax depicted in Figure 3. The solid line, $t + a$, which represents individuals' total payments under the regime with the inefficient legal rule, is copied from Figure 2. The dashed line, which represents the new income tax, $\hat{t}$, is obtained by subtracting $\hat{a}$ (which, recall, equals $1,000 for all income levels) from the line $t + a$. The two tax regimes are compared in Figure 4.[6]

We can now describe individuals' behavior and welfare under the efficient legal rule combined with the new income tax. The total effect of the tax and accident costs is given by the sum $\hat{t} + \hat{a}$. But, by construction, this expression is identical to $t + a$ for any income level. (After all, $\hat{t}$ is constructed by subtracting $\hat{a}$ from $t + a$. When $\hat{a}$ is added back, the result must equal $t + a$.) Thus, individuals who earn income y have

[6] The schedule $\hat{t}(y)$ is steeper than $t(y)$—that is, more redistributive—by precisely the amount by which $a(y)$ is steeper than $\hat{a}$, as depicted in Figure 1.

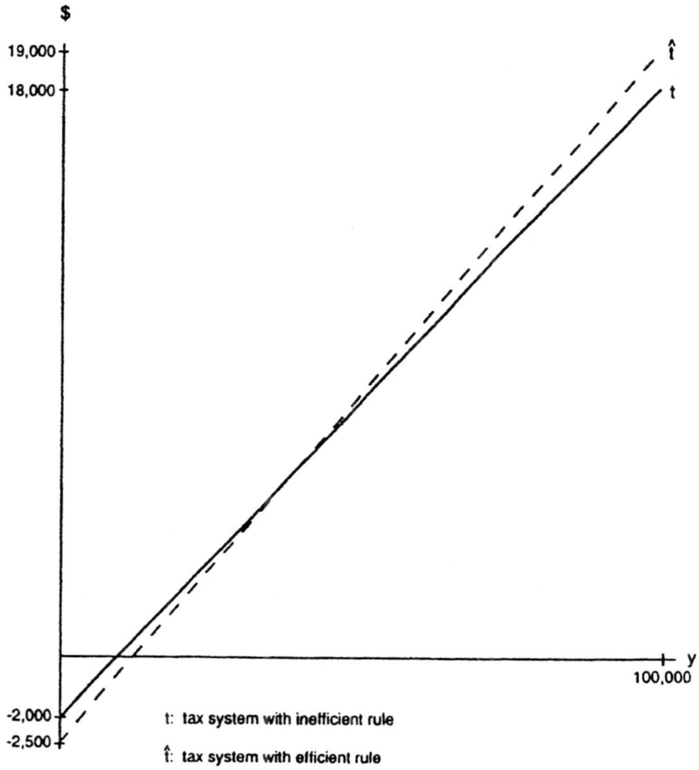

FIGURE 4

the same level of welfare under each regime. Moreover, each individual (whatever his ability) will choose to earn the same income under each regime because his incentives will be unchanged: a marginal dollar earned will result in the same incremental costs (taxes plus accident costs) under both regimes.

Although work effort and an individual's after-tax welfare are identical under the two regimes, the state collects more tax revenue in the new regime because it involves a more efficient legal rule. To see why this must be true, we first compare total available resources in each regime. Because individuals' work effort is unaffected by the new regime, total earnings will be the same. But the inefficient rule by definition wastes resources relative to the efficient rule, so total resources must be greater under the new regime. Yet the new income tax leaves individuals with the same income as in the initial regime. Thus, it must be that the new tax collects all the resources saved by the efficient legal rule. Indeed, the new tax was constructed precisely to produce this result.

To illustrate, consider the case in which individuals' income is uniformly distributed over the range from \$0 to \$100,000. It is straightforward to calculate that the per capita cost of the inefficient legal rule is \$250. The per capita revenue under the original income tax, t, is \$8,000, and per capita revenue under the modified income tax, $\hat{t}$, is \$8,250. Indeed, the modified tax collects greater revenue by an amount that just equals the resources wasted by the inefficient legal rule.

The conclusion is that adopting the efficient legal rule, with an appropriate change in the income tax, leaves all individuals equally well off but leaves the government with a surplus. With this additional revenue, the government can make each individual better off—for example, by lowering taxes (for the poor, increasing transfers) by a fixed amount for each individual or spending the funds on a public good that benefits everyone.[7]

II. Discussion

(*a*) *Factors bearing on redistribution through legal rules.* In this article, we have emphasized that redistribution through legal rules is less efficient than redistribution through the income tax. Other more familiar considerations of feasibility and accuracy also favor redistribution through the income tax system.[8] Specifically, the income tax system (including transfer programs) can redistribute from all the rich to all the poor,[9] whereas legal rules have substantially less redistributive potential. First, when parties are in a contractual relationship, it is well understood that redistribution usually is not accomplished because prices generally adjust to reflect the expected cost of legal rules.[10] Second, when redistri-

[7] In practice, redistribution through the income tax rather than through legal rules would not literally make everyone better off. Inevitably, some would gain more than others and a few might lose. Systematic distributive effects across income levels can be avoided by adjusting the income tax, which leaves the possibility of sporadic unequal treatment within income classes. There is, however, no reason that such inequality would be greater when using the income tax rather than legal rules to redistribute income. For reasons noted in Section II(*a*) one might expect legal rules to fare worse on this account.

[8] See, for example, A. Mitchell Polinsky, An Introduction to Law and Economics 124–27 (2d ed. 1989).

[9] Many exceptions, such as adjustments for numbers of dependents, presumably reflect aspects of distributional policy. Others, such as those that result from tax evasion and welfare fraud, may be addressed in many ways (increasing enforcement, augmenting income taxes with luxury taxes). It would be surprising, however, if courts could more accurately determine true income in, say, private tort disputes than in tax evasion or welfare fraud enforcement proceedings.

[10] Contract rules may affect distribution if prices are also regulated, but then the price regulation itself may be used to accomplish redistribution among such parties. Also, there may be some incidental distributive effects of contract rules, such as when some individuals must expend resources to opt out of default rules that are suitable for others.

bution is possible, it tends to be limited to those few who become parties to lawsuits. And even then, redistribution may be haphazard. (A pro-plaintiff rule may be redistributive if plaintiffs, on average, are poorer than defendants, but unless this is uniformly true, the redistribution will flow in the wrong direction in some cases.)[11] The latter problem can be avoided only if the legal rule depends directly on parties' incomes, a policy that few have proposed. Furthermore, if one is prepared to go that far, it becomes difficult to understand why one would administer redistribution in such an ad hoc and inefficient manner rather than through the income tax system.[12]

An argument sometimes offered in favor of redistribution through legal rules is that the tax system falls short of optimal redistributive taxation—perhaps because of the balance of political power in the legislature. This argument raises questions that we do not seek to address about the function of courts in a democracy. In any case, it seems unlikely that courts can accomplish significant redistribution through the legal system without attracting the attention of legislators. Also, much legal reform presently under consideration, such as tort reform, is in the jurisdiction of legislatures.

These points, combined with this article's efficiency argument, suggest that normative economic analysis of legal rules should be primarily concerned with efficiency rather than the distribution of income. Nonetheless, analyzing distribution may be important, because those formulating income tax policy need to be aware of any significant distributive effects of legal rules that would not otherwise be apparent, such as from studying information on the actual distribution of income. Distributive effects, of course, are identified by economic analysis that examines the costs and benefits of legal rules—the same sort of analysis used to determine which rules are efficient.

(*b*) *Is it ever efficient for legal rules to take account of parties' wealth?* We have argued that it is inefficient for legal rules to take into account parties' wealth in order to redistribute income. We now consider whether there may be other reasons for legal rules to depend on parties' wealth.

Because the poor are more risk-averse than the rich, the efficient allo-

[11] Even when a party appears to be rich, the redistributive effect may be more limited. For example, when corporations pay more for injuries to third parties, consumer prices and wages will be affected.

[12] Thus, although we did not consider the possible additional administrative costs of increasing the amount of redistribution through the income tax, it seems plausible that these costs would be less than those of achieving significant, well-targeted redistribution through legal rules.

cation of risk might appear to justify taking wealth into account in the design of legal rules. For example, poor injurers might be assessed lower damages, the law's generosity providing them implicit partial liability insurance. Yet, if liability insurance is available in the marketplace, it is inefficient to adjust damages to reflect risk aversion.[13] Insurance purchases will provide the optimal degree of risk mitigation; furthermore, imposition of damages fully equal to harm is necessary to induce potential injurers and their insurers to take complete account of harm that might be caused. Thus, any adjustment in legal rules due to parties' risk aversion, as evidenced by their wealth, must be premised on a failure in insurance markets.[14]

Nevertheless, it often is efficient for damages to reflect the victim's income. When an injury involves lost future earnings, the level of earnings indicates the extent of economic loss.[15] In addition, under a negligence rule, sometimes it is efficient for the standard of care to depend on parties' income. To illustrate, suppose that a precaution that reduces expected accident costs by $15 takes an hour of effort. This precaution would be efficient for individuals who can otherwise earn only $10 an hour but not for those whose opportunity cost is $20 an hour.[16]

[13] This is demonstrated in Steven Shavell, On Liability and Insurance, 13 Bell J. Econ. 120 (1982).

[14] Jennifer Arlen, *supra* note 3, argues that, when parties are risk-averse, their wealth should affect the level of liability—even in the presence of perfect insurance markets and complete insurance. Her result derives from the assumption that the rich value wealth less at the margin than the poor (which is formally equivalent to the assumption that individuals are risk-averse). Therefore, social welfare is advanced by using the legal system to transfer wealth from the rich to the poor; in her model, this is accomplished by imposing higher liability on the rich. Yet she describes the social desirability of higher liability on the rich as an aspect of optimal deterrence, not as the masked transfer of wealth that it is. In fact, a complete analysis of her model would lead to the conclusion that the socially ideal outcome involves damages that fully equalize the wealth of the victim and the injurer. Indeed, if the victim were rich, he would pay "damages" to the injurer! Obviously, it would not be socially desirable to take parties' wealth into account in the manner Arlen suggests unless the income tax were unavailable for redistributive purposes. For further discussion of Arlen's article, see Thomas J. Miceli & Kathleen Segerson, Defining Efficient Care: The Role of Income Redistribution, 24 J. Legal Stud. (1995, in press).

[15] The argument assumes that injurers have some advance knowledge of the economic loss they might cause. If they knew only average losses for all victims, a rule providing that damages equal average harm would be equally efficient. See Louis Kaplow & Steven Shavell, Accuracy in the Assessment of Damages (Working Paper No. 4287, National Bureau of Economic Research 1993).

[16] An implicit assumption in this argument is that it is not possible simply to hire someone else to undertake the precaution. Also, note that under a rule of strict liability, damages should equal $15 rather than assessing higher damages on the rich in order to induce them to take the same care that others take.

III. Conclusion

Redistribution is accomplished more efficiently through the income tax system than through the use of legal rules, even when redistributive taxes distort behavior. Redistribution through legal rules causes the same inefficiency as taxes with regard to the labor-leisure choice: the distortion is caused by the redistribution itself and is not particular to the mechanism by which it is accomplished. And when redistribution involves choosing less efficient legal rules, additional costs are incurred. This argument, along with others that are more familiar, suggests that it is appropriate for economic analysis of legal rules to focus on efficiency and to ignore the distribution of income in offering normative judgments.[17]

APPENDIX

Formal Proof and Remarks

The model parallels the illustration in Section I. Individuals exercise care x and cause accidents with probability $p(x)$, with $p' < 0, p'' > 0$. An accident causes harm of h, which is borne equally by all individuals.[18] Individuals differ in their ability α to earn income y through labor effort ℓ, where $y(\alpha) = \alpha\ell$ and (for notational simplicity) α is distributed uniformly on the interval [0,1]. Individuals who cause accidents pay damages of d. The income tax schedule is $t(y)$.

We begin with an inefficient legal rule in which damages are $d(y_I, y_V)$, where y_I is the injurer's income and y_V is the victim's income. (Allowing damages to depend on parties' incomes makes redistribution possible.) Each individual chooses labor effort, ℓ, and care, x, to maximize expected utility, which is

$$EU = y - \ell - t(y) - x - \bar{p}h - p(x)\int_0^1 d(y, y_V(\alpha))\,d\alpha + \int_0^1 p(x(y_I(\alpha)))\,d(y_I(\alpha), y)\,d\alpha, \qquad \text{(A1)}$$

where $\bar{p}$ is the average probability that others will cause a person harm and where, recall, $y = \alpha\ell$. The first four terms on the right side are income, work effort, income tax payments, and care. Next, utility is reduced by the expected harm a person suffers, $\bar{p}h$. The final two terms represent payments made and received under the legal rule. Payments are made when a person causes an accident, which has probability $p(x)$; damages, in turn, depend on a person's own income, y (when one is the injurer), and each possible victim's income ($y_V(\alpha)$ is the income earned by the type of individual who has ability α)—the integral measures the total over

[17] Conventional efficiency analysis of legal rules that abstracts from the distribution of income typically will yield the same result as an analysis that fully incorporates both the distributive effects of legal rules and adjustments to the income tax system. The conventional approach, however, is preferable on grounds of simplicity.

[18] Alternatively, it could be assumed that each individual bears harm with equal probability, so that the expected harm is the same for each individual.

all possible victims. Payments are received when one is injured; each type of individual causes an accident with probability $p(x(y_I(\alpha)))$ and pays damages reflecting his income—the integral measures the sum over all types who might injure a person.[19]

We now compare this regime to one with an efficient legal rule and a modified income tax system. The efficient rule is $\hat{d} = h$; as is well known, under strict liability when injurers pay damages equal to harm caused, all costs are internalized, so actors are induced to take the level of care that minimizes the sum of the cost of care and expected harm. We denote this efficient level of care as $\hat{x}$ and observe that it is independent of one's income level. It will be useful to denote the inefficiency caused by the damages rule $d(y_I, y_V)$ by

$$\pi = \int_0^1 \Big[[x(y(\alpha)) + p(x(y(\alpha)))h] - [\hat{x} + p(\hat{x})h] \Big] d\alpha. \tag{A2}$$

Because the damage rule d is inefficient, π is positive. (The integrand is positive whenever $x(y(\alpha))$ is unequal to efficient care $\hat{x}$.)[20]

In the regime with the efficient damages rule $\hat{d} = h$, let the modified income tax be

$$\hat{t}(y) = t(y) + \Big[x(y) + \bar{p}h + p(x(y)) \int_0^1 d(y, y_V(\alpha))\, d\alpha - \int_0^1 p(x(y_I(\alpha)))d(y_I(\alpha), y)\, d\alpha \Big] - \Big[\hat{x} + p(\hat{x})h \Big]. \tag{A3}$$

Note that, as in Section I, the new income tax, $\hat{t}(y)$, is constructed by beginning with the initial income tax, $t(y)$, adding total accident costs under the initial, inefficient regime and subtracting total accident costs under the efficient regime. The former total (under the inefficient rule) is the first term in large brackets: the cost of care, harm suffered, and expected damage payments, minus expected damage awards received. The latter (under the efficient rule) is the second term in large brackets: the cost of care and expected damage payments (harm suffered is precisely offset by expected damage awards received). As a result of the first adjustment, the new income tax changes with income in exactly the way that accident-related costs did under the inefficient liability rule. Thus, if higher-income individuals paid more in damages, now they pay more in taxes instead.

We next demonstrate that the expected utility of individuals will be the same under the new tax $\hat{t}(y)$ and the efficient legal rule as it is under the initial income tax and the inefficient rule. Recall that, under the efficient legal rule, all individuals (regardless of income) choose the same level of care, $\hat{x}$. Also, as just noted, expected harm suffered is just offset by expected damage awards received because damages equal harm. Hence, in the new regime, individuals choose labor effort ℓ to maximize expected utility, which is

[19] The last four terms together correspond to the expression $a(y)$ in the notation of Section I.

[20] In particular, whenever the damage rule d results in an expected payment exceeding h (as it would when injurers are relatively wealthy, if the rule is redistributive in a manner that favors the poor), injurers will take excessive care. Similarly, when the damage rule d results in an expected payment less than h (as when injurers are relatively poor), injurers will take too little care.

$$E\hat{U} = y - \ell - \hat{t}(y) - \hat{x} - p(\hat{x})h. \tag{A4}$$

If one uses (A3) to substitute for $\hat{t}(y)$ in (A4) and compares the result to (A1), the expression for expected utility in the initial regime, it is apparent that, for any income level y,

$$E\hat{U} = EU. \tag{A5}$$

Because expected utility is the same for any level of labor effort, ℓ, individuals of any given ability will choose the same labor effort under both regimes. This, in turn, implies that their welfare will be identical under both regimes.

Finally, we show that tax revenues are greater under the modified income tax. In particular,

$$\int_0^1 \hat{t}(y(\alpha))\,d\alpha = \int_0^1 t(y(\alpha))\,d\alpha + \pi. \tag{A6}$$

This follows directly from the definitions of $\hat{t}(y)$ in (A3) and π in (A2). After all, $\hat{t}(y)$ is constructed to equal $t(y)$, plus the total accident costs under the inefficient rule minus the total accident costs under the efficient rule. And π is defined to equal just this difference in accident costs. (The only difference between the bracketed expressions in [A3] and the right side of [A2] is that the former includes terms for damages individuals pay and receive. But when one integrates over all individuals, the total of damages paid and received are equal, so these components are precisely offsetting.)

One can define a new tax by $\hat{t}(y)-\pi$. (That is, the savings in accident costs are uniformly rebated, in a lump-sum manner, to the entire population.) Under this tax, labor effort will be unchanged (since the tax differs from $\hat{t}(y)$ by a constant),[21] so revenues will now be the same as under the initial tax, $t(y)$. Each individual is better off by π.

Remarks. (a) Generality of the result. It should be apparent that our result does not depend on the nature of the activity (for example, one could incorporate victim care), the form of the legal rule, the income tax system,[22] or the distribution of ability. The result might appear to depend on some features of the utility function—notably, risk neutrality, the lack of income effects, and care being independent of ability. Relaxing these assumptions would make determination of the efficient legal rule more complicated. It would remain true, however, that if the redistribution accomplished through an inefficient legal rule were instead achieved through a modification of the tax system, resources would be saved and all individuals could be made better off.

(b) Excise taxes versus legal rules as redistributive devices. Reasoning similar to that in our article suggests the superiority of excise taxes over legal rules as

[21] The utility function (A1) involves no income effects; if there were income effects, the argument would hold except that the amount of rebate that would restore budget balance would be less than π.

[22] For convenience, we examine the distribution of income with an income tax as the redistributive tool. In a dynamic analysis, one might wish to distinguish the distribution of consumption or wealth from the distribution of income (and consider consumption or wealth taxes in addition to an income tax), which would raise the issue of distorting savings. One can think of the labor-leisure distortion as exemplifying any distortion that results from a general redistributive tax.

redistributive tools. Suppose, for example, that there is an inefficient legal rule that requires excessive care by owners of yachts. Moreover, assume that this rule has desirable distributive features because yacht owners are usually wealthier than those injured by yachts. The inefficiency caused by this rule will have three components: excessive care is by definition more costly than the harm prevented; yachting is made more expensive, which distorts choices between yachting and other activities (for example, playing golf); and income buys less for the rich, which distorts their labor-leisure choices.

Consider the alternative of using an efficient legal rule combined with an appropriate excise tax on yachting, the proceeds to be distributed to low-income individuals (perhaps the victims of yachting accidents). Distortions of the amount of yachting and labor-leisure decisions would remain the same: the rich would pay more on account of the excise tax rather than on account of bearing higher accident costs (the sum of prevention costs and expected liability payments).[23] But the first inefficiency, excessive care, would be avoided. Thus, the excise tax would allow more efficient redistribution than the legal rule.

Observe, however, that an excise tax is a less efficient means of redistribution than the income tax, because the excise tax distorts the amount of yachting whereas the income tax does not.[24] Thus, if one wishes to redistribute income, the most efficient choice typically will be the income tax, the second choice would be an excise tax (as with luxury taxes), and the worst alternative would be an inefficient legal rule with desirable distributive consequences.

(c) Qualifications and the relationship between our result and those in the literature on optimal taxation. Our result is analogous to results on optimal taxation. In simple cases, specific commodity excises are inefficient in the presence of an optimal income tax.[25] This conclusion does not hold generally, however, because taxes or subsidies on particular commodities might have

[23] Analogous to the effects of excise taxes are subsidies for particular purchases. The familiar argument is that in-kind welfare assistance (for example, free housing rather than cash of equal market value) is inefficient because it distorts choices such as that between housing and food purchases, in addition to creating potential work disincentives for the poor that would result from cash assistance as well. Although one might justify in-kind welfare programs on other grounds—for example, because we paternalistically wish to force the poor to spend on food and housing—it is difficult to apply such arguments in the context of redistribution through legal rules. (We would not channel redistribution through a tort rule because we wished the poor to be in more accidents caused by the rich.)

[24] Under the Ramsey tax rule, the efficiency of such an excise tax would depend on the elasticity of demand for yachting. But, as explained in the following remark and note 25, this analysis is inapplicable in the presence of an income tax. An excise tax, however, may be superior if the amount of yachting were excessive, as it might be under a negligence rule. See Steven Shavell, Strict Liability versus Negligence, 9 J. Legal Stud. 1 (1980).

[25] For a useful survey of the literature and discussion of the ideas presented in this remark, see Joseph E. Stiglitz, Pareto Efficient and Optimal Taxation and the New New Welfare Economics, in 2 Handbook of Public Economics 991, 1023-27 (Alan J. Auerbach & Martin Feldstein eds. 1987). The survey explains why the familiar Ramsey tax rule—that tax rates on commodities should vary inversely with demand elasticities—is inapplicable in the presence of an income tax. (When an income tax is present, one can raise revenue without causing any distortion in choices among commodities. Hence, differential taxation of commodities is only useful when it reduces the labor-leisure distortion, as explained in the text.)

indirect effects that reduce the distortion of an income tax. In particular, by taxing complements of leisure and by subsidizing substitutes, one can reduce the labor-leisure distortion and thereby improve welfare by more than the inefficiency that results from distorted purchases of the taxed or subsidized commodities.

Analogously, if there were legal disputes involving activities that were strong complements of or substitutes for leisure, one might select rules that provided additional penalties or subsidies relative to what an efficient rule would involve. (As the excise tax discussion suggests, however, this would be the most efficient choice only if taxes or subsidies on the activities themselves were infeasible.) Such penalties and subsidies, however, are not conventionally redistributive: whether an activity should be penalized or subsidized depends on how the activity affects the labor-leisure choice, not on whether it is undertaken disproportionately by the rich. Thus, although a complete and sophisticated analysis does not demonstrate that it could never be efficient to change legal rules from what narrowly seem to be the most efficient ones, there is no general argument for adjustments of a conventionally redistributive type.[26]

[26] For discussion of other qualifications, see Kaplow, *supra* note 3.

Part II
Frontiers

Behavioural

[9]

ARTICLES

A Behavioral Approach to Law and Economics

Christine Jolls,* Cass R. Sunstein,**
and Richard Thaler***

Economic analysis of law usually proceeds under the assumptions of neoclassical economics. But empirical evidence gives much reason to doubt these assumptions; people exhibit bounded rationality, bounded self-interest, and bounded willpower. This article offers a broad vision of how law and economics analysis may be improved by increased attention to insights about actual human behavior. It considers specific topics in the economic analysis of law and proposes new models and approaches for addressing these topics. The analysis of the article is organized into three categories: positive, prescriptive, and normative. Positive analysis of law concerns how agents behave in response to legal rules and how legal rules are shaped. Prescriptive analysis concerns what rules should be adopted to advance specified ends. Normative analysis attempts to assess more broadly the ends of the legal system: Should the system always respect people's choices? By drawing attention to cognitive and motivational problems of both citizens and government, behavioral law and economics offers answers distinct from those offered by the standard analysis.

---

* Assistant Professor of Law, Harvard Law School.

** Karl N. Llewellyn Distinguished Service Professor of Jurisprudence, University of Chicago.

*** Robert P. Gwinn Professor of Economics and Behavioral Science, Graduate School of Business, University of Chicago.

We acknowledge the helpful comments of Ian Ayres, Lucian Bebchuk, Colin Camerer, David Charny, Richard Craswell, Jon Elster, Nuno Garoupa, J.B. Heaton, Samuel Issacharoff, Dan Kahan, Louis Kaplow, Lewis Kornhauser, Lawrence Lessig, Steven Levitt, A. Mitchell Polinsky, Eric Posner, Richard Posner, Richard Revesz, Steven Shavell, Jonathan Zittrain, Ari Zweiman, and participants at the American Law and Economics Association Annual Meeting, the Boston University Law School Faculty Workshop, the Columbia University Law and Economics Workshop, workshops at Harvard Law School on law and economics and on rationality, the NBER Behavioral Law and Economics Conference, the NYU Rational Choice Colloquium, and the University of Chicago Law and Economics Workshop. Todd Murtha and Gil Seinfeld provided outstanding research assistance. Nicole Armenta provided helpful material on criminal abstinence programs. This work was finished while Thaler was a Fellow at the Center for Advanced Study in the Behavioral Sciences; he is grateful for the Center's support.

INTRODUCTION

Objections to the rational actor model in law and economics are almost as old as the field itself. Early skeptics about the economic analysis of law were quick to marshal arguments from psychology and other social sciences to undermine its claims.[1] But in law, challenges to the rational actor assumption by those who sympathize with the basic objectives of economic analysis have been much less common. The absence of sustained and comprehensive economic analysis of legal rules from a perspective informed by insights about actual human behavior makes for a significant contrast with many other fields of economics, where such "behavioral" analysis has become relatively common.[2] This is especially odd since law is a domain where behavioral analysis would appear to be particularly promising in light of the fact that nonmarket behavior is frequently involved.

Our goal in this article is to advance an approach to the economic analysis of law that is informed by a more accurate conception of choice, one that reflects a better understanding of human behavior and its wellsprings. We build on and attempt to generalize earlier work in law outlining behavioral findings by taking the two logical next steps: proposing a systematic framework for a behavioral approach to economic analysis of law, and using behavioral insights to develop specific models and approaches addressing top-

1. *See, e.g.*, Mark Kelman, *Consumption Theory, Production Theory, and Ideology in the Coase Theorem*, 52 S. CAL. L. REV. 669 (1979); Duncan Kennedy, *Cost-Benefit Analysis of Entitlement Problems: A Critique*, 33 STAN. L. REV. 387 (1981); Arthur Allen Leff, *Economic Analysis of Law: Some Realism About Nominalism*, 60 VA. L. REV. 451 (1974).

2. *See, e.g.*, volume 112, issue 2 of the *Quarterly Journal of Economics*, which contains 11 articles related to behavioral economics.

ics of abiding interest in law and economics.[3] The analysis of these specific topics is preliminary and often in the nature of a proposal for a research agenda; we touch on a wide range of issues in an effort to show the potential uses of behavioral insights. The unifying idea in our analysis is that behavioral economics allows us to model and predict behavior relevant to law with the tools of traditional economic analysis, but with more accurate assumptions about human behavior, and more accurate predictions and prescriptions about law. Certainly a great deal of work would be necessary to justify a final evaluation of most of the topics pursued here; there is fertile ground for future research, both theoretical and empirical, and one of our principal goals is to suggest the directions in which that research might go.

We suggest that an approach based on behavioral economics will help with the three functions of any proposed approach to law: positive, prescriptive, and normative.[4] The positive task, perhaps most central to economic analysis of law and our principal emphasis here, is to explain both the effects and content of law. How will law affect human behavior? What will individuals' likely response to changes in the rules be? Why does law take the form that it does? A superior understanding of human behavior will improve answers to such questions.

The prescriptive task is to see how law might be used to achieve specified ends, such as deterring socially undesirable behavior. Much of conventional economic analysis is concerned with this sort of question. Explicit consideration of behavioral factors can improve the prescriptions offered by the analyst. For instance, instead of focusing only on the actual probability of detecting criminal behavior in considering whether offenders will be deterred, the analyst might also want to consider the *perceived* probability of detection and how it might differ in systematic and predictable ways from the actual probability.

The normative task is to assess more broadly the ends of the legal system. In conventional economic analysis, normative analysis is no different from prescriptive analysis, since the goal of the legal system is to maximize

---

3. The existing legal literature includes several articles that generally catalogue behavioral findings and suggest legal issues to which these findings might be relevant. *See* Ward Edwards & Detlof von Winterfeldt, *Cognitive Illusions and Their Implications for the Law*, 59 S. CAL. L. REV. 225 (1986); Melvin Aron Eisenberg, *The Limits of Cognition and the Limits of Contract*, 47 STAN. L. REV. 211 (1995); Robert C. Ellickson, *Bringing Culture and Human Frailty to Rational Actors: A Critique of Classical Law and Economics*, 65 CHI.-KENT L. REV. 23 (1989); Cass R. Sunstein, *Behavioral Analysis of Law*, 64 U. CHI. L. REV. 1175 (1997). The existing literature also includes a number of articles that use behavioral insights to analyze specific topics in the economic analysis of law—primarily the Coase theorem and behavior during bargaining. These articles are relevant to a few of the issues we discuss below, and we will draw on them in analyzing those issues.

4. For a similar distinction between positive, prescriptive, and normative analysis, see David E. Bell, Howard Raiffa & Amos Tversky, *Descriptive, Normative, and Prescriptive Interactions in Decision Making*, *in* DECISION MAKING 9 (David E. Bell, Howard Raiffa & Amos Tversky eds., 1988); Sunstein, *supra* note 3.

"social welfare," usually measured by people's revealed preferences, and prescriptive (in our sense of the term) analysis also focuses, for the conventional economist, on how to maximize social welfare. But from the perspective of behavioral economics, the ends of the legal system are more complex. This is so because people's revealed preferences are a less certain ground on which to build; obviously issues of paternalism become central here.

Each of these three strands of our project is deeply constructive. Behavioral economics is a form of economics, and our goal is to strengthen the predictive and analytic power of law and economics, not to undermine it. Behavioral economics does not suggest that behavior is random or impossible to predict; rather it suggests, with economics, that behavior is systematic and can be modeled. We attempt to sketch several such models here.

Part I below offers a general framework and provides an overview of the arguments for enriching the traditional economic framework. We see this enrichment as similar in spirit to the increased emphasis on asymmetric information in mainstream economic analysis in recent decades. Just as people often have imperfect information, which has predictable consequences for behavior, the departures from the standard conception of the economic agent also alter behavior in predictable ways.

Parts II and III of the article involve positive analysis. Part II examines how a behaviorally-informed law and economics analysis can help to explain the behavior of human agents insofar as that behavior is relevant to law. Our topics here include bargaining behavior and the effects of mandatory contract terms. Part III shifts to an explanation of existing legal rules and institutions. We suggest that many features of the legal landscape that are puzzling from a traditional law and economics perspective follow naturally from behavioral phenomena.

Part IV of the article examines prescriptive issues, offering a series of proposals that might seem surprising or controversial from a neoclassical economic perspective but that follow naturally from taking into account features of actual choice behavior. Our principal emphasis is on how people respond to information and how this point bears on the role of law.

Part V is more speculative and normative. We briefly outline the main problems—some familiar and others less so—with the idea that the legal system ought always to respect informed choice, and also with the idea that government decisionmakers—who after all are behavioral actors too—can be relied upon to make better choices than citizens. Because of the complexity of these issues, we emphasize three broad points: the framework that behavioral economics suggests for thinking about issues of paternalism; the possibility that some institutions—such as populist government—may be particularly bad at attempted correction of citizen error, while others may be better; and the prospect that some methods of correction (such as those that focus on debiasing rather than outright coercion) may be acceptable even if one thinks that citizen error is relatively unlikely.

I. FOUNDATIONS: WHAT IS "BEHAVIORAL LAW AND ECONOMICS"?

In order to identify, in a general way, the defining features of behavioral law and economics, it is useful first to understand the defining features of law and economics. As we understand it, this approach to the law posits that legal rules are best analyzed and understood in light of standard economic principles. Gary Becker offers a typical account of those principles: "[A]ll human behavior can be viewed as involving participants who [1] maximize their utility [2] from a stable set of preferences and [3] accumulate an optimal amount of information and other inputs in a variety of markets."[5] The task of law and economics is to determine the implications of such rational maximizing behavior in and out of markets, and its legal implications for markets and other institutions. Although some of Becker's particular applications of the economic approach might be thought of as contentious, that general approach underlies a wide range of work in the economic analysis of law.[6]

What then is the task of behavioral law and economics? How does it differ from standard law and economics? These are the questions we address below.

A. *Homo Economicus and Real People*

The task of behavioral law and economics, simply stated, is to explore the implications of *actual* (not hypothesized) human behavior for the law. How do "real people" differ from *homo economicus*? We will describe the differences by stressing three important "bounds" on human behavior, bounds that draw into question the central ideas of utility maximization, stable preferences, rational expectations, and optimal processing of information.[7] People can be said to display *bounded rationality*, *bounded willpower*, and *bounded self-interest*.

All three bounds are well documented in the literature of other social sciences, but they are relatively unexplored in economics (although, as we noted at the outset, this has begun to change). Each of these bounds represents a significant way in which most people depart from the standard eco-

5. GARY S. BECKER, THE ECONOMIC APPROACH TO HUMAN BEHAVIOR 14 (1976).

6. *See, e.g.*, A. MITCHELL POLINSKY, AN INTRODUCTION TO LAW AND ECONOMICS 10 (2d ed. 1989); RICHARD A. POSNER, ECONOMIC ANALYSIS OF LAW 3-4 (5th ed. 1998).

7. For a further elaboration of this view, see Richard H. Thaler, *Doing Economics Without* Homo Economicus, *in* FOUNDATIONS OF RESEARCH IN ECONOMICS: HOW DO ECONOMISTS DO ECONOMICS? 227, 230-35 (Steven G. Medema & Warren J. Samuels eds., 1996).

nomic model. While there are instances in which more than one bound comes into play, at this stage we think it is best to conceive of them as separate modeling problems. Nonetheless, each of the three bounds points to systematic (rather than random or arbitrary) departures from conventional economic models, and thus each of the three bears on generating sound predictions and prescriptions for law. They also provide the foundations for new and sometimes quite formal models of behavior.

1. *Bounded rationality.*

Bounded rationality, an idea first introduced by Herbert Simon, refers to the obvious fact that human cognitive abilities are not infinite.[8] We have limited computational skills and seriously flawed memories. People can respond sensibly to these failings; thus it might be said that people sometimes respond rationally to their own cognitive limitations, minimizing the sum of decision costs and error costs. To deal with limited memories we make lists. To deal with limited brain power and time we use mental shortcuts and rules of thumb. But even with these remedies, and in some cases because of these remedies, human behavior differs in systematic ways from that predicted by the standard economic model of unbounded rationality. Even when the use of mental shortcuts is rational, it can produce predictable mistakes. The departures from the standard model can be divided into two categories: judgment and decisionmaking. Actual judgments show systematic departures from models of unbiased forecasts, and actual decisions often violate the axioms of expected utility theory.

A major source of differences between actual judgments and unbiased forecasts is the use of rules of thumb. As stressed in the pathbreaking work of Daniel Kahneman and Amos Tversky, rules of thumb such as the availability heuristic—in which the frequency of some event is estimated by judging how easy it is to recall other instances of this type (how "available" such instances are)—lead us to erroneous conclusions. People tend to conclude, for example, that the probability of an event (such as a car accident) is greater if they have recently witnessed an occurrence of that event than if they have not.[9] What is especially important in the work of Kahneman and Tversky is that it shows that shortcuts and rules of thumb are predictable. While the heuristics are useful on average (which explains how they become adopted), they lead to errors in particular circumstances. This means that someone using such a rule of thumb may be behaving rationally in the sense of economizing on thinking time, but such a person will nonetheless make

8. Herbert A. Simon, *A Behavioral Model of Rational Choice*, 69 Q.J. ECON. 99 (1955).

9. Amos Tversky & Daniel Kahneman, *Judgment Under Uncertainty: Heuristics and Biases*, *in* JUDGMENT UNDER UNCERTAINTY 3, 11 (Daniel Kahneman, Paul Slovic & Amos Tversky eds., 1982).

forecasts that are different from those that emerge from the standard rational-choice model.[10]

Just as unbiased forecasting is not a good description of actual human behavior, expected utility theory is not a good description of actual decisionmaking. While the axioms of expected utility theory characterize rational choice, actual choices diverge in important ways from this model, as has been known since the early experiments by Allais and Ellsberg.[11] There has been an explosion of research in recent years trying to develop better formal models of actual decisionmaking. The model offered by Kahneman and Tversky, called prospect theory, seems to do a good job of explaining many features of observed behavior, and so we draw on that model (whose main features we summarize in Part IV.B below) here.[12]

We emphasize that bounded rationality is entirely consistent with modeling behavior and generating predictions based on a model, in line with the methodology of conventional economics. As Kenneth Arrow has explained, "[T]here is no general principle that prevents the creation of an economic theory based on other hypotheses than that of rationality. . . . [A]ny coherent theory of reactions to the stimuli appropriate in an economic context . . . could in principle lead to a theory of the economy."[13] Arrow's example here is habit formation; that behavior, he says, can be incorporated into a theory by supposing that people choose goods with an eye towards minimizing changes in their consumption.

> Though there is an optimization in this theory, it is different from utility maximization; for example, if prices and income return to their initial levels after several alterations, the final bundle [of goods] purchased will not be the same as the initial [bundle]. This theory would strike many lay observers as plausible, yet it is not rational as economists have used that term.[14]

10. For further discussion, see the recent survey of results in John Conlisk, *Why Bounded Rationality?*, 34 J. ECON. LITERATURE 669, 671, 682-83 (1996).

11. *See* Colin Camerer, *Individual Decision Making*, *in* HANDBOOK OF EXPERIMENTAL ECONOMICS 587, 619-20, 622-24 (John H. Kagel & Alvin E. Roth eds., 1995) (describing the Allais paradox); Daniel Ellsberg, *Risk, Ambiguity, and the Savage Axioms*, 75 Q.J. ECON. 643 (1961).

12. Daniel Kahneman & Amos Tversky, *Prospect Theory: An Analysis of Decision Under Risk*, 47 ECONOMETRICA 263 (1979). For a survey of empirical tests of this and other models, see Camerer, *supra* note 11, at 626-43. John D. Hey & Chris Orme, *Investigating Generalizations of Expected Utility Theory Using Experimental Data*, 62 ECONOMETRICA 1291 (1994), conclude that expected utility theory performs fairly well, but they do not consider prospect theory as an alternative. An alternative to prospect theory for modifying expected utility theory is offered by Itzhak Gilboa & David Schmeidler, *Case-Based Decision Theory*, 110 Q.J. ECON. 605 (1995).

13. Kenneth J. Arrow, *Rationality of Self and Others in an Economic System*, *in* RATIONAL CHOICE: THE CONTRAST BETWEEN ECONOMICS AND PSYCHOLOGY 201, 202 (Robin M. Hogarth & Melvin W. Reder eds., 1987).

14. *Id.*

2. *Bounded willpower.*

In addition to bounded rationality, people often display bounded willpower. This term refers to the fact that human beings often take actions that they know to be in conflict with their own long-term interests. Most smokers say they would prefer not to smoke, and many pay money to join a program or obtain a drug that will help them quit. As with bounded rationality, many people recognize that they have bounded willpower and take steps to mitigate its effects. They join a pension plan or "Christmas Club" (a special savings arrangement under which funds can be withdrawn only around the holidays) to prevent undersaving, and they don't keep tempting desserts around the house when trying to diet. In some cases they may vote for or support governmental policies, such as social security, to eliminate any temptation to succumb to the desire for immediate rewards.[15] Thus, the demand for and supply of law may reflect people's understanding of their own (or others') bounded willpower; consider "cooling off" periods for certain sales and programs that facilitate or even require saving.

3. *Bounded self-interest.*

Finally, we use the term bounded self-interest to refer to an important fact about the utility function of most people: They care, or act as if they care, about others, even strangers, in some circumstances. (Thus, we are not questioning here the idea of utility maximization, but rather the common assumptions about what that entails.) Our notion is distinct from simple altruism, which conventional economics has emphasized in areas such as bequest decisions.[16] Self-interest is bounded in a much broader range of settings than conventional economics assumes, and the bound operates in ways different from what the conventional understanding suggests. In many market and bargaining settings (as opposed to nonmarket settings such as bequest decisions), people care about being treated fairly and want to treat others fairly if those others are themselves behaving fairly. As a result of these concerns, the agents in a behavioral economic model are both nicer and (when they are not treated fairly) more spiteful than the agents postulated by neoclassical theory. Formal models have been used to show how people deal with both fairness and unfairness; we will draw on those models here.

15. *See* Deborah M. Weiss, *Paternalistic Pension Policy: Psychological Evidence and Economic Theory*, 58 U. CHI. L. REV. 1275 (1991).

16. *See* B. Douglas Bernheim, *How Strong Are Bequest Motives? Evidence Based on Estimates of the Demand for Life Insurance and Annuities*, 99 J. POL. ECON. 899, 899-900 (1991).

4. *Applications.*

The goal of this article is to show how the incorporation of these understandings of human behavior bears on the actual operation and possible improvement of the legal system. The appendix summarizes some key features of each of the three bounds on human behavior just described. It also indicates the law and economics issues we analyze under each category.

When is each bound likely to come into play? Any general statement will necessarily be incomplete, but some broad generalizations can be offered. First, bounded rationality as it relates to judgment behavior will come into play whenever actors in the legal system are called upon to assess the probability of an uncertain event. We discuss many examples below, including environmental legislation (Part III.C), negligence determinations (Part IV.A), and risk assessments (Parts IV.B and V.A.). Second, bounded rationality as it relates to decisionmaking behavior will come into play whenever actors are valuing outcomes; a prominent example here is loss aversion and its corollary, the endowment effect, which we discuss in connection with bargaining behavior (Part II.B), mandatory contract terms (Part II.D), prior restraints on speech (Part III.B), and risk assessments (Part IV.B). Bounded willpower is most relevant when decisions have consequences over time; our example is criminal behavior (Part IV.C), where the benefits are generally immediate and the costs deferred. Finally, bounded self-interest (as we use the term) is relevant primarily in situations in which one party has deviated substantially from the usual or ordinary conduct under the circumstances; in such circumstances the other party will often be willing to incur financial costs to punish the "unfair" behavior. Our applications here include bargaining behavior (Part II.B) and laws banning market transactions (Part III.A).

The three bounds we describe do not (at least as we characterize them here) constitute a full description of human behavior in all its complexity. Although we will have more to say about parsimony below, we will say for now that our goal is to sketch out an approach spare enough to generate predictions across a range of contexts, but not so spare that its predictions about behavior are often incorrect (as we will suggest is the case with conventional law and economics in some contexts). Many interesting features of behavior discussed by psychologists but not emphasized by our framework may also play a role in explaining specific forms of behavior relevant to law.[17] And it can be illuminating to attend in some detail to the role of social norms in

17. *See, e.g.*, Russell Korobkin & Chris Guthrie, *Psychological Barriers to Litigation Settlement: An Experimental Approach*, 93 MICH. L. REV. 107 (1994) (finding effects of "equity seeking" and "reactive devaluation" on settlement behavior); Mark Kelman, Yuval Rottenstreich & Amos Tversky, *Context-Dependence in Legal Decision Making*, 25 J. LEGAL STUD. 287 (1996) (describing effects of "compromise" and "contrast" behavior on jury decisionmaking).

various contexts[18] and to the place of shame, pride, and status,[19] especially insofar as an understanding of these variables helps give content to people's utility functions in ways that bear on the uses of law. Our principal purpose here, however, is to provide predictions, rather than to give full descriptions of individual motivations and self-understandings, and we will refer to these variables only occasionally and in passing. For similar reasons, we do not emphasize behavioral patterns that depart from standard economic assumptions but fail to point in systematic directions; such patterns would not generate distinct predictions (although they would of course matter to a full account of individual behavior). Our focus here is robust, empirically documented phenomena that have reasonably precise implications for legal issues.

B. *Testable Predictions*

Behavioral and conventional law and economics do not differ solely in their assumptions about human behavior. They also differ, in testable ways, in their predictions about how law (as well as other forces) affects behavior. To make these differences more concrete, consider the three "fundamental principles of economics" set forth by Richard Posner in his *Economic Analysis of Law*,[20] in a discussion that is, on these points, quite conventional. (Posner's discussion represents an application of the basic economic methodology set forth by Becker above.[21]) To what extent would an account based on behavioral law and economics offer different "fundamental principles"?

The first fundamental principle for the conventional approach is downward-sloping demand: Total demand for a good falls when its price rises.[22] This prediction is, of course, valid. There are few if any documented cases of Giffen goods (goods that are consumed more heavily at high prices, due to the fact that the price increase makes people unable to afford goods that are even pricier than the good in question). However, confirmation of the prediction of downward-sloping demand does not suggest that people are optimizing. As Becker has shown, even people choosing at random (rather than in a way designed to serve their preferences) will tend to consume less of a good when its price goes up as long as they have limited resources.[23] This

18. *See* Symposium, *Law, Economics & Norms*, 144 U. PA. L. REV. 1643 (1996).

19. *See* Lawrence Lessig, *The Regulation of Social Meaning*, 62 U. CHI. L. REV. 943 (1995); Richard H. McAdams, *Relative Preferences*, 102 YALE L.J. 1 (1992). McAdams' work draws on ROBERT H. FRANK, CHOOSING THE RIGHT POND (1985).

20. POSNER, *supra* note 6, at 4.

21. *See id.* at 3.

22. *See id.*

23. Gary S. Becker, *Irrational Behavior and Economic Theory*, 70 J. POL. ECON. 1, 4-6 (1962).

behavior has also been demonstrated with laboratory rats.[24] Thus, evidence of downward-sloping demand is not evidence in support of optimizing models.

The second fundamental principle of conventional law and economics concerns the nature of costs: "Cost to the economist is 'opportunity cost,'" and "'[s]unk' (incurred) costs do not affect decisions on prices and quantity."[25] Thus, according to traditional analysis, decisionmakers will equate opportunity costs (which are costs incurred by foregoing opportunities—say, the opportunity to sell one's possessions) to out-of-pocket costs (such as costs incurred in buying possessions); and they will ignore sunk costs (costs that cannot be recovered, such as the cost of nonrefundable tickets). But each of these propositions is a frequent source of predictive failures. The equality of opportunity costs and out-of-pocket costs implies that, in the absence of important wealth effects, buying prices will be roughly equal to selling prices. This is frequently violated, as is well known. Many people holding tickets to a popular sporting event such as the Super Bowl would be unwilling to buy tickets at the market price (say $1000), yet would also be unwilling to sell at this price. Indeed, estimates of the ratio of selling prices to buying prices are often at least two to one, yet the size of the transaction makes it implausible in these studies to conclude that wealth effects explain the difference.[26] As described below, these results are just what behavioral analysis suggests.

The traditional assumption about sunk costs also generates invalid predictions. Here is one: A theater patron who ignores sunk costs would not take into account the cost of a prepaid season pass in deciding whether to "rou[se] [him]self . . . to go out" on the evening of a particular performance;[27] the decision would be made purely on the basis of the benefits and costs from that moment forward. However, in a study of theater patrons, some of whom were randomly assigned to receive discounted prices on prepaid passes, the patrons who received discounts were found to attend significantly fewer performances than those who did not receive discounts, despite the fact that (due to random assignment) the benefit-cost ratio that *should* have mattered—benefits and costs going forward—was the same on average

24. JOHN H. KAGEL, RAYMOND C. BATTALIO & LEONARD GREEN, ECONOMIC CHOICE THEORY: AN EXPERIMENTAL ANALYSIS OF ANIMAL BEHAVIOR 8, 17-19, 24-25 (1995).

25. POSNER, *supra* note 6, at 6, 7.

26. *See* Daniel Kahneman, Jack L. Knetsch & Richard H. Thaler, *Experimental Tests of the Endowment Effect and the Coase Theorem*, 98 J. POL. ECON. 1325, 1327 tbl.1 (1990) (summarizing studies).

27. ROBERT NOZICK, THE NATURE OF RATIONALITY 22 (1993).

in the two groups.[28] In short, sunk costs mattered; again, the standard prediction proved invalid.

The third fundamental principle of conventional law and economics is that "resources tend to gravitate toward their most valuable uses" as markets drive out any unexploited profit opportunities.[29] When combined with the notion that opportunity and out-of-pocket costs are equated (see fundamental principle two), this yields the Coase theorem—the idea that initial assignments of entitlements will not affect the ultimate allocation of resources so long as transaction costs are zero.[30] Many economists and economically oriented lawyers think of the Coase theorem as a tautology; if there were really no transaction costs (and no wealth effects), and if an alternative allocation of resources would make some agents better off and none worse off, then of course the agents would move to that allocation. Careful empirical study, however, shows that the Coase theorem is not a tautology; indeed, it can lead to inaccurate predictions.[31] That is, even when transaction costs and wealth effects are known to be zero, initial entitlements alter the final allocation of resources. These results are predicted by behavioral economics, which emphasizes the difference between opportunity and out-of-pocket costs.

Consider the following set of experiments conducted to test the Coase theorem;[32] let us offer an interpretation geared to the particular context of economic analysis of law. The subjects were forty-four students taking an advanced undergraduate course in law and economics at Cornell University. Half the students were endowed with tokens. Each student (whether or not endowed with a token) was assigned a personal token value, the price at which a token could be redeemed for cash at the end of the experiment; these assigned values induce supply and demand curves for the tokens. Markets were conducted for tokens. Those without tokens could buy one, while those with tokens could sell. Those with tokens should (and do) sell their tokens if offered more than their assigned value; those without tokens should (and do) buy tokens if they can get one at a price below their assigned value. These token markets are a complete victory of economic theory. The equilibrium price was always exactly what the theory would predict, and the tokens did in fact flow to those who valued them most.

However, life is generally not about tokens redeemable for cash. Thus another experiment was conducted, identical to the first except that now half the students were given Cornell coffee mugs instead of tokens. Here behavioral analysis generates a prediction distinct from standard economic analy-

28. Hal R. Arkes & Catherine Blumer, *The Psychology of Sunk Cost*, 35 ORG. BEHAV. & HUM. DECISION PROCESSES 124, 127-28 (1985).

29. POSNER, *supra* note 6, at 11.

30. R.H. Coase, *The Problem of Social Cost*, 3 J. L. & ECON. 1 (1960).

31. *See* Kahneman et al., *supra* note 26, at 1329-42.

32. *See id.*

sis: Because people do not equate opportunity and out-of-pocket costs for goods whose values are not solely exogenously defined (as they were in the case of the tokens), those endowed with mugs should be reluctant to part with them even at prices they would not have considered paying to acquire a mug had they not received one.

Was this prediction correct? Yes. Markets were conducted and mugs bought and sold. Unlike the case of the tokens, the assignment of property rights had a pronounced effect on the final allocation of mugs. The students who were assigned mugs had a strong tendency to keep them. Whereas the Coase theorem would have predicted that about half the mugs would trade (since transaction costs had been shown to be essentially zero in the token experiments, and mugs were randomly distributed), instead only fifteen percent of the mugs traded. And those who were endowed with mugs asked more than twice as much to give up a mug as those who didn't get a mug were willing to pay. This result did not change if the markets were repeated. This effect is generally referred to as the "endowment effect"; it is a manifestation of the broader phenomenon of "loss aversion"—the idea that losses are weighted more heavily than gains—which in turn is a central building block of Kahneman and Tversky's prospect theory.

What are we to make of these findings? There are at least three important lessons. First, markets are indeed robust institutions. Even naive subjects participating at low stakes produce outcomes indistinguishable from those predicted by the theory *when trading for tokens*. Second, when agents must determine their own values (as with the mugs), outcomes can diverge substantially from those predicted by economic theory. Third, these departures will not be obvious outside an experiment, even when they exist and have considerable importance. That is, even in the mugs markets, there was trading; there was just not as much trading as the theory would predict. These lessons can be applied to other markets; we offer some examples below.

The foregoing discussion illustrates the point with which we began this section: The difference between conventional and behavioral law and economics is *not* just a difference in the validity of the assumptions about human behavior. While the assumptions of unbounded rationality, willpower, and self-interest are unrealistic, the force of behavioral economics comes from the difference in its predictions (for example, fewer trades for mugs than for tokens). In this sense, our analysis is consistent with the precept originally proposed by Milton Friedman: Economics should not be judged on whether the assumptions are realistic or valid, but rather on the quality of its predictions.[33] We share this view (or at least will accept it for purposes of this arti-

33. *See* MILTON FRIEDMAN, *The Methodology of Positive Economics*, *in* ESSAYS IN POSITIVE ECONOMICS 3, 14-16 (1953).

cle); as we have emphasized, our principal interest is predictive in character. A behavioral analysis would be of much less interest if conventional economic models did a satisfactory job of predicting the behavior of agents insofar as relevant to law. Unfortunately, they often do not.

C. *Partial and Ambiguous Successes of Conventional Economics*

What of all the well-known successes of conventional economics? Do they show that predictions about law based on the conventional assumptions tend to work? Consider some examples of the successes: (1) the inverse correlation between price ceilings and queues; (2) the inverse correlation between rent control and the stock of housing; (3) the positive correlation in financial markets between risk and expected return; (4) the relation between futures prices and spot-market prices.[34] The problem with the first three examples is that, as with tests of downward-sloping demand curves, they are quite undemanding; they ask simply whether the theory gets the direction of the effect right—and it does. But this is not a complete vindication of the theory, for the theory may misstate the *magnitude* of the effect. Consider (3), the positive relation between risk and return in financial markets. As predicted by this theory, stocks (equities) earn higher returns (on average) than do riskless assets such as treasury bills. But what can we say about the magnitude? Is this difference in return roughly what the theory would predict? This is precisely the question posed by Rajnish Mehra and Edward Prescott in their well-known paper on the "equity premium puzzle."[35] The equity premium is the difference in returns between equities and riskless assets. In the United States, the equity premium has been roughly six percent per year over the past seventy years.[36] This implies that a dollar invested in stocks in 1926 would, at the end of 1997, be worth over $1800, while a dollar invested in treasury bills would have accumulated to less than $15. This difference is remarkably large. Mehra and Prescott therefore ask whether it can possibly be explained by investor risk aversion. They conclude that it cannot. That is, no plausible value of risk aversion could explain such a big difference.[37] Although the theory gets the sign right in this case, the magnitude of the effect suggests that the theory is wrong. (And note that arbitrage, which we discuss just below, would not be expected to eliminate the equity premium; there are often significant costs of arbitrage in equity markets.[38])

34. *See* POSNER, *supra* note 6, at 18.

35. Rajnish Mehra & Edward C. Prescott, *The Equity Premium: A Puzzle*, 15 J. MONETARY ECON. 145 (1985).

36. *See* IBBOTSON ASSOCIATES, STOCKS, BONDS, BILLS AND INFLATION: 1997 YEARBOOK.

37. See Jeremy J. Siegel & Richard H. Thaler, *Anomalies: The Equity Premium Puzzle*, 11 J. ECON. PERSP., Winter 1997, at 191, 192, for a discussion.

38. *See* Jeffrey Pontiff, *Costly Arbitrage: Evidence from Closed-End Funds*, 111 Q.J. ECON. 1135 (1996); Andrei Shleifer & Robert W. Vishny, *The Limits of Arbitrage*, 52 J. FIN. 35 (1997).

Example (4) above, the relation between spot and futures prices, does better on magnitudes. Spot and futures prices are very closely related. However, this case is special in several respects. First, arbitrage is possible. If spot and futures prices get out of line, then investors can make sure profits by buying the contract that is too cheap and selling the one that is too expensive. Second, this context is one in which most of the activity is undertaken by professionals who will quickly lose their money and their jobs if they make frequent errors. Third, the markets in which these professionals operate offer frequent opportunities for learning. Under these circumstances, markets tend to work very well,[39] though not perfectly.[40] Essentially, these conditions render agents who do not conform to the standard economic assumptions irrelevant (because they will be bankrupt).

So, in some (fairly unusual) circumstances, such as futures trading, market forces are strong enough to make the three "bounds" irrelevant for predictive purposes. The point is important; it suggests that while human beings often display bounded rationality, willpower, and self-interest, markets can sometimes lead to behavior consistent with conventional economic assumptions. Then the question becomes when, exactly, do market forces make it reasonable to assume that people behave in accordance with those assumptions? What circumstances apply to most of the domains in which law and economics is used?

In this regard it is instructive to compare the market for futures contracts with the market for criminal activity. Consider the proposition that a potential criminal will commit some crime if the expected gains from the crime exceed its expected costs.[41] Suppose a criminal mistakenly thinks that the expected gains outweigh the expected costs, when in fact the opposite is true. First notice that no arbitrage will be possible in this situation. If someone is unfortunate enough to commit a crime with a negative expected value, then there is no way for anyone else to profit directly from his behavior. Outside of financial markets (and not always there), those who engage in low-payoff activities lose utility but do not create profit opportunities for others. Nor do they typically disappear from the market. (Even poorly run firms can survive for many years; consider GM.) Being a bad criminal is rarely fatal, and except possibly for organized crime, there is little opportunity for "hostile takeovers." Finally, the decision to enter a life of crime is not one that is made

39. *See* Thomas Russell & Richard H. Thaler, *The Relevance of Quasi Rationality in Competitive Markets*, *in* RICHARD H. THALER, QUASI RATIONAL ECONOMICS 239, 248-49 (1991).

40. For example, in a rational market, the relation between spot and futures contracts for foreign exchange are good forecasts of movements in exchange rates. In fact, these forecasts are systematically biased. *See* Kenneth A. Froot & Richard H. Thaler, *Foreign Exchange*, *in* RICHARD H. THALER, THE WINNER'S CURSE: PARADOXES AND ANOMALIES OF ECONOMIC LIFE 182, 185-86 (1992).

41. *See, e.g.*, Steven Shavell, *Criminal Law and the Optimal Use of Nonmonetary Sanctions as a Deterrent*, 85 COLUM. L. REV. 1232, 1235 (1985).

repeatedly with many opportunities to learn. Once a teenager has dropped out of high school to become a drug dealer, it is difficult to switch to dentistry.

Because law and economics is frequently applied to criminal behavior, the above argument is obviously germane. We think that the same analysis applies to many of the domains in which law and economics has been used. In fact, economic analysis of law seems to be a branch of economics in which the limits of arbitrage are particularly powerful, so special care should be taken not to push the standard economic model too far.

This is by no means to say that conventional law and economics has had no victories. One cannot look at the current state of antitrust law, or the use of market-based regulation in environmental law (to name just two of many examples), without acknowledging the important advances produced through the conventional approach. Often this approach points in the right direction and identifies flaws in noneconomic reasoning. Many advances in the positive and prescriptive understanding of law have come from the conventional assumptions. Attention to incentive effects can often reveal a great deal. (Thus, those who would argue that rent control helps tenants must contend with the obvious long-run supply effects of such laws.)

The project of behavioral law and economics, as we see it, is to take the core insights and successes of economics and build upon them by making more realistic assumptions about human behavior. We wish to retain the power of the economist's approach to social science while offering a better description of the behavior of the agents in society and the economy. Behavioral law and economics, in short, offers the potential to be law and economics with a higher "R^2"—that is, greater power to explain the observed data. We will try to highlight some of that potential (and suggest cases where it has been realized) in this article.

D. *Parsimony*

A possible objection to our approach is that conventional economics has the advantage of simplicity and parsimony. At least—the objection goes—it provides a theory. By contrast, a behavioral perspective offers a more complicated and unruly picture of human behavior, and perhaps that picture will make prediction more difficult, precisely because behavior is more complicated and unruly. Everything can be explained in an ex post fashion—some tool will be found that is up to the task—but the elegance, generalizability, and predictive power of the economic method will be lost. Shouldn't analysts proceed with simple tools? We offer two responses: First, simplicity and parsimony are indeed beneficial; it would be highly desirable to come up with a model of behavior that is both simple and right. But conventional economics is not in this position, for its predictions are often wrong. We will encounter many examples in addition to those already discussed.

Second, to the extent that conventional economics achieves parsimony, it often does so at the expense of any real predictive power. Its goal is to provide a unitary theory of behavior, a goal which may be impossible to achieve. By itself the notion of "rationality" (the centerpiece of traditional analysis) is not a theory; to generate predictions it must be more fully specified, often through the use of auxiliary assumptions.[42] Indeed, the term "rationality" is highly ambiguous and can be used to mean many things. A person might be deemed rational if her behavior (1) conforms to the axioms of expected utility theory; (2) is responsive to incentives, that is, if the actor changes her behavior when the costs and benefits are altered; (3) is internally consistent; (4) promotes her own welfare; or (5) is effective in achieving her goals, whatever the relationship between those goals and her actual welfare. We observe departures from most of these definitions; thus, with respect to (1), scholars have documented departures from expected utility theory for nearly fifty years, and prospect theory seems to predict behavior better.[43] With respect to (4) and (5), people's decisions sometimes do not promote their welfare or help them to achieve their own goals; and with respect to (3), behavioral research shows that people sometimes behave in an inconsistent manner by, for example, indicating a preference for X over Y if asked to make a direct choice, but Y over X if asked to give their willingness to pay for each option.[44] Many of our examples will thus show that people are frequently not rational if the term is understood to mean (1), (3), (4), or (5). As for (2), without some specification of what counts as a cost and a benefit, the idea of responsiveness to incentives is empty. If rationality is used to mean simply that people "choose" what they "prefer" in light of the prevailing incentives,[45] then the notion of rationality offers few restrictions on behavior. The person who drinks castor oil as often as possible is rational because she happens to love castor oil. Other self-destructive behavior (drug addiction, suicide, etc.) can be explained on similar grounds. It is not even clear on this view whether rationality is intended as a definition of "preference" or as a prediction.[46]

42. *See* Arrow, *supra* note 13, at 205-06.

43. *See* notes 11-12 *supra* and accompanying text.

44. Amos Tversky, *Rational Theory and Constructive Choice*, *in* THE RATIONAL FOUNDATIONS OF ECONOMIC BEHAVIOUR 185, 189-91 (Kenneth J. Arrow, Enrico Colombatto, Mark Perlman & Christian Schmidt eds., 1996).

45. *See, e.g.*, TOMAS J. PHILLIPSON & RICHARD A. POSNER, PRIVATE CHOICES AND PUBLIC HEALTH: THE AIDS EPIDEMIC IN AN ECONOMIC PERSPECTIVE 4 (1995).

46. Thus the idea is ambiguous between the notion of "revealed preferences," in which choices define preferences, and the notion of a maximization function that lies behind and helps explain choices. Both notions raise many difficult issues. *See* Cass R. Sunstein, *Social Norms and Social Roles*, 96 COLUM. L. REV. 903, 931-38 (1996).

If such a notion of rationality allowed for good predictions, then perhaps there would be no reason for complaint; the problem, however, is that so high a degree of flexibility leaves the theory with few a priori restrictions. A theory with infinite degrees of freedom is no theory at all. For example, consider whether it is a paradox (as many economists think) that so many people vote (despite the virtual certainty that no one person's vote will alter the outcome). If it is a paradox, so much the worse for the rationality assumption; if it is not a paradox, what does the assumption predict? Does it merely predict that people will respond to changes in conditions—for example, fewer people will vote when it is snowing? If so, the prediction is not bad, but surely it would be possible to say, after an unusually large vote amidst the storm, that more people voted simply because voting seemed especially valiant in those circumstances (so much for predictions based on this form of rationality). Conventional economics sometimes turns to stronger forms of rationality in response, and those forms provide stronger predictions in some cases; but those predictions are often inaccurate, as described above and as illustrated by the examples considered below.

We believe that a behavioral approach imposes discipline on economic theorizing because assumptions cannot be imported at will. In a behavioral approach, assumptions about behavior should accord with empirically validated descriptions of actual behavior. For example, in the case of "fairness," specifically defined and empirically verified patterns of behavior are used to generate predictions in new contexts. ("Fairness" is *not*, on this view, simply a catch-all to explain any observed behavior.) This is the approach we advocate for economic analysis of law. This approach, we believe, produces a better understanding of law and a better set of predictions about its effects.

We now turn to positive, prescriptive, and normative issues. Our purpose is not to settle all of them, but to show the promise of behavioral economics in casting light on a wide range of questions. A great deal of work would be necessary to justify authoritative judgments on most of these questions. What follows should be taken partly as a proposal, perhaps in the spirit of the early economic analysis of law, for a research agenda to be carried out with a new set of tools.

II. Behavior of Agents

A. *The Ultimatum Game*

1. *The game and its sunk-cost variation.*

We begin with bounded self-interest, the third bound described above. A useful first example of this bound is agents' behavior in a very simple bargaining game called the ultimatum game. In this game, one player, the Proposer, is asked to propose an allocation of a sum of money between herself and the other player, the Responder. The Responder then has a choice. He can either accept the amount offered to him by the Proposer, leaving the rest to the Proposer, or he can reject the offer, in which case both players get nothing. Neither player knows the identity of his or her counterpart, and the players will play against each other only once, so reputations and future retaliation are eliminated as factors.

Economic theory has a simple prediction about this game. The Proposer will offer the smallest unit of currency available, say a penny, and the Responder will accept, since a penny is better than nothing. This turns out to be a very bad prediction about how the game is actually played. Responders typically reject offers of less than twenty percent of the total amount available; the average minimum amount that Responders say they would accept is between twenty and thirty percent of that sum.[47] Responders are thus willing to punish unfair behavior, even at a financial cost to themselves. This is a form of bounded self-interest. And this response seems to be expected and anticipated by Proposers; they typically offer a substantial portion of the sum to be divided—ordinarily forty to fifty percent.[48]

Economists often worry that the results of this type of experiment are sensitive to the way in which the experiment was conducted. What would happen if the stakes were raised substantially, or the game was repeated several times to allow learning? In this case, we know the answer. To a first approximation, neither of these factors changes the results in any important way. Raising the stakes from $10 per pair to $100, or even to more than a week's income (in a poor country) has little effect; the same is true of repeating the game ten times with different partners.[49] (Of course, at some point raising the stakes would matter; probably few people would turn down an offer of five percent of $1,000,000.) We do not see behavior moving toward the prediction of standard economic theory.

Thus, the factors that many economists thought would change the outcome of the game did not. But, as we learned in a study conducted for this

47. *See* Werner Güth, Rolf Schmittberger & Bernd Schwarze, *An Experimental Analysis of Ultimatum Bargaining*, 3 J. ECON. BEHAV. & ORG. 367, 371-72, 375 tbls.4 & 5 (1982); Daniel Kahneman, Jack L. Knetsch & Richard H. Thaler, *Fairness and the Assumptions of Economics*, 59 J. BUS. S285, S291 tbl.2 (1986).

48. *See* Güth et al., *supra* note 47, at 371-72, 375 tbls.4 & 5; Kahneman et al., *supra* note 47, at S291 tbl.2.

49. *See* Colin Camerer & Richard H. Thaler, *Anomalies: Ultimatums, Dictators, and Manners*, 9 J. ECON. PERSP., Spring 1995, at 209, 210-11; Vesna Prasnikar & Alvin E. Roth, *Considerations of Fairness and Strategy: Experimental Data from Sequential Games*, 107 Q.J. ECON. 865, 873-75 (1992); Robert Slonim & Alvin E. Roth, *Learning in High Stakes Ultimatum Games: An Experiment in the Slovak Republic*, 66 ECONOMETRICA 569, 573 (1998). When repetition is combined with very high stakes, however, offers decrease somewhat, although they are still far above what the standard analysis would predict. *See* Slonim & Roth, *supra*, at 573, 588 fig.3A.

article, a factor that economic theory predicts will *not* have an effect, namely the introduction of a sunk cost, does have an effect. As noted above, economics predicts that decisionmakers will ignore sunk costs in making their choices (see fundamental principle two above); but in fact decisionmakers often do not behave in this way. Do sunk costs alter behavior in the ultimatum game? To find out, we asked classroom volunteers to bring $5—what would become a sunk cost for them—to class. Students were given a form asking them how they would play both roles in an ultimatum game in which the $10 to be divided was contributed half by the Proposer and half by the Responder. They were told that their role would be determined by chance, so they had to decide first what offer to make if they were chosen to be a Proposer and then what minimum offer they would be willing to accept if they were a Responder.[50] We also ran a version of the standard ultimatum game (without sunk costs by the students) as a control.

Although economic theory says that the sunk-cost variation of the ultimatum game will have no effect on behavior (since the $5 collected from each student is a sunk cost and should therefore be ignored by the players), we predicted that in this domain sunk costs would matter. In particular, we anticipated that Responders would feel that they had an "entitlement" to the $5 they had contributed to the experiment and would therefore be reluctant to accept less. This is precisely what we found. In the original version of the game, when the $10 to be divided was provided to subjects by the experimenter, the average minimum amount demanded by Responders was $1.94. In the sunk-cost version, where the students each paid $5 to participate, the average demand was $3.21 for a group of MIT MBA students, $3.73 for a group of University of Chicago (UC) MBA students, and $3.35 for a group of UC Law students. Each of these means is significantly different from the control value of $1.94 under any conventional measure of statistical significance. Looking past means, 61% of the MIT students demanded at least $4.00, and 32% demanded a full refund of their $5.00. For UC MBA students, 67% demanded at least $4.00, and 40% demanded $5.00. The UC Law students were slightly less extreme: 47% demanded at least $4.00, and 23% demanded $5.00.

50. This experiment is profitable for the experimenter if any offers are rejected by Responders (because the experimenter has collected $10 from each pair of bargainers, which the bargainers forfeit if the Proposer's offer is rejected). To solve this "problem," we conducted another experiment right after in which the winner of a game was awarded any profits earned by the experimenter in the first round.

ULTIMATUM GAME RESULTS

	Average Demand	Percent Demanding $4.00	Percent Demanding $5.00
MIT MBA	$3.21	61%	32%
UC MBA	$3.73	67%	40%
UC Law	$3.35	47%	23%

Note that our emphasis here, as well as in the ordinary ultimatum game, is on the fairness behavior of Responders, not on affirmative concerns for fairness on the part of Proposers. (As noted above, their behavior appears fully consistent with financially maximizing responses to Responders' fairness behavior; other experimental results support this conclusion.[51]) We do know, however, that in other contexts people appear to display affirmative concerns for fairness.[52]

The fairness results obtained in various experimental settings, such as the ultimatum game, cannot be explained on grounds of reputation. The parties are interacting anonymously and in a one-shot fashion. Of course, many real-world situations may reflect a combination of reputational and fairness factors. Thus, for example, firms that violate the norms of an industry are ostracized, presumably at some cost to the remaining firms, partly because of a rational fear that the offending party might be untrustworthy, and partly because of a spiteful tendency to punish unmannerly behavior, even when the punishment is costly to administer (as when Responders turn down small offers). Many of Robert Ellickson's examples in his pathbreaking book, *Order Without Law*, have precisely this flavor.[53] Often it is impossible to disentangle the two effects. The value of the experimental method is precisely that situations can be created in which the reputational factor is absent (because the transactions are anonymous and one-shot), allowing one to test directly for fairness. The ultimatum game results show that we find it: People will often behave in accordance with fairness considerations even when it is against their financial self-interest *and no one will know*. Thus, for instance,

51. *See* Elizabeth Hoffman, Kevin McCabe & Vernon L. Smith, *Social Distance and Other-Regarding Behavior in Dictator Games*, 86 AM. ECON. REV. 653, 653-54 & fig.1 (1996) (finding that Proposers typically offered no more than 10% of the sum to be divided—and over 60% offered nothing—when (1) the Responder had no choice but to accept the Proposer's offer and (2) anonymity was guaranteed).

52. *See* Ernst Fehr, Georg Kirchsteiger & Arno Riedl, *Does Fairness Prevent Market Clearing: An Experimental Investigation*, 108 Q.J. ECON. 437 (1993).

53. ROBERT C. ELLICKSON, ORDER WITHOUT LAW (1991).

most people leave tips in out-of-town restaurants that they never plan to visit again.

2. *Fairness, acrimony, and scruples.*

Theoretical considerations. How can economic analysis be enriched to incorporate the behavior observed in the ultimatum game and its sunk-cost variant? As we have indicated, the first step is to relax the assumption, common to most economic theorizing, of "unbounded self-interest." This assumption implies that Proposers should offer the smallest sum possible, and Responders should accept. An alternative view is offered in the following account:

> In the rural areas around Ithaca it is common for farmers to put some fresh produce on a table by the road. There is a cash box on the table, and customers are expected to put money in the box in return for the vegetables they take. The box has just a small slit, so money can only be put in, not taken out. Also, the box is attached to the table, so no one can (easily) make off with the money. We think that the farmers who use this system have just about the right model of human nature. They feel that enough people will volunteer to pay for the fresh corn to make it worthwhile to put it out there. The farmers also know that if it were easy to take the money, someone would do so.[54]

We emphasize that this is *not* a story of simple altruism. As noted above, such altruism is sometimes recognized in conventional economics; our account, in contrast, is a more complicated story of reciprocal fairness. A concern for fairness is part of most agents' utility function. The results of the ultimatum game, like the behavior of the Ithaca shoppers, cannot readily be explained on grounds of simple altruism. First of all, the games are played between anonymous strangers. What reason is there to believe that these people care about one another? (Most of us give little of our wealth to anonymous strangers whom we have no reason to believe are any worse off than we are. Similarly, most people driving by a farm do not pull over and stuff two dollars through the mail slot, even in Ithaca. Fairness behavior is probably reciprocal.) Second, we observe not only apparently "nice" behavior (generous offers) but also "spiteful" behavior (Responders turning down small offers at substantial cost to the Proposers). In the ultimatum game, people appear simultaneously nicer and more spiteful than conventional assumptions predict.

It is also no answer to say that the results of the ultimatum game are readily predictable on the conventional model on the ground that pride and self-conception are part of players' utility functions. The problem with this view is not that it is false but that it allows ad hoc, ex post additions to the

54. Richard H. Thaler & Robyn M. Dawes, *Cooperation*, *in* THALER, *supra* note 40, at 6, 19-20.

utility function, in such a way as to deprive the conventional model of the ability to make any predictions. The goal of the behavioral approach is to go back and forth between data and theory to generate predictions that will generalize.

The sort of balanced conception of human nature suggested by the ultimatum game results and the practices of farmers in Ithaca need not be informal or ad hoc. It is possible to incorporate material and nonmaterial motives, such as the desire to be fair (to those who have been fair) and also to be spiteful (to those who have not been fair), in a rigorous analysis. An elegant formal treatment is offered by Matthew Rabin in a model of fairness.[55] Rabin's framework incorporates three stylized facts about behavior. Stated simply and nonformally:

> (A) People are willing to sacrifice their own material well-being to help those who are being kind.
>
> (B) People are willing to sacrifice their own material well-being to punish those who are being unkind.
>
> (C) Both motivations (A) and (B) have a greater effect on behavior as the material cost of sacrificing becomes smaller.[56]

Rabin shows how these assumptions about behavior can explain the behavior observed in the ultimatum game as well as other games of cooperation such as the Prisoner's Dilemma. Related work, bearing on the appropriate role of law, has shown the role of such behavior in helping to produce norms that solve collective action problems.[57]

Rabin's theory can be viewed as a theory of manners and principles. Generalizing from Rabin's treatment, we might say that people can be understood as having preferences for (a) their own material payoffs and (b) those of some others they know well, and in addition they have preferences about (c) the well-being of some strangers whose interests are at stake, (d) their own reputation, and (e) what kind of person they wish to be. A person's willingness to cooperate or to help others can be seen as a function of these variables. The last factor is important and especially easy to overlook; the desire to think of yourself as an honest, principled person helps explain why most of us (though not all) do leave tips in strange restaurants and would leave money in the box at the road-side stand. As Rabin says, people are willing to sacrifice their own material well-being to help those who are being or have been kind. Of course, these desires compete with others in a world of scarce resources. We don't recommend that Mercedes dealers adopt the road-side stand selling technique.

55. Matthew Rabin, *Incorporating Fairness Into Game Theory and Economics*, 83 AM. ECON. REV. 1281 (1993).

56. *Id.* at 1282.

57. ROBERT AXELROD, THE EVOLUTION OF COOPERATION (1984); ROBERT AXELROD, THE COMPLEXITY OF COOPERATION (1997).

Thus behavioral economic agents have manners and scruples that can lead them to be "nice" in some settings. But, as we observe in the ultimatum game, people can also be provoked to be spiteful. Sometimes the fact that another person will lose, in a material or other sense, is a benefit to the agent; these are the conditions for spite. An agent may calculate that the costs of benefiting another person argue strongly against a deal, even if the agent would benefit materially. Thus Responders who receive (relatively) small offers are willing to decline them in order to punish the rude Proposers who tried to grab too much for themselves, even when the small offer is a substantial amount of money. Notice that this spiteful behavior is also "principled": People are willing to pay to punish someone who has been unfair. This is the same behavior that drives boycotts, where consumers refrain from buying something they normally enjoy in order to punish an offending party. Conventional economics has sometimes recognized such behavior, but it has received little attention in law and economics, where, unfortunately, it may often be quite relevant.[58]

Spiteful behavior is common under conditions of acrimony, such as during a fight or argument. Under these circumstances, even married couples will say and do things to hurt the other party; under bad conditions, the hurting, material or otherwise, is part of the agent's gain. A loss to another is a gain to oneself; even the idea of thinking of oneself as a certain kind of person (not a doormat or a dupe) can lead in the direction of inflicting losses. (Concern with not establishing a reputation as a doormat or a dupe may also play a role.) This is of course the converse of circumstances of cooperative behavior. Unfortunately, acrimony is particularly prevalent in many legal settings, before, during, and after litigation. Much protracted litigation—cases that fail to settle early and amicably—may arise precisely because the two sides were unable to deal with matters in a more friendly manner. (Divorces that end up in court are, almost by definition, acrimonious.) We suspect that spiteful behavior is frequently observed in conditions of acrimony even when reputational concerns are unimportant; for example, we think that the average contestant in a divorce case that ends up in court would be likely, in the role of Responder in the ultimatum game playing against his soon-to-be-ex-spouse, to reject low offers, not wanting the Proposer to benefit greatly.[59]

What is "fair"? Absent acrimony, spiteful behavior—such as rejection of small offers in the ultimatum game—is typically observed in situations

58. The concepts of revenge and retribution, which are related to spite, have been discussed by Posner. *See* Richard A. Posner, *Retribution and Related Concepts of Punishment*, 9 J. LEGAL STUD. 71 (1980).

59. *Cf.* Robert Gibbons & Leaf Van Boven, Multiple Selves in the Prisoners' Dilemma (Nov. 16, 1997) (unpublished manuscript, on file with the *Stanford Law Review*) (finding that subjects are more likely to engage in cooperative behavior in games when they have a positive impression of their opponent than when they have a negative impression).

where one party has violated a perceived "norm of fairness." This raises an obvious question: What is "fair"? In the ultimatum game, most people regard an offer of, say, a penny to the Responder as "unfair." This perception is an illustration of a more general pattern: People judge outcomes to be "unfair" if they depart substantially from the terms of a "reference transaction"—a transaction that defines the benchmark for the parties' interactions.[60] When the interactions are between bargainers dividing a sum of money to which neither is more entitled than the other (and this is common knowledge), the "reference transaction" is something like an equal split; substantial departures are viewed as unfair and, accordingly, punished by Responders. If parties are bargaining over the division of money and both have reason to view one side as more entitled than the other, then the "reference transaction" is a split that favors the more-entitled party.[61] And if the parties are a consumer and a firm in the market, the "reference transaction" is a transaction on the usual terms for the item in question.[62] We will have much more to say about this last context in Part III below. For now our goal is simply to offer our general definition of what is "fair" and to make clear that we do not view the term as a vague and ill-defined catch-all. Rather, we view it as having a reasonably well-specified meaning that can generate useful predictions across a range of contexts.[63]

Norms. Thus far the discussion has emphasized fairness, and we will stress this factor throughout. But fairness-related norms are a subset of a large category of norms that govern behavior and that can operate as "taxes" or "subsidies." An analysis like that above could be undertaken for many decisions in which people care not only about material self-interest but also about their reputations and their self-conception—for example, through purchasing books, suits, vacation spots, or through smoking, recycling, discriminating on the basis of race and sex, or through choosing friends, restaurants, and automobiles. A better understanding of the ingredients of individual utility could help a great deal with both the positive and prescriptive analysis of law. For example, it might help us understand more about (and be better able to predict in related contexts in the future) the massive changes

60. *See* Daniel Kahneman, Jack L. Knetsch & Richard Thaler, *Fairness as a Constraint on Profit Seeking: Entitlements in the Market*, 76 AM. ECON. REV. 728, 729-30 (1986).

61. *See* Elizabeth Hoffman & Matthew L. Spitzer, *Entitlements, Rights, and Fairness: An Experimental Examination of Subjects' Concepts of Distributive Justice*, 14 J. LEGAL STUD. 259, 261 (1985).

62. *See* Kahneman et al., *supra* note 60, at 729-30.

63. For a recent effort to incorporate a more general notion of "fairness" into the economic analysis of tort law, see Henrik Lando, *An Attempt to Incorporate Fairness into an Economic Model of Tort Law*, 17 INT'L REV. L. & ECON. 575 (1997). The relevant "fairness" notions there may be somewhat more "ad hoc," as Lando ultimately concludes, *id.* at 582, because, in contrast to the more market-oriented contexts we consider, there is no clear "reference transaction" in the tort context.

in behavior that have followed largely unenforced bans on smoking in public places—the phenomenon of "compliance without enforcement."[64]

B. *Bargaining Around Court Orders*

1. *Coasian prediction.*

As noted above, an important aspect of law and economics is the Coase theorem, which says that the assignment of a legal entitlement will not influence the ultimate allocation of that entitlement when transaction costs and wealth effects are zero. A straightforward application of this idea is that when a court enters a judgment, whether in the form of an injunction or a damage award, the parties are likely to bargain to a different outcome if that outcome is preferable to what the court did and the transaction costs and wealth effects are small. (Thus, for instance, if the court enters a prohibitively high damage award but the activity in question is efficient, the parties should bargain for a lower damage level, since this would increase the surplus to be shared between them.) To whom an entitlement is allocated after litigation, and how it is protected (by a property rule or a liability rule), are irrelevant to the ultimate allocation of the entitlement in these circumstances.

2. *Behavioral analysis.*

Influenced by behavioral economics, many legal commentators have observed that in light of the endowment effect described in Part I (an aspect of prospect theory, and thus an instance of bounded rationality), the assignment of a legal entitlement may well affect the outcome of bargaining, even when transaction costs (as conventionally defined) and wealth effects are zero.[65] This conclusion is suggested by the mugs experiments described in Part I, as well as by a substantial body of other evidence on the endowment effect.[66] The mugs results were obtained in circumstances that were the most favorable to the predictions of the conventional theory. Transaction costs were zero and the sort of emotional attachments that can grow over time in the real world were absent. Mug owners had become mug owners just minutes before the markets were run. Compare that with a homeowner who has been endowed with the right to have her homestead protected from noxious fumes being emitted nearby.

64. *See* Robert A. Kagan & Jerome H. Skolnick, *Banning Smoking: Compliance Without Enforcement*, *in* SMOKING POLICY: LAW, POLITICS, AND CULTURE 69 (Robert L. Rabin & Stephen D. Sugarman eds., 1993).

65. *See, e.g.*, Elizabeth Hoffman & Matthew L. Spitzer, *Willingness to Pay vs. Willingness to Accept: Legal and Economic Implications*, 71 WASH. U. L.Q. 59, 99 (1993).

66. *See* Kahneman et al., *supra* note 26, at 1327 tbl.1 (summarizing studies).

Although the endowment effect suggests generally that the assignment of a legal entitlement may affect the outcome of bargaining, such an effect is especially likely when the entitlement is in the form of a court order obtained after legal proceedings between opposing parties (our focus here). This is so for several reasons.

First, the process of going through litigation may strengthen the endowment effect. Experimental evidence suggests that there is an especially strong endowment effect when a party believes that he has earned the entitlement or that he particularly deserves it.[67] Of course someone who has received a court judgment in his favor will believe that he has earned it. Such a person may also believe strongly that this outcome is fair, based on the self-serving bias discussed in the following section.

Bounded self-interest, and specifically the acrimony notions developed above, provide an additional reason we might expect less bargaining in real world settings than in law and economics texts. Even if there are financial gains from making a deal, it is difficult to bargain without communication, and litigants are often not on speaking terms by the end of a protracted trial. Even if communication is possible, bargains are unlikely to be struck when both sides take pleasure in making the other side worse off; in such circumstances it can be difficult to reach agreements on settlements even if they would substantially improve the lot of both parties. For all of these reasons, behavioral research suggests that injunctions and damage awards may stick even with low transaction costs (as conventionally defined).

Note that another way of phrasing this conclusion is that the concept of transaction costs is broader than conventional analysis assumes. The costs of a transaction include not only the conventionally recognized ones (for example, the cost of assembling all of the relevant parties), but also costs such as the discomfort or displeasure of dealing with an adversary. If "transaction costs" are defined in this broader way, then, for the reasons given above, they will very often be substantial in the case of bargaining around court orders; hence, deals are unlikely to occur. This observation illustrates an important general point. Once the behavioral analysis is understood, it can often be incorporated into economic analyses using standard concepts such as transaction costs. This should not be taken to imply, however, that the behavioral analysis is superfluous. Under the usual account, transaction costs would have been assumed to be zero as long as the two sides could easily negotiate.

It is of course true that most cases settle, so that those which do not, and which thus produce court orders, may be atypical in some respects. But that does not mean they are unimportant objects of study for purposes of positive

67. *See* George Loewenstein & Samuel Issacharoff, *Source Dependence in the Valuation of Objects*, 7 J. BEHAV. DECISION MAKING 157, 159-61 (1994).

analysis. With conventional law and economics, behavioral analysis is concerned with the fact (and the consequences of the fact) that some cases proceed to trial.[68]

Although our focus in this section is on positive analysis, there is also a tricky normative issue: When people fail to reach bargains that would be reached in the absence of endowment effects and spiteful behavior, is there any problem from the standpoint of efficiency?[69] On one view, the answer is no; if the parties do not contract around a court-ordered outcome for these reasons, then the outcome must be efficient (even if another, different outcome—favoring the other side—would also have been efficient). An underlying question, however, is whether spite ought to count in the efficiency calculus. Some of the most prominent utilitarian philosophers believe that it should not.[70]

3. *Evidence.*

Conventional economic theory and behavioral analysis thus generate distinct predictions about what happens after trials. These theories can therefore be tested with empirical evidence. What happens once a court judgment has been entered? How often do the parties bargain to a different outcome? Consider the set of cases where the court has assigned an entitlement to the party who values it less. In these circumstances, the standard theory would predict contracting around the court order whenever transaction costs (as conventionally defined) and wealth effects are small. (The possibility of asymmetric information is discussed below in connection with the existing empirical findings.) The behavioral theory predicts that even in such cases, there will often be no recontracting. Since it is unlikely that court orders are, across the board, uniquely efficient, it should be possible to test these differing predictions.

Even without this detailed type of information, data gathered by Ward Farnsworth suggest that there is much less post-trial bargaining than the eco-

---

68. Conventional law and economics attributes failures to settle primarily to informational differences among parties. There is a large body of literature on this topic, which is summarized in Bruce L. Hay & Kathryn E. Spier, *Litigation and Settlement*, *in* THE NEW PALGRAVE DICTIONARY OF ECONOMICS AND THE LAW (forthcoming 1998).

69. For a discussion of various approaches to this question in the context of endowment effects, see Russell Korobkin, Note, *Policymaking and the Offer/Asking Price Gap: Toward a Theory of Efficient Entitlement Allocation*, 46 STAN. L. REV. 663, 675-97 (1994).

70. *See* John C. Harsanyi, *Morality and the Theory of Rational Behaviour*, *in* UTILITARIANISM AND BEYOND 39, 55-56 (Amartya Sen & Bernard Williams eds., 1982). A. Mitchell Polinsky and Steven Shavell have acknowledged this view in their analysis of punitive damages as a response to the socially illicit gains obtained by certain defendants. *See* A. Mitchell Polinsky & Steven Shavell, *Punitive Damages: An Economic Analysis*, 111 HARV. L. REV. 869, 908-10 (1998).

nomic model would predict.[71] Farnsworth interviewed attorneys from approximately twenty nuisance cases in which injunctive relief was sought and either granted or denied after full litigation before a judge. In not a single case of those Farnsworth studied did parties even attempt to contract around the court order, even when transaction costs were low, and even when an objective third party might think that there was considerable room for mutually advantageous deals. Conventional analysis might attribute failures to reach an ultimate agreement to asymmetric information;[72] but under such analysis it is difficult to explain the complete failure even to negotiate. It is also interesting to note that the lawyers interviewed said that the parties would not have reached a contractual solution if the opposite result had been reached. (This last point also means that the no-bargaining result cannot be explained by supposing that the court orders entered were uniquely efficient.)

The lawyers' explanations for these results are behavioral in character. Once people have received a court judgment, they are unwilling to negotiate with the opposing party, partly because of an unwillingness by victorious plaintiffs to confer advantages upon their opponents. Having invested a great deal of resources in pursuing the case all the way to court and through a trial, victors perceive themselves as having a special right to the legally endorsed status quo, and they are unlikely to give that right up, especially to their opponent, for all, or most, of the tea in China. Their investment in the entitlement gives it a distinctive character. Bargains are unlikely in the extreme; the plaintiff and the defendant tend not even to think about them. These tendencies are reinforced (according to the lawyers in Farnsworth's study) by the presence of acrimony between the parties; thus acrimony combines with the endowment effect to produce an absence of negotiation.

Here, as elsewhere in this article, our emphasis is on whether empirical evidence exists to test the predictions of the conventional and behavioral economic accounts, and, if more evidence would be helpful, what sort of study might be most useful. It is frequently remarked that law and economics is primarily theoretical or analytic, and rarely empirical. Victory is often declared based on a dataless model. We think that before victory can be declared for either conventional or behavioral law and economics, the fit of the theory with the available evidence must be assessed. For behavioral analysis, it is not enough to build a model consistent with behavior observed in an experimental setting (such as behavior in the ultimatum game or the mugs experiments); the model must be compared and tested against what we observe in the world. A good aspiration for both conventional and behavioral

71. Ward Farnsworth, Do Parties to Nuisance Lawsuits Bargain After Judgment? A Glimpse Inside the Cathedral (1998) (unpublished manuscript, on file with the *Stanford Law Review*).

72. *See, e.g.*, Louis Kaplow & Steven Shavell, *Property Rules Versus Liability Rules: An Economic Analysis*, 109 HARV. L. REV. 713, 734 & n.66 (1996) (discussing economic models in which asymmetric information leads to failed negotiations).

approaches is careful empirical work that provides reasonably definitive conclusions about predictive failures and successes.

The empirical data and future empirical research discussed in this section concern behavior after a court has entered a judgment. Of course, most cases settle before trial, and so it is also important to ask to what degree bargaining is likely to be successful prior to this point. This is a separate question; bargaining may be more likely in that setting because neither side has yet been endowed through a court judgment with a clear entitlement. On the other hand, self-serving bias and conditions of acrimony (as well as the background force of the "ordinary" endowment effect) may still preclude successful bargaining. The next section examines the effect of self-serving bias on successful pretrial bargaining (as well as other forms of bargaining) in more detail.

C. *Failed Negotiations*

1. *Self-serving conceptions of fairness.*

Even among the well-mannered, fair-minded agents that populate behavioral economics, self-interest is very much alive and well. For often there will be room for disagreement about what is fair (or, equivalently, what is the appropriate reference transaction)—and thus there will be the opportunity for manipulation by self-interested parties. These parties may tend to see things in the light most favorable to them; while people care about fairness, their assessments of fairness are distorted by their own self-interest. This is a form of bounded rationality—specifically, a judgment error; people's perceptions are distorted by self-serving bias.

This form of bias can help to explain the frequency of failed negotiations. It is quite common, in cases involving divorce, child custody, and even commercial disputes, to see protracted litigation in circumstances in which it might be expected that the parties would be able to reach negotiated solutions (although it of course remains the case that most suits settle). On the standard account, the existence of such protracted litigation is somewhat of a puzzle. With a good sense of the expected value of suit, parties should settle more than they do. It may be possible to explain some of the observed behavior in terms of asymmetric information and signaling, which may interfere with settlement prospects.[73] However, this account is difficult to test. By contrast, the effects of self-serving bias in negotiations have been tested empirically, as described below.

---

73. *See, e.g.*, POLINSKY, *supra* note 6, at 109-11.

2. *Evidence.*

The leading study in this area is one by Linda Babcock, Xianghong Wang, and George Loewenstein on the consequences of self-serving bias for negotiation impasse in public school teacher contract negotiations in Pennsylvania.[74] A common element of public sector labor negotiations is for both sides to invoke agreements in "comparable" communities, either as a measure of market conditions or as a characterization of what is fair. Do participants in a negotiation choose comparable communities in a rational manner? Babcock, Wang, and Loewenstein hypothesized that they may not; instead, both sides may adopt self-serving judgments about which communities are "comparable," and impasses may result from such judgments. They designed a survey of union and school board presidents in all school districts in Pennsylvania, in order to elicit judgments about comparable districts for purposes of salary negotiations. Respondents were asked to "list the districts they felt were comparable to their own."[75] Note that there is no strategic incentive here to misrepresent one's view of which districts are comparable, either to gain an advantage in negotiations or to curry public favor for one's negotiating position; the only audience for the responses in the study was the study's authors. Nonetheless, substantial differences between the two sides emerged. The average salary listed by union presidents for comparable districts was $27,633, compared to an average of $26,922 for school board presidents.[76] This difference was about 2.4% of the average teacher salary in a setting in which the last offers before teacher strikes were typically about one percent apart.[77]

By itself, this difference is highly suggestive; if the two sides have different views about comparable districts, bargaining impasses may well occur. But do these self-serving views (reported to the authors of the study in response to a survey question) correlate with actual behavior? Yes. The authors regressed the percentage of previous negotiations that ended in a strike against the difference between the two sides' lists of comparable districts. The regression showed that this difference had substantial explanatory power. In those school districts where the average salary of the union's list is $1000 greater than the board's list, a strike is forty-nine percent more likely than where the average salaries of the two lists are the same.[78] Thus self-serving biases can explain real-world bargaining impasses.

74. Linda Babcock, Xianghong Wang & George Loewenstein, *Choosing the Wrong Pond: Social Comparisons in Negotiations that Reflect a Self-Serving Bias*, 111 Q.J. ECON. 1 (1996).

75. *Id.* at 10.

76. *Id.* at 11.

77. *Id.*

78. *Id.* at 13.

As already noted, strategic behavior does not seem to provide a strong explanation for the empirical evidence on school-district negotiations. There was no incentive in the study (as there would often be in negotiations with the opposing party) for parties to choose comparable districts in a strategic manner.[79] The behavioral account seems to exhibit a higher "R^2"—a better ability to predict the observed data—than the standard account.

A fertile ground for future study of self-serving bias and its relationship to bargaining impasse may be negotiations between baseball players' agents and team management. It is common practice in these negotiations for both sides to use the contracts of "comparable" players as reference points, once again as a measure of market conditions and as a characterization of what is fair. Participants' selection of which players are comparable may well be colored by self-serving bias. Exploration of the impact of this behavioral factor on the success or failure of these negotiations seems far more promising than examining the role of informational asymmetry in this setting. For the participants have equal access to the information that defines what is a comparable player. Thus behavioral economics appears more likely than the conventional model to predict and account for those negotiations that fail and end up in the hands of an arbitrator.

In addition to the existing data on school district strikes, researchers have conducted experimental studies on the role of self-serving bias in preventing negotiated agreements.[80] The studies involved a tort case based on real litigation in Texas. Subjects—college and law students—were randomly assigned to the role of plaintiff or defendant; in this role they were asked to negotiate a settlement. They received a short summary of the case and also twenty-seven pages of materials from the original case. Subjects were told that the same case materials had been given to a judge in Texas, who had reached a judgment between $0 and $100,000. Before beginning to negotiate, subjects were asked to write down their guesses about what the judge awarded. They were also asked to say what they considered a fair amount for the plaintiff to receive in a settlement. The authors found quite substantial self-serving biases in subjects' assessments of the judge's award. The subjects acting as the plaintiffs guessed an average $14,527 higher than the defendants', and the plaintiffs' fair settlement values averaged $17,709 higher than those of the defendants.[81] Nonsettlement was strongly connected

---

79. For a fuller discussion than space here permits of the possibility of strategic behavior, and experimental evidence from other studies that points against such an explanation for the results, see *id.* at 17-18.

80. Linda Babcock, George Loewenstein, Samuel Issacharoff & Colin Camerer, *Biased Judgments of Fairness in Bargaining*, 85 AM. ECON. REV. 1337 (1995); George Loewenstein, Samuel Issacharoff, Colin Camerer & Linda Babcock, *Self-Serving Assessments of Fairness and Pretrial Bargaining*, 22 J. LEGAL STUD. 135 (1993).

81. Loewenstein et al., *supra* note 80, at 151.

to the discrepancy in predictions about the judge's likely award.[82] Note that the hypothetical, role-playing nature of this study in some ways strengthens the interpretation of the result. In the short time that it took to read all the materials, subjects adopted the point of view of their roles and the bias that comes with it. Of course, the fact that roles were only hypothetical, and the financial stakes small, means that we cannot be sure from these studies alone that parties would display self-serving bias in real-world settings; but the school district study suggests the importance of the bias in such settings.

3. *The role of lawyers.*

Are real lawyers immune from self-serving biases? There is some evidence that lawyers, as intermediators, are relatively less subject to various cognitive biases, in ways that can help promote settlement.[83] However, there is suggestive evidence that self-serving bias does affect lawyers and judges as well as other actors. A study of 205 bankruptcy lawyers and 150 bankruptcy judges found self-serving biases in responses to a wide range of questions involving how long it takes judges to rule on fee applications, the fairness of fees, and lawyers' fee awards in general.[84] Thus, for example, thirty-two percent of lawyers report that they never request court-ordered compensation in excess of normal hourly rates, but judges report that only eleven percent of lawyers never make such requests.[85] This evidence does not show that lawyers do not reduce self-serving bias in actual litigation, but it casts doubt on the proposition that this bias is eliminated by the involvement of professionals. To the extent that the bias is reduced through lawyers' involvement, it suggests that part of the appropriate role of lawyers may be to counter their clients' predictable inclination to overstate the fairness of their own cause. This may be difficult since clients are the ultimate decisionmakers and lawyers may have an economic interest in not settling. Thus, serious ethical issues may arise about the lawyer's obligations. To the extent that it is possible for clients to be "debiased" by their lawyers, behavioral research provides considerable guidance on which debiasing techniques are least likely to be successful, and which might actually work.[86]

82. *Id.*

83. *See* Russell Korobkin & Chris Guthrie, *Psychology, Economics, and Settlement: A New Look at the Role of the Lawyer*, 76 TEX. L. REV. 77 (1997).

84. Theodore Eisenberg, *Differing Perceptions of Attorney Fees in Bankruptcy Cases*, 72 WASH. U. L.Q. 979 (1994).

85. *Id.* at 988 tbl.3.

86. *See* Linda Babcock, George Loewenstein & Samuel Issacharoff, *Debiasing Litigation Impasse*, 22 J. L. SOC. INQUIRY. 913 (1997).

D. *Mandatory Contract Terms*

1. *Wage and price effects.*

One of the most frequent claims in the economic analysis of law is that the imposition of mandatory terms on parties to a contract will make both parties worse off; it will operate as an effective tax on their transaction. For example, rules granting employees a particular level of workplace safety, or tenants the right to a habitable apartment, will make employers and employees, or landlords and tenants, worse off.[87] In this section, we suggest that bounded rationality, in particular the endowment effect, casts doubt on the conventional law and economics claim. Our analysis here parallels that offered by Richard Craswell several years ago in the context of mandatory product warranties;[88] we build upon Craswell in emphasizing the employment setting and in drawing upon a recent empirical study of the effects of mandatory contract terms.

The conventional argument against mandatory terms such as those just mentioned has two steps. First, since the parties did not bargain for the term in question when left to their own devices, the cost of the term must exceed its benefit (otherwise they would have agreed to it on their own). Thus, for example, if a particular employment benefit is worth $100 per year to employees and costs the employer only $90 to provide, a mandate should not be necessary; but if we do not observe the parties agreeing to the benefit on their own, then the cost must exceed $100. The second step in the conventional argument is that imposing a mandatory term in these circumstances will operate as a tax on the parties, causing the wage to fall (or, in the case of a habitable apartment, the price to rise) by somewhere between the benefit and the cost of the term, and causing the number of profitable trades to fall.[89] Thus, in the example just given, if the cost of the benefit valued at $100 is $110, then the employer will reduce the wage rate by somewhere between $100 (the value of the benefit to employees) and $110 (the cost of the benefit); and the level of employment will fall. This analysis assumes an upward-sloping (not vertical) labor supply curve, but, at least for the worker group

87. *See* POSNER, *supra* note 6, at 363, 515-17; Richard A. Epstein, *In Defense of the Contract at Will*, 51 U. CHI. L. REV. 947, 954-55 (1984); Charles J. Meyers, *The Covenant of Habitability and the American Law Institute*, 27 STAN. L. REV. 879, 890 (1975); Edward H. Rabin, *The Revolution in Residential Landlord-Tenant Law: Causes and Consequences*, 69 CORNELL L. REV. 517, 558 (1984).

88. Richard Craswell, *Passing on the Costs of Legal Rules: Efficiency and Distribution in Buyer-Seller Relationships*, 43 STAN. L. REV. 361, 388-90 (1991).

89. *See* Lawrence H. Summers, *Some Simple Economics of Mandated Benefits*, 79 AM. ECON. REV., May 1989, Papers & Proceedings, at 177, 180-81 & fig.1.

discussed below in connection with the existing empirical evidence (female employees), this assumption is clearly reasonable.[90]

The conventional account thus offers sharp predictions about the effects of imposing mandatory contract terms. Do the data bear out these predictions? The leading study in this area is by Jonathan Gruber; Gruber examines the effects of imposing mandatory coverage of childbirth expenses in employer-provided insurance policies.[91] Imposition of the mandatory health-insurance term—which represented a substantial departure from the usual contractual arrangements prior to the mandate—caused the wages of affected workers (most prominently, married women of childbearing age) to fall by at least the cost of the mandated coverage according to most of the author's estimates.[92] The study also found that the hours of employment of these workers were either unchanged or slightly higher with the mandate and that their probability of being employed was either unchanged or slightly lower.[93] In sum, "[t]he findings consistently suggest shifting of the costs of the mandates on the order of 100 percent, with little effect on net labor input."[94] These findings are not easy to reconcile with the conventional account, which predicts a fall in wages less than the cost of the benefit. (If the wage were going to adjust by the full cost of the benefit, then some substantial fraction of employers should have offered the benefit even prior to the mandate.)

2. *Behavioral analysis.*

Departures from the assumptions of expected utility maximization by unboundedly rational agents suggest a different account of the effects of imposing mandatory contract terms, one that is consistent with the empirical findings just described. As noted above, the endowment effect implies that people are often less willing to sell entitlements that are given to them than to buy entitlements that they do not already possess; if given a mug, they will not sell it for three dollars, but if not given a mug, they will not buy one for that price. Thus, the fact that an employee (say) chooses not to purchase a particular workplace benefit if he is not granted an entitlement to it does not

90. *See, e.g.*, PAUL A. SAMUELSON & WILLIAM D. NORDHAUS, ECONOMICS 681 tbl.28-2 (13th ed. 1989).

91. Jonathan Gruber, *The Incidence of Mandated Maternity Benefits*, 84 AM. ECON. REV. 622 (1994).

92. *Id.* at 623, 630-31, 633, 636. Gruber performs a number of different regressions; one set did not yield statistically significant results, *id.* at 638, while the others yielded statistically significant results along the lines described in the text. The confidence intervals for the majority of these results also include values indicating less than full shifting of the cost—but also, of course, values indicating much more than full shifting of the cost.

93. *Id.* at 623, 633, 637.

94. *Id.* at 623.

imply that he would want to sell the entitlement (if he could) once it has been granted. The corollary of this observation is that imposing a mandatory term may have different effects than the standard analysis predicts. In supply-and-demand terms, imagine a labor supply curve prior to the imposition of the mandate, reflecting willingness to work at different wage levels given provision of the benefit; the consequence of the endowment effect may be that this curve is shifted to the right once the mandate is imposed, and this move may more than compensate for the backward shift in the employer's labor demand curve as a result of the mandate. If this occurs, then the wages of the affected worker will fall by as much as or more than the cost of the benefit. This is precisely what the Gruber study of mandated childbirth coverage finds.[95]

Three caveats are important here. First, while the endowment effect is consistent with complete or more than complete adjustment of the wage or price, it is also possible to have less than complete adjustment of the wage or price in the presence of the endowment effect. Perhaps workers are not any more willing to supply labor in exchange for a given wage plus the benefit in question once they have an entitlement to the benefit; it may be just that they would be even *less* willing to supply labor in the absence of the benefit. It is also possible that conventional economic analysis, by incorporating a market failure such as adverse selection (a possibility generally ignored by the above-mentioned critics of mandatory contract terms), can explain the empirical findings discussed above.[96] Our point is just the modest one that the behavioral account can predict an instance of observed behavior that is inconsistent with the standard law and economics account of mandatory terms. Future empirical work could attempt to address the adverse selection possibility by examining the effects of mandatory contract terms in a setting in which (in contrast to the health insurance context) adverse selection is unlikely to be a significant force.

The second qualification is that the endowment effect may not operate in contexts in which the beneficiaries of a mandatory term must give up a preexisting level of income, since they may be highly averse to such a loss.[97]

95. As noted above, Richard Craswell offers an analogous analysis in the context of mandatory product warranties for consumers. *See* Craswell, *supra* note 88, at 388-90. As Craswell describes, given the endowment effect, the mandatory term may cause the price paid by consumers to adjust by more than the cost of the term, and the quantity of the good demanded may rise. In addition to Craswell's discussion of mandatory terms, the endowment effect has been extensively discussed in the legal literature in connection with waivable contract terms and the Coase theorem. *See, e.g.*, David Charny, *Hypothetical Bargains: The Normative Structure of Contract Interpretation*, 89 MICH. L. REV. 1815, 1867-68 (1991) (discussing waivable terms); Kelman, *supra* note 1, at 678-95 (concerning the Coase theorem).

96. *See* Gruber, *supra* note 91, at 626 n.9.

97. *See* Kahneman & Tversky, *supra* note 12, at 277-79 (arguing that changes in welfare must be evaluated in terms of an initial reference point and that "losses loom larger than gains").

This qualification applies only to situations in which there is a financial loss relative to some preexisting expectation; thus it would not apply to, for example, a consumer's purchase of a durable good at a higher price due to the inclusion of a warranty. The final qualification here is that our analysis in this section is purely positive, concerned with the effects of imposing a mandatory contract term. The endowment effect does not necessarily imply that, from a normative perspective, mandatory terms are desirable; they may be efficient, in the sense that they would not be undone (if they could be) once imposed, but the situation without such terms is also efficient, for the same reasons given by the standard account, and there is no obvious means by which the two situations can be compared. Unlike several of the scenarios discussed in Part V below, in which we think there is often a relatively strong argument for choosing one normative benchmark over another (say because people are likely to underestimate certain objective probabilities based on some form of judgment error), here there does not seem to be a clear basis for such a decision.

Our emphasis, then, is the positive question of the effects of imposing mandatory contract terms. The primary point is that there is a substantial research agenda to test various hypotheses; what we wish to suggest is that the conventional view cannot be accepted a priori and that there is reason to think that behavioral law and economics points in helpful directions.

III. The Content of Law

One of the goals of law and economics is to explain the content of law—what the law allows and what it prohibits. The traditional approach provides two tools for this analysis. First, laws may be efficient solutions to the problems of organizing society.[98] Such laws can be thought of as solutions to optimal contracting problems with all of the affected parties at the table. Second, laws may come about because of the rent-seeking activities of politically powerful actors; many laws that benefit farmers and concentrated industries, for example, have been explained along these lines.[99] The positive theory of law reflected in the conventional account predicts that the legal rules we observe will be rules that either maximize social wealth (if they are judge-made rules) or redistribute wealth to interest groups able to influence the legislative process. Law and economics scholars who reject this account of the content of law have not offered any alternative account to explain and predict the rules we observe.

The notion that laws emerge from considerations of efficiency and conventional rent seeking would probably strike most citizens as odd. Instead,

98. *See* POSNER, *supra* note 6, at 569.

99. *See* George J. Stigler, *The Theory of Economic Regulation*, 2 BELL J. ECON. & MGMT. SCI. 3 (1971).

we suspect that most members of society—which is to say most of the people who are entitled to elect legislators—hold the view, undoubtedly naively, that the purpose of the law is to codify "right" and "wrong." Certainly many criminal statutes would be explained without reference to either of the above factors. In this section we argue that law and economics explanations of the content of law need to be modified by incorporating the ideas of bounded self-interest (in the form of fairness norms) and bounded rationality developed above. As we will try to show, many laws on the books appear to be difficult to justify on efficiency grounds (for example, those that prohibit mutually beneficial exchanges without obvious externalities) and seem to benefit groups that do not have much lobbying power (such as the poor or middle class). We argue that the explanation for the "anomalous" laws is typically a quite simple one: Most people think the result is fair. We also suggest that some laws we observe reflect neither efficiency nor conventional rent seeking but, instead, aspects of bounded rationality. Our point is not the general (and rather obvious) one that fairness concerns and bounded rationality may shape the content of law; we seek to show specifically how behavioral analysis has real predictive and explanatory power. We also do not claim that fairness concerns and bounded rationality explain every aspect of the content of law—just that they provide a useful supplement to existing explanations.[100]

The mechanisms underlying our behavioral economic account of the content of law are simple and conventional. With the existing analysis, we assume (for present purposes, and insofar as statutory rather than judge-made law is concerned) that legislators are maximizers interested in their own reelection. Legislators interested in their own reelection will be responsive to the preferences and judgments of their constituents and those of powerful interest groups. If constituents believe that a certain practice is unfair or dangerous, and should be banned or regulated, self-interested legislators will respond, even if they do not share these views. Likewise, if a mobilized group holds such views, legislators' response will be affected, in much the same way as if the group sought legislation to serve a narrowly defined financial self-interest, as posited by the standard account.

Mobilized groups may also attempt to manage and exploit the public's views, including views influenced by bounded self-interest and bounded rationality, to bolster their own efforts; a prime example discussed below is the "availability entrepreneur," who seeks to publicize an event in order to make

100. Our analysis in this part is similar in spirit to that offered by earlier work such as David Cohen & Jack Knetsch, *Judicial Choice and Disparities Between Measures of Economic Values*, 30 OSGOODE HALL L.J. 737 (1992) (seeking to explain various legal doctrines based on the endowment effect), and Sara Sun Beale, *What's Law Got To Do With It?*, 1 BUFF. CRIM. L. REV. 23 (1997) (seeking to explain criminal law based on the availability heuristic and other aspects of bounded rationality).

it more "available" to the general public, and thus to increase the public's demand for regulation. We suspect that a full account of the content of law would have to incorporate legislators' independent judgments about fairness or risk, which play an occasional role; but we do not discuss that point here because for the examples we consider, public and interest-group perceptions seem to provide a good (and the most parsimonious) account of the laws we observe.

A. *Bans on Market Transactions*

This section discusses the demand for the law insofar as that demand is affected by people's bounded self-interest and in particular by their taste for fairness as they understand it. We do not mean to defend the laws that we describe; we suggest more modestly that people's commitment to fairness is part of the causal mechanism that establishes those laws. Fairness norms interact with other forces to produce some of the seemingly anomalous laws we observe. "Fairness entrepreneurs" may play a role, mobilizing public judgments to serve their (selfish or nonselfish) interests.

1. *Bans on economic transactions.*

A puzzle. A pervasive feature of law is that mutually desired trades are blocked. Perhaps most puzzling amidst this landscape—which includes bans on baby selling and vote trading, discussed below—are bans on conventional "economic" transactions, such as usurious lending, price gouging, and ticket scalping. Usury, or charging an interest rate above a certain level, is prohibited by many states in consumer lending transactions.[101] Price gouging, or the charging of "grossly excessive" or "unconscionable" prices, is prohibited during "states of emergency" (as after a flood or other natural disaster) in many states that have had recent experience with such events.[102] Finally, ticket scalping, or the resale of tickets at prices well above face prices (in excess of a modest margin to cover ticket brokers' costs), is prohibited by roughly half of all states, including New York (with its heavy theater population).[103] What accounts for these laws, which impose constraints on gain-

101. *See* UNIF. CONSUMER CREDIT CODE § 2.201 (1974 Act).

102. *See* ALA. CODE § 8-31-3 (1997); 1997 ARK. ACTS 376; CAL. PENAL CODE § 396 (West 1998); CONN. GEN. STAT. § 42-232 (1997); FLA. STAT. ANN. § 501.160 (West 1998); GA. CODE ANN. § 10-1-393.4 (1997); LA. REV. STAT. ANN. § 29:732 (West 1988); N.Y. GEN. BUS. LAW § 396-r (McKinney 1997-1998); TEX. BUS. & COM. CODE ANN. § 1746(25) (1998).

103. *See* ARK. CODE ANN. § 5-63-201 (Michie 1997); CONN. GEN. STAT. § 53-289 (1997); FLA. STAT. ANN. § 817.36 (West 1998); GA. CODE ANN. § 10-1-310 (1997); KY. REV. STAT. ANN. § 518.070 (Banks-Baldwin 1997); LA. REV. STAT. ANN. § 4:1 (West 1997 & Supp. 1998); MD. CODE ANN., BUS. REG. § 4-318 (1992); MASS. GEN. LAWS ch. 140 §§ 185A, 185D (West 1994); MICH. COMP. LAWS ANN. § 750.465 (West 1991); MINN. STAT. ANN. § 609.805 (West 1987); MISS. CODE ANN. § 97-23-97 (1994); MO. ANN. STAT. § 578.395 (West 1995); N.M. STAT. ANN. §

producing transactions for ordinary commodities such as television sets and theater tickets?

Not surprisingly, economists and economically oriented lawyers often view these laws as inefficient and anomalous.[104] The laws also do not generally seem well explained in terms of conventional rent seeking by a politically powerful faction. One might argue that ticket-scalping laws are an exception to this last point, on the ground that ticket sellers (who may be politically powerful) might lobby in favor of the laws because moderate prices are necessary to create demand, which in turn certifies quality and makes the product more desirable.[105] (Thus, for example, the argument would be that restaurant owners do not raise prices when waits develop for tables, and if a secondary market in restaurant reservations were to develop with very high prices for tables, restaurateurs might wish to outlaw it.) The difficulty with this form of argument as applied here is that it cannot explain the application of ticket-scalping laws to perennially popular events whose quality is known from TV and whose attractiveness to the public would not decrease significantly even with some diminution in demand—a category that includes many professional sporting events. Our point here is actually a more general one: Although it may be possible to offer efficiency or conventional rent-seeking explanations for certain sorts of laws banning economic transactions,[106] there does not seem to be a general theory or set of theories that can explain all or even most of these laws on traditional grounds.

A behavioral account. By contrast, laws banning usurious lending, price gouging, and ticket scalping when such activities are prevalent are a straightforward prediction of the theory of perceived fairness developed in Part II.A above. (We assume here that self-interested legislators are responsive to citizens' or other actors' demand for the content of law.) In the case of each of these bans, the transaction in question is a significant departure from the usual terms of trade in the market for the good in question—that is, a significant departure from the "reference transaction." Behavioral analysis predicts that if trades are occurring frequently in a given jurisdiction at terms far from

30-46-1 (Michie 1997); N.Y. ARTS & CULT. AFF. LAW § 25.13 (McKinney 1984 & Supp. 1998) (effective June 1, 1998); N.C. GEN. STAT. § 14-344 (1997); 4 PA. CONS. STAT. ANN. §§ 211, 212 (West 1995); R.I. GEN. LAWS § 5-22-26 (1995); S.C. CODE ANN. § 16-17-710 (Law Co-op. 1985).

104. *See, e.g.*, John Tierney, *Tickets? Supply Meets Demand on Sidewalk*, N.Y. TIMES, Dec. 26, 1992, at A1 (quoting New York University economist William J. Baumol criticizing laws against ticket scalping).

105. *See* Gary S. Becker, *A Note on Restaurant Pricing and Other Examples of Social Influences on Price*, 99 J. POL. ECON. 1109, 1110 (1991) (offering quality-certification argument).

106. For an argument that usury laws can be explained on conventional economic grounds, see Eric A. Posner, *Contract Law in the Welfare State: A Defense of the Unconscionability Doctrine, Usury Laws, and Related Limitations on the Freedom to Contract*, 24 J. LEGAL STUD. 283 (1995). Peter Diamond has pointed out to us that ticket-scalping laws may be desirable to sports team owners who wish to engage in certain types of dynamic pricing strategies over the course of the season.

those of the reference transaction, there will be strong pressure for a law banning such trades. Note that the prediction is *not* that all high prices (ones that make it difficult or impossible for some people to afford things they might want) will be banned; what we predict will be banned are transactions at terms far from the terms on which those transactions *generally occur in the marketplace*.

Consider this example:

> A store has been sold out of the popular Cabbage Patch dolls for a month. A week before Christmas a single doll is discovered in a store room. The managers know that many customers would like to buy the doll. They announce over the store's public address system that the doll will be sold by auction to the customer who offers to pay the most.[107]

Nearly three-quarters of the respondents judged this action to be either somewhat unfair or very unfair, though, of course, an economic analysis would judge the auction the most efficient method of assuring that the doll goes to the person who values it most.[108] Although the auction is efficient, it represents a departure from the "reference transaction," under which the doll is sold at its usual price. (Of course, there would be no need for a law banning such behavior, since it does not appear to be prevalent.) As in the doll example, if money is loaned to individuals at a rate of interest significantly greater than the rate at which similarly-sized loans are made to other customers, then the lender's behavior may be viewed as unfair. Since lumber generally tends to sell for a particular price, sales at far higher prices in the wake of (say) a hurricane, which drives demand sky high, are thought unfair. Tickets to sporting events or the theater often sell for around the face price of the ticket, so large mark-ups over that amount are judged unfair. Consistent with this last suggestion, subjects asked whether a team should allocate its few remaining tickets to a key football game through an auction thought that this approach would be unfair; allocation based on who waited in line longest was the preferred solution.[109] Of course, waiting in line for tickets is precisely what happens with laws against ticket scalping. Thus, pervasive fairness norms appear to shape attitudes (and hence possibly law) on usury, price gouging, and ticket scalping.

"Conventional economic analyses assume as a matter of course that excess demand for a good creates an opportunity for suppliers to raise prices" and that "[t]he profit-seeking adjustments that clear the market are . . . as natural as water finding its level—and as ethically neutral," but "[t]he lay public does not share this indifference."[110] A system in which, for example, only fans able to pay $3000 could attend the Super Bowl would be a system

107. Kahneman et al., *supra* note 60, at 735.

108. *Id.*

109. Kahneman et al., *supra* note 47, at S287-88.

110. Kahneman et al., *supra* note 60, at 735.

characterized by the sort of severe departure from the reference transaction that people view as intolerable. As a letter-writer to the *New York Times* colorfully put it in responding to coverage of ticket-scalping laws: "With legalized scalping, lower- and middle-income consumers would be relegated to watching events at home or buying overpriced seats in the nosebleed section"; such a system of "entertainment Darwinism" would be a "raw deal" for the average consumer.[111]

We emphasize that we need not (and do not) find these views of fairness necessarily rational or compelling. Many of those who think "usurious" lenders are "unfair" might not have thought through the implications of their views (for example, that paying an outrageous price for a loan may be better than paying an infinite price, or that a loan to a riskier borrower is a product different in kind from a loan to a safer borrower). Still, if such views are widespread, they may underlie certain patterns in the content of law, such as the legal restrictions on usury, price gouging and ticket scalping. Our claim here is a positive one about the content of the law we observe, not a prescriptive or normative one about the shape practices or rules should take. As a positive matter, behavioral analysis predicts that if trades are commonly occurring with terms far from those of the reference transaction, then legal rules will often ban trades on such terms.

We do not claim to have offered a definitive explanation for the pattern of usury, price gouging, and ticket scalping laws we observe. Usury seems to be broadly prohibited, so one is not faced with the question of why we observe bans in some states but not others. The same cannot be said of price gouging and ticket scalping; each is prohibited only in certain states. Price gouging appears to be prohibited primarily by states that have recently experienced (or whose neighbors have recently experienced) natural disasters; and ticket scalping laws may be concentrated in states with very popular theater or sporting events. More in-depth empirical research would be required to determine if these patterns bear out, and whether conventional interest-group theories provide an alternative account. Our goal here is simply to suggest the likelihood, from the perspective of behavioral law and economics, that observed laws reflect, in systematic and predictable ways, fairness considerations as well as efficiency and conventional forms of rent seeking.

Private behavior. It is interesting to note that these transaction-banning laws often mimic, rather than constrain, the behavior of the firms they regulate. Consider first usury: It is a well-known puzzle of lending markets that lenders often refuse to loan money to risky borrowers even at above-market interest rates; rather, someone either qualifies for a loan at the offered rate or

111. Russ Haven & Amy Chester, Letter to the Editor, *Ticket-Scalping Laws Protect the Average Fan*, N.Y. TIMES, May 9, 1995, at A26.

does not qualify for a loan at all.[112] This is true even when a modest increase in the interest rate would not violate usury laws.[113] (Adverse selection considerations may also explain this behavior,[114] but they cannot easily explain the existence of *laws* against such behavior.) Price gouging and ticket scalping are similar in terms of private actors' behavior. Thus, when Hurricane Andrew hit Florida and the demand for lumber and other building supplies skyrocketed, Home Depot, a major national chain, continued to sell these goods at its usual prices, despite the fact that the stock could have been sold at an enormous (short-term) profit, and despite the fact that no law banned price increases.[115] More generally, economists have often remarked on the failure of firms to increase prices in response to temporary increases in demand.[116] Likewise, an interesting feature of ticket-scalping laws is that they will keep prices down only to the extent that firms choose to sell tickets at reasonable prices in the first place; but in fact firms routinely do this.[117] For example, during the 1997 NBA playoffs, the Chicago Bulls sold some tickets to the general public at prices that were somewhat higher than regular season games but a fraction of the price the tickets commanded on the (legal in Illinois) ticket broker open market. As the head of a major theater company explained, "there's a strong public relations argument" against raising prices for tickets for very popular shows (and presumably sporting events as well)—despite excess demand for seats at the going prices—because the public already believes "that Broadway ticket prices are too high."[118] "Even though we could sell tickets at $100," another theater owner said, "we'd be cutting our own throats because it would be a P.R. disaster for Broadway."[119] Why would it be a "P.R. disaster" if the market would allow them to sell

112. *See, e.g.*, Keith N. Hylton & Vincent D. Rougeau, *Lending Discrimination: Economic Theory, Econometric Evidence, and the Community Reinvestment Act*, 85 GEO. L.J. 237, 258 (1996) (discussing the residential mortgage lending market); BOARD OF GOVERNORS OF THE FEDERAL RESERVE SYSTEM, REPORT TO THE CONGRESS ON COMMUNITY DEVELOPMENT LENDING BY DEPOSITORY INSTITUTIONS 34 (1993) (same).

113. *See* Hylton & Rougeau, *supra* note 112, at 258 & n.85.

114. *See* Michael Klausner, *Market Failure and Community Investment: A Market-Oriented Alternative to the Community Reinvestment Act*, 143 U. PA. L. REV. 1561, 1566-68 (1995) (citing Joseph P. Stiglitz & Andrew Weiss, *Credit Rationing in Markets with Imperfect Information*, 71 AM. ECON. REV. 393 (1981)).

115. *See* Steve Lohr, *Lessons from a Hurricane: It Pays Not to Gouge*, N.Y. TIMES, Sept. 22, 1992, at D1, D5.

116. *See* David D. Haddock & Fred S. McChesney, *Why Do Firms Contrive Shortages? The Economics of Intentional Mispricing*, 32 ECON. INQUIRY 562, 562-63 (1994) (surveying the economic literature).

117. See Stephen K. Happel & Marianne M. Jennings, *Assessing the Economic Rationale and Legal Remedies for Ticket Scalping*, 16 J. LEGIS. 1, 8-9 (1989), for fairness explanations of this behavior.

118. Peter Passell, *If Scalpers Can Get So Much, Why Aren't Tickets Costlier?*, N.Y. TIMES, Dec. 23, 1993, at D2 (quoting Gerald Schoenfeld, head of the Shubert Organization).

119. Tierney, *supra* note 104, at D24 (quoting Rocco Landesman, president of Jujamcyn Theaters).

their tickets at $100? We think this would be so because a $100 ticket price for a very popular show would have been viewed as unfair by many members of the public given that the usual price for a ticket was below this.

Consistent with the foregoing analysis, recent evidence of price stickiness shows that firms' behavior seems to be affected greatly by their customers' perceptions of unfair price increases.[120] Note that this is not a standard reputation story; fairness considerations are the *reason* that raising prices harms the firm's reputation. None of this is to say that firms never raise prices in an opportunistic fashion; for instance, when sports teams sell playoff tickets to season ticket holders at below-market prices, it may be that the ticket holders paid a premium for the playoff tickets ex ante (through the purchase of season tickets). In each of the contexts we examine, our point is just the modest one that fairness norms often seem to constrain firms' behavior in much the same way that they shape laws against behavior violating those norms. Consistent with our analysis, it appears that firms typically support and even lobby for laws against ticket scalping.[121]

Why then are the laws necessary? Some of the relevant actors will not be constrained by fairness norms in the absence of a law. Noninstitutional lenders may be willing to lend at exorbitant rates; suppliers selling lumber out of the back of pick-up trucks will often charge whatever the market will bear (as occurred after Hurricane Andrew);[122] ticket scalpers, who are typically anonymous actors engaged in one-time transactions, have no reason to keep prices down. It is these actors who are regulated by the law. The more powerful mainstream firms will tend to support, or at least not oppose, rules banning unfair transactions. (Note, though, that their support would not be predicted by the standard account.)

2. *Other bans.*

Laws banning economic transactions are just a species of a broader form of regulation of transactions. Many deals are blocked, across a wide range of contexts. People may not buy and sell body parts.[123] They cannot sell their votes.[124] In some states, commercial surrogacy is prohibited,[125] and baby

120. ALAN BLINDER, ELIE R.D. CANETTI, DAVID E. LEBOW & JEREMY B. RUDD, ASKING ABOUT PRICES: A NEW APPROACH TO UNDERSTANDING PRICE STICKINESS 9-10, 149-64 (1998).

121. *See* Steve Kukolla, *Ticket Selling: One Big Unhappy Family*, INDIANAPOLIS BUS. J., June 20-26, 1994, at 36A; *Senate Committee OKs Bill to Legalize Scalping of Tickets*, ATLANTA CONST., Mar. 20, 1997, at 2.

122. *See* Lohr, *supra* note 115, at D1.

123. *See* 42 U.S.C. § 274e (1991).

124. *See, e.g.*, Richard A. Epstein, *Why Restrain Alienation?*, 85 COLUM. L. REV. 970, 987 (1985).

125. *See* Radhika Rao, *Reconceiving Privacy: Relationships and Reproductive Technology*, 45 UCLA L. REV. 1077, 1117 n.226 (1998) (citing state statutes).

selling is banned in all states.[126] People may not contract around bans on race and sex discrimination, as for example through written agreements.[127] Blocked trades can be found in every American jurisdiction.

Bans of this variety raise serious normative questions; those questions have been well-ventilated. Doubtless reasonable distinctions can be drawn between bans in different areas; sometimes externalities are readily apparent. We make a simple positive point here: Behavioral analysis suggests that pervasive judgments about fairness may account for many such bans on voluntary deals. Whether or not those judgments make sense, they seem to be widespread, and they help to explain the persistence of legislation that is often difficult to explain by reference to an efficiency or rent-seeking account. In banning certain deals, legislators may be responding to community sentiments about what kinds of things are properly subject to market arrangements. The reference transaction in these areas is generally "no transaction"; just as the norm or benchmark is the usual or face price of the ticket, or an equal division of the amount to be divided in the ultimatum game, the norm or benchmark here is "no market exchange." Departures from that norm are viewed as unfair and are prohibited.

How could this behavioral theory of law be tested? One idea is to determine, based on historical evidence, what sorts of transactions were generally not engaged in (despite their being technologically feasible—for example, baby selling) regardless of the existence of a law banning them. These transactions could be said to have a no-transaction benchmark. (The importance of looking to a pre-law benchmark is that the existence of a legal ban could itself produce a no-market-exchange reference point, in which case the reference point obviously could not account for the existence of the ban.) Behavioral analysis predicts that such transactions will be legally censured. The existing law and economics analysis, by contrast, predicts that such transactions will be banned only if a ban is either efficient or favorable to a politically powerful interest group.

B. *Prior Restraints on Speech*

Another instance in which fairness-related norms, and in addition bounded rationality, may affect law involves one of the enduring puzzles in First Amendment law: the special judicial hostility to "prior restraints" on

126. *See* Margaret Jane Radin, *What, If Anything, Is Wrong with Baby Selling?*, 26 PAC. L.J. 135, 135 (1995).

127. *See* Alexander v. Gardner-Denver Co., 415 U.S. 36, 51-52 (1974) (dicta). The specific issue presented in *Alexander*—the enforceability of agreements to arbitrate discrimination claims—has been considered in more recent cases. *See, e.g.*, Gilmer v. Interstate/Johnson Lane Corp., 500 U.S. 20 (1991). However, no court to our knowledge has suggested that *Gilmer* or any other recent case permits people to "sell" their substantive rights not to be subject to race and sex discrimination.

speech, most notably injunctions.[128] A court may well refuse to issue an injunction against speech even if it would allow subsequent punishment of that same speech. The puzzle is that a prior restraint involves subsequent punishment too; what an injunction means is that a violator will be subject to (subsequent) sanctions. Why is a criminal statute any less problematic than an injunction whose violation produces criminal penalties?

Conventional economic analysis provides no satisfying answer to this question. True, the injunction might be thought to create the prospect of a greater total punishment for the speech, but no one has suggested that the First Amendment imposes limits on the severity of punishment for speech that the government is entitled to criminalize. In any case, many criminal statutes impose greater punishments than many injunctions, and the latter are nonetheless more troublesome than the former.

Can behavioral analysis explain the law's special treatment of prior restraints? As noted in Part I.B above, court-ordered remedies are likely to create special forms of attachment for their beneficiaries; individuals will typically be reluctant to forego rights granted by such remedies, due to the perceived unfairness of that outcome and the type of attachment created by the endowment effect. This is apt to be as true for prosecutors as for everyone else. A prosecutor who has sought an injunction may be particularly insistent on ensuring that punishment occurs. A criminal statute, standing by itself and unaccompanied by an injunction, is likely to produce a different response on the part of the prosecutor. Reasonable defendants know the difference. Hence it is especially important for a court to ensure that any injunction imposed on speech is not issued *in advance of an accurate judgment that the speech involved is unprotected by the First Amendment.*

As it happens, this account matches the most sophisticated defenses of the special barrier to prior restraints.[129] Those defenses urge that the real purpose of the prior restraint doctrine is to ensure that no regulation is imposed without a reliable judgment that the First Amendment does not protect the speech at risk. The doctrine is difficult to explain on conventional economic principles but is a natural inference from behavioral ones.

128. *See, e.g.*, GEOFFREY R. STONE, LOUIS M. SEIDMAN, CASS R. SUNSTEIN & MARK V. TUSHNET, CONSTITUTIONAL LAW 1183-96 (3d ed. 1996).

129. *See* Martin H. Redish, *The Proper Role of the Prior Restraint Doctrine in First Amendment Theory*, 70 VA. L. REV. 53, 55 (1984).

C. *Anecdote-Driven Environmental Legislation (With Particular Reference to Superfund)*

1. *Estimating the likelihood of uncertain events.*

Thus far the discussion has focused on the role of bounded self-interest (specifically, fairness-related norms) and the endowment effect in predicting and explaining the content of law. But judgment errors by boundedly rational individuals also play a significant role here. In particular, people seek law in areas such as environmental protection on the basis of their judgments about the probabilities associated with certain harmful activities. Their judgments about probabilities will often be affected by how "available" other instances of the harm in question are, that is, on how easily such instances come to mind. In this section we offer an account of the Superfund statute, perhaps the most well-known and popular environmental statute, on this ground.

Here is a familiar example of availability: Individuals asked how many seven-letter words in a 2,000-word section of a novel end in "ing" give much larger estimates than individuals asked how many words in such a section have "n" as the second-to-last letter, despite the fact that objectively there are more words which satisfy the latter criterion than the former.[130] Reliance on how "available" instances of the event in question are is a form of judgment error, but the error is fully rational—in the sense of reflecting optimizing behavior—for people with limited information. Still, it can lead to systematic errors in probability assessment. In the context of environmental legislation, it encourages the well-known "pollutant of the month" syndrome, where regulation is driven by recent and memorable instances of harm.[131] When beliefs and preferences are produced by a set of probability judgments, made inaccurate by the availability heuristic, legislation will predictably become anecdote-driven. Many illustrations come to mind; consider the outcry over Agent Orange and Times Beach,[132] or the strict regulation of asbestos in schools after a large amount of media attention.[133] The same phenomenon may occur in other areas of regulatory law; an example here is the move to-

130. Amos Tversky & Daniel Kahneman, *Extensional Versus Intuitive Reasoning: The Conjunction Fallacy in Probability Judgment*, 90 PSYCHOL. REV. 293, 295 (1983).

131. *See* Sunstein, *supra* note 3, at 1188.

132. *See, e.g.*, Keith Schneider, *Fetal Harm Is Cited As Primary Hazard In Dioxin Exposure*, N.Y. TIMES, May 11, 1994, at A1, A20.

133. *See* Asbestos Hazard Emergency Act of 1986, 15 U.S.C. §§ 2641-56 (1994); Margo L. Stoffel, Comment, *Electromagnetic Fields and Cancer: A Legitimate Cause of Action or a Result of Media-Influenced Fear*, 21 OHIO N.U. L. REV. 551, 590 (1995) (referring to an ABC news special on how media reports "heightened anxiety over . . . asbestos in schools").

ward heavy regulation of school bus safety in the wake of media coverage of school bus accidents in which children were killed.[134]

What determines how available a particular environmental hazard is? Two factors are particularly important: the observed frequency of the hazard and its salience. Thus, if a particular hazard has materialized recently, people are likely to attach a higher probability to its occurring in the future. And this is particularly true if the hazard has a high degree of salience—as, for instance, with the discovery of asbestos in schools, where many children are present. Apart from the nature of the event, salience is heavily influenced by the way the event is packaged by the media, organized interest groups, and politicians.

Interested actors in the private and public sectors can be expected to exploit the availability heuristic for their own purposes. These actors are amateur behavioralists, operating strategically to promote their selfish or nonselfish goals. "Availability entrepreneurs" will thus focus attention on a specific event in order to ensure that this event will be salient and available to many members of the public.[135] Well-organized groups in the private sector very frequently use this strategy, thus showing that they are fine behavioralists. Self-interested politicians may use similar strategies to enhance their reelection prospects. Although self-serving behavior by such actors is an element of the conventional economic account, the role of such factors as availability is not; this is what is added by behavioral analysis.

The availability heuristic can lead to under- as well as over-regulation. People sometimes (although not always) underestimate the likelihood of low-probability or low-salience events because these threats simply do not make it onto people's "radar screens";[136] many health and environmental risks (such as the health threats from poor diet and exercise) may fit this description with some parts of the population. But when a particular threat, even an unlikely one, becomes available, as when, for example, asbestos is discovered in schools, then regulation will be demanded. The behavioral account thus predicts a patchwork of environmental laws characterized by both over- and under-regulation, with over-regulation when a particular risk has recently materialized, particularly if the harm in question is highly salient.

---

134. *See* JERRY L. MASHAW & DAVID L. HARFST, THE STRUGGLE FOR AUTO SAFETY 141-46 (1990).

135. *See* Timur Kuran & Cass R. Sunstein, Availability Cascades and Risk Regulation (Apr. 26, 1998) (unpublished manuscript, on file with the *Stanford Law Review*).

136. *See* Howard Kunreuther, *The Economics of Protection Against Low Probability Events*, *in* DECISION MAKING: AN INTERDISCIPLINARY INQUIRY 195, 209 (Gerardo R. Ungson & Daniel N. Braunstein eds., 1982); Howard Kunreuther, *Limited Knowledge and Insurance Protection*, 24 PUB. POL'Y 227, 235-36, 243-44 (1976). For a discussion of *over*estimation of the likelihood of low-frequency events, see Colin F. Camerer & Howard Kunreuther, *Decision Processes for Low Probability Events: Policy Implications*, 8 J. POL. ANAL. & MGMT. 565, 566 (1989).

2. *Superfund.*

The basic point that availability may affect the demand for environmental legislation is not new.[137] We wish to add two features to the analysis: first, an understanding of the mechanisms through which the availability heuristic may operate to produce environmental legislation (and here we emphasize the notion of "availability entrepreneurs"); and second, the fact that the behavioral account predicts the enactment of Superfund, a major piece of environmental legislation that is not readily explained on conventional grounds.[138]

Conventional approaches point to the important role of interest groups in shaping environmental law; these groups can use the law to redistribute resources in their preferred directions. Some of these groups are sincerely concerned with environmental protection; others have economic interests for which environmental issues operate as a smokescreen. Explanations of this kind have had some success, but they fail to account for Superfund.

Of course it is possible (as it always is) to generate post hoc accounts that show that some groups benefited from legislation, and to suggest that such legislation was passed *because* some groups benefited from it. Superfund is no exception. But an examination of the history of the statute shows that this explanation is extremely weak. Interest groups played little part in initiating its enactment. Instead the key actor, as described more fully below, was the Environmental Protection Agency, and the key mechanism was the availability heuristic.

Superfund was passed with substantial legislative and public support; in light of its crudely drafted character and uncertain empirical support, what is remarkable is how little opposition the statute provoked. What is even more remarkable is that for the last seventeen years, Americans have consistently ranked "abandoned toxic waste dumps" among the three most important environmental problems, even though experts believe that this is one of the least pressing environmental problems, if indeed it qualifies as a serious problem at all.[139] Experts contend that in terms of risks to human health, there are at least a dozen problems that are more serious; many of them receive less in the way of public (and legislative) support.

Availability provides a convincing explanation of Superfund's existence and its endurance. Its initial development occurred when officials within the

137. *See* W. KIP VISCUSI, RATIONAL RISK POLICY 96 (1998) (discussing role of availability); Roger G. Noll & James E. Krier, *Some Implications of Cognitive Psychology for Risk Regulation*, 19 J. LEGAL STUD. 747, 762 (1990) (same); Cass R. Sunstein, *Congress, Constitutional Moments, and the Cost-Benefit State*, 48 STAN. L. REV. 247, 265-66 (1996) (same).

138. We draw here from the more detailed discussion in Kuran & Sunstein, *supra* note 135.

139. *See, e.g.*, STEPHEN BREYER, BREAKING THE VICIOUS CIRCLE: TOWARD EFFECTIVE RISK REGULATION 21 (1993).

EPA, concerned about an apparent gap in federal law and eager to consolidate their authority over issues of public health, began to draft new legislation in order to respond to the existence of abandoned hazardous waste sites. But it is doubtful that the EPA could have succeeded if not for the fact that in August of 1978, national news began to focus on what was soon seen as a "ticking time bomb" at Love Canal, New York, consisting of apparent leaks from the disposal of 21,000 tons of chemical waste into the Canal between 1943 and 1952. In the middle and late 1970s, studies of groundwater and cancer incidence appeared to show that the leaks had created serious health risks, to the point where the New York Health Commissioner declared a public emergency on August 2, 1978. Within two weeks, President Carter declared an emergency in the area. A kind of cascade effect occurred, and hence in the period between August and October, 1978, the national news was saturated with stories of the risks to citizens near Love Canal.

The publicity continued in 1979 and 1980, the crucial years for Superfund's enactment. There can be no doubt that the Love Canal publicity was pivotal to the law's passage in 1980. In that year, Time magazine made the topic a cover story, and network documentaries followed suit. Polls showed that eighty percent of Americans favored prompt federal action to identify and clean up potentially hazardous abandoned waste sites. Congress responded quickly with the new statute. And to this date, American presidents and serious presidential candidates of both parties invoke abandoned hazardous waste dumps as a leading environmental problem. By the way, it remains unproven that Love Canal created significant health risks at any stage.

The behavioral account of Superfund is that the availability of "Love Canal" as a symbol for the problem of abandoned hazardous waste dumps greatly intensified public concern, to the point where a legislative response became nearly inevitable, no matter what the actual facts might be.[140] And there can be no doubt that proponents of Superfund self-consciously exploited the Love Canal incident. During crucial periods in the legislative debate, the prime proponent of the new legislation—the EPA—warned, very publicly, that hundreds of "Love Canals" could be found throughout the country. The EPA thus became an "availability entrepreneur," focusing attention on a specific event in order to ensure that this event would be highly available to many members of the public.

We do not say that conventional interest-group considerations played no role in the specific shape the Superfund statute took. The ultimate design of the statute surely owed a great deal to what relevant interest groups were willing to tolerate; though powerful private groups did not seek the legisla-

140. *Cf.* W. Kip Viscusi, *Alarmist Decisions with Divergent Risk Information*, 107 ECON. J. 1657 (1997) (finding that in the presence of divergent information about risks, people place inordinate weight on high risk assessments).

tion, they did influence its content and structure. But the enactment and continued popularity of Superfund are not predicted by the conventional account alone. The behavioral account, in contrast, suggests that the occurrence of an event such as Love Canal, particularly when played up and dramatized by the media and other actors, will produce a legislative response. Superfund is one example; regulatory responses to Agent Orange and asbestos in schools are others. Available instances of risk or threat seem to shape the content of law.

IV. PRESCRIPTIONS

In this part we shift our focus from the positive to the prescriptive. Instead of seeking to explain what the effects of law will be and why we have the laws we do, we now explore how the law can best be structured to achieve specified ends—deterring socially undesirable behavior through the tort system, encouraging measures that enhance human health, and so on. Our claim in each context we consider is that attention to behavioral insights can improve the law's ability to move society toward desired outcomes. Our primary emphasis is on problems in processing information, problems that create difficulties both for juries during trials and for those responding to information required by government or coming from government itself. Thus bounded rationality, in the form of both judgment errors and behavior in accordance with prospect theory rather than expected utility theory, are the central emphases in this part. Section A deals with juries, while section B deals with government information campaigns and mandatory disclosure. Section C emphasizes our second bound on human behavior, bounded willpower, and discusses its relevance to prescriptions directed toward deterring crime.

This part discusses only a small sample of the many areas in which sound prescriptive analysis may require us to consider possible bounds on jurors' or other actors' decisionmaking. Other authors have applied these insights to other topics in the economic analysis of law. Thus, for example, Daniel Kahneman and David Schkade, along with one of the present authors (Sunstein), have challenged the economic prescription for punitive damage awards recently offered by A. Mitchell Polinsky and Steven Shavell: that juries should be instructed to focus on the probability of nondetection of the tortfeasor's activities in order to achieve optimal deterrence through punitive awards.[141] From the behavioral point of view, this prescription fails to appreciate the cognitive and motivational limitations on jury decisionmaking. Because of the hindsight bias and overoptimism problems described below, juries will have difficulty making probability estimates, and in addition they

141. *See* Polinsky & Shavell, *supra* note 70, at 887-91.

appear to come to the task of awarding punitive damages with strong retributive instincts.[142] The goal of optimal deterrence may be best achieved through administrative agencies rather than juries.[143]

Another example of the application of behavioral economics to prescriptive analysis is Thomas Jackson's discussion of discharge policy in bankruptcy law. Although standard economic ideas of risk allocation would often support nondischargeability of debts, Jackson draws on aspects of what we have termed bounded rationality and bounded willpower to support the "fresh start" policy of discharge and to sketch the specific contours it should take.[144] Our goal in this part is to point to some additional topics in the economic analysis of law in which a more accurate understanding of decisionmaking can improve upon conventional law and economics prescriptions.

A. *Negligence Determinations and Other Determinations of Fact or Law*

1. *Background.*

Frequently juries are called upon to determine the probability of an event that ended up occurring; a prominent example is the negligence standard, which (in the formulation favored by the economic analysis of law) requires jurors to assess the costs and benefits of the defendant's course of action from an ex ante perspective, and thus to determine the probability that harm would end up coming of that action. These determinations are made with the "benefit" of hindsight; jurors know at the time they make their decision that the event in question did in fact occur. Jurors' determinations are thus likely to be afflicted by "hindsight bias"—the tendency of decisionmakers to attach an excessively high probability to an event simply because it ended up occurring.[145]

Hindsight bias has been observed in a large number of studies, including studies of "expert" actors such as physicians, who, when asked to assess the probabilities of alternative diagnoses, given a set of symptoms, offer significantly different estimates depending on what they are told the actual diagnosis turned out to be.[146] Hindsight bias also appears to occur in the specific

142. Cass R. Sunstein, Daniel Kahneman & David Schkade, *Assessing Punitive Damages (with Notes on Cognition and Valuation in Law)*, 107 YALE L.J. 2071, 2111-12 (1998).

143. *Id.* at 2122-25.

144. Thomas H. Jackson, *The Fresh-Start Policy in Bankruptcy Law*, 98 HARV. L. REV. 1393, 1394-95, 1399-1401 (1985).

145. *See* Baruch Fischhoff, *Hindsight ≠ Foresight: The Effect of Outcome Knowledge on Judgment Under Uncertainty*, 1 J. EXPERIMENTAL PSYCHOL. HUM. PERCEPTION & PERFORMANCE 288 (1975).

146. Hal R. Arkes, David Faust, Thomas J. Guilmette & Kathleen Hart, *Eliminating the Hindsight Bias*, 73 J. APPLIED PSYCHOL. 305, 306 tbl.1 (1988).

context of negligence determinations.[147] In the negligence studies, subjects in the role of jurors—armed with knowledge that harm had in fact occurred—were found to attach significantly higher probabilities to harm than subjects in the role of ex ante decisionmakers—those not informed of the occurrence of harm.[148] This is a straightforward prediction of the many prior studies on hindsight bias.[149] Although the negligence studies asked for individual rather than group probabilities (raising the question whether group interaction on an actual jury could dispel hindsight bias), other studies have found hindsight bias in group as well as individual settings.[150]

Hindsight bias will lead juries making negligence determinations to find defendants liable more frequently than if cost-benefit analysis were done correctly—that is, on an ex ante basis. Thus, plaintiffs will win cases they deserve to lose. This prediction is consistent with the frequently expressed (though difficult to verify) view that the tort system imposes too much liability.[151]

A threshold issue raised by the hindsight-bias account of negligence determinations is whether hindsight bias is simply a countervailing weight to a tendency on the part of defendants to underestimate the likelihood of being sanctioned. A common feature of human behavior is overoptimism: People tend to think that bad events are far less likely to happen to them than to others. Thus, most people think that their probability of a bad outcome is far less than others' probability, although of course this cannot be true for more than half the population.[152] If defendants exhibit such overoptimism, then they will be underdeterred by a correct application of the negligence stan-

147. *See* Kim A. Kamin & Jeffrey J. Rachlinski, *Ex Post ≠ Ex Ante*, 19 LAW & HUM. BEHAV. 89 (1995); Susan J. LaBine & Gary LaBine, *Determinations of Negligence and the Hindsight Bias*, 20 LAW & HUM. BEHAV. 501 (1996).

148. Kamin & Rachlinski, *supra* note 147, at 98; LaBine & LaBine, *supra* note 147, at 509-10.

149. *See, e.g.*, Arkes et al., *supra* note 146.

150. *See* Dagmar Stahlberg, Frank Eller, Anne Maass & Dieter Frey, *We Knew It All Along: Hindsight Bias in Groups*, 63 ORG. BEHAV. & HUM. DECISION PROCESSES 46 (1995); Ed Bukszar & Terry Connolly, *Hindsight Bias and Strategic Choice: Some Problems in Learning from Experience*, 31 ACAD. MGMT. J. 628 (1988).

151. *See, e.g.*, JEFFREY O'CONNELL, ENDING INSULT TO INJURY: NO-FAULT INSURANCE FOR PRODUCTS AND SERVICES 42-43 (1975); John G. Fleming, *Drug Injury Compensation Plans*, 30 AM. J. COMP. L. 297, 311 (1982); Stephen D. Sugarman, *Doing Away with Tort Law*, 73 CAL. L. REV. 555, 581-82 (1985).

152. *See* Neil D. Weinstein, *Unrealistic Optimism About Future Life Events*, 39 J. PERSONALITY & SOC. PSYCHOL. 806 (1980); Neil D. Weinstein, *Unrealistic Optimism About Susceptibility to Health Problems: Conclusions from a Community-Wide Sample*, 10 J. BEHAV. MED. 481 (1987) [hereinafter Weinstein, *Unrealistic Optimism*]. For discussion of the distinction between being below the average person's probability of a negative event and being below the average probability of that event (which could in fact be true for the majority of people), see Christine Jolls, *Behavioral Economic Analysis of Redistributive Legal Rules*, 51 VAND. L. REV. (forthcoming 1998).

dard; overestimation of the probability of harm based on hindsight bias might then be a desirable countervailing factor. We think that defendant overoptimism is likely to be a much smaller factor for firms than for individual defendants, since firms that make systematic errors in judgment will be at a competitive disadvantage. And for individuals, the role of overoptimism is likely to vary significantly with context. In a case in which the threat of being found liable is highly salient, individuals may tend to *overestimate* the likelihood of being sanctioned, for reasons discussed in connection with our account of Superfund above. Hindsight bias, in contrast, seems to be an across-the-board phenomenon; it has been observed in a wide range of contexts across many studies and is likely to be present whenever a jury makes a negligence determination.

It is also possible that the occurrence of harm itself provides genuine information about the probability of harm; this fact has led some to consider the possibility of an "ex post negligence" standard, under which negligence is assessed based on the information available ex post, rather than ex ante.[153] (However, if prospective defendants cannot easily ascertain (ex ante) the information that will be available ex post, then an ex post approach may be inefficient.[154]) But, even apart from situations in which the fact of harm provides new information about the probability of harm, hindsight bias suggests that decisionmakers will weigh the fact of harm heavily in assessing its probability.[155]

The findings on hindsight bias provide new empirical support for the old idea that such bias may distort negligence determinations. Despite the vast law and economics literature in the area of torts, no attention seems to have been paid to the potentially significant implications of hindsight bias for achieving optimal deterrence—the goal posited by that literature, and the goal on which we focus here. (Thus, we accept this goal for purposes of our prescriptive analysis; we do not necessarily endorse this goal from a normative perspective.) Law and economics scholars generally approve of the use of the negligence standard for achieving the goal of optimal deterrence; the negligence standard, if applied in an error-free fashion, leads to an efficient level of precaution (although other standards will as well; note that these other standards may be worse or better along other dimensions, such as encouraging victim precautions and inducing optimal activity levels).[156] These

153. Guido Calabresi & Alvin K. Klevorik, *Four Tests for Liability in Torts*, 14 J. LEGAL STUD. 585, 590 (1985).

154. *See* Omri Ben-Shahar, *Informed Courts, Uninformed Individuals and the Economics of Judicial Hindsight*, 151 J. INSTITUTIONAL & THEORETICAL ECON. 613 (1995).

155. For an example of a situation in which the fact of harm does not provide new information about its probability, see Calabresi & Klevorik, *supra* note 153, at 594-96.

156. *See* STEVEN SHAVELL, ECONOMIC ANALYSIS OF ACCIDENT LAW 8, 11, 14, 23-24 (1987) (analyzing rules of negligence and strict liability).

scholars have also analyzed reasons that legal rules, including the negligence standard, may be imperfectly applied, but they do not offer any clear prescriptions for addressing this problem, since as they see it, the problem does not have a clear direction; either underdeterrence or overdeterrence relative to correct application of the cost-benefit standard is possible.[157] In contrast, we can offer clear prescriptions because the hindsight bias points in only one direction: overdeterrence (again relative to what correct cost-benefit analysis would produce).

In fact the law in areas such as patent law already takes clear steps to address the problems caused by hindsight bias. Thus, as Jeffrey Rachlinski has recently pointed out, patent courts are required to guard against hindsight bias in determining whether an invention was "nonobvious" at the time of invention—despite its now (perhaps) seeming obvious—by looking to such "secondary considerations" as "commercial success, long felt but unsolved need, [and] failure of others";[158] this is in effect a limited form of debiasing of the decisionmaker. (Thus, the law seems to acknowledge that *judges*, like juries, may exhibit hindsight bias—although there is evidence that the bias is less for judges than juries.[159]) But in the area of tort law the existing responses are partial and incomplete at best.[160] Hindsight bias seems to be so deeply ingrained in the tort system that even when it is called to a court's attention, it may be difficult for the court (never mind a juror) to recognize or address it. A colorful example is provided by litigation in which one of the present authors (Thaler) was an expert witness. The litigation involved whether investment decisions involving $100 million in assets had been made in a negligent fashion. Although the court explicitly recognized that "[c]ase law . . . ties [this determination] to the circumstances extant at the time in question, rather than as they may appear in hindsight," the court characterized as "very imaginative" defendant's offer of testimony that "a decision based on information known at the time the decision was made can be evaluated as good or bad without regard to the outcome. In that way the evaluation is not biased by hindsight."[161] Although the judge was very active throughout the trial, he never suggested that the expert testimony offered by the plaintiff, which focused almost exclusively on the fact that the portfolio had lost money (rather than on the reasonableness of the investment decisions at the time they were made), was off-target or irrelevant. While the

157. *See, e.g.*, Jason S. Johnston, *Bayesian Fact-Finding and Efficiency: Toward an Economic Theory of Liability Under Uncertainty*, 61 S. CAL. L. REV. 137, 154-64 (1987).

158. Jeffrey J. Rachlinski, *A Positive Psychological Theory of Judging in Hindsight*, 65 U. CHI. L. REV. 571, 615 (1998) (quoting *Graham v. John Deere Co.*, 383 U.S. 1, 17-18 (1966)).

159. *See* Reid Hastie & W. Kip Viscusi, What Juries Can't Do Well: The Jury's Performance as a Risk Manager (May 21, 1998) (unpublished manuscript, on file with the *Stanford Law Review*).

160. Rachlinski describes several existing responses. *See* Rachlinski, *supra* note 158, at 615-18.

161. Johnson v. Johnson, 515 A.2d 255, 266-67 & n.17 (N.J. Super. 1986).

court ultimately accepted the "imaginative" argument of the defendant and ruled in his favor, its evident surprise at the nature of the argument suggests the pervasiveness of hindsight-based thinking in the tort system.

How might the law respond to hindsight bias in tort cases? An obvious response is the use of jury instructions that inform jurors of the bias and tell them to focus on the ex ante situation. Unfortunately, such debiasing techniques appear either to have no effect on decisions or to reduce hindsight bias by only a limited degree, leaving a significant gap between ex post and ex ante decisionmaking.[162] The findings on the limited effect of debiasing techniques suggest that attempts by lawyers to employ such techniques may also be of limited effectiveness, although there is room here for future research on the role of lawyers. Because of the apparent limits on debiasing, we propose two alternative prescriptions—one simple and clear-cut, but limited to certain sorts of cases, and the other general and giving rise to important avenues for future research.

2. *Prescriptions.*

First prescription: Manipulate the information given to jurors. One means of responding to the problem of hindsight bias in tort cases involves manipulating the set of information given to jurors. Suppose that a food-processing company is claimed to have decided in a negligent fashion to use a particular chemical in its production process; imagine that the chemical ended up causing cancer in a small number of residents who live near the company's plant. The company claims that *not* using the cancer-causing (as it turned out) chemical would have carried significant risks to residents in terms of bacterial contamination. We know that if jurors are told that the chemical was used and ended up causing cancer, they will be likely to overestimate the probability of harm from the chemical and, thus, hold the food-processing company liable even if liability is not in fact justified under an unbiased application of the cost-benefit standard. (Indeed, in this context the effects of hindsight bias may be exacerbated by the fact that the choice made by the defendant is an act of commission, rather than (as would have been the case had the chemical not been used) an act of omission.[163])

Imagine, however, that jurors are not told that the company decided to use the chemical; rather they are told only about the ex ante decision facing

162. *See, e.g.*, Martin F. Davies, *Reduction of Hindsight Bias by Restoration of Foresight Perspective: Effectiveness of Foresight-Encoding and Hindsight-Retrieval Strategies*, 40 ORG. BEHAV. & HUM. DECISION PROCESSES 40, 61-64 (1987); Baruch Fischhoff, *Perceived Informativeness of Facts*, 3 J. EXPERIMENTAL PSYCHOL. 349, 354-56 (1977); Kamin & Rachlinski, *supra* note 147, at 96-98.

163. *See* Ilana Ritov & Jonathan Baron, *Reluctance to Vaccinate: Omission Bias and Ambiguity*, 3 J. BEHAV. DECISION MAKING 263 (1990).

the company (whether to use the chemical). They learn about the benefits and costs of that strategy and must determine whether either pursuing it or failing to pursue it would have been negligent. In this scenario the jurors would be transformed into ex ante decisionmakers: They wouldn't know whether the "accident" that occurred (prompting the lawsuit) was harm from bacterial contamination or harm from the chemical. Because they would not know what harm ended up materializing, they would not be led by hindsight bias to overestimate the probability of that harm. Their probability estimates for each type of harm—and their resulting assessment of whether either decision by the company would have been negligent—would be untouched by hindsight bias. In this way it might be possible to eliminate the effect of hindsight bias on negligence determinations. (If the decision that the defendant actually made was one that the jury determined to be negligent, outcome information could be introduced for purposes of computing damages.)

It is important to note the structure of this example: The defendant faced a choice of options, *each of which* could have caused harm. In this sort of case, jurors assessing the defendant's conduct would not know (if they were not told) whether the harm that prompted the suit was caused by choice of the first option or choice of the second. It is also important to note that various procedural steps would have to be taken to protect the secrecy of the defendant's choice if outcome information were to be kept from the jury; lawyers' affiliations, for example, could not be revealed, and witnesses could not be identified as defense-side or plaintiff-side. (One might worry that the food-processing company's employees would testify in a way that revealed what choice the company made. But it would not be in the company's interests to have its employees testify in such a one-sided fashion, since then jurors would suspect which choice was made and would tend to engage in hindsight-biased decisionmaking to the defendant's detriment.)

In some cases, it might not be possible to keep the defendant's choice from the jury; the fact of the suit will make clear what that choice was. For example, in the well-known case of *Petition of Kinsman Transit Co.*,[164] in which a bridge operator failed to lift the bridge in time to prevent an accident, apparently because he was at a tavern, the fact of a suit may provide strong indication that the bridge was not lifted. In this sort of setting, a possible prescription (offered previously in the literature) involves bifurcation of trials, so that jurors deciding on liability do not learn any of the details of what happened until an initial determination of liability is made.[165] Although

164. 338 F.2d 708 (2d Cir. 1964).

165. Hal R. Arkes & Cindy A. Schipani, *Medical Malpractice v. the Business Judgment Rule: Differences in Hindsight Bias*, 73 OR. L. REV. 587, 633-36 (1994); Norman G. Poythress, Richard Wiener & Joseph E. Schumacher, *Reframing the Medical Malpractice Tort Reform Debate: Social Science Research Implications for Non-Economic Reforms*, 16 LAW & PSYCHOL. REV. 65, 105-11 (1992); David B. Wexler & Robert F. Schopp, *How and When to Correct for Juror Hindsight Bias*

we think this is a sensible prescription in such settings, we note that it will not eliminate the effects of hindsight bias, since (as proponents of bifurcated trials recognize) "the jury will undoubtedly *know* that they are not being asked simply to engage in an academic exercise,"[166] and that (because a trial is being held) "a bad outcome must have occurred."[167] In contrast, in cases in which jurors need not know (because they cannot infer from the fact of a lawsuit) what choice the defendant made, it may be possible to eliminate the hindsight bias completely. And there are many such situations: cases in which either of two options facing a physician could have caused harm or death to a patient; cases in which either the use or the failure to use a new technology could have led to harm; cases in which either revealing or failing to reveal suicide threats by a psychiatric patient could have resulted in suicide.

A further feature of our prescription here is that even if we are wrong about the effects of hindsight bias, the prescription seems unlikely to do significant harm (from the perspective of the specified goal of achieving correct application of the ex ante cost-benefit standard). If hindsight bias is unimportant, then whether jurors are told what outcome occurred should not matter; either way, they should be able to make a correct ex ante determination. Thus, the prescription should either have no effect on decisionmaking (if hindsight bias is not a problem) or represent an improvement over the current system (if hindsight bias is a problem).

Second prescription: Alter the evidentiary standard. The result of hindsight bias, as described above, is that jurors will overestimate the probability that harm will occur (since harm did, in fact, occur). The determination of the probability of harm would conventionally be made under a "preponderance of the evidence" standard: If jurors think it more likely than not, based on the evidence, that the probability of harm was above the threshold level required for liability, they are to find the defendant liable. One might imagine counteracting the effects of hindsight bias by raising the evidentiary standard (as an alternative, not in addition, to the previous proposal; the two together would produce overcorrection and, thus, underdeterrence). Thus, for example, if the jurors were to find the defendant liable only if the evidence suggested at least a seventy-five percent likelihood—rather than merely a fifty-one percent likelihood—that the critical harm probability threshold was met, then they might well reach the correct conclusion about liability: They would overestimate the likelihood attached to the critical threshold, but the overestimate might well be below the new required level.

---

in Mental Health Malpractice Litigation: Some Preliminary Observations, 7 BEHAV. SCI. & L. 485, 496 (1989).

166. Wexler & Schopp, *supra* note 165, at 494 (emphasis in original).

167. Arkes & Schipani, *supra* note 165, at 635.

The highest evidentiary threshold known to our legal system—the "beyond a reasonable doubt" standard—is used only in criminal cases. However, in civil cases an intermediate standard (higher than the preponderance standard, but less demanding than the "beyond a reasonable doubt" standard) is the "clear and convincing evidence" standard. This standard has been adopted by many states for punitive-damage determinations,[168] and a broadening of its use to all negligence determinations—or at least those in which hindsight bias seems most likely to present a significant problem—might provide a desirable counterweight to the tendency of jurors to overestimate the probability that harm will occur. (Of course, further study would be required before reaching a final conclusion here.) This, of course, would be likely to be a second-best solution; in some situations defendants might be found not liable when, under a perfectly functioning system with no hindsight bias and no heightened evidentiary standard, they would be found liable.[169] This need not be the case, however, and even if it is, we might well tolerate a crude measure that produced some errors so long as it represented an improvement over the current system. Most importantly, there is much room for research focused on determining whether altering the evidentiary threshold would represent a desirable response on balance—either across the board or in particular categories of cases. Our goal is to suggest the value of research on this issue, rather than to urge an immediate change in policy based on what we now know.

To fix ideas for purposes of exploring these points, imagine first that hindsight bias produces a similar increase across cases in a juror's perceived likelihood that the negligence threshold is met. (So, for example, suppose that jurors generally overestimate by fifty percent the likelihood that the negligence threshold is met, based on the evidence presented.) In this circumstance, the overestimation of the likelihood that the negligence threshold is met could in theory be precisely offset by a change in the evidentiary threshold. To see this point, imagine that the likelihood that the negligence threshold has been met is graphed as a function of the strength of the evidence. In the absence of hindsight bias, the function will cross the fifty-percent (preponderance) cut-off at a given level of evidentiary strength, and all cases in which the evidence is stronger than that should produce findings of liability. But with hindsight bias, jurors will overestimate the likelihood that the negligence threshold has been met, and this will produce an upward shift in the function we are imagining; as a result, too many cases will cross the preponderance line. But if that line itself is shifted up by an appropriate amount, the hindsight-influenced function will cross it at precisely the same level of evidentiary strength as the one at which the original function crossed

168. *See Developments in the Law—The Civil Jury*, 110 HARV. L. REV. 1408, 1531 (1997).
169. *See* Rachlinski, *supra* note 158, at 606-07.

the preponderance standard. For instance, if the likelihood that the negligence threshold has been met is a linear function of the strength of the evidence, half of all cases in the system meet the threshold under the preponderance standard, and jurors overestimate by fifty percent the likelihood that the threshold is met, then a move to a seventy-five-percent likelihood requirement would result in the jurors' finding negligence in precisely the half of cases in which it should be found.

If hindsight bias produces different degrees of distortion in jurors' probability estimates across different types of cases, then a shift to a higher evidentiary standard might result in underdeterrence of some defendants (specifically those whose actions will not be judged in a particularly hindsight-biased way). But as long as the increase in the evidentiary standard is modest relative to what hindsight bias in the *average* case warrants, the change would produce fewer "underdeterrence errors" (findings of no liability for defendants who should be found liable) than corrections of "overdeterrence errors" (findings of liability for defendants who should not be found liable). And the change from a move to the "clear and convincing evidence" standard would be a relatively modest one; a survey of federal district court judges found that in the judges' view that standard requires a likelihood of sixty to seventy percent, compared to the fifty-one percent threshold under the preponderance standard.[170] (Of course, more interesting would be data on how *jurors* view the two standards.)

One response to this analysis is that the reason jurors tend to find defendants liable even when liability is not legally warranted is *not* that jurors overestimate the probability of harm, but simply that they want to compensate tort victims. Our first prescription addresses the latter issue as well as the former, for if jurors do not know what harm occurred, it is difficult for them to engage in compensation-based decisionmaking. (In the case of the food-processing company discussed above, the jurors, to ensure compensation for the harm that occurred, would have to say that the company was negligent whether it used the chemical or refrained from using it—probably not a likely scenario.) But as far as the second prescription is concerned, the problem of compensation-based decisionmaking remains. So if this is what is going on, jurors may continue to find defendants liable, regardless of a higher evidentiary threshold. But there is no reason to think the existence of a higher threshold will make things worse in this situation, and so as long as there are some cases in which jurors try faithfully to apply the negligence standard, moving to the higher evidentiary threshold may improve decisionmaking. The same response may be offered to the objection that jurors' behavior is not sensitive to the evidentiary threshold—a point on which there is

170. United States v. Fatico, 458 F. Supp. 388, 410 (E.D.N.Y. 1978).

conflicting evidence;[171] as long as an increase in the threshold will matter in some cases, the change may be desirable, since there is no reason to think it will cause harm in cases in which it does not change jurors' behavior.

A final objection might be that altering the evidentiary standard would not (it is claimed) survive the Kantian-Rawlsian publicity condition, which means, roughly, that principles of justice must be defensible publicly, and that their basis and content must not be secret.[172] The question is whether it is coherent to tell jurors that: Although this case should be decided by the preponderance of the evidence, we know that you are likely to think irrationally, so therefore we raise the threshold to clear and convincing evidence. We do not believe that there is anything incoherent, or violative of the publicity condition, in an idea of this sort. In both private and public life, people, acting individually or in groups, take steps to ensure against their own tendencies to make mistakes. (We discussed in Part I.A the steps that people frequently take to deal with problems of bounded willpower.) Raising the standard of proof to prevent errors is consistent with much of the law of evidence, which is also designed to respond to cognitive errors. As just one example, consider the restrictions on admission of evidence of prior crimes.[173] A public defense of such steps is perfectly intelligible.

3. *Other applications.*

The discussion to this point has focused on tort cases decided under the negligence standard, but similar issues may arise in other areas of law in which juries (or judges) must determine whether an ex ante standard was met while armed with the knowledge that a negative event in fact materialized. One example is securities fraud litigation, whose perceived excesses prompted Congress to enact the Private Securities Litigation Reform Act of 1995.[174] In a typical securities fraud case, decisionmakers are confronted with a company whose stock price experienced a dramatic fall, and they are required to assess whether a particular issue or problem facing the company, whose disclosure prompted the fall, should have been disclosed at an earlier stage (typically before it had become an issue or problem). Decisionmakers in such a case are required to make an after-the-fact determination of whether a reasonable ex ante decisionmaker would have thought the prospective issue or problem "material" to the average shareholder based on the

171. *Compare* Dorothy K. Kagahiro & W. Clark Stanton, *Legal vs. Quantified Definitions of Standards of Proof*, 9 LAW & HUM. BEHAV. 159, 162-65 (1985) (finding no effect of different evidentiary thresholds), *with* SANFORD H. KADISH & STEPHEN J. SCHULHOFER, CRIMINAL LAW AND ITS PROCESSES 40 (6th ed. 1995) (citing studies that find such an effect).

172. JOHN RAWLS, A THEORY OF JUSTICE 133 (1971). This issue was raised by Jon Elster in comments on an earlier draft of this article.

173. FED. R. EVID. 404(b).

174. Pub. L. No. 104-67, 109 Stat. 737 (1995) (codified in scattered sections of 15 U.S.C.).

information available at the time.[175] The problem is that this determination must be made against the backdrop of knowledge that the issue or problem in fact materialized, and produced a large drop in the company's stock price. In this situation, a decisionmaker will likely find it difficult to see how a reasonable ex ante decisionmaker might have thought the prospective issue or problem other than material. Consistent with this analysis, the main predictor of whether a securities fraud action is brought seems to be whether there has been a large change in the company's stock market value, not whether the company's behavior was reasonable from an ex ante perspective.[176]

Another example here involves damage suits for violations of the Fourth Amendment. A risk in such suits is that if the allegedly illegal search did in fact produce damaging evidence (say, drugs or other contraband), then decisionmakers are likely to conclude that the law enforcement agency's behavior was reasonable. This will be true even if, from an ex ante perspective (without knowing the eventual outcome), this behavior would not have been found reasonable.

B. *Information Disclosure and Government Advertising*

1. *Background.*

Suppose it is agreed that individuals lack adequate information on a given subject—for example, workplace safety, appliance energy efficiency, or the effects of drug use. In some such instances the government may seek to foster comparison shopping and informed decisionmaking (as in the federal truth-in-lending law, which requires lenders to announce interest rates, measured the same way[177]); in other instances the government may have a specific policy goal (reducing drug use, encouraging the use of energy-efficient refrigerators). Conventional economics acknowledges the possible desirability of each of these goals (the second in the case of phenomena such as externalities), and it often advocates, as a means of achieving them, providing additional information to citizens, either through a mandate to the relevant private actors (for instance, employers), or through provision of information by the government itself.[178]

The prescription to "provide more information" is striking in its spareness. Behavioral analysis suggests that this prescription is far *too* spare.

175. *See* ROBERT CHARLES CLARK, CORPORATE LAW § 8.10.4 (1986).

176. *See* Janet Cooper Alexander, *Do the Merits Matter? A Study of Settlements in Securities Class Actions*, 43 STAN. L. REV. 497, 511-13 (1991); James Bohn & Stephen Choi, *Fraud in the New-Issues Market: Empirical Evidence on Securities Class Actions*, 144 U. PA. L. REV. 903, 935-40, 979-80 (1996).

177. *See* Edward L. Rubin, *Legislative Methodology: Some Lessons from the Truth-in-Lending Act*, 80 GEO. L.J. 223, 235-36 (1991).

178. *See, e.g.*, JOSEPH E. STIGLITZ, ECONOMICS OF THE PUBLIC SECTOR 90-91 (1986).

"Provide more information" says nothing about the *way* in which the information will be provided, and yet we know from much of what has been said already, as well as from empirical work by scholars such as W. Kip Viscusi, that this will matter a great deal.[179] Thus, for example, we know that people's perceptions of the probability of uncertain events is influenced by the salience of the presentation of these events.

That presentation matters has several implications. One is "antiprescriptive": Prescriptions directed toward fostering comparison shopping—the first government goal mentioned above—will often be incomplete and may even be paralyzing, since there is often no "neutral" way to present information. The second implication is that effective prescriptive strategies for achieving the second goal mentioned above—discouraging particular types of behavior—must take behavioral factors into account. It is not enough simply to "provide information." We discuss several examples of this below.

2. *Antiprescription.*

Consider the following example of a government attempt to foster informed decisionmaking: In the case of defined contribution plans such as 401(k)s, the Labor Department, the relevant government authority, has ruled that employers must give employees investment alternatives, and must provide information about those alternatives (such as risk and returns); but firms are not allowed to offer "advice" as to how to invest.[180] We think that such spare guidelines place employers in a very difficult position. The reason is that the way firms decide to describe and display information on investment alternatives will have a powerful impact on the choices employees make.

Consider in this connection a recent study of the division of retirement savings by university staff employees between two different funds, a safe one (bonds) and a risky one (stocks).[181] All the employees were shown actual historical data on the returns of the two funds, but this information was displayed in two different ways; one group was given the distribution of one-year rates of return, while the other was given a simulated distribution of thirty-year rates of return. Those shown the thirty-year returns elected to invest nearly all their savings in stocks, while those shown the one-year returns invested a majority of their funds in bonds. Our point is not that one of

179. *See, e.g.*, W. Kip Viscusi, *Individual Rationality, Hazard Warnings, and the Foundations of Tort Law*, 48 RUTGERS L. REV. 625, 630-36 (1996); W. Kip Viscusi, Wesley A. Magat & Joel Huber, *An Investigation of the Rationality of Consumer Valuations of Multiple Health Risks*, 18 RAND J. ECON. 465, 477-78 (1987).

180. *See* Christine Williamson, *Defined Contribution; DOL Moves Help Sponsors; But New Proposals Raise Concerns at P&I Conference*, PENSIONS & INVESTMENTS, Feb. 5, 1996, at 27.

181. Shlomo Benartzi & Richard H. Thaler, Risk Aversion or Myopia? Choices in Repeated Gambles and Retirement Investments (Nov. 8, 1997) (unpublished manuscript, on file with the *Stanford Law Review*).

these outcomes is better. Our point is simply that in the real world, she who provides information ends up giving advice.

This is an example in which the prescription to "provide more information" may be paralyzing; in other instances it may simply be incomplete. Thus, suppose that the prescription is that certain private actors be required to provide "information"; what does this mean? If it means that those who expose people to a dangerous substance or product in the workplace (say benzene) must provide them with accurate information about the danger, this leaves open a tremendous range of possibilities. The actors subject to the mandate will often have an interest in providing the least scary, most pallid version of the information possible (for example, "benzene has been associated with a statistical increase in risk"), while regulators might want the most scary, salient message available (say, "exposure to benzene will increase your risk of getting CANCER and other FATAL diseases"). Of course, the best message in this case, if the goal is accurate knowledge, may well be somewhere in between. An important goal of the analyst's task in making prescriptions in this area is to say *how* the information should be provided — not just *that* it should be provided.

In still other contexts, such as ones in which the presentation of information will affect people's preferences rather than just their perceptions of risk, it is not even clear in theory what is meant by ensuring "informed decisionmaking." It is not even clear that there are steady or stable background preferences that might be "informed." The preferences can themselves be an artifact of the method of informing. For instance, one of the central features of Kahneman and Tversky's prospect theory is that people evaluate outcomes based on the change they represent from an initial reference point, rather than based on the nature of the outcome itself; also, losses from the initial reference point are weighted much more heavily than gains.[182] This aspect of prospect theory (like its other features) is based on evidence about actual choice behavior.[183] The evaluation of outcomes in terms of gains and

182. *See* Kahneman & Tversky, *supra* note 12, at 277-79.

183. *See id.* at 273 (outcomes are viewed differently depending on whether they come in the form of gains or losses from a perceived status quo); *id.* at 279 (citing Eugene Galanter & Patricia Pliner, *Cross-Modality Matching of Money Against Other Continua*, *in* SENSATION AND MEASUREMENT 65 (Howard R. Moskowitz, Bertram Scharf & Joseph C. Stevens eds., 1974)) (losses are weighted more heavily than gains). Another feature of how outcomes are viewed, both empirically and under prospect theory, is that a given change produces less reaction the further a decisionmaker is from her reference point. Thus, for example, the value difference between $10 and $20 is greater than the value difference between $1000 and $1010, both for gains and for losses, assuming a reference point of $0. *See id.* at 278. In terms of the shape of the "value function" for decisionmakers (a function giving the value of each outcome–this is prospect theory's counterpart to the utility function), this suggests a function that is concave for gains and convex for losses; only with that shape are both gains and losses viewed as less significant the further the decisionmaker is from her reference point. *See id.* This shape of the value function is further supported by evidence of attitudes toward risk: People appear generally (though there are exceptions) to exhibit risk-

losses from an initial reference point, coupled with the special aversion to losses, means that it matters a great deal whether something is presented as a gain or a loss relative to the status quo; a perceived threat of a loss relative to the status quo weighs more heavily than a perceived threat of foregoing a gain. In such cases it is difficult to say which individual is "informed"—the one who is told of the perceived threat of a loss or the one who is told of the perceived threat of foregoing a gain. In this and other contexts, preferences are not preexisting but rather "constructive, context-dependent," analogous to the balls or strikes that do not predate the situation of choice and that "ain't nothing till" the umpire calls them.[184]

3. *Prescriptions.*

Suppose now that the agreed-upon goal is not to foster "informed decisionmaking," but to discourage particular types of behavior. Conventional economics would view this as a desirable goal at least to the extent that fully-informed consumers would not engage in the behavior in question, and to an even greater extent if the behavior in question produces externality effects. And to achieve this goal, conventional economics would again prescribe, as one possible means, "more information." (Other, probably more usual, means include taxation and regulation designed to discourage the unwanted behavior.) Quite obviously, though, some ways of providing information are more effective than others. There is nothing surprising about this statement. Presumably, when firms pay millions of dollars to advertising agencies to create splashy new ad campaigns, they think they are getting something for their money. Likewise, there is of course an enormous marketing literature about how best to shape people's behavior in desired directions. These points apply equally to the government. Below we develop briefly some specific prescriptions for achieving goals that involve changing people's behavior.

First prescription: Exploit loss aversion. As just noted, individuals tend to weight losses far more heavily than gains. As a result, framing consequences in terms of losses rather than gains is likely to be far more effective in changing behavior.[185] A well-known illustration of this sort of framing

averse attitudes towards gains but risk-seeking attitudes toward losses, and these attitudes imply concavity of the value function for gains and convexity for losses. *See id.* This pattern of concavity and convexity has received considerable empirical support. *See id.* at 268, 278; Peter C. Fishburn & Gary A. Kochenberger, *Two-Piece Von Neumann-Morgenstern Utility Functions*, 10 DECISION SCI. 503, 509-10 (1979).

184. Amos Tversky & Richard H. Thaler, *Preference Reversals*, *in* THALER, *supra* note 40, at 79, 91.

185. *Cf.* Edward J. McCaffery, Daniel J. Kahneman & Matthew L. Spitzer, *Framing the Jury: Cognitive Perspectives on Pain and Suffering Awards*, 81 VA. L. REV. 1341 (1995) (finding effect of gain versus loss framing on magnitude of damage awards).

effect is a study involving breast self-examination; pamphlets describing the positive effects of breast self-examination (for example, women who undertake such examinations have a greater chance of finding a tumor at a treatable stage) are ineffective, but there are significant changes in behavior from pamphlets that stress the negative consequences of a refusal to undertake self-examinations (women who fail to perform such examinations have a decreased chance of finding a tumor at a treatable stage).[186] Note that this example illustrates how the provision of information may be a more natural tool than taxation or regulation for discouraging some forms of behavior (such as the failure to perform a self-examination).

Second prescription: Exploit salience. Effective prescriptive strategies need to take account of the fact that vivid and personal information will often be more effective than statistical evidence. This sort of information has a high degree of salience, and, as a result of the availability heuristic, people will tend to respond to it by attaching a higher probability to the event in question. Thus an antidrug advertisement, showing a frying egg with the announcer's voice claiming, "this is your brain on drugs," appeared to have a significant effect on behavior.[187] Availability suggests that the ad produced a higher perceived probability of negative effects than a flatter ad would have.

Third prescription: Avoid the pitfalls of overoptimism. As noted in the previous section, a common feature of human behavior is overoptimism.[188] This behavior is not specific to the young, although it may be diminished as people move beyond middle to old age, as Richard Posner has suggested.[189] What does this feature of behavior imply about government provision of information? Consider the choice between a safe-driving campaign focused on drivers' own driving and the ingenuous campaign actually adopted by the government: "Drive defensively: Watch out for the other guy."[190] The government's campaign, perhaps self-consciously, responded to the fact that most people tend to believe that they are unusually safe drivers. This is a model of the sort of prescriptive approach advocated by behavioral analysis.

186. Beth E. Meyerowitz & Shelly Chaiken, *The Effect of Message Framing on Breast Self-Examination: Attitudes, Intentions, and Behavior*, 52 J. PERSONALITY & SOC. PSYCHOL. 500, 505 (1987).

187. *See* Douglas Herring, Comment, *Getting High from South of the Border: Illicit Smuggling of Rohynol as an Example of the Need to Modify U.S. Response to International Drug Smuggling After NAFTA*, 18 LOY. L.A. INT'L & COMP. L.J. 841, 863 (1996) (citing Mathea Falco, *Toward a More Effective Drug Policy*, 1994 U CHI. LEGAL F. 9, 15).

188. *See* note 152 *supra* and accompanying text.

189. *See* Weinstein, *Unrealistic Optimism*, *supra* note 152 (overoptimism apparent in the general public); RICHARD A. POSNER, AGING AND OLD AGE 104-06 (1995).

190. *See* Sunstein, *supra* note 3, at 1177.

C. *Behavior of Criminals*

1. *Background.*

Our discussion of prescriptive analysis has thus far focused on bounded rationality. But bounded willpower may also play a role. Consider the question of deterring criminal behavior. Economic analysis of this question typically starts from the premise that potential offenders will be deterred from criminal acts if the expected costs of those acts exceed their expected benefits.[191] Potential offenders are imagined to make at least a rough calculation of these costs and benefits in the process of making their decisions. Bounded rationality suggests that people may make systematic (as opposed to random) errors in computing these costs and benefits; for example, as described above, individuals tend to judge the likelihood of uncertain events (such as getting caught for a crime) by how available such instances are to the human mind, and this may depend on factors unrelated to the actual probability of the event. This analysis suggests the desirability, from a prescriptive standpoint, of making law enforcement highly visible, holding constant the actual probability that offenders will be caught; it suggests, for example, the good sense of the familiar method of parking-ticket enforcement—sticking large, brightly-colored tickets that read "VIOLATION" in large letters on the drivers' side window, where they are particularly noticeable to drivers passing by—as opposed to a less costly approach (putting small, plain tickets under the windshield wiper on the curb side of the street, convenient for the parking officer to reach). Another example here is "community policing," now widely practiced across the country; by making more visible and memorable the presence of police (as, for example, by having them walk their beats rather than ride in patrol cars), authorities can, it is suggested, increase the deterrence of potential criminals without altering the actual probability of apprehension.

But even if one assumes that potential offenders can accurately compute the costs and benefits of crime, bounded willpower suggests that they will often behave in ways at odds with conventional economic analysis, due to problems of self-control. A central feature of much criminal behavior is that the benefits are immediate, while the costs (if they are incurred at all) are spread out over time—often a very long time. Economic analysis assumes that such future costs are discounted to present value, and A. Mitchell Polinsky and Steven Shavell have recently suggested that potential criminal offenders may have unusually high discount rates, so that years in prison far in

---

191. *See* Shavell, *supra* note 41, at 1235.

the future will be discounted very heavily.[192] Behavioral economic analysis carries this idea further by incorporating self-control issues often emphasized by criminologists.[193]

2. *Prescriptions.*

As just noted, the existing economic analysis assumes a constant discount rate (although perhaps a high one); this means that the difference between the attractiveness or aversiveness of a reward or punishment today versus tomorrow is the same as the difference between a year from now and a year and one day from now. In contrast to this theory, there is considerable evidence that people display sharply declining discount rates.[194] This means that impatience is very strong for near rewards (and aversion very strong for near punishments) but that each of these declines over time—a pattern referred to as "hyperbolic discounting."[195] Such attitudes reflect "dynamic inconsistency"; one's present desires for the future are at odds with one's future desires for the future.[196] In an illuminating overstatement, Jon Elster has referred to this as the "absolute priority of the present"—akin to the "absolute priority [of the self] over other persons: I am I—while they are all 'out there.'"[197] Richard Posner has recently applied these ideas to issues of aging and old age,[198] and their application to criminal offenders is supported by the idea that such offenders often behave "impulsive[ly]" and then have to "exaggerat[e] the benefits of crime" in order to justify their behavior to themselves later.[199] Such a need for justification would not occur with the ordinary discounting assumed by most conventional economic analysis; decisions would not be regretted later because with that form of discounting there is no dynamic inconsistency of preference.[200]

What does hyperbolic discounting imply for effective deterrence of criminal behavior? With this sort of bounded willpower on the part of po-

192. A. MITCHELL POLINSKY & STEVEN SHAVELL, ON THE DISUTILITY AND DISCOUNTING OF IMPRISONMENT AND THE THEORY OF DETERRENCE 12-13 (Harvard Law School, John M Olin Center for Law, Economics, and Business, Discussion Paper No. 213, 1997).

193. *See, e.g.*, MICHAEL R. GOTTFREDSON & TRAVIS HIRSCHI, A GENERAL THEORY OF CRIME 85-120 (1990) (emphasizing role of lack of self-control in criminal behavior); James Q. Wilson & Allan Abrahamse, *Does Crime Pay?*, 9 JUST. Q. 359, 372-74 (1992) (similar).

194. *See* George Loewenstein & Richard H. Thaler, *Intertemporal Choice*, *in* THALER, *supra* note 40, at 92, 95-96 (discussing studies).

195. *See* David Laibson, *Golden Eggs and Hyperbolic Discounting*, 112 Q.J. ECON. 443, 445-46 (1997).

196. *See id.*

197. JON ELSTER, ULYSSES AND THE SIRENS: STUDIES IN RATIONALITY AND IRRATIONALITY 71 (1979).

198. POSNER, *supra* note 189, at 84-94, 281-82.

199. Wilson & Abrahamse, *supra* note 193, at 374.

200. *See* Laibson, *supra* note 195, at 445.

tential offenders, the difference between not getting caught and being imprisoned for, say, a year differs dramatically from the difference between being imprisoned for ten years and being imprisoned for eleven years (even apart from any fixed costs that may accompany the fact of conviction). While the standard theory says that these two things differ only insofar as the costs of imprisonment in year eleven must be discounted to present value in order to be compared with the loss of wages and personal freedom in year one, behavioral economic analysis (and basic common sense) tells us that this is not so. Short punishments will thus have much more effect than long punishments as a result of the "priority of the present"; adding years onto a sentence will produce little additional deterrence.[201] This idea is reflected in policy recommendations such as Mark Kleiman's "coerced abstinence" proposal, under which drug offenders on probation or parole would be swiftly and automatically punished, but with modest sanctions, for any positive drug result.[202] Short punishments are also desirable under Polinsky and Shavell's approach, but for a different reason.

Our analysis is consistent with empirical evidence suggesting that criminal behavior is correlated with high levels of self-control problems. It appears, for example, that drunk-driving behavior is significantly correlated with not wearing a seat belt—itself a behavior that seems to suggest a very high weight on the present, and thus a lack of self-control in the sense used here.[203] Another interesting piece of empirical evidence concerns offenders' views of sentences of different lengths. One study found that they view a five-year term of imprisonment as, on average, only twice as bad as a one-year term; the five-year term had a perceived severity of 200, compared to 100 for the one-year term.[204] This alone is also consistent with a high discount rate—a rate of roughly 0.5. But with that discount rate, the difference between a five- and ten-year term should be quite small (approximately 6 on the severity measure); in fact, the difference was 300.[205] This difference is also somewhat higher than hyperbolic discounting would suggest; if the difference between 100 and 200 represents a .25 weight on all years after the first year (so that the five-year term's severity is 100 + 25 + 25 + 25 + 25 = 200), then the ten-year term's severity would be 325—much closer than the

---

201. *Cf.* Robert D. Cooter, *Lapses, Conflict, and Akrasia in Torts and Crimes: Towards an Economic Theory of the Will*, 11 INT'L REV. L. & ECON. 149, 154 (1991) (concluding that short but highly probable sentences are optimal in a model in which potential offenders experience "lapses" in self-control).

202. Mark A.R. Kleiman, *Coerced Abstinence: A Neopaternalist Drug Policy Initiative*, *in* THE NEW PATERNALISM 182, 203, 205-08 (Lawrence M. Mead ed., 1997).

203. *See* Martin Friedland, Michael Trebilcock & Kent Roach, *Regulating Traffic Safety*, *in* SECURING COMPLIANCE: SEVEN CASE STUDIES 165, 192 (1990).

204. William Spelman, *The Severity of Intermediate Sanctions*, 32 J. RES. CRIME & DELINQ. 107, 113 (1995).

205. *Id.*

206 predicted by the nonhyperbolic approach, although still less than the actual severity rating of 500. These data are of course only suggestive; we have not shown that the bounded willpower approach leads to improved predictions of actual criminal behavior. Empirical work on actual behavior of this sort is notoriously difficult, but scholars such as Steven Levitt have begun to demonstrate the possibilities in this area.[206] A full analysis of criminal behavior would also need to incorporate other factors not considered here (such as the role of community); our goal is only to sketch some of the many ways in which conventional economic analysis of criminal law can be usefully extended using the tools of behavioral economics.

V. Normative Analysis: Anti-Antipaternalism

In its normative orientation, conventional law and economics is often strongly antipaternalistic. The idea of "consumer sovereignty" plays a large role; citizens, assuming they have reasonable access to relevant information, are thought to be the best judges of what will promote their own welfare. Yet many of the instances of bounded rationality discussed above call this idea into question—and also, as we will emphasize below, call into question the idea that intervention by government actors, who themselves may face the same cognitive or motivational problems as everyone else, can improve matters. In this way bounded rationality pushes toward a sort of anti-antipaternalism—a skepticism about antipaternalism, but not an affirmative defense of paternalism.[207] We also note (although we do not explore this point here) that while bounded rationality may increase the need for law (if government's failings are less serious than citizens'), bounded self-interest may reduce it, by creating norms that solve collective action problems even without government intervention.[208]

A. *Citizen Error*

Many of the forms of bounded rationality discussed above call into question the idea of consumer sovereignty. For example, overoptimism leads most people to believe that their own risk of a negative outcome is far lower than the average person's. Similarly, the effect of salience may lead to substantial underestimation of certain risks encountered in everyday life (for example, the risks from poor diet), since these harms may not be very salient.

206. Steven D. Levitt, *Using Electoral Cycles in Police Hiring to Estimate the Effect of Police on Crime*, 87 AM. ECON. REV. 270 (1997); Steven D. Levitt, *The Effect of Prison Population Size on Crime Rates: Evidence from Prison Overcrowding Litigation*, 111 Q.J. ECON. 319 (1996).

207. *See* Sunstein, *supra* note 3, at 1178.

208. A standard argument for law under the conventional economic approach is that self-interested people will create collective irrationality; if people are boundedly self-interested, however, this problem may tend to disappear.

When overoptimism is combined with salience, people may underestimate risks substantially. We emphasize that these problems are not ones of insufficient information per se; they are ones of insufficient ability to process accurately the information one possesses insofar as that information bears on one's own risks. Thus, for example, people may have reasonably adequate information about the risks of smoking,[209] but this does not at all imply that they have adequate perceptions of the risks of smoking that *they themselves face*.[210] Even if people can obtain accurate statistical knowledge, statistical knowledge may not be enough to inform actual choices.[211] It does not follow from this that information is useless; it is just that having information per se does not automatically imply optimal behavior.

Further questions about the idea of consumer sovereignty arise from the gap between "decision" and "experience" utility. The utility of actual experience may diverge from the anticipated utility as revealed by people's decisions.[212] The identity of decision and experience utility in conventional economics is often treated as an axiom, or at least as a proposition that could not be falsified. But behavioral research shows that people's judgments about their future experience at the time of decision can be mistaken, in the sense that people are sometimes unable (even apart from the sorts of informational issues recognized by conventional economics) to assess what the experience will actually be like. Thus, for example, people appear not to predict accurately the consequences of becoming seriously ill or disabled.[213] They tend to underestimate their ability to adapt to negative changes, a point that may bear on law and policy in such areas as global climate change.[214]

But this suggestion about adaptation raises a complex normative question: Is a person's measure of welfare after (for example) becoming ill the appropriate measure of value? Perhaps people, through coping mechanisms, are able to adapt to disease better than they anticipate in advance, but does this mean that disease is a less severe problem than prior attitudes would

209. *See* W. KIP VISCUSI, SMOKING 4 (1992).

210. *See* Paul Slovic, *Do Adolescent Smokers Know the Risks?*, 47 DUKE L.J. (forthcoming 1998).

211. *See* Sunstein, *supra* note 3, at 1184.

212. *See* Daniel Kahneman, *New Challenges to the Rationality Assumption*, *in* THE RATIONAL FOUNDATIONS OF ECONOMIC BEHAVIOUR 203 (Kenneth J. Arrow, Enrico Colombatto, Mark Perlman & Christian Schmidt eds., 1996).

213. *See* Philip Brickman, Dan Coates & Ronnie Janoff-Bulman, *Lottery Winners and Accident Victims: Is Happiness Relative?* 36 J. PERSONALITY & SOC. PSYCHOL. 917 (1978); George Loewenstein & David Schkade, *Wouldn't It Be Nice? Predicting Future Feelings*, *in* HEDONIC PSYCHOLOGY: SCIENTIFIC APPROACHES TO ENJOYMENT, SUFFERING, AND WELL-BEING (Ed Diener, Norbert Schwartz & Daniel Kahneman eds., forthcoming 1998).

214. *See* George Loewenstein & Shane Frederick, *Predicting Reactions to Environmental Change*, *in* ENVIRONMENT, ETHICS, AND BEHAVIOR: THE PSYCHOLOGY OF ENVIRONMENTAL VALUATION AND DEGRADATION 52, 64-65 (Max H. Bazerman, David M. Messick, Ann E. Tenbrunsel & Kimberly A. Wade-Benzoni eds., 1997).

have suggested? On conventional utilitarian grounds, the answer is probably affirmative; the subjective experience is what counts. But a well-established challenge to utilitarian analysis suggests the possibility of a negative answer, on the ground that subjective experience may not be all that counts.[215] What we mean to suggest here is a simple point: People sometimes do mispredict their utility at the time of decision, and on conventional grounds, this phenomenon raises serious problems for the idea of consumer sovereignty.

B. *Behavioral Bureaucrats*

Any suggestion that the government should intervene in response to people's mistakes raises the question whether the government will be able to avoid such errors. The prospects for productive and useful intervention may be smallest in the case of populist government; the actions of such a government, based heavily on pressures coming from citizens, may tend to be subject to the very same biases and errors that afflict citizens. (Thus behavioral analysis complements existing accounts of the problems with populism.) An example of the effects of populism is the Superfund statute, discussed in Part III.C; irregular perceptions of risk by ordinary people may tend to produce irregularities in regulation, as the cognitive errors that ordinary people make are replicated in statutory and administrative law.[216] The effects of social interaction may even make government action worse, and more dangerous, than individual errors. Our earlier discussion suggests a possible mechanism: Availability entrepreneurs in the private sector can heighten the demand for regulation, and public sector availability entrepreneurs can take advantage of, and heighten, this effect, by advocating anecdote-driven policy. Thus public choice accounts of legislation can work productively with behavioral accounts; there is a good deal of synergy between behavioral mechanisms and interest group leaders, many of whom are amateur (or professional?) behavioral economists. The pollutant-of-the-month syndrome in environmental law is paralleled by many measures responding to the crisis-of-the-month. These difficulties with populist government also point to problems with the referendum process.

But populist government is not the only worry. Government will often be subject to cognitive and motivational problems even if it is not populist. (Bureaucrats may also lack appropriate incentives to make decisions in the public interest.[217]) Thus, for example, there is no necessary reason to think

215. *See* JON ELSTER, SOUR GRAPES: STUDIES IN THE SUBVERSION OF RATIONALITY (1983); AMARTYA SEN, COMMODITIES AND CAPABILITIES (1985).

216. *See* W. KIP VISCUSI, FATAL TRADEOFFS: PUBLIC AND PRIVATE RESPONSIBILITIES FOR RISK 149 (1992); VISCUSI, *supra* note 137, at 85-88, 94-97; Noll & Krier, *supra* note 137, at 760-72.

217. *See* Robert C. Clark, *Contracts, Elites, and Traditions in the Making of Corporate Law*, 89 COLUM. L. REV. 1703, 1719-20 (1989).

that government officials are, by virtue of their offices, able to avoid overoptimism or predict experience utility. On the other hand, a degree of insulation from populist pressures, combined with knowledge of behavioral economics, might produce some improvement. New institutions may play a role; consider Justice Breyer's plea for an insulated body of specialized civil servants, entrusted with the job of comparing risks and ensuring that resources are devoted to the most serious problems;[218] Howard Margolis' behaviorally-informed suggestion that government should be required to ensure that all initiatives "do no harm";[219] even proposals for cost-benefit analysis, understood in a behavioral light as an attempt to overcome biases and confusions in both perception and motivation.[220] We also emphasize that government intervention need not come in highly coercive forms; perhaps distortions in people's decisionmaking can be overcome by information campaigns falling well short of coercion. For instance, in the contexts of risks such as smoking, might debiasing techniques work to link the statistical evidence with the personal reality?

All of the foregoing ideas raise many complexities; and we have not even touched upon the complicated philosophical literature on the legitimacy of paternalism. Application of these ideas to any specific topic in law would require a much fuller development of many issues than the space in this article permits. But we need not leave the ideas in purely abstract form; consider the following simple illustration of their application. Imagine that sunlamps are being sold in an unregulated market and that it is learned that many consumers fall asleep under the lamps, burning themselves badly. Consumers make this mistake in spite of warnings included on the package and in the instructions, perhaps because they fail to anticipate that lying in a warm place with one's eyes closed is likely to induce sleep. Let's call this an "unintended risk," meaning a risk that consumers fail to appreciate. The existence of this unintended risk leaves open the possibility of welfare-enhancing regulation. Suppose, for example, that an automatic timer can be added to the sunlamp at a cost of twenty-five cents, and that manufacturers have not included this feature because consumers do not anticipate that they will need it. We do not discuss here the issues raised by the possibility that a government mandate of the timer interferes with freedom, rightly conceived. Nor do we address possible distributive issues (all will pay more for sunlamps, although perhaps only some failed to appreciate the risks of falling asleep). All we suggest is that an important part of the analysis involves asking whether the cost of requiring this safety-promoting feature (twenty-five cents per customer) is less than the cost of the unanticipated burns.

218. BREYER, *supra* note 139, at 55-81.

219. HOWARD MARGOLIS, DEALING WITH RISK 165-89 (1996).

220. RISK VS. RISK (John D. Graham & Jonathan Baert Wiener eds., 1995). Each of the solutions stated in the text may also be attractive to conventional economists on a variety of grounds.

A central point of this example is that from the perspective of behavioral law and economics, issues of paternalism are to a significant degree empirical questions, not questions to be answered on an a priori basis. No axiom demonstrates that people make choices that serve their best interests; this is a question to be answered based on evidence. Of course the case for intervention is weakened to the extent that public institutions are likely to make things worse rather than better. What we are suggesting is that facts, and assessment of costs and benefits, should replace assumptions that beg the underlying questions.

CONCLUSION

Traditional law and economics is largely based on the standard assumptions of neoclassical economics. These assumptions are sometimes useful but often false. People display bounded rationality: They suffer from certain biases, such as overoptimism and self-serving conceptions of fairness; they follow heuristics, such as availability, that lead to mistakes; and they behave in accordance with prospect theory rather than expected utility theory. People also have bounded willpower; they can be tempted and are sometimes myopic. They take steps to overcome these limitations. Finally, people are (fortunately!) boundedly self-interested. They are concerned about the well-being of others, even strangers in some circumstances, and this concern and their self-conception can lead them in the direction of cooperation at the expense of their material self-interest (and sometimes spite, also at the expense of their material self-interest). Most of these bounds can be and have been made part of formal models.

In this article we have sketched some of the implications of enriching the traditional analysis by incorporating a more realistic conception of human behavior. We have insisted on the value and importance of using the three bounds in the economic analysis of law; more tentatively, we have explored a series of legal problems in which the bounds may be significant. Obviously there is a great deal of research to be done, and one of our principal goals has been to outline areas that could benefit from further work, both analytic and empirical.

We do not doubt that replacing the simple maximizing model of economics with a more complicated psychological treatment comes at some cost. Solving optimization problems is usually easier than describing actual behavior. It has been said (we believe by Herbert Simon) that economics makes things hard on agents, but easy on economists; behavioral economics, we suggest, does the opposite. We recapitulate here some of the reasons we think the enriched model is worth the trouble for those interested in the economic analysis of law.

1. Some of the predictions of the standard model are simply wrong. For example, people can be both more spiteful and more cooperative than traditional analysis predicts, and this matters a great deal to law. It is also important to know that even in a world without transaction costs and wealth effects, the assignment of property rights alters the ultimate allocation of those rights, and that this may be particularly true for certain forms of property-rights assignment (such as court orders). These features of the world matter greatly for making predictions and formulating policy.
2. In other cases economics makes no predictions (or incorrect predictions of no effect). Prominent in this category are the effects of presentation; since economic theory assumes that choices are invariant to the manner in which a problem is framed, it falsely predicts that the language of a media account or advertisement has no effect on behavior, holding the information content constant. In contrast, it is well established that people react differently to potential outcomes depending on whether they are perceived as foregone gains or out-of-pocket costs (losses), and that they are likely to think, mistakenly, that salient events are more common than equally prevalent but more subtle ones. These points bear on the supply of and the demand for law, and on the behavior of agents in their interactions with the legal system.
3. Standard economic theories of the content of law are based on an unduly limited range of potential explanations, namely optimal (or second-best) rules set by judges and rent-seeking legislation determined by self-interested log-rolling. Behavioral economics offers other sources of potential explanation—most prominently, perceptions of fairness. We have tried to show that many laws which are seemingly inefficient and do not benefit powerful interest groups may be explained on grounds of judgments about right and wrong.
4. A behavioral approach to law and economics offers a host of novel prescriptions regarding how to make the legal system work better. Some stem from the improved predictions mentioned in point 2 above. Cognitive difficulties and motivational distortions undermine or alter conventional economic prescriptions about the jury's role, most notably in the context of assessing negligence and making other determinations of fact or law. We have taken some preliminary steps in suggesting ways to reduce the costs of some of these problems.
5. A behavioral approach to law and economics produces new questions about possible mistakes by private and public actors. On the one hand, it raises serious doubts about the reflexive antipaternalism of some economic analysis of law. On the other hand, it raises equivalent questions

about whether even well-motivated public officials will be able to offer appropriate responses to private mistakes and confusion.

We hope that this article will encourage others to continue the inquiry and research, both theoretical and empirical, that will be needed to flesh out the behavioral approach for which we have argued here. This approach will use traditional economic tools, enhanced by a better understanding of human behavior. Thirty years from now, we hope that there will be no such thing as behavioral economics. Instead we hope that economists and economically oriented lawyers will simply incorporate the useful findings of other social sciences, and in so doing, transform economics into behavioral economics, and economic analysis of law into one of its most important branches.

APPENDIX: FRAMEWORK AND SUMMARY OF APPLICATIONS

This appendix summarizes our framework for behavioral law and economics. It also lists the law and economics issues we analyze within each category of the framework. The specific behavioral mechanisms we draw upon, which are summarized here, do not constitute an exhaustive list of the mechanisms that might be relevant to law and economics; they simply reflect the mechanisms we have used here. For each mechanism, we provide a reference to the literature, as an overview of or entry to the existing research; we refer the interested reader to the text of our article for additional references on each topic.

A. *Bounded rationality*

Judgment errors

1. *self-serving bias*

   reference: Linda Babcock & George Loewenstein, *Explaining Bargaining Impasse: The Role of Self-Serving Biases*, 11 J. ECON. PERSP., Winter 1997, at 109.

   our applications: bargaining around court orders; failed negotiations.

2. *availability heuristic*

   reference: Amos Tversky & Daniel Kahneman, *Judgment Under Uncertainty: Heuristics and Biases*, *in* JUDGMENT UNDER UNCERTAINTY 3 (Daniel Kahneman, Paul Slovic & Amos Tversky eds., 1982).

   our applications: environmental legislation, government advertising, anti-antipaternalism.

3. *hindsight bias*

   reference: Baruch Fischhoff, *Hindsight ≠ Foresight: The Effect of Outcome Knowledge on Judgment Under Uncertainty*, 1 J. EXPERIMENTAL PSYCHOL. HUM. PERCEPTION & PERFORMANCE 288 (1975).

our applications: negligence determinations; other determinations of fact or law.

4. *omission bias*

reference: Ilana Ritov & Jonathan Baron, *Reluctance to Vaccinate: Omission Bias and Ambiguity*, 3 J. BEHAV. DECISION MAKING 263 (1990).

our applications: negligence determinations; other determinations of fact or law.

5. *overoptimism*

reference: Neil D. Weinstein, *Unrealistic Optimism About Future Life Events*, 39 J. PERSONALITY & SOC. PSCYHOL. 806 (1980).

our applications: government advertising, anti-antipaternalism.

6. *inability to predict experience utility*

reference: Daniel Kahneman, *New Challenges to the Rationality Assumption*, *in* THE RATIONAL FOUNDATIONS OF ECONOMIC BEHAVIOUR 203 (Kenneth J. Arrow, Enrico Colombatto, Mark Perlman & Christian Schmidt eds., 1996).

our applications: anti-antipaternalism.

Decisionmaking behavior

1. *loss aversion*

reference: Daniel Kahneman & Amos Tversky, *Prospect Theory: An Analysis of Decision Under Risk*, 47 ECONOMETRICA 263 (1979).

our applications: government advertising.

2. *endowment effect (a corollary of loss aversion)*

reference: Daniel Kahneman, Jack L. Knetsch & Richard H. Thaler, *Experimental Tests of the Endowment Effect and the Coase Theorem*, 98 J. POL. ECON. 1325, 1327 (1990).

our applications: bargaining around court orders, mandatory contract terms, prior restraints on speech.

B. *Bounded willpower*

1. *"hyperbolic" discounting*

reference: David Laibson, *Golden Eggs and Hyperbolic Discounting*, 112 Q.J. ECON. 443 (1997).

our applications: criminal behavior.

C. *Bounded self-interest*

1. *fairness behavior and spitefulness*

reference: Colin Camerer & Richard H. Thaler, *Anomalies: Ultimatums, Dictators, and Manners*, 9 J. ECON. PERSP., Spring 1995, at 209.

our applications: bargaining around court orders; bans on market transactions; prior restraints on speech.

Social Norms

[10]

SYMBOLS, SIGNALS, AND SOCIAL NORMS IN POLITICS AND THE LAW

ERIC A. POSNER*

ABSTRACT

This article uses a signaling model to explain the role of symbols in people's behavior and beliefs, with special attention to legal manipulation of symbols. It is argued that certain actions become symbolic because they have the proper cost structure and because they are, for historical or psychological reasons, focal. The government can in theory use standard legal instruments (which mainly affect the cost of the signal) to change equilibrium behavior and belief. The use of the law in this way is likely to have unpredictable effects because of multiple equilibria and of the sensitivity of behavior to parameters, but it occurs frequently because lobbying and other actions that influence lawmaking can become signals themselves, and the law is simply an equilibrium outcome. The analysis is used to discuss flag desecration, censorship, voting, and antidiscrimination laws.

I. INTRODUCTION

SYMBOLS dominate American politics and permeate the law, but they are poorly understood. The lone protestor who burns an American flag on the steps of the courthouse also ignites a political firestorm, and when the smoke finally clears, it reveals a political and legal system in great disarray: political leaders condemning the perpetrator in the strongest terms, prosecutors struggling to bring him to justice, legislators scrambling to outlaw flag desecration, commentators wringing their hands beneath the looming shadow of constitutional amendment. By any standard, this is an extraordinary uproar. And yet the burning of the American flag harms no one in any way. In a country where the dominant political view holds that the state's main purpose is to prevent coercive harm, the attention lavished on the question whether a person should be allowed to burn an American flag—an action that does not coerce or harm anyone—can only be called an em-

* Professor of Law, University of Pennsylvania. My thanks to Matthew Adler, Douglas Baird, Steve Coate, Jason Johnston, Timur Kuran, Richard McAdams, Geoffrey Miller, Eric Rasmusen, and participants at this conference and at a talk at the American Law and Economics Association annual meeting, Toronto, 1997. Karen Schoen provided valuable research assistance.

[*Journal of Legal Studies,* vol. XXVII (June 1998)]

barrassment. True, people are offended at the desecration of a symbol. But why is the American flag a symbol? And why do symbols matter?

That they do matter is beyond dispute. A little research reveals a multitude of controversies over symbols both in this country and abroad. Examples from the United States include the placement of crèches and other religious symbols on public property, the display of the Confederate flag in certain southern universities,[1] the refusal by some citizens to use social security numbers and license plates with patriotic slogans on them, marches by Nazis and Klan members, "hate speech" on university campuses, and presidential apologies to victims of harsh government policies. Overseas, examples include controversies over the respect owed to the deutsche mark, the kangaroo, and the Emperor of Japan.[2] The first response of citizens to the fall of the communist regimes in Eastern Europe was not the privatization of industry and the reform of the secret police, but the destruction of statues, the renaming of streets, and the redesign of national flags.

Many of these examples seem trivial, but the influence of symbols on substantive policies and legal change cannot be doubted. The politician commits political suicide who supports a "wrong" (in his supporters' eyes) modification of laws relating to abortion, affirmative action, Social Security, gun control, and other highly charged policies, no matter how trivial the proposed modification. When voters interpret support for a political program as a symbol of a politician's commitment to their values and interests, political compromise becomes difficult, even impossible.[3]

What accounts for the prominence of the flag desecration issue and other issues of pure symbolism? One theory is that the violation of symbols causes "psychic harm," another is that the violation of symbols conflicts with "social norms." But these theories do not explain why one behavior has symbolic resonance that causes psychic harm or violates social norms, while some other behavior does not. Acknowledgment of a right to be free of any psychic harm, moreover, would throw all traditional liberal rights—to speech, religion, privacy, conscience—into doubt. To provide a foundation for a legal order that protects people from some psychic harms and not others, one must explain how such harms arise.

This article uses a signaling model to explain why symbols matter. Sym-

[1] Kevin Sack, Symbols of Old South Feed a New Bitterness, N.Y. Times, February 8, 1997, at 1.

[2] Nathaniel C. Nash, The New Symbol of Germany: Faith in a Scrap of Paper, N.Y. Times, June 25, 1995; Philip Shenon, Battling over a National Symbol: It's on the Menu, N.Y. Times, July 10, 1995; Nicholas D. Kristof, Japan's State Symbols: Now You See Them . . . , N.Y. Times, November 12, 1995.

[3] A detailed discussion of this problem can be found in Michael J. Piore, Beyond Individualism, ch. 2 (1995).

bols matter because a person's manifested attitude toward symbols tells others something about that person's character. People rely heavily on this information when deciding whether to engage in cooperative behavior in all realms of life. Indeed, because symbols matter so much, people's efforts to show respect for them lead to significant forms of conformity that can be described as "social norms." When symbols change, some people obtain advantages in forming cooperative relationships while other people lose advantages they had. Because changes in symbols can thus result in material loss for some people, these people resist when the government or other people challenge a particular system of symbols. Moreover, because cooperative behavior can be highly sensitive to symbols, there are great incentives for the government to regulate symbols, and dangers, too.

II. Analysis

A. *Games of Cooperation*

In ordinary life people engage in symbolic behavior all the time. They shake hands, applaud in theaters, salute the flag, wear stylish clothes, exchange wedding rings, bow, present gifts, observe diplomatic protocol, and show deference to superiors. In every case, the symbolic behavior is intended as a signal that the agent has a characteristic that the agent wants the receiver of the signal to believe that the agent has, but that the receiver cannot directly observe. When the symbolic action serves no obvious private, "substantive" interest, as is the case of the actions listed above, everyone understands its symbolic nature. One does not applaud a performance because the act of bringing one's hands together is pleasurable but because applause signals to the performer and the other audience members that one enjoyed the show. Much behavior, however, has both symbolic and substantive purposes. One might discriminate against members of a minority group both because one dislikes them and because one wants to show others that one dislikes members of the minority group. One might obtain an education both because one believes that an education will improve one's skills and because one wants to show employers that one is smart enough to be able to earn a degree. One might participate in a patriotic parade both because one enjoys the spectacle and because one wants to show one's neighbors that one has patriotic feelings.

To capture these ideas and their implications for the legal system, I use a signaling model. The model will be referred to as the "cooperation game." Cooperation refers to any kind of cooperative relationship that can be modeled as a repeat prisoner's dilemma, including business, family, and social relationships. I should mention that in the space I have I can no more than sketch out the way the argument would proceed. A more detailed analysis must await future work.

In the cooperation game citizens of the high type ("cooperators") care about future gains relative to present gains and earn more through joint action with others than they earn by acting alone. In contrast, citizens of the low type ("cheaters") care more about the present and have adequate private opportunities for gain. Both types would cheat in a one-shot prisoner's dilemma, but in a repeated version of this game that has no definite ending and appropriate payoffs, the cooperators would never cheat while the cheaters would cheat on the first move. The reason is that the cooperators care enough about future payoffs that they would want the game to continue, whereas the cheaters value the immediate payoffs more than the (highly discounted) stream of future payoffs.

Somewhat artificially, we imagine that the two types ("senders") seek to cooperate with members of another group ("receivers"). The receivers cannot distinguish the senders by type. If the receivers cooperate with anyone who approaches them, they will sometimes gain and sometimes lose. The cooperators do not cheat them on the first round, so the receivers know that they are cooperators, and the two players then can cooperate indefinitely and obtain mutual gains. The cheaters cheat the receivers on the first round, and the receivers then decline to cooperate further, but they already have sustained a one-time loss. Depending on the fraction of cheaters in the population and the difference between the payoffs from cooperation and from cheating, receivers might be willing to cooperate with anyone, but they would refuse to cooperate with everyone whenever the expected losses exceed the expected gains.

To avoid the possibility that receivers will not cooperate with them, high types try to provide credible evidence of their type by sending a signal to the receivers. A signal is any costly action that, if successful, reveals the type of the sender. A signal can distinguish a cooperator and a cheater only if the cooperator can afford to issue the signal and the cheater cannot. Examples of signals discussed in the literature include gift giving, advertising, the acquisition of education that has no value, and consumption of luxury goods or fashionable items.[4] The person who engages in these actions shows others that he expects to earn high returns from cooperation, for if he did not, he would not be able to afford the signal. It should be empha-

[4] A. M. Spence, Market Signaling (1974); Colin Camerer, Gifts as Economic Signals and Social Symbols, 94 Am. J. Soc. S180 (1988); Benjamin Klein & Keith B. Leffler, The Role of Market Forces in Assuring Contractual Performance, 89 J. Pol. Econ. 615 (1981); Wolfgang Pesendorfer, Design Innovation and Fashion Cycles, 85 Am. Econ. Rev. 771 (1995); Laurie Simon Bagwell & B. Douglas Bernheim, Veblen Effects in a Theory of Conspicuous Consumption, 86 Am. Econ. Rev. 349 (1996).

sized that signals may be ambiguous: gift giving, for example, may reflect a person's generosity or altruism rather than his discount rate.[5] And it should be emphasized that signals that have the wrong cost structure—that are too cheap or too costly—fail to distinguish the cooperaters and the cheaters, leading to equilibria in which everyone sends the signal or everyone abandons it. Cooperators send signals in order to reveal their type; to the extent that the signals have the wrong cost structure, cheaters will mimic the signals in order to avoid revealing to the receiver that they belong to the low type. If the cooperators distinguish themselves from cheaters, receivers will cooperate with the cooperators; if they fail to do so, the receivers will not cooperate with them (or if the payoffs are appropriate, they will cooperate with cooperators and cheaters to an equal extent).

Several kinds of signals have received little attention in the literature but are of great significance. When a person shows respect for the national flag, performs civic obligations like voting and jury duty, and avoids people who are considered enemies of the state but are in fact desirable cooperative partners in the short term, this person engages in actions that are costly. If receivers interpret these actions as a means of revealing one's type, and if the actions are cheap enough that cooperators can recover their costs through payoffs from cooperation, but costly enough that cheaters cannot recover their costs by defecting in the first round, the actions may serve as signals. Why *these* actions serve as signals, rather than any other costly action (such as sitting on a pillar for one month), will be discussed subsequently. When focusing on these kinds of signals, as opposed to gift giving, advertising, and the like, I will sometimes refer to the cooperation game as the "patriotism game," although the games are formally identical.

To give the reader a more precise sense of the influence of signaling incentives on behavior, I will just sketch the main points, using a simple numerical example.[6] For the purpose of the example, I will refer in a stylized way to the signal of "saluting the flag" on appropriate occasions, but this behavior, which might seem too cheap to serve as a signal, should be taken as a synecdoche for the patriotic behaviors mentioned above, and it will be placed in its proper context in succeeding sections of this article.

Senders are either cooperators or cheaters. The probability that a sender is a cooperator is 0.9. In the first move Nature determines a sender's type.

[5] See Eric A. Posner, Altruism, Status, and Trust in the Law of Gifts and Gratuitous Promises, 1997 Wis. L. Rev. 657.

[6] The model resembles advertising models. See, for example, Klein & Leffler, *supra* note 4; Paul Milgrom & John Roberts, Price and Advertising Signals of Product Quality, 94 J. Pol. Econ. 796 (1986). Also compare the model of symbols in Jack L. Carr & Janet Landa, The Economics of Symbols, Clan Names, and Religions, 12 J. Legal Stud. 135 (1983).

The sender learns his type, then chooses either to salute or not to salute. The receiver initially does not know the senders' types but does know the distribution of types. The receiver observes whether the sender salutes, then decides either to cooperate with the sender or reject him. If the receiver rejects the sender, everyone receivers \$0. If the receiver cooperates, and the sender is a cheater, then the sender cheats the receiver and obtains a gain (\$2), and the receiver incurs a loss (−\$2). If the receiver cooperates, and the sender is a cooperator, then the receiver and the cooperator embark on a long-term relationship of mutual cooperation from which they both receive a stream of relatively small payments, though large in the aggregate (\$6 for each). Technically, the same stream of payments is available to the cheater and the cooperator, but because the cheater and the cooperator have different discount rates, the cheater values it at less than \$2 (the defection payoff) while the cooperator values it at \$6. It costs both types of senders \$3 to salute the flag and \$0 not to salute the flag.

A separating equilibrium occurs under the following conditions. The receiver believes that anyone who salutes the flag is a cooperator and anyone who fails to salute the flag is a cheater. Therefore, the receiver cooperates with anyone who salutes the flag (expecting a payoff of \$6 > \$0) and rejects anyone who fails to salute the flag (\$0 > −\$2). The cooperator receives \$3 from saluting the flag (\$6 − \$3), which exceeds his payoff from failing to salute the flag (\$0). The cheater receives \$0 from failing to salute the flag, which exceeds the payoff from saluting the flag (\$2 − \$3 = −\$1). Therefore, neither sender deviates from his strategy. The receiver has no reason to revise his assumption that all flag saluters are cooperators, because in equilibrium this is true. The equilibrium is a perfect Bayesian equilibrium.

Another perfect Bayesian equilibrium is "passive pooling," by which I mean a pooling equilibrium in which no one issues the signal. Suppose no one salutes the flag, and the receiver correctly estimates the proportion of types in the population. The receiver cooperates with everyone, since the gain (.9(\$6) + .1(−\$2) = \$5.2) exceeds the gain from rejecting everyone (\$0). The cooperator will not salute the flag (\$6 > \$6 − \$3); nor will the cheater (\$2 > \$2 − \$3). It does not matter what the receiver's beliefs are off the equilibrium path: even if he thinks that only cooperators salute the flag, no sender gains by doing so. Accordingly, passive pooling is a perfect Bayesian equilibrium.

"Active pooling," in which everyone issues the signal, is not a perfect Bayesian equilibrium: the cheater does better by deviating and failing to salute (\$0) than by saluting (\$2 − \$3 = −\$1). But we can create an active pooling equilibrium by adjusting the numbers. Suppose that the cheater gains \$4 from cooperation, and suppose that the receiver believes that the probability that a person who salutes is a cooperator is 90 percent. Suppose also that if someone does not salute the flag, the receiver believes that he is a cheater. If everyone salutes the flag, the receiver will cooperate rather than reject (.9($6) + .1(−$2) = $5.2 > 0). The cooperator will not deviate: the gain from signaling ($6 − $3 = $3) exceeds the gain from not signaling ($0). The cheater will not deviate ($4 − $3 = $1 > $0).

There are many other possible equilibria, including equilibria in which people of one type randomize among signals. To keep the discussion simple, I avoid these issues.[7] The example suffices for my main purpose, which is to analyze the effect of legal interventions on symbolic behavior. For now I focus on three kinds of legal interventions. (A fourth is introduced in the next section.)

Changes in the Cost of Signaling. Consider again the original example. Suppose that the cost of saluting the flag falls to $1 for both types of sender. The cheater now gains $1 from saluting the flag ($2 − $1 = $1 > $0), and so the separating strategies are no longer a perfect Bayesian equilibrium. Passive and active pooling equilibria are now possible: passive, because when both types fail to salute, the receiver nevertheless cooperates ($5.2 > $0), so neither type gains enough by distinguishing himself as a cooperator to justify the cost of the signal ($6 > $5, $2 > $1); active, because when both types salute and the receiver believes that all nonsignalers are cheaters, neither type gains by failing to salute, being perceived as a cheater, and being rejected by the receiver ($5 > $0, $1 > $0).

Changes in the Senders' and the Receiver's Gains from Cooperation. We saw in our discussion of the active pooling equilibrium that an increase in the cheater's payoff from cooperation from $2 to $4 will sustain an active pooling equilibrium. In general, the higher the senders' gains from cooperation (relative to being rejected), the greater are their incentives to signal, to avoid being thought a cheater and rejected. Similarly, if the

[7] The complications arise from the difficulty of arriving at satisfactory equilibrium concepts. As an illustration, one could argue that the active pooling equilibrium is not plausible. The cooperator would prefer to deviate if the receiver would cooperate with those who deviate, because the cooperator would then save the cost of the signal (earning $6 rather than $3). The receiver might in fact believe that anyone who deviates would be 90 percent likely a cooperator, because the cooperator and the cheater both do better by deviating than by signaling, assuming the receiver would in fact cooperate with someone who deviates, and given that both would do better, the receiver has no reason to believe that only a cheater would deviate. If the receiver did believe that anyone who deviates is 90 percent likely a cooperator, he would cooperate; therefore, the cooperator would, anticipating this, deviate. For a discussion of the equilibrium refinement used here, see Douglas G. Baird, Robert H. Gertner, & Randal C. Picker, Game Theory and the Law 255 (1994). If the cost from an unsuccessful deviation is high enough, however, the cooperator might find unacceptable the risk that the receiver would mistakenly reject him.

receiver's payoff from cooperating with a cheater is reduced by a sufficient amount, passive and active pooling can no longer be equilibria.

Changes in the Receiver's Beliefs about the Ratio of Types. Suppose there is a passive pooling equilibrium in which cooperation occurs. We saw that this is possible with the numbers used in the original example, and the result continues to hold if the receiver's payoff from cooperating with the cheater is even lower than in the original example, say, −$6. Suppose that a shock causes receivers to believe that 60 percent of all senders are cheaters, rather than 10 percent. In response, receivers will refuse to cooperate when types are not distinguishable (.4($6) + .6(−$6) = −$1.2 < 0). Now cooperators will deviate and salute the flag ($6 − $3 > 0). Cheaters will not deviate ($0 > $2 − $3). As a result, a separating equilibrium is formed. Receivers will not in the future correct their beliefs: since they cooperate only with those who salute the flag, and all those who salute the flag are cooperators, they will not learn the correct ratio.

B. *The Norm Entrepreneur*

The cooperation game requires that the signal be costly, but nothing about the game dictates the form of the signal. As long as an action is both actually and apparently costly, it can serve as a signal that the sender belongs to the high type. As noted above, gift giving, advertising, the purchase of fashions, and other forms of conspicuous consumption can serve as signals in the cooperation game. But signals can be ambiguous. Giving a gift or attending a parade does not reveal a person's discount rate if he or she enjoys these activities. The question is, then, how do certain behaviors take on symbolic value?

One answer draws on the idea of focal points.[8] Historical coincidence, physical qualities, and other attributes of a behavior can cause people to associate it with certain qualities of character. For example, April 19 has arisen, purely by chance, as a date on which an opponent of the government can distinguish himself by blowing up a building or engaging in other forms of protest. The coincidental occurrence of several significant conflicts between the government and right-wing opponents on that date has given it salience.

Other signals are fabricated. Martin Luther King Day, for example, was created by the federal government; it did not arise spontaneously. Once it was created, people could signal their loyalty to the civil rights movement by making gestures of respect on that day, in a publicly visible way.

Truly fabricated signals are rare. Usually, when the government or pri-

[8] See Thomas Schelling, The Strategy of Conflict 57 (1960).

vate individuals succeed in establishing certain actions as signals, they do so by drawing the public's attention to one of several conflicting focal points. To show respect for civil rights, should one have a holiday or some other celebration? Should it be in honor of King or another leader? Should it be on the date of King's birth or death or on the date of one of his accomplishments? History supplies a number of focal points; authoritative individuals enable citizens to coordinate around one.

To analyze these points more formally, we embed the cooperation or patriotism game in a larger game. Prior to the first move of the cooperation game, a "norm entrepreneur"[9] announces that a particular action will be a signal. The norm entrepreneur states that a particular action, for example, voting, will be understood as a signal of cooperativeness.[10] The cooperation game is modified in the following way. Each sender chooses among all possible signals. The sender might choose the signal recommended by the norm entrepreneur or might choose another signal. After the cooperation game is played, the norm entrepreneur receives a payoff that is a function of the number of people who issue the signal that he recommends. In some contexts it makes sense to say that the norm entrepreneur receives payoffs if he eliminates an active pooling equilibrium; in other contexts it makes sense to say that he receives payoffs if he transforms a passive pooling equilibrium into a separating equilibrium. The norm entrepreneur does not, ex ante, have full information about the payoffs of the parties in the cooperation game, so he cannot invariably choose the signal that maximizes his payoff. Because the game repeats itself, however, the norm entrepreneur can invent new signals in future rounds if earlier signals fail to yield high payoffs.[11]

In choosing among signals senders have only a rough idea of which signals will allow them to distinguish themselves from cheaters and which signals will not. They must also worry about whether the receiver will recognize the signal as an effort to distinguish oneself, as opposed to simply a pleasurable form of behavior. This is a coordination problem: as long as everyone, or most people, believe that certain behaviors serve as signals, and as long as these behaviors actually have the right cost structure, then

[9] The term is from Cass R. Sunstein, Social Roles and Social Norms, 96 Colum. L. Rev. 903, 909 (1996).

[10] This is cheap talk; see Joseph Farrell & Matthew Rabin, Cheap Talk, 10 J. Econ. Persp. 103 (1996).

[11] This approach is loosely related to Pesendorfer's model, in which a designer manufactures goods that will be used by consumers to signal status; the designer's payoff results just from the fact that many consumers will want to buy the goods, and some consumers will pay a premium for them, because their exclusivity allows them to signal status. See Pesendorfer, *supra* note 4.

these behaviors can act as signals. Senders will rely on custom (for example, gift giving on holidays), but also on meanings provided by the Zeitgeist (for example, anticommunism), and the suggestions of authoritative norm entrepreneurs narrow down the pool. As long as enough senders follow the suggestion of a person, he will become an authentic norm entrepreneur. (An important condition is salience: that is why even politically ignorant celebrities can make influential political and cultural announcements, and the descendants of royalty, no matter how undistinguished their abilities, could always find a following.)

The significance of the NE game, as I will call it, is that it shows that if a signal fails to create a separating equilibrium or an active pooling equilibrium, the norm entrepreneur has an incentive to create a new signal, in the hope that it will be more successful. But it also should be emphasized that signaling can arise spontaneously around random events that become focal (like April 19), with norm entrepreneurs playing no role. In either case, we will refer to the creation of new symbols to replace old symbols that fail to produce the appropriate equilibrium, as *symbol transformations.*

More realistically, many people—including politicians, academics, novelists, journalists, and other cultural players—compete to be a successful norm entrepreneur in the first round of the NE game. They propose signals; cooperators use the signal that seems most likely to create a separating equilibrium. There will be conflict and confusion, but pooling around a single signal may emerge, with benefits redounding to the norm entrepreneur(s) who proposed it.

We can now add a fourth alternative to the three methods for influencing signaling equilibria. When the state or a private norm entrepreneur successfully publicizes a new signal, people may substitute from an old signal to the new signal, and the new signal may change the equilibrium.[12]

C. *Why Patriotism?*

Unlike signals such as gift giving and advertising, patriotic signals appeal to national values. But the differences between these actions are superficial. Actions can be interpreted as a signal of one's desire to cooperate when they have some connection to the well-being of the receiver. When the pool of players consists of people in a social or business relationship, signals typically are actions that appeal to the pleasures and interests of the members of the group, which can be quite local and idiosyncratic (barbecues, fishing expeditions, ritual fasting and feasting, exchanges of gifts, and so

[12] This is analytically the same as changing the cost of the signal; only the interpretation differs.

on). When the pool of players consists of a nation, the actions must be thinner—they must not cause signficant offense or cost to most of the people in the country. In such circumstances, one finds two kinds of symbolic behavior: "pure" symbols, such as saluting the flag, whose benefits are entirely nonmaterial; and "impure" symbols, such as voting and discriminating against enemies of the country, which produce public goods that benefit all or most citizens. The latter are more focal, in the sense that we all recognize that a person who sacrifices himself for the country is a patriot; the former require a concerted effort to create and disseminate a tradition that everyone understands.

To explain why demonstrations of patriotism can serve as signals, it helps to use a stylized example. The McCarthy era arose suddenly after the successful explosion by the Soviet Union of a hydrogen bomb and the exposure of Soviet spies in the American government, events that heightened fears about the security of the United States and provoked concern about national cohesiveness. Even in ordinary business and social relationships far removed from international events, citizens will think that any person who engages in an action that weakens American security, however remotely, may be a "cheater." After all, cheaters prefer short-term gains to long-term payoffs, and the decline of a country is usually a slow and insidious thing. But it is not necessary to assume that people believe that any person who is a remote threat to the overall security of the United States cannot be trusted to deliver widgets on time or to help construct a new fence. It is enough to assume that some people will draw attention to their own loyalty by ostentatiously avoiding (or ostracizing) people who engage in actions that may be interpreted as unpatriotic, no matter how small and unthreatening these actions. If successful, anyone who wants to avoid being thought a cheater will pool around the actions, including ostracism of people thought to be cheaters, resulting in conformity to supposedly patriotic norms.

As the Soviet threat increased, then, people felt they could distinguish themselves from cheaters by refusing to criticize the government (or at least the hawks in the government), engaging in ostentatious patriotic displays, casting suspicion on immigrants and others whose connection to the United States was attenuated, and criticizing people who criticized American values and especially those who supported the communist ideology of the Soviet Union.

Notice that the significance of world events was twofold. First, they supplied the focal point, thus suggesting the form of the signal. If the Soviet Union is the threat, and the Soviet Union is controlled by communists, then maybe American communists are also a threat. Avoiding American communists thus reveals one's commitment to cooperation with noncommunist citizens. Second, world events may have enhanced the perceived need to avoid cheaters. In times of peace, entering a relationship with a cheater may not be so dangerous: they may cheat you, but little is at stake anyway. In times of war, entering a relationship with a cheater is dangerous: in cheating you, they make you vulnerable to heightened scarcity in the wartime economy if not also to hostile powers. McCarthy, a classic norm entrepreneur, exploited these fears. He did not fabricate the association between communism and subversion, but he did provide theories and "evidence" to strengthen people's suspicions. Before the McCarthy era, avoiding communists was not a powerful signal of loyalty. During the McCarthy era, it became such a powerful signal of loyalty that a separating equilibrium was created. Only after some years did this equilibrium collapse, when it became believed that the Soviet threat was exaggerated, or that the threat from cheaters was exaggerated, or that the cost of erroneously ostracizing people who were not cheaters was too high. As a result, it was not worthwhile to incur the cost of sending a patriotic signal, since one would obtain similar gains whether one did or not, and the separating equilibrium converted to a pooling equilibrium in which no one (or few people) sent patriotic messages and no one (or few people) inferred from the failure to send such a message that a particular person would be an unreliable partner.[13]

D. *Assumptions and Qualifications*

Senders and Receivers. One inelegant aspect of the model is the division of the population into receivers and senders, when in fact everyone is both a receiver and a sender. The rationale is that when deciding whether to signal, a person takes the rest of the population as given. The receiver can be thought of as the average person a sender expects to deal with, given that in any functional society most of the population consists of cooperators and a small fraction of the population consists of cheaters. The artificiality of these assumptions could be avoided by using a model in which everyone sends and receives signals,[14] but such a model would produce unnecessary complexity.

Cheaters. A person might gain little from cooperation because he has a high discount rate; but he also might gain little from cooperation because he does not desire that which others can offer or because the others demand as a signal of cooperativeness an action that this person finds unusually costly. Thus, the principled communist or liberal might refuse to show re-

[13] A brief overview of the McCarthy era can be found in McCarthyism (Thomas C. Reeves ed., 3d ed. 1989).

[14] See, for example, Pesendorfer, *supra* note 4; Camerer, *supra* note 4.

spect for the flag, or to engage in other supposedly patriotic actions, because he or she believes that the truly patriotic person is one who points out the deficiencies in the existing political system. The difference between a real cheater and, say, a principled liberal is crucial: the former does not care about the future while the latter cares about the future but believes that the required symbolic behavior is repugnant. But the two types are lumped together by the cooperator who is persuaded of the value of the signal. We return to this problem—the crudeness of signals—subsequently.[15]

The Reason for Signaling: The Payoff from Private Cooperation. The cooperation and patriotism models assume that citizens issue signals, even self-consciously political signals, in order to induce other citizens to cooperate with them. An alternative purpose for issuing political signals is to reveal one's political preferences to the government and other private citizens, in the hope of influencing the decisions of the former and the voting of the latter.[16] A third purpose for issuing political signals is to reveal one's costs to potential competitors.[17] These motives are probably important, but for simplicity I ignore them.

Note also that it is better to think of receivers cooperating *more* or *less* with citizens, rather than making an all or nothing choice.

Discrete versus Continuous Types and Actions. An alternative model might assume that people fall along a range of continuous types, with a few people being supercooperators and a few people being supercheaters, and everyone else clustering around a moderate position. It might also assume that people could send a range of patriotic or cooperative signals, from the very cheap to the very expensive. A model that made these assumptions rather than assuming dichotomous types and actions would probably not result in substantially different conclusions, for our purposes, though the model has not yet been well developed in the literature. A particularly nice aspect of such a model, however, is that it might show how continuous preferences result in discontinuous behavior, a result that is artificially generated in dichotomous models. The result is more persuasive also, as it suggests that if people do not fully conform, their behavior will still reflect the

[15] A further confusion arises because in a subcommunity people signal their loyalty to each other by engaging in actions that violate the dominant norms. Thus, a person may burn a flag in order to show other critics of the government that he is deeply committed and a worthy ally.

[16] See Susanne Lohmann, Information Aggregation through Costly Political Action, 84 Am. Econ. Rev. 518 (1994); Eric Rasmusen, Lobbying When the Decisionmaker Can Acquire Independent Information, 77 Pub. Choice 899 (1993).

[17] Glazer and Konrad argue that firms lobby for protective regulations as a way of signaling to a potential entrant that they have low marginal costs, thus deterring entry. Amihai Glazer & Kai A. Konrad, Strategic Lobbying by Potential Industry Entrants, 7 Econ. Pol. 167 (1995).

influence of the conformity of others.[18] This result is consistent with observed behavior; its significance will be discussed subsequently.[19]

III. State Regulation of Symbolic Behavior

When the state announces some prohibition, for example, a prohibition on the burning of American flags, we can distinguish two kinds of effect that the prohibition may produce. First, the law has an effect on behavior: it increases or decreases the amount of flag burning. This effect will be called the *behavioral* effect of the law. Second, the law might change people's understanding of the behavior it influences. For example, those who continue to burn flags after the law is enacted may be thought to be unpatriotic, whereas prior to the law they might have been thought less unpatriotic or just odd; or, conversely, those who continue to burn flags may be admired as civil libertarians, whereas prior to the law they might have been thought to be unpatriotic. The law's effect on people's beliefs about the kind of person who engages in a particular action will be called that law's *hermeneutic* effect.

The cooperation game shows the various ways in which a law's behavioral and hermeneutic effects are generated. We mentioned the four methods earlier. First, the law can modify the cost of sending a signal. Second, the law can modify the payoffs from cooperation. Third, the law can modify receivers' beliefs about the proportion of types in the population. Fourth, the law can modify the norm entrepreneur's payoff from constructing a signal or the law can construct a signal itself. These four effects in combination may produce a change in the equilibrium: the behavior in this new equilibrium represents the law's behavioral effect; the beliefs in this equilibrium represent the law's hermeneutic effect.

The following examples illustrate these phenomena. No effort is made to be systematic, however; the examples focus on different aspects of the models. Section IV draws together the threads.

A. *Flags*

One way to signal one's cooperativeness is to show respect for the flag. I will call "saluting the flag" any of a range of actions, including actually saluting the flag when the opportunity arises, displaying the flag, especially when done consistently with the complicated rituals, and so on. I will call "denigrating the flag" any gesture perceived as disrespect to the flag, from

[18] See B. Douglas Bernheim, A Theory of Conformity, 102 J. Pol. & Econ. 841 (1994).

[19] See Section IVA.

ignoring the flag when one should show respect for it, to burning it on the steps of the courthouse. Saluting a flag is costly. Although cooperators and cheaters incur the same cost in saluting the flag, cooperators earn higher returns when flag saluting functions as a signal, because receivers do not cut off relations when they discover the cooperators' type, whereas they do end relations with the cheaters. The cooperation game shows why enthusiasm for the flag waxes and wanes. In times of crisis the cost of being ostracized is so great that no one would risk the punishment that might result from deviation from active pooling. In times of security because receivers lose little from cooperating with cheaters, they will cooperate with anyone, so cheaters do not bother to salute the flag. But if receivers will cooperate with people who do not salute the flag, cooperators will not incur the cost of saluting the flag. In times of tension separating may occur, as only the cooperators find it profitable to salute the flag.

Does it make sense for receivers to believe that people who fail to show respect for the flag are not good cooperative partners? Yes, because of the association with soldiers who fight and die for the flag in a just war. Soldiers are the preeminent cooperators, sacrificing themselves for the sake of the nation. No, because soldiers do not fight for the flag (but, say, for the King), and the flag is (say) simply a means of identifying property of the country; or no, because the flag is associated with a particular *government,* not the nation, and that government is despised. Thus, in many countries the idea of a sacred flag is ridiculous, as is the idea of burning it, and indeed few national flags are burned outside the United States. The flag has become in the United States a focal point of cooperativeness at the national level (that is, patriotism) as a result of purely contingent circumstances and traditions that do not exist in most other countries.[20]

Any of the equilibria mentioned above may be desirable or not, because saluting the flag is an imperfect signal of propensity to engage in cooperation. Consider the separating equilibrium. Some people will show respect for the flag in order to obtain cooperative gains but still cheat when the time is right. People who believe that patriotism, rightly understood, requires nonparticipation in patriotic displays will decline to show respect for the flag because of the intrinsic costliness of doing so, and the gains from cooperating with them will be lost. As long as error is low enough that receivers gain by cooperating only with those who salute the flag, the equilibrium will be sustained. Notice also that when everyone salutes the flag to avoid being rejected, but it is generally believed that not everyone is a patriot,

[20] Another example comes from Turkey, where flag-waving and burning have recently become important political symbols. See Günter Seufert, The Sacred Aura of the Turkish Flag, 16 New Persp. on Turkey 53 (1997).

people will realize that some flag-wavers must be cheaters and that flag-waving is not a reliable signal of patriotism. Instead, flag-waving becomes a hollow ritual, and this may drive cooperators over time to abandon this signal—and the norm entrepreneur to create new ones (this is an example of *symbol transformation*).

The state, considered exogenously, can influence the flag-waving game in a variety of ways. First, the state can modify the cost of saluting the flag. Consider a law that not only illegalizes the burning of flags but requires people to show respect for the flag in various ways. (A law that *simply* banned the burning of flags would not impose any cost on the vast majority of people; its importance will be discussed in Section IVC.) Suppose that before the law is passed, a separating equilibrium exists. Cooperators show respect for flags; cheaters denigrate or even burn them. The law decreases the citizens' cost of saluting the flag by increasing the cost of substitutes, denigrating or ignoring the flag. Most plausibly, this change would create an active pooling equilibrium. Now that it costs so much *not* to send the signal, cheaters are forced to mimic the cooperators and send the signal.

However, the law could have a different effect on behavior. When the cost of *not* sending the signal rises, the receivers may anticipate that everyone—cooperators and cheaters alike—will show respect for the flag. This being the case, the receivers no longer can rely on respect for the flag as a reliable indicator of a person's type. If the receiver's loss from cooperating with a cheater is high enough, the receiver will refuse to cooperate with anyone when both types can afford to salute the flag. But if the senders anticipate this reaction, they will not bother to incur the cost of showing respect for the flag, even though the law has reduced this cost. Why incur this cost, if the receiver is not going to respond by cooperating? Accordingly, the law results in a passive pooling equilibrium, in which no one shows respect for the flag and no one cooperates with anyone else.

An additional complication arises when members of a deviant subcommunity show their commitment to each other by desecrating the flag. This action serves as an effective commitment mechanism because those who publicly desecrate the flag and are subsequently ostracized by members of the dominant community reduce the value of their opportunities outside their group, increase their incentive not to free ride on the group, and thus enhance their trustworthiness within the group. Thus, a law that punishes flag desecration could result in more, not less, flag desecration, and in the greater effectiveness of the antisocial activities of deviant groups.

Predicting the law's behavioral effect is impossible: it could increase the amount of respect shown for the flag or reduce it. The defender of flag desecration laws, however, might argue that the purpose of the law is to change beliefs, not behavior—to instill in people feelings of respect for the flag. But the hermeneutic effect of the law is likewise impossible to predict. Respect for the flag increases when people increasingly believe that only cooperators show respect for the flag. If the status quo equilibrium is passive pooling, and if the law creates a separating equilibrium, then the law might cause people to abandon their belief that flag saluters are odd or idiosyncratic people and accept the belief that they are cooperators and patriots. But if the status quo equilibrium is a separating equilibrium, and the purpose of the law is to enhance people's respect for the flag, the law may well fail. If it produces a passive pooling equilibrium, people will no longer associate saluting the flag with any character type. If the law produces an active pooling equilibrium, people will believe that everyone who waves a flag may be a cooperator *or* a cheater. We term this phenomenon *reification.* The law in this case ambiguates the meaning of the symbol, rather than increasing respect for the symbol. If the law's purpose is to enhance respect for the flag, then the law is self-defeating.

The complexity of predicting the effect of a flag-burning law on behavior and beliefs should be evident. One should doubt, then, the claim that a law against flag burning would have any predictable effect that would be socially desirable. Then why is there so much support in the United States for a law against flag burning? This question is answered in Section IV*C*.[21]

B. *Self-Censorship*

Self-censorship, like respect for the flag, may emerge as a signal of cooperativeness. In the struggle to find ways of distinguishing themselves as cooperators, people accuse critics of the government of being cheaters, while drawing attention to their own support of the government, by implication a signal of their patriotism. The average person may like to criticize the government or feel an obligation to do so; thus, not doing so will usually be a cost. But cooperators recover their cost through cooperation with receivers; cheaters may not. The association between self-censorship and patriotism arises frequently in countries, no doubt in part because of traditions of deference to authority, and no doubt in part because of the threat posed by internecine conflict to national survival in times of war. Norm entrepreneurs frequently exploit these circumstances.

The difference between self-censorship and respect for the flag is just a difference in the cost structure of the action. Some people might find self-censorship more costly, others might find respect for the flag more costly.

[21] For a different analysis of flag desecration issues, see Eric Rasmusen, The Economics of Desecration: Flag Burning and Related Activities, 27 J. Legal Stud. 245 (1988).

In any event, whether one action, the other, or both actions emerge as signals of cooperativeness depends on the various costs faced by the different types and the extent to which each signal is made focal by tradition and other circumstances.

The problem with self-censorship equilibria is that they may reduce the well-being of the population. This point is explored at length by Timur Kuran in a recent book,[22] so I will be brief. When the reputational costs are high enough, cheaters and serious-minded cooperators, who care deeply about the state but disagree with prevailing views, may avoid publicly criticizing the government, in which case valuable information is lost.[23] During the McCarthy era, when the cost of criticizing the government (or, at any rate, McCarthy and the policies he supported) became extremely high, many people—cooperators and cheaters alike—stopped criticizing the government, and in this equilibrium not only was socially valuable patriotic criticism lost, so was the valuable exposure of cheaters.

One of the most striking aspects of McCarthyism was that this campaign resulted from McCarthy's entrepreneurial modification of focal points, not from changes in the law. But we can also analyze the effect of a law, such as a censorship law. Imagine that a passive pooling equilibrium exists: no one censors himself. The state enacts a censorship law. If the law provides for the correct level of sanctions, it creates a separating equilibrium. The law has two effects one might care about: it reveals cheaters (the *internal* effect) and it discourages criticism of the government (the *external* effect). This is characteristic of all the laws under consideration. The pro-flag law reveals cheaters and it encourages respect for the flag. The censorship law may be more effective than the pro-flag law at exposing cheaters, but it may also cause more harm than the pro-flag law, because speech has valuable external effects that showing respect for the flag, for the most part, lacks.

The state can also produce or maintain separating equilibria or active pooling equilibria by influencing the receivers' beliefs about the fraction of cheaters in the population. Suppose that receivers believe that almost all people are cooperators and cooperate with everyone, so no one sends the signal of not criticizing the government. The government now warns the receivers that a lot of people are in fact cheaters. If the government is persuasive, the receivers may refuse to accept new cooperative partners (or, more realistically, they take precautionary measures that lower the gains to the sender); in response, the cooperators distinguish themselves as coopera-

[22] See Timur Kuran, Private Truths, Public Lies (1995).

[23] When the relevant community is not the nation, but a smaller community, such as the university or the small town, a similar result obtains. See, for example, Glenn C. Loury, Self-Censorship in Public Discourse, 6 Rationality & Soc. 428 (1994).

tors by declining to criticize the government. If cheaters would not be able to recover their costs, they will not mimic the cooperators, and a separating equilibrium is produced. Because receivers learn the types of only the senders they cooperate with, they will have no grounds for later revising their beliefs despite their inaccuracy.

Propaganda can be analyzed in another way. In the NE game the state can take the role of norm entrepreneur by issuing propaganda. By issuing propaganda the state creates an opportunity for people to signal their patriotism or subversion. The signal is self-censorship—resisting one's impulse to disagree with the propaganda. The more baldly untruthful the propaganda, the more clearly does a person signal his patriotism by declining to disagree with it. Official lies are in this way like a flag or a national holiday: they provide the opportunity for demonstrating one's loyalty to the government.

C. *Voting and Other Forms of Civic Participation*

Rational choice theorists have not produced a satisfactory explanation of why people vote. Given the vanishingly small chance of influencing the outcome of an election and the relatively high and certain cost of taking time from work and standing in line at the voting booth, one would expect people never to vote. Positing a "taste" for voting turns the problem into a tautology; other efforts to play with utility functions have not been satisfactory.[24] One might just assume a social norm in favor of voting, and work from there,[25] but this strategy transforms the question, Why do people vote? to the question, Why does a social norm require people to vote?

An adequate theory of voting behavior would take us too far afield, but we can sketch its outlines. The signal is the act of voting in the voting booth, not the vote in favor of one person or another. Voting is observable, even if the casting of the vote is not: one's friends, associates, and family members know that one voted, because one took time off work or simply told them that one did when duplicity would risk one's reputation or because one is seen waiting in line. The act of voting is costly both for the cooperator and for the cheater, but the cooperator recovers his costs through repeated rounds of cooperation with the receiver, while the cheater does not. In the separating equilibrium the voter is believed to be a cooperator, and the nonvoter is believed to be a cheater. This explanation turns the voting paradox on its head: voting functions as a signal precisely because the

[24] See Donald P. Green & Ian Shapiro, Pathologies of Rational Choice Theory 70 (1994).

[25] See, for example, Richard L. Hasen, Voting without Law? 144 U. Pa. L. Rev. 2135 (1996).

costs exceed the material gains. If voting were profitable, as would be the case if people were paid to vote or severely punished for not voting, or if everyone derived "expressive utility" from voting, then cooperators and cheaters would all vote. The motive for voting, on this theory, is not to satisfy some taste for voting, or for expressing one's views, or even for helping one's country—although all these motives would strengthen the patriot's incentive to vote—but to obtain cooperative returns from other private actors. Patriotism is relevant only as a theory of the origin of the psychological association of voting and cooperation.

One would expect a separating equilibrium in which the more cooperative people vote and the less cooperative decline to vote. In the United States many people disapprove of those who do not vote and admit it. This reaction is inexplicable under the theory that posits a taste for voting, whereas it follows from the signaling model: the disapproval expresses the receiver's view that you may not be a trustworthy person. Times of national emergency could stimulate a pooling equilibrium in which everyone (or nearly everyone) votes. The main reason for voting at such times is not that your single vote now matters (it still does not) but that it now matters if people think you are a cheater.

I do not have space to survey the evidence for and against the signaling theory of voting, but let me briefly mention a few pieces of evidence. First, the fact that voting increases with wealth and education[26] supports the signaling theory but contradicts the taste theory: an action can serve as a signal only if it is costly, and the cost of voting increases with one's opportunity costs. Second, voting increases with membership activity in organizations like parent-teacher associations, charitable organization, neighborhood organization, business organizations, interest groups, and unions[27]—all organizations that require cooperative behavior from their members. Third, respondents' frequent exaggeration of their voting behavior to pollsters suggests an embarrassment about admitting failure to vote, embarrassment that may express their concern about their reputation.[28]

[26] See Jan E. Leighley & Jonathan Nagler, Individual and Systematic Influences on Turnout: Who Votes? 1984, 54 J. Pol. 718 (1992); Garey C. Durden & Patricia Gaynor, The Rational Behavior Theory of Voting Participation: Evidence from the 1970 and 1982 Elections, 53 Pub. Choice 231 (1987).

[27] See Stephen Knack, Civic Norms, Social Sanctions and Voter Turnout, 4 Rationality & Soc. 133, 143 (1992). In one poll 41 percent of regular voters agreed with the following reason for voting: "My friends and relatives almost always vote and I'd feel uncomfortable telling them I hadn't voted." *Id.* at 137.

[28] Stanley Presser & Michael Traugott, Little White Lies and Social Science Models, 56 Pub. Opinion Q. 77 (1992); see also Hasen, *supra* note 25, at 2160–61.

Some countries penalize nonvoters with small fines; Italy posts the names of nonvoters in a public area. All of these countries enjoy a high voting rate.[29] But while both kinds of law effectively reduce the relative cost of the signal, voting, the first method relies on the legal bureaucracy whereas the latter exploits social sanctions that exist independently of the law.

Hand-wringing about low voter turnout is often scoffed at, because it could mean that people are relatively satisfied with the political status quo. The problem, however, is that because of peace and prosperity, it matters less if one is believed to be a cheater, so people do not bother to vote as a signal of patriotism. If, as a result, voter turnout falls, there will be undersupplied information about the preferences of citizens, leading to mistaken actions by politicians. However, equilibria in which many or all people vote are not necessarily desirable, either. People who vote solely for reputational reasons will not take their vote seriously, failing to inform themselves about the various candidates and voting instead on the basis of the mellifluousness or familiarity of the candidates' names.

D. *Discrimination on the Basis of Race, Ethnicity, and Religion*

Discrimination against members of a minority group can serve as a signal of cooperativeness or "patriotism." Because members of the out-group have skills and other desirable qualities, refusal to deal with them commercially or socially is costly for a member of the in-group. As long as other members of the in-group recognize that discriminatory action constitutes self-sacrifice for the sake of their group, a separating or active pooling equilibrium can emerge.[30]

But why would people think that discrimination against minorities is a signal of cooperativeness? Sometimes, the answer is simply that the members of the outcast group have social or ancestral connections with a group that is unambiguously a threat to the majority group. Examples include Americans of Japanese origin after the bombing of Pearl Harbor, and people of Serbian ancestry living in Croatia or Bosnia. Sometimes, the answer is that the members of the outcast group compete with members of the majority group for scarce resources. If black migration threatens the power of whites in the labor market, then whites can demonstrates their loyalty to each other by discriminating against blacks. Sometimes, a minority group

[29] Hasen, *supra* note 25, at 2169–71.

[30] The theory does not assume a "taste for discrimination" (Gary S. Becker, The Economics of Discrimination (2d ed. 1973)), or that physical traits are used as a proxy for unobservable characteristics (Kenneth J. Arrow, The Theory of Discrimination, in Discrimination in Labor Markets (Orley Ashenfelter & Albert Rees eds. 1973)).

prospers while the majority does poorly, and the source of the minority group's prosperity is not understood but can be loosely connected to the majority's problems. Jewish dominance of the credit market and other important markets in European history gave Jews political power out of proportion to their numbers, a result that was used to justify theories of their harmful influence. These phenomena are self-reinforcing: when members of an out-group do well in a market or in a society, they become suspect, and members of the larger society discriminate against them to show their loyalty to each other, but this makes it even more important for out-group members to rely on each other, enhancing their trust and their mutual gains, leading to further discrimination against them by the insiders.[31]

Discrimination against groups for purely self-interested motives is often rationalized. A common rationalization that supports the use of discrimination is a theory of racial or ethnic superiority, and such theories are endlessly supplied by norm entrepreneurs. That these theories are transparently false (it cannot be the case that the Serbs are superior to the Croats, as the Serbs believe, and that the Croats are superior to the Serbs, as the Croats believe, or that the Aryans are superior to the Slavs, as the Nazis believed, and yet that Slavs are superior to everyone else, and so on) shows that the forces that drive people into signaling equilibria are more powerful than the desire for truth. Just as one shows one's patriotism in a totalitarian country by endorsing its obviously wrong propaganda (the more obviously wrong, the more effective the signal), one shows one's patriotism in a fascist country by participating in collective discrimination against minorities even when one has warm feelings toward them or the minorities are defined in an obviously arbitrary way.[32] The signaling theory thus emphasizes the arbitrariness of state ideologies, be they ethnic, religious, or nationalistic. What counts as a signal depends on the importance of cooperation for individuals (which rises and falls with fluctuations in economic and political circumstances), the historical accidents that create associations between certain kinds of behavior and certain kinds of people, and the relative costs of the actions that are made salient by these associations. This is in contrast with views that people with certain characteristics, such as ethnicity and race, "naturally" belong together under one government. Indeed, the signaling

[31] See Eric A. Posner, The Regulation of Groups: The Influence of Legal and Nonlegal Sanctions on Collective Action, 63 U. Chi. L. Rev. 133 (1996).

[32] Compare Richard H. McAdams, Cooperation and Conflict: The Economics of Group Status Production and Race Discrimination, 108 Harv. L. Rev. 1003, 1039–40 (1995). He relies on an assumption that people seek status, that is, they derive utility from being wealthier than other people. The signaling theory does not make this assumption, instead relying on the usual assumptions about preferences. Status, in this model, is endogenous: one has status if one has the reputation for being a desirable cooperative partner.

theory shows how ethnicity and race are inventions that respond to the demand for criteria that facilitate cooperation against potential threats.[33]

The social cost of this behavior is obvious, but it is worth mentioning that, unlike the examples of flag burning, self-censorship, and voting, the signal is an injury to a third party who is not a player in the game. The members of the minority are not the "cheaters"; those who fail to discriminate against them are the "cheaters." Although any theory that justifies the view that people who fail to discriminate against a certain group are cheaters will almost certainly conclude that members of that group are cheaters as well, special venom is directed to the insider who breaks ranks and treats outsiders with respect.[34]

It is unnecessary to repeat the analysis of equilibria, and instead I will quickly mention examples of each of the four kinds of laws described above. First, antidiscrimination laws raise the cost of sending the signal, thus possibly reducing the amount of discrimination. Second, because whites were required to ostracize a white who treated blacks as equals in the South[35] (this was a social norm, not a law), a receiver's payoff from cooperating with a white person who cooperated with blacks would decline by the expected sanction to the receiver for violating the norm of ostracism. Third, the use of propaganda to convince citizens of an internal threat from people *not* belonging to the minority (that is, the cheaters) could enhance incentives to engage in discrimination as a way of showing people that one is not such a cheater. Fourth, the state can, as a norm entrepreneur, attempt to establish the signal in the first place—for example, endorsing or rejecting doctrines of racial superiority and placing religious symbols on public property.

The signaling theory helps explain the rapidity with which norms of discrimination change. Jews had been assimilated in German society decades before the rise of Hitler; a few years later, they were outcasts. Blacks had been outcasts in American society centuries before the civil rights movement; within a generation, the most obvious forms of discrimination had vanished. It is possible that these changes were due to fundamental changes in attitude, but the rapidity of the change, and the widespread feeling, especially among minorities, that the changes have been shallow, suggest the influence of signaling equilibria.

[33] The theory is thus consistent with the view that nations are "imagined communities"; see Benedict Anderson, Imagined Communities (1983); and historiography that emphasizes the contingency of the nation-state, for example, Eric J. Hobsbawm, Nations and Nationalism since 1780 (1990).

[34] See McAdams, *supra* note 32, at 1039–40; Timur Kuran, Ethnic Norms and Their Transformation through Reputational Cascades, in this issue, at 623.

[35] See McAdams, *supra* note 32.

More should be said about the state's role as a norm entrepreneur. Official pronouncements play an important role, because officials enjoy the attention of the nation and thus can cheaply create focal points—for example, Hitler spinning out theories of Jewish influence. The effectiveness of politicians in this way accounts for the heavily symbolic content of so much political behavior. Officeholders and candidates for office must endlessly shake hands with, march in parades with, and attend the ceremonies of people who belong to powerful ethnic organizations, because once a politician associates himself with a minority group, attempts by him later to exploit circumstances and blame national problems on that group will lack credibility. If the group were so evil, the politician's earlier association with it would count against him.

The norm entrepreneur recognizes that a threat to the social order is presented when the minority becomes invisible: laws defining the minority can prevent the signal from becoming too costly. The yellow star in Nazi Germany and antimiscegenation laws in the United States minimize the cost of signaling by eliminating ambiguity about whom one should discriminate against. Jim Crow laws enabled whites to signal racial discrimination, by giving them an opportunity, never taken, to publicly display their rejection of racial norms. These laws do not so much enforce segregation as constantly remind everyone that everyone else is sending the signal. Otherwise, bad memory, the potential gains from cooperating with minorities, and the ambiguity of behavior would over time diminish the effectiveness of the signal.

When any of these factors eliminates the effectiveness of a signal at identifying cheaters, while the felt need to identify cheaters remains, the norm entrepreneur will search out new signals.[36] The most striking examples of the resulting symbol transformation come, again, from the history of anti-Semitism in Europe. In Spain in the fourteenth century and again in Germany and elsewhere in the nineteenth century, discrimination on the basis of the Jewish religion lost its effectiveness at causing separation. In Spain the reason was that persecution drove Jews to emigrate or convert to Christianity; in Germany the reason was that theological grounds for discrimination lost their plausibility as the influence of religion declined generally. But the great need in both countries for national unity provoked a demand for a method for distinguishing the loyal from the disloyal, and this demand stimulated the development of a new theory. The new theory would be based on race, not religion. People who used to practice Jewish rituals or whose parents practiced Jewish rituals were classified as racial Jews. This

[36] The politicization of race by political entrepreneurs is discussed in Jennifer Roback, Racism as Rent Seeking, 27 Econ. Inquiry 661 (1989).

approach dealt with the problems created by demographic and theological trends by redefining the body of people who could be the subject of discrimination. Norm entrepreneurs promoted racial theories to supplement (in Spain) or replace (in Germany) the religious theories.[37]

IV. Some Themes

A. *Positive Implications*

As noted earlier, the laws and official pronouncements of the state can influence equilibria in four ways. First, a law typically influences the relative costs of sending a signal. An antidiscrimination law increases the cost of signaling patriotism through discrimination; a censorship law reduces the cost of signaling patriotism by not criticizing the government. Second, a law may influence the cooperative payoffs for sender and receiver. An example would be a law that taxes employers who hire critics of the government or people who violate widespread norms of racial exclusion. Third, a law may influence the receiver's beliefs about the proportion of types in the population. Propaganda produces this effect through persuasion; other laws, such as laws that deport or imprison people who belong to the wrong type, change the receiver's beliefs by changing the actual proportion of types. Fourth, a law may influence or crowd out efforts by norm entrepreneurs to construct new signals; laws and official acts create new signals or refine existing ones by providing opportunities to send the signal or by increasing its visibility.

In predicting the effect of a law, one must take account of several complications. First, the effect of a law depends on the status quo equilibrium. A censorship law imposed on an active pooling equilibrium may have no effect on behavior; but imposed on other equilibria, it may cause a significant change in behavior. Second, the effect of a law even on a given equilibrium may be unpredictable: as we saw in Section IIIA, a law that reduces the cost of a signal may produce an active pooling equilibrium, but it also may produce a passive pooling equilibrium. Third, a single law may influence equilibrium behavior through more than one of the four routes mentioned in the prior paragraph. A law against flag burning may both reduce

[37] See B. Netanyahu, The Origins of the Inquisition in Fifteenth Century Spain 1052–54 (1995). Netanyahu puts more emphasis on the interest of the majority in seizing economic and political power from the Jews (in Spain, the conversos), than on the importance of cooperating on a national level, but he does elsewhere identify the demand for national unity in Spain as an important cause of the persecution of the conversos. *Id.* at 1004. Spain united around its opposition to the Jews; when religious Jews vanished, racial Jews had to be invented.

the relative cost of flag-waving and increase the cost of flag-waving (for cheaters) by more firmly associating it with patriotic activity. The effects can thus be offsetting, but they can also be reinforcing. Fourth, a law designed to eliminate undesirable signaling equilibria in the dominant community may have perverse effects on behavior in deviant communities. This is the paradox illustrated most vividly by laws that punish discrimination and flag desecration. By increasing the cost of these activities, the law makes them viable commitment mechanisms in deviant or alienated groups, resulting in an increase in the undesirable activity rather than a reduction, at least among the members of those groups.

Two other complications are discontinuity and symbol transformation. To understand the problem of discontinuity, imagine an active pooling equilibrium in which everyone discriminates against members of a minority group. Assume that "tastes" for discrimination are distributed uniformly: many people would like not to discriminate but suppress their inclinations to avoid being ostracized. A law is enacted that prohibits discrimination against minorities. If the sanction is small, it is unlikely to affect behavior: the cost of ostracism exceeds the cost of the sanction. As the sanction is gradually increased, discrimination does not change by much. As long as the reputational sanction exceeds the legal sanction, behavior is unaffected except for those with the most extreme preferences. But at some threshold, when the legal sanction exceeds the reputational sanction, the amount of discrimination will decline discontinuously. The reason is that once people with the stronger preferences against discrimination deviate from the active pooling equilibrium in sufficient numbers, the reputational sanction disappears, and all the people who would cooperate with the members of the minority group but for the existence of the reputational sanction will stop discriminating.[38] This phenomenon means that a law that has a small sanction (or even no sanction, like an announcement by an official) may have a disproportionate influence on behavior, and a law that has a large sanction may have little or no influence on behavior. Social norms are robust, but they are also delicate.[39]

Symbol transformations occur because exogenous changes cause old signals to fail, eliminating the ability of receivers to distinguish cooperators and cheaters and thus giving cooperators and norm entrepreneurs an incentive to discover new signals to replace the old signals. We have already discussed the substitution from discrimination on the basis of religion to discrimination on the basis of race, the latter becoming a signal of loyalty

[38] Compare Bernheim, *supra* note 18; Kuran, *supra* note 34.

[39] See Sunstein, *supra* note 9, at 909.

when the former lost its effectiveness. Another example, which is presented in stylized form, comes from the McCarthy period. At roughly the same time McCarthy was making the connection between communism and subversion, others were asserting a connection between homosexuality and subversion. Thanks to the widely read Kinsey report and the social and demographic dislocations caused by World War II, it suddenly became evident that a lot of people engaged in homosexual behavior, just as a lot of people supported communism. Because refusing to cooperate with identifiable homosexuals is costly, discrimination could serve as a signal of cooperativeness. But for this signal to function properly, it was necessary for people to believe that discrimination expressed a desire to signal cooperativeness rather than a moral conviction, prejudice, or taste. Norm entrepreneurs had to draw the connection between homosexuality and subversion, and this was done in a variety of ways—by appealing to traditional moral and religious antipathy to homosexual behavior while claiming the importance of unity for national security and by claiming that homosexuals corrupted youth on whose ''manliness'' the nation relied.[40] But because homosexuals were no more a threat than anyone else, and because it was therefore not much more costly for a real cheater to discriminate against a homosexual than it was for a patriot, something like an active pooling equilibrium resulted. Sweeping legal and nonlegal attacks on homosexuality paralleled the mostly unofficial attacks on communists.[41]

Symbol transformation occurs when one signal (self-censorship) fails to expose cheaters, perhaps because of exogenous changes in payoffs, resulting in the substitution to or the addition of another signal (discrimination against homosexuals). The irony is that if any American citizens posed a threat to the United States in the 1950s, it is more likely that communists and other political critics did than homosexuals, and yet discrimination against homosexuals proved to be a far more powerful equilibrium than discrimination against communists. The reason is probably that this country's traditions prior to the 1960s supported political freedom and religious conformity much more than sexual freedom, so self-censorship was a less reliable indication of patriotism—indeed, could be interpreted as a failure of patriotism—than discrimination against homosexuals.

B. *Normative Implications*

When a law generates a new signaling equilibrium, one evaluates the law by comparing the new equilibrium with the old equilibrium. In doing so,

[40] John D'Emilio, Sexual Politics, Sexual Communities: The Making of a Homosexual Minority in the United States, 1940–1970 (1983).

[41] *Id.*

one should take account of both the behavioral and hermeneutic effects of the law.

1. *The Behavioral Effect.* It is well known that signaling equilibria cannot be ranked according to their contribution to social welfare without information about the costs and benefits of each kind of equilibrium. A separating equilibrium might at first appear to be superior to a pooling equilibrium because information is revealed, and information is often valuable; but it is possible that the gains from information disclosure in a given separating equilibrium are less than the costs of signaling. It is also possible that an active pooling equilibrium is superior to the separating equilibrium, since revelation of information may reduce incentives to generate value.[42] Because one cannot generalize about the costs and benefits of each kind of equilibrium with any accuracy, I have resisted making conclusions about the overall welfare gains from converting one equilibrium into another.

Still, we can draw three useful generalizations. First, there is a tension between the motive that causes a person to take an action and that action's contribution to a public good; and there is a tension between two kinds of public goods produced by an action—the revelation of information, on the one hand, and the production of some other public good, on the other. For example, a person may vote or engage in self-censorship from the motive of signaling his cooperativeness or patriotism. Voting, happily, produces an *external* public good (revelation of political preferences); self-censorship produces an external public bad (concealment of political preferences). Both kinds of action produce an *internal* public good, namely, the exposure of cheaters. But even here the cost of signaling may exceed the benefits of that information. There is nothing intrinsically socially beneficial about signaling: sometimes it is beneficial, sometimes it is not.

Second, signals are crude, and even equilibria that might be considered broadly socially beneficial result in some undesirable behavior. Some politically uninformed people vote to avoid reputational sanctions. It would be more desirable if they followed their nonreputational preferences and did not vote. When self-censorship equilibria arise, political stability is established, and this may be important in times of war, but cooperators with valid criticisms of the government will be silenced along with the cheaters.

Third, when signaling equilibria are beneficial, we can expect them to occur too rarely. The reason is that a signal is a public good. (This is not true in standard signaling models, but they do not account for the ambiguity of actions that may serve as signals.) To be established, everyone has to recognize that certain actions are cheaper for some types than for others;

[42] See Andreu Mas-Colell, Michael D. Whinston, & Jerry R. Green, Microeconomic Theory 455–57 (1995).

but because the benefits of the signal are enjoyed by everyone, whereas the costs of making this connection are born by a few (the norm entrepreneurs, the gossips), there will be too few kinds of signals that are available for use.[43] For similar reasons, harmful equilibria occur more rarely than they would if signals were not produced through collective efforts.

2. *The Hermeneutic Effect: The Creation of Social Meaning and the Problem of Reification.* When the law changes a separating equilibrium into an active pooling equilibrium, people stop associating the signal with cooperativeness or patriotism and instead associate the signal with not-being-a-cheater. If we care about the "social meaning" of the action that serves as a signal, this result may be undesirable. This is the difference between putting an American flag on your house in an American suburb and raising it in a hostile foreign country, or the difference between criticism of the authorities in a democracy and criticism of the authorities in a dictatorship, or the difference between wearing a pink triangle on a college campus in the 1990s and doing so in the 1970s or early 1980s. Because everyone or almost everyone issues the signal, it no longer distinguishes some people from others. The "social meaning" of an action, which can be defined as the belief that the average receiver has about the type of person who engages in that action,[44] has become *reified.*

When the law changes a separating equilibrium into a passive pooling equilibrium, the signal disappears. Veterans of wars complain that people do not take the flag as seriously now as they used to. Then, the signal, though reified, was not meaningless: few people failed to salute the flag, but those who did fail to salute the flag were necessarily cheaters, so those who did not were at least possibly cooperators. Now, in many circles saluting the flag is almost meaningless. The observer assumes that the person who salutes the flag is old-fashioned or even a bit dotty—a person with strange tastes. When so few people issue a signal that the observer no longer associates that signal with a particular type, the social meaning has been *destroyed.*

When the state converts a passive pooling equilibrium into a separating equilibrium, it produces social meaning. An action that previously had little significance now has a great deal. Saluting a piece of cloth displaying stars and stripes had no significance prior to the Revolutionary War; later, it would have a great deal. Discrimination against those who engage in homosexual behavior is seen initially as a reaction to a practice believed to be

[43] See Lawrence Lessig, The Regulation of Social Meaning, 62 U. Chi. L. Rev. 943 (1995).

[44] Compare *id.*

immoral; after state action it is seen as an expression of patriotism. A social meaning is *created.*[45]

But for all the emphasis of the role of the state, social meanings can emerge and disappear spontaneously, and often in the face of state efforts to regulate them. To see why, suppose at time 1 there is a separating equilibrium, and cooperators salute the flag just to show that they are cooperators. At time 2 the state enacts a law that punishes people who fail to salute the flag. At time 3 there is an active pooling equilibrium, created by the cheaters' desire to avoid the punishment. But at time 3 saluting the flag is no longer a reliable signal of patriotism. If many people salute the flag just to avoid the sanction, then those who salute the flag are not necessarily cooperators; the salute becomes reified. In the patriotism game, both types continue to salute the flag, the cooperators fearing that if they fail to salute they will be mistaken for cheaters. But over time many people, cooperators or not, will begin to recognize saluting the flag as the empty ritual that it has become. Saluting the flag becomes an embarrassment, because everyone knows that people salute the flag just to avoid legal punishment. Some will conceal their embarrassment behind a mask of irony, but under such conditions the meaning of the salute may eventually *flip,* becoming instead a signal of fear of legal punishment rather than a signal of patriotism.[46] The person who salutes is slavishly obedient, fearful to offend the authorities or other people; the person who declines to salute has integrity and independence—has an authentic cooperative nature. Failing to salute the flag becomes a better signal of patriotism than saluting the flag, and I believe that in some circles this is the case.

The *politicization* of behavior occurs with the creation of a law that requires people to engage in some behavior in which previously they had engaged voluntarily. People already salute the flag or pray at ceremonies; then a law is created that requires exactly the same behavior. At first sight, one would expect the law not to affect behavior, perhaps even to intensify it. But the law may flip the signal, so that the sender fears that others will

[45] The creation of social meanings through spontaneous behavior on the part of the masses, but guided and exploited by norm entrepreneurs, helps explain the phenomenon of "invented traditions." The paradoxical connotation arises because old behaviors provide focal points which people use to signal their devotion to a new political entity. Wearing a kilt is distinctively Scottish in the sense that people in no other nations wear a kilt; but it only becomes a symbol of Scottish nationalism after later changes in social conditions made possible a Scottish "community," through which cooperative gains could be obtained. Then, norm entrepreneurs create further refinements of the signal by, for example, elaborating (entirely fictionally) on the connection between tartans and clans. See The Invention of Tradition (Eric J. Hobsbawm & Terence Ranger eds. 1983), especially Trevor-Roper's chapter on Scottish traditions.

[46] Compare Kuran, *supra* note 22.

think that he engages in the behavior to comply with the law, rather than to express patriotism or religious fervor. The result may or may not be that people stop engaging in the behavior—that depends on the size of the sanctions and other parameters. The important conclusion for present purposes is that politicization destroys important social meanings by legally compelling behavior that derives its meaning in part from the fact that it is not required by law. This argument is an analogy to the argument that the *commodification* of goods and services through the market destroys social meanings when a behavior derives its meaning from the fact that it is given freely.[47]

C. *Endogenizing the State*

Several recent articles argue that the state has an important role in managing norms and social meanings. Norms, social meanings, and similar phenomena create externalities that cannot be bargained over. Because the market should thus be expected to undersupply socially desirable norms and social meanings, the state should either supply them itself or encourage their supply through legal incentives.[48]

To see a problem with this argument, suppose that everyone engages in self-censorship in order to avoid being labeled a cheater. This active pooling equilibrium does not serve the interest of most people, but every citizen is afraid to deviate. Now we might say that here is a collective action problem that the government could solve: for example, by subsidizing the publication of newspapers and journals, giving politicians free air time, enacting special legal immunities against charges of libel and slander, and granting other privileges and subsidies. The question is why we should expect the government to engage in any of these actions. The problem is not just that government officials may enjoy the lack of criticism. The problem is that if the government officials proposed these laws, their support for them would be taken as a signal that they are cheaters. Citizens will not lobby the government to enact these laws, because they fear that their lobbying—a violation of the self-censorship norm—would be taken as a signal that they are cheaters. We cannot expect the government to change socially undesirable social meanings when these meanings are sufficiently powerful.

These considerations return us to the question raised at the start of this article: why do people seek laws against flag burning when flag burning

[47] Compare Margaret Jane Radin, Market-Inalienability, 100 Harv. L. Rev. 1849 (1987).

[48] Lessig, *supra* note 43; Sunstein, *supra* note 9; Richard H. Pildes, The Unintended Cultural Consequences of Public Policy: A Comment on the Symposium, 89 Mich. L. Rev. 936 (1991).

causes no "real" harm? One answer is that citizens signal their patriotism not only by engaging in patriotic activity but by lobbying or at least passively showing support for laws that punish people who engage in unpatriotic activity. The second follows from the first as a matter of logic, and since the signal, political support, is still relatively cheap, an active pooling equilibrium can result. Once *support* for a law against flag burning is taken as a signal of one's patriotism, elected government officials cannot afford the political consequences of opposing such a law, nor can legal academics who hope for appointment to an important government position.[49]

A problem with government-led norm entrepreneurship is that it produces wasteful competition for government resources. Competing groups treat the government as an instrument for conveying their symbols. An important example concerns the placement of religious symbols on public property. The problem is that observers understand that the symbol represents the successful lobbying efforts of one religious group and thus that this religious group has significant political influence. This inference causes receivers to assume that members of the religious group exist in great numbers or that they have great power—in either case, they are likely to be attractive (or unavoidable) cooperative partners. Thus, attempts by members of the majority to use discrimination against members of this group as a signal of loyalty or patriotism will fail. It is thus in the interest of religious groups to compete for influence over the government's decision to use religious symbols. Constitutional restrictions on establishment deter wasteful competition among religious groups over the use of the government as an instrument for recruiting members through its endorsement of their beliefs.[50] The free exercise clause and equal protection rules, to some extent,

[49] These observations may be used to lay the foundation of a more general theory of ideology, which would state the conditions under which people endorse (even in great numbers) political positions that are contrary to their interests. The germ of such a theory can be found in Kuran, *supra* note 22; and Loury, *supra* note 23; and see also Timur Kuran, Preference Falsification, Policy Continuity and Collective Conservatism, 97 Econ. J. 642 (1987). But this must be the subject of future research. A brief discussion can be found in Eric A. Posner, The Strategic Basis of Principled Behavior: A Critique of the Incommensurability Thesis, 146 U. Pa. L. Rev. (1998), in press.

[50] For a general discussion, see Eric A. Posner, The Regulation of Religious Groups, 2 Legal Theory 33 (1996). Objections to certain forms of "expressive" conduct by the government are thus derived from basic fears that such conduct will lead to changes in beliefs of private citizens that will reduce one's ability to enter into cooperative relationships. A person opposes legal endorsements of the views of a particular group, even if this law does not cause a direct injury to him, because the legal endorsement may stimulate a shift in attitudes that will injure him. This motivation more likely lies behind objections to race-based gerrymandering than general moral objections to "value reductionism." See Richard H. Pildes & Richard G. Niemi, Expressive Harms, "Bizarre Districts," and Voting Rights: Evaluating Election-District Appearances after Shaw v. Reno, 92 Mich. L. Rev. 483 (1993).

protect members of minority religions against the kind of discrimination that would stimulate the pursuit of political power in the first place.

V. Conclusion: Symbols and Social Norms

Because the term, "social norm," is used in ordinary language to refer to many different kinds of behavior, understanding social norms requires the use of different models in different contexts.[51] In this article, I have argued that an important class of social norms arises from signaling games in which people choose actions that signal loyalty to states and communities. Because people often engage in a particular behavior only in order to show that they are loyal, that behavior has the peculiarly empty quality of a symbol: people take little or no pleasure from the behavior, but engage in it for the sake of reputation. Notice that the social norm is endogenous to the model: the social norm describes the behavior that arises in equilibrium. It is not that X punishes Y for violating a social norm; rather, X (and many other people) avoids Y because Y's behavior reveals to X that association with Y will not serve X's interests. Although in common speech we say that Y's behavior violates a social norm, the punishment is endogenous, not imposed by an external force.[52]

The article contributes to the literature on law and social norms in three ways. First, it incorporates symbolic behavior in the general analysis. Second, it shows the ways in which a signaling model sheds light on the relationship between laws and social norms. The article argues that signaling is crucial to understanding social norms. The main alternative, the repeat game model, can explain how cooperation is possible, but it does not explain how patterned or norm-influenced behavior arises. Most other discussions of social norms in the legal literature differ in two important ways: by making exogenous assumptions about why people cooperate, and by *endogenizing* preferences.[53] For reasons that should be clear, I claim that this approach is backward. One can make a great deal of progress in explaining

[51] For a discussion of different possible models, see Eric A. Posner, Efficient Norms, in The New Palgrave Dictionary of Economics and the Law (Peter Newman ed. 1998), in press.

[52] Thus, one avoids the second-order prisoner's dilemma (see Jon Elster, The Cement of Society: A Study of Social Order, 132–33 (1989)) that results from the theory, rejected here, that social norms are enforced by purposive collective action.

[53] For example, Sunstein, *supra* note 9; Lessig, *supra* note 43. See also Robert Cooter, Structural Adjudication and the New Law Merchant: A Model of Decentralized Law, 14 Int'l Rev. L. & Econ. 215 (1994); and Robert Cooter, Normative Failure Theory of Law, 82 Cornell L. Rev. 947 (1997), which combine an evolutionary theory of behavior and a theory of internalization of norms. Another approach derives social norms from the assumption that people desire status for its own sake. See Richard H. McAdams, The Origin, Development, and Regulation of Norms, 96 Mich. L. Rev. 338 (1997); see also Bernheim, *supra* note 18.

law and behavior without resorting to arguments about preferences, which are notoriously difficult to analyze. Third, the article shows several ways in which social norms can be pathological or inefficient.[54]

The latter point suggests, of course, the possibility of desirable state intervention, but we have also seen several reasons for skepticism about proposals to involve the state in self-conscious efforts to "regulate" social meaning. First, government officials do not stand outside the signaling game. They, like citizens, are prisoners of symbols when the symbols are sufficiently powerful. Truman and Eisenhower were powerless to resist McCarthy at his height, because any effort to criticize McCarthy would have been interpreted as a signal of the presidents' pusillanimity, even sympathy, toward America's enemies. Second, the results of government efforts to change or sustain symbols, whether through legal devices or official exhortation, are inherently unpredictable. Thus, government efforts to change signals can backfire, leading to a strengthening of symbols that the government sought to change (a possible example is Clinton's efforts to increase acceptance of gays in the military), or to reification of the desired symbol (a possible effect of a law banning flag desecration). And when government efforts, whether deliberately or not, destroy or reify existing symbols, norm entrepreneurs will propose new symbols that may have worse effects than the old ones. When searching for examples of successful government-led efforts to exploit symbolic behavior, one repeatedly finds the most vivid triumphs in the histories of fascist and totalitarian states—not attractive models for the United States, a country in which the most striking successes in norm entrepreneurship have been achieved by nongovernmental movements such as civil rights, feminism, and religious evangelism.

[54] Compare Eric A. Posner, Law, Economics, and Inefficient Norms, 144 U. Pa. L. Rev. 1697 (1996); Posner, *supra* note 51; but compare Robert Ellickson, Order without Law: How Neighbors Settle Disputes (1991).

Positive Political Theory

[11]

The Article I, Section 7 Game

WILLIAM N. ESKRIDGE, JR.*
AND JOHN FEREJOHN**

Article I, Section 7, Clause 2 of the Constitution provides that "[e]very Bill which shall have passed the House of Representatives and the Senate, shall, before it becomes a law, be presented to the President of the United States" who may veto the bill; a vetoed bill can become law only if two-thirds of those voting in both chambers of Congress approve the bill, notwithstanding the President's objections.[1] This provision, together with Clause 3, codify the so-called bicameralism and presentment requirements for statute-making under the Constitution. For most of our history, bicameralism and presentment played little role in constitutional discourse. That changed in the 1980s. Article I, Section 7 figured prominently in several important constitutional debates in the Supreme Court during the last ten years.

Early in the decade, the Supreme Court in *INS v. Chadha*[2] held that a single-chamber legislative veto of an adjudicative decision violates Article I, Section 7. The Court rested its holding in *Chadha* upon the Framers' "original intent" that "the bicameral requirement and the Presentment Clauses would serve essential constitutional functions" that would be violated by "lawmaking" through action of only one chamber of Congress *or* without presentment to the President.[3] Confirmed by subsequent summary disposi-

---

* Professor of Law, Georgetown University Law Center.

** Patrick Suppes Family Professor in Humanities and Social Sciences, Stanford University; Senior Fellow, Hoover Institution, Stanford University.

We are grateful to Frank Easterbrook, Dan Farber, Jack Knight, Jerry Mashaw, Roger Noll, Andrew Rutten, Edward Schwartz, Peter Strauss, and Barry Weingast for comments on earlier versions of this article.

1. U.S. CONST. art. I, § 7, cl. 2:

> Every Bill which shall have passed the House of Representatives and the Senate, shall, before it become a Law, be presented to the President of the United States; If he approve he shall sign it, but if not he shall return it, with his Objections to that House in which it shall have originated, who shall enter the Objections at large on their Journal, and proceed to reconsider it. If after such Reconsideration two thirds of that House shall agree to pass the Bill, it shall be sent, together with the Objections, to the other House, by which it shall likewise be reconsidered, and if approved by two thirds of that House, it shall become a Law. But in all such Cases the Votes of both Houses shall be determined by Yeas and Nays, and the Names of the Persons voting for and against the Bill shall be entered on the Journal of each House respectively. If any Bill shall not be returned by the President within ten Days (Sundays excepted) after it shall have been presented to him, the Same shall be a Law, in like Manner as if he had signed it, unless the Congress by their Adjournment prevent its Return, in which Case it shall not be a Law.

2. 462 U.S. 919 (1983).

3. *Id.* at 951. This statement followed the Court's historical analysis of Article I, Section 1,

tions, this reasoning suggested the constitutional invalidity of two-house legislative vetoes and of legislative vetoes of agency rulemaking. So interpreted, *Chadha* nullified hundreds of federal legislative vetoes. That, in turn, stimulated litigation over whether legislative vetoes are "severable" from the underlying statutes and, hence, whether their invalidity voided the statutes as well. The Court in *Alaska Airlines v. Brock*[4] applied the standard severability test in a way that rendered all or virtually all legislative vetoes severable from their statutes.[5]

Chadha aroused great interest in the bicameralism and presentment requirements of Article I, Section 7, yet the Court's treatment of those requirements both before and after *Chadha* is not entirely consistent with the broad reasoning in that decision. For example, in *Bowsher v. Synar,*[6] the Court invalidated the Gramm-Rudman Act's[7] delegation of budget-cutting authority to the Comptroller General, an official removable by Congress.[8] In light of the reasoning of *Chadha,* the delegation would appear to be invalid as a violation of the required procedures for congressional "lawmaking" under Article I, Section 7.[9] Instead, the Court rested its decision upon the general constitutional structure of separate powers, holding that Congress's action was an effort to usurp executive powers (vested in the President under Article II) by assigning them to an official "controlled" by Congress.[10]

More troubling than the Court's waffle in *Bowsher* is its apparent sacrifice of bicameralism and presentment in *Dames & Moore v. Regan.*[11] There, the Court held that presidential orders suspending federal litigation against the Islamic Republic of Iran had the force of "law"—notwithstanding Congress's failure to authorize such action in the International Emergency Economic Powers Act (IEEPA),[12] which authorizes and regulates presidential actions during foreign affairs emergencies, and further notwithstanding the inconsistency of such a presidential power with the Foreign Sovereign Immunities Act (FSIA),[13] which comprehensively regulates lawsuits brought in

---

Clauses 2-3. *Id.* at 946-50. The historical analysis, in turn, was taken almost entirely from THE FEDERALIST. *Id.*

4. 480 U.S. 678 (1987).

5. *Id.* at 684-87.

6. 478 U.S. 714 (1986).

7. 2 U.S.C. §§ 901-909 (1988 & Supp. 1990).

8. *Bowsher,* 478 U.S. at 736.

9. Justices Marshall and Stevens took this approach in their votes to invalidate the statute. *Id.* at 736, 753-59 (Stevens & Marshall, JJ., concurring in the judgment).

10. *Id.* at 721-26, 732-34 (opinion of the Court). The opinion of the Court, by Chief Justice Burger (who authored *Chadha*), was joined by four other Justices. Justices Marshall and Stevens concurred in the judgment, based upon the *Chadha* analysis. Justices White and Blackmun dissented.

11. 453 U.S. 654 (1981).

12. 50 U.S.C. §§ 1701-1706 (1988).

13. 28 U.S.C. §§ 1601-1611 (1988).

United States courts against foreign states and their instrumentalities.[14] The Court relied on Congress's "acquiescence" in prior executive agreements settling claims by United States companies against foreign states. Because Congress did not object to this longstanding practice and passed legislation consistent with the practice, the Court held that "Congress has implicitly approved the practice."[15]

This reasoning, similar to that in many of the Court's other constitutional as well as statutory precedents, seems inconsistent with Article I, Section 7, at least as interpreted two years later in *Chadha:* If "law" cannot be made by the vote of a single chamber of Congress (or even by the vote of both chambers, without presentment), how can it be made by the failure of either chamber to act? Another Article I, Section 7 puzzle is presented by Justice White in his *Chadha* dissent: If Article I "law" requires bicameral approval and presentment, why should agency "lawmaking" not be illegitimate for some of the same reasons as the legislative veto?[16]

The Court's apparent response to this concern is that delegation to an agency is valid under Article I so long as the agency is merely administering the "law" and not making it up. Theoretically, this idea is enforced by the nondelegation doctrine, which requires that Congress cannot delegate tasks to agencies without laying down an "intelligible principle" to which the agency must conform.[17] This idea might reconcile broad delegations to agencies with Article I, Section 7, and in the early 1980s a few Justices signaled a willingness to enforce the nondelegation doctrine.[18] In 1988, however, a unanimous Court rejected application of the nondelegation doctrine in *Mistretta v. United States,* with some suggestion that the doctrine is basically unenforceable.[19] This seems anomalous in light of *Chadha*'s commitment of the Court to enforcing bicameralism and presentment as prerequisites to constitutional lawmaking.

The ability of agencies to make "law" might also be reconciled with Arti-

---

14. *Id.* §§ 1604-1605.

15. *Dames & Moore,* 453 U.S. at 680. The Court also relied on the President's "inherent power" to enter into executive agreements. *Id.* at 682. But this argument might not provide much support for the Court's holding that the executive order suspending the lawsuits should be given the force of "law."

16. *Chadha,* 462 U.S. at 984-89 (White, J., dissenting).

17. J.W. Hampton, Jr., & Co. v. United States, 276 U.S. 394, 409 (1928) (Taft, C.J.); *see also* A.L.A. Schechter Poultry Corp. v. United States, 295 U.S. 495, 541-42 (1935).

18. Justice Rehnquist endorsed it in American Textile Mfrs. Inst., Inc. v. Donovan, 452 U.S. 490. 543 (1981) (Rehnquist, J., dissenting); Industrial Union Dep't, AFL-CIO v. American Petroleum Inst., 448 U.S. 607, 685-86 (1980) (Rehnquist, J., concurring in the judgment). Future Justice Scalia endorsed it by joining the per curiam opinion of the three-judge court in Synar v. United States, 626 F. Supp. 1374, 1383-85 (D.D.C. 1986), *aff'd sub. nom.* Bowsher v. Synar, 478 U.S. 714 (1986).

19. 488 U.S. 361, 371-79 (1989).

cle I, Section 7 by subjecting agency law to judicial review, ensuring that the agency-made law would reflect the legislative preferences that yielded the legislation. Paradoxically, however, the Supreme Court has gone in the opposite direction, holding in *Chevron U.S.A. Inc. v. Natural Resources Defense Council,*[20] that courts must defer to agency interpretations of statutes they are charged with enforcing, unless the agency interpretation is "manifestly contrary to the statute."[21] Assuming a broad and legal delegation of lawmaking power to the agency, the Court reasoned that aggressive judicial review of the agency's action would be inconsistent with the democratic values underlying Article I.[22]

Decisions in the late 1980s reveal that the Court is even split on the issue of whether it should consult a statute's legislative history when deciding whether an agency interpretation is "manifestly contrary to the statute" under *Chevron*.[23] Indeed, a few Justices argue from Article I, Section 7 that there are constitutional problems with the Court's reliance on legislative history (especially committee reports) as "authoritative" evidence of statutory meaning in any case.[24] Under this line of argument, a court's consideration of legislative history (e.g., committee reports) violates bicameralism because the whole Congress does not vote on the legislative history, and violates presentment because the President is usually not represented in the legislative history and is not presented with it when he or she signs the bill into law.

In spite of—or because of—all this doctrinal debate in the Court's opinions, the import of Article I, Section 7 for lawmaking in the modern administrative state is unclear. The Court does not seem to have a well-developed conceptual framework for Article I, Section 7. The closest the Court has come to such a framework is *Chadha,* where the Court hearkened back to the Framers' reasons for the bicameralism and presentment requirements.[25] But *Chadha*'s conceptual framework is in tension with the results or the reasoning of the Court's practice in other areas: it is strikingly inconsistent with *Dames & Moore*; arguably inconsistent with *Alaska Airlines, Mistretta, Chevron,* and the Court's frequent endorsements of legislative history; and suggests a different analysis than that followed by the Court in *Bowsher*.

More importantly, *Chadha*'s conceptual framework is an unsatisfactory analysis and application of the Framers' original expectations for the creation of law pursuant to Article I, Section 7. It is unsatisfactory in three different ways. First, although *Chadha* adverts to the purposes the Framers

20. 467 U.S. 837 (1984).
21. *Id.* at 844.
22. *Id.* at 865-66.
23. *Id.* at 844.
24. In particular, Justice Scalia has criticized reliance on committee reports. *See infra* Part II.E.
25. 462 U.S. at 946-51.

envisioned for bicameralism and presentment, its understanding of those purposes is impoverished; the opinion seems unaware of how bicameralism and presentment fit into the overall vision of government, which the Framers saw as a dynamic balance between popular republican governance and "energetic" stable governance. Second, *Chadha* assumes a wooden and unnecessarily formalist operation of bicameralism and presentment, as simply hoops that bills must jump through before they become law. A better way to understand Article I, Section 7 is to view it as setting up a dynamics (rather than a statics) of power, ultimately subserving the constitutional balance just noted. Third, *Chadha*'s reliance on the very specific statements of the Framers is ahistorical, given the vast changes in United States government in the modern administrative state. Those changes engulf the narrow constitutional vision offered by *Chadha* and suggest the superiority of an understanding of the Framers' expectations that is pitched at a more general level.

What we want to do in this piece is to rethink Article I, Section 7 in a way that is both more attentive to the Framers' expectations and goals and more comprehensible in the modern administrative state. Drawing upon formal models developed by positive political theory, Part I analyzes Article I, Section 7 as a sequential game, in which lawmaking is conceptualized as a dynamic interaction between the preferences of the House and Senate (bicameralism) and the President (presentment). The advent of the administrative state, in which much "lawmaking" is accomplished by agencies dominated by the President, has altered the game in an important way. From the perspective of the Framers' original expectations, interpretation of Article I, Section 7 must meet this challenge, adapting the dynamic game to preserve its original value.

Part II applies the Framers' original game, updated to account for agency lawmaking, as a way of evaluating modern constitutional doctrine. Much of it is found lacking, especially *Mistretta*'s apparent abandonment of the nondelegation doctrine, *Chadha*'s invalidation of all legislative vetoes, *Alaska Airlines*' unrealistic approach to severability, *Dames & Moore*'s acceptance of lawmaking by acquiescence, and *Chevron*'s deference to agency decisionmaking. The conclusion of Part II is that if the Court takes the Framers' intent seriously, its reasoning in *Chadha* is flawed and its decisions in other cases incorrect.

Part III steps back and asks whether the Framers' original goals and values have meaning for the modern administrative state. In other words, should our conceptualization of Article I, Section 7 be persuasive to a nonoriginalist, that is, a judge or scholar who does not care what the Framers expected, or who feels that their expectations have been so overtaken by subsequent developments as to be irrelevant today? Rather tentatively, we believe the model does have some value for nonoriginalists because the balance sought by the Framers remains normatively attractive today. We develop this insight through reconsideration of the validity of the Supreme Court decisions analyzed in Part II.

I. A GAME THEORETIC MODEL OF THE ORIGINAL CONSTITUTIONAL UNDERSTANDING OF BALANCED LAWMAKING

The plain meaning of Article I, Section 7 is that the Constitution does not contemplate a unicameral parliamentary model of statute creation in which statutes reflect the preferences of the median legislator. Instead, the model is a bicameral presidential one in which statutes simply reflect some accommodation of the preferences of the median legislator in two different chambers and of the President.

This bicameral presidential model of legislation is not in the Constitution by accident. It reflects a carefully considered judgment by the Framers about how lawmaking should be structured.[26] The Framers admired the legitimacy of popular republican decisionmaking, but rejected systems of lawmaking by simple majority votes, either in the form of direct democracy[27] or of a unicameral parliamentary system,[28] because they feared that temporary alliances would establish short-sighted policies not in the public interest. Their decision to require both bicameral approval and presentment of legislation before it becomes law represents the Framers' judgments about the need for balance between republican liberty, in which popular preferences would generate laws, and stability, in which laws would reflect deliberation among many perspectives and would not yield abrupt changes in social policy.[29]

The Constitution's requirements for lawmaking can be modeled as a sequential game, which we dub the "Article I, Section 7 game." The starting point for the game is the status quo, which prevails in the absence of legislation. If the median legislator in both chambers can agree on a similar policy to replace the status quo, the legislature will want to pass a statute implementing the legislative preference. In a parliamentary system, this would be the end of the game. In our presidential system, the President may not prefer the policy preferred by the median legislator to the status quo and, hence, might veto the legislation. The final move would then be that of Congress, to

26. This discussion is mainly informed by THE FEDERALIST NO. 51 (James Madison), and NO. 73 (Alexander Hamilton), especially as interpreted in DAVID F. EPSTEIN, THE POLITICAL THEORY OF THE FEDERALIST 133-46, 176-79 (1984).

27. THE FEDERALIST NO. 10, at 80-82 (James Madison) (Clinton Rossiter ed., 1961).

28. THE FEDERALIST NO. 51, at 322-23 (James Madison), NO. 73, at 441-47 (Alexander Hamilton) (Clinton Rossiter ed., 1961).

29. THE FEDERALIST NO. 37, at 226 (James Madison), NO. 70, at 423-24 (Alexander Hamilton) (Clinton Rossiter ed., 1961); *see* EPSTEIN, *supra* note 26, at 162-76.

override the veto, if two-thirds of the legislators in each chamber prefer the median chamber preference to that of the President.

Positive political theory suggests a formal model for this sequential game.[30] For purposes of constructing the model, we assume that information is complete, in that the preferences of the players, the structure of the game, and the rationality of the actors are all common knowledge. We also assume that the players perfectly anticipate the future course of play, that no one is able to commit to future courses of action, and that all the actors in the model prefer that their decisions not be overturned. We employ the following notation:

SQ	=	Existing policy (status quo), the default position if no legislation is enacted to deal with a social problem
H and S	=	Preferences of the median legislator in the two chambers of the bicameral legislature
P	=	Preferences of the President
h and s	=	Preferences of the pivotal legislator in the House and Senate, whose vote is needed for the two-thirds majority needed to override a presidential veto.
x	=	Statutory policy resulting from the game

In determining whether a statute will be enacted, and where policy will be set under our game, the critical factor is the relationship of SQ to P, S, H, h, and s. Consider the following three cases.[31]

Case 1: $P < H, S < SQ$. We start with a case in which the status quo is objectionable from the perspectives of both Congress and the President, and their preferences for changing the status quo run in the same direction, but the President would like to change the status quo more drastically than would either chamber in Congress. Figure 1 maps the relevant preferences:

---

30. The sequential game model used *infra* is similar to the models used in William N. Eskridge, Jr., *Reneging on History? Playing the Court/Congress/President Civil Rights Game,* 79 CAL. L. REV. 613 (1991); John Ferejohn & Charles Shipan, *Congressional Influence on Administrative Agencies: A Case Study of Telecommunications Policy, in* CONGRESS RECONSIDERED 393 (Lawrence C. Dodd & Bruce I. Oppenheimer eds., 4th ed. 1989); Rafael Gely & Pablo T. Spiller, *A Rational Choice Theory of Supreme Court Statutory Decisions with Applications to the* State Farm *and* Grove City *Cases,* 6 J.L. ECON. & ORGANIZATION 263 (1990); Brian Marks, A Model of Judicial Influence on Congressional Policymaking: *Grove City College v. Bell* (1989) (unpublished Ph.D. dissertation, Washington University) (copy on file at *The Georgetown Law Journal).*

31. Please note that these three cases do not exhaust the possible preference alignments, but other variations would be analyzed similarly to one of our three variations. For example, the Framers expected the Senate and President to be much more inclined to the status quo than the House (as in $H < S, P < SQ$). This alignment is similar to Case 1 below, and statutory policy would be set at $x = S$. If the President were particularly protective of the status quo (as in $H < S < P < SQ$), the alignment of preferences would be similar to Case 3, with statutory policy being set at $x = P$. If the House wanted to change the status quo in ways different than the President and the Senate ($H < SQ < S, P$), the alignment of preferences would be similar to Case 2, with no statute being enacted.

x

P H S SQ

FIGURE 1. Statutory policy H $\leq$ x $\leq$ S when P $<$ H, S $<$ SQ.

In such a case there is no problem enacting a statute,[32] since both chambers and the President prefer a range of policies to the status quo. The ultimate statutory policy will fall somewhere between the preferences of the two legislative chambers (*H* and *S*), and the preferences of the President will be irrelevant.[33] Note here the tendency of the game to avoid drastic shifts away from the status quo (*SQ*). The President's preference for a somewhat more significant policy shift will have little if any effect on statutory policy under the circumstances described in Figure 1, for it is Congress that must take the initial action. And the President cannot credibly threaten to veto any bill acceptable to Congress because the President prefers any action moving policy to the left of the status quo.

Case 2: h < SQ < S. Consider how the game changes when the actors' preferences for changing the status quo run in different directions. Figure 2 maps one illustration of such preferences:

H SQ S

FIGURE 2. No statute when H $<$ SQ $<$ S.

If *SQ* is anywhere between *H* and *S,* Congress would be unable to agree on statutory policy because the House would prefer the status quo to any point to the right of *SQ,* and the Senate would prefer the status quo to any point to the left of *SQ*. The Framers expected that such a legislative stalemate would not be uncommon, and the requirement of bicameral approval reflects the constitutional presumption in favor of the status quo. Note that for the game diagrammed in Figure 2, we have left the President out of the Article I, Section 7 game. The President's preferences are irrelevant when Congress cannot agree on a statute changing the status quo.

32. We are of course assuming no transaction costs for statutory enactment and frictionless bargaining among the players. We are also for the present assuming away internal congressional barriers such as committees. We take up the role of committees in Part II.

33. That is, even though the President would like to adopt a major shift in policy from the status quo, neither chamber in Congress is willing to adopt a major shift. Since bicameralism requires the consent of both chambers, the two chambers will work out a compromise of their preferences ($H \leq x \leq S$). Presentment does not require the President's consent to legislation, unless his veto can be backed up by more than a third of one chamber. In the configuration described by Figure 1, the President cannot credibly threaten to veto the legislature's preferred policy (*x*), in large part because a successful veto would leave policy at the status quo (*SQ*), which the President hates even more than Congress does.

Even when Congress can agree on a change in the status quo (as in *SQ* < *H, S*), it still may be unable to enact a statute, if the President prefers the status quo to any change Congress would like to make. Figure 2A maps one example of such a situation:

---

h P s SQ H S

FIGURE 2A. No statute when h < P < SQ < H, S.

The same outcome (no statute) results from the game in Figure 2A as in Figure 2, but because of the presentment and not the bicameralism requirement. That is, even though *H* and *S* will agree on a statutory policy located somewhere between their preferences, the President will be able to sustain a veto because *h,* the voters at or near the veto median of the more pro-President chamber, will prefer *SQ* to *x*. If *SQ* is anywhere between *h* and *S,* it is clear that any statutory proposal would have to move policy to the right of *SQ* to satisfy the Senate and that any statute that had this effect would be vetoed by the President. The supporters of the statute would be unable to produce sufficient votes in *H* to override the veto, again because *h* would prefer *SQ* to *x*. Thus, there would be no legislation and policy would remain at $x = SQ$. Again, the Framers anticipated this possibility, approvingly, for they placed the executive veto in Article I, Section 7 to prevent abrupt shifts in policy even when both chambers of Congress desired it.

Case 3: SQ < h. The President's ability to block legislation ends, of course, when two-thirds of the legislators in each chamber disagree with the President about how the status quo should be changed. Figure 3 illustrates this situation:

x

P SQ h h(SQ) s H S

FIGURE 3. Policy set at x ≈ h(SQ) when SQ < h.

Although the President does not have enough votes in Congress to sustain a veto, the threat of a veto significantly affects the location of statutory policy. The threat of a veto induces the median legislator, *H,* to introduce legislation at about point *h(SQ)*. Recall that *h* represents the pivotal legislator for veto purposes—namely, the legislator whose vote is needed for the two-thirds majority needed to override a presidential veto. For that "veto median" legislator, *h(SQ)* is the point at which she would be indifferent to the choice between the status quo, *SQ,* and the proposed policy, *h(SQ)*. By setting policy just a little to the left of *h(SQ), H* will be able to attract the pivotal voter, *h,* needed to override a presidential veto. If the status quo is located exactly at the preferences of the pivotal voter of the more pro-President chamber ($SQ = h$), policy will be set at $x = SQ$, and no statute will be passed. The further the status quo is to the left of the veto median, the further to the right Congress will set statutory policy and not risk a veto. Again, the Framers anticipated many Case 3 situations, where the President would oppose Congress's desire to change the status quo. The majority required in each chamber of Congress to override a presidential veto would ensure a more moderate change in the status quo than Congress acting alone would have enacted.

The Framers contemplated the following consequences from the model of lawmaking described above: First, most social and economic problems would not generate legislation at all. The Framers expected the House, Senate, and President to have widely dispersed preferences about the status quo, and therefore the no-statute game (Case 2) was most likely in the short term.[34] Nevertheless, the Framers expected that, if the problem persisted over time, a solution in the common interest would emerge and preferences would realign (from Case 2 to Case 1 or 3) so that a statute could pass.[35] Second, if a social or economic problem were to stimulate legislative action, the structure of the Article I, Section 7 game would militate in favor of moderate rather than radical shifts from the status quo.[36] The games suggested in Cases 1 and 3 push policy away from extreme preferences. Third, once legislation was enacted into law, it would be interpreted over time to reflect the original policy balance.[37] This point requires some elaboration of the Framers' expectations about law implementation (as opposed to lawmaking, explored above).

The Constitution separates lawmaking (Article I) from law implementation (Articles II and III). The Framers believed that Congress would be less likely to pass "tyrannical" laws if there were the possibility that such laws could be applied to members of Congress or their supporters.[38] But the Framers also believed that the policy balance achieved in a given statute would not be disturbed by the President's "execution" of laws or the Court's "interpretation" of laws.[39] The reason for the Framers' belief was their understanding that Congress-with-the-President (the lawmaking process in Ar-

34. *See* THE FEDERALIST NO. 73, at 443-44 (Alexander Hamilton) (Clinton Rossiter ed., 1961).

35. *See* EPSTEIN, *supra* note 26, at 177-78.

36. *See* THE FEDERALIST NO. 63, at 384-85 (James Madison) (Clinton Rossiter ed., 1961).

37. *See* THE FEDERALIST NO. 78, at 468-69 (Alexander Hamilton) (Clinton Rossiter ed., 1961).

38. THE FEDERALIST NO. 47, at 302-03 (James Madison) (Clinton Rossiter ed., 1961); *see* EPSTEIN, *supra* note 26, at 129-30 (tracing idea from Locke and Montesquieu to the Framers, and explaining Madison's probable understanding of Montesquieu to be that "if the legislators cannot ensure a tyrannical execution, i.e., one which favors themselves, they will be less likely to make tyrannical laws for fear that they themselves will be tyrannically ruled by them.").

39. THE FEDERALIST NOS. 70, 78 (Alexander Hamilton).

ticle I, Section 7) is the constitutionally required process for deliberation and choice regarding statutory policy, and their further understanding that the processes of execution and interpretation would be faithful to the policy choices of the lawmaking process.[40]

II. The Original Understanding of the Article I, Section 7 Game and the Modern Administrative State: Implications for Constitutional Doctrine

The world of the Framers is not our world. The modern administrative state in which we live is much more complicated than the republic envisioned by the Framers. This complexity has engendered an amount of lawmaking and legal regulation inconceivable to the Framers. More important, in the modern administrative state most "lawmaking" is accomplished by agencies under the authority of statutory delegations. Most important, this shift to agency lawmaking has been accompanied by an overall shift of lawmaking authority from Congress to the President.

These modern developments are in tension with the specific as well as general balance sought by the Framers through Article I, Section 7. Specifically, the modern developments have shifted statutory policy away from the compromise among House, Senate, and presidential preferences reflected in the game set up by Article I, Section 7. Since agency heads are appointed by the President and many agencies are located within the executive department, presidential preferences are now much more important to lawmaking than the Framers originally intended. Generally, the modern developments—especially the increased lawmaking power of the President—have unsettled the balance between popular government and stability, to the detriment of both.[41]

If the Court is truly serious about the Framers' original expectations as to the meaning of Article I, Section 7, as the Court claimed to be in *Chadha*,[42] the Court should be more attentive to the ways in which agency lawmaking unsettles those expectations. In the remainder of this Part, we consider the ways in which the game outlined in Part I provides insight into the validity of several constitutional doctrines: the nondelegation doctrine, the legislative

---

40. THE FEDERALIST NO. 78, at 468-69 (Alexander Hamilton) (Clinton Rossiter ed., 1961) ("It can be of no weight to say that the courts, on the pretense of a repugnancy, may substitute their own pleasure to the constitutional intentions of the legislature."); *see* EPSTEIN, *supra* note 26, at 173 ("[E]xecution does not really require much deliberation, perhaps because it does not present many choices. To execute well means to execute vigorously whatever laws there are against whatever lawbreakers there are. The choices which require deliberation are apparently made by the legislature.").

41. We reserve to Part III discussion of the practical problems involved with unstable policy in modern society.

42. 462 U.S. 919, 945-51 (1983).

veto and its severability from the underlying legislation, congressional acquiescence as lawmaking, congressional efforts to control agencies, judicial deference to agency interpretations, and the use of legislative history in interpreting statutes. We emphasize that the normative perspective for this Part's analysis is that of *Chadha,* namely, the original expectations of the Framers. We reserve for Part III discussion of these doctrines from a nonoriginalist perspective.

A. THE NONDELEGATION DOCTRINE AND THE CONSTITUTIONAL DILEMMA POSED BY THE MODERN ADMINISTRATIVE STATE

Modern American government is structurally quite different from the government envisioned by the Framers. A great deal of national lawmaking has been delegated[43] by Congress to administrative agencies, with little or no specific standards to guide the agencies. As a result, most initial efforts at statutory interpretation are now done by agency rulemaking and adjudication, rather than in the context of judicial adjudication.[44] There are numerous reasons for Congress's willingness to delegate significant lawmaking power to agencies, including the institutional advantages agencies have in developing detailed policy prescriptions and the congressional inclination to avoid or defer controversial policy decisions. Whatever the reasons, such delegation is in tension with the original constitutional understanding that lawmaking would be accomplished by Congress-with-the-President, and with the policies underlying that understanding. Specifically, the Framers did not expect the President to have an active role in lawmaking and in changing the law; the executive's role, reflected in the veto power, was only reactive, protecting the presidency against congressional usurpation or the status quo against immediate popular change.[45]

In the federal system, the nondelegation doctrine is, theoretically, supposed to police standardless congressional delegations to agencies. But the nondelegation doctrine has not been invoked by the Supreme Court to strike down legislation since the New Deal.[46] For example, in 1989 a unanimous

---

43. By "delegation," we are mainly thinking of delegation on the face of the statute, to the effect that the agency is affirmatively charged with developing regulations to fill out the framework as well as the details of statutory policy. This is the way delegation is usually used in the legal literature. We would also include statutes that charge an agency with implementing vague statutory mandates, even when there is no formal language delegating lawmaking tasks to the agency.

44. *See* Edward L. Rubin, *Law and Legislation in the Administrative State,* 89 COLUM. L. REV. 369, 372-85 (1989).

45. *See* THE FEDERALIST NO. 73, at 442-43 (Alexander Hamilton) (Clinton Rossiter ed., 1961) (dual purpose of veto is to enable the President to "defend himself against the depredations" of Congress *and* to prevent "the passing of bad laws, through haste, inadvertence, or design").

46. *See* WILLIAM N. ESKRIDGE, JR. & PHILIP P. FRICKEY, CASES AND MATERIALS ON LEGISLATION: STATUTES AND THE CREATION OF PUBLIC POLICY 473-76 (1988).

Supreme Court in *Mistretta v. United States*[47] held that Congress could delegate federal sentencing guidelines to a commission made up of seven presidential appointees (three of whom must be federal judges).[48] The Court applied the "intelligible principle" test but prefaced it with observations that, "in our increasingly complex society, replete with ever changing and more technical problems, Congress simply cannot do its job absent an ability to delegate power under broad general directives"[49] and that virtually any broad standard has been held to pass the "intelligible principle" test.[50] Justice Scalia's separate opinion, agreeing with the Court on this issue (and disagreeing on every other issue in the case), opined that the nondelegation doctrine is as unenforceable as it is important to the constitutional scheme.[51]

Notwithstanding *Mistretta* and other precedents, an enforceable nondelegation doctrine is not only consistent with but required by any serious effort to respect the original constitutional understanding about lawmaking in our polity. By requiring Congress-with-the-President to set statutory policy (x) on the face of the statute, the nondelegation doctrine curtails the freedom of agencies to move statutory policy, and hence might be a useful means for enforcing the original understanding of Article I, Section 7 in the modern administrative state. This is the first normative lesson of our game theoretic model: when it fails to make clear its policy choices in statutes delegating lawmaking to agencies, Congress has violated a most fundamental rule and policy in Article I of the Constitution. Unpoliced delegation of lawmaking authority to agencies represents a major amendment in the Constitution's procedures for lawmaking, and such an amendment has important consequences for the balance and allocation of national power. Because agencies are influenced or even controlled by the President,[52] the transfer of lawmaking authority from Congress-with-the-President (the Article I, Section 7 structure) to agencies significantly increases the importance of the President's preferences in the lawmaking process.

Consider the alignment of preferences in Case 1 (see Figure 1), in which

---

47. 488 U.S. 361 (1989).

48. *Id.* at 371-79.

49. *Id.* at 372.

50. *Id.* at 373.

51. *Id.* at 415-16 (Scalia, J., dissenting from the Court's opinion but joining the Court on this single issue).

52. Many agencies are within the executive branch (e.g., the Internal Revenue Service, the Immigration and Naturalization Service) and hence under the direct thumb of the President, who can fire top officials. Other agencies are "independent" of the executive branch (e.g., the Federal Trade Commission, the Federal Communication Commission); although their top officials cannot be fired at will by the President, they are appointed by the President for limited terms. And in the 1980s the Office of Management and Budget took on authority to oversee rulemaking by independent as well as executive branch agencies. *See* Peter L. Strauss & Cass R. Sunstein, *The Role of the President and OMB in Informal Rulemaking*, 38 ADMIN. L. REV. 181 (1986).

the Article I, Section 7 structure for lawmaking would yield a statutory policy falling somewhere between the preferred policies of the two legislative chambers ($H < x < S$). In the modern administrative state, Congress often will not pass a statute setting policy precisely at *x*, but will instead pass a statute delegating the policy-setting function to an agency (*A*), with the expectation that the agency will implement policy at *x*, or thereabouts. In that event, the agency can (perhaps over time) set policy virtually anywhere it wants, unless Congress would be stimulated to override the agency's choice by enacting new legislation. Thus, in Case 1 situations the agency with policy preferences near those of the President can propose any policy, *x'*, at or to the right of the veto median of the more pro-President chamber, and Congress cannot successfully challenge this interpretation. Any attempt to do so would be vetoed and the veto could not be overridden because the pivotal voter for an override, *h*, likes the agency policy, $x = h$, more than any other policy choice. Thus, instead of *x*—the policy that would have been adopted under the Article I, Section 7 procedures—the administrative state produces x'. This is reflected in Figure 1A below:

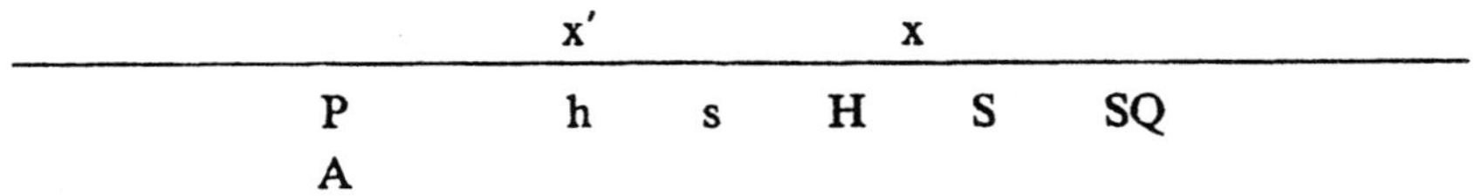

FIGURE 1A. Statutory policy shifts from $H < x < S$ to $x' = h$, if Congress delegates lawmaking authority to agency.

Obviously, this represents a substantial shift in policy toward the preferences of the President and away from those of most members of Congress.

A less dramatic story occurs in Case 3.[53] Again, because the starting point for the lawmaking game is the agency's and not Congress's decision, the agency can set statutory policy at the more favorable veto median ($x' = h$) rather than the point ($x = h(SQ)$) that would have prevailed under the original structure for lawmaking. While in Case 3 Congress's position as policymaker induced it to set *x* as far to the right of *h* as it could, Congress will not respond to the agency's moving policy further to the left, because any effort to overrule the agency's interpretation will be met by a presidential

53. Case 2, which did not yield a statute in the first place, does not concern the present analysis. But note that a Presidency with substantial lawmaking power, which might fuel further lawmaking ambitions, can be expected to assert lawmaking authority over areas where there has never been enough political consensus to pass a statute. For example, there will be situations where the President will try to assert his "inherent powers" to cover Case 2 situations. Or the President/agency may try to interpret the jurisdictional limits of related statutes broadly, in order to impose their interpretations into areas essentially covered by Case 2. This is what the President argued, and the Court accepted, in *Dames & Moore*.

veto that cannot be overridden in one of the chambers. Figure 3A diagrams this version of the game:

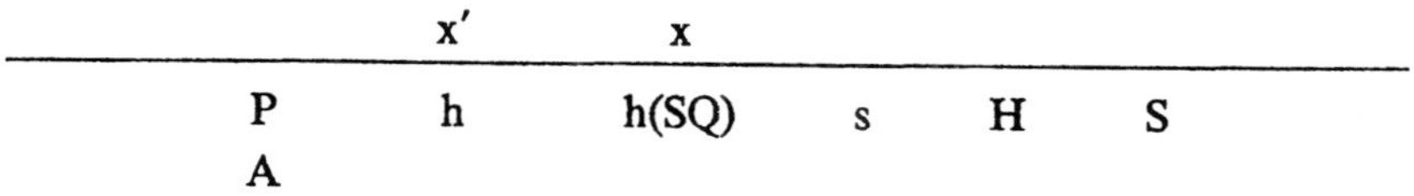

FIGURE 3A. Statutory policy shifts from h < x = h(SQ), to x' = h when Congress delegates lawmaking authority to agency.

The shift in statutory policy here is less dramatic than in Case 1, from $x = h(SQ)$ to $x' = h$, but it is still potentially significant. Indeed, the more Congress originally wanted to change the status quo in Case 3 situations (and therefore the greater the gulf between h and SQ), the bigger will be the movement from x to x'. These are the situations where Article I, Section 7 lawmaking would have reflected a particularly striking compromise of congressional preferences, and delegation of lawmaking authority to an agency makes the compromise more acute.

Thus far, our discussion has assumed that congressional and presidential preferences do not change over time. Of course, those preferences do change, and electoral politics has produced dramatic shifts in presidential preferences in particular.[54] Figure 3B maps the shift in statutory policy in Case 3 statutes when there is a dramatic left-to-right switch in presidential preferences (as there was in 1981):

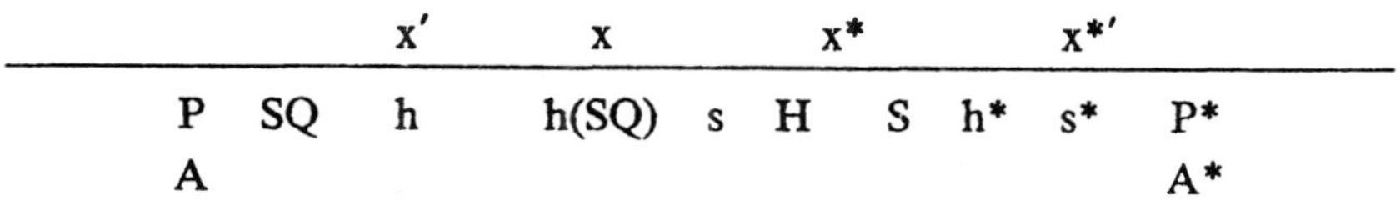

FIGURE 3B. Administrative policy moves from x' = h to x*' = s* when President shifts from P to P*.

54. *Vide* the dramatic shifts in 1953 from Truman to Eisenhower, in 1961 from Eisenhower to Kennedy, in 1969 from Johnson to Nixon, in 1977 from Ford to Carter, and in 1981 from Carter to Reagan. In contrast, congressional elections have yielded remarkably few abrupt policy shifts during this period. The only dramatic shifts occurred in 1959 (slender Democratic majorities in Congress to substantial Democratic majorities), and 1981 (Democratic Senate to Republican Senate, with working Republican majority in the House on some issues). Less dramatic shifts occurred in 1953 (slim Democratic majorities to slim Republican majorities in Congress), 1955 (switch back to Democratic Congress), and 1987 (Democrats regain control of Senate). Note here that this experience is contrary to the Framers' expectations, which were that the preferences of the popularly elected House of Representatives would fluctuate more dramatically than those of the indirectly elected Senate and President.

Consider Figures 3, 3A, and 3B as a sequential pattern. The Case 3 statute that should result from lawmaking by Congress-with-the-President (the Article I, Section 7, Clause 2 procedures) already strongly reflects the President's preferences (policy would be set at $x = h(SQ)$), but if an agency is given lawmaking authority, then policy is pushed more strongly toward the President's preferences ($x' = h$). After an election that shifts presidential preferences to P^* (such as the 1952, 1968, or 1980 elections), lawmaking that followed Article I, Section 7 procedures could amend the statute to shift policy to a position like x^*, between H and S, but lawmaking originally delegated to a presidentially controlled agency shifts policy much more dramatically to $x^{*\prime} = s^*$. This sequence suggests that agency lawmaking can sometimes result in drastic shifts in policy from one Presidency to the next (from x' to $x^{*\prime}$)—much more dramatic shifts than would be observed within the framework of the original understanding (from x to x^*).

In our model, the introduction of agencies as delegated lawmakers shifts policy deliberation in our bicameral presidential system away from the original constitutional understanding: not only is it often difficult for one or both chambers of Congress to enact statutes reflecting their preferences (Case 3) as the Framers originally intended, but even when statutes are enacted in situations where congressional preferences ought to be dominant (Case 1), Congress's tendency to delegate ultimate policymaking choices to agencies pushes policy in these situations toward presidential preferences as well (Figure 1A). And over time, the original agency policy choice, wherever situated, is vulnerable to abrupt change in response to shifting presidential preferences (Figure 3B).

Stated another way, the Framers' modest restraints on congressional power to enact statutes reflecting legislative preferences has in the modern state given way to a substantial transfer of legislative power from Congress to the President. Whatever the modern normative justifications for such a transfer of power, this phenomenon is a significant abandonment of fundamental choices made by the Framers regarding lawmaking, as expressed in Article I, Section 7. The failure of the modern Supreme Court to enforce the nondelegation doctrine has significant consequences for the allocation of national power between the branches.

Positive political theory suggests that Congress would try to find ways around the reallocation of lawmaking power outlined above, and Congress has in fact been responding to this phenomenon for the last fifty years. Indeed, once Congress became aware of the constitutional dilemma outlined above, Congress should have factored that problem into its overall willingness to pass statutes delegating lawmaking authority to agencies. For example, we should expect that Congress would not pass general delegation statutes in Case 1 situations unless it had some assurance that the implementing agency would not immediately seek to move policy from the probable congressional preferences, x, to the veto median, x' (see Figure 1A).

Unfortunately (for Congress), many of the broad delegating statutes were enacted in periods when Congress was either not aware of this phenomenon or had policy preferences similar to those of the President (e.g., the New Deal and the Great Society). Because statutes have an indefinite life, a broad delegation in 1937 (when the preferences of Congress and the President were congruent on many issues) still had important consequences in 1987 (when the political preferences of Congress and the President were very different). Relatedly, Congress may underestimate the erosion of its power over time. Even if Congress and the agency in year one have an understanding about where policy will be set, that understanding does not necessarily bind the agency in year twenty-one (this is one lesson of *Chevron*). This phenomenon creates a long-term constitutional dilemma, in which Congress over time loses lawmaking authority to the President. How might Congress respond to the constitutional dilemma?

The traditional congressional response to the dilemma has been to try to prevent the agency's preferences from reflecting those of the President—in other words, to ensure that $P < A$. To the extent that Congress can pressure the agency to implement the statutory policy as originally agreed, it will do so. Congress is not without means to influence agency preferences. Congress can monitor agencies by oversight hearings, budgetary constraints, and informal contacts. Congress can also structure the agency to reduce the President's power to affect agency preferences; an agency located outside of the executive department (namely, an independent administrative agency) is headed by officials who cannot be easily removed by the President and who may be more responsive to congressional monitoring.[55]

These responses surely have an effect on agency preferences in many (and probably most) instances, but are not a panacea for the constitutional dilemma described here. To begin with, agencies located within the executive branch ought to be less susceptible to congressional monitoring because the President has direct control over the agency: the President can fire its leaders. Thus, when the President has a firm preference on the policy issue, that preference will often exercise a more powerful constraint on the agency than congressional monitoring. Moreover, the congressional monitoring is done not by Congress as a whole, but by its committees. Many committees are not representative of their chamber, and when committee preferences run in the same direction as presidential and agency preferences there will be less effective monitoring. Finally, it is not clear that even vigorous and effective con-

55. Also, the Senate can sometimes affect agency policy by its confirmation power. It can head off presidential nomination of "extreme" agency chiefs. The confirmation power is more useful for controlling independent agencies, whose heads cannot be fired by the President.

gressional monitoring can move agency preferences all the way to the statutory policy that would have been adopted pursuant to the Article I, Section 7 procedures. In other words, Congress can shift *A* to the right of *P* in most cases, but can it shift *A* all the way to the original statutory equilibrium ($H < A < S$, for Case 1 statutes)? This seems most unlikely, especially for agencies that are part of the executive department.

The problems with congressional monitoring, especially for executive agencies, suggest that a Congress concerned with the constitutional dilemma described in the previous Section would find other ways to correct for this pro-President bias in agency lawmaking. Again, this is what we find, historically. Congress has sought to offset agency bias in at least three other ways—the legislative veto of agency rulemaking, delegation of responsibilities to congressionally-dominated agents, and procedural checks on agency rulemaking, especially the availability of judicial review to correct pro-President agency interpretations. The remainder of this Part will explore the validity of constitutional restrictions the Supreme Court placed on these strategies in the 1980s. The analysis we have introduced in this article makes us more sympathetic to these mechanisms than the Supreme Court has been.

B. THE LEGISLATIVE VETO AS A RESPONSE TO THE CONSTITUTIONAL DILEMMA: *CHADHA*

A legislative veto is a provision that an agency rule or action can be voided by the action of Congress without presentment (two-house veto), or of one chamber of Congress (one-house veto), or of one committee of Congress (committee veto). By avoiding presentment, the legislative veto makes it easier for Congress, or a subgroup, to respond to agency interpretations which push statutory policy toward the President's preferences. In the 1930s, at precisely the time when the modern administrative state was aborning, Congress began to attach legislative vetoes to statutes delegating lawmaking functions to agencies. By 1982 there were hundreds of legislative vetoes in federal statutes,[56] and thousands more in state statutes.[57]

In 1983, the Supreme Court invalidated a one-house veto of an agency adjudication in *Chadha*,[58] and subsequent summary dispositions expanded the holding to two-house vetoes and vetoes of agency rulemaking.[59] As noted in the introduction to this article, *Chadha*'s reasoning rested upon the

---

56. *See* Joseph Cooper, *The Legislative Veto in the 1980s, in* CONGRESS RECONSIDERED, supra note 30, at 364, 367; *see also* Jacob K. Javits & Gary J. Klein, *Congressional Oversight and the Legislative Veto: A Constitutional Analysis,* 52 N.Y.U. L. REV. 455-58, 496 (1977).

57. *See* L. Harold Levinson, *Legislative and Executive Veto of Rules of Administrative Agencies: Models and Alternatives,* 24 WM. & MARY L. REV. 79, 81-83 (1982).

58. 462 U.S. at 959.

59. *See, e.g.,* Process Gas Consumers Group v. Consumer Energy Council of Am., 463 U.S. 1216 (1983) (summary invalidation of one-house veto of independent agency rulemaking); United States

original intent of the Framers.[60] But *Chadha*'s focus on the original constitutional understanding is unhelpful because it ignores the ways in which delegation of lawmaking power to agencies has already destroyed the original constitutional balance. To the extent that the Court is concerned with protecting—or restoring—some of the original balance of lawmaking influence suggested by Article I, Section 7, the two-house veto is constitutionally defensible, as is the one-house veto under certain assumptions.

In the short term, a legislative veto would have little consequence for the statutes described in Case 3 above, in which $SQ < h$. In these situations, the advent of agency rulemaking shifts statutory policy only slightly toward the President's preferences (from $h < x = h(SQ)$ to $x' = h$).[61] Because a veto of the agency's rule ($x' = h$) would leave Congress with a status quo that it likes even less than the agency's rule ($SQ < h$), Congress would not rationally exercise its veto authority. This scenario reflects a fundamental limitation of the legislative veto as a policy tool: unlike override legislation, which can not only negate the agency's rule but can implement the rule Congress wants, the legislative veto merely negates the agency's rule, leaving the status quo in its place.

The effect of the legislative veto is more readily apparent for statutes described in Case 1, namely, those statutes whose policy direction was supported by all the actors, with the President favoring a more radical change in the status quo than the Congress. Recall Figure 1A, which revealed a dramatic shift in statutory policy from delegation of lawmaking to agencies (from $H < x < S$ to $x' = h$). The introduction of a two-house legislative veto in these statutes would reverse this dramatic shift, though it is doubtful that it would restore policy to the original Article I, Section 7 balance ($H < x < S$). Figure 1B maps the new game introduced by a two-house veto:[62]

FIGURE 1B. Statutory policy shifts from x' = h to x'' = H(SQ) when two-house veto is introduced.

Letting *H(SQ)* stand for the point that the median member of the House—the chamber closer to the position of the President—regards as indifferent to

Senate v. FTC, 463 U.S. 1216 (1983) (summary invalidation of two-house veto of independent agency rulemaking).

60. 462 U.S. at 945-51.

61. *See supra* Figure 3A.

62. The effect of congressional monitoring of administrative agencies discussed in Part II.A is represented in this and subsequent figures as $P < A$.

SQ, we see that if the agency sets policy at $x'' < H(SQ)$, both chambers of Congress would veto the agency's decision and overturn it in favor of *SQ*. The agency can avoid a two-house veto by setting its rule at the point where the more pro-President chamber is indifferent as to that point and the status quo ($x'' = H(SQ)$).[63] For Case 1 statutes, the introduction of a two-house legislative veto shifts the outcome "weakly" in the direction of the equilibrium position suggested by Article I, Section 7.

The introduction of a one-house veto would yield a more pronounced shift toward the original legislative preferences for Case 1 statutes, in some cases yielding a policy not so distant from the Article I, Section 7 equilibrium position. Consider Figure 1C:

x' x'' x

P A h s S(SQ) H S SQ

FIGURE 1C. Statutory policy shifts from x' = h to x'' = S(SQ) when one-house veto is introduced.

Under a one-house veto, the agency would have to set statutory policy at or to the right of the points where both legislative chambers are indifferent between the agency's policy and the status quo ($x'' = S(SQ)$).

Finally, consider the effect of a legislative veto for a Case 1 statute in the longer term. Figure 1D maps the effect of a radical change in presidential preferences compared with a legislative veto for a Case 1 statute:

x' x'' x* x*'

P A h s S(SQ) H S h* SQ s* A* P*

FIGURE 1D. Statutory policy shifts from x'' = S(SQ) to x* = SQ with legislative veto, when presidential preferences shift globally.

Whereas without a legislative veto, a shift in the President's position from P to P^* would shift policy from $x' = h$ to $x^* = s^*$, with a one-house legislative veto, the outcomes would shift only from $x'' = S(SQ)$ to $x^* = SQ$. Therefore, the change in policy following a large shift in presidential position is generally smaller under a one-house veto than without a veto. Similar reasoning would show that the two-house veto has intermediate effects.

To summarize our argument at this point: The rise of the administrative

63. Note that if *SQ* is sufficiently far to the right, *H(SQ)* will be to the left of *h*. In that event, the agency would set policy at $x'' = h$; it would not set policy to the left of the veto median, *h*, because Congress would then enact veto-proof corrective legislation. For a discussion of how and why this movement occurs, see *supra* Part I, Case 3.

state has substantially subverted the original constitutional understanding by vesting much lawmaking in agencies. Congressional monitoring of agencies (especially those located in the executive department) is not a completely effective remedy for this constitutional dilemma. The introduction of a two-house legislative veto has the effect of moving policy outcomes back toward those that would occur under the original understanding. These effects are most significant in Case 1 statutes, where the President and Congress both object to the status quo and favor reform in the same direction, but have different preferences about how much the status quo should be changed. The effects are less significant in Case 3 statutes, but often ameliorate the constitutional dilemma there as well. Moreover, the two-house veto's effects hold for both the short term (in which preferences remain the same) as well as the long term (in which the President's preferences change but Congress's remain stable). In all cases, the two-house veto works to offset the President's power to change statutory policy through his control of agencies (especially executive agencies), though it does not completely restore the original statutory compromise.

Under the perspective of the original constitutional understanding adopted in *Chadha,* there are also good arguments for one-house legislative vetoes, because such vetoes can move statutory policy back much closer to the original equilibrium, notwithstanding agency bias. On the other hand, our analysis suggests at least one argument against one-house legislative vetoes. If the preferences of one chamber of Congress change drastically over time, while those of the President and the other chamber remain stable, then the new "outlier" chamber may veto statutory policies that precisely envision the original policy choices, x. We do not consider this a likely scenario, in part because congressional preferences in the post-World War II era do change more slowly than those of the President, and they usually change in conjunction with a change in presidential preferences.[64] But this is a potential drawback to the one-house veto in particular.

In short, although *Chadha* itself was correctly decided, for the reasons set out in Justice Powell's opinion concurring in the judgment,[65] the opinion's reasoning misinterprets the original constitutional understanding, and summary decisions striking down legislative vetoes of agency rulemaking are incorrect, from the perspective of the original understanding.

64. The only time in the post-New Deal era that one chamber of Congress has shifted from one party to another, without a corresponding shift in the other chamber, was in 1980, when President Reagan's coattails pulled in a Republican Senate, with the House of Representatives remaining Democratic (though a little more conservative). The Senate shifted back to the Democrats in 1986.

65. 462 U.S. at 959-67 (Powell, J., concurring). Justice Powell would not have reached the question of the validity of legislative vetoes. Instead he reasoned that the one-house veto in this case was a judicial act beyond the scope of Congress's constitutionally prescribed authority.

C. CONGRESSIONALLY DOMINATED AGENTS AS A SOLUTION TO THE CONSTITUTIONAL DILEMMA: *BOWSHER* AND *METROPOLITAN WASHINGTON*

A second approach to the constitutional dilemma outlined above would be for Congress to delegate lawmaking power to agencies that the President does not dominate. This is probably one reason for the growth of "independent" agencies. Although independent agencies have been questioned as inconsistent with the Constitution's separation of powers in Articles I-III, they are positively useful in ameliorating the tension between Article I, Section 7 and the extensive delegation of lawmaking responsibilities by Congress, and hence are a constitutionally permissible response to the constitutional dilemma. Such agencies are most useful to Congress when they are not slanted toward the President. Unhappily, that is not necessarily the case. The President's power to appoint and (with statutory qualifications) remove agency commissioners gives the President substantial influence over many "independent" agencies.

Disappointed with the performance of independent agencies, Congress has sometimes delegated important lawmaking responsibilities to agencies that it, rather than the President, could control. This was an important issue in *Bowsher v. Synar*,[66] in which the Court invalidated the Gramm-Rudman Act's[67] plan for eliminating the federal budget deficit over time. Under the Act, the President's Office of Management and Budget and the Congressional Budget Office jointly determine how much the anticipated federal budget must be cut to meet the Act's targets. Then, the Act directs the Comptroller General to decide exactly where budget cuts should be made in order to meet the deficit reduction targets each year. The constitutional challenge grew out of Congress's potential control over the Comptroller General, who is appointed from a list supplied by Congress and can be removed "for cause" by Congress, and not by the President. The Court majority in *Bowsher* invalidated this plan on general separation of powers grounds, as a legislative usurpation of executive powers.[68] Concurring in the judgment, Justices Stevens and Marshall believed the plan violated Article I, Section 7 because it delegated important legislative powers to an agent of Congress.[69]

Justice Stevens recently wrote on this issue for a majority of the Court in *Metropolitan Washington Airports Authority v. Citizens for the Abatement of Aircraft Noise, Inc.*[70] The case involved a statutory transfer of federal con-

66. 478 U.S. 714 (1986).
67. 2 U.S.C. §§ 901-909 (1988 & Supp. 1990).
68. 478 U.S. at 721-27.
69. *Id.* at 737-41 (Stevens, J., concurring in the judgment).
70. 111 S. Ct. 2298 (1991).

trol of Dulles and National Airports to a regional authority (the MWAA), conditioned upon its supervision by a board of review having veto power over its decisions and composed of nine members of Congress.[71] The Court held that this statutory scheme was invalid however the board of appeals is described.[72] If its duties were executive, the scheme would violate separation of powers as analyzed in *Bowsher*. If its duties were legislative, the scheme would violate Article I, Section 7 as analyzed in *Chadha*.

Our game theoretic model of the original understanding provides a basis for criticizing the Court's approach and result in *Bowsher* and in *Metropolitan Washington*. The analysis turns on what kind of statute is at stake. *Bowsher* involved a Case 1 statute, in which both Congress and the President very much wanted to change the status quo, but the President wanted a more dramatic change than Congress. The Gramm-Rudman Act reflected congressional preferences to cut the budget deficit (*SQ*), as well as Congress's desire to delegate authority to make specific cuts (because Congress wanted flexibility in the plan but did not want to revisit the issue itself every year). On the other hand, Congress did not want to delegate that authority to the President, because Congress feared that the President would use any budget-cutting authority to delete programs Congress wanted. This created a dilemma for Congress: How could it achieve its goal of reducing the deficit without ceding critical budget policy decisions to the President? Congress's solution was to delegate to the Comptroller General—not the President or an executive agency—the power to make the specific decisions. The President did not like this and objected to it, but he did not veto the law because he preferred the congressional solution to the status quo.

For Case 1 statutes like the Gramm-Rudman Act, Congress's delegation of lawmaking responsibilities to an agent it, rather than the President, controls is responsive to, rather than contrary to, the equilibrium required by Article I, Section 7. Recall Figure 1, which maps the equilibrium policy for Case 1 statutes at a compromise point between House and Senate preferences. Presidential preferences do not figure prominently because the President cannot credibly threaten to veto legislation which moves policy away from the status quo and toward presidential preferences (even if just a little bit). In enacting such a statute, Congress realizes that it cannot anticipate all the hard choices over the years and that it will have to delegate. But Congress in the 1980s was aware of Figure 1A: if it delegates decisionmaking power to the President or an executive agency, statutory policy will shift toward the veto median of the more pro-President chamber. To avoid that result and preserve the original equilibrium, the Gramm-Rudman Act dele-

71. *Id.* at 2301.
72. *Id.* at 2312.

gated to an agent more responsive to Congress, thereby preserving the equilibrium mapped in Figure 1 and suggested by Article I, Section 7. Hence, Justice Stevens was wrong to argue in *Bowsher* that the statute violated Article I, Section 7. Indeed, since the delegation was an effort by Congress to preserve the equilibrium mandated by Article I, Section 7, the *Bowsher* majority was wrong to conclude that the delegation represented a congressional "usurpation" of executive power.[73]

In the short term, for Case 1 statutes, the Court would be faithful to the original dynamics of lawmaking to permit Congress to exercise some control over the agency implementing policy. As with the one-house legislative veto, the main constitutional problem with such an arrangement is that congressional preferences will change over time, and the agent's implementation will change with it, as mapped in Figure 1E:

x x* x*′

P h s H S h* s* H* A S*

FIGURE 1E. Statutory policy shifts from H < x < S to H* < x*′ < S* when Congress controls agency and congressional preferences shift globally.

If there is a global shift in congressional preferences to the right, congressionally controlled implementation will shift statutory policy ($x^{*\prime}$) far away from the original policy (x), much further away than presidentially controlled implementation (x^*).

This scenario is the only legitimate risk that *Bowsher* prevents, but we doubt it is much of a risk. The reason is that when congressional preferences shift so markedly, the shift has usually been presidentially led—that is, the biggest shifts in congressional preferences have been in connection with landslide victories for similarly minded Presidents (1932, 1948, 1952, 1964, 1980). While off-year elections also yield shifts, usually against the President, they do not tend to be so global and important (1938, 1946, 1950, 1954, 1958, 1966, 1982, 1986). If the President shifts along with Congress, then Figure 1E would show a new Presidential position (P^*) also located along the righthand part of the spectrum. In that event, Congress could reach the new equilibrium point ($x^{*\prime}$) following normal Article I, Section 7 procedures.

Case 3 statutes present a much more favorable field for Justice Stevens's analysis in *Bowsher* and *Metropolitan Washington* because congressional control over the implementing agency would dramatically shift statutory policy from the Article I, Section 7 equilibrium point, as mapped in Figure 3C:

73. *See supra* text accompanying note 68.

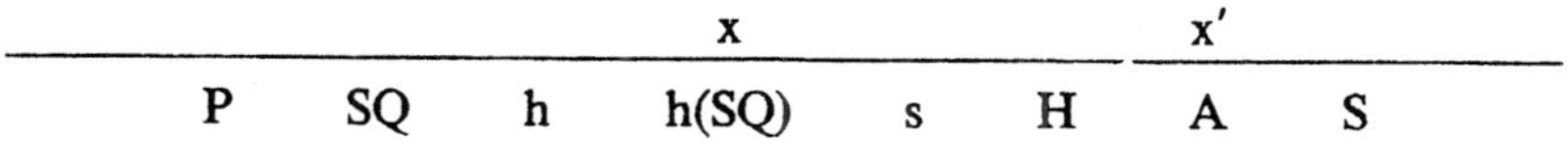

FIGURE 3C. Policy shifts from x = h(SQ) to H < x' < S, if Congress delegates lawmaking authority to congressional agent.

This is obviously a dramatic shift in the equilibrium policy, from a point close to the veto median of the more pro-president chamber (*h(SQ)*) to a point reflecting a compromise between the two chambers but ignoring the President's preferences. For Case 3 statutes, the shift in statutory policy represented by delegation to a congressionally dominated agency is more dramatic than the shift represented by delegation to a presidentially dominated agency (compare Figure 3C to Figure 3A above). This is the sort of situation the Court should discourage, and Justice Stevens's analysis seems appropriate for Case 3 statutes.

Unhappily, this same analysis suggests that Case 3 statutes will rarely include a provision for congressionally dominated agencies. Because such a provision would negate the President's preferences in the statute's implementation, the President could successfully veto any bill creating such an agency, thereby forcing Congress to back down in order to obtain a statute. Partly for this reason, it appears that the statute in *Metropolitan Washington* was not a Case 3 statute; the President (having Air Force One and Andrews Air Force Base to land it) had no stake in the ultimate policy equilibrium and probably would have gone along with a wide range of congressional policy choices, including the review board provision. This makes the case look pretty much like *Bowsher;* therefore, Article I, Section 7 was not seriously implicated, contrary to the Court's opinion in *Metropolitan Washington*.

D. JUDICIAL REVIEW OF AGENCY ACTION AS A RESPONSE TO THE CONSTITUTIONAL DILEMMA: *CHEVRON*

In the 1930s, at the same time that legislative vetoes were being introduced into legislation, the legal and political community was also debating the scope of judicial review of agency rulemaking (a debate that long predated the 1930s). One consequence of this debate was the Administrative Procedure Act of 1946 (APA),[74] which assured that agency rulemaking would ordinarily be subject to judicial review. What was not thoroughly addressed by the APA was how scrutinizing courts should be of agency lawmaking, and Supreme Court practice and doctrine has run in many different directions. In 1984, however, the Court clarified its position on review of agency

74. 5 U.S.C. §§ 551-559, 701-706 (Supp. 1989-1990).

rulemaking[75] in *Chevron U.S.A. Inc. v. National Resources Defense Council.*[76]

In reasoning that the Court has broadly applied since 1984, *Chevron* held that constitutional separation of powers requires courts to defer to any reasonable agency interpretation of statutes it is charged with implementing,[77] and that such deference is not undermined by an agency's changing positions in response to presidential preferences.[78] *Chevron* has been subjected to keen criticism by at least some legal commentators,[79] and we join the critics of *Chevron*. From the perspective of the original constitutional design, aggressive judicial review of agency rulemaking ameliorates the constitutional dilemma, under which the modern administrative state has witnessed a shift of lawmaking power from Congress to the President.

If there is sufficient evidence in the statute or the legislative history for the original policy equilibrium in the statute, and if judges saw their role as enforcing such statutory guidance, then judicial review becomes a powerful mechanism for redressing at least some of the constitutional imbalance. Under these circumstances, the effect of judicial review is obviously beneficial, because courts then become mechanisms for moving usurpative agency-set policy (x') back to the original statutory policy (x) set by Congress-with-the-President. Under these circumstances, it is easy to say that *Chevron* is wrong, or at least should be narrowly read, from the perspective of the original understanding embodied in Article I, Section 7. *Chevron* suggests, however, that for many cases the statutory equilibrium will be unknowable to the Court, and under conditions of uncertainty the agency's preferences are more legitimate than the Court's preferences because the former is more electorally accountable.

But our game theorctic account of the original understanding embodied in Article I, Section 7 suggests that judicial review is valuable even when the statute or its legislative history provide little guidance and when the judge only seeks to read her own preferences into the statutory policy. To explain

75. We distinguish among judicial review of (1) the correctness of agency rulemaking and statutory interpretation, where the inquiry is whether the agency's interpretation of the statute is correct; (2) the correctness of agency adjudications, which focuses on whether a trial-like result is supported to the extent required by the appropriate evidentiary standard but may also evaluate the correctness of agency interpretations of statutes; and (3) agency adherence to proper procedures in either type of proceeding. Although some agencies do their lawmaking only through adjudication (e.g., the National Labor Relations Board), most do it through rulemaking, and we limit our analysis in this Section to rulemaking.

76. 467 U.S. 837 (1984).

77. *Id.* at 842-45.

78. *Id.* at 865-66.

79. *See, e.g.*, Cynthia R. Farina, *Statutory Interpretation and the Balance of Power in the Administrative State*, 89 COLUM. L. REV. 452 (1989).

this argument, we now include the Court[80] (*J*) as a player in the Article I, Section 7 game. That is, judges have exogenous preferences about the statutory policy and try to impose them on the statute in place of the agency's preferences, but are willing to compromise their preferences to the extent necessary to prevent being overruled.

The Court's participation as a political player affects the game's equilibrium in different ways, depending upon the location of the Court's own preferences. We shall develop this point by reference to three possible positions for judicial preferences, mapped out for Case 1 statutes.[81]

Variation 1: $J > S$. Figure 4 maps the configuration of preferences where those of the Court, *J*, are to the right of the chamber median in both the House and Senate ($J > S > H$):

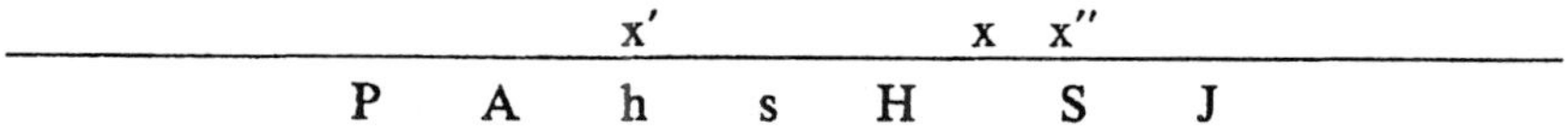

FIGURE 4. Statutory policy shifts from x' = h to x'' = S, with judicial review where J > S.

Judicial review introduces the Court as a decisionmaker that can create a new default position, much as the agency has done in our earlier examples. The agency thereby loses its policymaking advantage. If the agency sets statutory policy anywhere to the left of the Senate median, *S*, the Court will want to override the agency interpretation with its own preferred policy. Anticipating future moves of the other players, the Court will not set policy to the right of the chamber median, *S*, because in that event both the House and Senate would favor legislation set at or to the left of the Senate median, *S*, which the President would sign, because they all prefer *S* to *J*. As a result, the Court will override any agency policy set to the left of the Senate median, *S*. Knowing this could be the result of unconstrained judicial review, the agency will then set policy at the chamber median, *S*, to avoid a judicial overruling that would be accepted by Congress. The equilibrium result, $x'' = S$, is much closer to the original statutory policy, *x*, than was the result without judicial review, $x' = h$.

Variation 2: $h < J < S$. If the Court's policy preferences fall between the

80. We are using "Court" to mean any reviewing court, ultimately including the Supreme Court, whose preferences would often govern what we are calling "*J*".

81. We use Case 1 statutes since those statutes represent the most dramatic erosion of the original equilibrium in the modern administrative state. Most of the points made in this section for Case 1 statutes would apply also, but with lesser force, to Case 3 statutes. For a more technical version of this analysis that also considers the role of committees, see William N. Eskridge, Jr. & John Ferejohn, *Making the Deal Stick: Enforcing the Original Constitutional Structure of Lawmaking in the Modern Regulatory State*, J.L. ECON. & ORGANIZATION (forthcoming 1992) (special issue).

Senate median, *S*, and the House veto median, *h*, the introduction of judicial review ameliorates the constitutional dilemma, though not as much as in Variation 1. Consider Figure 4A:

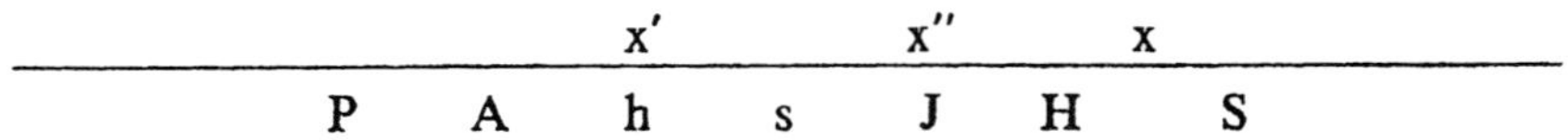

FIGURE 4A. Statutory policy shifts from x' = h to x'' = J, with judicial review where h < J < S.

Under this configuration of preferences, the Court has maximum freedom, for wherever it sets policy (such that $h < x'' < S$), its policy will be protected from override. If the Court's preferences are anywhere between those of the two chambers ($H < J < S$), one of the chambers will always object to any shift away from the new default position, *J*. Bicameralism protects the Court from override. If the Court's preferences are to the left of both chamber medians but not to the left of the veto median of the more pro-President chamber ($h < J < H$), both chambers of Congress might want to override the Court's decision, but the President would veto the override and one or both chambers would not be able to override the veto. Presentment then protects the Court's position from override.

Given these dynamics, and not wanting to be overridden itself, the agency will anticipate the Court's power and will set policy at $x'' = J$. Note here that the extent to which judicial review ameliorates the constitutional dilemma depends upon how close the Court's preferences are to those of the chamber medians.

Variation 3: $J < h$. The final variation locates the Court's preferences at or to the left of those of the veto median of the more pro-President chamber, as in Figure 4B:

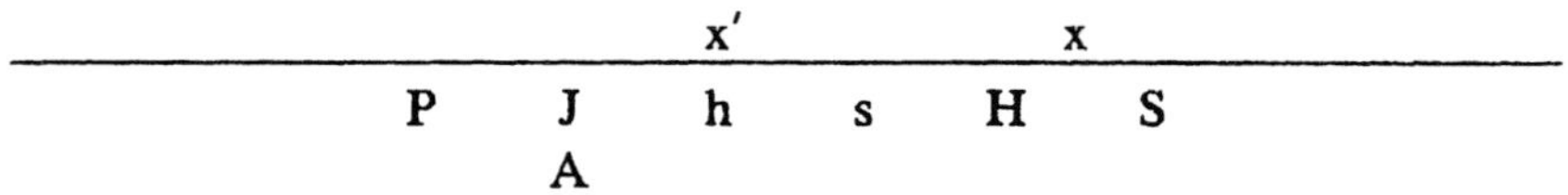

FIGURE 4B. Statutory policy remains at x' = h, with judicial review where J < h.

Under this configuration of preferences, the agency will set statutory policy at the House veto median, *h*, and the Court will affirm on judicial review, because both realize that any policy to the left of the veto median can be overridden by Congress, with veto-proof margins.

The introduction of aggressive judicial review of agency action does ameliorate the constitutional dilemma—sometimes substantially—under all variations, except when the Court's preferences are at or to the left of the veto median, and in that variation the introduction of judicial review has no effect on the dilemma (i.e., it does not aggravate it). Contrary to *Chevron*, aggressive judicial review of agency rulemaking is not countermajoritarian in the context of the Article I, Section 7 game. Instead. it is *Chevron* that may be countermajoritarian under the circumstances of the modern administrative state.

More importantly, this analysis suggests that aggressive judicial review is a better way for congressional preferences to reassert themselves, than is the legislative veto. To the extent that the Court sees itself as enforcing the original statutory "deal" (namely, the original equilibrium result of Article I, Section 7 game), judicial review offers the possibility of enforcing that deal precisely against efforts by agencies to shift statutory policy. Even if the Court sees its role as imposing its own preferences onto statutory policy, its role will tend to push policy back toward the original deal. The Court's independence from presidential as well as congressional pressure suggests a greater randomness of its preferences that will affect the pro-President agency bias, but without the potential pro-Congress bias of the one-house legislative veto (in particular).

E. THE DEBATE OVER THE COURT'S USE OF LEGISLATIVE HISTORY

As emphasized in the prior section, aggressive judicial review of agency decisions works best to restore the Article I, Section 7 equilibrium if the reviewing court has access to information permitting it to locate the original equilibrium point, x. We are here equating "information" with what is conventionally known as "legislative history." However, the Court's longstanding use of legislative history to interpret ambiguous statutes came under intense criticism in the 1980s from within the judiciary itself. The main critics have been Justice Scalia and Judge Easterbrook.[82] Their view is that the Court's traditional use of legislative history is in tension with Article I, Sec-

---

82. For Justice Scalia, see Antonin Scalia, Speech on Use of Legislative History (delivered between fall 1985 and spring 1986 at various law schools) (transcript on file with *The Georgetown Law Journal)* (role of court to interpret statutory language, not to reconstruct intentions of Congress), and the cases and materials collected in William N. Eskridge Jr., *The New Textualism*, 37 UCLA L. REV. 621, 650-56 (1990) (summary of Justice Scalia's criticisms of the use of legislative history and Justice Scalia's proposed alternative); Nicholas S. Zeppos, *Justice Scalia's Textualism: The "New" New Legal Process*, 12 CARDOZO L. REV. 1597 (1991). For Judge Easterbrook, see *In re* Sinclair, 870 F.2d 1340, 1344 (7th Cir. 1989) (Easterbrook, J.) (legislative history "may not be used to show an 'intent' at variance with the meaning of the text."); Frank H. Easterbrook, *The Role of Original Intent in Statutory Construction*, 11 HARV. J.L. & PUB. POL'Y 59, 62-66 (1988) (courts should "look at the statutory structure and hear the words as they would sound in the mind of a skilled, objectively reasonable user of words."). Their views are the basis for the extensive analysis in U.S. DEP'T OF JUSTICE OFFICE OF LEGAL POLICY, USING AND MISUSING LEGISLATIVE HISTORY: A

tion 7. "Committee reports, floor speeches, and even colloquies between Congressmen, are frail substitutes for bicameral vote upon the text of a law and its presentment to the President. It is at best dangerous to assume that all the necessary participants in the law-enactment process are acting upon the same unexpressed assumptions."[83] Justice Scalia has been particularly critical of the Court's reliance on committee reports as support for a particular statutory interpretation, and he strongly objects to their use to rebut the deference owed to agency rules under *Chevron*.[84] Justice Scalia's views may have had some influence on the Court, which in the last several years has been prone to ignore legislative history in applying *Chevron*'s deference to agency decisionmaking.[85]

Justice Scalia's formalist objection to legislative history in general and committee reports in particular is that the Court's reliance on such materials is tantamount to a *Chadha*-like delegation of lawmaking power to a congressional subgroup (i.e., committees) and therefore suffers from the same constitutional infirmity as the legislative veto. What is correct about Justice Scalia's point is that the Court should not give committee reports the same authority as the statute itself. What is questionable about his point is that he fails to make out a case for ignoring committee reports altogether, as the Court has recently noted in *Wisconsin Public Intervenor v. Mortier*.[86] Justice Scalia himself slavishly relies on dictionaries to interpret statutes, upon the view that the members of Congress and the President would take dictionary meanings as an "unexpressed assumption" of what the bill means.[87] But the participants in the lawmaking process treat committee reports that way, as an "unexpressed assumption" that participants rely on much more than they rely on dictionaries. For this and other reasons, Justice Scalia's attack has

---

RE-EVALUATION OF THE STATUS OF LEGISLATIVE HISTORY IN STATUTORY INTERPRETATION (1989) (arguing for narrow role for legislative history).

83. Thompson v. Thompson, 484 U.S. 174, 191-92 (1988) (Scalia, J., concurring).

84. *See* Eskridge, *supra* note 82, at 650-52.

85. The leading case is K Mart Corp. v. Cartier, Inc., 486 U.S. 281, 291-92 (1988) (Kennedy, J.) (to determine consistency of Customs Service regulation with implementing statute, Court looks to particular statutory language at issue and design of statute as a whole). *See also* Sullivan v. Everhart, 494 U.S. 83, 89 (1990) (to determine consistency of Health and Human Services department regulations with implementing statute, look to particular statutory language and language and design of statute as a whole); Sullivan v. Zebley, 493 U.S. 521, 528-29 (1990) (to determine consistency of HHS decision with implementing statute look to statutory language and structure of statute); Mead Corp. v. Tilley, 490 U.S. 714, 723-24 (1989) (rejecting reliance on legislative history of ERISA in favor of plain meaning of statute).

86. "[C]ommon sense suggests that inquiry benefits from reviewing additional information rather than ignoring it. Legislative history materials are not generally so misleading that jurists should never employ them in a good faith effort to discern legislative intent." Wisconsin Pub. Intervenor v. Mortier, 111 S. Ct. 2476, 2485 n.4 (1991).

87. *See, e.g.,* Chisom v. Roemer, 111 S. Ct. 2354, 2372 (1991) (Scalia, J., dissenting) (dictionary definition of "representative" used to interpret its meaning in Voting Rights Act).

drawn few allies.[88]

Positive political theory provides an interesting structural argument for Justice Scalia's position. Early positive political theory argued that congressional committees would tend to be populated with "outliers," that is, members of Congress whose preferences are very unrepresentative of those of Congress as a whole.[89] Members from farm districts would cluster around the Agriculture Committee, those with strong union constituencies around the Labor Committee, and so forth. Since most authoritative history is created by committees (through their hearings and reports, and floor statements by key members), this poses a danger that such history is systematically biased and not representative of congressional preferences generally. If important congressional committees are indeed populated by outliers, then Justice Scalia's criticism of committee reports has greater bite.

The Scalia critique can be expressed in the argot of our Article I, Section 7 game, simplified to focus on only one chamber in the context of a Case 1 statute. Consider Figure 5, which includes the relevant committee (C) as a new player in the Article I, Section 7 game.

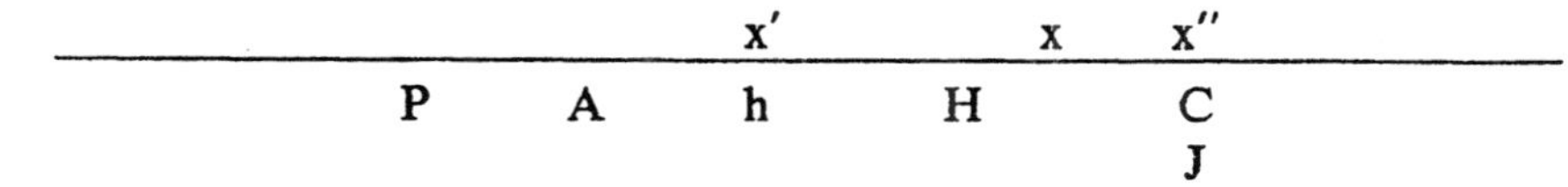

FIGURE 5. Statutory policy shifts to x'' = C, where Court follows committee report to overturn agency interpretation of statute.

Justice Scalia's fear is that slavish adherence to committee reports and other legislative history generated by outlier committees will lead the reviewing Court to a position, x'', very far away from the agency interpretation, (x'), without being any closer to the original Article I, Section 7 equilibrium (x). This strikes us as a legitimate concern for any outlier situation, including those where the outlying committee is to the left of the chamber (and aligned with the agency).

Nevertheless, the doctrinal implications of this point are not as harsh as those suggested by Justice Scalia. To begin with, recent positive political theory scholarship suggests that the danger of outlier committees is not as great as once believed. That is, Congress has few incentives to defer decision-making responsibilities to subgroups that will systematically subvert overall congressional preferences. And Congress has not only incentives but effec-

88. Academics have been unimpressed with Justice Scalia's arguments. *E.g.*, Daniel A. Farber & Phillip P. Frickey, *Legislative Intent & Public Choice*, 74 VA. L. REV. 423 (1988); Stephen Ross, *Reaganist Realism Comes to Detroit*, 1989 U. ILL. L. REV. 399, 420-33.

89. The leading work is KENNETH A. SHEPSLE, THE GIANT JIGSAW PUZZLE (1978).

tive means to monitor and discourage outlying committees. For these reasons, a recent empirical work reports that most House committees are not preference outliers.[90]

Even if congressional committees were preference outliers, it is not clear that legislative history is valueless. The import of Article I, Section 7 is that committee reports themselves are not "law" and are at best one type of evidence to figure out the original statutory policy. To the extent there is an outlier danger, the Court should be reluctant to follow a committee report over an equally clear statutory provision and should seek confirming or rebutting suggestions in the remainder of the legislative history before following the committee report.[91] In other words, the Court should use committee reports "critically," which has been the Court's practice in fact.[92] If the outlier phenomenon supports any theory of legislative history, it supports, not Justice Scalia's harsh exclusionary approach, but "imaginative reconstruction," in which the Court develops a history of the statute from all sorts of evidence and derives a probable answer from the reconstructed policy preferences suggested by the history.[93] The opinions of Justice Stevens are textbook examples of deft and judicious reconstruction of Article I, Section 7 policy equilibria.[94]

F. THE LEGISLATIVE ACQUIESCENCE DOCTRINE: *DAMES & MOORE*

Also controversial in the 1980s has been the Court's legislative acquiescence doctrine. Under this doctrine of statutory interpretation, the Court will often presume that Congress "acquiesces" in settled interpretations of the statute by the Supreme Court, lower court consensus, or administrative

---

90. KEITH KREHBIEL, INFORMATION AND LEGISLATIVE ORGANIZATION 105-50 (1991) (most congressional committees are not preference outliers and are roughly "representative" of their chambers).

91. For example, the views of the President can be gleaned from the committee hearings, which almost always focus on the views of executive branch officials. Hearings also may reflect early deals that are struck. Floor colloquy represent an opportunity for members objecting to committee report language to set forth their views, and presidential signing statements have been used for this purpose as well.

92. *See* Eskridge, *supra* note 82, at 626-40 (describing the Court's traditional practice).

93. This theory is associated with Judge Learned Hand. *See, e.g.,* Lehigh Valley Coal Co. v. Yensavage, 218 F. 547, 553 (2d Cir. 1914), *cert. denied,* 235 U.S. 705 (1915) (statutes such as one so strictly defining the word employee as to work an injustice on an injured contractor, "should be construed, not as theorems of Euclid, but with some imagination of the purposes which lie behind them"). It has been further popularized by Judge Richard Posner. *E.g.,* RICHARD A. POSNER, THE FEDERAL COURTS: CRISIS AND REFORM 286-87 (1985) (in deciding application of statute to case, judge should "put himself in the shoes of the enacting legislators").

94. *See, e.g.,* Green v. Bock Laundry Mach. Co., 490 U.S. 504, 511-24 (1989) (Stevens, J.) (interpretation of FED. R. EVID. 609 through thorough examination of history leading to rule's enactment); INS v. Cardoza-Fonseca, 480 U.S. 421, 432-43 (1987) (Stevens, J.) (interpretation of Immigration and Nationality Act through examination of legislative history).

agencies.[95] The Court invoked the acquiescence doctrine in several notable statutory interpretation cases during the 1980s,[96] and in at least one constitutional case.

In *Dames & Moore v. Regan,*[97] the Court relied on the acquiescence doctrine to hold that the President has authority to enter into executive agreements with foreign states that "suspend" U.S. lawsuits against those states in U.S. courts. Although the Court held that the International Emergency Economic Powers Act[98] does not authorize suspension of lawsuits,[99] the Court held that the Act "invited" presidential initiatives to settle claims and that the President was empowered to suspend lawsuits by "a history of congressional acquiescence in conduct of the sort engaged in by the President."[100] The Court's holding was an amalgam of constitutional and statutory interpretation: the "inviting" character of the statute, the President's prior settlement of foreign claims by shifting them to claims settlement tribunals together with Congress's acquiescence in the President's actions, and the President's own inherent authority to deal with foreign affairs emergencies, combined to persuade the Court that the President had authority to suspend claims without an explicit statutory grant of power.

First suggested by the dissenting and concurring opinions in the Steel Seizure Case,[101] the acquiescence rule as applied in *Dames & Moore* amounts to a constitutional doctrine of adverse possession, through which the President can expand upon his inherent powers by a longstanding practice in which Congress acquiesces. Relying on Article I, Section 7, in the pure statutory interpretation context, Justice Scalia has claimed that "vindication by congressional inaction is a canard."[102] The argument would be that only Congress acting through the Article I, Section 7 procedures[103] can alter ap-

---

95. For a doctrinal and critical account of the acquiescence rule, see William N. Eskridge, Jr., *Interpreting Legislative Inaction,* 87 MICH. L. REV. 67, 71-78 (1988).

96. *E.g.,* Johnson v. Transportation Agency, Santa Clara County, 480 U.S. 616, 629 n.7 (1987) (congressional acquiescence to Title VII ruling); School Bd. v. Arline, 480 U.S. 273, 277-80 (1987) (congressional acquiescence to HHS regulations); Bob Jones Univ. v. United States, 461 U.S. 574, 599-602 (1983) (congressional acquiescence to IRS ruling); North Haven Bd. of Educ. v. Bell, 456 U.S. 512, 535 (1982) (congressional acquiescence to construction of Title IX). *See generally* Eskridge, *supra* note 95, at 125-28 (app.1, collecting relevant cases).

97. 453 U.S. 654 (1981).

98. 50 U.S.C. §§ 1701-1706 (1988).

99. 453 U.S. at 675-76. The Court also held that the "Hostage Act," 22 U.S.C. § 1732 (1988), does not authorize suspension of lawsuits either. 453 U.S. at 676-77.

100. 453 U.S. at 678-79.

101. Youngstown Sheet & Tube Co. v. Sawyer, 343 U.S. 579, 701-04 (1952) (Vinson, C.J., dissenting); *id.* at 593-614 (Frankfurter, J., concurring); *id.* at 634-55 (Jackson, J., concurring).

102. Johnson v. Transportation Agency, Santa Clara County, 480 U.S. 616, 672 (1987) (Scalia, J., dissenting).

103. Or, as in *Dames & Moore,* through Article II, Section 2 procedures for making treaties (proposal from the President, ratification by the Senate).

parent statutory rights.

The Article I, Section 7 game developed here lends support to Justice Scalia's critique of the acquiescence doctrine generally—and in particular with regard to *Dames & Moore*. *Dames & Moore* is a classic Case 1 situation, where the President wants to change the status quo (a dispute with a foreign state) much further than Congress has signified. Based upon the President's prior practice in settling claims, the Court is willing to assume that Congress has "acquiesced" in the President's having that power. But the Article I, Section 7 game suggests that Congress's failure to object means virtually nothing. Recall the game mapped by Figure 1A: the President only has to satisfy the veto median of the more pro-President chamber in order to avoid a congressional reaction to policies set by the President. Thus, even though the President sets policy far away from that which would result from the Article I, Section 7 game envisioned by the Framers, Congress will not respond. This is obviously not legislative acquiescence; it is executive usurpation.

III. THE ARTICLE I, SECTION 7 GAME TODAY: ADAPTING THE FRAMERS' VALUES TO THE MODERN ADMINISTRATIVE STATE

The game played out in this Article seeks to understand the dynamics behind the bicameralism and presentment requirements of Article I, Section 7 as originally understood by the Framers. The main point of our analysis thus far has been to present an originalist theory of Article I, Section 7 that better accounts for the Framers' expectations in the modern administrative state (where there is unpoliced delegation to executive agencies) than the originalist theory adopted by the Court in *Chadha*. We have suggested that our originalist theory is superior to that of *Chadha* because it better accounts for the overall goals of the Constitution in general and of Article I, Section 7 in particular.[104] We have also suggested that the Court itself has not been able to apply *Chadha*'s originalist theory in a coherent way. Our Article I, Section 7 game offers an originalist theory that can be logically applied to various structural constitutional problems, though our game would reverse the approach taken by the Court in a number of important constitutional cases, from *Dames & Moore* to *Bowsher* to *Chadha* itself.

A central problem with our Article I, Section 7 game is that it, like *Chadha*, only seeks to enforce the Framers' original values and expectations. Many constitutional theorists reject originalist theories of constitutional ad-

104. And *Chadha* offers no countervailing advantages. The Court and some of its defenders believe that *Chadha* offers the advantage of being faithful to the "plain meaning" of Article I, but that is unsupportable: as Justice White argued in dissent, a legislative veto is part of legislation that is enacted by both chambers of Congress (bicameralism) and presented to the President (presentment), and so satisfies the plain meaning of Article I, Section 7.

judication, and the Justices themselves invoke such theories selectively. What relevance does the Article I, Section 7 game have for the modern regulatory state in light of current post-New Deal values? This is an important question, to which we now turn.

A. THE DIFFICULTIES OF PURE ORIGINALISM: FROM 1789 TO THE NEW DEAL TO THE ERA OF DIVIDED GOVERNMENT

What ultimately makes our dynamic theory of Article I, Section 7 superior to that in *Chadha* is that it provides a framework within which we can understand the effects of historical change upon the constitutional structure. The result and reasoning in *Chadha* make the most sense if our polity were exactly like the one in 1789 (represented in Figures 1-3): Congress-with-the-President enact statutes, which are applied to specific situations by the executive and judicial branches. In such a polity, the legislative veto would be unnecessary to any nonusurpative congressional policy.

The massive and often standardless delegation of lawmaking power to agencies (recall Figures 1A, 3A, and 3B) both gives rise to the legislative veto as a nonusurpative congressional response and destroys the analytical foundation of *Chadha*-like reasoning. That is, once "lawmaking" in the federal government becomes agency decisionmaking authorized by broad congressional authorization (*Chevron*), or even presidential decisionmaking authorized by congressional acquiescence (*Dames & Moore*), the Article I, Section 7 game changes. No longer is it the simple game assumed by the Framers (Figures 1-3), but it is a more complicated game in which the equilibrium policy adopted by Congress-with-the-President is immediately subject to significant shifts (Figures 1A, 3A, and 3B).

This was the point of Justice White's dissenting opinion in *Chadha*:[105] the New Deal changed Article I, Section 7 and generated the constitutional legitimacy of the legislative veto as a nonusurpative congressional response to the new imbalance created by the President's influence over post-enactment lawmaking. To deal with an enormous crisis, the New Deal Congress willingly delegated—gave away—enormous lawmaking power to agencies. The agency-generated policies generally mirrored those that would have been adopted by the normal Article I, Section 7 procedures because the preferences of the President (Franklin Roosevelt) and Congress (lopsided Democratic majorities, usually very supportive of Roosevelt) were similar on most issues. Since agencies were implementing Article I, Section 7 policy with greater speed and expertise than Congress itself could have done, progressive legal thought found the massive delegation unproblematic. The result was the almost immediate death of the nondelegation doctrine. Few mourned it,

105. 462 U.S. 919, 967-74 (1983) (White, J., dissenting).

but with its demise was a semipermanent transfer of power from Congress to agencies dominated or influenced by the President.

That transfer of power became more problematic during periods of conflict between the President and Congress, especially after 1968. Since then, our national government has (except for the Carter years) been divided between a Republican President and a Democratic Congress.[106] Not surprisingly, during this period, each institution has been more aggressive about self-consciously protecting its turf. Congress, in particular, found that much of its power had been given away by prior Congresses and sought to avoid or reverse that phenomenon through mechanisms such as the legislative veto, delegation to congressionally controlled agencies, and reliance on judicial review of agency action.

The implications of this historical analysis for *Chadha* are significant: the Court's invocation of a static model of Article I, Section 7 oversimplifies the constitutional problem. Once Article I, Section 7 procedures and policies have been sacrificed—and sacrificed with the Court's constant approval (most recently in *Mistretta*[107])—by the nonenforcement of the nondelegation doctrine, the Court cannot then pretend that the Article I, Section 7 of the Framers' time still exists today. Yet that is what the Court tried to do in *Chadha*.

But only "tried" to do. The Court's results and reasoning in other constitutional cases suggest that the Court itself has not internalized its *Chadha* understanding of Article I, Section 7, even at a formal level.[108] The most telling contrasts are *Alaska Airlines* and *Dames & Moore*. In the former case, the Court held that a *Chadha*-invalidated legislative veto of regulations governing the administration of a plan to aid airline employees dislocated by deregulation was severable from the underlying substantive statute, because Congress "would have enacted" the statute even without the legislative veto.[109] Our Article I, Section 7 game exposes the error in this reasoning. Once Congress becomes aware that the Article I, Section 7 game becomes a progressive diminution in congressional power whenever Congress delegates rulemaking to an agency it does not control (an awareness that is acute by the 1970s), Congress becomes unwilling to delegate unless it can have some assurance that agency policy will not wander away from the original equilibrium. The legislative veto was one such assurance—a clear quid pro quo for legislative delegation to an agency Congress wants to monitor. Without the veto, Congress would certainly want to enact a more specific statute, or no statute at all. On the one hand, therefore, *Alaska Airlines* is almost certainly

106. Or, between 1981 and 1987, a Republican President and Senate and a Democratic House.

107. 488 U.S. 361 (1988).

108. See our analysis in the Introduction to this article.

109. Alaska Airlines v. Brock, 480 U.S. 678, 691 (1987).

wrong in concluding that Congress would have enacted the same statutory delegation, even if there were no legislative veto. On the other hand, because of the obviousness of this flaw in its reasoning, *Alaska Airlines* is a clue as to what *Chadha* itself is all about: *Chadha* is no rigorous formalist effort to enforce Article I, Section 7 as written, for otherwise the Court would have invalidated entire statutes under its traditional severability test. Instead, *Chadha* is the Court's expression of concern that the legislative veto "goes too far" in protecting Congress's interests and creates a new imbalance favoring Congress's preferences.

This hypothesis is also supported by the Court's action in *Dames & Moore*. The President's unilateral suspension of federal lawsuits pursuant to an executive agreement is, if anything, a more significant breach of the formal structures of lawmaking in the Constitution than the legislative veto. The President's action added to presidential powers under IEEPA[110] and amended the FSIA,[111] all without going through the Article I, Section 7 procedures for lawmaking.[112] Yet the Court did not even pause to analyze Article I, Section 7. The reason for the Court's obliviousness is surely that the Court found the President's action justified by the needs of the modern administrative state. Indeed, the point of the Court's acquiescence discussion is that there is a tradition of presidential involvement in settling foreign claims, and that tradition is productive and workable. This suggests *either* that the Court is willing to sacrifice originalist values when they are unworkable in the modern administrative state *or* that the Court does not really believe in *Chadha*'s stringent articulation of those originalist values. We think that both propositions are true.

B. THE ARTICLE I, SECTION 7 GAME, UPDATED FOR THE MODERN ADMINISTRATIVE STATE

The game developed in this article is, we think, superior to the *Chadha* framework for analyzing Article I, Section 7 to effectuate the Framers' original values in the modern administrative state. But, for a nonoriginalist, that hardly makes our Article I, Section 7 game a viable one for the modern administrative state. One key difficulty is that our game adopts several assumptions made by the Framers that are not easily defensible today. Specifically, the Framers sought a balance between popular desires and policy stability across time. The modern regulatory state seeks a balance among at least three things: popular desires, stability, and accommodation of prior policy

110. 50 U.S.C. §§ 1701-1706 (1988).

111. 28 U.S.C. §§ 1601-1611 (1988).

112. The President's action, as enforced by the Court, can in the alternative be viewed as the creation of a "treaty" enforceable as the "law of the land" under the Supremacy Clause, U.S. CONST. art. VI, without obtaining Senate ratification, as explicitly required by Article II.

choices to changing circumstances and new problems. The modern regulatory state values stability less than the Framers did and introduces dynamic policy evolution as part of the balance.

Moreover, the Framers envisioned a very different Congress and Presidency than the institutions we now observe. For the Framers, the House of Representatives embodied popular desires but threatened stability with its mercurial sentiments. Bicameralism and presentment were mechanisms by which the often volatile House could be restrained by the indirectly elected and longer-termed (and therefore not so responsive to We the People) Senate and President. Today, all three institutions are essentially elected by We the People and might be said to reflect "popular" desires. Indeed, with its overwhelming reelection percentages election after election, the House is the least likely body to reflect popular preference changes, while the Presidency is more likely to reflect such changes.

We are sympathetic to arguments that these changes in twentieth-century America simply render Article I, Section 7 irrelevant to modern constitutional theory, much as the Contracts Clause has been.[113] But we think that our Article I, Section 7 game provides a heuristic method by which the original balance can be understood and updated in light of modern developments. The Framers' notion that lawmaking needs to balance popular desires with stability should be updated to reflect a third value, that of dynamic policy evolution. This third value is critical to the modern acceptance of massive and often standardless delegation of lawmaking responsibilities to administrative agencies, which we endorse. What we urge is that the modern version of the Article I, Section 7 game react to this delegation of lawmaking in such a way as to preserve a balance among the three popularly elected national institutions.

Thus, too, the Framers' specific ideas about Congress need to be reconsidered. For example, their notion that the House is the seat of popular desires needs to give way to the notion that the House, Senate, and President all reflect popular desires, but with different constituencies: the President is the main nationally elected official, Senators hail from the states, and House members are elected from small, internally more homogeneous districts. The different constituencies of the different officials justify the Article I, Section 7 game today: while in 1789 the Article I, Section 7 structure was mainly justified by the need for the more stable institutions (Senate and President) to rein in the House, today that structure is justified by the desirability that no one constituency dominate lawmaking.[114] James Madison's notion that

113. Or, indeed, as Article I, Section 7, Clause 1, the "Origination Clause," has been. Clause 1's requirement that all bills raising revenue originate in the House of Representatives is easily evaded and virtually never enforced.

114. This insight has been supported from various pluralist political perspectives, including pub-

"ambition must be made to counteract ambition"[115] is still a sound precept for republican governance.

Consider some tentative implications of this updated Article I, Section 7 balance for constitutional doctrine:

1. The Nondelegation Doctrine as a Principle of Statutory Interpretation

Experience suggests that the needs of the modern administrative state have overtaken the nondelegation doctrine. The key reason for extensive congressional delegation is that modern regulation requires both detailed and flexible rules that Congress cannot easily produce on a regular basis.[116] Agencies can do so, and Article I, Section 7 should accommodate agency lawmaking. Although contrary to the Framers' apparent understanding in 1789, we agree with *Mistretta*[117] that the nondelegation doctrine is essentially unenforceable as a constitutional doctrine. Its essential test, that the delegation be accompanied by an "intelligible principle" to which the agency must conform its implementation, is quite elastic and has been applied creatively.

While *Mistretta* correctly considers the nondelegation doctrine to be a largely toothless constitutional instrument, the opinion suggests that it may have some teeth as a precept of statutory interpretation.[118] We endorse and expand upon this suggestion as one way to maintain balanced lawmaking. Our proposed rule of statutory interpretation: when agency rules go beyond the clear commands of the statutory text, the agency has the burden of justifying its rule as one advancing the congressional intent or purpose.

This rule of responsible delegation is inconsistent with the Court's reasoning in *Chevron* and *Dames & Moore,* though not necessarily the Court's result in either case. We would reinterpret *Chevron,* not as a virtual carte blanche for agencies to make policy judgments when Congress has broadly delegated lawmaking to them, but as an invitation for agencies to justify policy initiatives based upon sensitivity to congressional signals and reasoned application of the statutory policies.[119] We would reinterpret *Dames &*

---

lic choice theory. *See* JAMES M. BUCHANAN & GORDAN TULLOCK, THE CALCULUS OF CONSENT: THE LOGICAL FOUNDATIONS OF DEMOCRACY (1962).

115. THE FEDERALIST NO. 51, *supra* note 28, at 322.

116. Congress's experience in producing detailed rules for environmental regulation has not been promising. *See, e.g.*, BRUCE A. ACKERMAN & WILLIAM T. HASSLER, CLEAN COAL, DIRTY AIR (1981); William M. Eichbaum & Hope M. Babcock, *A Question of Delegation: The Surface Mining Control and Reclamation Act of 1977 and State-Federal Relations*, 86 DICK. L. REV. 615 (1982).

117. 488 U.S. 361, 371-80 (1988).

118. *Id.* at 371-80 n.7 ("In recent years, our application of the nondelegation doctrine principally has been limited to the interpretation of statutory texts, and, more particularly, to giving narrow constructions to statutory delegations that might otherwise be thought to be unconstitutional.").

119. This, by the way, is the way *Chevron*'s author, Justice Stevens, reads the decision. *See* INS v. Cardoza-Fonseca, 480 U.S. 421, 445-48 (1987) (Stevens, J.). *But see id.* at 454 (Scalia, J., concurring in judgment) (much stronger reading of *Chevron*).

Moore, not as a delegation to the President by reason of Congress' inaction and acquiescence, but as a decision that the President has at least some inherent powers to settle claims under Article II of the Constitution.[120]

2. Relevance of Legislative History for Statutory Interpretation

In addition to the rule of responsible delegation, we propose that judicial review of agency action be aggressive and not deferential, that review be particularly scrutinizing when the agency is departing from established prior rules, and that such judicial review consider legislative history as a basis for overturning the agency's policy balance. The first two suggestions are both contrary to the reasoning in *Chevron,* but are justified by the analysis in Part II.D above: according to our Article I, Section 7 game, aggressive judicial review of agency action is not countermajoritarian at all; by creating a new default position, judicial review makes it more likely that congressional preferences will be honored by the agency.

The third suggestion (legislative history) makes it more likely that the reviewing court will be enforcing the policy equilibrium reached in the Article I, Section 7 game, or some updated version of that equilibrium. This is consistent with *Chevron,* which examined the statute's legislative history and found it unilluminating, but inconsistent with subsequent applications of *Chevron* by the Court.

3. Congressional Influence over Agency Rulemaking

Congress already has some influence over agency rulemaking through informal channels such as appropriations pressure, hearings, and the like. This is useful, but we also endorse more formal congressional input into agency rulemaking. The legislative veto was a promising mechanism for such input. We agree with *Chadha* on its facts (no one-house vetoes of agency adjudications) but not in its implications (no legislative vetoes of any sort). Our updated Article I, Section 7 game would allow—indeed encourage—two-house vetoes of agency rulemaking, which would give Congress opportunities to negate agency rules, after deliberation by two different bodies. We consider the validity of one-house vetoes much less clear under modern assumptions, and do not necessarily oppose *Chadha*'s preclusion of them, because of the danger that an outlying chamber will unsettle the stability and continuity of agency policy.

---

120. *Dames & Moore* discusses briefly the President's inherent powers in this area. 453 U.S. 654, 677-78 (1981). Even under such a reinterpretation of the decision's reasoning, we think it is a questionable decision, for it flies in the teeth of two clear federal statutes, with no sufficient justification for the President's not seeking Senate ratification of his action as a treaty entitled to Article VI authority.

C. CONCLUSION: THE BAIT-AND-SWITCH GAME

Our vision of Article I, Section 7 is, we think, a realistic updating of the Framers' original lawmaking game to the modern regulatory state where most lawmaking is by agencies under legislative grants of authority. In this article we have demonstrated that the Court does not have a vision of Article I, Section 7, and that its main attempt to define a vision—*Chadha*—is an unsuccessful attempt at originalist analysis because it is historically incomplete, ignores the impact of the regulatory state upon the Framers' vision, and has not even been applied consistently by the Court itself.[121]

There is a final line of criticism of the Court's practice that is suggested by our analysis. By invalidating the legislative veto and weakening judicial review of agency interpretations, the Supreme Court in the 1980s was systematically reversing congressional expectations that were necessary parts of dozens and perhaps hundreds of statutory deals in the last several decades. In other words, the existence of legislative vetoes (in some statutes), the possibility of judicial review (in virtually all statutes), and the assumption that reviewing courts would consult legislative history were necessary conditions to Congress's willingness to enact a variety of regulatory statutes. Without those provisions protecting against the movement of statutory policy too much toward the President's preferences over time, Congress would not have been willing to pass those statutes. In this way, the Supreme Court's decisions in *Chadha, Alaska Airlines,* and *Chevron* can be viewed as constitutional "bait and switch." That is, Congress enacts legislation with certain controls on agency lawmaking that the Court has done nothing to discourage, and then later on the Court changes the rules so that the statutes are left in place but with fewer constraints for the implementing agencies.

While Congress is certainly not without means to respond to such a constitutional bait and switch, these decisions represent a perhaps unconscious preference on the part of the Supreme Court in the 1980s to shift lawmaking power from the Congress to the President. Our analysis suggests, normatively, that the Court's action was deeply inconsistent with the Constitution. Our analysis suggests, descriptively, that the Court was itself behaving like

121. Justice Scalia has outlined a theory of Article I, Section 7 that might avoid the last pitfall. Justice Scalia accepts the unenforceability of the nondelegation doctrine as a practical matter. "Precisely because the scope of delegation is largely uncontrollable by the courts, we must be particularly rigorous in preserving the Constitution's structural restrictions that deter excessive delegation." *Mistretta,* 488 U.S. at 416-17 (Scalia, J., dissenting). Thus, Justice Scalia would stringently enforce what he sees to be the "plain meaning" of Article I, Section 7: legislative vetoes, delegation to congressionally controlled agents, and efforts by members of Congress and committees to influence statutory interpretation through legislative history are all invalid and unconstitutional. Agencies must as a matter of constitutional doctrine be given full discretion to do what they want with statutory policy, so long as they do not violate the plain meaning of the statutory language adopted according to Article I, Section 7.

an agent of the President in the 1980s. After all, Republicans of varying degrees of conservatism have occupied the White House all but continuously since 1969, and all but one Justice on the current Court have been appointed by those Republican Presidents. Congress, in contrast, has been just as continuously dominated by liberal Democrats. In *Chadha* and *Chevron* the Court has implemented its preference for presidential rather than congressional policymaking.

This is quite rational for the Court to do. Recall Figure 4B, in which a Court with preferences close to those of the President would permit the agency to set policy at the veto median ($x' = h$), far away from the original statutory compromise ($H < x < S$). Figure 4B assumed that the Court was reviewing a single agency interpretation. Figure 4B also models the current Court, in which the ruling is no longer an isolated review of a single agency interpretation but is instead the systemic rules by which lower courts approach agency rulemaking. And x is no longer statutory policy, but constitutional policy, which the Supreme Court of the 1980s has shifted from the Framer's dynamics (x, with the center of lawmaking power in Congress), to the President's dynamics (x', with the center of lawmaking power with the President).

In short, the game played by the Court in the 1980s was in one respect a simple game: the President wins, at the expense of Congress. We believe that this very feature of the Court's game is its greatest weakness, for by contributing to the aggrandizement of presidential power the Court is contributing to unbalanced governance, which was the greatest value animating Article I, Section 7.

Experimental

[12]

FEAR AND LOATHING IN THE COASE THEOREM: EXPERIMENTAL TESTS INVOLVING PHYSICAL DISCOMFORT

*DON L. COURSEY, ELIZABETH HOFFMAN, and MATTHEW L. SPITZER**

I. Introduction

THE Coase Theorem, originally suggested by Ronald Coase, predicts that changing a liability rule will leave the production and consumption decisions of individuals (people and corporations) unchanged and will allow perfectly operating markets to perform efficiently.[1] In previous papers, Hoffman and Spitzer have suggested that the Coase Theorem's results may apply more broadly.[2] They reported the results of experiments confirming the Coase Theorem in settings precisely mimicking per-

* School of Business, Washington University; Department of Economics, Purdue University and the University of Wyoming; and the Law Center, University of Southern California. The authors gratefully acknowledge the financial support of National Science Foundation grant SES-8201865. Earlier versions of this paper were presented at the Experimental Social Choice Workshop in Logan, Utah; the Department of Decision Sciences of the University of Pennsylvania; the Public Choice Society; and the California Institute of Technology.

[1] The full set of sufficient conditions for the Coase result include (1) two individuals to each bargain, (2) both individuals have perfect knowledge of each other's (convex) production and profit (or utility) functions, (3) competitive markets, (4) zero transactions costs, (5) a costless, perfectly accurate court system, (6) profit-maximizing procedures and utility-maximizing consumers, (7) no wealth effects, and (8) individuals will strike mutually advantageous bargains in the absence of transactions costs. Coase did not state these assumptions explicitly in his original work, The Problem of Social Cost, 3 J. Law & Econ. 1 (1960), but they may be inferred from his discussion.

[2] Elizabeth Hoffman & Matthew L. Spitzer, Experimental Tests of the Coase Theorem with Large Bargaining Groups, 15 J. Legal Stud. 149 (1986) (hereinafter cited as Experimental Tests); Elizabeth Hoffman & Matthew L. Spitzer, Entitlements, Rights, and Fairness: An Experimental Examination of Subjects' Concepts of Distributive Justice, 14 J. Legal Stud. 259 (1985) (hereinafter cited as Entitlements, Rights, and Fairness); and Elizabeth Hoffman & Matthew L. Spitzer, The Coase Theorem: Some Experimental Tests, 25 J. Law & Econ. 73 (1982) (hereinafter cited as The Coase Theorem).

[*Journal of Legal Studies*, vol. XVI (January 1987)]
 0047-2530/87/1601-0004$01.50

fect markets and in extensions designed to stress the Coase Theorem by modeling more realistic circumstances. Included in these extensions were studies involving disputes with as many as thirty-eight parties and disputes where the parties had less-than-perfect information.

The original Hoffman and Spitzer experimental design, which is only briefly summarized here, informed two subjects that they had to choose a number and that, depending on which number was chosen, the monitor would pay each of them some money in cash. Table 1 is a sample payoff chart. Spitzer and Hoffman constructed the payoffs so that the interests of the subjects were completely opposed; any chosen outcome number that increased the payoff to one subject would decrease the payoff to the other. The outcome number was chosen by designating one of the subjects as the "controller." The controller could choose whatever outcome number he or she wished. However, the other subject could attempt to persuade the controller to enter into a contract, specifying the outcome number chosen and any reallocation of payoff money from one party to the other.

The Coase Theorem predicts that subjects will agree to choose the joint-profit-maximizing outcome number[3] regardless of whether A or B is the controller. Subjects did pick the joint-profit-maximizing outcome number in well over 90 percent of the experiments. Hoffman and Spitzer also conducted several variations of this basic experiment. In a series of "full information" experiments the subjects each knew the other's payoff schedule, while in "partial information" experiments they were told only their own. Second, the number of parties to the dispute was increased in steps from two to three, four, ten, and twenty parties. Finally, the controller was determined by using different methods. Sometimes a coin was flipped, and other times subjects played a preliminary game with the winner of the game earning the right to be the controller. None of these variations made much difference in the basic result: the Coase Theorem predicted the outcome in 93 percent of all experiments. It was even more powerful in large (ten- and twenty-subject) experiments, where it predicted 100 percent of the outcomes.

Hoffman and Spitzer contended that these results produce substantial insights for legal policy, supporting a "presumption in favor of the Coase Theorem."[4] In disputes involving substantial numbers of parties (as many as thirty-eight), a court should presume that the parties will bargain to produce an efficient outcome through voluntary agreement. Thus one who contends that bargaining breakdown is likely must produce argu-

[3] That would be outcome number 1 in Table 1.

[4] See Hoffman & Spitzer, Experimental Tests, *supra* note 2.

TABLE 1

SAMPLE PAYOFF CHART

Outcome Number	Subject A ($)	Subject B ($)
0	0	12
1	4	10
2	6	6
3	8	4
4	9	2
5	10	1
6	11	0

ments and data that support the contention that the Coase Theorem will not apply. This presumption in favor of the Coase Theorem produces powerful results for the choice of remedies in property, tort, and bankruptcy, leading courts to prefer "property" rules to "liability" rules. Property rules give the right holder the final say in whether to transfer his right to anyone else, while liability rules allow third parties to force the right holder to transfer his interest on payment of a court-determined amount of money to the right holder. Hoffman and Spitzer argued that, where courts can depend on parties to correct inefficient decisions through bargaining, they should rely on property rules rather than on liability rules.[5] These results were applied to legal disputes in nuisance, contract, and bankruptcy law.

II. ASYMMETRY AND THE DIGNITY HYPOTHESIS

Two possible sources of concern might substantially limit the applicability of these results. First, the payoffs in the original experiments were quite symmetrical and provided the subjects little ground on which to differentiate themselves. This design feature might ease the formation of bargains and possibly remove any opportunity for divergent strategic behavior (where each subject "sees" a strategy for walking away with the lion's share of the profits). With symmetric positions, each subject might quickly come to realize the futility of any strategic behavior, understanding that the same strategy can be used against him. The central theme of this argument is that, when nonsymmetric payoffs are used, subjects might fail to reach the efficient outcome. Second, the externality between

[5] For a more complete treatment and explanation of the reasoning behind these results, see text at notes 32–39 *infra;* Guido Calabresi & A. Douglas Melamed, Property Rules, Liability Rules and Inalienability: One View of the Cathedral, 85 Harv. L. Rev. 1089 (1972); and A. Mitchell Polinsky, An Introduction to Law and Economics (1983).

our subjects was entirely folded into a single-dimension payoff function. However, many of the conflicts to which these results have been applied, such as home owners living next to waste-disposal sites, involve physical discomfort.[6]

Perhaps there is something special that would prevent value-increasing bargains when one of the parties to the dispute might suffer physically. There are three obvious possibilities. First, if only one of the parties must suffer, the payoffs are asymmetric. The role of symmetry in the reward structure has already been discussed. Second, depending on which party owns the right, the physical sufferer may put different values on the externality. If the sufferer owns the right to avoid the externality, he must be paid some money to agree to accept the physical discomfort. Call the minimum amount that he would voluntarily accept his "willingness to accept" (WTA). If the sufferer does not own the right to avoid the discomfort, he must pay to avoid the externality. Call this maximum amount that the sufferer would pay his "willingness to pay" (WTP). One's WTA might differ from one's WTP either because of wealth effects or because of various psychological reasons such as strategic behavior or framing of the value-solicitation technique.[7]

Third, the process of bargaining over accepting physical discomfort—particularly the ingestion of noxious gases, liquids, and so forth—may involve such an affront to dignity as to stymie bargain formation. This "dignity hypothesis" is independent of the point concerning WTA values differing from WTP values. This hypothesis focuses on the exchange concept itself, and it captures the same idea as is found in the following

[6] See generally Parker v. City of Mountain Brook, 286 Ala. 241, 238 So.2d 868 (1970); and Suther v. Jefferson Cty. Board of Health, 456 So.2d 769 (Ala. 1984). Both cases involve complaints in which garbage dumps are attacked as nuisances.

[7] Wealth effects will tend to force WTA to be greater than WTP if freedom from physical discomfort is a normal good. Those who start with the right to be free from discomfort are wealthier than are those who have no such right, other things being equal. These two groups of people would purchase freedom from physical discomfort by refusing to accept payment for giving up the right to be free from discomfort or by paying to be free of the discomfort, respectively. If freedom from discomfort is a normal good, then those who are wealthier will pay more for it, and WTA will be greater than WTP. See generally David S. Brookshire, Don L. Coursey, & William D. Schulze, Experiments in the Solicitation of Private and Public Values: An Overview, in Advances in Behavioral Economics (L. Green & J. Kagel eds., in press) (discussed below in text); Mark Kelman, Consumption Theory, Production Theory, and Ideology in the Coase Theorem, 52 S. Cal. L. Rev. 669 (1979) (detailing some theories for the divergence; attacked on methodological grounds in Matthew L. Spitzer & Elizabeth Hoffman, A Reply to Consumption Theory, Production Theory, and Ideology in the Coase Theorem, 53 S. Cal. L. Rev. 1187 (1980)); and Jack L. Knetch & J. A. Sinden, Willingness to Pay and Compensation Demanded: Experimental Evidence of an Unexpected Disparity in Measures of Value, 99 Q. J. Econ. 507 (1984) (strongly suggesting that there is a divergence in some consumer contexts).

joke. Two people meet at a party, and the first asks the second, "Will you have sex with me in exchange for $1,000,000?" The second thinks for a minute and then responds, "Yes." The first then counters, "Will you do it for $50?" And the second immediately responds, "Of course not, what do you think I am?" The first replies, "We have already determined *what* you are. Now the question is price." In other words, there are some things that one is not supposed to sell. In such circumstances, the refusal to bargain at all would upset the Coase Theorem.

The role of asymmetric payoffs, discussed above, may also interact with the dignity hypothesis. People may feel that agreeing to accept physical discomfort when others do not have to agree to the unpleasant experience may heighten the affront to dignity. One would be agreeing, in essence, to be part of a class with less dignity. This argument focuses on the quality of one's treatment relative to the treatment of others, whereas the first discussion of dignity focused on the absolute quality of treatment. For example, residents in the area of Kiev may feel somewhat indignified at the prospect of having to drink radioactive water. The affront to dignity may be increased, however, when they learn that the residents of Moscow can drink clean water. The necessity of drinking radioactive water would represent the absolute affront to dignity, while being placed in an inferior class may heighten the insult.[8]

III. Experimental Design

This paper reports results of experiments testing the first and the third hypotheses (asymmetry and the dignity hypothesis) but excluding the second (that WTA and WTP values might be different).

A. *Asymmetry*

Our experiment that tested the first hypothesis was quite simple, replicating the two-person experiment described above but substituting an asymmetric payoff function. The payoffs are shown in Table 2. Subjects contracted to the efficient point 100 percent of the time, thereby disposing of the first hypothesis.

B. *The Dignity Hypothesis*

Constructing a test of the third hypothesis was far trickier. We have found no direct test of the dignity hypothesis in the experimental social psychology literature on which to build. Indeed the last thirty years of

[8] Nothing in this paper should be taken to suggest that the Ukrainians, if given a free choice, would choose to submit to this sort of treatment at the hands of the Russians.

TABLE 2

ASYMMETRIC PAYOFF CHART

Outcome Number	A's Payoff ($)	B's Payoff ($)
1	11	0
2	9	13
3	3	15

research in social psychology has put heavy emphasis on the situational determinants of behavior rather than on internal norm determinants of behavior, which has culminated in the current deluge of work on "attribution error."[9]

Several areas of work seem tangentially relevant. For example, the literature on cognitive dissonance suggests that, if subjects can be led to behave at variance with internal norms (that is, in an "undignified" fashion, for purposes of our work), then subjects will either deny the quality of their acts or revise their internal norms so as to reduce a type of psychic friction.[10] However, in these experiments subjects are almost always induced to behave in some fashion, and then the experimenter monitors changes in beliefs, affect, attitude, and the like. These experiments do not create markets and then observe subjects' willingness to bargain over rights.

Many works in experimental social psychology (including some on cognitive dissonance) induce subjects to do undignified things such as agree to be placed in a closet, blindfolded, tied to a chair, and shocked for twenty minutes;[11] to administer dangerous, high-voltage shocks to another subject who is screaming with pain and demanding to be released;[12] to drink bitter quinine solution;[13] or to choose to eat caterpillars.[14] But none of these experiments observes these choices as the result of explicit,

[9] See Hoffman & Spitzer, Entitlements, Rights, and Fairness, *supra* note 2; and Andrew Baum, Jeffrey D. Fisher, & Jerome E. Singer, Social Psychology 84–85 (1985).

[10] See generally Robert A. Wicklund & Jack W. Brehm, Perspectives on Cognitive Dissonance (1976).

[11] Gary P. Frieden, Masochistic Behavior as an Outcome of Role Confusion (unpublished Ph.D. dissertation, Univ. Southern California, June 1978).

[12] Stanley Milgram, Obedience to Authority (1974).

[13] E. Aronson, J. M. Carlsmith, & J. M. Darley, The Effects of Expectancy on Volunteering for an Unpleasant Experience, 66 J. Abnormal & Soc. Psychology 220 (1963).

[14] J. Foxman & R. C. Radtke, Negative Expectancy and the Choice of an Aversive Task, 15 J. Personality & Soc. Psychology 253 (1970).

economic bargaining for monetary payment, and none of the mechanisms most important to the social psychology work, such as purposefully confusing the subjects about their own preferences, seem to be present in our design.

To design our own test of the dignity hypothesis, we were forced to rely heavily on previous experimental work by Brookshire, Coursey, and Schulze,[15] who devised bidding mechanisms (termed "incentive compatible") for leading subjects to reveal their true WTP and WTA values for holding a one-ounce cup of sucrose octa-acetate (SOA)—a safe but very bitter-tasting, unpleasant liquid—in their mouths for twenty seconds. Each subject in these experiments was allowed to sample a drop or two.

The WTP experiments proceeded, in essence, by asking each subject to state his willingness to pay to avoid tasting the SOA. The four highest bids were accepted by the experimenter, thereby enabling the high bidders to avoid tasting the SOA. (The remaining subjects had to taste the SOA.) But these four high bidders had to pay the experimenter only the amount of the fifth highest bid. Under these circumstances it is in the self-interest of each subject to reveal his true value for tasting the SOA because the size of his bid determines only whether it will be accepted, not how much he will have to pay if it is accepted.[16] The WTA experiments were run in the identical fashion, except that subjects were asked to reveal their willingness to accept payment for agreement to taste the SOA, and only the four low bids were accepted. The four low bidders were paid the amount of the fifth lowest bid.

Brookshire, Coursey, and Schulze also collected survey data from their subjects regarding their hypothetical WTA and WTP values. Some of the surveys first allowed the subjects to sample a drop or two of the SOA, while others just described the SOA to the subjects. In both types of hypothetical surveys, WTA averaged between $7.00 and $15, but WTP averaged only $3.00–$4.50. In contrast, in the incentive-compatible bidding experiments described in the paragraph above, WTA and WTP values converged to about $4.00.[17]

The experiments reported in this paper incorporate the use of SOA into the basic Coase Theorem experiment so as to provide a test with a true

[15] Brookshire et al., *supra* note 7.

[16] See Dennis C. Mueller, Public Choice 72–84 (1979). Brookshire, Coursey, and Schulze utilized an iterative process designed to ensure that these theoretical properties could be "learned" during the experiment.

[17] The WTA averages stayed slightly above the WTP averages even in the bidding experiments, but statistical tests showed that the difference was not sufficient to reject the null hypothesis that WTA equals WTP.

negative externality. Most of the basic institutional features included in the original Coase Theorem experiments are used here so as to provide the cleanest possible test of Coase's hypothesis in the presence of physical discomfort, uncluttered by degradation of the Coase Theorem's other assumptions.

In all the experiments, subjects bargained face-to-face in the presence of a monitor for more money than most students can earn for an hour's work in their next-best alternative employment. Side payments were allowed, and contracts were in writing and strictly enforced. All payments were made in public. Subjects were not told what their objectives should be in choosing a number or in forming contracts.

We placed each bargaining group in a separate room (with the monitor being the only other person present) and randomly assigned payoff charts to the subjects. The monitor provided the subjects with the instructions contained in the Appendix. The subjects first read the instructions silently and then listened as the monitor read then aloud. After reading the instructions, subjects played a game to determine which one earned the right to be the controller. As before, the controller had the right to choose whatever outcome number he wished. The other subject was free to try to persuade the controller to choose another number by offering to pay part or all of his payoff money to the controller.

The instructions revealed the basic design reflected in the payoff chart in Section IV of the Appendix. If outcome number 1 was chosen, A received $10 and did not have to taste the SOA, and B received nothing. If number 2 was chosen, A received $10 and had to hold one ounce of the SOA in his mouth for twenty seconds, and B received $20. As above, one of the parties, called the controller, could choose whatever number he wished. Therefore, if A was the controller, he could choose outcome number 1 and avoid tasting the SOA. If B was the controller, he could choose number 2, thereby forcing A to taste the SOA.

Such a design provides a fairly clean test of a rather mild version of the dignity hypothesis because holding an extremely bitter, unpleasant liquid in one's mouth for twenty seconds is a very personal and moderately obnoxious experience. It seems to be as close to the quintessential "thing" that one is not supposed to sell as one can persuade human-subject review boards to let one test in the laboratory. And, just as important, it models the milder forms of noise, muck, grime, odors, and ugliness often involved in nuisance (pollution) disputes, such as the disturbance to a single-family dwelling next to an apartment building's extremely noisy air-conditioning unit, which is discussed at length below.

Such a design attempts to heighten the insult to dignity by making the game asymmetric: A may have to taste the SOA, but B need never do so.

Hence, if A were to agree to taste the SOA when he did not otherwise have to do so, he would be agreeing to have relatively less dignity than B.

This design also avoids testing the second hypothesis because any possible divergence between WTP and WTA values should not impede bargaining to the same, efficient outcome. Brookshire, Coursey, and Schulze's bidding results showed that WTP and WTA values both approximated $4.00. With this value, number 2 is clearly the joint-profit-maximizing outcome. However, even in their surveys, the maximum average hypothetical WTA value recorded was $15. Even if we were to use this figure for the WTA value, number 2 remains the joint-profit-maximizing outcome.

When testing the dignity hypothesis, the degree of information possessed by each subject about the prospective experience may be crucial. After all, if the SOA were to taste like an expensive Chardonnay (which it most certainly does not), the decision to taste would involve little affront to dignity.[18] There are many degrees of information that a potential sufferer might have about a particular discomfort, ranging all the way from complete familiarity with the discomfort, to having sampled a bit of the discomfort, to having only had the discomfort described, to confronting the dreaded "unknown unknown." Modeling all these information conditions was well beyond the scope of our investigation. Instead we focused on only two of them. We decided to allow some of our subjects to sample a drop or two of the SOA, while others learned of the SOA only by reading a description in the instructions. Crossing A (sampling or not) with B (sampling or not) produced four variations:

1. *Both Sample.* This condition models a dispute between an owner of a small house located next to a large apartment complex. The owner of the apartment is about to install a large, noisy air-conditioning unit in a place that will disturb the residents of the house but not the apartment house's owner. During this period of time both the residents of the small house and the owner of the apartment house visit another site where the same type of air-conditioning unit has already been installed and listen to the noise for a minute or two. In this way, both parties will have sampled the noise, but only one of them, the owner of the small house, actually will have to hear it once the air-conditioning unit is installed.[19]

2. *A Samples Only.* This represents the same conflict described in the paragraph above, except that only the owner of the small house, not the owner of the apartment house, went to another site to hear the same type

[18] This brings up the interesting theoretical question (not addressed in this paper) of whether being ordered to do something that one would have voluntarily chosen to do would be an affront to dignity.

[19] This case corresponds to the instructions found in the Appendix.

of air-conditioning unit. The owner of the small house then tells the owner of the apartment building that the air conditioner will be very noisy.[20]

3. *B Samples Only*. This models the same conflict in the two conditions above, except that only the owner of the apartment building has heard a similar, already-installed air conditioner. The owner of the apartment building tells the owner of the small house that the air conditioner will be very noisy.[21]

4. *Neither Samples*. This models the conflict in the first three conditions, except that neither the owner of the small house nor the owner of the apartment house has listened to a similar, installed air conditioner at another site, and a third party has described the noise to each of them as being very noisy.[22]

In which condition is bargaining breakdown most likely? The following pair of arguments suggests that bargaining breakdown probability will be maximized when only A samples. First, the dignity hypothesis probably gets its best chance to prevent bargain formation when A samples, which will be the case in conditions 1 and 2 above, for then A knows the true, bitter nature of the SOA. The dignity hypothesis predicts that, when A knows the truth and is the controller, he will refuse to choose number 2. (Note that when B is the controller, A is powerless to refuse number 2 because his agreement is not needed.) If neither samples, the subjects can only guess at its qualities,[23] while, if only B samples, B can tell A that the SOA is not so bad.[24]

Second, we hypothesize that strategic behavior is most likely to cause bargaining breakdown in experiments in which either A or B samples but not both because the obvious asymmetry in the experiment creates opportunities for mutually inconsistent strategies. When we put together the predictions from the dignity hypothesis and the predictions from asymmetry, we derive an overall prediction that bargaining breakdown will be

[20] The instructions for this case were identical to those in the Appendix, except that we added the sentence "Before the experiment begins participant A will sample a few drops of the bitter liquid" to the end of the second paragraph of Section II*B* of the Appendix.

[21] The instructions for this case were identical to those in condition 2 except that they stated, "Before the experiment begins participant B will sample a few drops of the bitter liquid."

[22] The instructions for this condition were identical to those in conditions 2 and 3, except that the crucial sentence "Before the experiment begins you will sample a few drops of the bitter liquid" was omitted.

[23] We are assuming, in essence, that the subjects are not extremely timid souls whose active imaginations lead them to fear the SOA experience more than the reality would warrant.

[24] We frequently observed this form of behavior in the experiments in which only B sampled.

greatest when only A samples, least when neither samples, and somewhere between in the other two conditions.[25]

C. *Subjects*

Subjects were undergraduate economics and management students at the University of Wyoming. They were recruited in class, were told only that they would participate in an economics decision, and were promised $3.00 for participating. Friends were not allowed to participate together. All subjects were inexperienced with this type of experiment. After each experiment we explained the nature and purpose of the experiment and asked them, in the name of "science," not to reveal anything about the experiment to future subjects. Later subjects seemed to be initially naive about the purpose and conduct of the experiment, and there was no time trend in the results.

IV. Results

The most striking aspect of the results is the overwhelming choice of number 2, the efficient outcome. In the twenty-two experiments in which B was the controller, number 2 was chosen every time. In the eighteen experiments in which A was the controller, number 2 was chosen sixteen times. Thus, in general, using a physical externality does not seem to interfere with subjects' ability to reach the efficient outcome. In general, the dignity hypothesis is rejected, and the Coase Theorem is accepted.

Table 3 summarizes results according to experimental treatment, showing how many experiments out of the number possible joint-profit maximized when A was the controller.

Our hypothesis was that, when only A sampled, the probability of bargaining breakdown would be maximized. These results, however, provide no support for our hypothesis. This table suggests instead that the treatment in which both A and B sample may be different from the other conditions. However, there are not enough events in that quadrant to be statistically certain. For the remainder of this paper, however, we will assume that there is no difference, in part because our working hypothesis was that bargaining breakdown was most likely when only A sampled, and in that case four out of four bargaining groups chose efficiently. Clearly, only initial, tentative conclusions can be made regarding this point.

Figure 1 summarizes the distribution of money between A and B when

[25] We will discuss hypotheses about the distribution of money within the discussion of results *infra*.

TABLE 3

EXPERIMENTAL RESULTS WITH A AS CONTROLLER

	A Not Sample	A Sample
B not sample	5/5	4/4
B sample	5/5	2/4

number 2 was chosen. The vertical axis represents the number of observations at a particular payoff amount, and the horizontal axes of the two panels represent the total payoffs to A. Notice that, with one exception, if number 2 was chosen, A never received more than $15 when B was the controller or less than $15 when A was the controller himself. This indicates quite strongly that the distribution of rights had a significant effect on the distribution of payoffs, even though some B controllers did not impose individually rational divisions. In fact, when A was the controller and chose number 2, A received on average $19.06. When B was the controller, A received only $10 in eleven of the twenty-two experiments and an average of $14.36 in the other eleven for an overall average of only $12.18. This is consistent with data from Hoffman and Spitzer's game-trigger experiments,[26] in which individual rationality was generally observed, but some controllers were still somewhat altruistic.

Looking first at the top panel of Figure 1, where A is the controller, received Coasian theory predicts that A will not accept less than his WTA value for choosing number 2. And if we use the $4.00 figure for WTA generated by Brookshire, Coursey, and Schulze, it seems clear that no A did so. We cannot use either the $5.00 minimum accepted or the $9.06 average accepted as a measure of the WTA of our subjects for this experiment, however, because there was no market mechanism enforcing convergence to the true WTA. What we can say is that these results are consistent with the hypothetical WTA values obtained by Brookshire, Coursey, and Schulze.

It also appears that A succeeded in negotiating for less when only B sampled. This is consistent with the process of bargaining in these experiments. The B's who had sampled alone tended to tell the A's that it was "not so bad." On the other hand, when only A sampled, he would typically complain about how horrible it tasted.

Turning now to the bottom panel, where B is the controller, the core of a game with self-interested parties is that B gets $20 and A $10. The fact that in eleven of the twenty-two B-controlled experiments the controller

[26] Hoffman & Spitzer, Entitlements, Rights, and Fairness *supra* note 2.

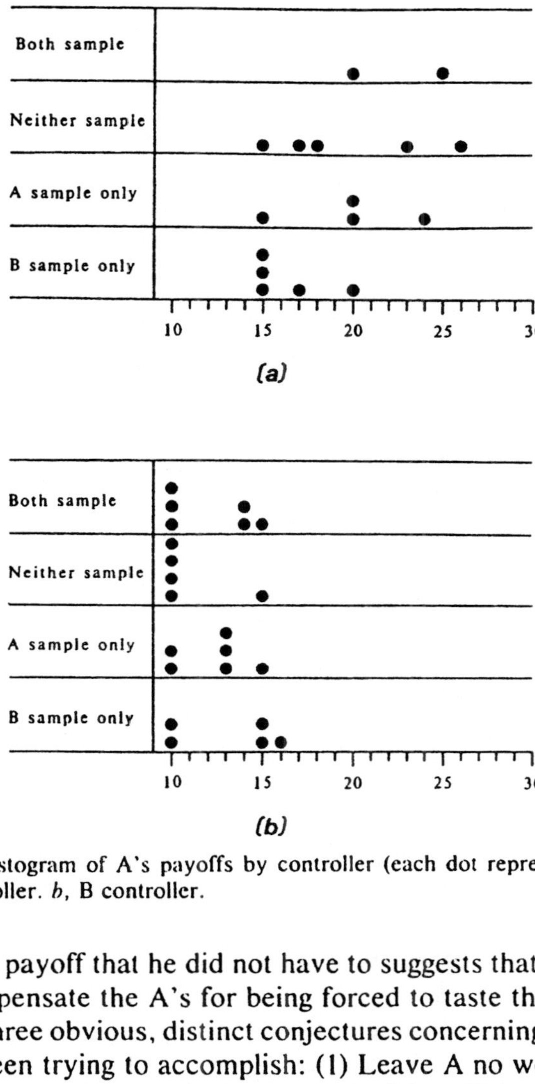

FIGURE 1.—Histogram of A's payoffs by controller (each dot represents one observation). *a*, A controller. *b*, B controller.

gave up some payoff that he did not have to suggests that some B's were trying to compensate the A's for being forced to taste the SOA.[27]

There are three obvious, distinct conjectures concerning what these B's might have been trying to accomplish: (1) Leave A no worse off than he would have been had he not had to taste the SOA. This would produce a distribution of (A, B) = $(10 + \alpha, 20 - \alpha)$, where α is B's estimate of the monetary equivalent of the disutility from tasting the SOA. (2) Equalize the money earned from the experiment. This would produce (15, 15).

[27] There may be some interaction between the position of the controller and altruism. When A was the controller, the B's were willing to tell the A's that the SOA was "not so bad" if only the B's sampled—not a particularly altruistic act. But when the B's were the controllers, about half gave the A's some money. We might resolve this by saying that the B's that claimed that the SOA was "not so bad" were the same sort of folks who would fail to give the A's some money when the B's had control.

(3) Equalize the subjective utility from the experiment. This would produce (15 + [α/2], 15 − [α/2]), where α is again B's estimate of the monetary equivalent of the disutility from tasting the SOA.[28]

Because we did not independently measure the α values of the B's and because we have no strong theory that all (or most) of the subjects were trying to accomplish any one of these things, we can offer no firm conclusions. However, if we introspectively hypothesize that the B's were using α's of approximately $4.00—which was the convergence figure derived by Brookshire, Coursey, and Schulze for WTA and WTP values—then we can immediately rule out the third alternative. However, both the first and the second alternatives fit the data reasonably well. Or we can run this logic backward. If we assume that the B's are trying to leave the A's no worse off than before, then we would conclude that the B's, through introspection, determine on average the same figures for α that Brookshire, Coursey, and Schulze's experiments produced.

The data also suggest that there is a relation between the information conditions and the empathy of the B's for the A's. When B only sampled and B was the controller, B actually gave up more than he did in the other three treatments where B was the controller. Those B's who shared when only A sampled the SOA averaged a $3.50 payment to A, but when only B sampled, the sharing B's transferred an average of $5.33. This is in contrast to the case in which A was the controller and only B sampled. In that case, A was able to negotiate for less on average than when A was controller and only A sampled.

Perhaps what is happening in these experiments when only B tastes is that B forms an opinion of the proper WTP and WTA values, which is not affected by any information gained by A. But, having been the only one to taste, B may feel greater responsibility toward the unwitting A. In this case, those controlling B's who do share may actually give up little less than noncontrolling B's when A is controller. In these cases, B tells A that it is not so bad and argues for a smaller payment when A is the controller but, feeling somewhat responsible, is willing to give a larger payment when B is the controller.

V. Implications for Naturally Occurring Environments

Before we can analyze the implications of our experiment for nonlaboratory settings, we must ask what types of nonlaboratory environments were (or were not) modeled well by our experiment.

[28] All these results assume that B assumes equal utility of money.

A. Applicability of Results

There are two lines of reasoning that would argue against applying these results to a nonlaboratory setting. First, subjects might behave differently in the laboratory than they would elsewhere. Second, the experiments may have failed to capture the essential features of particular natural settings. Many of the arguments governing the extent to which the results of such laboratory experiments may be applied to natural environments have been considered extensively by Hoffman and Spitzer and will be only briefly reviewed at this juncture.[29]

1. *Laboratory Effects.* What are the most likely laboratory effects in our experiments? The subjects might have regarded money differently, or they might have had different attitudes toward bargaining. They also might have had a different attitude toward tasting the SOA. These differences might have been produced either by important differences between our subject pool and the target population or by observer effects.

Is there any evidence of laboratory effects in the data? The willingness of some of the subjects to share their monetary payoffs should suggest some initial concern. We usually presume that people who are not close friends or family members will behave in a self-interested fashion in natural settings. Perhaps the frequent sharing behavior indicates that subjects were not taking the experiment seriously.

Three insights suggest that this line of argument is mistaken and that it should not prevent applying our results to nonlaboratory settings. First, subjects appeared to take the bargaining and the resulting outcome very seriously. Second, recent experimental work has shown that subjects behave in a self-regarding fashion when they independently regard as morally justified the entitlements that the experimenter allows them to exercise.[30]

This work has shown that, if experimenters randomly distribute rights to control a purely monetary externality, the right holders will not exercise those rights to maximize their own profit. Instead the right holders exercise the rights so as to maximize joint profits and then split all money equally with the other subject, thereby "giving away" money. If the experimenter instead distributes the rights by allowing the right holder to both "earn" them and regard the rights as morally justified under a

[29] Hoffman & Spitzer, The Coase Theorem, *supra* note 2.

[30] Hoffman & Spitzer, Entitlements, Rights, and Fairness, *supra* note 2; Glenn Harrison & Michael McKee, Experimental Examination of the Coase Theorem, 28 J. Law & Econ. 653 (1985).

Lockean labor-desert theory, subjects tend to be much more self-regarding.

The experiments reported in this paper differ from previous work because rights holders are asked to exercise the right to inflict physical discomfort. Subjects may require a greater degree of perceived moral justification before they are willing to exercise such rights in a self-regarding way. It is entirely possible that many of the B's did not feel morally justified to invoke the right to force A to taste the SOA without compensation. Pending some additional work on the circumstances providing moral justification for exercising a right to inflict physical discomfort, we will presume that the non-self-regarding behavior of the subjects does not suggest that the subjects were behaving frivolously.

Third, the Coase Theorem received overwhelming support regardless of whether or not the subjects were self-regarding.[31] More than half of the experiments produced self-regarding outcomes when B was the controller, and all of these supported the Coase Theorem by choosing number 2. The Coase Theorem, then, gets strong support in the laboratory from our results.

Despite our strong laboratory support of the Coase Theorem, however, observer effects, attitudes of subjects, and differences between our subject pool and target populations could prevent applying our results to natural settings. Observer effects would be present if subjects were to bargain to efficient outcomes because they were being watched and wished to be thought of as "nice" or "worthy." Most important for our test of the dignity hypothesis, subjects might have been more willing to bargain over something disgusting such as tasting the SOA because they were being observed.

Would we expect this to be true? A number of images from natural settings argue for this observer effect, but others argue against it. In support of this observer effect, consider the "Ugly George Hour of Truth, Sex, and Violence" on CATV in New York City, in which George Urban routinely persuades young, middle-class women to strip off all their clothes in front of a television camera, when few, if any, of these women would otherwise have given George Urban the time of day. In a similar vein, for example, on the "Gong Show" and other television game shows, people debase themselves for money in front of cameras and large studio audiences.

On the other hand, people may be less willing to tolerate obnoxious

[31] This is true not only for the experiments reported in this paper but also for literally hundreds of experiments previously reported. See Hoffman & Spitzer, Experimental Tests, *supra* note 2.

odors, tastes, and so forth if they are being observed. Consider someone who runs home to clean up his or her house, removing filth and rotten food with which the person is otherwise content to live because the boss or a date is going to arrive. In sum, there is no single a priori hypothesis about the observer effect.

Fortunately, regardless of which way this issue is resolved, it will not preclude applying our results to natural settings. Most of the disputes to which our results would apply (such as odors) involve discomforts that must be suffered in public (in the sense that everyone knows you are experiencing the discomfort) and involve public bargaining over settlement of the disputes. Few externalities involving physical discomfort take place in complete secret. Therefore, these observer effects should occur in natural settings as well as in the laboratory.

Attitudes of the subjects toward the experiment might also preclude applying our results to nonlaboratory environments. To the extent that the subjects regarded the duty to taste the SOA as a perverse sort of thrill or recreation and therefore fundamentally different from physical discomforts encountered in the naturally occurring world, our test of the dignity hypothesis would be impeached. Did the subjects regard the experiment as "fun" and bargain over the duty to taste the SOA out of a desire to be sociable? This is a very difficult question to answer, for the bargaining was face-to-face between college students. Our observation of the subjects did not bring to light anything that would directly suggest that this would be a problem. However, we had no control over this sort of attitude variable, nor can we imagine an effective one apart from inflicting physical discomfort so intense that no human-subject review board would ever approve of the experiment. For this reason we emphasize that we have provided a test of only a rather mild form of the dignity hypothesis, but probably about the best test that one could do in the laboratory.[32]

Differences, if any, between our subject pool and target populations also provide no reason to refrain from using our results. Our subjects tended to be undergraduate students, about twenty years old, who will very soon be adult citizens who may get involved in the types of lawsuits that the Coase Theorem models. Did their relative youth make a difference? Probably not. They seemed to be adept at bargaining, took the experiment very seriously, and routinely bargained to the efficient out-

[32] The subjects may also have had a different, more permissive attitude toward bargaining because we gave them contract forms and told them that we would enforce bargains, thereby giving implicit approval to the act of bargaining. Previous research by Milgram has shown that people may be willing to commit morally repugnant acts if they are ordered to commit those acts by an experimenter. Milgram, *supra* note 12. This effect may extend as well to acts that an experimenter indicates are permitted.

come. If we were to expect subjects to become less likely to bargain to efficient outcomes as they grow older, we would have grounds to suspect our results. But why expect this? In the long run, people are more likely to learn that bargaining breakdown is costly for everyone and thus to learn to be proficient at making deals. Indeed a large number of our subjects, having come to the University of Wyoming from ranch or farm backgrounds, probably have experienced more of the processes associated with auctioning and bargaining than have other individuals their age.

2. *Experimental Treatment Effects on the Efficiency Result.* A policymaker should refrain from applying our results to any natural setting if the essential features of that setting were not incorporated into our design. There are four important sources of bargaining breakdown that were not incorporated into our design.

First, we excluded most sources of transactions costs by bringing the parties together, modeling only two parties to the dispute, paying the subjects for their time, and providing standard form contracts that were perfectly enforced. This eliminated most sources of such friction in the natural world.[33] Examples include situations in which the parties do not know each other, there are hundreds of thousands of parties to the dispute, bargaining is very costly, or the parties are uncertain that their agreements will be enforced. The problem of acid-rain deposition provides the quintessential example where all these elements are present to some extent. Many polluters' activities combine to produce serious environmental blight across thousands of miles and across international borders. Many other examples of large-scale pollution also involve many of these elements, and our results should not be applied to them.

As we explained in our introduction, previous work has shown that with purely monetary externalities even moderately large groups (those as large as thirty-eight) can be expected to bargain efficiently. We would have to run additional experiments to be certain that this result would carry over to externalities with physical discomfort, but for the remainder of this paper we will assume that it would.

Second, we excluded most informational deficiencies that might cause bargaining breakdown by making all payoffs, including A's duty (or lack thereof) to taste the SOA, common knowledge. The only informational

[33] We also eliminated one feature of the naturally occurring world that may ameliorate transactions costs, that is, the iterative nature of some conflicts. Recent work suggests that when conflicts are repeated between the same parties over and over the chances for cooperation may be increased. See Robert Axelrod, The Evolution of Cooperation (1985); David M. Kreps & Robert Wilson, Sequential Equilibria, 50 Econometrica 863 (1982); David M. Kreps & Robert Wilson, Reputation and Imperfect Information, 27 J. Econ. Theory 253 (1982); and Robert C. Ellickson, Of Cattle and Coase: Dispute Resolution among Neighbors in Shasta County, 38 Stan. L. Rev. 623 (1986).

asymmetry that we included involved sampling of the SOA. This excluded situations in which the parties did not know their own profit functions or in which they did not know that their own decisions interfered with another's well-being. A reformulated Coase Theorem including these informational constraints would produce different behavioral predictions.[34] We would need to test these new predictions with appropriate experiments. But until that time we should be chary of applying our results to situations involving great uncertainty, such as the acid-rain example.

Third, someone might value a right he owns more than he would value the right if he had to buy it either because of "wealth effects" or for other psychological reasons. As we explained in detail above, we took great pains not to test this hypothesis.[35]

Fourth, and most important for a test of the dignity hypothesis, tasting the SOA was unpleasant. But it was neither dangerous nor completely debasing; tasting the SOA is akin neither to eating a bar of plutonium for lunch nor to having sexual intercourse in front of a full house at Yankee Stadium. The willingness of individuals to sell risk of death or their complete degradation are the core elements of the dignity hypothesis that cannot be tested in an experimental setting.[36] Again we emphasize that we have provided a mild test of the dignity hypothesis, but one that is as good as can be provided in the laboratory.

Notwithstanding all these caveats, we feel that there is a substantial class of conflicts to which our results may be applied. This class would include disputes involving moderate numbers of parties and noxious (but not dangerous) sights and smells. For example, small nuisances, such as dog kennels,[37] or neighborhood aesthetics, such as ugly houses or funeral parlors,[38] would be included. (Obviously, there is nothing in our results to disturb the strength of previous studies supporting the Coase Theorem with purely monetary externalities.) In such disputes a court should

[34] Then again, it might not. Reformulation of the standard economic model of behavior under a negligence standard with uncertainty produces no simple behavioral prediction at all. See John E. Calfee & Richard Craswell, Some Effects of Uncertainty on Compliance with Legal Standards, 70 Va. L. Rev. 965 (1984); and Richard Craswell & John E. Calfee, Deterrence and Uncertain Legal Standards (unpublished manuscript, Federal Trade Comm'n, September 1985).

[35] See discussion at note 7 *supra*.

[36] See Elizabeth Hoffman & Matthew L. Spitzer, An Introduction to Experimental Law and Economics, 85 Colum. L. Rev. 991 n.36 (1985), noting that fear of death cannot be modeled in an experiment.

[37] See, for example, Ensign v. Walls, 323 Mich. 49, 34 N.W.2d 549 (1948).

[38] See, for example, Matthewson v. Primeau, 64 Wash. 2d 929, 395 P.2d 183 (1964); and C. Gregory, H. Kalven, Jr., & R. Epstein, Cases and Materials on Torts 524 (1977).

choose legal remedies by presuming that the parties can and will bargain efficiently. Again, one who contends that bargaining breakdown is likely must bear the burden of proof. Only if the person who bears the burden can sustain it should the court presume that bargaining breakdown is likely.

3. *Distributional Considerations.* Can we expect the willingness of the B's to share their money and provide a form of voluntary compensation to the A's to apply in natural settings? If so, then a court might be able to assign a property right to a polluter and worry little about the equity of the situation, depending on the polluter to provide voluntary compensation to the victims. Our results suggest that in two-person, face-to-face bargaining situations, such as those over neighborhood nuisances, the parties to the bargain might be able to resolve such equity considerations themselves.

Unfortunately, there are many reasons to expect that behavior will be different in natural settings involving impersonal bargaining and bargaining over market transactions. First, natural settings would often involve disputes where the polluter would not have to watch his victim suffer. More important, polluters and sometimes victims will often be corporations, which are subject to the discipline of competitive markets. Any management that tried to pursue a truly charitable policy (and not merely one that traded short-run profits for long-run goodwill that translates into higher long-run profits) would depress the share value of its corporation and raise its costs, thereby risking shareholder displeasure and implicitly inviting takeover by new management. Therefore, in the long run, managements that do not try to give away substantial amounts of money will probably be more successful.

B. *Implications for Legal Policy*

1. *Nuisance Law.* The most obvious application of our results would be to legal doctrines governing disputes over pollution among moderate numbers of actors. For example, when neighboring landowners create externalities that interfere with each other's "use and enjoyment" of the land, the law of nuisance determines the rights and remedies of the parties.[39] These interfering uses might be, for example, an oil refinery that

[39] Analogous problems between a landlord and his tenants, such as the landlord creating a stench that annoys several of his tenants, is controlled by the "covenant of quiet enjoyment," which, under certain circumstances, regards the landlord's behavior as a breach of his relationship with the tenants. See Jesse Dukeminier & James E. Krier, Property 266–83 (1981). The discussion of choice of remedies based on efficiency concerns, at least when the rental contract does not allocate rights between the parties, would parallel the discussion in the text.

produces odors that bother neighbors,[40] an apartment building with an extremely noisy air-conditioning unit that disturbs a single-family dwelling next door,[41] a dog kennel that produces both bad odors and loud noises that disturb the landowners in the immediate vicinity,[42] or a waste-disposal site.[43] In all these cases the court must choose between injunctive remedies and damages remedies. We will use the example of the noisy air-conditioning unit in the discussion that follows.

There are two extreme forms of injunctive remedies. (1) The apartment owner's right; that is, the apartment owner may make as much noise with his air-conditioning unit as he wishes, and the single family must secure his voluntary agreement to reduce the noise. (2) The single family's right; that is, the single family may obtain an order from the court directing the apartment owner to make no noise with his air conditioner. The apartment owner must secure the voluntary agreement of the single family to be released from the obligation of silence.

The law of nuisance actually would tend to use a rule that looked like a combination of the two above rules: the apartment owner may make noise with impunity up to some critical level, and, if the apartment owner makes more than the critical level of noise, the single family may obtain an order of the court directing the apartment owner to reduce the noise down to the critical level. This means the court would apply rule 1 up to the critical level and rule 2 thereafter. By choosing the critical level appropriately, a court could increase the efficiency of its decision.[44]

There are also two damages remedies. (*a*) The apartment owner's right; that is, the single family may obtain an order directing the apartment owner to reduce the noise level, but the single family must pay the apartment owner all increased expenses from reducing the noise. (*b*) The single family's right; that is, the apartment owner may make as much noise as he likes but must compensate the single family for all damage from the noise.

Traditional wisdom has noted that the risks associated with both injunctive and damages remedies depend on whether one can depend on the parties to form contracts and hence "correct" any mistakes that the court might make. If the parties cannot be trusted to make contracts, then both

[40] Morgan v. High Penn Oil Co., 238 N.C. 185, 77 S.E.2d 682 (1953).

[41] Estancia Dallas Corp. v. Schultz, 500 S.W.2d 217 (1973).

[42] Ensign v. Walls, 323 Mich. 49, 34 N.W.2d 549 (1948).

[43] See sources cited in note 6 *supra*.

[44] See Richard A. Epstein, Nuisance Law and Its Utilitarian Constraints, 8 J. Legal Stud. 49 (1979); and Dukeminier & Krier, *supra* note 39, at 924–28. In addition, courts can grant injunctions conditioned on one of the parties adopting some harm-avoiding technology and also retain jurisdiction over disputes for many years to administer remedies. Our experimental results hold no implications for such techniques.

injunctive and damages remedies threaten large efficiency losses. Injunctive remedies risk large efficiency losses if the court grants the entitlement to the party who values it least and if the parties cannot agree to rearrange the rights by contract. Damages remedies might produce large efficiency losses if the court charges too little (or too much) for the injuries done, thereby inducing too much (or too little) of the nuisance.

If bargaining breakdown is extremely unlikely, a court may choose either an injunctive remedy or a damages remedy without fear of causing large efficiency losses; the parties will correct the court's "mistakes" by contract. In such circumstances the court should choose between remedies on the basis of minimizing administrative costs, that is, the sum of the costs of fashioning and enforcing the remedy plus the costs of bargaining to correct any errors. In any particular case, damages or an injunction might be better. However, if we make three basic assumptions, injunctive remedies will be preferred. First, assume that the costs of bargaining to correct the court's mistakes will be very similar for injunctive and damages entitlements because the contracts will involve the same parties bargaining over very similar issues. Second, assume that the court has about the same chance of making substantial errors with injunctive or damages remedies.[45] Third, assume that evaluating damages is more costly and time consuming than is getting an injunction, for the court must take and assess particularized evidence on harms suffered by each plaintiff. Under such circumstances, injunctive remedies will be preferred to damages remedies because damages remedies have higher administrative costs. When a court is faced with such a situation, and it often will be, it should choose an injunctive remedy, that is, rule 1 or 2. In terms of our example above, if the court were to find that the noise was a nuisance, it should choose rule 2, but if the noise was not a nuisance, it should choose rule 1.

Our results have little to say, however, about disputes involving very large numbers of parties or risk of death. For example, the oil refinery mentioned above might produce pollutants that not only smell terrible but that also greatly increase the risk of cancer to thousands of people. In such a situation, a court may presume that there is a substantial risk of bargaining breakdown. If the refinery's noxious fumes constitute a nuisance and the court grants the neighboring landowners injunctive entitlements, it might have to close down, for it would not likely be able to secure the consent of all the thousands of right holders that would be needed for continued operation. If the court were to grant the refinery an

[45] If the court is much more accurate at choosing one remedy rather than the other, then using the more accurate remedy will reduce the expected bargaining costs to correct errors.

injunctive right instead, strategic problems would likely stymie the efforts of the adjoining landowners to buy the refinery's cooperation to reduce pollution.

These considerations might prompt a court to choose damages remedies instead. If the refinery is a nuisance, it would be required to pay the landowners all damages from the pollution.[46] But if the court were to decide instead that the refinery is not a nuisance, a damages remedy becomes more problematic. For example, the court might set a price schedule for pollution reductions and then let the landowners work out for themselves whether to purchase an injunction against some of the pollution. To do so they would also have to decide how much each would contribute to the total purchase price. The allocation of payment to reduce the risk of death might involve coordination and strategic problems, leading to bargaining breakdown.

To get around these problems, the court would have to invent some method for determining the marginal benefit that each landowner would receive from the purchase of cleaner air. But the courts do not traditionally concern themselves with estimating the marginal benefits accruing to individual plaintiffs in such suits. Moreover, determination of marginal benefits is subject to notorious practical and theoretical problems associated with the individual incentive to strategically misrepresent in hopes of reducing individual assessments.[47] These problems might prompt the court to find the refinery to be a nuisance and grant neighboring landowners a damages entitlement.[48]

2. *Inalienability.* In many circumstances the law refuses to allow or enforce consensual transfers of rights even where it allows particular individuals to have those rights in the first place. Obvious examples include the law's prohibitions against prostitution and against an individual's resale of prescription drugs. In both cases the law will enforce the

[46] Actually, compensation to the people living on the land would likely be only partial, for the damage to the landowners is to their interests in the land and not to the individuals themselves.

[47] This is generally referred to as the "free-rider problem" in economics and is discussed in most microeconomic theory texts as well as in books on public finance, welfare economics, and public choice. See, for example, Mancur Olson, The Logic of Collective Action (1965).

[48] The court's presumption that, for some people, greatly increased risk of cancer is something to which the dignity hypothesis properly applies—that this is something someone just would not sell—might complicate this analysis. By finding the refinery to be a nuisance but granting the landowners a damages entitlement, the court allows the refinery to force a sale. Should a court do this? Tort law allows this sort of sale ex post all the time when some costly interaction has already produced the harm (for example, a broken leg) and then compensation is required. But should a court allow the sale to be made ex ante? The resolution of these issues is beyond the scope of this paper.

individual's rights to use the resources in question. In the case of sexual services there are laws against rape and sexual assault, and in the case of prescription drugs the law of theft protects the individual's right to keep and take his lawfully prescribed medications. A substantial amount of recent writing has focused on the justifications for rules of inalienability, concentrating on arguments grounded in utility,[49] politics,[50] and liberty.[51] But for our purposes, the most important justification for inalienability centers on personhood and the loss of dignity. There may be a class of transactions in which the transfer of the rights would so alter and debase them that the parties to the bargain and perhaps the rest of us as well would suffer by the degradation of our true dignity, which is necessary to be a whole person.[52]

The most famous recent example of such legislation occurred in Indianapolis, which passed a city regulation prohibiting "trafficking" in pornography.[53] Pornography was defined to be "the graphic sexually explicit subordination of women, whether in pictures or in words, that also includes one or more" specific elements of domination and degradation.[54] Trafficking included the "production, sale, exhibition, or distribution" of pornography.[55] Such an ordinance constituted a type of inalienability because those who would have voluntarily performed in such material may not legally distribute their performances by word, picture, or videotape. This restriction is made regardless of the apparent voluntariness of the

[49] Richard A. Epstein, Why Restrain Alienation? 85 Colum. L. Rev. 970 (1985); Susan Rose-Ackerman, Inalienability and the Theory of Property Rights, 85 Colum. L. Rev. 931 (1985); Calabresi & Melamed, *supra* note 5.

[50] Rose-Ackerman, *supra* note 49.

[51] Calabresi & Melamed, *supra* note 5.

[52] See Margaret J. Radin, Property and Personhood, 34 Stan. L. Rev. 957 (1982); and Margaret J. Radin, Inalienability (unpublished manuscript, Univ. Southern California Law Center 1985).

[53] See Indianapolis Code §§ 16-3(q), 16-3(g)(4), declared unconstitutional in American Booksellers Ass'n v. Hudnut, 771 F.2d 323 (1985), aff'd, 106 S. Ct. 1172 (1986).

[54] These elements were defined as follows. "(1) Women are presented as sexual objects who enjoy pain or humiliation; or (2) Women are presented as sexual objects who experience sexual pleasure in being raped; or (3) Women are presented as sexual objects tied up or cut up or mutilated or bruised or physically hurt, or as dismembered or truncated or fragmented or severed into body parts; or (4) Women are presented as being penetrated by objects or animals; or (5) Women are presented in scenarios of degradation, injury, abasement, torture, shown as filthy or inferior, bleeding, bruised, or hurt in a context that makes these conditions sexual; or (6) Women are presented as sexual objects for domination, conquest, violation, exploitation, possession, or use, or through postures or positions of servility or submission or display." Indianapolis Code § 16-3(q).

[55] *Id.* § 16-3(g)(4). Indianapolis also outlawed "coercing" people into performing in pornography, *id.* § 16-3(g)(5), or "forcing pornography on a person," *id.* § 16-3(g)(5).

performance, the willingness of others to view, and the legality of pretending to engage in the depicted behaviors.[56]

Although the ordinance was passed by a rather unusual coalition that included fundamentalist Christians, radical Right politicians, and Marxist/feminist left-wingers, we will analyze the Indianapolis ordinance as though it was passed for the reasons recounted by one of its drafters, Catharine A. MacKinnon.[57] She argues that those who are in power in society create the concepts and ideas by which we all come to know and understand the world. To the extent that phenomena cannot be appreciated or understood within the accepted epistemology, the phenomena will be ignored or misunderstood. To MacKinnon, women's subordination and debasement in our society is propped up and reinforced by the epistemology of sex that is propagated by pornography. Because pornography (as defined in the Indianapolis statute) teaches that women want to be hurt and humiliated, particularly within sexual relations, men (and some women) come to regard women as masochists and learn to misinterpret sexual domination and humiliation as natural and healthy. This is played out in all areas of life. For example, sexual assault is misinterpreted to be foreplay, rape is misinterpreted to be love, denial of opportunity to women to work is misinterpreted as protecting the weaker sex, and so on. To break the epistemological and political cycle of subordination, repression, and humiliation, MacKinnon drafted the antipornography ordinance described above and then worked for its passage.[58]

Do our results provide any implications for the debate over inalienability, at least to the extent that inalienable rights are justified by reference to dignity, oppression, and domination? We think not for issues such as pornography, although for other (less topical) issues they might. To explain our conclusions, we will sketch the steps in an argument that are needed to connect our results to normative conclusions regarding inalienability.

[56] Do not, at this stage, confuse the legality of actually engaging in behaviors such as rape, sodomy, and so on with the legality of pretending to engage in those behaviors for the purpose of performance.

[57] See Catharine A. MacKinnon, Pornography, Civil Rights, and Speech, 20 Harv. Civ. Rts. & Civ. Liberties L. Rev. 1 (1985). We apologize in advance for the shortcomings of our encapsulation of MacKinnon's argument. We have attempted to boil down a rather complex seventy-page published article into one paragraph, and much must be lost in the process.

[58] Radin argues against allowing prostitution in similar terms. She claims that, if we all were to start selling sexual services instead of engaging in sex out of love, we would learn to think of sex in monetary terms, and the link between sex and love would be broken, leaving us all personally warped and degraded. To avoid this result, Radin argues, the law should not enforce contracts for sexual services. In this way, sex becomes "inalienable." See Radin, *supra* note 52.

Three crucial assumptions provide the link between a subject's behavior and normative conclusions:

ASSUMPTION 1. The behavior of subjects tends to reveal their true beliefs about what is morally permissible for them to trade for money.

ASSUMPTION 2. Subjects do not tend to regard as permissible trading away things necessary for their own true dignity.

ASSUMPTION 3. The beliefs of subjects about what is necessary for their true dignity generally tend to reveal (or accurately describe) what is truly needed for dignity.

The first assumption corresponds to theories about how "true" preferences motivate observed behavior.[59] The only change is that the first assumption links their behavior to true beliefs about what is morally permissible to trade for money.

The second assumption requires only that conceptions of personhood and dignity help to shape the conceptions of subjects as to what is morally permissible. No explicit internal dialogue using these concepts is required to justify this assumption, however. As long as subjects have this type of concept, regard it as important, and implicitly refer to it, the assumption will be satisfied.

The second and third assumptions together deny any significant role for "false consciousness" arguments. These arguments contend, in general, that social pressures so mold and warp the psychological process of people, particularly those living in capitalist societies, that they no longer know their "true" desires or interests. They also claim that honestly held preferences for racism, sexism, selfish materialism, and so forth are strong items of evidence for the inability to know one's true preferences and interests. People who have not been warped would not want such things. As a result, these arguments contend, even honest preferences of the "wrong" sort should be given no weight either in treating individuals or in formulating policies for society. Only if people exhibit the right types of preferences—that is, egalitarian, unselfish, antiracist, antisexist, and communitarian—should we regard their preferences as "true."

In particular, the second and third assumptions rule out MacKinnon's arguments about the epistemology of debasement and the misunderstanding of phenomena that do not fit into the prevailing set of approved concepts. MacKinnon's arguments form, in essence, a false consciousness based on cognitive error.

[59] Such theories may be found in philosophy, for example, David Blumenfeld, Free Action and Unconscious Motivation, 56 Monist 426 (1972); and in economics, particularly under the rubric of revealed-preference theory, Eugene Silberberg, The Structure of Economics: A Mathematical Analysis 324–42 (1978).

In contrast, the second and third assumptions allow that people can and do know, on average, their true preferences. As applied to MacKinnon's argument, the second and third assumptions state that, in general, people can differentiate between that which is and that which is not truly debasing and can distinguish between relationships between the sexes that have dignity and relationships that do not.[60] The third assumption represents the position of conventionalists (also known as relativists), who believe that there is a strong link between the real beliefs of individuals about morality and the moral truths that those beliefs describe.[61] This assumption also rebuffs those who believe that values and facts are completely separate and that values, such as a healthy personality, exist totally apart from any factual contexts in which they are applied.

We find our three-assumption link between behavior and values quite plausible, although by no means certain, when applied to disputes involving physical discomfort, such as the example of the noisy air conditioner discussed in the previous section. And for people like us, our data provide some evidence of what is needed for true dignity in such situations. Our results, based on a sample of eighty subjects, suggest that seemingly healthy college students are willing to taste something nasty (but not life threatening) if they are paid enough to do so. On the basis of this observation we would infer that it is more likely than not that a healthy person, with full regard for his dignity, would be willing to sell the duty to taste bad things. We would suggest that anyone who would argue for making inalienable the right to refrain from tasting bad (but not life-threatening) things should bear the burden of proof.

How far can we generalize this result? It probably extends to rights to endure other unpleasant sensations. We therefore suggest that a similar burden of proof should attach to making inalienable the right to be free from similar harms, such as listening to loud air conditioners. A landowner should probably be allowed to sell an adjoining landowner the right to build a large, ugly structure that will block a beautiful view of a valley below. People also should be allowed to agree to endure unpleasant

[60] See generally Barry Holden, Liberal Democracy and the Social Determination of Ideas, in 25 Nomos: Liberal Democracy 289 (J. Roland Pennock & John W. Chapman eds. 1983).

[61] Stephen Morse, for example, has argued for such an approach in defining the insanity defense in criminal law by asking the members of the jury (or judge) if "craziness so substantially affected the criminal behavior that the defendant does not deserve to be punished." Stephen J. Morse, Excusing the Crazy: The Insanity Defense Reconsidered, 58 S. Cal. L. Rev. 777, 820–21 (1985).

noises and odors, such as those emanating from neighboring dog kennels or garbage dumps, in exchange for money.

However, as applied to performing pornography, as defined in the Indianapolis ordinance, we can take no such position on the basis of our experiments. First, we suspect that agreeing to taste SOA and agreeing to be sodomized while someone films the experience are two very different things. The routine willingness of our subjects to agree to the former implies nothing about their willingness to agree to the latter. Second, even if some of our subjects would agree to perform pornographic acts (something about which we have our doubts), we would be unable to dismiss as easily the false-consciousness arguments. Perhaps, as MacKinnon claims, epistemological impediments would prevent people from seeing the true nature of actions, or maybe some warping experience would have produced "false" preferences in our subjects. We take no stand on these possibilities in this paper except to note that they seem to be substantial enough concerns to prevent us from making the link between our results and any normative conclusions about pornography.

We repeat one last time a qualification that we have repeated throughout this paper: we have provided a mild test of the dignity hypothesis. We express no opinion on the basis of our results about whether people should be allowed to endure great danger, such as increased risk of cancer from a leaking toxic waste dump, or extreme humiliation, such as prostitution.

VI. Conclusion

Our results clearly dispose of asymmetric payoffs as a source of bargaining breakdown and to some extent dispose of the dignity hypothesis as well. The Coase Theorem has been reaffirmed, and courts should choose legal rights and remedies in many situations under a presumption that parties can and will exhaust all gains from trade. However, we have a strong hunch that tasting SOA is qualitatively different from risking death or engaging in much more degrading conduct, so our results cannot be extended to such issues.[62]

[62] Usually, at this point, an article concludes with a call for further research. However, a human-subjects-experiment review board probably would not approve of experiments asking subjects to risk death or to do terribly degrading things regardless of how feasible the experimental design might be. At any rate, we will certainly try no such experiments, and we suspect that no one else will either.

APPENDIX

Experimental Instructions for the Design, Both Sample SOA

I. Consent for Participation

We invite you to participate in an experiment in economic decision making. Part of the decision-making process may involve tasting a displeasurable stimulus. This stimulus is not harmful for human consumption. In fact, the stimulus is a sucrose derivative. However, some taste or oral discomfort may result if you taste the substance because of its bitter qualities. Efforts will be made to shorten any such period of discomfort by providing water for rinsing your mouth. There is a risk to diabetics; no diabetics may participate. No other predictable health risks are foreseen.

This experiment was developed to explore how individuals, such as yourself, react to natural hazards such as contamination of water supplies. Since we obviously cannot use contaminated water in the experiment, the bitter, unharmful liquid is substituted.

You are free to withdraw from participation in this study at any time without prejudice. If you decide to participate in the experiment, you may earn a considerable amount of money. This will be paid to you in cash at the end of the session. Your signature at the bottom of this page indicates that you have decided to participate and have read the above information. You may deny consent if desired.

The nature and general purpose of the experimental procedure have been explained to me. The experiments are authorized to proceed on the understanding that I may terminate participation at any time. I understand that it is not possible to identify all potential risks in an experimental procedure, but I believe that reasonable safeguards have been taken to minimize both known and potential health risks.

Participant ________

Date ________

II. Instructions

A. *General*

You are about to participate in an experiment in decision making. The purpose of the experiment is to gain insight into certain features of complex economic processes. If you follow the instructions carefully, you might earn a considerable amount of money. You will be paid in cash at the end of the experiment.

B. *Specific Instructions to Participants*

You are person A in this experiment. You will make an economic decision with *one* other person, who is person B.

This experiment requires that one decision be made. This decision involves choosing a number. The number chosen will correspond to an actual dollar amount, which will be paid to you at the end of this experiment. In addition, person A may have to hold a one-ounce cup of the bitter liquid in his or her mouth for twenty seconds. The number, corresponding payoffs, and whether A has to taste the bitter liquid are tabulated on page 6 of these instructions. Page 6 lists not only the value of each number to you (under column A), but also the value of each number to the other participant (under column B). Before the experiment begins you will sample a few drops of the bitter liquid.

Before the decision, both participants A and B will play a game. Whoever wins this game earns the right to be designated the "controller." The rules of this preliminary game are as follows.

/ / / / / / / / / / / / / / / / /

Above is a picture of seventeen vertical hash marks. Each player must, on each turn, cross out one, two, three, *or* four hash marks. After a player has crossed out as many hash marks as he or she wishes, it is the other player's turn to cross out one, two, three, *or* four hash marks. The game continues until all hash marks have been crossed out. The person who crosses out the last hash mark *loses* the game. For simplicity, the person who goes first will be the person whose last name would appear first in the dictionary.

Example

A goes first and crosses out four marks:

+ + + + / / / / / / / / / / / / /

Then B crosses out four marks:

+ + + + + + + + / / / / / / / / /

Then A crosses out four marks:

+ + + + + + + + + + + + / / / / /

Then B crosses out four marks:

+ + + + + + + + + + + + + + + + /

A must cross out the last mark on his turn, so A loses the game, and B has earned the position of controller.

If you win the game and are designated the controller, you may, if you wish, choose any number you like by filling out the form on page 7 and giving it to the monitor. However, if you lose the preliminary game and are not designated controller, you may still attempt to influence the controller to form a *joint agreement* and choose some other number. In order to induce the controller to reach an acceptable *joint agreement,* you may offer to pay part of your earnings to the controller.

Example

Assume that A wins the preliminary game and earns the position of the controller. Assume also the following payoffs for A and B. (These payoffs are different from the ones you will have in the actual experiment.)

Outcome Number	A's Payoff ($)	A Tastes?	B's Payoff ($)
1	4	No	0
2	4	Yes	6

Once A has become controller, he or she may choose number 1 without consulting B. However, B may attempt to persuade A to join in a joint decision to choose number 2 instead of number 1. If a joint agreement is reached, *both* parties must sign the agreement form on page 7, stating both what the chosen number will be and how much money will be transferred from one participant's earnings to the other's. For example, A and B might sign the agreement form on page 7, choosing number 2 and directing that $2.00 be paid from B to A. Once the agreement form is signed the monitor will note that, for this decision, A is to be paid $6.00, representing the $4.00 original payoff for number 2 plus the $2.00 transferred from B, and must taste the bitter liquid at the end of the experiment. B is paid $4.00, representing the $6.00 original payoff less the $2.00 transferred to A.

The monitor can only enforce written decisions recorded on the form set out on page 7. You are, however, free to make any other sort of informal agreement that you wish.

No physical threats are allowed. If any party makes a physical threat, the threatened party will get his or her maximum payoff, and the threatening party will get nothing. In addition, if number 2 is chosen and A refuses to taste the bitter liquid, for whatever reason, he or she will get nothing, and B will get his or her maximum payoff.

Are there any questions? We ask you to answer the questions on the attached sheet to make sure you understand the instructions. While you are answering the questions, each participant will go individually into a separate room to sample the bitter liquid. Sampling the bitter liquid will involve flowing a few drops over the tip of your tongue. The monitor will use a dropper and allow the drops to fall off your tongue. Thus only a very small sample will be tasted, and this sample will not remain in your mouth for any length of time. Remember that tasting the liquid in the actual experiment involves holding a full one-ounce cup in your mouth for twenty seconds.

III. Questions

(Refer to your actual payoffs listed on p. 6.)

1. Number ______ is the best alternative for me. Number ______ is the worst alternative for me.

2. If number ______ is chosen, A must taste the bitter liquid.

3. If I become controller, I can make $______ even if the other person doesn't agree.

4. If A is controller, he or she may avoid tasting the bitter liquid by picking number 1. True or False? ______.

5. If A and B reach a joint decision to choose number 2 and B pays A $2.00, I make $______.

6. If I am the controller, I may choose the number that corresponds to my maximum payoff without making a joint agreement with the other participant. True or False? ______.

IV. Payoff Sheet

Outcome Number	A's Payoff ($)	A Tastes?	B's Payoff ($)
1	10	No	0
2	10	Yes	20

V. Agreement Form

Number chosen: _____

$_____ to be paid from _____ to _____

Signed: ________
A

____
B

Computer Models

[13]

ARTICLE

Simple Games in a Complex World: A Generative Approach to the Adoption of Norms

Randal C. Picker†

Uncovering the boundaries of legal rules and defining their proper limits have traditionally vexed students of the law. When must we regulate? When will behavior coalesce in an appropriate way without the intervention of law? These are big questions, as the recent explosion of norms literature makes clear.[1] I do not try to answer these questions here. Instead, I introduce a particular approach to examining these questions, stepping beyond the formal tools that law professors often use. Applying this methodology could ultimately produce a much richer feel for the possibilities and risks in these situations.

---

† Professor of Law, The University of Chicago. I thank the Sarah Scaife Foundation and the Lynde & Harry Bradley Foundation for their generous research support; Seth Chandler, Dick Craswell, Bob Ellickson, Eric Posner, Mark Ramseyer, Matt Spitzer, and participants at workshops at the American Law and Economics Association Annual Meeting, Caltech, Chicago, Georgetown, and Stanford for comments; and Cass Sunstein for enthusiasm and helpful discussion. The title of this article obviously "borrows" from Richard A. Epstein, *Simple Rules for a Complex World* (Harvard 1995), and appropriate apologies (I hope) are hereby made.

A note about reading this paper. The computer simulations presented here are inherently dynamic, and the best way to grasp the dynamics is to see them. The published version of this paper includes a color insert that sets out snapshots of these dynamics. A CD-ROM version of the paper is also available from The University of Chicago Law Review. Requests should be directed in writing to Dawn M. Matthews, Business Manager, The University of Chicago Law Review, The University of Chicago Law School, 1111 East 60th Street, Chicago, Illinois 60637 or by phone at 773-702-9593. Finally, the simulations are also posted at <http://www.law.uchicago.edu/Picker/aworkingpapers/norms.html>.

[1] See, for example, *Symposium: Law, Economics, & Norms*, 144 U Pa L Rev 1643 (1996).

In looking at this traditional question of how and when must we regulate, I confine the focus of this article. This article examines norm competition: identifying the circumstances under which one norm will drive out a second norm or the conditions that will allow two norms to co-exist in a stable outcome. Put differently, this paper investigates the scope of collective action problems in the adoption of norms. I will generate a wide variety of outcomes that might result in norm competition; I will not, however, generate the norms themselves. It is possible that we might create these norms in models of the sort described in this paper, but I will not do so and will take particular norms as simply given and wholly outside the formal model. Understanding where we get competing norms will certainly require painstaking investigation into particular institutions and situations.[2]

This paper has three purposes. First, I want to step beyond simple game-theoretic formulations of norms to examine a larger, more realistic setting. Simple two-by-two games are a principal focus of analysis in game theory generally and in game theory and the law more particularly. This focus is quite understandable: these games are tractable and provide a familiar framework. Nonetheless, simplicity is both a vice and a virtue. These models seem almost naked, stripped of a meaningful strategy space and shorn of the multiplicity of players that typify real-life situations. The adoption of a particular norm is quintessentially a problem of more than small numbers, and we need to move beyond freestanding two-by-two games.

Second, I want to use the computer as a laboratory and run experiments in self-organization. Computer modeling of interactive situations has exploded. There are many labels associated with this work, including: "complexity," "artificial life," "artificial societies," "agent-based modeling," and "massively parallel microworlds." The common elements of this work, however, are straightforward: identify a situation with a substantial number of actors, specify rules for their actions, and let the system rip to see what happens. Results emerge, patterns form, and the system organizes on its own. Central to this work is the idea of self-organization, but this concept is hardly new. Friedrich von

[2] See, for example, Lisa Bernstein, *Merchant Law in a Merchant Court: Rethinking the Code's Search for Immanent Business Norms*, 144 U Pa L Rev 1765, 1768 (1996) (studying merchant practice and challenging the idea that courts should seek to discover and apply "immanent business norms"); J. Mark Ramseyer, *Products Liability Through Private Ordering: Notes on a Japanese Experiment*, 144 U Pa L Rev 1823 (1996) (studying the decision of many Japanese firms to subject themselves voluntarily to strict products liability at a time when Japan did not mandate it).

Hayek emphasized self-organization,[3] and Adam Smith's invisible hand is its defining metaphor. Moreover, scholars have already used computers to test notions about basic social phenomena. Robert Axelrod's classic, *The Evolution of Cooperation*,[4] did exactly that more than a decade ago. Nonetheless, recent changes in computer modeling techniques make it possible to test *in silico*, as the phrase goes, the circumstances under which a society will evolve on its own to a desired social outcome. These tests in societal self-organization are essential first steps before we can understand the possible domain for laws.

Finally, I try to contextualize my game theoretic results. Game theory—on its own and as applied to law—has generated little more than "possibility" results. A given model will show that a particular outcome is possible in the context of a coherent rational framework, but will not reveal the empirical importance of the phenomenon. A given result may be quite brittle, obtainable only if the key parameters are tuned just so, but lost if the values do not line up precisely. To understand whether the possibility result matters, we need to understand the full range of the relevant parameter space. The computer models described here allow us to test a wide range of possibilities directly and in so doing judge how robust our outcomes are.

My computer models lead to several conclusions. Under a broad set of assumptions, my model societies exhibit strong self-organization in the presence of shared values about norms. When norms are competing—when two norms are in play simultaneously—the individuals in the society successfully coalesce around the Pareto-superior norm. This is not to say that the good norm is invariably entrenched or that we cannot influence whether the good equilibrium is obtained. The set of starting conditions that leads to the superior norm—the basin of attraction for that norm—depends on the scope of connectedness among neighbors, the amount of information available to neighbors when making decisions, and the rules they use to assess that information. Each of these is a possible instrument for action as the government seeks to funnel a larger chunk of the possible initial conditions into the desired outcome. Think of each outcome as being associ-

---

[3] Hayek identified the concept of spontaneous order with the market and with common law. See, for example, F.A. Hayek, *Studies in Philosophy, Politics and Economics* 96-105 (Chicago 1967). Hayek traced the belief in control planning to Cartesian rationalism, in reaction to which Adam Smith and other British philosophers of the eighteenth century "provided a comprehensive theory of the spontaneous order of the market." Id at 98-99. See also A.I. Ogus, *Law and Spontaneous Order: Hayek's Contribution to Legal Theory*, 16 J L & Soc 393 (1989).

[4] Robert Axelrod, *The Evolution of Cooperation* (Basic 1984).

ated with a funnel. Making the mouth of the funnel for the good equilibrium relatively larger—expanding its basin of attraction—then emerges as an important way for the government to implement policy.

Furthermore, the results suggest that we should be less sanguine about sequential norm competition, as occurs when a new norm competes with an old, entrenched norm. The old norm will likely continue to survive, notwithstanding that its useful life has expired.[5] The seeding of norm clusters might jump-start the transition from old to new, causing a "norm cascade."[6] In this scenario, the government—or, for that matter, charities, for-profit organizations, or you and I—would encourage experimentation; and, if the conditions were right, the seeded norms would take root and spread, and society would successfully move from the old norm to the new norm. If the old norm really should survive, the experiment fails, and society loses very little.

Thus, to some extent, the collective action problem faced in norms and social meaning analysis has been overstated. I no longer lose sleep over this problem when we have simultaneous competition between two competing norms. Of course, in many social settings, the choice of norms may not be a binary on/off or yes/no choice. For example, in some tort and commercial settings, more than two norms may compete simultaneously, but my models will say nothing about this situation.[7] And competition over time still remains a genuine problem, although to understand this problem, we need first to understand the circumstances that drive experimentation with new norms.

This article has five sections. Section I sets out the basic problem of norm competition and norm adoption and discusses the prior related literature. Section II lays out the basic frame-

---

[5] Compare the problem of "excess inertia" in the network externalities literature. See Douglas G. Baird, Robert H. Gertner, and Randal C. Picker, *Game Theory and the Law* 209-11 (Harvard 1994) (illustrating excess inertia in the context of network externalities). See also Michael Klausner, *Corporations, Corporate Law, and Networks of Contracts*, 81 Va L Rev 757, 763-64 (1995) (arguing that because the value of a corporate contract term is related to the number of firms that adopt it, decentralized individual decisionmaking in the market may fail to produce a socially optimal equilibrium).

[6] Cass R. Sunstein, *Social Norms and Social Roles*, 96 Colum L Rev 903, 909 (1996) (explaining that norm cascades occur when there are rapid shifts in norms, perhaps as a result of fragile social conditions). Compare Sushil Bikhchandani, David Hirshleifer, and Ivo Welch, *A Theory of Fads, Fashion, Custom, and Cultural Change as Informational Cascades*, 100 J Pol Econ 992, 994 (1992) (presenting a model and examples of individuals rapidly converging on one action despite imperfect information).

[7] For an argument based on cultural evolution that suggests that commercial norms will not likely be optimal, see Jody S. Kraus, *Legal Design and the Evolution of Commercial Norms*, 26 J Legal Stud 337 (1997).

work of the analysis. Section III discusses the simulation results. Section IV ties these results to approaches that the law might take vis-à-vis norms. Section V concludes the paper, discusses its key limitations, and suggests directions for future work.

I. ORIENTATION: THE PROBLEM AND THE LITERATURE

The idea of norms is sufficiently well understood that I will introduce it only briefly before moving to consider the relevant literature. Consider three situations:

- You go to lunch with a business associate. It is Friday and the end of a long week. The waiter approaches your table and asks whether you would like to order a drink. You hesitate. You would like a drink, but at the same time you do not want your lunch partner to think ill of you for having a drink. Of course, she may be hoping that you will order a drink so that she can order one as well. What do you do? What does she do?
- During a speech you want to mention the substantial role played in your business by members of a particular racial group. Do you refer to these employees as "African-Americans"? "Blacks"? "People of Color"? You know of course that past terms for this racial group are no longer acceptable, notwithstanding continued use by organizations such as the NAACP and the United Negro College Fund. You do not want to be seen as following what might be seen as the new political orthodoxy, but at the same time you also do not want to offend these valued employees. What do you do?
- You are negotiating the terms of your employment with a new employer. You care about the parental leave policy, as you hope to have children soon. You are nonetheless reluctant to ask about this policy, because you fear that your new employer may doubt your commitment to the new job. What do you do?

These are situations in which the background context—whether described as a norm, a social meaning, or a social role—matters in an important way. The lunch presents a situation where neither person wants to move first. Other cases similar to this include asking first for a prenuptial agreement, which could be seen as a sign of doubts about the marriage, and moving to color-blind hiring unilaterally in a community dominated by discriminatory norms.[8] A social norm may exist that will resolve these situations in ways that benefit all interested parties. These norms could easily change over time or be subject to geographical or class variation.[9]

The second situation is more complex. It demonstrates clearly that norms can evolve and presents a clear example of a "norm entrepreneur."[10] Who used the term "African-American" before Jesse Jackson embraced it? Once Jackson did so, the norm shifted away from "Black," and this created a complex range of possible social meanings reflected in the use of the phrase "African-American." Initial use of the term could be seen as embracing Jesse Jackson personally or perhaps the broad set of social goals that he favored.

The third situation might be seen as just a problem in signaling theory,[11] but can also be understood as an issue embedded in a web of social roles and social norms. Mothers are expected to be quite involved with their children, fathers in the 90s increasingly so, and thus how one answers the question almost certainly depends on gender. Norms matter as well: if everyone routinely asks this question, it loses its signaling punch.

The issues raised by norms have generated a substantial literature. This literature establishes the context in which I will create my computer simulations. Accordingly, the following sections review the literature concerning norms and game theory; social norms, social meanings, and collective action problems; custom; social learning and social computation; agent-based computer simulations; and, finally, evolutionary and spatial games.

---

[8] Eric A. Posner, *Law, Economics, and Inefficient Norms*, 144 U Pa L Rev 1697, 1730 (1996).

[9] Indeed, the daily arbiter of American business life claims that the norm has shifted recently in favor of drinks at lunch, so enjoy. See Stephanie N. Mehta, *Lunch Hour Is Becoming Happy Hour Again*, Wall St J B1 (Sept 23, 1996).

[10] See Sunstein, 96 Colum L Rev at 909 (cited in note 6) (defining "norm entrepreneurs" as people interested in changing social norms).

[11] See Philippe Aghion and Benjamin Hermalin, *Legal Restrictions on Private Contracts Can Increase Efficiency*, 6 J L Econ & Org 381 (1990) (arguing that restrictions on contracts that correct distortions when one party signals information to another can be valuable). See also Baird, Gertner, and Picker, *Game Theory and the Law* at 143 (cited in note 5) (suggesting that a law requiring employers to offer parental leave could solve the problem of potential employees not bargaining for parental leave because of the other inferences that the employer might draw about them before hiring them. In this case, the mandatory law could lead to a more efficient result by prohibiting signaling).

A. Norms and Game Theory

Simple two-by-two games provide much of the formal apparatus at work in the norm theory literature. For example, Sugden's masterful book *The Economics of Rights, Co-operation and Welfare*[12] establishes the two-by-two game as his central tool in studying the evolution of conventions and the rise of spontaneous order. Ellickson also sustains much of his theoretical analysis of norms in the two-by-two framework.[13] As he makes clear up front, he views his inquiry into norms as seeking "to integrate three valuable—but overly narrow—visions of the social world: those of law and economics, sociology, and game theory."[14] A survey of recent articles also reveals that the tools of game theory—and, in particular, free-standing two-by-two games—remain the formal vehicle of choice for understanding norms.[15]

B. Social Norms, Social Meanings, and Collective Action Problems

Recent theoretical work on social norms and social meaning advocates a substantial role for government in cultivating appropriate norms. Much of this analysis is rooted in the collective action problem faced by individuals in the adoption of a particular norm or social meaning.

For example, Cass Sunstein has recently mounted a vigorous defense of "norm management" by the government.[16] He focuses on the context in which individuals make choices and identifies the important, if not pervasive, role that social norms play in de-

---

[12] Robert Sugden, *The Economics of Rights, Co-operation and Welfare* vii (Basil Blackwell 1986) (The book's object is "to show that if individuals pursue their own interests in a state of anarchy, order—in the form of conventions of behavior that it is in each individual's interest to follow—can arise spontaneously.").

[13] Robert C. Ellickson, *Order without Law* 156-66 (Harvard 1991). Indeed, Ellickson devotes Chapter 9 of *Order without Law* entirely to game theory.

[14] Id at 1.

[15] See, for example, Robert D. Cooter, *Decentralized Law for a Complex Economy: The Structural Approach to Adjudicating the New Law Merchant*, 144 U Pa L Rev 1643, 1657-77 (1996) (explaining how social norms arise and persist without state intervention); Posner, 144 U Pa L Rev at 1713-19 (cited in note 8) (examining the mechanisms by which preferences for various rules are transformed into a rule that governs behavior); Jason Scott Johnston, *The Statute of Frauds and Business Norms: A Testable Game-Theoretic Model*, 144 U Pa L Rev 1859, 1859 (1996) (analyzing the relationship between Article 2 of the Uniform Commercial Code and business norms). Compare Rajiv Sethi, *Evolutionary stability and social norms*, 29 J Econ Behav & Org 113 (1996) (examining the emergence of stable patterns of behavior that correspond to observed social norms such as vengeance and cooperation); Peter H. Huang and Ho-Mou Wu, *More Order without More Law: A Theory of Social Norms and Organizational Cultures*, 10 J L Econ & Org 390, 391 (1994) (modeling formally the control of corruption in principal-supervisor-agent relationships).

[16] Sunstein, 96 Colum L Rev at 907 (cited in note 6).

fining choices. These norms will change the cost of a possible choice and thus will exert a substantial influence over observed choices.[17] For example, Sunstein notes that social norms regarding smoking have changed over time.[18] Behavior that once may have been admired is now seen as a sign of weakness and is a source of stigmatization. The social price of smoking has risen over time, and, like the direct cost of buying cigarettes or the health costs of cigarettes, should reduce the amount of smoking.[19]

Given the important way in which social norms influence the costs and benefits of particular choices, we need to understand how norms arise. Sunstein notes that individuals typically have little control over the content of a particular norm and almost no ability to push society from one norm to another.[20] This individual impotence raises the specter of a collective action problem where society cannot coalesce around a beneficial norm.[21] Given this collective failure, direct government cultivation of particular norms—"norm management" in Sunstein's phrase[22]—appears to be a plausible response.

Larry Lessig also has emphasized the collective action problem in his defense of social meaning regulation.[23] Again, social meanings are purely contextual. An action that might give offense in a cab in Hungary—putting on a seat belt, to pursue one of Lessig's examples[24]—might go completely unnoticed in France. An individual is essentially powerless to alter the prevailing meaning associated with a particular act. She may take steps to mute that meaning, but her act has already spoken for her. In this framework, it is certainly imaginable that society will get stuck on a destructive convention.[25]

C. Custom

Scholars also examine the same issues under the guise of custom, often in the context of evaluating reasonable behavior in

---

[17] Id at 939-40.

[18] Id at 905-06, 940.

[19] Id at 950-51.

[20] Id at 911.

[21] Id. See also the related discussion of coordination problems as a justification for legal intervention in Cass R. Sunstein, *After the Rights Revolution* 49-52 (Harvard 1990).

[22] Sunstein, 96 Colum L Rev at 913 (cited in note 6).

[23] See Lawrence Lessig, *The Regulation of Social Meaning*, 62 U Chi L Rev 943, 991-1016 (1995). See also Lawrence Lessig, *Social Meaning and Social Norms*, 144 U Pa L Rev 2181, 2189 (1996) (asserting that norm analysis supplements traditional economics and should focus not just on describing behavior but also on the social meaning of norms).

[24] Lessig, 62 U Chi L Rev at 998.

[25] See also Dan M. Kahan, *Social Influence, Social Meaning and Deterrence*, 83 Va L Rev 349 (1997).

both commercial[26] and tort[27] settings. We used to say "customs" when we were talking about norms; now the norm, of course, is to say "norm." Bad jokes aside, we might distinguish customs and norms based on the roles assigned by the legal system. Customs might be used to describe practices that have legal significance. They might be seen as norms that have been incorporated by reference into the law, statutory or otherwise. If so, then norms are assigned a role by the legal system only by negative inference. For example, Section 547(c)(2) of the Bankruptcy Code embraces a triple-ordinariness standard to insulate some prebankruptcy payments from avoidance as preferences. The standard looks to the practices between the parties but also to "ordinary business terms." Embracing custom or current trade practices means, of course, that a court needs to figure out what those practices are, and that endeavor can be quite difficult.[28] In any event, nothing that I do in this paper distinguishes customs from norms.[29]

D. Social Learning and Social Computation

This work examines the circumstances under which widely held information will be aggregated efficiently so that the right social outcome is reached. For example, imagine a new technology of uncertain quality. Individuals receive information about the technology through its use, but they receive a noisy signal. Aggregating these separate signals into an integrated framework is the work of social learning or social computation.[30]

---

[26] See generally Bernstein, 144 U Pa L Rev 1765 (cited in note 2); Richard Craswell, *Do Trade Customs Exist?*, in Jody Kraus and Steven Walt, eds, *The Jurisprudential Foundations of Corporate and Commercial Law* (forthcoming Cambridge 1998); Kraus, 26 J Legal Stud 337 (cited in note 7).

[27] See generally Richard A. Epstein, *The Path to* The T.J. Hooper: *The Theory and History of Custom in the Law of Tort*, 21 J Legal Stud 1 (1992).

[28] See Craswell, *Trade Customs* at 2 (cited in note 26) (arguing that custom is based more on individual case-by-case judgments than bright-line rules). See also *In the Matter of Tolona Pizza Products Corp*, 3 F3d 1029, 1033 (7th Cir 1993) (holding that "ordinary business terms" refers to practices in which similarly situated firms engage).

[29] A third and overlapping literature addresses conventions. For an introduction, see H. Peyton Young, *The Economics of Convention*, 10 J Econ Perspectives 105 (Spring 1996).

[30] See generally Glenn Ellison and Drew Fudenberg, *Rules of Thumb for Social Learning*, 101 J Pol Econ 612 (1993) (examining learning environment models where players consider the experience of their neighbors in deciding which technology to use); Glenn Ellison and Drew Fudenberg, *Word-of-Mouth Communication and Social Learning*, 110 Q J Econ 93, 93-97 (1995) (studying the way that word-of-mouth communication aggregates the information of individual agents and may lead to the socially efficient outcome). For work from the perspective of cultural evolution, see Kraus, 26 J Legal Stud 337 (cited in note 7).

E. Agent-Based Computer Simulations

The study of the social patterns that arise when individuals interact using simple decision rules dates back at least as far as Thomas Schelling's classic work, *Micromotives and Macrobehavior*.[31] In his characteristically low-tech fashion using only a checkerboard and dimes and pennies, Schelling showed how even relatively mild associational preferences could give rise to substantial segregation.[32] The coins were randomly placed on the squares of the checkerboard. They then were given simple preferences and rules for moving around the checkerboard. For example, each coin wanted at least one-third of its neighbors to be like it. If they were not, it would move to the nearest empty square that met its demands.[33] Schelling demonstrated that segregation could emerge quite naturally even if none of the participants had an affirmative taste for discrimination.[34]

An emerging literature reports on the uses of computers to study self-organization in social systems. These developments spill over from the complexity and artificial life research in biology and the physical sciences, which maintains a similar emphasis on computer simulations of complex adaptive systems.[35] Mitchell Resnick's *Turtles, Termites, and Traffic Jams*[36] is a wonderful introduction to the possibilities in these large, decentralized models. But Resnick's focus is on epistemology, rather than on the detailed study of particular social phenomena. Joshua Epstein's and Robert Axtell's *Growing Artificial Societies*[37] represents the most sustained treatment to date in the social sciences. It describes the Sugarscape, an artificial society constructed with more than twenty thousand lines of computer

[31] Thomas C. Schelling, *Micromotives and Macrobehavior* (Norton 1978).

[32] Id at 147-55.

[33] Id at 148.

[34] Id at 153-54. For recent applications of this work, see generally Joshua M. Epstein and Robert Axtell, *Growing Artificial Societies* 165-71 (Brookings/MIT 1996); Paul Krugman, *The Self-Organizing Economy* 15-22 (Blackwell 1996); Mitchell Resnick, *Turtles, Termites, and Traffic Jams* 81-88 (MIT 1994).

[35] For representative work, see generally Stuart Kauffman, *At Home in the Universe: The Search for Laws of Self-Organization and Complexity* vii (Oxford 1995) (arguing that self-organization is the root source of order in the natural world); John H. Holland, *Hidden Order: How Adaptation Builds Complexity* xviii-xix (Addison-Wesley 1995) (providing an overview of "complex adaptive systems"); Per Bak, *How Nature Works* xi (Springer-Verlag 1996) (viewing nature as "self-organized criticality"—perpetually out of balance, but organized in a poised state, the critical state, where anything can happen within well defined statistical laws).

[36] Resnick, *Turtles* (cited in note 34).

[37] Epstein and Axtell, *Artificial Societies* (cited in note 34).

code.[38] Behavior in the Sugarscape mimics several key elements of behavior in society: agents are born, accumulate wealth, trade, reproduce, and die. The book offers a vision of social science as seeking to replicate—or to generate—particular macro patterns from well defined initial microspecifications.[39] This vision gives rise to a generative approach—hence the use of the term in the title of this article—to modeling.[40] The move from micro to macro itself is not new; leading macroeconomics theorists have spent the last two decades building rigorous micro foundations for macroeconomic phenomena.[41] The use of explicit computer simulations with detailed specifications of decision rules as the means to fine-tune these micro-generated macro principles is, however, innovative.[42]

Growing Artificial Societies provides a leading example of the possibilities of agent-based computer models, but also makes apparent the weaknesses of the best models to date. The book is bereft of institutional features: notwithstanding the desire to grow everything "from the bottom up," the authors fail to generate the norms, contracts, laws, and organizations that constitute the basic institutional framework. Of course, the same criticism applies to this article: I model norm competition, but not the creation of the competing norms themselves. As noted above, I believe that modeling the creation of these institutions (or the norms) is at least an order of magnitude more complex than the problem tackled here.[43]

F. Evolutionary and Spatial Games

Game theory is built up from a handful of key concepts. Perhaps most important is the notion of a Nash equilibrium. A Nash

---

[38] Id at 181.

[39] Id at 1.

[40] Id at 4.

[41] See, for example, Robert E. Lucas, Jr., *Expectations and the Neutrality of Money*, 4 J Econ Theory 103, 121-22 (1972) (modeling why real output might sputter with monetary disturbances); Thomas J. Sargent, *Dynamic Macroeconomic Theory* 1 (Harvard 1987) (describing general equilibrium models that have been built to help interpret time series observations of economic aggregates).

[42] Though even here macro theorists have worked with automatons—agents acting under bounded rationality—to investigate macro phenomena. See, for example, Thomas J. Sargent, *Bounded Rationality in Macroeconomics* (Oxford 1993).

[43] See text accompanying note 2. For additional discussion of Sugarscape and for a general introduction to agent-based simulations, see John L. Casti, *Would-Be Worlds* 170-79 (Wiley 1997). And, for a recent effort to apply models of self-organization to economic phenomena, see Krugman, *The Self-Organizing Economy* at vi (cited in note 34) (showing, for example, how the principle of "order from instability," which explains the growth of hurricanes and embryos, can also explain the formation of cities and business cycles).

equilibrium is a set of self-consistent strategy choices, in the sense that each player prefers no other strategy in response to the strategy of the other players. So, for example, in a two-player simultaneous-move game where each player has two choices, say, left or right, (left, left) forms a Nash equilibrium if player 1 would have no reason to deviate from left if player 2 were to play left, and the same holds for player 2 were player 1 to play left. Put this way, I hope to highlight a key problem with the Nash idea: it is far from obvious how the players actually effectuate a Nash equilibrium. It is one thing to say that player 1 would play left if she knew that player 2 would play left and that player 2 would play left if he knew that player 1 would play left; it is something else to say how the players choose when they do not know what the other player will do. Much of the recent work in game theory has examined the circumstances under which play by boundedly rational players using simple decision rules converges on Nash equilibria.[44] This is conventionally labeled as work in evolutionary game theory, notwithstanding the use of that phrase to describe an earlier, somewhat related literature typically associated with the work of John Maynard Smith.[45] The areas of overlap between this work and the current paper will be noted throughout the paper.

In addition to this literature, Luca Anderlini and Antonella Ianni use cellular automata to explore success in a pure coordination game, where the players are indifferent to two possible equilibria.[46] They use these models to examine the relationships between absorbing states—fixed equilibrium points given the decision rules used in the model—which may or may not be strategically optimal—and Nash equilibria, which are in some sense strategically optimal.[47] Finally, the scholarship that most clearly

---

[44] See George J. Mailath, *Economics and Evolutionary Game Theory* (manuscript on file with U Chi L Rev); Drew Fudenberg and David K. Levine, *Theory of Learning in Games* (manuscript on file with U Chi L Rev); Michihiro Kandori, George J. Mailath, and Rafael Rob, *Learning, Mutation, and Long Run Equilibria in Games*, 61 Econometrica 29 (1993); Glenn Ellison, *Learning, Local Interaction, and Coordination*, 61 Econometrica 1047 (1993); Siegfried K. Berninghaus and Ulrich Schwalbe, *Evolution, Interaction, and Nash Equilibria*, 29 J Econ Behav & Org 57 (1996).

[45] John Maynard Smith, *Evolution and the Theory of Games* (Cambridge 1982).

[46] Luca Anderlini and Antonella Ianni, *Path Dependence and Learning from Neighbors*, 13 Games & Econ Behav 141, 142 (1996) (studying evolutionary learning in a locally interactive system). See also Luca Anderlini and Antonella Ianni, *Learning on a Torus* (forthcoming Cambridge) (investigating the behavior of locally interactive learning systems for a finite population playing a coordination game).

[47] Anderlini and Ianni, 13 Games & Econ Behav at 142. See also Lawrence E. Blume, *The Statistical Mechanics of Strategic Interaction*, 5 Games & Econ Behav 387, 389 (1993) (presenting dynamic models of strategic interaction in a population of players whose direct interaction is local but indirect interaction is global).

parallels the approach taken here uses a spatial version of the prisoner's dilemma model to look at questions in evolution and biology.[48] I discuss this literature in Section II below.

II. THE BASIC SETUP

A. Physical Setup

The two-by-two interactions considered in this article will have the following form:

	Player 2	
Player 1	Left	Right
Left	a,a	c,b
Right	b,c	d,d

Payoffs: (Player 1, Player 2)

These are symmetric games, meaning that exchanging player 1 for player 2 (or vice versa) changes nothing. In that sense, only one type of player plays these games. This strategy space is a natural starting point, but also excludes some well-known games, including the Battle of the Sexes.[49]

I will embed this game in a spatial framework, and to do so, I will lay out an nxn grid.[50] Focusing on just one block of nine players in a 10x10 version of this framework, we would have the following:

[48] See generally Martin A. Nowak and Robert M. May, *Evolutionary games and spatial chaos*, 359 Nature 826 (1992) (studying model in which players have no memory and either always defect or always cooperate); Martin A. Nowak and Robert M. May, *The Spatial Dilemmas of Evolution*, 3 Intl J Bifurcation & Chaos 35 (1993) (similar extension of evolutionary game theory to include spatial dimensions); Martin A. Nowak, Robert M. May, and Karl Sigmund, *The Arithmetics of Mutual Help*, Scientific American 76 (June 1995) (examining various cooperative strategies and reciprocal help in the biological world); Martin A. Nowak, Sebastian Bonhoeffer, and Robert M. May, *More Spatial Games*, 4 Intl J Bifurcation & Chaos 33 (1994) (extending earlier work).

[49] See Baird, Gertner, and Picker, *Game Theory and the Law* at 41-42 (cited in note 5). In the traditional "Battle of the Sexes," there is a conflict between two people who want to spend the evening together but have different preferences about whether to go to a fight or to the opera. Both would rather go together to their less preferred event than go alone to their preferred event. Neither is able to communicate with the other, however, so each must guess what the other will do. This game exemplifies coordination games where there are multiple Nash equilibria and conflicts over the equilibria. Both players want to coordinate their actions, but each player wants a different outcome. Id at 302.

[50] For an introduction to the issues raised by embedded games, see id at 191-95.

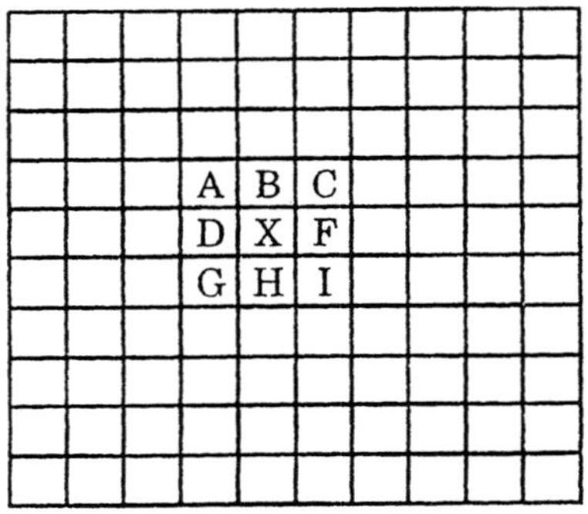

Diagram 1

Player X interacts with her immediate eight neighbors. She plays the free-standing two-by-two game with each neighbor, but she plays only one strategy per round. In other words, she will play either left or right, and that strategy will be the single play for each of the eight interactions. Player X's payoff is determined from the payoff function defined by the two-by-two game, given the plays of her neighbors.

For example, if our player played right, while all eight of her neighbors played left, she would receive a payoff of 8b. If seven played left, while one played right, she would get a payoff of 7b + d. This model is a natural extension of the two-by-two game to a somewhat more general framework. Note also that there are no boundaries here, notwithstanding the picture. Players at the top are treated as neighbors of the players at the bottom, at the left edge with those on the right edge. (Put differently, the layout is a doughnut, or a torus.) In the actual runs of the model, the grid is 101x101, giving a total of 10,201 cells (and 10,201 players).

1. Payoff neighborhood.

I will discuss two kinds of neighborhoods in this article: payoff neighborhoods and information neighborhoods. A payoff neighborhood is the local area that directly impacts one player's payoffs. Once a player's strategy is chosen, the strategy choices made by the other players in the payoff neighborhood will determine the original player's payoffs and thus these strategies define the neighborhood's impact. In a basic two-by-two game, the payoff neighborhood for one player is simply the other player. In the game set forth in Diagram 1, the payoff neighborhood is player X's eight neighbors.

While the notion of a payoff neighborhood is quite abstract, it would be a mistake to think that it does not track something quite real. The payoff neighborhood is akin to a measure of community connectedness, or how linked we are to our neighbors. Of course, linkage could operate over many dimensions: linkage could be a sense of how much I care about my neighbor's welfare, or it could be much more instrumental, in the sense that your decisions help create the environment in which I operate. My payoff neighborhoods, however, are purely instrumental: my neighbor's strategy decisions set the environment, which, when coupled with my decision, create the consequences that flow to all of us.

Any number of payoff neighborhoods are possible, but I will work with the two standard neighborhoods from the cellular automata literature:

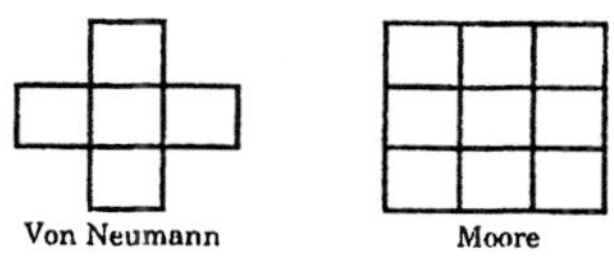

Diagram 2

The grouping on the left is the Von Neumann neighborhood, the grouping on the right is the Moore neighborhood. Focus on the cell at the center of each neighborhood. In the Von Neumann version, the payoff of each player is determined by her strategy choice and the choices of her neighbors to the immediate East, West, North, and South. The Moore neighborhood starts with the Von Neumann neighborhood and adds the four diagonal cells. The payoff of the center player is given by her decision and the decision of her eight neighbors. (Diagram 1 above thus represents a Moore neighborhood.) Of course, each player will be treated as centered at a payoff neighborhood, so the mosaic created is one of overlapping payoff neighborhoods.[51]

2. Information neighborhood.

An information neighborhood is the area in which a player observes results. One might think of it as the "vision" of the player. This information will form the basis for the player's strategy choice in the next round of the model. In many cases, the payoff neighborhood and the information neighborhood will

[51] For a general introduction to the Von Neumann and Moore neighborhoods, see Richard J. Gaylord and Kazume Nishidate, *Modeling Nature* 4-7 (Springer-Verlag 1996). Also note, as Bob Ellickson did in a letter to me, that each individual in this model has a unique reference group, as the overlap is imperfect. These social groups are therefore different from kinship or professional groups where each person has the same "neighbors."

be identical. But, as a general matter, it would be a mistake to assume that these neighborhoods need be coextensive. Information has a natural flow to it. Information also is a natural instrument for changing results in the models. Creating an ethic of welfare connectedness—what many would label a sense of community—is certainly extraordinarily difficult. Even creating instrumental connectedness is probably difficult, given the ability of individuals to isolate themselves from the consequences of the decisions of others. In contrast, information connectedness is much easier: it is relatively straightforward to provide information about others (though getting the recipients to listen is another hurdle).

To examine this divergence between payoff and information neighborhoods, I will vary the information neighborhoods. I will begin by looking at the coextensive cases and then move to cases in which the information neighborhood is larger than the payoff neighborhood. I will first embed a Von Neumann payoff neighborhood in a Moore information neighborhood. The player at the center will still have her payoffs determined by the choices made by her North, South, East, and West neighbors, but when she chooses her strategy for the next round, she will have seen the outcome of the prior round for her eight Moore neighbors. Next, I will embed the Moore neighborhood in a double Moore neighborhood, letting the player at the center see out a distance of two cells in all directions instead of just one cell. Finally, I will look at one version of a global information neighborhood, where players see all of the outcomes. Lest this be thought silly, information sources such as newspapers and stock markets may play exactly this kind of aggregation role.

B. Strategy Choice

Next, we need to specify some rules regarding strategies. In most of the models, initial strategies will be assigned at random. I will vary the distribution of initial left and right players and test how these initial conditions influence outcomes. As is conventional in this literature, I will use a color-coding scheme to track strategy changes between rounds. This scheme will be used in the color insert associated with this article and the website where videos of simulations are available.[52] Other than in the initial round, a cell will be coded as blue if the player occupying it has played left in two consecutive rounds and will be coded as

[52] The website is at <http://www.law.uchicago.edu/Picker/aworkingpapers/norms.html>.

red if the player has played right in these same rounds. A player who switches from left to right is coded as yellow, and one who makes the reverse switch—from right to left—is coded as green. (In the initial random distribution, any cell playing left is coded as blue, playing right as red.) To review the color-coding for the strategy choices per round:

COLOR	**STRATEGY**
Blue	Two Rounds of Left
Red	Two Rounds of Right
Yellow	Switch from Left to Right
Green	Switch from Right to Left

Turn next to the substantive question of how we define strategy choice, which determines how the model will evolve from round to round, generation by generation. Contrast three frameworks for looking at decisionmaking and knowledge:

- *The Full Information/Full Rationality Model*: Players know the strategy space of the game, know the function giving rise to the payoffs, and have the ability to assess optimal strategy. This model tracks the usual assumption that the players have full knowledge of the rules of the game that they are playing and the ability to use that information in the best possible way.
- *The Biological Model*: Two types of players exist, one can only cooperate, one can only defect (that is, one plays left only, one plays right only). Thus, these "players" make no decisions at all; nature and instinct have programmed their "decisions." The situation evolves by tying reproductive success in the next generation to payoffs in the current generation. A given cell is occupied in the next round by a player of the type that received the highest payoff among the nine cells centered on the cell in question. This model is a natural interpretation of the Darwinian model of adaptive success generating reproductive success.
- *The Limited Information/Incomplete Rationality Model*: Players lack full information regarding the strategy space or the way strategies interact to give rise to payoffs. For example, they might know that they are playing a two-by-two game, but they do not know which one. They may learn this information through the play of the game, though the approach to learning needs to be specified. Incomplete rationality may mean that the players' abilities are bounded or

that rationality analysis is insufficient to guide behavior. Some heuristic rule is required for decisions, but this rule is not generated internally from the rationality assumptions. Examples might include selecting the strategy that does best among those observed by a player or playing a spatial version of tit-for-tat.[53]

It is important to understand where these approaches converge and diverge. Consider a spatial version of the prisoner's dilemma. Given its overall prominence, I would be remiss in not addressing the prisoner's dilemma, though for reasons that will become clear, I think the spatial prisoner's dilemma is a dead-end for the law and economics crowd. Start with a free-standing version of the game that fits the general scheme described above:

	Player 2	
Player 1	Left	Right
Left	a,a	c,b
Right	b,c	d,d

Payoffs: (Player 1, Player 2)

Assume that b > 1. If we analyze this game, we should expect both players to play right. If player 1 expected player 2 to play right, player 1 would be indifferent between playing left or right because her payoffs are the same (0) under either strategy. But if player 1 expected player 2 to play left, she would clearly play right, as b > 1. This reasoning holds for both players, so we should expect (right, right) with a payoff of (0,0). Obviously, the players would both be better off with (left, left), as they each would receive a payoff of 1. This result replicates the essential feature of the prisoner's dilemma.

1. Full information/full rationality model.

Now look at the same prisoner's dilemma in the spatial context in each of our three frameworks. Start with the full information/full rationality model. Players know exactly what game they are playing and assess strategies in an individually rational way. As in the free-standing prisoner's dilemma, all players should defect. To see this result, walk through the possibilities one-by-one

[53] See Baird, Gertner, and Picker, *Game Theory and the Law* at 171-72 (cited in note 5). "Tit-for-Tat" is the strategy in a repeated game in which a player cooperates in the first period and, in all subsequent periods, defects if the other player defected in the immediately preceding period, but otherwise cooperates. Id at 316.

and assume again that b > 1. First, what should you do if you know that all eight of your neighbors are going to cooperate? If you cooperate you receive a payoff of 8, but if you defect you receive a payoff of 8b, so clearly you should defect. Next, suppose that seven neighbors were going to cooperate and one was going to defect. You get 7 from cooperating, but 7b from defecting, so you defect. Now, approach the other extreme. Suppose that seven of your neighbors were going to defect and one intended to cooperate. You will get nothing from your defecting neighbors, regardless of whether you cooperate or defect, but you will get 1 from your cooperating neighbor if you cooperate and b from him if you defect. So you defect. Finally, suppose that all eight of your neighbors were going to defect. You would get 0 from cooperating, and 0 from defecting, so you are indifferent. Taking all of this analysis together, you never do worse by defecting and often do better, so you will defect. Everyone defects, just as in the free-standing model.

The spatial feature adds nothing in the full information/full rationality setting. The analysis does show that the central failure of the free-standing prisoner's dilemma—individually rational behavior is collectively foolish—carries over to the spatial setting, but we should have guessed that anyhow. So switch frameworks, and consider how the spatial version of the prisoner's dilemma fares if we use a biological model instead.

2. Biological model.

In the biological model, the spatial prisoner's dilemma is little more than a payoff function for the two strategies of cooperation and defection. Recall that no decisions are made in the biological model: actors simply have a preordained type. There is no obvious reason to think that this model will evolve in any particular way, and indeed, as Nowak, May, Bonhoeffer, and Sigmund show,[54] a rich variety of behavior emerges. In some cases, the model converges to the all-defection outcome that we saw in the full information/full rationality model. In other cases, the model cycles forever through a handful of states, all of which involve a mix of cooperation and defection. In yet other cases—and these are arguably the most interesting—the model appears to be almost chaotic. The model cycles only over a long time period, and the cycle will be all but undetectable to you or me.[55]

---

[54] See note 48.

[55] To see an example of this, set b = 1.65, and start with an initial random distribution of 10 percent defectors and 90 percent cooperators. A movie showing the first hun-

This result is a dramatic change from the full information/full rationality model, which locks into the defection equilibrium immediately and is bereft of interesting behavior. In contrast, the biological framework provides an embarrassment of riches. Where does this result put us? Biology is a great subject, but we want models in which people make decisions and their behavior is not simply instinctive and preordained. To achieve this setting, switch to the limited information/limited rationality framework.

3. Limited information/limited rationality model.

In this framework, players know only that they are playing a two-by-two game and thus have a choice between two strategies. We now need to consider learning quite carefully. Suppose that our players learn nothing, and make decisions based on a simple observation. In each round, each player observes the payoffs that she receives and those received by her neighbors and the strategies that the neighbors play. Given this information, she adopts the strategy that did best—the strategy that resulted in the single highest payoff in the nine cells that she sees.

This strategy choice matches the biological framework exactly; indeed, that is the point of this exercise. The absence of learning means that our player never assesses whether defection is a dominant strategy. Instead, she uses a more basic decision rule that tracks exactly the reproductive success rule used in the biological model. By introducing limited information and limited rationality, we seem to have made the spatial prisoner's dilemma interesting for us.

But this outcome does not hold if we advance the model just a bit. It does not take much for our players to learn what game they are playing. A little experimentation and a little variation coupled with some simple calculations will let our players convert this limited information game to the full information version. Suppose, for example, that our test player cooperates in one round, while six of her neighbors cooperate and two defect. She will receive a payoff of 6, which she knows to be derived in the following way:[56]

$$6p_{cc} + 2p_{cd} = 6$$

Obviously, an infinite number of pairs will satisfy this equation, including (1,0) and (0,3). She does not yet know much. Sup-

dred generations of this model is available at my web site (cited in note 52).

[56] The symbols p_{cc} and p_{cd} represent the payoffs in the model when, respectively, both players cooperate, and player 1 cooperates and player 2 defects.

pose that in the next round, she again cooperates, while five of her neighbors cooperate and three defect. She now gets a payoff of 5, which she again knows to be generated in the following way:

$$5p_{cc} + 3p_{cd} = 5$$

Our player now has two equations with unknowns, and can solve them to learn that $p_{cc} = 1$ and $p_{cd} = 0$. Given this information, she can defect in the next round and learn the value of p_{dd}.[57] She now enjoys full information regarding the game, and can determine that defection is her dominant strategy.

The limited information model therefore tracks the interesting biological model when players do not learn, but quickly converts into the full information model when players begin to learn. To give a richer sense of this outcome, I have simulated the model one hundred times on the assumption that 25 percent of the players learn the game and defect. Moreover, I assumed that 25 percent of the remaining players defect initially, while 75 percent of this same group cooperate. After that, this predetermined group chooses the strategy that yields the highest payoff in the nine cells that they see. Under those parameter settings, eighty-five out of one hundred games ended in the all-defection equilibrium. In the other fifteen simulations, cooperation did poorly.

For me, this analysis yields the following results. We can generate complex, interesting behavior in the spatial prisoner's dilemma, and this behavior may have important implications in contexts in which individuals do not learn. Nonetheless, relatively simple learning converts the limited information framework to the full information framework, and only a modest fraction of the players need to master this learning for the interesting behavior to vanish. For most circumstances of interest to us, the spatial prisoner's dilemma should look a lot like the freestanding prisoner's dilemma. That result is worth noting, but it also means that playing the spatial prisoner's dilemma reveals nothing new.

This discussion has been an extended look down a dead-end. I started by emphasizing the need to be precise about the rationality and information assumptions used to generate strategies from generation to generation. The traditional assumptions of full information and full rationality make the spatial prisoner's dilemma an uninteresting vehicle for studying norm problems. Relatively simple learning converts a limited information/limited

---

[57] The symbol p_{dd}, of course, represents payoffs when both players defect.

rationality approach into the traditional rationality approach. We should therefore look elsewhere to model norm competition.

III. How Norm Competition Evolves

Turn now to the traditional coordination game. I will focus on a particularly simple version of it:

Player 1	Player 2: Left	Player 2: Right
Left	1,1	0,0
Right	0,0	b,b

Payoffs: (Player 1, Player 2)

As is generally known, we have little interesting to say about this model even when we use our full rationality assumptions. Dominance arguments will not solve this game. If Player 1 plays left, Player 2 wants to play left, and vice versa; if Player 1 plays right, Player 2 wants to play right, and vice versa. Neither player has a single best strategy to play. In the parlance of game theory, both (left, left) and (right, right) are Nash equilibria: neither player wants to switch strategy given the other player's strategy. Nonetheless, game theory provides no good way of choosing between these equilibria. We do not reach a determinate result, meaning that we cannot explain how the players would actually make decisions.[58] We must therefore use our limited information/limited rationality framework. Once we are in this framework, we can weaken our usual information assumptions without changing results in any material way.

Assume that players know only that they are playing a spatial two-by-two game. They know nothing about the payoffs and nothing about the strategy space. They are endowed with an initial strategy at random from all of the available strategies. They know only one strategy, and they play it. Round by round, players will observe the strategies played by their neighbors and thereby learn new strategies. Players will also observe the consequences of those strategies. Some players will learn the full payoff function, just as our players in the prior section learned that they were playing the spatial prisoner's dilemma. In this model,

[58] This overstates somewhat. Harsanyi and Selten have emphasized the idea of risk dominance to resolve these games. This idea focuses on the consequences of failing to coordinate and therefore the relative risk associated with each choice. See John C. Harsanyi and Reinhard Selten, *A General Theory of Equilibrium Selection in Games* 82-89 (MIT 1988).

the same linear learning will be fully informative about the payoff functions defined by the particular coordination game being played. But—and this is the key difference from the spatial prisoner's dilemma—full knowledge of the strategies and the payoffs will not render this game uninteresting. In the spatial prisoner's dilemma, learning converted the limited information framework into the full rationality framework and distanced us from the biological model. In contrast, here, because we do not have a determinate way of playing coordination games, we necessarily must reach outside the model for an operational decision rule. Learning does not convert the limited information framework into the full rationality model, and indeed, we remain quite close to the biological approach.

This discussion lays out the game and its setup. Next, we need to specify a choice rule for the players. For now, I will assume that each player uses the same rule. In Section III.D, I will look at an alternative choice rule, but I will start with the rule that has received the most study in the literature: In the next round, the player will adopt the strategy that did the best, as measured by how her strategy performed and how her neighbors did in the previous round. Each player looks at the payoffs she obtained as well as those of her eight neighbors, figures out which payoff is the highest, and then adopts the strategy used by that player. As noted before, this scheme does not work in the first round—there are no prior payoffs to evaluate—so strategy choices will be assigned at random. While perfectly plausible, to me at least, this decision rule is created out of whole cloth. I do not justify it as emerging out of some other generally accepted framework.

A. Initial Examples

Before looking at the examples, note that all-left and all-right are both Nash equilibria and absorbing states (meaning that the model will not change from the state once it is reached). As will become clear, Nash equilibria and absorbing states are not interchangeable: we will have absorbing states in the models that are clearly not Nash equilibria. To see that all-left and all-right are Nash, if a given player thought that every other player was going to play right, she clearly would play right. She would get zero if she played left and a payoff of 8b from playing right. The same holds for left: if the player expected everyone else to play left, she would play left and get 8 rather than play right and get zero. Obviously, these two Nash equilibria in the spatial coordination game track those seen in the free-standing game.

All-left and all-right are also absorbing states—fixed points given the decision rules used. If everyone has played right, each player observes only how right has done, and therefore chooses right. If everyone plays left, each player observes only left outcomes, and chooses only left. As should be clear, the extent of initial variation in the number of players playing left or right will be important. To see this result, I will start with a few examples to give you a sense of the variety of behavior seen in this framework. Start with b = 1.05 and assume that the equal number of players initially play the left and right strategies. Figures P1 to P6 on the color insert show six snapshots of the evolution of this model.[59]

As is evident, this model converges to a mixed equilibrium, with large numbers of players adopting each strategy.[60] Of course, this mixed equilibrium is inefficient, as the social optimum is achieved when all players play right. Nonetheless, this result is not too surprising. The value of getting to the right equilibrium is low—1 versus 1.05—and the initial starting conditions do not tilt the tables significantly in favor of one of the equilibria.

Consider a second example. Bump b up to 1.25 and again assume that left and right are initially played in equal numbers. Figures P7 to P12 on the color insert show six snapshots of the evolution of this model.[61] All we have done is increase the value of coordinating on the second equilibrium, and now the model converges to the social optimum. Nonetheless, simply increasing b to 1.25 is not enough to assure convergence to the right equilibrium. Let 80 percent of the players start with the left strategy and 20 percent with the right, and consider the five snapshots of the model given on the color insert as Figures P13 to P17. Once again, the model fails to converge completely.[62]

This outcome highlights the difference between absorbing states—fixed points—and Nash equilibria. The result in Figure P17 is an absorbing state, but it is not a Nash equilibrium. The diagram below sets out the relevant chunk of the final result:

---

[59] To see this evolution directly, play the video at my website (cited in note 52).

[60] I mean "mixed" in the sense of having both strategies played at the same time by different players; I do not mean "mixed" in the sense of one player playing both strategies with some positive probability. For a discussion of mixed strategies played by single players, see Baird, Gertner, and Picker, *Game Theory and the Law* at 37-39 (cited in note 5).

[61] See the website (cited in note 52).

[62] Id.

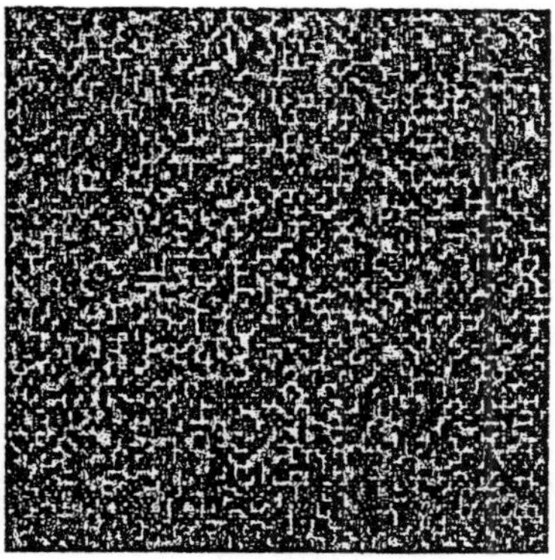

Figure P1

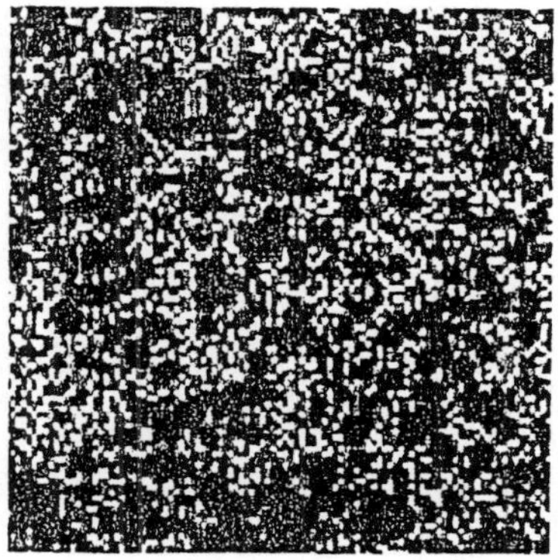

Figure P2

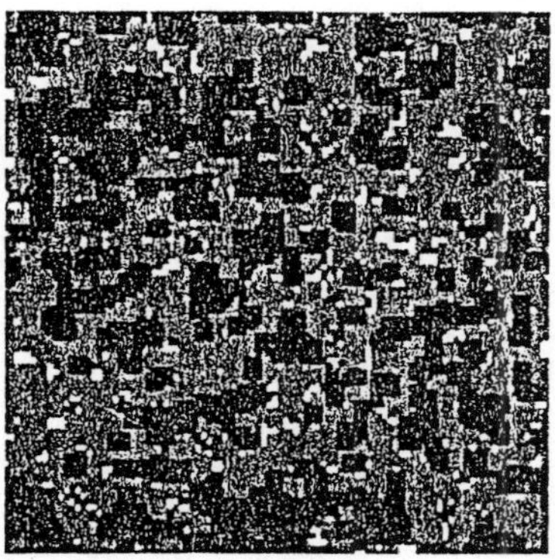

Figure P3

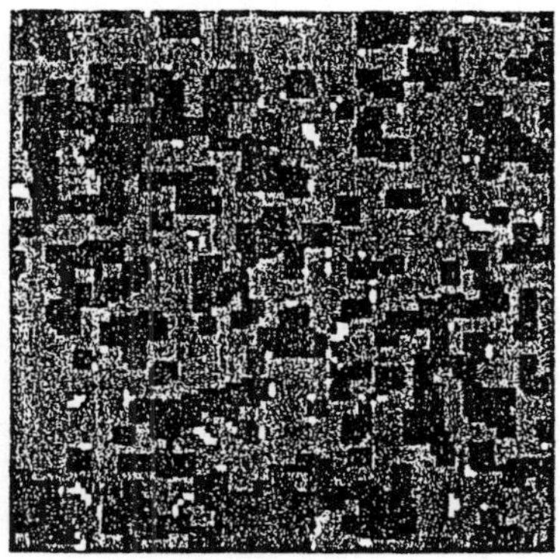

Figure P4

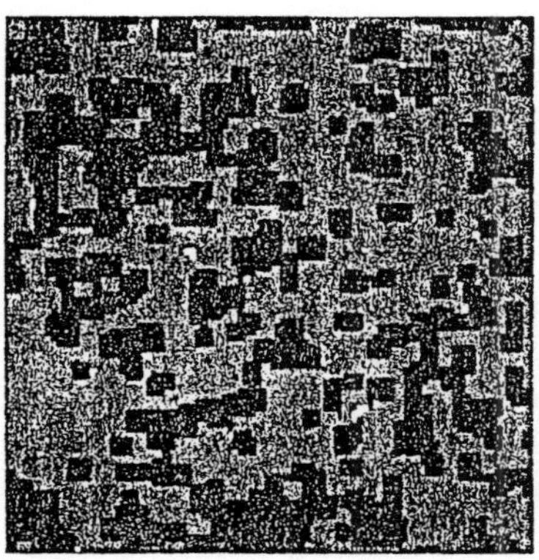

Figure P5

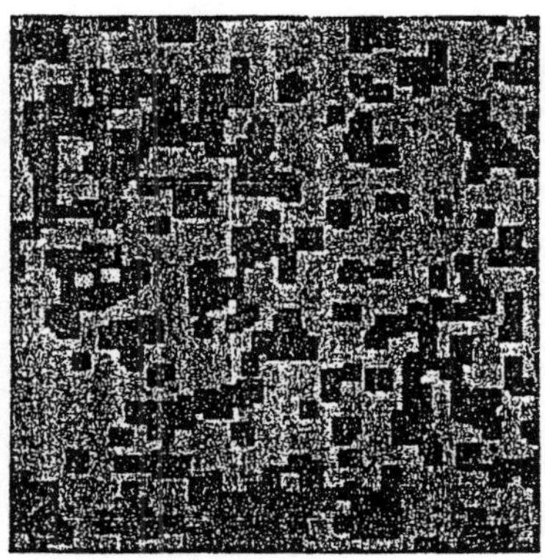

Figure P6

b = 1.05, Initial Setup: 50% Left, 50% Right

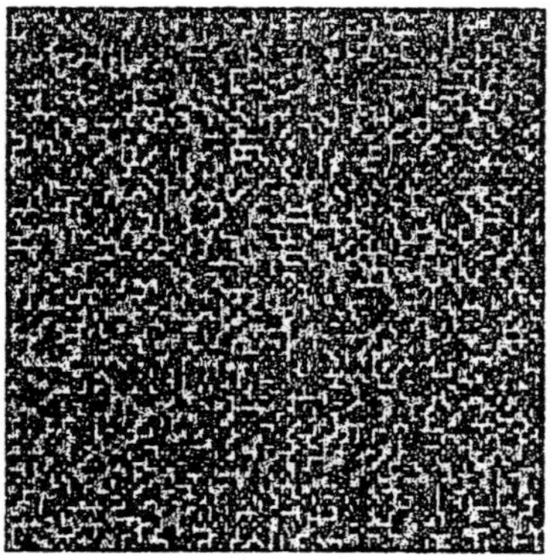

Figure P7

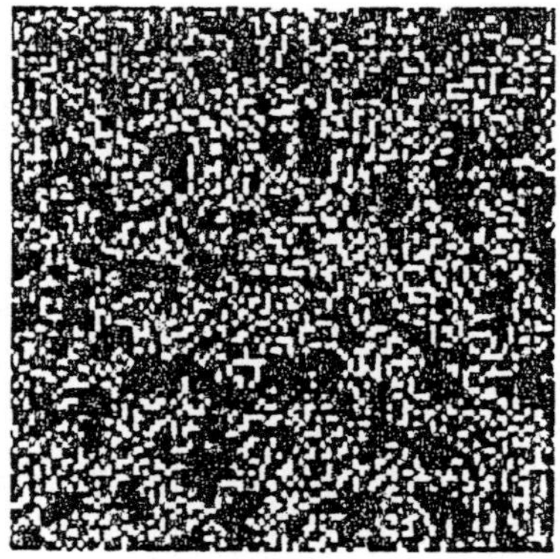

Figure P8

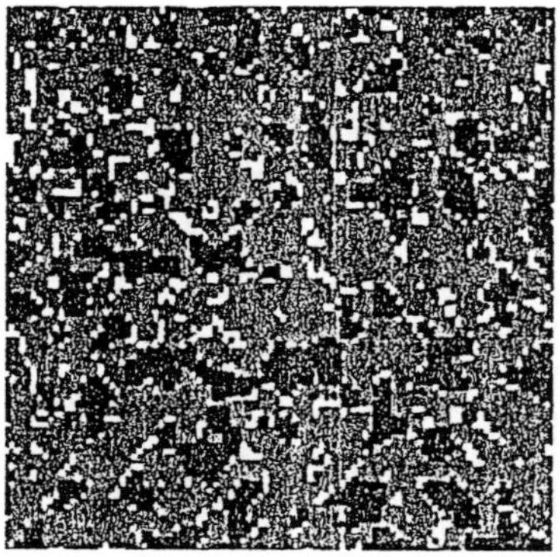

Figure P9

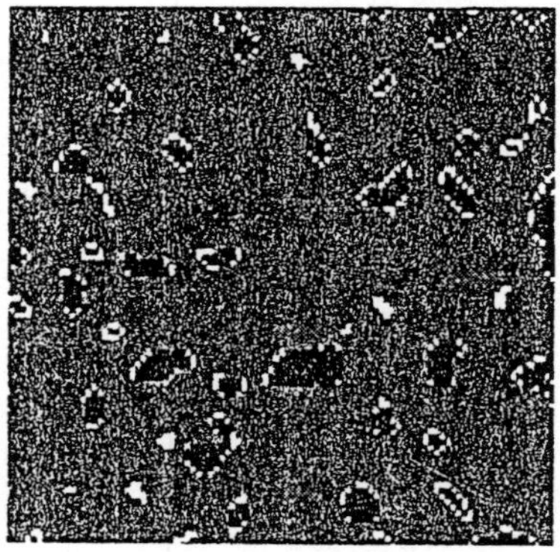

Figure P10

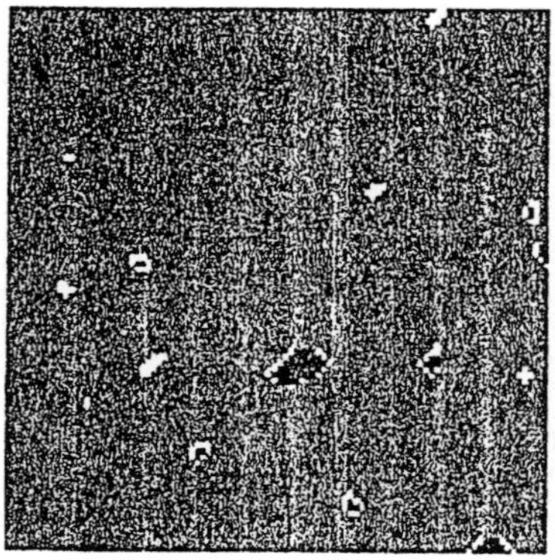

Figure P11

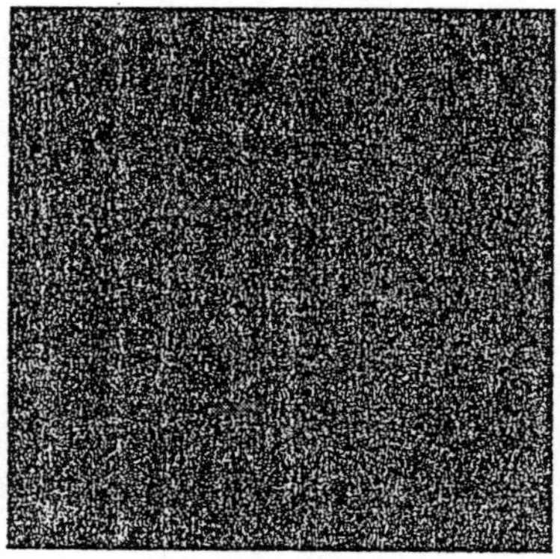

Figure P12

b = 1.25, Initial Setup: 50% Left, 50% Right

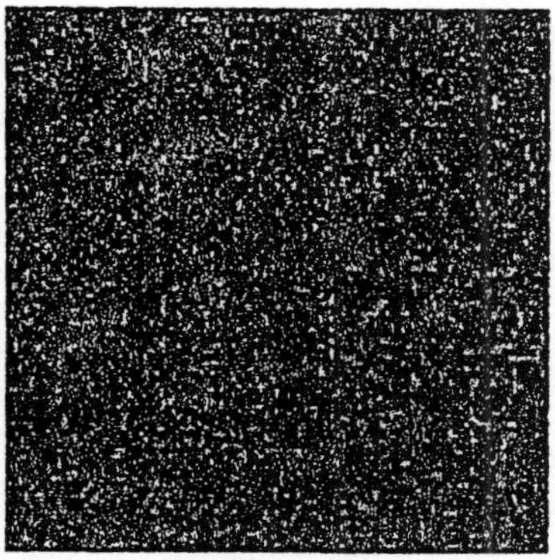

Figure P13

Figure P14

Figure P15

Figure P16

Figure P17

b = 1.25, Initial Setup: 80% Left, 20% Right

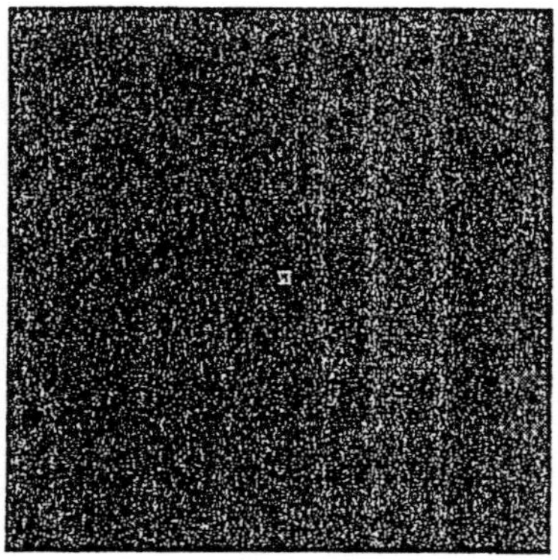
Figure P18

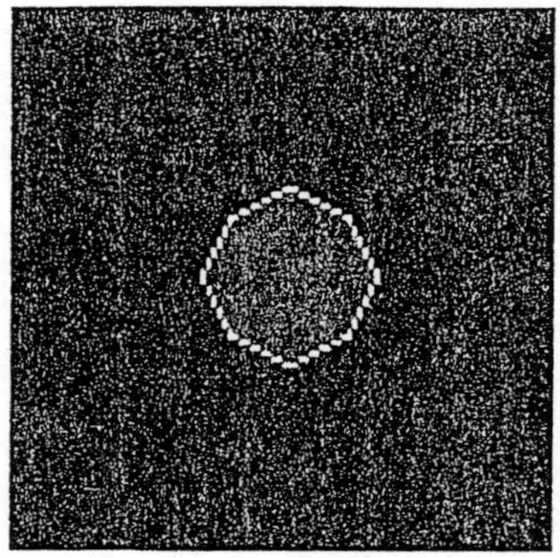
Figure P19

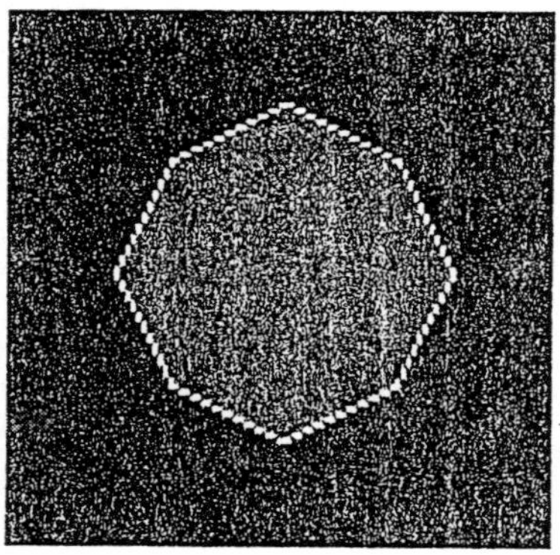
Figure P20

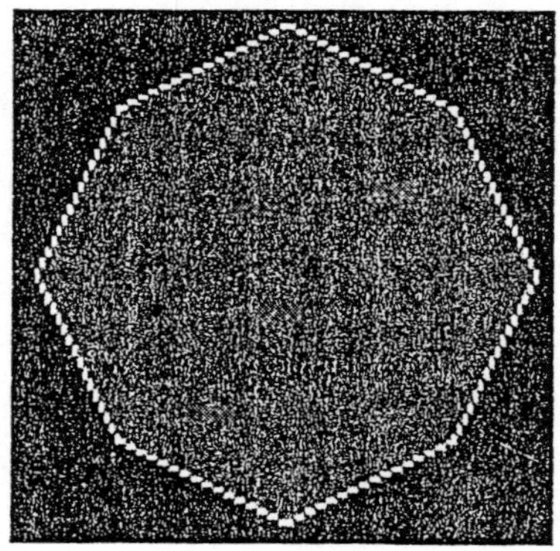
Figure P21

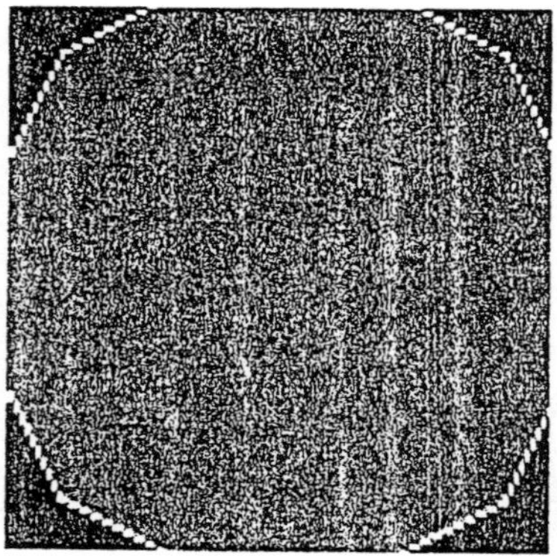
Figure P22

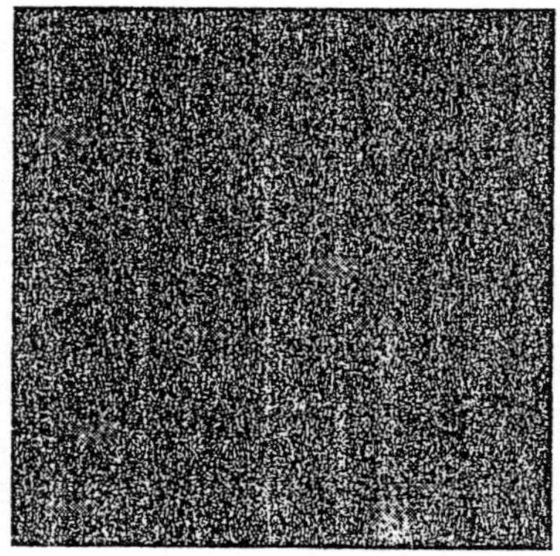
Figure P23

Norm Seeding: b = 1.65, Nine Cluster Start

B	B	B	B	B	B	B	B	B
B	B	B	B	B	B	B	B	B
B	B	B	B	B	B	B	B	B
B	B	B	R	R	R	B	B	B
B	B	B	R	R	R	B	B	B
B	B	R	R	R	R	R	B	B
B	B	B	B	B	R	R	B	B
B	B	B	B	B	B	B	B	B
B	B	B	B	B	B	B	B	B

Diagram 3

To understand why this equilibrium is not Nash, focus on the red (R) cell at the corner of the cluster of nine reds. Round after round in this model, this cell continues to play right and remains red because it observes the red at the center of the cluster of nine reds receiving a payoff of 8b. This payoff, of course, is the best possible outcome in the model, and, on my assumed strategy for making decisions, any player who observes that outcome adopts right as her strategy. Nonetheless, this strategy cannot be a Nash equilibrium unless right is the best strategy for this player given all of the other strategies. Our corner red expects, however, three of her neighbors to play right, and five to play left. Given those strategies, she gets a payoff of 3b if she played right and a payoff of 5 from playing left, so she should switch strategies, so long as $b < 1.67$.

What should we make of this outcome? This particular mixed play absorbing state is sustainable only if we have "irrational" play round after round. Our corner red continues to play red because the center red is doing so well, even though the context in which the center red plays is quite different from corner red's own setting. We might feel the need to abandon Nash approaches initially because they depend on highly refined introspection driven by high-level reasoning abilities. Nonetheless, we should be equally uncomfortable about results that depend on seemingly implausible play into perpetuity. Some middle ground may be more appropriate,[63] but, in any event, the approach taken in this paper builds or constructs an absorbing state based on a minimal set of key ideas. This generative approach may offer a more plausible account of how equilibria are actually achieved.[64]

---

[63] See the suggested directions for future research at text following note 93.

[64] This parallels—indeed, overlaps with—the recent work in evolutionary game theory. See note 44.

B. The Emergence of a Phase Transition

The preceding examples give a flavor for the range of behavior that arises in the model. To get more systematic, I set b = 1.65 and ran sets of 100 simulations of the model for different initial densities. The results are set forth in Figure 1. To be clear on the meaning of the figure, I ran 100 simulations of the model with b = 1.65 for each of the initial densities shown along the x-axis (9900 simulations total). The three graphs in Figure 1 capture three possible results. All of the players could converge on playing right ("Red"); all could converge on left ("Blue"); and some could converge on left while others played right ("Mixed").

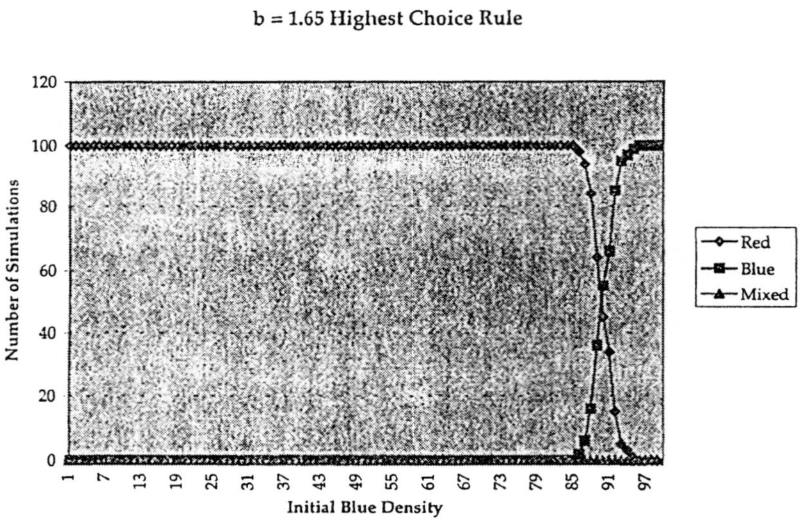

Figure 1

The graphs chart the number of times each possible outcome occurs in the 100 simulations for each initial value. If we start with 1 percent of the players playing left and 99 percent playing right, then in 100 times out of 100, the play of the game converged on the right-right (or all-red) equilibrium. In contrast, if we start with 99 percent of the players playing left and 1 percent playing right, then in 100 percent of the cases we converged on the inferior all-left equilibrium.

Neither of these results is surprising. The good (right) equilibrium, however, is particularly robust. Even if we start in tough conditions—say with 80 percent of the players playing left and 20 percent playing right—we still converge on the good equilibrium in 100 percent of the cases. As we push the initial density of players playing the inferior choice ever higher, however, we run into problems. Some fraction of the simulations converge to the inferior equilibrium. By the time we reach just a bit more than 89 percent of the players playing left initially, the graphs cross: as many simulations converge on the bad equilibrium as converge on the good equilibrium. If we have more players choose initially the inferior strategy, more and more of the simulations converge on the inferior equilibrium. As we reach our maximal densities, the rout is complete, and all of our simulations converge on the inferior equilibrium.

The shape of these graphs is characteristic of a phase transition in physics or a model of punctuated equilibria in biology.[65] The system has two natural equilibria and shifts from one to the other occur over a narrow band. The combination of a standard two-by-two game and some neighborhood effects results in this phase transition.

What is going on here? Why is it that this system converges so well and why do we start to encounter trouble when 85 percent of the players initially choose the inferior play? To understand this phenomenon, start with a cluster of nine red cells surrounded by a sea of blue:

B	B	B	B	B	B	B	B	B
B	B	B	B	B	B	B	B	B
B	B	B	B	B	B	B	B	B
B	B	B	R	R	R	B	B	B
B	B	B	R	R	R	B	B	B
B	B	B	R	R	R	B	B	B
B	B	B	B	B	B	B	B	B
B	B	B	B	B	B	B	B	B
B	B	B	B	B	B	B	B	B

Diagram 4

Focus on decisionmaking by the players in the red cells. Each border red will observe the payoff of the center red, who will be getting 8b (that is, the center red interacts with eight players playing the strategy that she has played, so she is perfectly coordinated with her neighbors). The best blue cell that our border red could see has a payoff of 7. No border red will switch.

[65] See, for example, Stuart Kauffman, *At Home in the Universe* 57, 116-18 (Oxford 1995); Stephen Jay Gould and Niles Eldredge, *Punctuated Equilibria: The Tempo and Mode of Evolution Reconsidered*, 3 Paleobiology 115 (1977).

The center red, of course, has received the best payoff possible, and will see no reason to switch given the decision rule.

Now focus on the blue cells bordering the cluster of nine reds. There are four corner blues. A corner blue will see the best blue cell receiving a payoff of 8. The only red cell that it sees receives 3b. Given our numbers, a corner blue will switch only if b > 8/3 or 2.66. Of the remaining blue cells, there are eight off-center border blues. Each will see a blue cell receiving 8, while the best red cell seen—the middle border red—will be getting 5b. The off-center border blue will switch if b > 8/5 or 1.6. Finally, the analysis for the four center border blues tracks the analysis for the other border blues. Accordingly, if b > 2.66, all of the border blues will switch strategies; if 1.6 < b < 2.66, all of the non-corner blues will switch, while if b < 1.6, no blue cells will change over.

Already, under this decision rule, we can have pockets of players playing blue and red simultaneously, if the benefits of coordinating on strategy right are not sufficiently great. This situation will give rise to clusters of blue cells and clusters of red cells and we will see a model in which multiple norms, conventions, or decentralized rules are in use at the same time.

Consider the intermediate case and roll over the cells to the next generation.

B	B	B	B	B	B	B	B	B
B	B	B	B	B	B	B	B	B
B	B	B	Y	Y	Y	B	B	B
B	B	Y	R	R	R	Y	B	B
B	B	Y	R	R	R	Y	B	B
B	B	Y	R	R	R	Y	B	B
B	B	B	Y	Y	Y	B	B	B
B	B	B	B	B	B	B	B	B
B	B	B	B	B	B	B	B	B

Diagram 5

Nothing has changed for the red cells: the original cluster of nine play as before. Each yellow cell—recall that these are players who had been playing strategy left and who have now switched to strategy right—will see a red cell receiving a payoff of 8b. Each yellow cell will therefore play strategy right again (and will turn red in the next round).

Now examine the blue cells as we did before: cell by cell. The former corner blues still see a blue cell playing with eight neighboring blues, but will now see the best red cell playing with seven neighboring reds. The old corner blue will thus switch if 7b > 8, or if b > 1.14. The new non-corner border blues will each see a red playing with five reds, and thus will switch if b > 1.6. The new corner blues will compare 8 with 4b, and will switch if b > 2. The second iteration thus plays out in one of two fashions depending on whether b is less than or equal to 2.[66]

Where b > 1.6, there is a powerful drive in the system to converge on the correct equilibrium. The model, however, does not necessarily get there. I started the cluster analysis with a block of nine red cells, but the relative scarcity of right strategy players may prevent the use of such a starting cluster. For example, suppose that the largest cluster of red cells is a square block of four cells, surrounded by a sea of blue. Each red cell will receive a payoff of 3b, or 4.95 if b = 1.65. The best blue cell seen by each red cell will be the blue cell cater-corner to it. The blue cell will touch seven other blues and one red cell, and thus will receive a payoff of 7. Each red cell will switch strategies in the next round. This cluster is too small to support growth and it dies.[67]

When b = 1.65, our cluster of nine red cells grows until it spreads throughout the entire domain, while our cluster of four red cells withers. A little bit more analysis makes clear that a two-by-three cluster of six red cells survives and grows when b = 1.65. Again, surround our cluster of six red cells with blue cells and consider the choices that each will make. Each red cell sees another red cell that received 8.25 (or 5b) in the previous round. (In other words, each red cell sees at least one other red cell that has five red neighbors.) The payoff of 8.25 exceeds the highest payoff that a blue cell could enjoy—namely 8—and thus no red cell will switch in the next round. What will the neighboring blue cells do? Each of these neighboring blue cells sees a red cell receiving the 8.25 payoff. Again, they will see no blue doing better, so they will all switch. We now have a cluster of nine red cells, and the above analysis applies.[68] Finally, to complete the analysis, consider a cluster of five red cells. The best red payoff will be 4b, or 6.6. Four of the five red cells will see a blue cell receiving a payoff of 7, and they will switch, then the fifth red cell will follow

[66] To see this pattern directly, play the video with a nine red cell starting point at my website (cited in note 52).

[67] To see this pattern directly, play the video with a four red cell starting point at my website (cited in note 52).

[68] To see this pattern directly, play the video with a six red cell starting point at my website (cited in note 52).

in the next round.[69] Six cells thus sustain growth while five cells do not when b = 1.65.

We can now make a bit more sense of Figure 1. The charts represent exercises in applied probability. We know now that a cluster of six grows indefinitely until every player plays the socially preferred strategy. If we initially assign strategies at random, what is the probability that we will have one or more of the growth clusters? We could answer this question algebraically, but the chart itself provides the answer. For example, when we start with 90 percent of the players playing left and 10 percent playing right, then 55 times out of 100, we do not get at least one of our growth clusters. Absent a growth cluster, the small, scattered clusters of red die, and we converge to the inefficient blue equilibrium.[70]

To put this in a different language—that of dynamic systems—we have mapped the basin of attraction for each of our point attractors. The basin of attraction for an attractor—or the catchment basin—is that chunk of the possible set of starting conditions that leads to that attractor.[71] (The attractors in this example are the two Nash equilibria.) Think of a ball rolling over an undulating surface: at some point, the ball falls into a steep depression—this is a physical description, obviously, and not a statement of the ball's state of mind—and eventually comes to rest in that hole. That hole is an attractor and the starting points on the surface that result in the ball coming to rest in that particular hole form the basin of attraction for the hole. So, to return to the diagram, the basin of attraction for the red equilibrium includes initial distributions of 1 percent left to 85 percent left, while the corresponding basin of attraction for the blue equilibrium covers 96 percent left to 99 percent left. Initial distributions between 86 percent left to 95 percent left are as if our ball is running along an edge that separates the two basins of attraction and a slight nudge in one direction or the other pushes the ball into one equilibrium or the other.

[69] To see this pattern directly, play the video with a five red cell starting point at my website (cited in note 52). Note that there is not a unique way of laying out the five cells. This observation was true for our prior examples as well, but I have emphasized relative compactness of the cluster, and that gave a simple representation of the cluster.

[70] To see an example of this pattern, play the video at my website (cited in note 52). As both Dan Klerman and Seth Chandler noted in e-mails to me, this is one place where the size of the lattice matters. The bigger the lattice, the greater the chances of a growth cluster forming in the initial set of random plays.

[71] For an introduction to these ideas, see I.M.T. Thompson and H.B. Stewart, *Nonlinear Dynamics and Chaos* 9-12 (Wiley 1986).

Step back and now ask what we should make of this discussion. First, this game is path dependence writ large. The convergence of this system largely depends upon the initial starting conditions. The literature on path dependence grows by the day,[72] and this model gives a crisp example of this phenomenon. Second, and perhaps of more interest given what we already know about path dependence, this setup converges on the superior equilibrium even in the face of tough starting conditions. If we just started with our free-standing coordination game, we could say very little about the likelihood that we would converge on the right equilibrium. Now, we should take some comfort that this system will get to where we want it to go.[73] In real situations, we might think of the initial choice of strategy as indeed random. This example says if these choices are essentially coin flips—a 50/50 chance—the model will always converge to the right norm. Even if the choice is substantially biased against the good strategy, we still converge on the best norm. (If we replace the coin with a single die, and play right only if six comes up, we still get to the good equilibrium.) And my intuition says that the bias should run in favor of the good strategy if players are choosing between both strategies at the same time. I have offered no other story of salience here other than the potential value that results from successful coordination. We should think that the extra value available would push us away from a 50/50 chance to odds favoring the good strategy.

This outcome is good news. We see a good chance of successful coordination on the right norm. We also see that it is easy to overstate the problems that define the coordination game and justify legal intervention. At least in this particular framework and on these values, I believe that it is highly unlikely that we would end up in the inferior equilibrium. For the inferior equilibrium to win over our players, we need either extremely bad luck or something that makes the inferior strategy especially salient.

Before leaving this particular example, we should look at one other variable of interest. The graph of the red outcomes in Figure 1 appears to be one of unremitting sameness until we get to particularly skewed distributions of initial choices at the end.

---

[72] See, for example, W. Brian Arthur, *Competing Technologies, Increasing Returns, and Lock-In By Historical Events*, 99 Econ J 116 (1989) (exploring "the dynamics of allocation under increasing returns in a context where increasing returns arise naturally: agents choosing between technologies competing for adoption").

[73] Substantially more general results in a related model of coordination games regarding the success of convergence to the good equilibrium are obtained in Kandori, Mailath, and Rob, 61 Econometrica at 44 (cited in note 44). See also Ellison, 61 Econometrica at 1066-67 (cited in note 44).

Value after value ends up in the same place. But this graph omits the path of convergence to the social equilibrium. These paths actually look quite different, as Figure 2 should make clear. Figure 2 charts the average number of periods that the model used to converge to the red equilibrium. These numbers increase steadily, but slowly, for an extended period before reaching a region of a sharp increase in the time to convergence. Unsurprisingly, the initial distribution of strategy choices sets the ultimate rate of convergence to the good social equilibrium. Still, more comfort is found here. For values in the middle of the distribution, the time to convergence is relatively modest.[74]

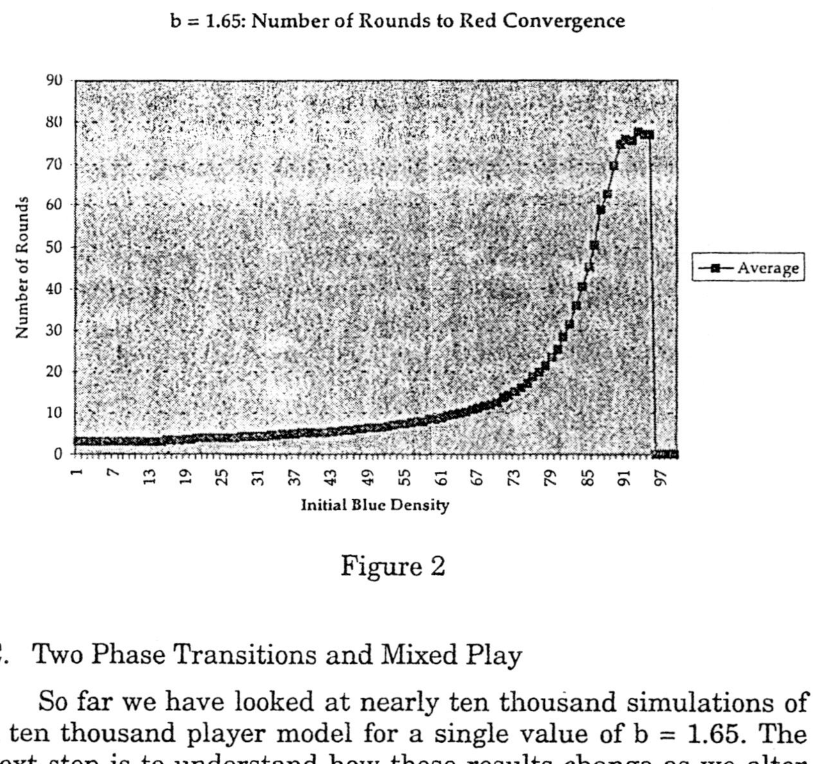

Figure 2

C. Two Phase Transitions and Mixed Play

So far we have looked at nearly ten thousand simulations of a ten thousand player model for a single value of b = 1.65. The next step is to understand how these results change as we alter the value of b. Start by noting that there is an inverse relation between the value of b and the minimal cluster required to assure convergence to the social optimum. Larger b values will

[74] The convergence times are also determined by the rules used to match players of the coordination game. The model used here fixes these matches in the initial nxn grid. Other matching rules might very well alter this pattern of convergence. Compare Ellison, 61 Econometrica at 1060-62 (cited in note 44).

support smaller initial growth clusters; smaller b values will require larger initial clusters. For example, a cluster of four red cells will survive and grow if b > 2.66. Each of the red cells receives a payoff of 3b, which is greater than 8 if b > 2.66. These red cells will thus stay red. Adjacent blue cells will switch strategies, as they will see a red cell receiving more than 8 while no blue cell can do better than 8. We can still end up in the inefficient norm equilibrium, but that result would occur only if no cluster of four red cells formed in our initial distribution of strategies. As we increase b beyond 1.65, we keep pushing toward the right edge of the figures, until virtually all of the models converge to the good norm equilibrium.

So move b in the other direction and return to our discussion of the cluster of nine red cells. As noted above, when b < 1.6, the neighboring blue cells do not switch over. The blue cell most likely to switch sees at least one blue earning 8, while the best red cell seen will earn 5b. When b < 1.6, the payoff for 5b is less than 8, and the blue cell stands pat. This situation raises the possibility of a mixed outcome, where some players play perpetual left, while other players play perpetual right. Indeed, were we to start with a single cluster of nine red cells and all other cells blue, the model would not move an inch. To see the latter point more clearly, I reran the model above with b = 1.55 and obtained the results in Figure 3. The setup here is the same as before, save for the revised value of b, but the results change substantially. As predicted, we see a region in which the model converges to an outcome in which some players are playing left, while others play right.

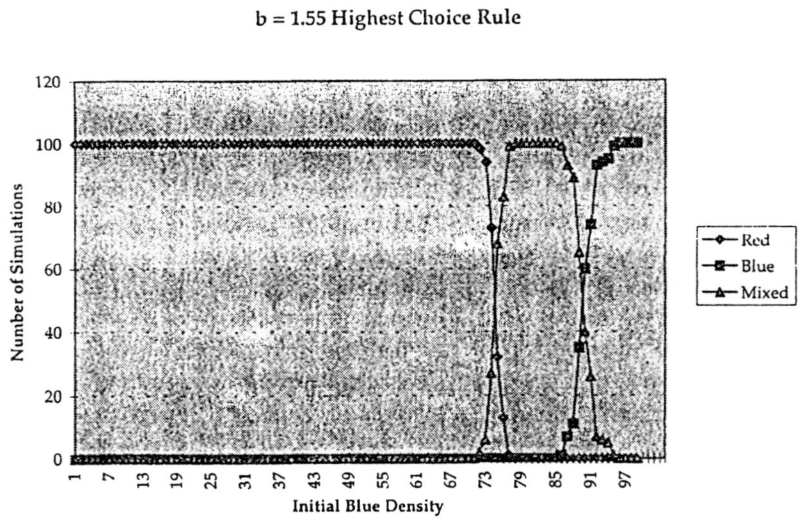

Figure 3

Figure 3 again graphs the number of all-red outcomes, all-blue outcomes and mixed outcomes against the initial blue densities. In broad terms, there are five distinct bands of behavior and two different phase transitions. For initial blue densities of 1 to 73, the model converges to the all-red equilibrium. The time to convergence is influenced by density—I do not set this chart out but it looks like the one in Figure 2—but we eventually get to the right steady state. We then reach our first phase transition: we move from the good all-red equilibrium to a mixed absorbing state, where the model locks on a mixture of left and right players. This transition occurs between initial blue density values of 74 and 76. For initial blue densities of 77 to 86, we converge to the mixed equilibrium. The second phase transition kicks in at an initial blue density of approximately 87 and is over by the time we get to 92. At that point, we move away from the mixed absorbing states to the bad all-blue equilibrium. Finally, for initial blue densities of 92 to 99, we converge to the blue equilibrium.[75]

The existence of three different steady-state regions and two phase transitions is an important change from the prior analysis. Convergence on all-blue or all-red means that we eventually see

[75] I should note that at an initial density of 76, four of the one hundred simulations did not converge before reaching the then-applicable limit of two hundred and fifty generations.

society using only one norm. The good norm drives out the bad norm (or vice versa). We do see both norms in use out of equilibrium when b = 1.65, but only until we move to fixed, uniform play. In contrast, when we reduce b just slightly, we see a region in which we have two norms at work, in perpetuity. If our focus is on whether we will converge to the good norm, we should be reasonably confident that we will: so long as the initial density of players playing left is less than 74 percent, we converge to the good norm 100 percent of the time. Certainly this outcome represents a substantial drop from the results when b = 1.65, as we converged successfully in 100 percent of the cases up to an initial left density of 85 percent. But again, absent something that makes the left strategy particularly salient, we should expect to reach the good equilibrium.

Figures 4 through 8 set out runs of the same model with b set at, respectively, 1.35, 1.15, 1.14, 1.10, and 1.05. Remember that these values for b do not upset our rule that the all-right equilibrium is always better than the all-left equilibrium, but when b = 1.05, the differences are quite small. A quick glance at these figures reveals several facts. First, in each figure, we get three final state regions: all-red, all-blue, and mixed. Second, we see sharp phase transitions from region to region; change in the ultimate equilibrium is driven by a small fraction of the entire parameter space. Third, the location of these regions moves systematically as we reduce b. The right-most point where 100 percent of the simulations converges to the good norm decreases from 65 percent when b = 1.35 to 60 percent when b = 1.15; to 17 percent when b = 1.14; to 16 percent when b = 1.10; and then finally jumps up a bit to 17 percent when b = 1.05. Again, to return to the language of dynamic systems, the basins of attraction for the two point attractors change systematically as we reduce b. The basin of attraction of the good equilibrium shrinks steadily and then dramatically, while that for the bad equilibrium grows slowly over time.

b = 1.35 Highest Choice Rule

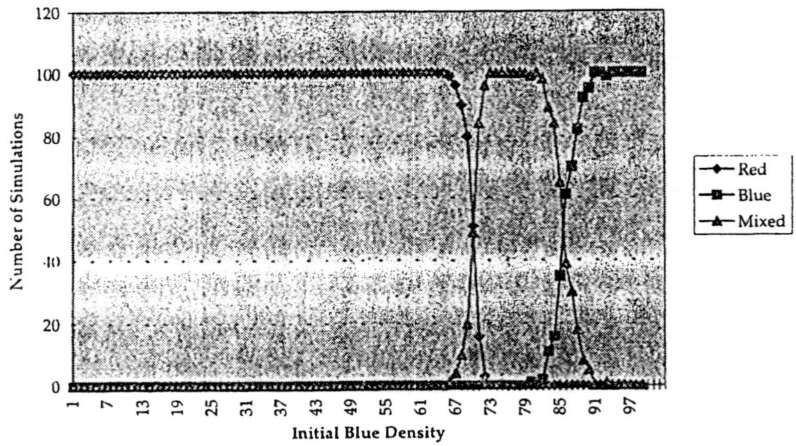

Figure 4

b = 1.15 Highest Choice Rule

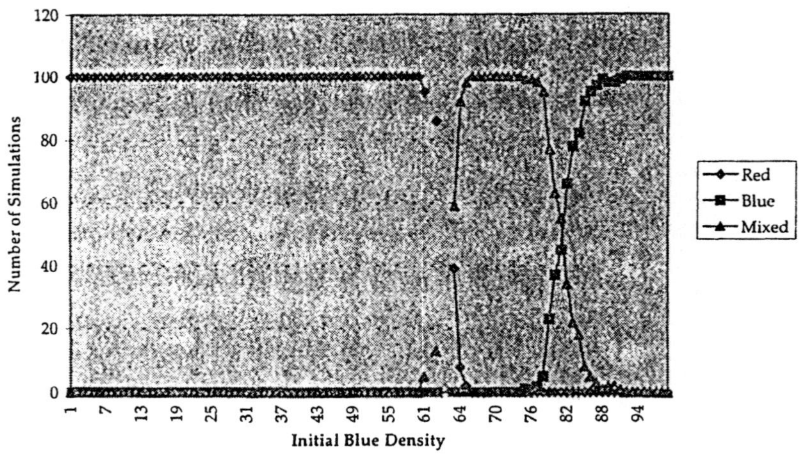

Figure 5

b = 1.14 Highest Choice Rule

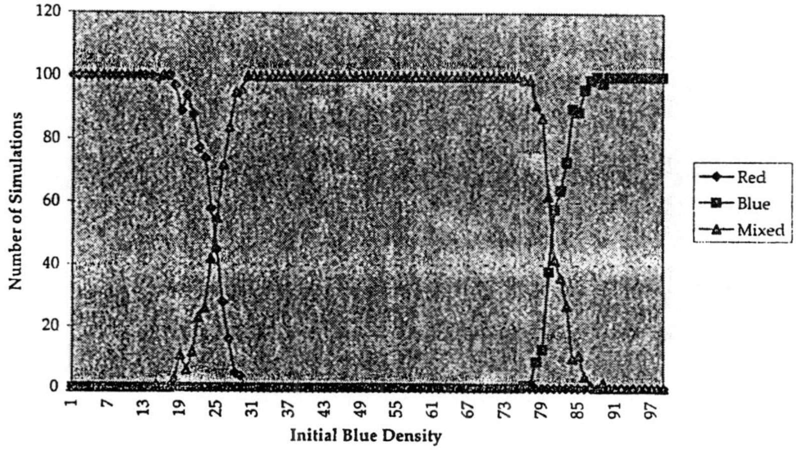

Figure 6

b = 1.10 Highest Choice Rule

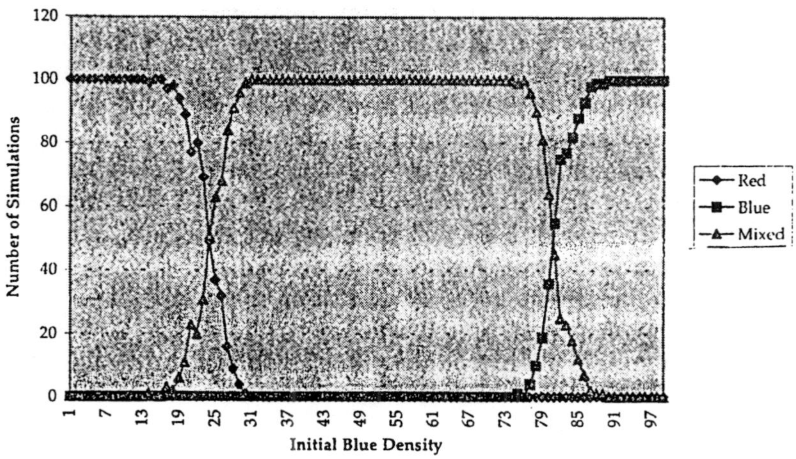

Figure 7

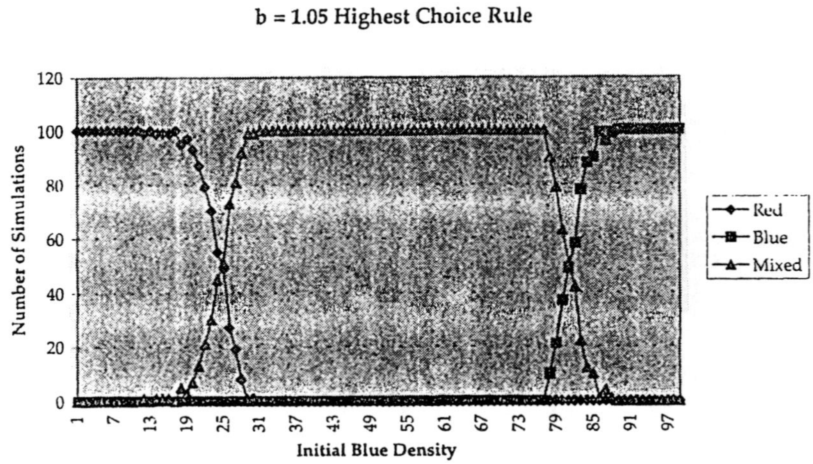

Figure 8

As this analysis should make clear, we can remain fairly confident that the model will converge on the good norm so long as b is at least equal to 1.15. The chance that we will end up elsewhere, in one of the mixed play outcomes or the all-blue outcome, does rise as the value of b falls. But so long as not more than 60 percent of the players play left initially, we will converge on the good norm even if b = 1.15. This outcome again should be quite reassuring. If two norms are competing and one norm is better for everyone than the other by at least 15 percent, we will converge on the good equilibrium. Put differently, if the gains from getting to the right equilibrium are sufficiently large, we will get there. We could not get that result out of our free-standing coordination game, where we could only identify our two Nash equilibria and then punt. Moving to the good equilibrium when there is a substantial advantage to doing so instinctively seems right and it is comforting to see this result emerge in the model.

Note also the sharp break between 1.15 and 1.14. The probability of ending up in the good norm equilibrium in all cases plummets within this twilight zone of b values. The best bet here is that we will end up in a mixed play region. We will see both norms extant in the society, and perhaps in significant numbers. And this result holds as we move b toward 1. There are two natural questions. First, why the sharp change at this point? Second, are all the mixed outcomes identical, or are there meaningful differences for different initial densities, even if we know that we end up in mixed play in 100 percent of the cases? Start with the second question and consider Figure 9:

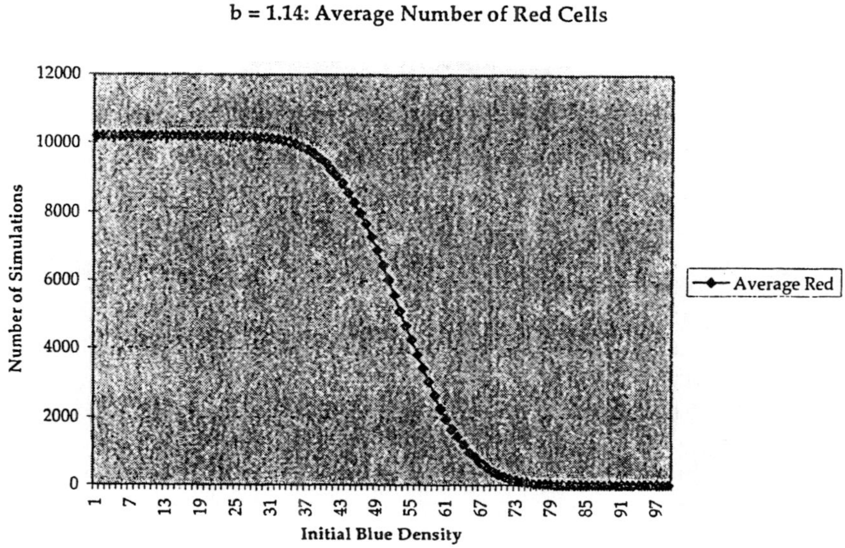

Figure 9

Figure 9 charts the average number of red cells in the eventual end state for the one hundred simulations for each initial density. Obviously, if all one hundred simulations converge to the all-red equilibrium, the average is the entire board of 10,201 cells. And, if each of the simulations converges to all-blue, there will be no red cells. The regions of interest are the two phase transitions and the mixed play region. As inspection of Figure 9 makes clear, all mixed play outcomes are not created equal. Indeed, these outcomes systematically move from being mainly red, to being a fair mix of both blue and red, to being almost exclusively blue. Again, this outcome represents substantial and unsurprising path dependence.

Now consider the first question: why the sharp transition between 1.15 and 1.14? The simple answer is that 7 times 1.14 is 7.98, which is less than 8, while 7 times 1.15 is 8.05, which is more than 8. To see why this difference matters, consider a cluster of nine blue cells surrounded by a sea of red (this is the flip of our prior example, where we started with a cluster of nine red cells):

R	R	R	R	R	R	R	R	R
R	R	R	R	R	R	R	R	R
R	R	R	R	R	R	R	R	R
R	R	R	B	B	B	R	R	R
R	R	R	B	B	B	R	R	R
R	R	R	B	B	B	R	R	R
R	R	R	R	R	R	R	R	R
R	R	R	R	R	R	R	R	R
R	R	R	R	R	R	R	R	R

Diagram 6

The red cells are all rock-solid here, so long as b > 1. Each red cell either will see a red receiving 8b or be such a red, and the best blue cell that could be observed can do no better than 8. No red cell will switch.

Next consider the blue cells, and start with a corner blue as that is the one most likely to switch. A corner blue will see the center blue receiving a payoff of 8 and the best red cell—the one cater-corner to it—receiving a payoff of 7b. That blue will stay blue if 7b < 8, or b < 8/7. The corner blue thus remains blue at b = 1.14 and switches at b = 1.15. In other words, a cluster of nine blue cells cannot be invaded if b < 8/7, and a mixed play outcome will result. In contrast, if b > 8/7, the four corner blues will switch to red, and the remaining blues will soon follow in subsequent rounds.

What should we make of this analysis? In one way, it should be quite comforting. If we have "reasonable" initial blue densities and sufficient benefit from the superior equilibrium, we converge to the good equilibrium. These circumstances may be present in many cases. For example, if two norms or standards are competing at the same time, with both trying to emerge as the accepted convention, we should anticipate that the middle initial densities will be most important. In contrast, if norms are competing over time—if one standard is the convention, and the situation evolves so that a new convention is socially preferable—society will be at either end of the initial densities. The low values in the parameter space will give us a sense of how successful a new standard will be in displacing a preexisting standard. In that case, we should be much less sanguine that our model will get to the right outcome.

D. Variations on the Model

Altering basic features of the model allows us to evaluate if and how these features drive the results of the model. In this section, I will discuss four variations of the original model: (1) a different decision rule; (2) a different payoff neighborhood; (3) different information assumptions; and (4) an alternative approach to parallel decision processing. Take these variations one by one.

1. Different decision rule.

Thus far, I have used a particular decision rule without offering any particular justification for the choice. I believe it a plausible rule, but not the only rule. It might be worth exploring the choice of decision rules systematically, but, to provide just one source of comparison, consider the following rule. Suppose that instead of choosing the strategy with the highest payoff from the nine observed results, our players choose the strategy with the highest *average* payoff. This rule imposes a much more severe calculation burden, but not one that we should deem too daunting.[76] How do the results change with the new decision rule?

Figures 10 to 14 set out the results when b is set to, respectively, 1.65, 1.35, 1.15, 1.10 and 1.05. A quick look reveals that the basic shape of the results is quite similar, but the precise break points do change in important ways. The one change in shape that we do see is mixed play regions at all values of b, even when b = 1.65. Again, if we believe that mixed play is important, the revised decision rule validates that possibility. The other interesting change is that we sustain 100 percent convergence to the good norm for lower values of b. For example, when b = 1.10, we get 100 percent convergence even with initial blue densities of 54 percent. Recall that under the highest decision rule, when b was 1.10, we lost 100 percent convergence when the initial blue density exceeded 16 percent. This difference is substantial, not only in absolute terms, but relative to where we think we are likely to be. If you believe that at least 50 percent of the players should adopt the good strategy, the highest average rule provides

[76] To see an example of this, return to Diagram 4 and focus on the decisionmaking of a corner red. Under the highest payoff rule, the corner red bases its decision on the payoff of the center red, as that will be the highest observed payoff. Under the highest average payoff rule, the corner red is red, obviously, sees three other reds, and sees five blue cells. The blue cells receive payoffs of 5,6,7,6, and 5 for an average payoff of 5.8. In contrast, the observed red cells have payoffs of 5b, 8b, 5b, plus the cell itself obtaining a payoff of 3b. The average red payoff is 21/4b or 5.25b. The corner red will switch if 5.8 > 5.25b, or b < 1.105, and will stay otherwise.

real evidence that we will converge on the good norm even when the good strategy provides relatively insignificant benefits (10 percent). We lose this result when b drops to 1.05—100 percent convergence to the good norm occurs last at an initial density of 43 percent—but this change is still a substantial improvement over the original decision rule. Again, altering the decision rule changes the relative size of the basins of attraction for our equilibria.

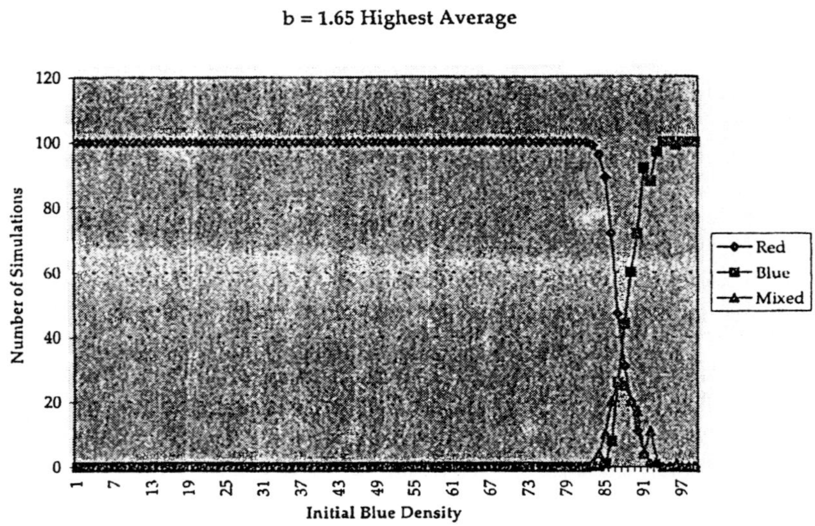

Figure 10

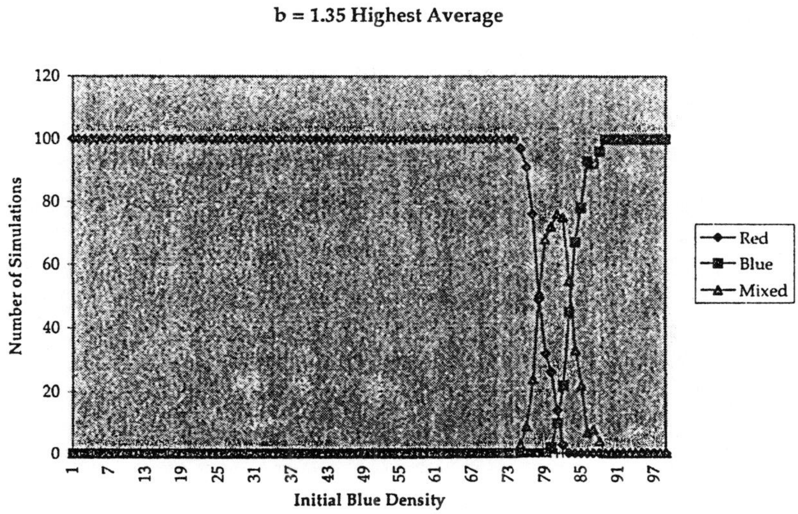

Figure 11

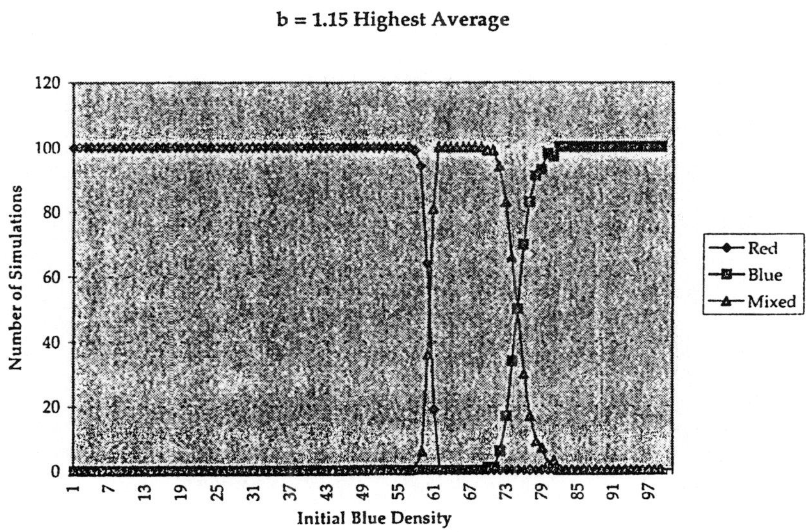

Figure 12

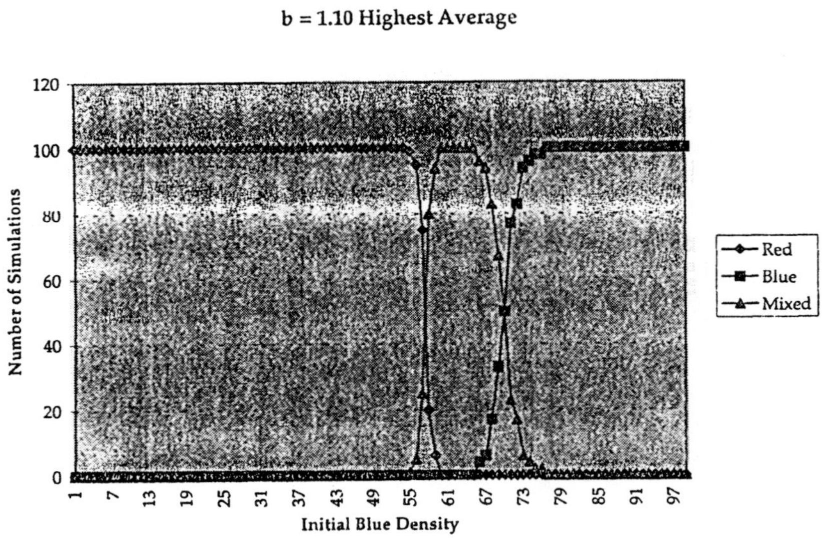

Figure 13

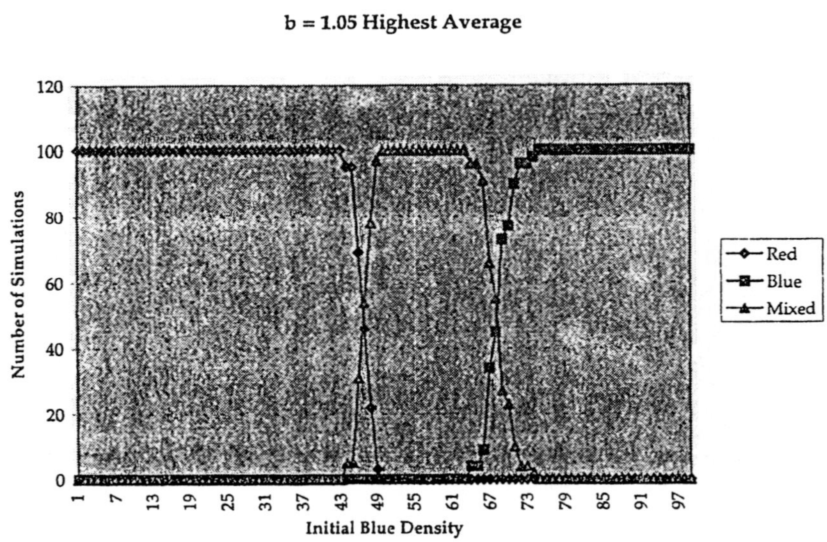

Figure 14

2. Different payoff neighborhood.

A second way to change the model is to switch payoff neighborhoods. We have focused on the Moore neighborhood, which likely drives particular features of the results. The significance of 1.6 and the breakpoint between 1.14 and 1.15 are both functions of having eight neighbors. As discussed before, the second prominent neighborhood used in the cellular automata literature is the Von Neumann neighborhood (see Diagram 2). This payoff neighborhood starts with a center cell and adds its North, South, East, and West neighbors. Figures 15 to 18 set out results for the Von Neumann version of the model with b set at, respectively, 1.65, 1.35, 1.30, and 1.15:

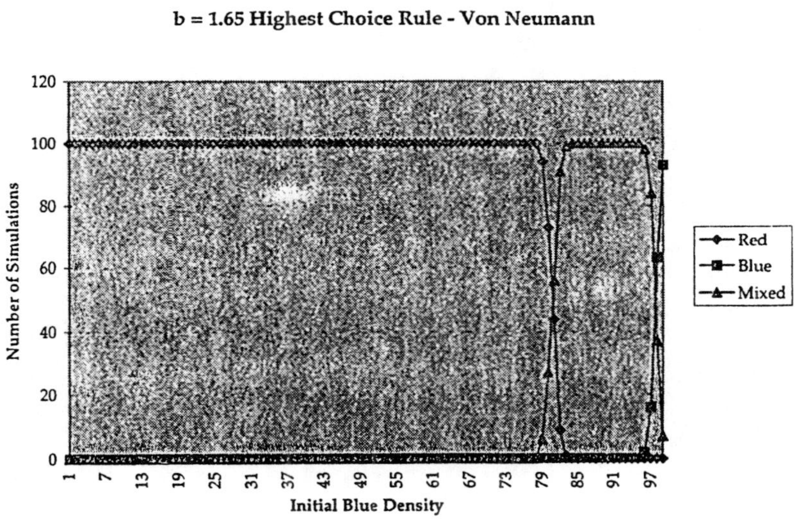

Figure 15

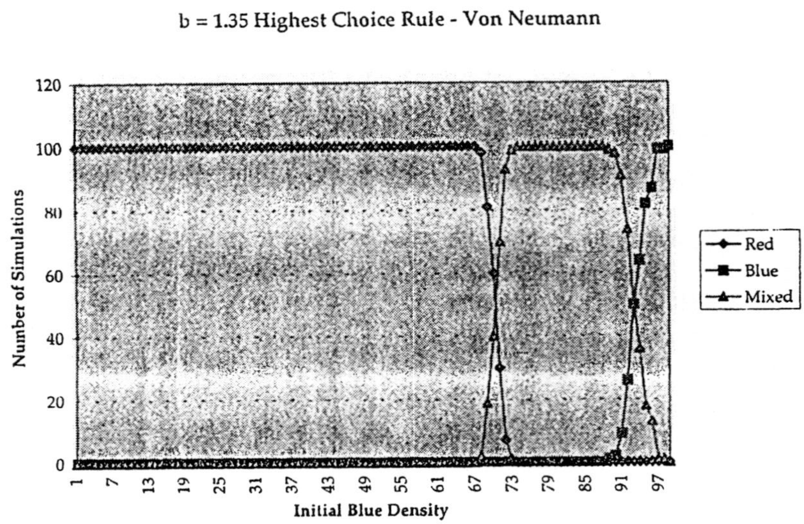

Figure 16

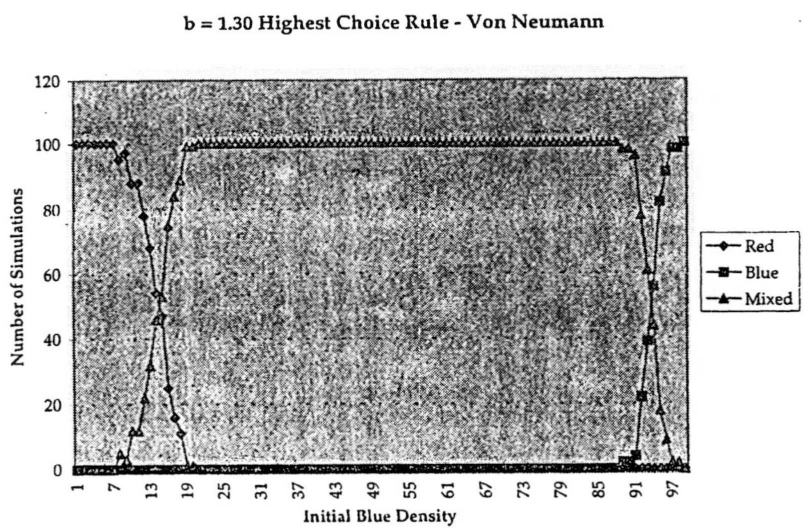

Figure 17

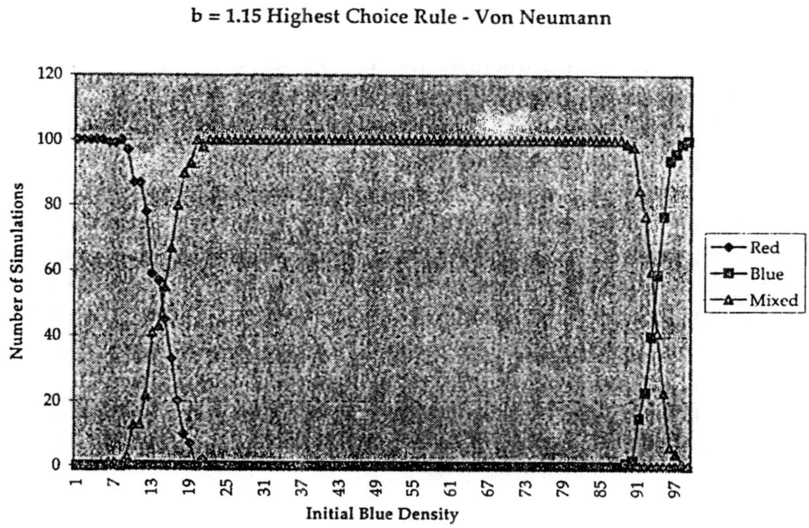

Figure 18

We do see important differences in the results. The mixed play region exists even when b = 1.65, and the last 100 percent convergence to the good norm drops from 85 percent in the original Moore version to 78 percent in the Von Neumann version. The results at b = 1.35 are almost identical for the two neighborhood versions. Note also that we get a break point at 1.33 rather than 1.14, so when b = 1.30, we find that a large mixed play region emerges. Again, this outcome is important, because it suggests that even with gains as large as 30 percent—with b = 1.30 the good norm is that much better—we cannot be confident that the model will converge on the good equilibrium.[77] Comparing the results of the Von Neumann and Moore neighborhoods therefore suggests that a bigger payoff neighborhood increases the chance that the model will converge on the good norm.[78]

3. Different information assumptions.

To see a simple example of how a small change can alter the results of a model substantially, alter the information neighborhood. Recall that the payoff neighborhood is made up of the

---

[77] As to why b = 1.33 matters, see note 81.

[78] This result needs more analysis. Berninghaus and Schwalbe reach the opposite conclusion in a related model: "The smaller this reference group, the higher the probability that an efficient equilibrium will be reached." See Berninghaus and Schwalbe, 29 J Econ Behav & Org at 79 (cited in note 44).

neighboring cells whose actions directly influence payoffs. The information neighborhood is the neighborhood that a given cell observes and provides information that players can use to formulate the choice of strategy in the next round. In all of the prior examples, the payoff neighborhood and the information neighborhood have been coextensive.

Now switch the assumptions. Set the payoff neighborhood as the Moore neighborhood and let the information neighborhood be the five-by-five cluster of twenty-five cells centered around the payoff neighborhood. Put differently, the payoff neighborhood starts with a single cell and extends out one cell in all directions. The information neighborhood starts with a center cell and extends out two cells in all directions. Payoffs are determined as before, but now each player chooses her next strategy based on the strategy yielding the single highest return in the twenty-five cells that the player observes. Figures 19 through 21 reflect the runs with b set at, respectively, 1.65, 1.35, and 1.10:

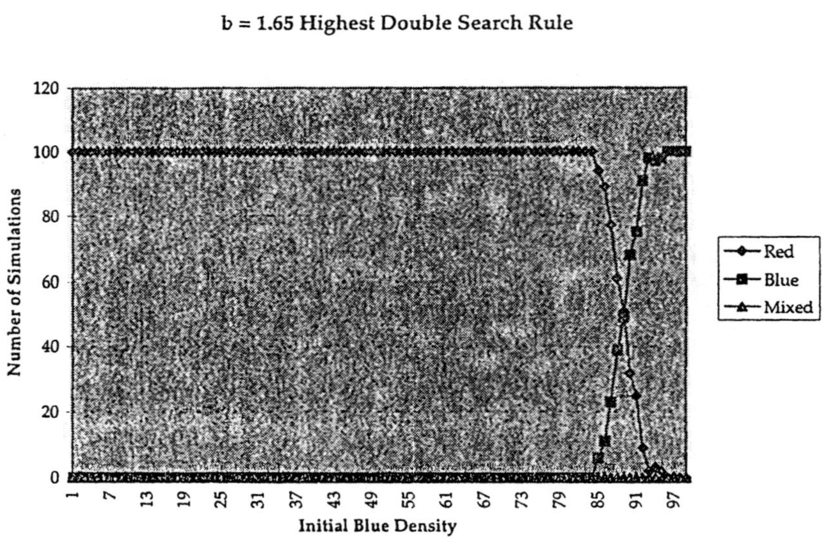

Figure 19

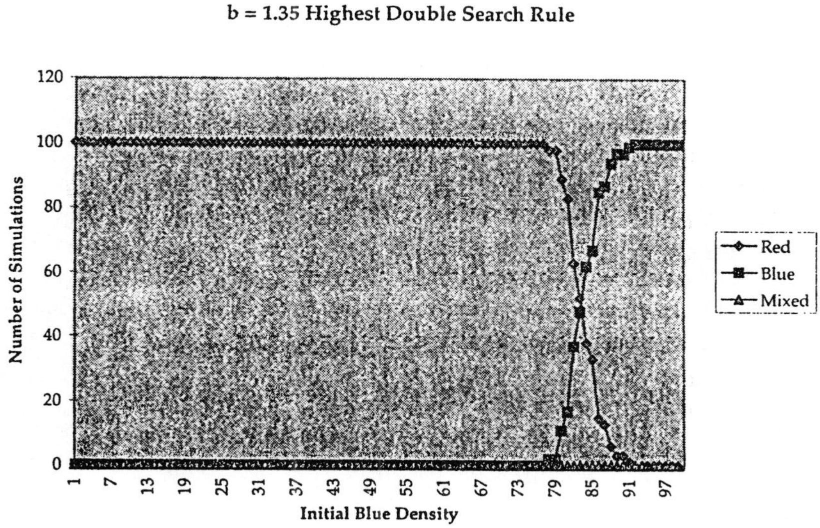

Figure 20

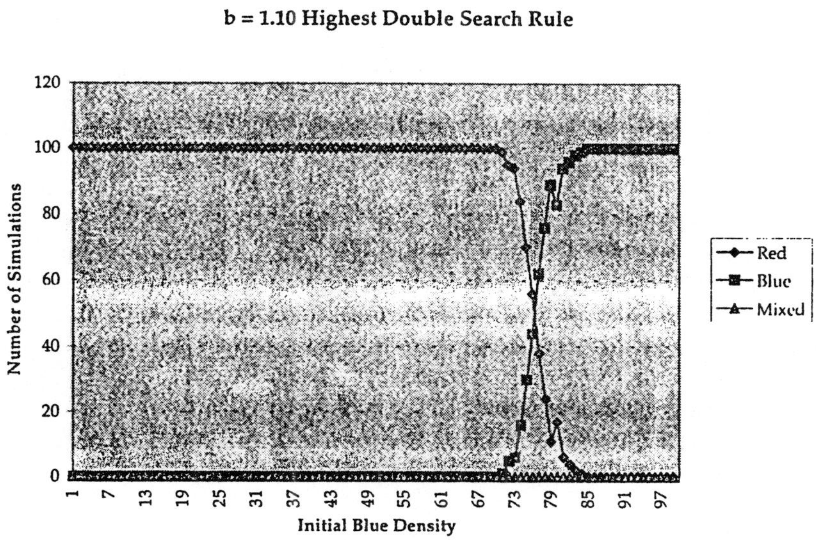

Figure 21

How does this model compare to our prior results? In the new results, when b = 1.65, there is little change, but when b < 1.6, the results change dramatically. We lose the mixed equilibrium outcomes, and there is a single phase transition, moving from the superior equilibrium to the inferior equilibrium. The superior equilibrium is also reached much more often. In the original example, when b = 1.10, the region of 100 percent convergence on all-red ended at 16 percent, but with more information, that changes to 70 percent. Adding the additional layer of information enlarges the basin of attraction for the good equilibrium. A much larger set of initial conditions funnels into the good equilibrium.

Why the dramatic shift? Return to Diagram 4, where we had a cluster of nine red cells surrounded by blue cells. We noted before that the red cells would not change, so long as b > 1. Each red cell sees the center red receiving a payoff of 8b, and no player can do better than that. Whether the neighboring blue cells turned over depended on how b compared to 1.6. If b > 1.6, the adjacent blue cells flipped over, but if b < 1.6, they all held firm. In the first case, the model would converge to the all-red equilibrium; but in the second, we reached a mixed outcome.

Now think about extending the information seen by the players. The cluster of nine red cells is as before: Each sees the center red receiving 8b, and no one will switch. But the border blue cells now see the red cell in the center of the cluster of nine. When the blue cells could see out only one level, they saw only their immediate neighbors. Seeing out two levels brings the center red cell within view. The red cell does the best that anyone could do, and the blue cells shift. Note that this outcome holds regardless of how big b is, so long as b > 1.[79]

We do not always reach the good equilibrium, nor is the size of the gain from getting to that equilibrium irrelevant. The graphs make clear that if we start with too many players playing the inferior strategy, we will converge on the inferior equilibrium. The size of the minimum cluster necessary to sustain growth is still determined by b. So long as we have at least one cluster of nine red cells, however, the model will converge to the right social norm whenever b > 1. Whether such a cluster exists is purely a question of probability and is independent of the size of b, but does depend on the size of the lattice itself.

There is one other point of interest. Figure 22 sets out a comparison of the results for convergence to the good equilibrium as a function of the information available when b = 1.65:

[79] To see this pattern, play the video that starts with a single cluster of nine red cells and b = 1.01 at my website (cited in note 52).

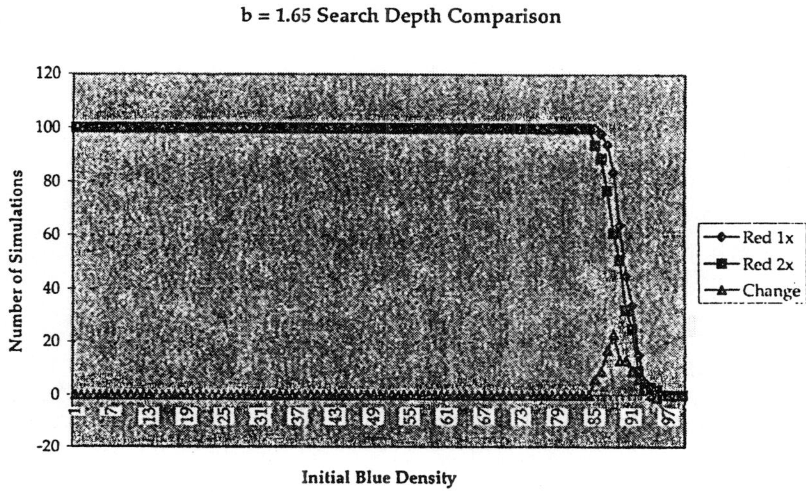

Figure 22

The first two graphs—labeled "Red 1x" and "Red 2x"—just repeat the results from before when we set the information neighborhood equal to, respectively, the Moore neighborhood and the double Moore neighborhood. The third graph subtracts the number of times the model converged to the good equilibrium for the double Moore test from the single Moore test. Save for one density, we converge to the good equilibrium more frequently when we have less information. Believe it or not, when we give the players more information, we end up at the wrong equilibrium more often.

The double Moore results move to the inefficient blue equilibrium more often, sometimes substantially so (look, for example, at the spike in Figure 22 when initial blue density is 88). This result looks like a herd behavior in action,[80] but is less obviously tied to hidden information. Our players are not necessarily worse off with the additional information, as the double Moore model converges much more quickly (see Figure 23). This speed-

[80] Herd behavior arises when dispersed information is aggregated inappropriately. A chain of inferences arises that, while individually rational, leads the society—the herd—down the wrong path. In real life, you see this behavior frequently at traffic lights, where a few pedestrians trying to cross against the light lead an entire group into the street. See generally Abhijit V. Banerjee, *A Simple Model of Herd Behavior*, 107 Q J Econ 797, 798 (1992) (defining herd behavior as "everyone doing what everyone else is doing, even when their private information suggests doing something quite different"); Baird, Gertner, and Picker, *Game Theory and the Law* at 213-17 (cited in note 5).

ier convergence is a good thing, and we need to explicitly weigh faster outcomes against the possibility of more wrong outcomes.

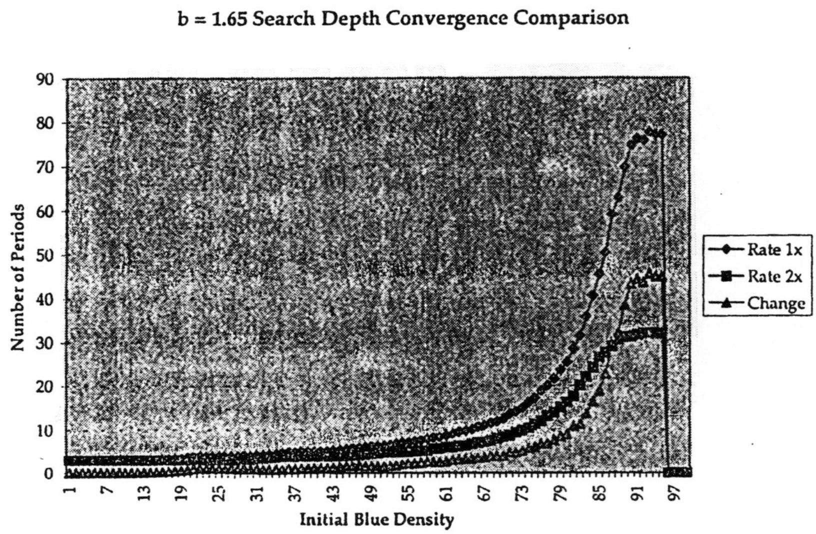

Figure 23

As a second example of how changes in information alter the results of our model, consider Figures 24 to 26. These runs use a Von Neumann payoff neighborhood and a Moore information neighborhood. Payoffs are therefore determined by the North, South, East, and West neighbors, but players receive information about strategy results from all eight of their immediate neighbors. The figures report results for b = 1.65, 1.35, and 1.15. Again, note how increasing information makes it more difficult for mixed play to be sustained. Recall (see Figure 15) that in the original Von Neumann run with b = 1.65, we had a substantial mixed play region, and we lost 100 percent red convergence at an initial blue density of 78 percent. The revised model (see Figure 24) has no mixed play region at all and converges successfully to the good equilibrium 100 percent of the time up to an initial left density of 89 percent.

b = 1.65 Highest Choice - Von N Payoff/Moore Info

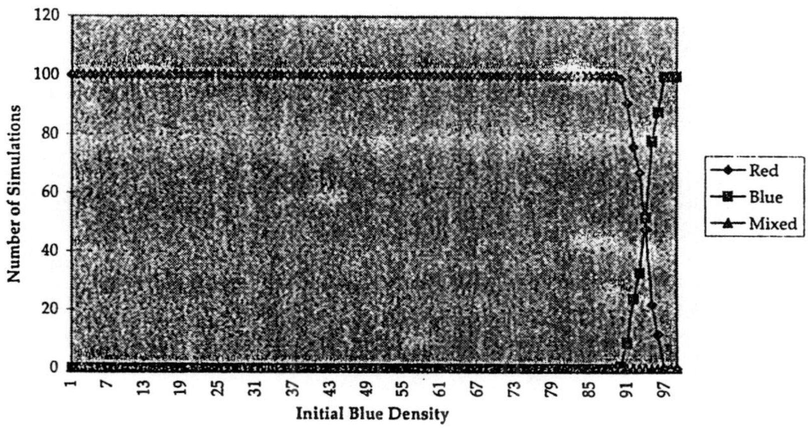

Figure 24

b = 1.35 Highest Choice - Von N Payoff/Moore Info

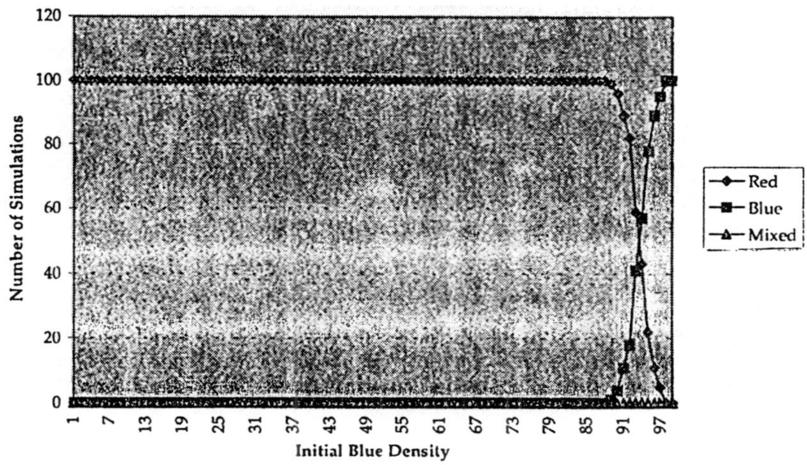

Figure 25

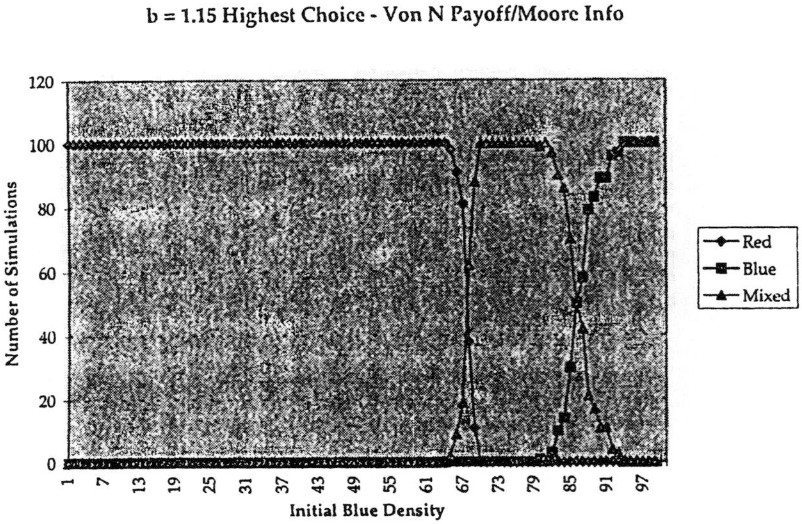

Figure 26

The same result holds at b = 1.35. Before (see Figure 16), we had mixed play and 100 percent red convergence through 67 percent. In the revised model (see Figure 25), no mixed play occurs and 100 percent red convergence runs through 88 percent. But these are not general results, as Figure 26 makes clear. With b = 1.15 and the Von Neumann/Moore fusion, there is a mixed play region, and we lose all-red convergence at 64 percent. This change in the basin of attraction for the good equilibrium is a sizable improvement over the purely Von Neumann run (see Figure 18), where all-red convergence was lost at 8 percent.[81]

[81] If you have followed this analysis so far and care why the results change with the switch to the Moore neighborhood, the key point to note is that when b > 1.33, a red Von Neumann cluster will be a growth cluster when the model uses a Moore information neighborhood. When we start with five red cells in the form of a cross, none of the red cells will change. The four red cells forming the arms of the cross will observe the center red, who receives a payment of 4b, the best possible payoff. None of the red cells will switch. Focus next on the four blue cells that complete the Moore neighborhood. Each of these cells now observes the center red. Note importantly that they would not have seen this red with Von Neumann vision, as the center red is on their diagonal and thus would be out of their sights. With the Moore information neighborhood, they too see the center red, and they switch over. This switch creates a cluster of nine red cells, surrounded by sixteen blue cells. The non-corner blue cells—all but four obviously—will each see one red cell receiving a payoff of 3b, the center-edge red. The best blue cell that they observe will receive a payoff of 4, and the non-corner border blue cells will switch if 3b > 4, or b > 1.33. This iteration drives the model round after round to the red equilibrium. To see the evolution of this model directly, play the video at my website (cited in note 52).

Finally, consider one last information comparison. Suppose that we let each player observe all of the other players' payoffs. Also assume that each player adopted the strategy with the single highest payoff that the player observed. As should be clear, each player will adopt the same strategy immediately, and the model converges to an all-blue or all-red absorbing state almost immediately. Figures 27 and 28 do just this for b = 1.65 and b = 1.35. The graph labeled "Global" charts the outcomes just described. These outcomes are compared with the outcomes from the double Moore information neighborhood. The results are quite close. The extended local information is almost equivalent to having information about the entire board, at least where each player decides based upon the single highest observed payoff.

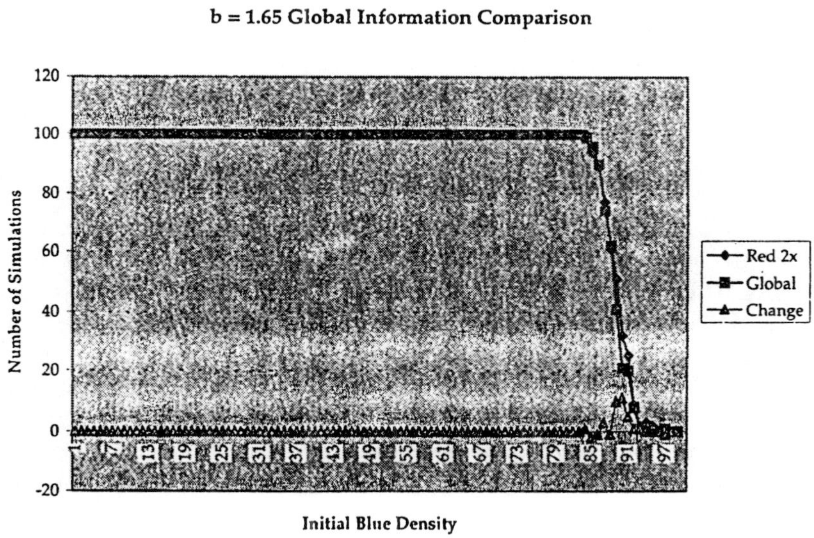

Figure 27

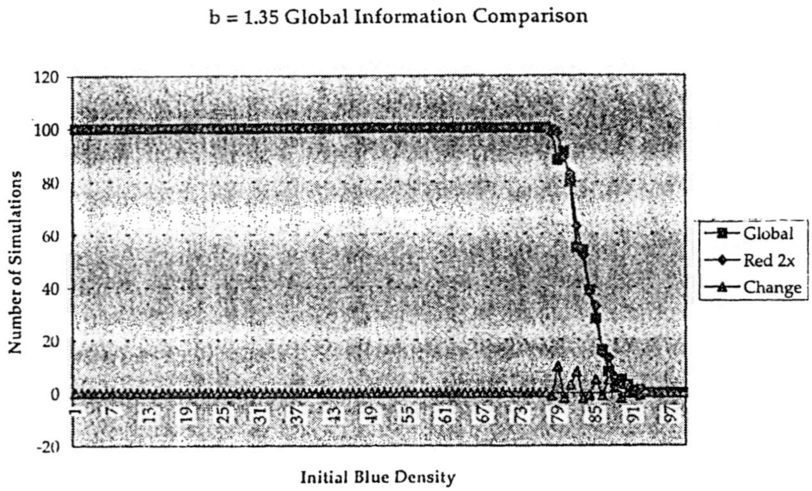

Figure 28

4. Parallel decision processing: SIMD v MIMD.

What appears to be the name of an obscure case, turns out to be an important issue in approaching parallel programming. "SIMD" is an abbreviation for single-instruction, multiple-data; "MIMD" is multiple-instruction, multiple-data. Putting technical niceties to one side, the key issue is whether all of the players remain in perfect sync. If you think of the players as executing a computer program—as they actually do in the computer simulations—does each player execute the same instruction at exactly the same time? In a SIMD scheme they do; in a MIMD scheme, they do not. (In reality, the setup is more complicated than this explanation, as we are using a single processor machine to simulate a multiple processor scheme, but this really is just a computational point.)

What turns on whether the players act exactly at the same time? Turn to Figure 29 and compare it to Figure 4:

b = 1.35 Highest Choice Rule MIMD Version

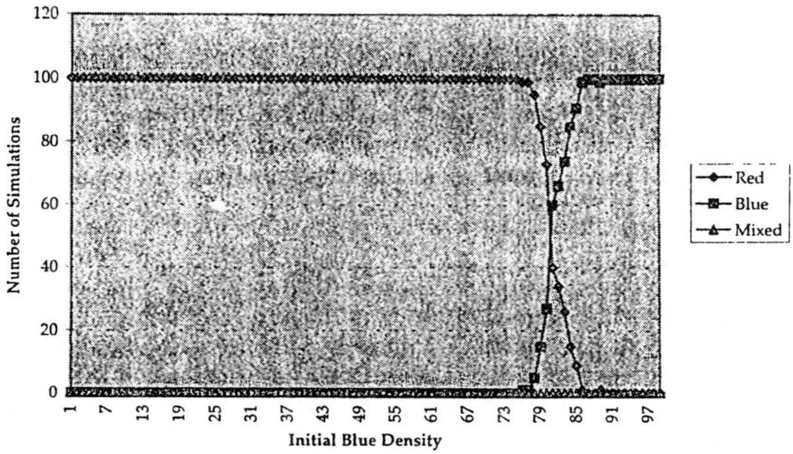

Figure 29

Both models set b = 1.35; both use the same highest choice decision rule; and both use the Moore payoff and information neighborhoods. What differs are the results. The MIMD version (see Figure 29) has a single phase transition, no mixed play region, and 100 percent convergence on the good social norm at an initial density for the inferior strategy at 75 percent. In contrast, our original SIMD version (see Figure 4) has two phase transitions, a mixed play region, and the final 100 percent convergence on the good social norm at an initial inferior density of 65 percent.

These findings represent mixed to good results. We actually do better on reaching the good norm equilibrium and should be even more confident in our prior forecast that if b = 1.35, we will converge on the good equilibrium. That result, however, comes at the expense of losing the mixed play region.[82]

[82] The natural thing to do is to run more versions of the MIMD model to see whether the mixed play region reappears at lower values of b. Unfortunately, the single run presented in the paper took twenty-four days of computer time. And, there is substantial reason to doubt in any event the overall stability of the mixed play region. A large level of mutations in the players would tend to disrupt the boundaries that define the mixed play outcomes. Compare Kandori, Mailath, and Rob, 61 Econometrica 29 (cited in note 44).

IV. SPECULATIONS ON LAW: DECENTRALIZED RULEMAKING, NORMS AND SOCIAL MEANING

I want to be cautious about inferring too much about the relative roles of government and the private sectors in these models. I have said nothing about sources of market failure or of inadequacies in private ordering, nor have I addressed the range of infirmities associated with government action. With that caveat issued, I will nonetheless offer the following few speculative thoughts.

A. Echoing the Free-Standing Coordination Game

The basic coordination game has been the model of choice for illustrating the problem of coalescing around a Pareto-superior norm. I had very little to say about the original free-standing coordination game, but, for better or worse, quite a bit to say about the spatial version of this game. The extended analysis of the basic spatial game and possible variations reveals that the results do depend on particular settings of the model. The Von Neumann variation suggested that the basic problem of the coordination game might persist, as we faced mixed play outcomes with b as high as 1.33. To fail to converge on the good norm with this much at stake is disappointing. Still, the more general message has to be quite positive, at least for the case of simultaneous norm competition. The basic Moore model did quite well, and the revised versions did even better. Moving to the highest average decision rule and adding information typically led to better outcomes. Whether we think that the government should intervene depends on quite a lot—see the caveat above—but the model does suggest that the possible loss of value from inadequate coordination is naturally self-limiting.[83] This outcome makes me much less concerned about the problem seen in the free-standing coordination game.

B. The Importance of Phase Transitions for Policymakers

I find it striking how small ranges matter for the outcomes in these models. The vast majority of the parameter space is completely irrelevant to whether the model gets to the right steady state. I think, on the whole, that the small ranges should comfort us. If a policymaker were to try to switch this system

[83] Again, see the prior results to this effect in Kandori, Mailath, and Rob, 61 Econometrica at 44 (cited in note 44); Ellison, 61 Econometrica at 1066-67 (cited in note 44).

from one equilibrium to the other, the narrow band effect would work in our favor. If we were near the phase transition, a policymaker who mistakenly sought to switch from the red equilibrium to the blue equilibrium, and who took blue density as the variable on which to work, might do real damage. Such proximity, however, would arise from exceedingly bad luck—unless we have a story as to why these systems should gravitate toward the point of a phase transition.[84] Instead, we would expect to be at some distance from the transition, and one would hope that our policymaker would get quite discouraged before getting to the transition point. After all, our policymaker could push blue densities from 50 to 60 to 70 to 80 and accomplish nothing. Few policymakers would persevere for so long in the face of such apparent failure.[85]

In contrast, the narrow band effect should work to our benefit if our policymaker sought to move us from the bad blue equilibrium to the good red equilibrium. In this case, a policymaker might correctly want to try to trigger a norm cascade, which looks a lot like swooshing down the phase transition to the good equilibrium. Here, little effort would be rewarded quickly, and the reward might be vastly disproportionate to the effort expended.

When might this analysis be relevant? Imagine norms competing over time. A norm or standard becomes entrenched at one time, and appropriately so: it represents the socially efficient outcome. We converge on the red equilibrium and everyone plays red. Things change. A new norm or standard is now superior to the old standard, but everyone is still playing the old standard. (Recorded video technology, with VCR tapes representing the old, locked-in standard, and DVD the new superior technology, may represent this situation today.)

Indeed, the law itself may help entrench a particular standard and thereby make it more difficult for our players to move to a new, superior equilibrium. For example, if custom is a good defense against a charge of negligence, there will be little reason for a new custom to evolve. Indeed, the status attached to the pre-existing custom further entrenches it against newcomers.

The models proper will not let us get from the old standard to the new standard, and even if a small number of folks start to

---

[84] We do get stories in the chaos literature of models that move to the edge of chaotic behavior, see Kauffman, *At Home in the Universe* at 26-29 (cited in note 65), but that is a far cry from where we are now.

[85] Of course, my guess is that politicians at either end of the spectrum would say that their worthy opponents routinely display such bullheadedness in promoting policies!

experiment with the new option, they may be too few and too dispersed to move the system to the new, better equilibrium. To track our charts, it is as if we have 98 percent or 99 percent playing the old, inferior standard, and only 1 percent or 2 percent playing the new standard. As the charts demonstrate, even in the face of a substantial improvement—remember that when b = 1.65, it represents 65 percent more value compared to 1—we might end up in the wrong equilibrium. Our policymaker now may be able to push us down the phase transition to the new equilibrium, where only a small shift in densities will be required.

C. Seeding Norm Clusters

If we take the model literally, the government may use a more direct route to effect the transition: seed norm or standard clusters. Given a cluster of the right size—for example, when b = 1.65 start with six red players clustered together in a sea of 10,195 blue players—the model will converge to the appropriate social equilibrium, even if the absolute number of players of the strategy in issue is almost zero. Look at the development of the model as seen in the six snapshots of its evolution in the color insert at Figures P18 to P23.[86]

Gerry Mackie provides a striking example of the power of seeding norm clusters in an account of the end of footbinding in China.[87] Mackie argues that footbinding should be understood as a Schelling convention at work in the marriage market. China appears to have been locked into this convention for centuries, notwithstanding recognition of the harmful consequences of the practice. The practice, however, vanished in a generation. Mackie cites data showing, for example, that in Tinghsien, 99 percent of the women were footbound in 1889, 94 percent in 1899, and virtually none in 1919. This dramatic shift is easily understood as a rapid shift from an inferior to a superior equilibrium, a norm cascade as we have described it.

What accounts for the change? Local missionaries in China established the first antifootbinding society in 1874. Families pledged that they would not footbind their daughters and that they would not let their sons marry the footbound. This local convention created sufficient density to make it self-sustaining—this is our norm cluster—and these clusters grew until the old

[86] To see this evolution directly, play the video at my website (cited in note 52).

[87] Gerry Mackie, *Ending Footbinding and Infibulation: A Convention Account*, 61 Am Sociological Rev 999, 1015 (1996).

convention was overrun. This is a dramatic example of the power of seeding norm clusters, but it also emphasizes that the government need not play a unique role in creating these clusters. Any number of groups can play this role: the government certainly can, but so can charities and for-profit entities.[88]

This approach is probably more important in cases in which the established, but appropriate, norm or meaning changes, and we need to navigate from the formerly appropriate norm to the new norm. Norm seeding is a low-risk strategy. If the government seeds an inefficient cluster, it will die, and little will be lost. If the new norm is superior to the old norm, however, the artificially created norm cluster will thrive and spread. This analysis suggests that the government should embrace test policies or norms or take steps to foster social meanings in particular local contexts as a way of testing whether a superior approach can take root and spread.

D. Instruments for Policymakers

Finally, the analysis of the variations on the model suggests possible instruments to facilitate adoption of good norms. These are all directed at expanding the basin of attraction for the superior equilibrium, so that the initial starting conditions are less likely to influence the ultimate outcome of the system. First, larger payoff neighborhoods appear to do a better job of converging on norms that represent modest improvements (say, $1.15 < b < 1.33$).[89] As discussed before,[90] creating instrumental connectedness among individuals within a neighborhood may be difficult, but this model suggests that success yields substantial returns. Second, more refined decisionmaking—averages rather than a single, highest value—also supported success for lower values of b. Third, additional information usually increases the likelihood of success for the good norm. A strategy of providing information from beyond the boundaries of the payoff neighborhood generally increases the chance of converging on the good norm.

---

[88] Anti-dueling societies played a similar role in the decline of dueling in Europe, see V.G. Kiernan, *The Duel in European History* 216-17 (Oxford 1988), cited in Posner, 144 U Pa L Rev at 1740 n 108 (cited in note 8); and in the Old South, see Jack Kenny Williams, *Dueling in the Old South: Vignettes of Social History* 64 (College Station 1980), cited in Warren F. Schwartz, Keith Baxter, and David Ryan, *The Duel: Can These Gentlemen Be Acting Efficiently?*, 13 J Legal Stud 321, 329 n 27 (1984).

[89] But see Berninghaus and Schwalbe, 29 J Econ Behav & Org 57 (cited in note 44).

[90] See Section II.A.2.

CONCLUSION: LIMITS AND FUTURE DIRECTIONS

The recent interest in norms and law almost certainly dates from Bob Ellickson's important work on Shasta County.[91] This work started as an inquiry into the Coasean Irrelevance Proposition and emerged as a separate Ellicksonian Irrelevance Proposition. The bastardized version of the Coase result states that the allocation of property rights is irrelevant, as parties will recontract efficiently. Law plays very little role, at least in a world of low transactions costs. Now Coase himself would probably contend that the point of *The Problem of Social Cost* was precisely that transaction costs were important, and that the role for law needed to be understood in a particularized context of preexisting transaction costs. In contrast, Ellickson's investigation of cattle in Shasta County led him to conclude that law was irrelevant when robust local norms could evolve.[92] Neighbors did not know the law, did not use it to their advantage or disadvantage, and resolved their disputes in full sunlight—no bargaining in the shadow of the law for these folks. Law simply did not matter in a community with well developed norms.

More recent work takes as a given that norms, social meanings, and social roles matter enormously, and turns to the role that government might play in shaping these essential features of society.[93] The central concern of this work is that too often society will end up with weak norms, or, even worse, norms that are affirmatively harmful. Individuals who recognize the problem will be trapped and will lack a mechanism to move the collective to the superior norm.

This is certainly possible, but the computer experiments described here suggest local interactions will often lead to convergence on the superior norm. The benefits obtained by clusters of individuals who successfully embrace the better norm will often lead that norm to be propagated throughout the entire population of players. Again, this is not to say the government is irrelevant. The simulations identify at least three policy instruments of interest—the scope of local connectedness (my payoff neighborhoods); the information available to the players (the information neighborhoods); and the manner in which individuals process available information (the decision rule)—plus a strategy of seeding norm clusters so as to perturb an existing equilibrium to test whether a superior equilibrium will take root and spread.

---

[91] See Ellickson, *Order without Law* §§ 1-6 (cited in note 13).

[92] Id.

[93] See Section I.B.

The current paper suffers from at least five weaknesses, all of which suggest directions for future work:

- The players do not contest the choice of norm. How many potential norms benefit everyone identically? In contrast, how often will the norm chosen have substantial consequences for individual players (or player types) even if all benefit from a single norm? The traditional Battle of the Sexes is exactly this situation: the players want to coordinate on a single choice but each cares about the particular choice made.[94] Migration will also become an important feature of these models, as players may reduce the conflict over norms through separation by type.
- Competition between norms has been restricted to only two norms at a time. As suggested before, this model may capture many social contexts accurately, but it almost certainly does not track all commercial dealings.[95]
- My models are awfully static for dynamic models. There is no baseline of change, either through replacement of players or spontaneous mutation or experimentation. The zone of mixed play may not be as sustainable when baseline change is introduced.
- The spatial game setup itself tends to obscure the way that information is transmitted in these models. There are no holes in the lattice, meaning that there is a player at every spot. Connectedness may matter in important ways. Full connectedness maximizes the chances that a good strategy will propagate throughout the entire lattice. Separation of clusters would introduce physical barriers to the spread of a good strategy, and might create situations in which both strategies would thrive in physically distinct locations. Whether a good strategy would percolate throughout the entire lattice will undoubtedly depend on how connected our lattice is. At the same time—and this works in the other direction—the players in the spatial game do not move about. Movement serves as another way in which information is transmitted—in which strategies are spread. A richer model

---

[94] For a discussion of the "Battle of the Sexes," see note 49.

[95] See text accompanying note 7. Moving to a continuous strategy space has been shown to have substantial consequences for the results in spatial games. See Bernardo A. Huberman and Natalie S. Glance, *Evolutionary games and computer simulations*, 90 Proc Natl Acad Sci 7716, 7717-18 (1993) (showing that the results of digital simulations regarding territoriality and cooperation in the prisoner's dilemma differ greatly when time is continuous rather than discrete).

would incorporate holes in the lattice (and thus explicitly introduce something akin to networks and the extent of connectedness) and allow movement by the players. This would allow a more refined analysis of information and strategy transmission.

- Finally, there is no cost of switching strategies in these games. In real life, switching strategies is costly (have you switched from a Macintosh to a Wintel machine lately?). Friction of this sort would certainly slow down the move to new strategies. Whether it would alter the outcomes in other important ways awaits more work.

As this suggests, this article is just a first step down a path of uncertain length. The silicon models set forth here make it possible to test the importance of a variety of factors for the evolution of norms. Given the pervasive role that norms play in shaping the contexts in which we act, it is hardly surprising that norms have become the focus of so much attention. It may be possible for the law to play a role in shaping norms and thereby alter the backgrounds against which much activity takes place. Whether we think legal intervention in norms is appropriate should turn on whether we believe that private ordering will result in inefficient or positively harmful norms. The message of this article, where individuals have a shared interest in the norms, is that large-scale intervention is unjustified, as individual decisions turn out to aggregate nicely and to coalesce around the appropriate norms. Small-scale intervention—norm perturbation—may be appropriate, and a strategy of norm seeding may be an effective way for the government to test at little cost whether a norm improvement should be and can be effectuated.

Name Index